Embedded Systems with ARM Cortex-M Microcontrollers in Assembly Language and C

Dr. Yifeng Zhu

Third edition

June 2017

Book covered designed by Andrew Hayford

Library of Congress Control Number: 2017944799

ISBN 978-0-9826926-6-0

Preface

"I hear and I forget. I see and I remember. I do and I understand."

Confucius (Chinese philosopher, 551–479 BC)

Modern embedded systems exploit a single, highly integrated chip consisting of one or more general-purpose processor core, memories, advanced peripherals, digital logic, and miniaturized sensors. Due to small power dissipation, low fabrication cost, and small size, System-on-Chips (SoC) become increasingly more prevalent in many embedded applications, including cell phones, MP3 players, GPS, smart watches, medical devices, fitness gadgets, and automobile control. ARM Cortex processors are one of such successful SoC chips in the industry.

Significant changes in the third edition include updated serial communication description (UART, SPI, and I²C), new serial communication examples, incorporation of GNU gcc compiler, low power modes, modification of example programs from STM32L1 (Cortex-M3) to STM32L4 (Cortex-M4).

The book introduces basic programming of ARM Cortex-M cores in assembly and C at the register level, and the fundamentals of embedded system design. It presents basic concepts such as data representations (integer, fixed-point, floating-point), assembly instructions, stack, and implementing basic controls and functions of C language at the assembly level. It covers advanced topics such as interrupts, mixing C and assembly, direct memory access (DMA), system timer (SysTick), multi-tasking, SIMD instructions for digital signal processing (DSP), and instruction encoding/decoding. The book also gives detailed examples of interfacing peripherals, such as general purpose I/O (GPIO), LCD driver, keypad interaction, stepper motor control, PWM output, timer input capture, DAC, ADC, real-time clock (RTC), and serial communication (USART, I²C, SPI, and USB).

The book has the following features:
- Focusing on register-level programming on bare metal hardware, with no or minimum usage of STM, CMSIS, and ARM APIs
- Emphasis on structured programming and top-down modular design in both C and assembly language
- Line-by-line translation and comparison between C and ARM assembly
- Mixture of C and assembly languages, such as a C program calling assembly subroutines, and an assembly program calling C subroutines
- Balance between theory and practical examples
- Valuable knowledge that prepares students for the courses of computer architecture and operating systems

Although assembly languages are used relatively less in modern embedded systems, learning assembly languages is still crucial.

- First, assembly is not another programming language. It is a low-level interface between hardware and software. It provides a better understanding of how a processor executes a program. Assembly programming is the prerequisite knowledge of compilers, operating systems, and computer architecture.
- Secondly, assembly programs can potentially run faster than C programs. Compilers sometimes cannot fully utilize hardware features of a particular processor, especially when the processor provides some specific operations of which compilers are not aware. Therefore, we often use assembly languages to develop some speed-sensitive portion of an application.
- Thirdly, some operations have to be performed in assembly language because there is no equivalent statement in C. Consequently, assembly programs are often in the kernel codes of operating systems to implement low-level tasks, such as booting and CPU scheduling.
- Finally yet importantly, understanding how to translate high-level constructs into low-level assembly instructions can help programmers to write more efficient codes in high-level languages.

The audience for this book includes those who want to gain knowledge of the inner working of a System-on-Chip (SoC), and experiences of programming embedded systems at the register level. This book would serve better as text or reference material if readers have learned some basic C programming. The book covers both fundamental concepts and advanced topics, suitable for a broad range of audience.

I would like to thank all the people who have helped me greatly. My colleague Prof. Duane Hanselman has offered excellent guidance and advice on book publishing. I would like to thank Kaishuang Li for encouragement and help. I would like to thank Elyse Kahl and Nolan Gagnon for proofreading and Andrew Hayford for the cover design. I appreciate all the students of ECE 271 Microcomputer Architecture and Applications class who have helped me correct many errors and gave me significant improvement suggestions in the first and second edition.

Last but most importantly, I acknowledge the profound debt of gratitude I owe to my mother and father. I cannot thank them enough for all the support and love they have given to me.

Yifeng Zhu
June 1, 2017
Orono, Maine, USA

Table of Contents

See a Program Running

This chapter shows how a machine program is generated and executed. If you do not fully understand every detail presented, do not feel discouraged. It is merely meant to be a general introduction. The following chapters explain the assembly programming concepts in detail.

1.1 Translate a C Program into a Machine Program

Compilers translate a human-readable source program written in a high-level programming language such as C, into a low-level machine-understandable executable file encoded in binary form.

Executable files created by compilers are usually platform dependent. An executable file compiled for one type of microprocessors, such as ARM Cortex-M3, cannot directly run on a platform with a different kind of microprocessors that support a different set of machine instructions, such as PIC or Atmel AVR microcontrollers. When we migrate a program written in a high-level language to a processor of a different instruction set, we usually have to modify and recompile the source programs for the new target platform.

One exception is Java executables, which are platform independent. The Java compiler converts a Java program to bytecodes. A Java virtual machine (JVM) translates bytecodes into machine instructions at runtime. Because each platform has its JVM, Java executables become platform-independent. Currently, Java is not popular in embedded systems yet because it needs more memory and cannot control peripherals flexibly.

Compilers first perform some analysis on the source program, such as extracting symbols and checking syntax, and then create an *intermediate representation* (IR). Compilers make some transformations and optimizations to the IR to improve the program execution speed or reduce the program size. For C compilers, the intermediate program is similar to an assembly program, as shown in Figure 1-1. Finally, compilers translate the assembly program into a *machine program*, also called a binary executable, which can run on the target platform. The machine program consists of computer instructions and data symbols.

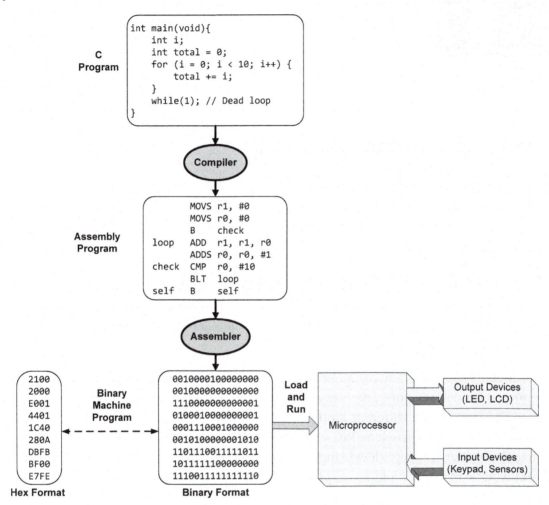

Figure 1-1. Compiling a C program into a binary executable

An assembly program includes the following five key components. Chapter 3.5 shows a simple assembly program that annotates these components.

1. A *label* represents the memory address of a data variable or an assembly instruction.
2. An *instruction mnemonic* is an operation that the processor should perform, such as "ADD" for adding integers.
3. *Operands* of a machine operation can be numeric constants or processor registers.

4. A ***program comment*** aims to improve inter-programmer communication and code readability by explicitly specifying programmers' intentions, assumptions, and hidden concepts.
5. An ***assembly directive*** is not a machine instruction, but it defines the data content or provides relevant information to assist the assembler.

The binary machine program follows a standard called *executable and linkable format* (ELF), which most Linux and UNIX systems use. The UNIX System Laboratories developed and published ELF to standardize the format for most executable files, shared libraries and object code. *Object code* is an intermediate file that a compiler generates at the compiling stage. Compilers link object code together at the linking stage to form an executable or a software library. Most ARM-based embedded systems support ELF.

> *Three popular UNIX executable file formats: ELF, a.out, and COFF.*

ELF, as its name suggests, provides two interfaces to binary files:

- a ***linkable interface*** that is used at static link time to combine multiple files when compiling and building a program, and
- an ***executable interface*** that is utilized at runtime to create a process image in memory when a program is loaded into memory and then executed.

Since we want to see how a program is loaded and executed, we focus only on the executable interface in the following discussion.

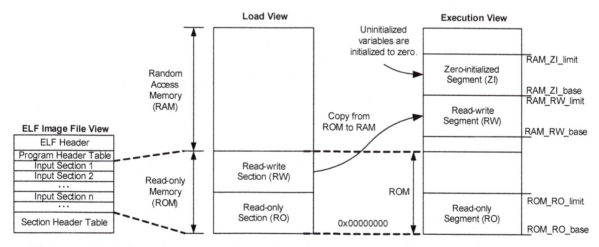

Figure 1-2. Interface of an executable binary file in the executable and linking format (ELF). An ELF file provides *load view* and *execution view*. The load view specifies how to load data into the memory. The execution view instructs how to initialize data regions at runtime.

In ELF, similar data, symbols, and other information are grouped into many important input sections. The executable interface provides two separate logic views: the load view and the execution view, as shown in Figure 1-2.

- The *load view* classifies the input sections into two regions: read-write section and read-only section. The load view also defines the base memory address of these regions so that the processor knows where it should load them into the memory.
- The *execution view* informs the processor how to load the executable at runtime. A binary machine program includes four critical sections, including:
  - a *text segment* that consists of binary machine instructions,
  - a *read-only data segment* that defines the value of variables unalterable at runtime,
  - a *read-write data segment* that sets the initial values of statically allocated and modifiable variables, and
  - a *zero-initialized data segment* that holds all uninitialized variables declared in the program.

1.2 Load a Machine Program into Memory

Binary executable programs are initially stored in non-volatile storage devices such as hard drives and flash memory. Therefore, when the system loses power, the program is not lost, and the system can restart. The processor must load the instructions and data of a machine program into main memory before the program starts to run. Main memory usually consists of volatile data storage devices, such as DRAM and SRAM, and all stored information in main memory is lost if power is turned off.

1.2.1 Harvard Architecture and Von Neumann Architecture

There are two types of computer architecture, *Von Neumann* architecture, and *Harvard architecture*, as shown in Figure 1-3.

In the Von Neumann architecture, data and instructions share the same physical memory. There are only one memory address bus and one data transmission bus, as shown in Figure 1-4. A bus is a communication connection, which allows the exchange of information between two or more parts of a computer. All sections of an executable program, including the text section (executable instructions), the read-only data section, the read-write sections, and the zero-initialized section, are loaded into the main memory. The data stream and the instruction stream share the memory bandwidth.

In the Harvard architecture, the instruction memory and data memory are two physically separate memory devices. There are two sets of data transmission buses and memory address buses. When a program starts, the processor copies at least the read-write data section and the zero-initialized data section in the binary executable to the data memory. Copying the read-only data section to the data memory is optional. The text section usually stays in the non-volatile storage. When the program runs, the instruction stream and the data stream transfer information on separate sets of data and address buses.

Von Neumann Architecture   **Harvard Architecture**

Figure 1-3. Two types of computer architecture. In the Von Neumann architecture, data and instructions are stored in the same memory. In the Harvard architecture, data and instructions are stored in two physically separate memory devices.

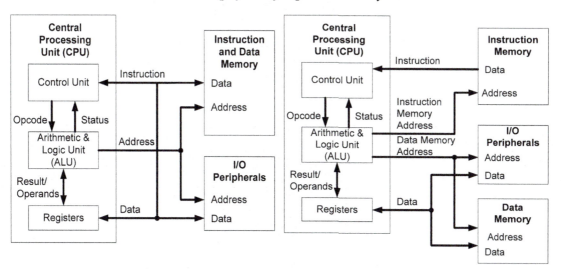

Figure 1-4. Von Neumann computer architecture. Instructions and data share the memory device. It has only one set of data bus and address bus shared by the instruction memory and the data memory.

Figure 1-5. Harvard computer architecture. Instructions and data are stored in different memory devices. It has a dedicated set of data bus and address bus for the instruction memory and the data memory.

In the Harvard architecture, the instruction memory and the data memory are often small enough to fit in the same address space. For a 32-bit processor, the memory address has 32 bits. Modern computers are byte-addressable (*i.e.*, each memory address identifies a byte in memory). When the memory address has 32 bits, the total addressable memory space includes 2^{32} bytes (*i.e.*, 4 GB). Table 1-1 lists a few metric prefixes, with their numerical equivalents. A 4-GB memory space is large enough for embedded systems.

Name	Abbr.	Size
Kilo	K	2^{10} = 1,024
Mega	M	2^{20} = 1,048,576
Giga	G	2^{30} = 1,073,741,824
Tera	T	2^{40} = 1,099,511,627,776

Table 1-1. Metric prefixes of memory size

Because the data and instruction memory are small enough to fit in the same 32-bit memory address space, they often share the memory address bus, as shown in Figure 1-5. Suppose the data memory has 256 kilobytes (2^{18} bytes), and the instruction memory has 4 kilobytes (2^{12} bytes). In the 32-bit (*i.e.*, 4 GB) memory address space, we can allocate a 4KB region for the instruction memory and a 256KB region for the instruction memory, as shown in Figure 1-6. Because there is no overlap between these two address ranges, the instruction memory and the data memory can share the address bus.

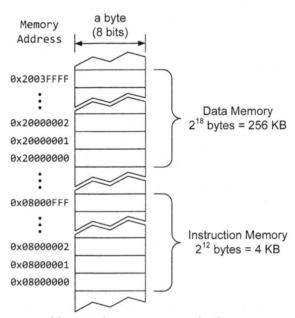

Figure 1-6. Data memory and instruction memory are in the same memory address space in Harvard Architecture in many embedded systems. Accordingly, the instruction memory and the data memory can share the same address bus.

Each type of computer architecture has ...

- The Von Neumann architecture is relatively inexpensi...
- The Harvard architecture allows the processor to access the data mem...
  instruction memory concurrently. By contrast, the Von Neumann arch...
  allows only one memory access at any time instant; the processor either rea...
  instruction from the instruction memory or accesses data in the data memory
  Accordingly, the Harvard architecture often offers faster processing speed at the
  same clock rate.
- The Harvard architecture tends to be more energy efficient. Under the same
  performance requirement, the Harvard architecture often needs lower clock
  speeds, resulting in a lower power consumption rate.
- In the Harvard architecture, the data bus and the instruction bus may have
  different widths. For example, digital signal processing processors can leverage
  this feature to make the instruction bus wider to reduce the number of clock cycles
  required to load an instruction.

1.2.2 Creating Runtime Memory Image

ARM Cortex-M3/M4/M7 microprocessors are
Harvard computer architecture, and the
instruction memory (flash memory) and the
data memory (SRAM) are built into the
processor chip, as shown in Figure 1-7. The
microprocessor employs two separate and
isolated memories. Separating the instruction
and data memories allows concurrent accesses
to instructions and data, thus improving the
memory bandwidth and speeding up the
processor performance. Typically, the
instruction memory uses a slow but non-
volatile flash memory, and the data memory
uses a fast but volatile SRAM.

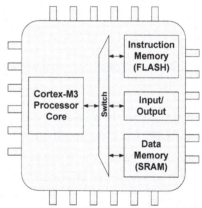

**Figure 1-7. The instruction memory and
the data memory are built into the
processor chip.**

Figure 1-8 gives a simple example that shows how the Harvard architecture loads a
program to start the execution. When the processor loads a program, all initialized global
variables, such as the integer array *a*, are copied from the instruction memory into the
initialized data segment in the data memory. All uninitialized global variables, such as
the variable *counter*, are allocated in the zero-initialized data segment. The local variables,
such as the integer array *b*, are allocated on the stack, located at the top of SRAM. Note
the stack grows downward. When the processor boots successfully, the first instruction

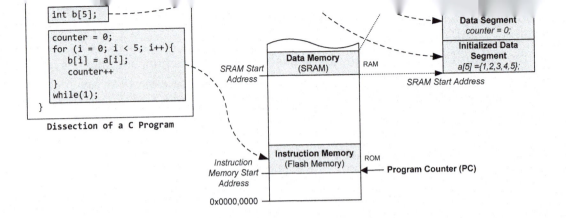

```
int b[5];

counter = 0;
for (i = 0; i < 5; i++){
    b[i] = a[i];
    counter++
}
while(1);
}
```

Dissection of a C Program

SRAM Start Address

Data Memory (SRAM)   RAM

Data Segment
counter = 0;

Initialized Data Segment
a[5] ={1,2,3,4,5};

SRAM Start Address

Instruction Memory Start Address

Instruction Memory (Flash Memory)   ROM

Program Counter (PC)

0x0000,0000

Figure 1-8. A processor of Harvard architecture loads a program into the instruction memory and the data memory.

At runtime, the data memory is divided into four segments: initialized data segment, uninitialized data segment, heap, and stack. The processor allocates the first two data segments statically, and their size and location remain unchanged at runtime. The size of the last two segments changes as the program runs.

The *initialized data segment* contains global and static variables that the program gives some initial values. For example, in a C declaration, "int capacity = 100;", if it appears outside any function (*i.e.*, it is a global variable), the processor places the variable *capacity* in the initialized data segment with an initial value when the processor creates a running-time memory image for this C program.

- The *zero-initialized data segment* contains all global or static variables that are uninitialized or initialized to zero in the program. For example, a globally declared string "char name[20];" is stored in the uninitialized data segment.
- The *heap* holds all data objects that an application creates dynamically at runtime. For example, all data objects created by dynamic memory allocation library functions like *malloc()* or *calloc()* in C or by the new operator in C++ are placed in

the heap. A *free()* function in C or a *delete* operator in C++ removes a data object from the heap. The memory space allocated to this data object is freed up. The heap is placed immediately after the zero-initialized segment, and it grows upward (toward higher addresses).

- The **stack** stores local variables of subroutines, including *main()*, saves the runtime environment and passes arguments to a subroutine. A stack is a *first-in-last-out* (FILO) memory region, and the processor places it on the top of the data memory. When a subroutine declares a local variable, the variable is saved in the stack. When a subroutine returns, the subroutine should pop from the stack all variables it has pushed. Additionally, when a caller calls a subroutine, the caller may pass parameters to the subroutine via the stack. As subroutines are called and returned at runtime, the stack grows downward or shrinks upward correspondingly.

The processor places the heap and the stack at the opposite end of a memory region, and they grow in different directions, as shown in Figure 1-8. In a free memory region, the stack starts from the top, and the heap starts from the bottom. As variables are dynamically allocated or removed from the heap or stack, the size of the heap and stack changes at runtime. The heap grows up toward the large memory address, and the stack grows down toward the small memory address. Growing in opposite directions allows the heap and stack to take full advantage of the free memory region. When the stack meets the heap, free memory space is exhausted.

Figure 1-9 shows an example memory map of the 4GB memory space in a Cortex-M3 microprocessor. The memory map is pre-defined by the chip manufacturer and is not programmable usually. Within this 4GB linear memory space, the address range of instruction memory, data memory, internal and external peripheral devices, and external RAM has no overlap with each other.

- The on-chip flash memory, used for the instruction memory, has 4 KB, and its address starts at `0x08000000`.
- The on-chip SRAM, used for the data memory, has 256 KB, and its memory address begins at `0x20000000`.
- The external RAM allows the processor to expand the data memory capacity.

The processor allocates memory addresses for each internal or external peripheral. This addressing scheme enables the processor to interface a peripheral in a convenient way. A peripheral typically has a set of registers, such as data registers for data exchange between the peripheral and the processor, control registers for the processor to configure or control the peripheral, and status registers to indicate the operation state of the peripheral. A peripheral may also contain a small memory.

The processor maps the registers and memory of all peripherals to the same memory address space of the instruction and data memory. To interface a peripheral, the processor uses regular memory access instructions to read or write to those memory addresses predefined for this peripheral. This method is called *memory-mapped I/O* (See Chapter 14.6 for details). The processor interfaces all peripheral in the way as if they were part of the memory.

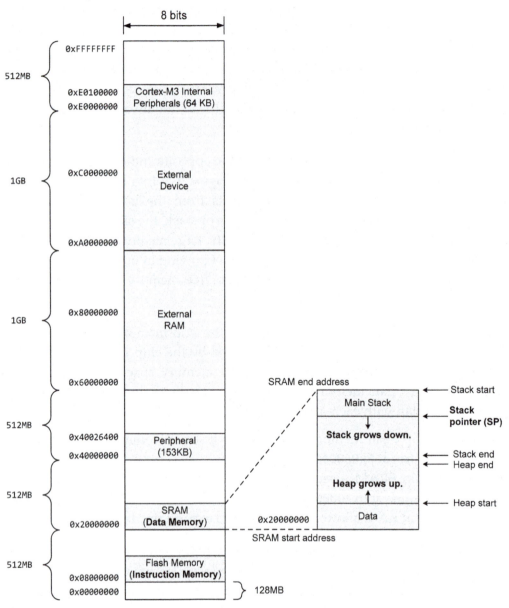

Figure 1-9. Example memory map of a 4GB memory space. The instruction memory, the data memory, and all peripherals share the same memory address space. The memory map is fixed and contains unused region.

1.3 Registers

Before we illustrate how a microprocessor executes a program, let us first introduce one important component of microprocessors - *hardware registers*. A processor contains a small set of registers to store digital values. Registers are the fastest data storage in a computing system.

All registers are of the same size and typically hold 16, 32, or 64 bits. Each register in Cortex-M processors has 32 bits. The processor reads or writes all bits in a register together. Chapter 4.6 presents how to check or change individual bits in a register. A register can store the content of an operand for a logic or arithmetic operation, or the memory address or offset when the processor access data in memory.

A processor core has two types of registers: **general-purpose registers** and **special-purpose registers**. While general-purpose registers store the operands and intermediate results during the execution of a program, special-purpose registers have a predetermined usage, such as representing the processor status. Special-purpose registers have more usage restrictions than general-purpose registers. For example, some of them require special instructions or privileges to access them.

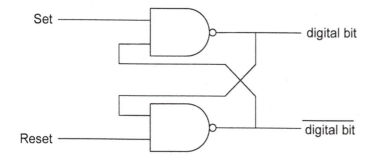

Set	Reset	Digital Bit
1	0	1
0	1	0
0	0	not allowed
1	1	hold state

Figure 1-10. Logic diagram and truth table of a basic flip-flop constructed by using two Negated AND (NAND) gates

A register consists of a set of flip-flops in parallel to store binary bits. A 32-bit register has 32 flip-flops side by side. Figure 1-10 shows a simple implementation of a flip-flop by using a pair of Negated AND (NAND) gates. A flip-flop usually has a clock input, which is not shown in this example.

The flip-flop works as follows. When the set or the reset is true, a digital value of 1 or 0 is stored, respectively. When both the set and the reset are false, the digital value stored remains unaffected. The set and reset signals cannot be true simultaneously. Otherwise, the result produced would be random.

1.3.1 Reusing Registers to Improve Performance

Accessing the processor's registers is much faster than data memory. Storing data in registers instead of memory improves the processor performance.

- In most programs, the probability that a data item is accessed is not uniform. It is a common phenomenon that a program accesses some data items much more frequently than the other items. Moreover, a data item that the processor accesses at one point in time is likely to be accessed again shortly. This phenomenon is pervasive in applications, and it is called *temporal locality*. Therefore, most compilers try to place the value of frequently or recently accessed data variables and memory addresses in registers whenever possible to optimize the performance.
- Software programs also have *spatial locality*. When a processor accesses data at a memory address, data stored in nearby memory locations are likely to be read or

> *Analogy Example*
>
> *Temporal Locality: You tend to read the same book repeatedly in the library when preparing an exam.*
>
> *Spatial Locality: You tend to read books on the same bookshelf in the library when preparing an exam.*

written shortly. Processor architecture design (such as caching and prefetching) and software development (such as reorganizing data access sequence) exploit spatial locality to speed up the overall performance.

The number of registers available on a microprocessor is often small, typically between 4 and 32, for two important reasons.

- First, many experimental measurements have shown that registers often exhibit the highest temperature compared to the other hardware components of a processor. Reducing the number of registers helps mitigate the thermal problem.
- Secondly, if there are fewer registers, it takes fewer bits to encode a register in a machine instruction. A small number of registers consequently decrease the code size and reduce the bandwidth requirement on the instruction memory. For example, if a processor has 16 registers, it requires 4 bits to represent a register in an instruction. To encode an assembly instruction with two operand registers and one destination register, such as "add r3, r1, r2" (r3 = r1 + r2), the binary machine instruction uses 12 bits to identify these registers. However, if a processor has only eight registers, encoding three registers in an instruction takes only 9 bits.

Register allocation is a process that assigns variables and constants to general-purpose registers. It is often the case that a program has more variables and constants than registers. Register allocation decides whether a variable or constant should reside in a processor register or at some location in the data memory. Register allocation is performed either automatically by compilers if the program is written in a high-level language (such as C or C++), or manually if the program is in assembly.

For a given program, finding the optimal register allocation that minimizes the number of memory accesses is a very challenging problem. Register allocation becomes further complicated in Cortex-M processors. For example, some instructions can only access registers with small addresses (low registers). Some instructions, such as multiplication, place a 64-bit result into two registers.

When writing an assembly program, we can follow three basic steps to allocate registers. Chapter 7.2 gives a detailed example.

1. We inspect the live range of a variable. A variable is live if the program accesses it again at some later point in time.
2. If the live range of two variables overlaps, we should not allocate them into the same register. Otherwise, we can assign them to the same register.
3. We map the most frequently used variables to registers and allocate the least frequently used variables in the data memory if necessary to reduce the number of memory accesses.

1.3.2 Processor Registers

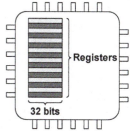

As shown in Figure 1-11, registers are divided into two groups: general-purpose registers and special-purpose registers. Register names are case-insensitive.

*   There are 13 general-purpose registers (r0 - r12) available for program data operations. The first eight registers (r0 - r7) are called *low registers*, and the other five (r8 - r12) are called *high registers*. Some of the 16-bit assembly instructions in Cortex-M can only access the low registers.
*   *Stack point* (SP) r13 holds the memory address of the top of the stack. Cortex-M processors provide two different stacks: the *main stack* and the *process stack*. Thus, there are two stack pointers: the main stack pointer (MSP) and the process stack pointer (PSP). The processor uses PSP when executing regular user programs, and uses MSP when serving interrupts or privileged accesses. The stack pointer (SP) is a shadow register of either MSP or PSP, depending on the processor's mode setting. When a processor starts, it assigns MSP to SP initially.
*   *Link register* (LR) r14 holds the memory address of the instruction that needs to run immediately after a subroutine completes. It is the next instruction after the

instruction that calls a subroutine. During the execution of an interrupt service routine, LR holds a special value to indicate whether MSP or PSP is used.

- *Program counter* (PC) r15 holds the memory address (location in memory) of the next instruction(s) that the processor fetches from the instruction memory.
- *Program status register* (xPSR) records status bit flags of the application program, interrupt, and processor execution. Example flags include negative, zero, carry, and overflow. Chapter 4.1 gives a detailed introduction.
- *Base priority mask register* (BASEPRI) defines the priority threshold, and the processor disables all interrupts with a higher priority value than the threshold. A lower priority value represents a higher priority (or urgency).
- *Control register* (CONTROL) sets the choice of the main stack or the process stack, and the selection of privileged or unprivileged mode. Chapter 23 discusses the CONTROL register.
- *Priority mask register* (PRIMASK) is used to disable all interrupts excluding hard faults and non-maskable interrupts (NMI). If an interrupt is masked, the processor disables this interrupt. Chapter 11 introduces interrupts in detail.
- *Fault mask register* (FAULTMASK) is used to disable all interrupts excluding non-maskable interrupts (NMI).

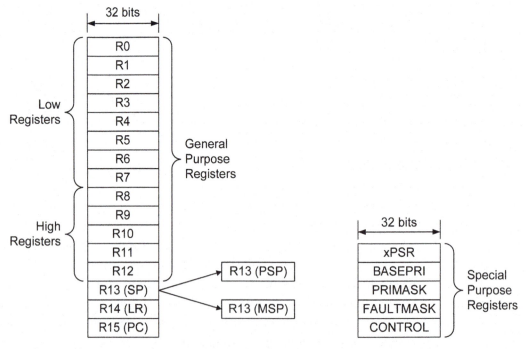

Figure 1-11. Registers of ARM Cortex-M processor.
PC = program counter, LR = link register, SP = stack pointer, MSP = main stack pointer, PSP = process stack pointer, xPSR = program status register

The program counter (PC) stores the memory address at which the processor loads the next instruction(s). Instructions in a program run sequentially if the program flow is not changed. Usually, the processor fetches instructions consecutively from the instruction memory. Thus, the program counter is automatically incremented, pointing to the next instruction to be executed.

Each instruction in Cortex-M has either 16 or 32 bits. Typically, the processor increases the program counter by four automatically. The processor retrieves four bytes (*i.e.,* 32 bits) from the instruction memory in one clock cycle, as shown in Figure 1-12. Chapter 13.2 discusses how the processor decodes these 32 bits and finds out whether they represent one 32-bit instruction or two 16-bit instructions.

$$PC = PC + 4$$
after each
instruction fetch

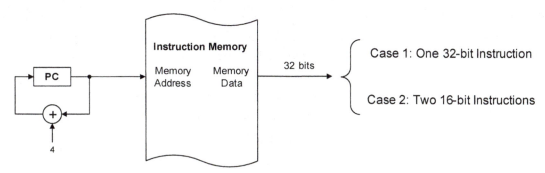

Figure 1-12. The program counter (PC) is incremented by 4. PC holds the memory address of the next instruction(s) to be fetched from the instruction memory. When the program reads PC, the returned value is the address of the current instruction plus 4.

Normally, assembly instructions in a program run in a sequential order. However, branch instructions (see Chapter 6), subroutines (see Chapter 8), and interrupts (see Chapter 11) can change the sequential program flow by setting PC to the memory address of the target instruction.

For Cortex-M0/M3/M4, each instruction takes three stages, as shown in Figure 1-13.

- At the first stage, the processor fetches 4 bytes from the instruction memory and increments the program counter by 4 automatically. After each instruction fetch, the program counter points to the next instruction(s) to be fetched.
- At the second stage, the processor decodes the instruction and finds out what operations are to be carried out.
- At the last stage, the processor reads operand registers, carries out the designated arithmetic or logic operation, accesses data memory (if necessary) and updates target registers (if needed).

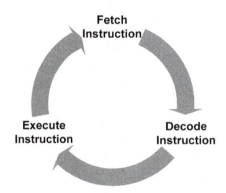

Figure 1-13. Life cycle of an instruction. An instruction pointed by the program counter is fetched, decoded, and executed. The processor increments PC automatically after it loads an instruction from the instruction memory.

This *fetch-decode-execution* process repeats for each instruction until the program finishes. As shown in Figure 1-14, the processor executes each instruction in a pipelined fashion. This pipeline is like an automobile assembly line. Pipelining allows multiple instructions to run simultaneously. Thus, it increases the utilization of hardware resources and improves the processor's overall performance. To execute programs correctly, a pipeline processor should take special considerations to branch instructions. For example, when a branch instruction changes the program flow, any instructions that the processor has fetched incorrectly should not complete the pipeline.

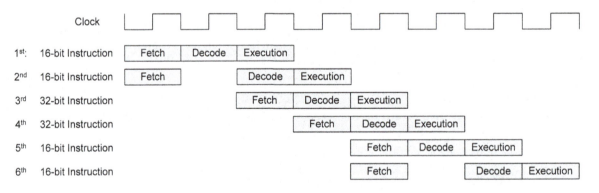

Figure 1-14. Three-stage *fetch-decode-execution* pipeline in Cortex-M4. Pipelining makes hardware resources fully utilized. Each time the processor fetches 4 bytes from the instruction memory, which includes two 16-bit instructions or one 32-bit instruction (See Chapter 13.2 for details). Therefore, after each fetch, PC is incremented by 4.

While Cortex-M0, Cortex-M3, and Cortex-M4 have three pipeline stages, Cortex-M0+ has only two stages, including instruction fetch and execution. As well, Cortex-M0+ is based on Von Neumann Architecture, instead of Harvard Architecture. Cortex-M7 is much more complicated, and it has multiple pipelines, such as load/store pipeline, two ALU pipeline, and FPU pipeline. It allows more instructions to run concurrently. Each pipeline can have up to six stages, including instruction fetch, instruction decode, instruction issue, execute sub-stage 1, execute sub-stage 2, and write back.

1.4 Executing a Machine Program

This section illustrates how a Cortex-M processor executes a program. We use a simple C program given in Table 1-2 as an example. The program calculates the sum of two global integer variables (*a* and *b*) and saves the result into another global variable *c*. Because most software programs in embedded systems never exit, there is an endless loop at the end of the C program.

C Program	Assembly Program		Machine Program	
			Binary	Hex
	AREA myData, DATA			
	ALIGN			
int a = 1;	a	DCD 1	0000000000000000	0x0000
			0000000000000001	0x0001
int b = 2;	b	DCD 2	0000000000000000	0x0000
			0000000000000010	0x0002
int c = 0;	c	DCD 0	0000000000000000	0x0000
			0000000000000000	0x0000
	AREA myCode, CODE			
	EXPORT __main			
	ALIGN			
	ENTRY			
int **main**(){	__main PROC			
c = a + b;	LDR r1, =a		0100100100000011	0x4903
while(1);	LDR r2, [r1]		0110100000001010	0x680A
}	LDR r3, =b		0100101100000011	0x4B03
	LDR r4, [r3]		0110100000011100	0x681C
	ADDS r5, r2, r4		0001100100011001	0x1915
	LDR r6, =c		0100111000000011	0x4E03
	STR r5, [r6]		0110000000111001	0x6035
	stop B stop		1110011111111110	0xE7FE
	ENDP		0000000000000000	0x0000
	END		0010000000000000	0x2000
			0000000000000100	0x0004
			0010000000000000	0x2000
			0000000000001000	0x0008
			0010000000000000	0x2000

Table 1-2. Comparison of C program, assembly program, and machine program

A compiler translates the above C program into an assembly program like the one given in Table 1-2. Different compilers may generate assembly programs that differ from each other. Even the same compiler can generate different assembly programs from the same C program if different compilation options (such as optimization levels) are used.

The assembler then produces the machine program based on the assembly program. The machine program includes two parts: data and instructions. Table 1-2 only lists the instructions. The prefix "0x" represents a hexadecimal number. A number represented in hexadecimal format is more readable than its representation in binary. Chapter 2 introduces the representation and conversion of integers in detail.

Note that the assembly program uses instruction "ADDS r5, r2, r4", instead of "ADD r5, r2, r4", even though the processor does not use the N, Z, C, and V flags updated by the ADDS instruction in this program (see Chapter 4.2). The ADD instruction has 32 bits, and ADDS has only 16 bits. The compiler prefers ADDS to ADD to reduce the binary program size.

1.4.1 Loading a Program

When the program runs on Harvard architecture, its instructions and data are loaded into the instruction and data memory, respectively. Table 1-3 gives an example image of the instruction and data memory.

Memory Region	Memory Address	Binary Instruction	Assembly Instruction	Comments
Data Memory	0x20000000	0x0001	DCW 0x0001	
	0x20000002	0x0000	DCW 0x0000	; 0x00000001
	0x20000004	0x0002	DCW 0x0002	
	0x20000006	0x0000	DCW 0x0000	; 0x00000002
	0x20000008	0x0000	DCW 0x0000	
	0x2000000A	0x0000	DCW 0x0000	; 0x00000000
	. . .	. . .	. . .	
Instruction Memory	0x08000160	0x4903	LDR r1, [pc,#12]	; @0x08000170
	0x08000162	0x680A	LDR r2, [r1]	; r2 = a
	0x08000164	0x4B03	LDR r3, [pc,#12]	; @0x08000174
	0x08000166	0x681C	LDR r4, [r3]	; r4 = b
	0x08000168	0x1915	ADDS r5, r2, r4	; r5 = a + b
	0x0800016A	0x4E03	LDR r6, [pc,#12]	; @0x08000178
	0x0800016C	0x6035	STR r5, [r6]	; save c
	0x0800016E	0xE7FE	B 0x0800016E	; stop
	0x08000170	0x0000	DCW 0x0000	
	0x08000172	0x2000	DCW 0x2000	; 0x20000000
	0x08000174	0x0004	DCW 0x0004	
	0x08000176	0x2000	DCW 0x2000	; 0x20000004
	0x08000178	0x0008	DCW 0x0008	
	0x0800017A	0x2000	DCW 0x2000	; 0x20000008
	. . .	. . .	. . .	

Table 1-3. Memory image when the processor loads the instructions and data of a program into the instruction memory and the data memory, respectively.

Depending on the processor hardware setting, the starting address of the instruction and data memory might differ from this example. Each instruction in this example happens to take two bytes in the instruction memory. The global variables are placed in the data memory when a program runs, as shown in Figure 1-8.

By default, the address of the RAM, used as data memory starts at 0x20000000 (see Figure 1-9). Therefore, as Table 1-3 shows, these three integer variables (*a*, *b*, and *c*) are stored in the RAM, and their starting address is 0x20000000. Each integer takes four bytes in memory.

Each instruction takes three clock cycles (fetch, decode, and execute) to complete on ARM Cortex-M3 and Cortex-M4 processors:

(1) Fetch the instruction from the instruction memory,
(2) Decode the instruction, and
(3) Execute the arithmetic or logic operation, update the program counter for a branch instruction, or access the data memory for a load or store instruction.

The assembly instruction "LDR   r1, =a" is a pseudo instruction, and the compiler translates it to real machine instructions, as discussed in detail in Chapter 5.4.4. This instruction sets the content in register r1 to the memory address of variable *a*. The pseudo instruction is translated to "LDR   r1, [pc, #12]". The memory address of variable *a* is stored at the memory location "[pc, #12]". This PC-relative addressing scheme is a general

> *Pseudo instructions are not real machine instructions.*

approach to loading a large irregular constant number into a register. Chapter 3 explains PC-relative addressing.

1.4.2 Starting the Execution

After the processor is booted and initialized, the program counter (PC) is set to 0x08000160. After executing an instruction, the processor increments PC automatically by four. PC points to the next 32-bit instruction or the next two 16-bit instructions to be fetched from the instruction memory. In this example, each instruction happens to take only two bytes (16 bits). Many instructions take four bytes (32 bits), as discussed in Chapter 13. Consequently, the processor fetches two instructions each time in this example.

Each processor has a special program called *boot loader*, which sets up the runtime environment after completion of self-testing. The boot loader sets PC to the first instruction of a user program. For a C program, PC points to the first statement in the main function. For an assembly program, PC points the first instruction of the __main function (See Table 1-2).

Figure 1-15 shows the values of registers, the layout of instruction memory and data memory after the processor loads the sample program. When the program starts, PC is set to 0x08000160. Note each memory address specifies the location of a byte in memory. Because each instruction takes 16 bits in this example, the memory address of the next instruction is 0x08000162. Variables a, b, and c are declared as integers, and each of them takes four bytes in memory.

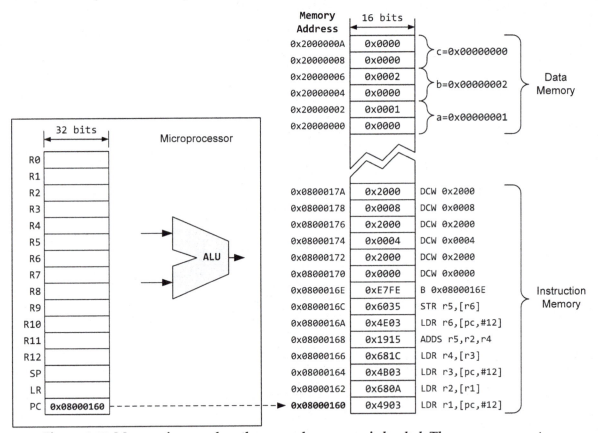

Figure 1-15. Memory image when the example program is loaded. The program counter points to the next instruction to be loaded. Variables a, b, and c are stored in the data memory.

Registers hold values to be operated by the arithmetic and logic unit (ALU). All registers can be accessed simultaneously, without causing any extra delay. A variable can be stored in memory or a register. When a variable is stored in the data memory, the value of this variable must be loaded into a register because arithmetic and logic instructions cannot directly operate on a value stored in memory. The processor must carry out the *load-modify-store* sequence to update this variable:

1. **Load** the value of the variable from the data memory into a register,
2. **Modify** the value of the register by using ALU, and
3. **Store** the value of this register back into the data memory.

> *A load-modify-store sequence is required to update a memory value.*

This assembly program given in Table 1-2 involves the following four key steps:

1. Load the value of variable *a* from the data memory into register r2.
2. Load the value of variable *b* from the data memory into register r4.
3. Calculate the sum of r2 and r4 and save the result into register r5.
4. Save the content of register r5 to the memory where variable *c* is stored.

The following explains the execution of each assembly instruction line by line. To facilitate the discussion, we list the memory address where the instruction is stored, the binary machine instruction, the assembly instruction that the binary machine instruction represents, the execution result, and comments in sequential order.

```
    Address: Binary Code ⇒ Assembly Instruction ⇒ Execution Result
1. 0x08000160:  0x4903  ⇒  LDR r1, [pc, #12]  ⇒  r1 = 0x20000000
   ; Load memory address of global variable a into register r1
```

A 16-bit binary instruction stored at 0x08000160 in the instruction memory is 0x4903. The processor decodes it as "LDR r1, [pc, #12]".

- This instruction loads a 32-bit data (a word) stored at the address PC + 4 + 12 into register r1. PC is the base memory address. The constant number 12 is an offset, which denotes the distance between the base address and the target address.

- Note that the target memory address is PC + 4 + 12, not PC + 12. PC is automatically incremented by four. Reading the program counter always returns PC + 4.

- Because PC at this moment is 0x08000160, the memory address of the target data in this load instruction is PC + 4 + 12, *i.e.*, 0x08000170.

- The 32-bit data stored at the memory address 0x08000170 is 0x20000000.

- After executing this instruction, register r1 is set to 0x20000000.

In this program, the memory address of variable *a* is directly stored in the binary code, and this instruction uses PC-relative addressing to load the memory address of *a* into r1.

2. `0x08000162:` | `0x680` | ⇒ | `LDR r2, [r1]` | ⇒ | `r2 = 0x00000001`
   `; Load the value of global variable a from the data memory into r2`

The 16-bit binary instruction stored at the memory address `0x08000162` is `0x680A`. In C, each integer variable takes four bytes in memory. In this example, the value of the integer variable *a* is stored at the address `0x20000000` in the data memory. This instruction loads the value of variable *a* into register r1. After this instruction completes, the content in register r2 is `0x00000001`.

3. `0x08000164:` | `0x4B03` | ⇒ | `LDR r3, [pc, #12]` | ⇒ | `r3 = 0x20000004`
   `; Load the memory address of global variable b into register r3`

The next 16-bit instruction is `0x4B03`, which is decoded as "`LDR r3, [pc, #12]`". It loads the memory address of variable *b* into register r3. PC is `0x08000164` and thus the target memory address is PC + 4 + 12, *i.e.*, `0x08000174`. After loading 32-bit data located at `0x08000174`, r3 is `0x20000004`.

4. `0x08000166:` | `0x681C` | ⇒ | `LDR r4, [r3]` | ⇒ | `r4 = 0x00000002`
   `; Load value of global variable b into register r4`

The machine instruction `0x681C` instructs the processor to load 32-bit data at memory location `0x20000004` into register r4. Register r3 holds the memory address of variable *b*. After the execution, r4 is `0x00000002`.

5. `0x08000168:` | `0x1915` | ⇒ | `ADDS r5, r2, r4` | ⇒ | `r5 = 0x00000003`
   `; Add the values of a and b`

The machine instruction `0x1915` asks the processor to add two integers stored in register r2 and r4, and save the result into register r5, *i.e.*, `r5 = r2 + r4`.
   - Register r2 and r4 hold the values of variable *a* and *b*, respectively.
   - After the add operation completes, r5 is `0x00000003`.
   - Because ADD is a 32-bit instruction and ADDS is a 16-bit instruction, ADDS is preferred to increase the code density. In this example, "`ADD r5, r2, r4`" allows the program to run correctly, but increases the size of the binary code by two bytes.

6. `0x0800016A:` | `0x4E03` | ⇒ | `LDR r6, [pc, #12]` | ⇒ | `r6 = 0x20000008`
   `; Load memory address of global variable c into register r6`

This instruction loads the memory address of variable c into register r6. After completion, r6 is 0x20000008.

7. 0x0800016C: | 0x6035 | ⇒ | STR r5, [r6] | ⇒ | mem[0x20000008] = 0x00000003 |
   ; Store sum into variable c located in the data memory

This instruction stores the 32-bit content in register r5 into the memory address pointed by register r6. It saves the content of variable c into the data memory located at 0x20000008. After completion, the content of the data memory located at 0x20000008 is 0x00000003.

8. 0x0800016E: | 0xE7FE | ⇒ | B 0x0800016E | ⇒ | PC = 0x0800016E |
   ; Dead loop

This instruction (0xE7FE) is a branch instruction that sets PC to 0x0800016E, which points to the instruction itself. The 11-bit branch offset is 0x7FE (*i.e.,* -2). Thus, PC = PC + 4 + 2 × offset = PC + 4 − 4 = PC. Consequently, the same instruction is repeatedly executed, which creates an endless loop. This corresponds to the *while(1)* loop of the C program.

1.4.3 Program Completion

Figure 1-16 shows the values of all registers and the data memory when the program reaches the dead loop.

- The instruction memory remains unchanged because it is read only.
- The data memory stores computed values that may change at run time.
- The program saves the result in the data memory. Variable c stored at the data memory address 0x20000008 has a value of 3, which is the sum of *a* and *b*.
- The program counter (PC) is kept at 0x0800016E, pointing to the instruction 0xE7FE repeatedly. PC keeps pointing to the current instruction, which forms a dead loop. In embedded systems, most applications do not return and consequently places a dead loop at the end of the *main* function.

During the computation, values stored in the data memory cannot be operands of ALU directly. To process data stored in the data memory, the processor must load data into processor's general-purpose registers first. Neither can the processor save the result of ALU to the data memory directly. The processor should write the ALU result to a general-purpose register first and use a store instruction to copy the data from the register to the data memory.

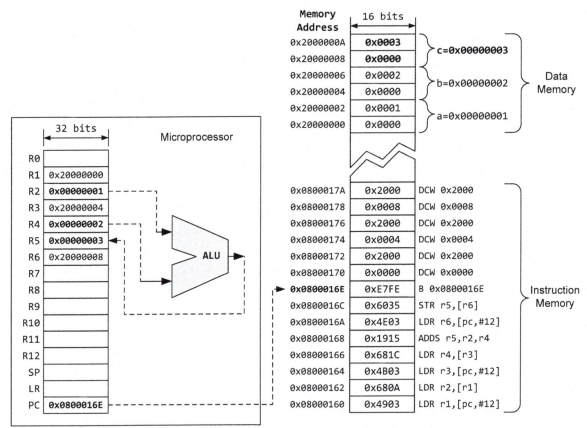

Figure 1-16. Processor and memory status when the program reaches the dead loop. The program counter (PC) points to the branch instruction. The ALU can take any general-purpose registers as the source operands and the destination operand. To change the value stored in the data memory, the processor must perform a sequence of load-modify-store.

1.5 Exercises

1. Identify the processor type and manufacturer of five different devices, excluding servers, laptops, and desktops. Answer the following questions for each processor.

    a) How many bits does a machine instruction have? How many bits does the memory address have?
    b) What is the maximum memory capacity they can support?
    c) Do they have Harvard architecture and Von Neumann architecture?

2. The program counter (PC) points to the memory address of the next instruction(s) that the processor load from memory.

   a) How does the PC value change after fetching a 32-bit instruction?
   b) How does PC change after executing a 16-bit instruction?

3. The arithmetic and logic unit (ALU) performs integer and logic operations. Implement the logic of a simple ALU that performs 2-bit addition and subtraction. Assume that the operands are A_1A_0 and B_1B_0, and the output is C_1C_0. The operation code O has only one bit, which selects addition or subtraction.

4. A register is the fastest data storage element within a processor. A 32-bit register consists of a set of flip-flops to store 32 bits of information. Design a 4-bit register by using flip-flops and answer the following questions.

   a) How many bits does the address bus have?
   b) How many bits does the data bus have?
   c) What else should input signals the register have?

5. Suppose the memory address in most embedded systems has 32 bits.

   a) How many unique memory locations can a 32-bit address access?
   b) Desktops and servers usually have virtual memory, which allows a process to allocate and use a memory space that is larger than the physical memory. Why do not embedded systems use virtual memory usually?

6. What are the advantages and disadvantages of Von Neumann architecture and Harvard architecture?

7. Executable and Linkable Format (ELF) is a standard used for Linux operating systems and many other embedded systems. Compile a C program in Linux into a binary executable and use the *readelf* command to display the information of a binary executable. Identify the data sections and instruction/data sections of a binary executable program.

8. Suppose a processor of the Harvard architecture has 4MB instruction memory and 32MB data memory. If the instruction memory and the data memory shares the same address bus, design a memory allocation scheme for this processor (*i.e.,* give an example address range for the instruction memory and the data memory).

9. Why can instruction memory and data memory share the same address bus in Cortex-M3, Cortex-M4, and Cortex-M7? In other words, why can we put the instruction memory and data memory in the same memory address space?

10. Cortex-M0+ is the most energy-efficient processor in the Cortex-M family. Suppose a Cortex-M0+ processor takes 100 μA in the active mode, and 48 μA in the sleep mode. If the application puts the processor 50% of the time in active mode and 50% in sleep mode, and two button cell batteries power the processor, with a total capacity of 600 mAh. How long can the batteries last? (Rule of thumb: Battery Life = Battery Capacity in mA per hour / Load Current in mA * 0.70)

11. A mov assembly instruction copies the value of the source register to the destination register. What is the value of the destination register r1 after the following instruction completes?

Memory Address	Assembly Instruction
...	...
0x08000166	MOV r1, pc
...	...

12. Suppose a pipeline processor has three stages, as shown in Figure 1-14. Assume in a perfect scenario (such as no branch instructions, no data dependence between instructions, and no memory I/O waiting).

   a) How many clock cycles does it take to execute 10 instructions? What is the throughput (measured in instructions per cycle)?
   b) How many clock cycles does it take to execute n instructions? If n is sufficiently large, what is the throughput in terms of instructions per cycle?

13. If two processors given below run the same binary program, which processor runs faster and how many times faster?

Processor	Clock Frequency
Non-pipeline Processor A	10 MHz
Three-stage Pipeline Processor B	28 MHz

Data Representation

Computers store data as a sequence of binary bits. This chapter focuses on digital representations of integers and text strings. Chapter 11 explains digital representations of real numbers.

2.1 Bit, Byte, Halfword, Word, and Double-word

A *bit* is the smallest quantity of information. Each bit has a value of either one or zero, and thus it is called a binary bit. However, it is more efficient for computers to load, process, store, and transmit a group of bits simultaneously. Therefore, bits are divided into a sequence of fixed-length logic units.

As shown in Figure 2-1, a byte is a group of 8 bits, a *halfword* consists of 16 bits (or 2 bytes), a *word* has 32 bits (or 4 bytes), and a *double-word* contains 64 bits (or 8 bytes). The most significant bit (MSB) and the least significant bit (LSB) of a byte are the bit at the leftmost and rightmost position, respectively. Usually, this is also true for halfword, word, and double-word. However, MSB and LSB may be located at some other positions in these units (See *big endian* and *little endian* in Chapter 5.2 for details).

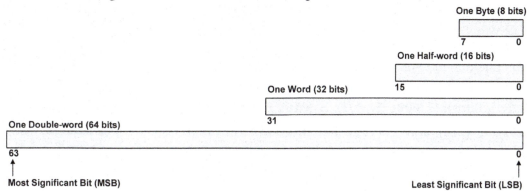

Figure 2-1. Number of bits in a byte, halfword, word, and double-word

The C standard specifies the minimum size of basic data types. The actual size of a variable relies on the implementation of C compilers. Table 2-1 gives the typical size of some data bytes. A pointer in a C program is a special variable that holds the memory address of a variable stored in memory. On 32-bit processors, a pointer has 32 bits. Each register in Cortex-M processors has 32 bits. Accordingly, a register can hold a pointer or all basic data types listed except double. A `double` variable takes two registers.

Basic data type of C language	Typical size in memory
char	1 byte
short	2 bytes or 1 halfword
signed/unsigned integer	4 bytes or 1 word
signed/unsigned long	4 bytes or 1 word
signed/unsigned long long	8 bytes or 1 double word
float	4 bytes or 1 word
double	8 bytes or 1 double word

Table 2-1. Size of C variables in memory

A byte is the smallest unit that can be transferred into or out of memory. Each byte in memory has a memory address. A halfword, word, and double-word span 2, 4, and 8 consecutive bytes in memory, respectively. By convention, if a variable takes multiple bytes in memory, the processor uses the lowest memory address of these bytes as the memory address of this variable. For example, if a C integer variable takes four bytes in memory (0x20000000 - 0x20000003), the memory address of this integer variable is 0x20000000. To modify a bit in memory, in general, a processor should load at least a byte from memory and then operate on the target bit. ARM Cortex-M processors provide a performance-enhancement technique called bit banding, which allows the processor to store directly or modify a bit (See Reference [17] for details).

History of Binary Representation

Modern binary systems were inspired from *"Yi Jing"* (also known as *Book of Changes*), one of the oldest classic texts dating back to 2852 - 2738 B.C. It used *Yin* (a broken line, --) and *Yang* (a solid line, —) to represent two contrast but complementary natural phenomena, such as heaven and earth, fire and water, and wind and thunder. It uses a set of eight special symbols (called trigrams): ☷ (000), ☶ (001), ☵ (010), ☴ (011), ☳ (100), ☲ (101), ☱ (110), and ☰ (111). Two trigrams from this set form a hexagram. Therefore, there are 64 possible hexagrams, forming sophisticated tools in analyzing and predicting patterns applicable to all human affairs.

Figure 2-2. Yin Yang Ba Gua.
Courtesy: Image from
wikipedia.org

2.2 Binary, Octal, Decimal, and Hexadecimal Numbers

We can represent an integer with different base values. Four commonly used bases are binary (base 2), octal (base 8), decimal (base 10), and hexadecimal (base 16). In general, an n-digit integer N in the base b has the following form:

$$a_{n-1}a_{n-2}a_{n-3}\cdots a_1 a_0$$

We can calculate its equivalent decimal value N as follows:

$$N = a_{n-1}{\times}b^{n-1} + a_{n-2}{\times}b^{n-2} + a_{n-3}{\times}b^{n-3} + \cdots + a_1{\times}b + a_0$$

For example, in the decimal system (base 10), the number 2014_{10} means

$$2014_{10} = 2{\times}10^3 + 0{\times}10^2 + 1{\times}10^1 + 4$$

Similarly, in the octal system (base 8), the number 1375_8 represents

$$1375_8 = 1{\times}8^3 + 3{\times}8^2 + 7{\times}8^1 + 5 = 765_{10}$$

Table 2-2 shows the conversion of a decimal number between 0 and 15 to its equivalent in decimal, binary, octal, and hexadecimal (hex for short). Because binary numbers are verbose, programmers often use hex numbers in programs.

We can convert a binary number to its hex equivalent by separating binary bits into groups of four and then using Table 2-2 to replace each group of four binary digits with its equivalent hex digit.

Decimal	Binary	Octal	Hexadecimal
0	0000	00	0x0
1	0001	01	0x1
2	0010	02	0x2
3	0011	03	0x3
4	0100	04	0x4
5	0101	05	0x5
6	0110	06	0x6
7	0111	07	0x7
8	1000	010	0x8
9	1001	011	0x9
10	1010	012	0xA
11	1011	013	0xB
12	1100	014	0xC
13	1101	015	0xD
14	1110	016	0xE
15	1111	017	0xF

Table 2-2. Conversion between decimal, binary, octal, and hexadecimal

In C, a prefix "**0**" represents octal, and a prefix "**0x**" or "**0X**" represents hexadecimal. The following gives examples of defining constant numbers in C. Most C compilers do not support directly declaring a binary number. This book uses "**0b**" to represent binary.

```
int k;
k = 0xA;      // hex constant, k = 10 in decimal
k = 0XA;      // 0X is the same as 0x
k = -0xA;     // hex constant, k = -10 in decimal
k = 012;      // octal constant, k = 10 in decimal
k = 0b1010;   // binary constant. Most compilers do not support it.
```

2.3 Unsigned Integers

How many unique symbols can n binary bits represent? Because each bit has two possible values, either one or zero, n bits can represent a total of 2^n different symbols. For example, with 5 bits, we can have 2^5 (*i.e.*, 32) symbols, including **0b00000**, **0b00001**, **0b00010**, ..., and **0b11111**. To use these symbols to represent numbers, we need to establish a mapping between each symbol and the number it represents.

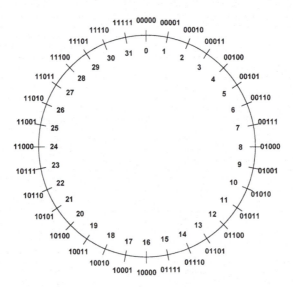

Figure 2-3. Representing unsigned numbers in a five-bit system

Let us first look at unsigned numbers. Since each unsigned number can be represented in binary, it is natural for computers to store them using their binary representation directly. Figure 2-3 shows the mapping between unsigned numbers and all binary symbols in a five-bit system. If a n-bit string represents an unsigned number, the representable range is $[0, 2^n - 1]$, including zero and $2^n - 1$ positive integers.

Converting a binary number to an unsigned integer

Since binary numbers have a base of 2, the conversion from binary to unsigned decimal is the same as the one presented in Chapter 2.2. The equivalent unsigned decimal integer of a binary number is the sum of the product of each binary digit and the power of 2 this binary bit represents. The exponent of each power is incremented by 1 for each binary digit, starting from the rightmost digit. For example, the binary value 0b1011 represents:

$$1011_2 = 1\times2^3 + 0\times2^2 + 1\times2^1 + 1\times2^0$$
$$= 8 + 2 + 1$$
$$= 11$$

Converting an unsigned integer to a binary number

We can convert an unsigned decimal to its binary equivalent by repeatedly dividing the decimal number by 2 until the quotient becomes zero. The binary equivalent is the combination of all remainders, with the first remainder as the least-significant bit (LSB). For example, the binary of 52 and 32 are 0b110100 and 0b100000 respectively, as shown below.

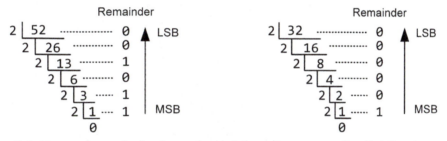

Figure 2-4. Converting a decimal number to binary by repeatedly dividing it by 2. Read the binary from the bottom to the top (52_{10} = 110100_2, and 32_{10} = 100000_2).

2.4 Signed Integers

There are different ways to map binary symbols to signed integer numbers. Examples include sign-and-magnitude, one's complement, and two's complement. One common characteristic of these numeral systems is that the most significant bit (also called the rightmost bit) indicates the sign of the number. The most significant bit is also known as the sign bit. The number is non-negative if the sign bit is zero and negative if it is one.

Table 2-3 shows three different approaches to mapping 4-bit binary symbols to different signed integers. These mapping schemes are sign-and-magnitude, one's complement, and two's complement. While we present these three different representations for signed numbers in detail later, the following gives a summary.

- *Sign-and-magnitude* uses the most significant bit to represent the sign, and the rest of the bits to represent the magnitude.
- *One's complement* denotes a negative number by inverting every bit of its positive equivalent.
- *Two's complement* represents a negative number by adding one to the equivalent one's complement.

Binary Bit String	Sign-and-Magnitude	One's Complement	Two's Complement
0000	+0	+0	0
0001	1	1	1
0010	2	2	2
0011	3	3	3
0100	4	4	4
0101	5	5	5
0110	6	6	6
0111	7	7	7
1000	-0	-7	-8
1001	-1	-6	-7
1010	-2	-5	-6
1011	-3	-4	-5
1100	-4	-3	-4
1101	-5	-2	-3
1110	-6	-1	-2
1111	-7	-0	-1

Table 2-3. Decimal values represented by a four-bit binary string

Based on Table 2-3, we make the following summary, if the bit string has n bits. The range means the largest and the smallest values that these bit strings can represent.

	Sign-and-Magnitude	One's Complement	Two's Complement
Range	$[-2^{n-1}+1, 2^{n-1}-1]$	$[-2^{n-1}+1, 2^{n-1}-1]$	$[-2^{n-1}, 2^{n-1}-1]$
Zero	Two zeros (± 0)	Two zeros (± 0)	One zero
Unique Numbers	$2^n - 1$	$2^n - 1$	2^n

Table 2-4. Data range of three different representation methods

In C, the range that a signed integer variable can represent depends on its data type. An integer variable of "signed char," "signed short," "signed int," and "signed long long" has at least 8, 16, 32, and 64 bits in size, respectively. The C standard only specifies the minimum size of integer types, and their actual size varies by implementation.

Two's complement is the one used in almost all modern computers to represent signed integers because it simplifies the hardware design from two aspects:

(1) the hardware for two's complement subtraction is the same as two's complement addition, and

(2) the hardware implementation for addition, subtraction, and multiplication of signed numbers are identical to those for unsigned numbers.

2.4.1   Sign-and-Magnitude

The sign-and-magnitude is a straightforward way to represent signed integers. It uses the most significant bit to indicate the sign, with one being negative and zero being positive. The remaining n-1 bits represent the value.

Sign-and-Magnitude

$$value = (-1)^{sign} \times Magnitude$$

For example, in a five-bit system shown in Figure 2-5, 0b10111 is -7, and 0b00111 is 7.

There are two ways to represent zero: 0b00000 for +0 and 0b10000 for -0.

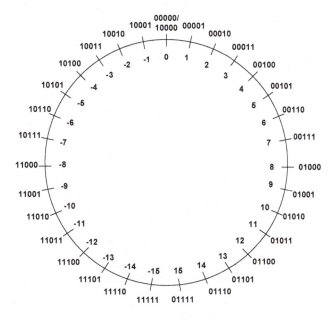

Figure 2-5. Sign-and-magnitude representation in a five-bit system

Many computer systems do not use the sign-and-magnitude due to two shortcomings.

- First, it is difficult for the hardware to perform addition or subtraction because hardware should consider the sign of both operands. If we add two numbers in a straightforward way, such as `00011` (3) + `11011` (-3), we get a wrong answer, `11110` (-14).

- Second, there are two representations of zero: positive zero and negative zero. A system with two zeros complicates the circuit for checking for equality.

2.4.2 One's Complement

The one's complement representation of a negative number (denoted as ã) is bitwise NOT of its positive counterpart (denoted as α). For example, in a five-bit system, the one's complement of -1 is `0b11110` (see Figure 2-6). Arithmetically, we have:

$$\tilde{\alpha} = 2^n - 1 - \alpha.$$

> **One's Complement ($\tilde{\alpha}$):**
>
> $$\alpha + \tilde{\alpha} = 2^n - 1$$

The word "complement" means that two counterparts complete the whole. Specifically, the one's complement ã and its counterpart α add to 2^n-1. For example, adding `0b00001` (+1) and `0b11110` (-1) leads to `0b11111`, which is in fact negative zero.

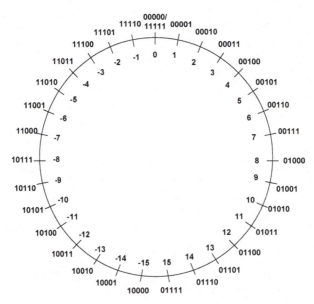

Figure 2-6. One's complement representation in a five-bit system

A simple way to find the one's complement ã is to toggle every bit in its counterpart α. In C, the bitwise NOT operator (~) is also called the one's complement operator.

```
y = ~y;    // Take one's complement in a C program
```

Earlier processors, such as CDC Cyber 18 developed in the 1980s, use one's complement. However, modern computer systems rarely use it.

2.4.3 Two's Complement

The two's complement (TC) representation of a negative number ($\tilde{\alpha}$) is bitwise NOT of its positive counterpart (α) plus one.

The opposite is also true. If we take bitwise NOT of a negative number and then add 1 to the result, we obtain the two's complement representation of its positive counterpart.

> *Two's Complement*
>
> $\alpha + \bar{\alpha} = 2^n$

We say $\bar{\alpha}$ and α are a complement to each other with respect to 2^n. Mathematically, we have

$$\bar{\alpha} = \tilde{\alpha} + 1 = 2^n - \alpha.$$

Figure 2-7 shows a five-bit system in two's complement form. For an n-bit system, the representable range is $[-2^{n-1}, 2^{n-1} - 1]$. There is only one representation for zero.

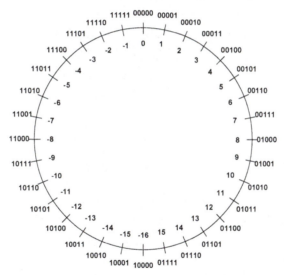

Figure 2-7. Two's complement representation in a five-bit system

The following clarifies two confusing terms:

- *Convert x to two's complement*: Find the two's complement representation of x without changing its value.
- *Calculate or take two's complement of x*: Compute the negative of x.

For example, the following C program calculates two's complement of x.

```
y = ~x;     // Toggle every bit
y += 1;     // Obtain two's complement
```

The following gives two examples of calculating two's complement.

Example 1. Calculate the two's complement of 0b00011.

	Binary	Decimal
Original number	0b00011	3
Step 1: Invert every bit	0b11100	
Step 2: Add 1	+ 0b00001	
Two's complement	0b11101	-3

Example 2. Calculate the two's complement of 0b11101.

	Binary	Decimal
Original number	0b11101	-3
Step 1: Invert every bit	0b00010	
Step 2: Add 1	+ 0b00001	
Two's complement	0b00011	3

2.4.4 Carry Flag for Unsigned Addition or Subtraction

Cortex-M processors maintain the application program status register (APSR). It holds important flags such as a carry flag (C), an overflow flag (V), a zero flag (Z), a negative flag (N), and a saturation flag (Q). Chapter 4.1 gives detailed information on these flags.

Processors rely on these flags to evaluate whether any abnormal phenomenon occurs at runtime. For example, when two unsigned numbers are added, the carry flag indicates whether the sum is too large to fit into a 32-bit register.

Moreover, processors rely on these flags to implement branch instructions. In Example 2-1, the compiler translates the *if-else* statement into conditional branch instructions, which check the flag bits to decide whether the processor should execute "$c = a - b$" or "$c = b - a$" (see Chapter 6.1).

```
if ( a > b ) {
    c = a - b;
} else {
    c = b - a;
}
```

Example 2-1. Depending on whether variables *a* and *b* are signed or unsigned, the compiler uses different assembly instructions to implement the *if-else* statement.

The following focuses only on how a processor sets up the carry flag and the overflow flag when adding and subtracting integers. The carry flag is for operations on unsigned integers, and the overflow flag is for operations on signed integers.

Let us first review simple addition and subtraction of two integers with only one bit. The carry/borrow flag is set as shown in Table 2-5.

Addition	Subtraction
0 + 0 = 0, Carry = 0	0 - 0 = 0, Borrow = 0
1 + 0 = 1, Carry = 0	1 - 0 = 1, Borrow = 0
0 + 1 = 1, Carry = 0	0 - 1 = 1, Borrow = 1
1 + 1 = 0, Carry = 1	1 - 1 = 0, Borrow = 0

Table 2-5. Settings of carry and borrow on 1-bit binary addition and subtraction. Cortex-M processors use the same bit in the APSR register to store the carry and the borrow flag.

In an n-bit system, a carry or borrow occurs under the following scenarios.

- When two unsigned integers are added, a carry event takes place if the result is larger than the maximum representable unsigned integer (*i.e.*, $2^n - 1$).

- When two unsigned integers are subtracted, a borrow event occurs if the result is negative, smaller than the smallest expressible unsigned integer (*i.e.*, 0).

While addition can modify the carry flag, subtraction can change the borrow flag. However, on ARM Cortex-M processors, the carry flag and the borrow flag are physically the same flag bit in the *application program status register* (APSR). Thus, the borrow flag is in fact called the carry flag.

> *For unsigned subtraction,*
> *Carry = NOT Borrow*

On Cortex-M, the carry flag is set as follows:

- When adding two unsigned integers, the processor sets the carry flag if a carry occurs, *i.e.*, the sum is too large ($\geq 2^{32}$, *i.e.*, 4,294,967,296) to be stored in a 32-bit register). Otherwise, the carry flag is cleared.

- When subtracting two unsigned integers, the processor sets the carry flag if no borrow occurs, implying the difference is positive or zero. Otherwise, the carry bit is cleared.

Figure 2-8 and Figure 2-9 show two examples of finding the value of the carry flag. We can obtain the result of addition and subtraction by traversing the number circle clockwise and counter-clockwise, respectively.

The carry flag follows this rule:

> *If the traversal crosses the boundary between 0 and $2^n - 1$, the carry flag is set on addition and is cleared on subtraction.*

Example: 28 + 6

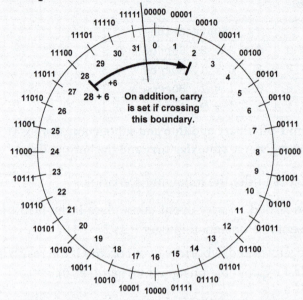

Figure 2-8. Carry flag is set if the result of the unsigned addition is larger than $2^5 - 1$.

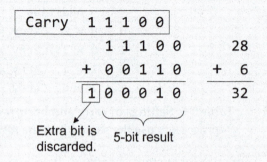

- Carry flag = 1, indicating carry has occurred on unsigned addition.
- The carry flag is 1 because the result crosses the boundary between 32 and 0.

Example: 3 – 5

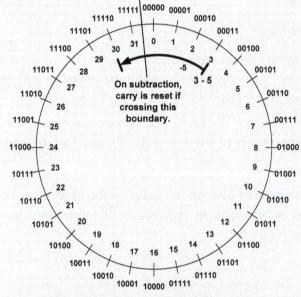

Figure 2-9. Carry flag is cleared if the result of the unsigned subtraction should be negative.

```
Borrow  1 1 1 0 0
          0 0 0 1 1      3
        - 0 0 1 0 1    - 5
          1 1 1 1 0     30
```

5-bit result

- Carry flag = 0, indicating borrow has occurred on unsigned subtraction.
- For subtraction, carry = NOT borrow.

2.4.5 Overflow Flag for Signed Addition or Subtraction

While the carry flag is for unsigned arithmetic operations, the overflow flag is for signed arithmetic operations. Overflow occurs when the result produced by an arithmetic operation falls outside the representable range $[-2^{n-1}, 2^{n-1} - 1]$ of two's complement.

When adding signed numbers, overflow occurs only in two scenarios:

- Adding two positive numbers produces a non-positive result, or
- Adding two negative numbers yields a non-negative result.

Similarly, when subtracting signed numbers, overflow occurs in two scenarios:

- Subtracting a positive number from a negative one creates a positive result, or
- Subtracting a negative number from a positive one makes a negative result.

Overflow cannot occur when operands with different signs are added or when operands with the same sign are subtracted. Checking sign bits can detect overflow on addition. Overflow occurs on addition if the signs of the operands are the same, but the sum has a sign different with the operands.

We can also use the number circle to illustrate the concept. On the number circle, if the boundary between -2^{n-1} and $2^{n-1} - 1$ is crossed on addition, the overflow flag is set, as shown in Figure 2-10 and Figure 2-11.

Example: 12 + 5

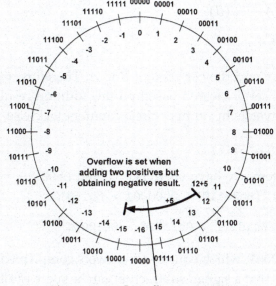

$$
\begin{array}{r}
0\ 1\ 1\ 0\ 0 \\
+\ 0\ 0\ 1\ 0\ 1 \\
\hline
1\ 0\ 0\ 0\ 1
\end{array}
\qquad
\begin{array}{r}
12 \\
+\ 5 \\
\hline
-15
\end{array}
$$

5-bit result

- On addition, overflow occurs if $sum \geq 2^4$ when adding two positives.
- On addition, overflow never occurs when adding two numbers with different signs.

Figure 2-10. Overflow example

Example: (−13) + (−7)

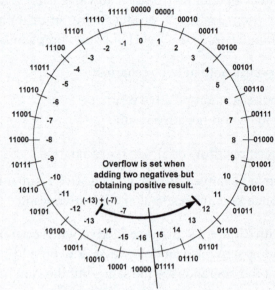

$$10011 \qquad -13$$
$$+ \; 11001 \qquad + \; -7$$
$$\boxed{1}\,01100 \qquad 12$$

Extra bit is discarded.   5-bit result

On addition, overflow happens if $sum < -2^4$ when adding two negatives.

Figure 2-11. Overflow example

In two's complement arithmetic, the problem of detecting overflow on subtraction can be converted to the issue of detecting overflow of addition. We can transform a subtraction operation into an addition operation. Algebraically, we have

$$A - B = A + (-B)$$
$$= A + TC(B)$$

where *TC(B)* takes the two's complement of *B*.

Thus, instead of performing subtraction, we add the negation of *B* to *A*. Therefore, the overflow flag of the original subtraction is set or cleared based on the addition result. When adding a negative integer, we can traverse the number circle counter-clockwise.

Subtraction example: 0b10111 - 0b00110 (*i.e.*, -9-6)

In a five-bit two's complement system, we have 0b10111 = -9 and 0b00110 = 6. The two's complement of -6 is *invert*(0b00110) + 0b00001 = 0b11010.

$$-9 - 6 = -9 + (-6) = 0b10111 + 0b11010 = 0b10001$$

The hardware adder produces 0b10001, which equals -15 in two's complement, as shown in Figure 2-12. This shows that a signed subtraction can be successfully converted to a signed addition by taking the two's complement of the second source operand. When adding `0b10111` and `0b11010`, no overflow has occurred. Therefore, the overflow flag for the signed subtraction `0b10111` - `0b00110` is 0.

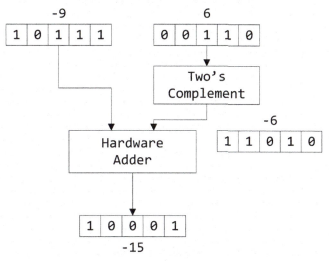

Subtracting two numbers

Figure 2-12. Signed subtraction can be converted to signed addition. No overflow occurs on the addition in this example. Therefore, the overflow flag of the signed subtraction is 0.

Below is another method to detect overflow on signed addition.

> *Overflow occurs on signed addition, if the carry into the sign bit differs from the carry out of the sign bit. Otherwise, there is no overflow.*

Example: 12 + 5

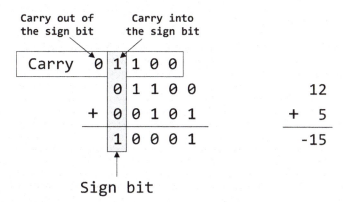

Figure 2-13. When adding 12 and 5, the carry into the sign bit is 1, but the carry out of the sign bit is 0. Thus, an overflow has occurred.

Example: (− 13) + (− 7)

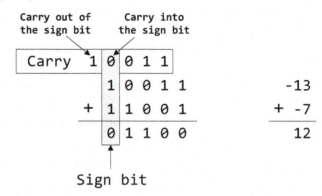

Figure 2-14. When adding -13 and -7, the carry into the sign bit is 0,
but the carry out of the sign bit is 1. Thus, an overflow has occurred.

2.4.5.1   Interpreting the Carry and Overflow Flags

Suppose in a five-bit system, the binary values of two variables are set as follows:

$$a = 0b10000$$
$$b = 0b10000$$

When adding these two numbers in an assembly program, should these two binary values represent signed or unsigned integers?

> *Is 0xFFFFFFFF a signed or unsigned number?*
>
> *You and compilers know the answer. But the processor does not know it at runtime.*

- If a and b are unsigned integers, we have:
  $a = 16$,
  $b = 16$, and
  $a + b = 32 > 2^5 - 1$.

  Thus, carry has occurred if a and b are unsigned integers.

- If a and b are signed integers, we have:
  $a = -16$,
  $b = -16$, and
  $a + b = -32 < -2^4$.

  Thus, overflow has occurred if a and b are signed integers.

Should the processor set up the carry flag or the overflow flag when a and b are added?

In fact, when adding these two numbers in an assembly program, the processor does not know whether a and b are signed or unsigned integers. Thus, the processor simply sets both the overflow flag and the carry flag. It is the assembly programmer's responsibility to interpret the flag results.

> *A processor modifies both the carry flag and the overflow flag.*

Assembly programs should appropriately choose to check either the overflow flag or the carry flag in assembly instructions, depending on the software's intention of using them as signed or unsigned integers. For example, to evaluate the logical expression $a + b > 10$, we should use different assembly instructions to check either the carry or overflow flag depending on whether a and b are unsigned or signed integers (see Chapter 6.1).

	Carry Flag	Overflow Flag
Objective	For unsigned arithmetic, assuming a, b, and c are all unsigned numbers	For signed arithmetic, assuming two's complement is used to represent a, b and c
Addition $c = a + b$	**Method 1**: Carry = 1 if true result > 2^n-1. **Method 2**: Both a and b are unsigned. Carry is set if $c < a$ or $c < b$.	**Method 1**: Overflow = 1 if true result > $2^{n-1}-1$ or true result < -2^{n-1}. **Method 2**: Overflow = 1 if • $a > 0$ and $b > 0$ but $c < 0$ • $a < 0$ and $b < 0$ but $c > 0$
Subtraction $c = a - b$	Carry = Not Borrow. Carry is set if $a \geq b$. (meaning no borrow)	**Method 1**: Subtraction is transformed into addition. Overflow is set based on addition. **Method 2**: Overflow = 1 if • $a > 0$ and $b < 0$ but $c < 0$ • $a < 0$ and $b > 0$ but $c > 0$
Correctness	If the carry is 1 on unsigned addition, the result is incorrect; otherwise, it is correct. If the carry is 1 on unsigned subtraction, the result is correct; otherwise, it is wrong.	Overflow flag has the same meaning for signed addition and signed subtraction. If the overflow is 1, the result is incorrect.
Shift operations	Shift operations can change the carry flag.	Shift operations cannot modify the overflow flag.

Table 2-6. Summary of the carry flag and the overflow flag

When interpreting the carry flag and overflow flag, one must be careful because they have different meanings for different operations. If the carry flag is set, it means the result is incorrect for addition, but correct for subtraction. If the overflow is set, it means the result is wrong for both addition and subtraction. Table 2-6 summarizes the carry flag and the overflow flag for unsigned and signed addition/subtraction.

In C, variables *a* and *b* are declared explicitly either signed or unsigned by the programmer, such as "unsigned int a" or "int a," and thus the corresponding assembly program translated from the C program can correctly choose either the carry flag or the overflow flag to interpret the result.

Example: Translating the C statement "if (a > b)" into assembly

An *if*-statement in C is translated into a set of assembly instructions involving comparison and conditional branch. When translating "if (a > b)," C compilers must choose appropriate branch instructions by considering whether the logic expression compares two signed numbers or two unsigned numbers. When performing the comparison, the processor does not know whether they are signed or unsigned. Therefore, the processor hardware will write a value to the carry flag by assuming they are unsigned and simultaneously write a value to the overflow flag by assuming they are signed numbers. The software should choose the appropriate instructions to evaluate the carry flag or the overflow flag, based on the following rules. (Chapter 6.2 gives a detailed explanation.)

- If variables *a* and *b* are declared as *unsigned* in C, the compiler appends the HI condition suffix to the branch instruction (*i.e.*, BHI), which checks the carry flag.
- If *a* and *b* are declared as *signed*, the compiler appends the GT suffix to the branch instruction (*i.e.*, BGT), which checks the overflow flag.

Although an *if*-statement is correctly translated to assembly instructions, most C compilers ignore the occurrence of the overflow and carry when an integer result falling out of the representable range is stored during data operations. In Example 2-2, the leading bytes of the variable *i* are truncated, but the compiler might not generate any error message to abort compiling. This often leads to an unexpected or erroneous result. Failing to consider overflow and carry is a software bug often made by programmers.

```
signed int i = 0x89ABCDEF; // 32-bit signed integer
signed short s = i;        // overflow, s = 0xCDEF, variable i is truncated
signed char c = i;         // overflow, c = 0xEF, variable i is truncated
...
```

Example 2-2. Overflow and carry are ignored in C.

2.4.5.2   Two's Complement Simplifies Hardware Implementation

Two's complement simplifies the logic implementation of arithmetic functions. Binary data to be processed may be signed or unsigned integers. If two's complement is used to represent signed numbers, the hardware implementation becomes simple. The hardware does not need to worry about whether these operands are signed or unsigned, performs the same addition, subtraction, or multiplication operation, and still obtains the correct result.

Two's complement addition

The hardware adder designed for adding two unsigned numbers also works correctly for adding two signed numbers. For example, if two binary numbers, 0b10111 and 0b00110, are added in a five-bit system, the hardware adder performs a simple addition by treating them as unsigned numbers, such as the ones shown in Figure 2-15. We obtain the sum as 0b11101.

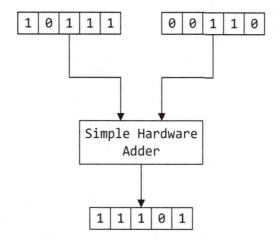

Figure 2-15. A simple adder works for both unsigned addition and signed addition.

In fact, the binary number 0b11101 equals 29 if it is an unsigned number, and -3 if it represents a signed number in two's complement. This implies that a simple adder, which does not distinguish the sign of its operands, can obtain the correct result. Therefore, the same hardware adder works correctly for both signed addition and unsigned addition.

```
  Simple Addition    Unsigned    Signed
  (ignore the sign)  Addition   Addition
      1 0 1 1 1          23         -9        addend
   +  0 0 1 1 0       +   6      +   6      + addend
      1 1 1 0 1          29         -3          sum
```

Proposition 1. Suppose X and Y are two unsigned integers that two n-bit strings represent, and x and y are two signed integers that these bit strings represent in two's complement. Prove the following:

$$X + Y = x + y \quad (\text{modulo } 2^n).$$

Proof. We give the proof in four cases.
1. If $x \geq 0$ and $y \geq 0$, apparently $X + Y = x + y$ (modulo 2^n);
2. If $x < 0$ and $y \geq 0$, then $X + Y = (2^n + x) + y = x + y$ (modulo 2^n);
3. If $x \geq 0$ and $y < 0$, apparently $X + Y = x + (y + 2^n) = x + y$ (modulo 2^n);
4. If $x < 0$ and $y < 0$, apparently $X + Y = (x + 2^n) + (y + 2^n) = x + y$ (modulo 2^n);

Two's complement subtraction

The same subtraction hardware works correctly for both signed subtraction and unsigned subtraction. For example, when we subtract 0b00110 from 0b10111, in a five-bit system, we obtain 0b10001, as shown in Figure 2-16.

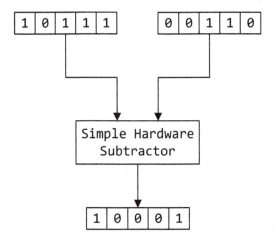

Figure 2-16. A simple subtractor works for both unsigned subtraction and signed subtraction.

The binary result 0b10001 represents 17 if it is unsigned and -15 if it is signed in two's complement. As illustrated below, the simple subtraction hardware can successfully achieve the correct result, no matter whether the operands are signed or unsigned.

```
Simple Subtraction      Unsigned        Signed
 (ignore the sign)    Subtraction    Subtraction
    1  0  1  1  1            23            -9          minuend
 -  0  0  1  1  0         -   6         -   6        - subtrahend
 ─────────────────       ──────        ──────
    1  0  0  0  1            17           -15          difference
```

Proposition 2. Suppose X and Y are two unsigned integers that two n-bit strings represent, and x and y are two signed integers that these bit strings represent in two's complement. Prove the following:

$$X - Y = x - y \quad \text{(modulo } 2^n\text{)}.$$

Proof. We give the proof in four cases.
1. If $x \geq 0$ and $y \geq 0$, apparently $X - Y = x - y$ (modulo 2^n);
2. If $x < 0$ and $y \geq 0$, then $X - Y = (2^n + x) - y = x - y$ (modulo 2^n);
3. If $x \geq 0$ and $y < 0$, apparently $X + Y = x - (y + 2^n) = x - y$ (modulo 2^n);
4. If $x < 0$ and $y < 0$, apparently $X + Y = (x + 2^n) - (y + 2^n) = x - y$ (modulo 2^n);

Two's complement multiplication

If the product is required to keep the same number of bits as operands, unsigned multiplication hardware works correctly for signed numbers. Given two binary numbers: 0b00011 and 0b11101, the hardware performs a simple multiplication, as shown follows. Since the product must be five bits, the product obtained is 0b10111, with extra leading bits truncated.

- If both operands are signed, then in two's complement we have two operands as 0b00011 = 3, 0b11101 = -3, and the result as 0b10111 = -9.

- On the other hand, if both operands are unsigned, then we have two operands 0b00011 = 3 and 0b11101 = 29, and the result 0b10111 = 23. While the result is incorrect, it does not mean the hardware has failed. It is only because the result is too large and cannot be fully expressed with 5 bits. To avoid this issue, software should use a more complex multiplication instruction to multiply two large numbers, as discussed in Chapter 4.4 (Refer to UMULL and SMULL instructions).

```
              0  0  0  1  1             multiplicand
         × 1  1  1  0  1          ×     multiplier
              0  0  0  1  1
           0  0  0  0  0
        0  0  0  1  1
     0  0  0  1  1
  0  0  0  1  1
  0  0  1  0  1  0  1  1  1             product
```

On many processors, multiplication instructions do not affect the carry and overflow flags. On ARM Cortex-M, a multiplication instruction leaves the carry flag undefined and the overflow flag unchanged.

Proposition 3. Suppose X and Y are two unsigned integers that two n-bit strings represent, and x and y are two signed integers that these bit strings represent in two's complement. Prove the following:

$$X \bullet Y = x \bullet y \quad (\text{modulo } 2^n).$$

Proof. There are only four possible cases.

1. If $x \geq 0$ and $y \geq 0$, apparently $X \bullet Y = x \bullet y \quad (\text{modulo } 2^n)$;
2. If $x < 0$ and $y \geq 0$, then $X \bullet Y = (2^n + x) \bullet y = 2^n \bullet y + x \bullet y = x \bullet y \quad (\text{modulo } 2^n)$;
3. If $x \geq 0$ and $y < 0$, apparently $X \bullet Y = x \bullet (y + 2^n) = x \bullet y + 2^n \bullet x = x \bullet y \quad (\text{modulo } 2^n)$;
4. If $x < 0$ and $y < 0$, apparently $X + Y = (x + 2^n) \bullet (y + 2^n) = x \bullet y + 2^n \bullet x + 2^n \bullet y + 2^{n+1} = x \bullet y \quad (\text{modulo } 2^n)$;

Two's complement division

However, signed and unsigned division cannot directly share the same division hardware. For example, we divide -10 (`0b10110` in two's complement) by 2 (`0b00010` in two's complement) by using a traditional division technique, the quotient obtained is 11 (`0b01011` in two's complement). Apparently, the conventional division for unsigned integers does not work for signed integers.

```
                       0  1  0  1  1      quotient
        divisor   1  0 |1  0  1  1  0      dividend
                       1  0
                       ─────
                          0  1
                          0  0
                          ─────
                             1  1
                             1  0
                             ─────
                                1  0
                                1  0
                                ─────
                                   0      remainder
```

Signed division is harder than unsigned division. A general method of signed division is first to convert both signed numbers to positive numbers, then execute unsigned division, and finally change the result into signed form.

Therefore, there are two 32-bit integer division instructions in Cortex-M processors. The SDIV instruction is signed division, and the UDIV instruction is unsigned division (see Chapter 4.4).

Summary of two's complement arithmetic operations

Two's complement can simplify the hardware design. The same addition, subtraction, and multiplication hardware work for both signed and unsigned integers.

1. When adding or subtracting two integers, the hardware does not know whether they are signed or unsigned. Accordingly, the hardware will set up both the overflow and carry flags.
   a. The hardware assumes both operands are unsigned and sets the carry flag to the appropriate value.
   b. At the same time, the hardware also assumes both operands are signed and sets up the overflow flag.

2. It is the software's responsibility to decide whether to use either the carry flag or overflow flag in the assembly code. Whether the carry flag or the overflow flag should be utilized depends on the programmer's intention.
   a. If the programmer intends to use the binary value stored in a register as an unsigned integer, then the carry flag should be used.
   b. If the programmer intends to use it as a signed integer, then the overflow flag should be used.
   c. When programming in high-level languages such as C, the compiler automatically chooses to use the carry or overflow flag based on how this integer is declared in the source code ("int" or "unsigned int").

3. The same multiplication hardware works for both signed and unsigned multiplication if the product obtained has the same length as the operands.

4. The same division hardware cannot function correctly for both signed division and unsigned division.

2.5 Character String

The American Standard Code for Information Interchange (ASCII) defines the 7-bit encoding standard for 128 characters, including 33 control characters (0x00-0x19, plus 0x7F) and 95 printable characters (0x20-0x7E). The ASCII value 0x20 represents the space character, which is a printable character. The first ASCII was published in 1963, and many of these control characters have become obsolete. However, ASCII is still widely used for computers to store text documents and data, such as a C or assembly programs.

A string consists of an array of ASCII characters determined by the NULL character. NULL is a reserved character used to signify the termination of a string. Note that NULL differs from 0. ASCII of ZERO is 0x30 while ASCII of NULL character is 0x00.

Dec	Hex	Char	Dec	Hex	Char	Dec	Hex	Char	Dec	Hex	Char
0	00	NUL	32	20	SP	64	40	@	96	60	`
1	01	SOH	33	21	!	65	41	A	97	61	a
2	02	STX	34	22	"	66	42	B	98	62	b
3	03	ETX	35	23	#	67	43	C	99	63	c
4	04	EOT	36	24	$	68	44	D	100	64	d
5	05	ENQ	37	25	%	69	45	E	101	65	e
6	06	ACK	38	26	&	70	46	F	102	66	f
7	07	BEL	39	27	'	71	47	G	103	67	g
8	08	BS	40	28	(	72	48	H	104	68	h
9	09	HT	41	29	)	73	49	I	105	69	i
10	0A	LF	42	2A	*	74	4A	J	106	6A	j
11	0B	VT	43	2B	+	75	4B	K	107	6B	k
12	0C	FF	44	2C	,	76	4C	L	108	6C	l
13	0D	CR	45	2D	-	77	4D	M	109	6D	m
14	0E	SO	46	2E	.	78	4E	N	110	6E	n
15	0F	SI	47	2F	/	79	4F	O	111	6F	o
16	10	DLE	48	30	0	80	50	P	112	70	p
17	11	DC1	49	31	1	81	51	Q	113	71	q
18	12	DC2	50	32	2	82	52	R	114	72	r
19	13	DC3	51	33	3	83	53	S	115	73	s
20	14	DC4	52	34	4	84	54	T	116	74	t
21	15	NAK	53	35	5	85	55	U	117	75	u
22	16	SYN	54	36	6	86	56	V	118	76	v
23	17	ETB	55	37	7	87	57	W	119	77	w
24	18	CAN	56	38	8	88	58	X	120	78	x
25	19	EM	57	39	9	89	59	Y	121	79	y
26	1A	SUB	58	3A	:	90	5A	Z	122	7A	z
27	1B	ESC	59	3B	;	91	5B	[	123	7B	{
28	1C	FS	60	3C	<	92	5C	\	124	7C	|
29	1D	GS	61	3D	=	93	5D	]	125	7D	}
30	1E	RS	62	3E	>	94	5E	^	126	7E	~
31	1F	US	63	3F	?	95	5F	_	127	7F	DEL

Table 2-7. ASCII table

When a C program declares a string, the compiler automatically adds a NULL terminator at the end of the string. Each character takes one byte in memory, and all characters are stored in consecutive memory addresses. The first character of the string is stored at the lowest memory address.

Example 2-3 shows the memory layout of a string "ARM Assembly." Because of the NULL terminator, the string size is 13.

Characters are compared based on their ASCII values. For example,

- 'B' > 'A' because ASCII of 'B' is 0x42 and ASCII of 'A' is 0x41.
- Similarly, 'z' > 'a' > 'Z' > 'A' > '9' > '1' > '0' > '!' > ' '.

	Memory Address	Memory Content	Letter
	str + 12 →	0x00	\0
	str + 11 →	0x79	y
	str + 10 →	0x6C	l
	str + 9 →	0x62	b
	str + 8 →	0x6D	m
	str + 7 →	0x65	e
	str + 6 →	0x73	s
	str + 5 →	0x73	s
	str + 4 →	0x41	A
	str + 3 →	0x20	space
	str + 2 →	0x4D	M
	str + 1 →	0x52	R
	str →	0x41	A

```c
char str[13] = "ARM Assembly";

// The array should have at least 13
// bytes even though the string has
// only 12 letters. The NULL
// terminator takes one byte.
//
// strlen() returns the length
// excluding the NULL terminator
//
// sizeof() returns the length
// including the NULL terminator
```

Example 2-3. All strings are null-terminated. While "ARM Assembly" has 12 characters, the string str should be declared with a length of 13 characters to include NULL.

Strings are compared in alphabetical order by following three steps.

1. If two strings are of different length, the shorter one is assumed to have one or more NULL (0x00) characters appended to make the length equal.

2. Then the strings are compared character by character starting with the first one.

3. When a character in one string is smaller than the corresponding one in the other string, the former string is then smaller than the latter one.

For example, we have the following string comparison results:

- "j" < "jar" < "jargon" < "jargonize"
- "CAT" < "Cat" < "DOG" < "Dog" < "cat" < "dog"
- "12" < "123" < "2" < "AB" < "Ab" < "ab" < "abc"

The following gives a few commonly used string functions in C.

isDigit tests for a decimal digit (0 through 9). If the given character is one of the 10 decimal digits, the function returns 1; otherwise, returns 0. The ASCII values of decimal digits are from 48 to 57, with 48 representing '0' and 57 representing '9'.

C Implementation	Simplified C Implementation

`int isDigit(char c){`
  `if(c >= '0' && c <= '9')`
    `return 1;`
  `return 0;`
`}`
	`int isDigit(char c){`
	  `return (c >= '0' && c <= '9');`
	  `// or: return (c >= 48 && c <= 57);`
	`}`

isLower exams for a lower-case character (a through z). The ASCII values of lower-case characters are between 97 and 122.

```
int isLower(char c){
    return(c >= 'a' && c <= 'z');       // or: return (c >= 97 && c <= 122);
}
```

isUpper checks for an upper-case character (A through Z). The ASCII values of upper-case characters are between 65 and 90.

```
int isUpper(char c){
    return(c >= 'A' && c <= 'Z');       // or: return (c >= 65 && c <= 90);
}
```

isWhitespace searches for a whitespace character, including space (ASCII 32), horizontal tab (ASCII 9), line feed (ASCII 10), and form feed (ASCII 12).

```
int isWhitespace(char c) {
    return(c == ' ' || c == '\t' || c == '\n' || c == '\12');
    // or: return(c == 32 || c == 9 || c == 10 || c == 12);
}
```

strlen finds the length of a string, excluding the null terminator. It checks all characters of a string array one by one. If the loop reaches the end of the string array, *pStr[i]* has a value of 0, making the while condition false and thus terminating the loop.

```
int strlen(char *pStr){
    int i = 0;
    while(pStr[i]){ i++; }  // loop until pStr[i] is NULL
    return i;
}
```

toUpper converts all alphabetic characters to lower case. The difference between the ASCII value of a lower-case character and its corresponding upper case is 32. Below are two different implementations, one based on dereferencing a pointer (*i.e.*, get the value stored at the pointer address), and the other based on a numeric index.

Pointer dereference operator *	Array subscript operator []

<pre>void toUpper(char *pStr){
  for(char *p = pStr; *p; ++p){
    if(*p >= 'a' && *p <= 'z')
      *p -= 'a' - 'A';
      //or: *p -= 32;
  }
}</pre>
	<pre>void toUpper(char *pStr){
	  char c = pStr[0];
	  for(int i = 0; c; i++, c = pStr[i];) {
	    if(c >= 'a' && c <= 'z')
	      pStr[i] -= 'a' - 'A';
	      // or: pStr[i] -= 32;
	  }
	}</pre>

toLower changes all alphabetic characters in a string to its upper case. Adding 32 to the ASCII value of a lower-case character converts it to its corresponding upper case. Like the toUpper function, the following provides two different implementations.

Pointer dereference operator *	Array subscript operator []
| ```
void toLower(char *pStr){
  for(char *p = pStr; *p; ++p) {
    if(*p >= 'A' && *p <= 'Z')
      *p += 'a' - 'A';
      // or: *p += 32;
  }
}
``` | ```
void toLower(char *pStr){
  int i;
  char c = pStr[0];
  for(i = 0; c; i++, c = pStr[i]) {
    if(c >= 'A' && c <= 'Z')
      pStr[i] += 'a' - 'A';
      // or: pStr[i] += 32;
  }
}
``` |

2.6 Exercises

1. For the six-bit binary values given below, find the equivalent decimal values when the data is interpreted as signed or unsigned integers, respectively.

   010000, 100001, 010111, 111000, 111001,
   001111, 101011, 110110, 101010, 100011

2. Complete the following arithmetic operations in two's complement representation. What are the value of the carry flag and the overflow flag? (Assume a six-bit system)

   a) $-7 + (-29)$
   b) $31 + 11$
   c) $15 - 19$
   d) $-7 \times (-3)$
   e) $-7 \times (3)$
   f) $21 \div 3$
   g) $21 \div (-3)$

3. To check for the signed greater or equal (GE) condition, we evaluate whether the negative flag is equal to the overflow flag. If they are equal, then GE condition is true. Explain the reasons why this works.

4. For Cortex-M, there are separate division instructions for signed integers and unsigned integers. Does the same division instruction work for both signed and unsigned integers? If yes, prove it. If not, show an example.

5. What are the overflow and carry flags in the following operations in a four-bit system?

	Carry	Overflow
1101 + 1100		
1101 - 1100		
1100 + 1010		
0100 - 0110		
0100 + 0010		
0100 + 0110		
1100 - 0110		

6. Given the following two 32-bit binary unsigned numbers A and B, find the logic expression of the carry flag when A and B are added. The result is R.

    $$A = a_{31}a_{30}a_{29} \cdots a_2 a_1 a_0$$

    $$B = b_{31}b_{30}b_{29} \cdots b_2 b_1 b_0$$

    $$R = r_{31}r_{30}r_{29} \cdots r_2 r_1 r_0$$

7. Find the logic expression of the carry flag when B is subtracted from A, where A and B have the same format as Question 6.

8. Suppose A and B are signed numbers, and they have the same format as Question 6, find the logic expression of the overflow flag when A and B are added.

9. Suppose A and B are signed numbers, and they have the same format as Question 6, find the logic expression of the overflow flag when B is subtracted from A.

10. If a string is stored at the memory address 0x20008000 and the string is "Cortex-M", show the memory content in hex format starting at 0x20008000. How many bytes does this string take in memory?

11. Write a C program that implements the standard function
    ```
    char * strrchr(const char *str, int c)
    ```
    that returns the memory address of the last instance of c in the string *str*. Return a NULL pointer if c is not found in the string.

12. Write a C program that implements the standard function
    ```
    char * strstr(char *str1, char *str2)
    ```
    that returns the memory address of the first instance of string *str2* in string *str1*. Return a NULL pointer if string *str2* is not found in string *str1*.

ARM Instruction Set Architecture

This chapter gives an overview of ARM assembly instructions and presents basic instruction formats.

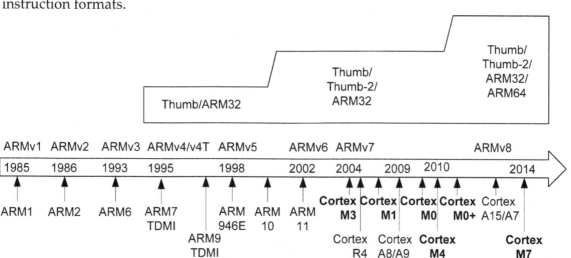

Figure 3-1. History of ARM architecture and instruction sets

3.1 ARM Assembly Instruction Sets

ARM processors support mainly four different assembly instruction sets: Thumb, Thumb-2, ARM32, and ARM64. Figure 3-1 shows their history.

- *Thumb*. The objective of the Thumb instruction set is to improve the code density. Because an instruction in Thumb has only 16 bits in length, the size of their executable files is small. The space saving is achieved by reducing the possibilities of operands and limiting the number of registers that are accessible by an instruction. Reducing the size of instruction memory benefits many embedded systems demanding for low cost and long battery life.

- *ARM32*. Each instruction in ARM32 has 32 bits and provides more coding flexibility than a Thumb instruction. More operand options, more flexible memory addressing schemes, larger immediate numbers, and more addressable registers can be encoded in a 32-bit word. Furthermore, ARM32 instructions run faster than Thumb because an instruction can perform more operations or include more operands. However, the disadvantage is its code density.

- *Thumb-2*. It provides an outstanding compromise between ARM32 and Thumb. It optimizes the tradeoff between code density and processor performance. It consists of 16-bit Thumb instructions and a subset of 32-bit ARM32 instructions. The goal of Thumb-2 is to achieve higher code density like Thumb and fast performance comparable to ARM32.

- *ARM64*. ARM 64-bit processors are often used in desktops and servers. These processors have a set of 64-bit assembly instructions.

One prominent ARM family is Cortex processors, which have three groups:

- *Cortex-M* series for microcontrollers (*M* stands for microcontroller),
- *Cortex-R* series for real-time embedded systems (*R* stands for real-time), and
- *Cortex-A* series for high-performance applications (*A* stands for application).

Cortex-A processors are specially designed based on the ARMv7-A or ARMv8-A architecture to provide fast performance for sophisticated devices, such as smartphones and tablets. They often support full-fledged operating systems such as Linux, iOS, and Android.

Cortex-R processors are designed for mission-critical real-time systems that require high reliability, fault-tolerance, and most importantly, deterministic real-time responsiveness. Example systems include factory automation and automobile engine control. In real-time systems, the correctness of computation is determined not only by the logical correctness but also by whether it is consistently completed within certain time constraints.

Cortex-M processors offer an excellent tradeoff between performance, cost, and energy efficiency. Therefore, they are suitable for a broad range of microcontroller applications, such as home appliances, robotics, industrial control, smart watch, and internet-of-things (IoT). In contrast to general-purpose processors in desktops, a microcontroller is a small processor with a processor core, memory, and many integrated I/O peripherals such as timers, analog-to-digital converter, serial communications, and LCD driver.

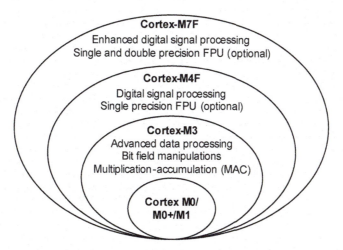

Figure 3-2. ARM Cortex-M family

The Cortex-M family includes Cortex-M0, Cortex-M0+, Cortex-M1, Cortex-M3, Cortex-M4, and Cortex-M7. The former three are Von Neumann architecture, and the latter three are Harvard architecture. Moreover, Cortex-M0/M0+/M1 are ARMv6-M, and Cortex-M3/M4/M7 are ARMv7-M.

Cortex-M processors are backward compatible, and Figure 3-2 compares the instructions supported by each processor group. For example, a binary program compiled for Cortex-M3 can run on Cortex-M4 without any modification.

The floating-point unit (FPU), which is a coprocessor for floating-point operations, is optional on Cortex-M4 and Cortex-M7. Cortex-M4 and M7 also provide single-instruction multiple-data (SIMD) and multiply-and-accumulate (MAC) instructions for digital signal processing applications (DSP).

This book focuses on the ARMv7-M architecture, including Cortex-M3, Cortex-M4, and Cortex-M7. ARMv7-M only supports the Thumb-2 instruction set and is not compatible with ARM32. Conventional ARM processors are required to switch to the Thumb state to execute a 16-bit instruction and to the ARM state to run a 32-bit instruction. Cortex-M processors can run a mix of 16-bit and 32-bit Thumb-2 instructions without changing the processor state, thus eliminating the overhead of state switching.

Thumb-2 optimizes the tradeoff between code density and application speed.

This book also presents assembly instructions for floating-point operations and digital signal processing, which are available on Cortex-M4 and M7 but not available on the other Cortex-M processors.

3.2 ARM Cortex-M Organization

An ARM Cortex-M processor chip consists of a Cortex-M core licensed by ARM, on-chip peripheral devices implemented by chip manufacturers, and buses and bridges for the communication between the core and peripheral devices.

Examples of peripheral devices integrated into a Cortex-M chip are LCD controllers, serial communication (I²C, SPI, and USART), USB, digital-to-analog converters (DAC), and analog-to-digital converters (ADC). Different manufacturers may add various peripheral devices to the chip.

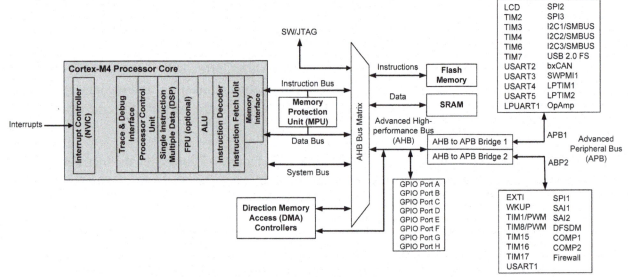

Figure 3-3. Organization of STM32L4 ARM Cortex-M4 processor

Figure 3-3 shows the core and peripheral devices integrated into the STM32L4 Cortex-M4 processor chip.

- The core processor communicates with the flash memory (typically used as instruction memory), SRAM (generally used as data memory), Direct Memory Access (DMA) controller, and general-purpose input/output (GPIO) ports via a bus matrix (also called crossbar switch).

- The bus matrix is an interconnection scheme, which allows concurrent data streams between components connected to the bus matrix, thus providing a high communication bandwidth. The bus matrix connects high-speed components, such as the processor core, Flash, SRAM, DMA controllers, and GPIO ports.

- Peripheral devices are connected to the bus matrix via the bus bridges that links the advanced high-performance bus (AHB) and the advanced peripheral bus

(APB). Generally, AHB is for high-bandwidth communication, and APB is for low-bandwidth communication. AHB and APB are connected via bridges, which buffers data and control signals to fill the bandwidth gap between these two buses, and ensure that there is no data loss.

- Each GPIO pin has multiple functions usually. Software can change its function, even at runtime. We can use a pin simply for digital input or digital output, or we can use it for more advanced functions such as analog-to-digital conversion (ADC), serial communication, timer functions, and so on. Different SoC chips may have different GPIO functions, depending on the chip manufacturers.

- Most peripheral components, such as timers, ADC and I2C, are connected to APB.

A bus is a set of physical wires for transferring data or control signals between two or more hardware components. A communication protocol or agreement must be in place to coordinate the use of a bus. The bandwidth of a bus depends on the width of the bus (usually specified in bits) and the clock speed supported. A processor has various buses for communicating 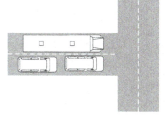 internal and external hardware components. A bus bridge connects two different buses together.

Fundamental components of a Cortex-M processor core include the arithmetic logic unit (ALU), the processor control unit, the interrupt controller (NVIC), the instruction fetching and decoding unit, and the interfaces for memory and debug.

- ALU carries out logical (such as logic AND), and integer arithmetic operations (such as add). ALU has two data inputs (called operands) and one data output.

- The processor control unit generates control signals for internal digital circuits (such as the selection signal of the multiplexers, the control signals of the ALU) and coordinates all components of the processor core.

- The interrupt controller (NVIC) allows the processor core to stop the execution of the current task and immediately respond to special events or signals generated by software or by peripheral devices. Chapter 11 introduces interrupts.

- The instruction fetching and decoding unit reads one machine instruction from the instruction memory address pointed by the program counter and decodes the instruction to figure out what operations the processor core should perform. The processor control unit then generates corresponding control signals based on the decoding result. Chapter 13 introduces how to encode and decode an instruction.

- The memory interface supports the access to memory devices (such as SRAM and flash).

- The debug interface allows a programmer to use a host computer to start or stop a software program on a Cortex-M processor, and monitor or modify processor registers, peripheral registers, and memory in real-time.
- Cortex-M4 supports digital signal processing (DSP) and can optionally have a single-precision floating processing unit (FPU). Cortex-M0/M0+/M1/M3 has no support to DSP and FPU. Compared with Cortex-M4, the optional FPU on Cortex-M7 can support both single-precision and double-precision operations.

3.3 Going from C to Assembly

Before we study the syntax (grammar) and semantics (meaning) of assembly instructions, let us first examine the key differences between C and assembly.

C, like many other high-level programming languages, makes powerful abstraction of computer hardware to hide from programmers the details of how computation is implemented. High-level languages make program codes more concise, more portable, and easier to develop and debug.

However, the assembly language, a low-level programming language, offers programmers not only almost complete and fine-grained control of the underlying hardware, but also the flexibility of specifying how a computation should be carried out. Hence, it is often that a well-written assembly program is more efficient than its C counterpart is. Besides abstracting a microprocessor at different levels, some assembly instructions have no equivalent implementation in C, as we shall see later in this book.

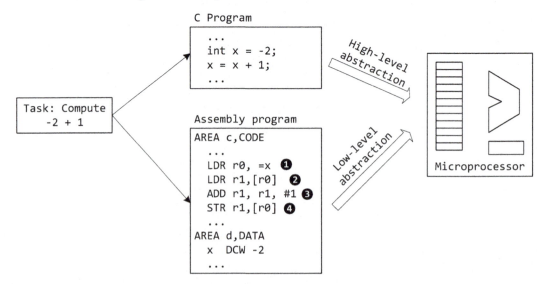

Figure 3-4. Comparison of C and assembly in abstracting microprocessors

In Figure 3-4, we use a simple example, which computes the sum of two signed integers (1 and -2), to compare the hardware abstraction of C and assembly. We assume the variable x is stored in memory. Note that a variable may be stored in a register instead of in memory to improve the computation speed.

- C abstracts away much detail of complex low-level computing operations. Accordingly, C provides a friendly and convenient programming interface to programmers. Because of strong abstraction, the same C program can be recompiled for two different hardware platforms, as given below:

	Platform 1	Platform 2
Signed integer representation	Two's complement	One's complement
Size of an integer (bits)	32	16
Operate on immediate numbers?	No	Yes
Data endian (see Chapter 5.1)	Big endian	Little endian

Table 3-1. A C program can be compiled for two different hardware platforms.

- In contrast, assembly language requires programmers to understand low-level details of the instruction set that this specific microprocessor supports. For example, how many bits does an integer take in memory? What is the data layout of the signed integer x in memory? How are memory locations specified? How is the integer x retrieved from memory? How many operands can an addition support? How is an overflow or carry handled on an addition?

In general, there are three types of instruction set architecture (ISA).

- **Accumulator-based instruction set**. One of the ALU source operands is implicitly stored in a special register called accumulator, and the ALU result is saved into the accumulator. The programmer does not have to specify this operand and the destination register in the program. The accumulator-based instruction set was popular in the 1950s.

- **Stack-based instruction set**. All ALU operands are assumed to be on top of the stack, and the ALU result is also placed on top of the stack. The stack is a special region of memory. Thus, programmers need to push the value of operands onto the stack before an ALU operation is called. The stack-based instruction set was used in the 1960s.

- **Load-store instruction set**. ALU source or destination operands can be any general-purpose registers. ALU cannot directly use data stored in memory as operands. ALU can only access data in memory by using load or store instructions. Most modern processors are based on a load-store instruction set.

In the load-store instruction set, many arithmetic and logic instructions typically support two source operands that are stored in registers. The second operand of some instructions can also be a constant number, encoded directly in the instruction.

Load-store instruction set allows effective use of registers.

Compared with the other two types of instruction sets, the load-store instruction set is faster in performance. The accumulator-based instruction set must make an extra copy to store one of the source operands in the accumulator. The performance of a stack-based instruction set is undermined by the performance of memory because ALU must access the memory repeatedly. However, because there are many general-purpose registers available, the load-store instruction set can take full advantage of temporal locality exhibited in almost all applications, effectively reducing the number of accesses to slow memory.

In a load-store instruction set, data stored in memory cannot be ALU operands directly. Therefore, if we want to change some data in memory, software needs to perform a sequence of *load-modify-store* operations. Software (1) loads target data from memory to a register, (2) modifies the value in the register, and (3) stores the new value in the register back to the memory.

As Figure 3-5 shows, to increment the value of variable x stored in memory by one, a load-modify-store sequence is carried out in four steps in a sequential order: (1) set up the memory address, (2) load data from memory, (3) perform addition, and (4) store new value back to memory.

While we will examine the detailed syntax of assembly instruction later, we can briefly show the assembly program to illustrate the load-modify-store concept.

```
LDR r0, =x      ; Step 1: Set up address (Load memory address of x into r0)
LDR r1, [r0]    ; Step 2: Load (Register r0 holds the memory address of x)
ADD r1, r1, #1  ; Step 3: Modify (Increase the value in register r1 by 1)
STR r1, [r0]    ; Step 4: Store (Save the content in register r1 into memory)
```

Note an integer takes four bytes in memory. The 32-bit two's complement of -2 is 0xFFFFFFFE. Assume this number is stored in contiguous memory locations, starting at 0x20000000. The second LDR instruction loads this 32-bit integer into register r0 (LDR stands for load register). The last step is to save the 32-bit result (0xFFFFFFFF, *i.e.*, -1) back to the memory region. After these four steps, the byte stored at memory location 0x20000003, 0x20000002, 0x20000001 and 0x20000000 is 0xFF, 0xFF, 0xFF, and 0xFF.

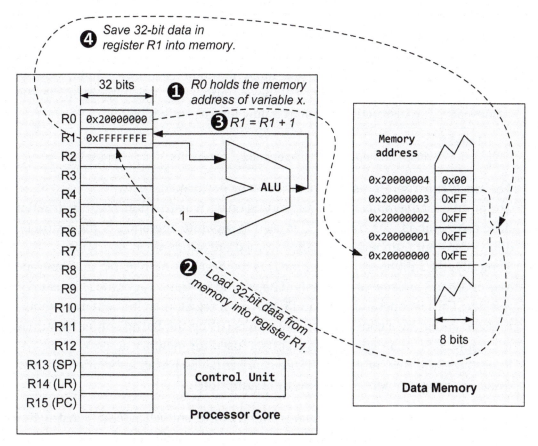

Figure 3-5. A sequence of load-modify-store in assembly equivalent to "x = x + 1;" in C. The variable *x* has an initial value of -2 (*i.e.*, 0xFFFFFFFE) in two's complement.

3.4 Assembly Instruction Format

A machine instruction consists of:

- a binary operation code (opcode) denoting a specific operation to be carried out
- zero or more operands specifying the inputs of the operation

In an assembly program, each binary opcode is replaced by its symbolic abbreviation, called instruction *mnemonic*. Using human-readable mnemonics instead of binary opcode makes developing an assembly program simpler and more convenient.

The general format of an assembly instruction for ARM Keil compilers is as follows:

```
label          mnemonic operand1, operand2, operand3    ; comments
```

- The *label* in the above instruction is a reference to the memory address of this instruction. The assembler either replaces the label with the actual numeric memory address or memory address offset when generating the binary executable. The label is optional and must be unique within the same assembly program file. The label should start at the beginning of a line, without any leading whitespace. The instruction can start a new line, as shown below:

```
label
        mnemonic operand1, operand2, operand3    ; comments
```

- The *mnemonic* represents the operation to be performed.
- The number of *operands* varies, depending on each instruction. Some instructions have no operands. The comma "," is used to separate operands. Some instruction allows constant numbers (also called immediate numbers) as operands.
- Typically, the first operand (operand1) is the *destination register*, and operand2 and operand3 are *source operands*. The second operand (operand2) is usually a register. The last operand (operand3) may be a register, an immediate number, a register shifted by a constant amount of bits (using the Barrel shifter introduced in Chapter 4.5), or a register plus an offset (used for memory access).
- Everything after the semicolon ";" is a *comment*, which is an annotation explicitly declaring programmers' intentions or assumptions.

For GNU compilers, the instruction format is slightly different. All assembly instructions presented in this book follow the ARM format. The GNU format is shown below.

```
label: mnemonic operand1, operand2, operand3    /* comment */
```

The following gives five examples of ARM assembly instructions.

Example 1: Adding two registers

```
        ADD r0, r2, r3      ; r0 = r2 + r3
```

"ADD" is a mnemonic for arithmetic addition, register r0 is the destination operand, and registers r2 and r3 are two source operands. Register names are case-insensitive. We can also write r0 as R0, r1 as R1, and so on.

Example 2: Subtracting an immediate number

```
        SUB r3, r0, #3      ; r3 = r0 - 3
```

"SUB" is mnemonic for subtraction, register r3 is the destination operand, register r0 is the minuend, and the immediate number 3 is the subtrahend.

Example 3: Setting the value of a register

```
MOV r0, #'M'          ; r0 = ASCII value of 'M' (i.e., 0x4D)
```

"MOV" instruction sets the value of r0 to the ASCII value of character M. A constant number has the prefix '#'.

Example 4: Variants of the ADD instruction

```
ADD r1, r2, r3     ; r1 = r2 + r3
ADD r1, r3         ; r1 = r1 + r3
ADD r1, r2, #4     ; r1 = r2 + 4
ADD r1, #15        ; r1 = r1 + 15
```

The number of operands in an instruction varies. If the destination operand (operand1) is the same as the first source operand (operand2), the destination operand can be omitted. The second operand (operand2) can have some variations (such as using Barrel shifter, see Chapter 4.5, and memory addressing, see Chapter 5.4), and it is often written as Op2 in the instruction description. For example, the add instruction is described as follows:

```
ADD {Rd,} Rn, Op2    ; Rd = Rn + Op2
```

The curly brackets "{ }" mean the destination operand Rd is optional if Rn is the same as Rd.

Example 5: Inline Barrel shifter

```
ADD r0, r2, r1, LSL #2   ; r0 = r2 + r1 << 2 = r2 + 4 × r1
MOV r0, r2, ASR #2       ; r0 = r2/4 (signed division)
MOV r0, r0, ROR #16      ; Swap the top and bottom halfword
```

In many instructions, the last operand (operand2 or operand3) can have different formats. We can use the Barrel shifter to shift or rotate the last operation. Refer to Chapter 4.5 for details.

3.5 Anatomy of an Assembly Program

Let us take a quick look at a complete assembly program, as shown in Figure 3-6. The program copies a string to another string. An assembly program includes labels, directives, assembly instructions, and program comments.

1. A *label*, such as *strcpy*, *stop*, *srcStr*, and *dstStr*, represents the memory address of the data or instruction marked with that label. The assembler replaces each label with its memory address or its memory address offset when generating the

executable. *A label must start with the beginning of a line without any leading space.* A label can be a function name (such as "__main" as in the example), which is the memory address of the first instruction of a function. The "__main" label is exported to allow the linker to find it and resolve this label.

2. The *directives* provide valuable information for assisting the assembler. The example in Figure 3-6 uses the following directives. PROC and ENDP declare the start and the end of a function (or called a subroutine). END indicates the end of an assembly program file. AREA defines code or data regions. ENTRY designates the initial entry into the program. ALIGN specifies the requirement of memory address alignment. DCB allocates and defines data.

3. An *assembly instruction* is a machine command that controls the program flow or manipulates data. Some instructions are pseudo instructions, which are not real machine commands but are allowed in assembly language code. The assembler translates a pseudo instruction, such as "LDR r1, =srcStr" in the example code, into a real instruction. Pseudo instructions make the job of writing assembly language programs easier.

4. A *comment* is a text annotation that explains the programmer's intentions or assumptions. It aims to improve inter-programmer communication and code readability. A comment in an assembly program starts with a semicolon. Assemblers ignore everything after the semi-colon in that line.

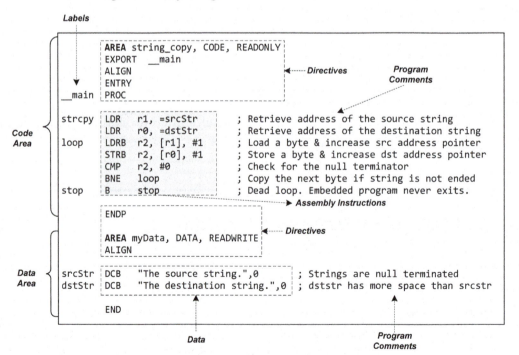

Figure 3-6. An example assembly program

The example assembly program in Figure 3-6 has two areas: a data area and a code area.

- The *data area* defines two strings: *srcStr* and *dstStr*. The program allocates memory space for both strings and gives them initial values. The NULL character terminates a string.
- The *code area* includes a function named __main, which is equivalent to the main() function in a C program. This program copies string *srcStr* to string *dstStr*.

Most assembly instructions of Cortex-M3 can be classified into the following four categories:

- arithmetic, shift, and logic instructions (see Chapter 4),
- data movement instructions (see Chapter 5),
- compare and branch instructions (see Chapter 6), and
- miscellaneous instructions for various functions such as debugging.

In addition to these instructions, Cortex-M4 and M7 also support

- digital signal processing instructions (see Chapter 24), and
- floating-point instructions (see Chapter 12.4).

(1) Arithmetic, shift, and logic instructions

Shift, logic, and bit instructions	*Shift*: **LSL** (logic shift left), **LSR** (logic shift right), **ASR** (arithmetic shift right), **ROR** (rotate right), **RRX** (rotate right with extend)
	Logic: **AND** (bitwise and), **ORR** (bitwise or), **EOR** (bitwise exclusive or), **ORN** (bitwise or not), **MVN** (move not)
	Bit set/clear: **BFC** (bit field clear), **BFI** (bit field insert), **BIC** (bit clear), **CLZ** (count leading zeros)
	Bit/byte reordering: **RBIT** (reverse bit order in a word), **REV** (reverse byte order in a word), **REV16** (reverse byte order in each halfword independently), **REVSH** (reverse byte order in the bottom halfword, and sign extend to 32 bits)

Arithmetic instructions	*Addition*: **ADD, ADC** (add with carry)
	Subtraction: **SUB, RSB** (reverse subtract), **SBC** (subtract with carry)
	Multiplication: **MUL** (multiply), **MLA** (multiply with accumulate), **MLS** (multiply with subtract), **SMULL** (signed long multiply), **UMULL** (unsigned long multiply), **SMLAL** (signed long multiply, with accumulate), **UMLAL** (unsigned long multiply, with subtract)

	Division: **SDIV** (signed), **UDIV** (unsigned)
	Saturation: **SSAT** (signed), **USAT** (unsigned)
	Extension: **SXTB** (sign-extend a byte), **SXTH** (sign-extend a halfword), **UXTB** (zero-extend a byte), **UXTH** (zero-extend a halfword)
	Bit field extract: **SBFX** (signed extraction), **UBFX** (unsigned extraction)

(2) Data movement instructions

Memory access instructions	*Read data memory*: **LDRB** (load byte), **LDRH** (load halfword), **LDR** (load word), **LDRD** (load double-word), **LDRSB** (load signed byte), **LDRSH** (load signed halfword), **LDM, LDMDB, LDMFD** (load multiple words) **LDREXB, LDREXH, LDREX** (load register exclusive with a byte, halfword, and word), **LDRT** (load in privileged modes), **POP** (load from stack)
	Write data memory: **STRB** (store byte), **STRH** (store halfword), **STR** (store word), **STRD** (store double-word), **STRSB** (store signed byte), **STRSH** (store signed halfword), **STM, STMDB, STMFD** (store multiple words), **STREXB, STREXH, STREX** (store register exclusive with a byte, halfword, and word), **STRT** (store in privileged modes), **PUSH** (store into stack)
Data copy instructions	**MOV** (move), **MOVT** (move top), **MOVW** (move halfword), **MRS** (move from coprocessor), **MSR** (move to coprocessor)

(3) Compare and branch instructions

Data compare instructions	**CMP** (compare), **CMN** (compare negative), **TST** (test), **TEQ** (test equivalent), **IT** (if-then)
Branch instructions	**B** (branch), **CBZ** (compare and branch on zero), **CBNZ** (compare and branch on non-zero), **TBB** (table branch byte), **TBH** (table branch halfword)
Subroutine instructions	**BL** (branch with link), **BLX** (branch with link and exchange), **BX** (branch and exchange)

(4) Miscellaneous instructions

Miscellaneous instructions	**BKPT** (breakpoint), **NOP** (no operation), **SEV** (set event), **WFE** (wait for event), **WFI** (wait for interrupt), **CPSID** (interrupt disable), **CPSIE** (interrupt enable), **DMB** (data memory barrier), **DSB** (data synchronization barrier), **ISB** (instruction synchronization barrier)

3.6 Assembly Directives

In assembly programs, directives are not actual commands. Instead, they are used to provide key information to compile the source program, such as declaring constants and symbolic names, defining data layout, allocating memory space, and specifying the program structure and entry point. Table 3-2 lists some commonly used directives.

AREA	Make a new block of data or code
ENTRY	Declare an entry point where the program execution starts
ALIGN	Align data or code to a memory boundary
DCB	Allocate one or more bytes (8 bits) of data
DCW	Allocate one or more halfwords (16 bits) of data
DCD	Allocate one or more words (32 bits) of data
DCFS	Allocate single-precision (32 bits) floating-point numbers
DCFB	Allocate double-precision (64 bits) floating-point numbers
SPACE	Allocate a zeroed block of memory
FILL	Allocate a block of memory and fill with a given value
EQU	Give a symbol name to a numeric constant
RN	Give a symbol name to a register
EXPORT	Declare a symbol and make it referable by other source files
IMPORT	Provide a symbol defined outside the current source file
INCLUDE/GET	Include a separate source file within the current source file
PROC	Declare the start of a procedure
ENDP	Designate the end of a procedure
END	Designate the end of a source file

Table 3-2 Directives commonly used in ARM assembly language

Table 3-3 gives a typical skeleton frame of an assembly program.

```
       AREA myData, DATA, READWRITE ; Define a data section
Array  DCD 1, 2, 3, 4, 5                ; Define an array with five integers

       AREA myCode, CODE, READONLY   ; Define a code section
       EXPORT   __main                ; Make __main visible to the linker
       ENTRY                          ; Mark the entrance to the entire program
__main PROC                           ; PROC marks the beginning of subroutine
       ...                            ; Assembly program starts here.
       ENDP                           ; Mark the end of a subroutine
       END                            ; Mark the end of a program
```

Table 3-3. Skeleton of an ARM assembly program.

(1) AREA

An application consists of one or multiple data and code areas. The AREA directive indicates to the assembler the start of a new data or code section. A code section contains a list of instructions, and a data section includes the declaration and initialization of variables.

An area is a basic independent and indivisible unit processed by the linker. Each area should have a name, and areas within the same source file cannot share the same name. An assembly program must have at least one code area. By default, a code area can only be read (READONLY), and a data area may be read from and written to (READWRITE).

(2) ENTRY

The ENTRY directive marks the first instruction to be executed within an application. There must be one and only one entry directive in an application, no matter how many source files the application has. When there is no entry directive, the linker generates an error message. When there are multiple entry directives, the assembler gives an error message.

> *There should be only one entry for the whole application, even if it has multiple source files.*

For applications written in C or C++, the entry point is in the C library's initialization function, not directly visible to programmers.

(3) END

The END directive indicates the end of a source file. Each assembly program file must end with this directive. Suppose we have two assembly source files *A* and B. When *A* uses either GET or INCLUDE to include B, the assembler returns to *A* after reaching END in B, and continues to assemble the rest of *A*. The END directive of the top-level file informs the assembler to complete the application.

(4) Function or subroutine definition: PROC and ENDP

PROC and ENDP mark the beginning and the end of a function (also called a subroutine or procedure), respectively. PROC stands for "procedure" and ENDP means "end of procedure."

A single source file can contain multiple subroutines. However, PROC and ENDP cannot be nested. We cannot define a subroutine within another subroutine.

A C program must have at least one function named main(). Similarly, an assembly program must have at least one subroutine named __main.

(5) Data allocation directive: DCB, DCW, DCD, DCQ, SPACE, and FILL

An assembly program needs to reserve space in the data memory for variables and set their initial contents. Table 3-4 lists commonly used data allocation directives.

Directive	Description	Memory Space
DCB	Define Constant Byte	Reserve 8-bit values
DCW	Define Constant Half-word	Reserve 16-bit values
DCD	Define Constant Word	Reserve 32-bit values
DCQ	Define Constant Doubleword	Reserve 64-bit values
SPACE	Defined Zeroed Bytes	Reserve some zeroed bytes
FILL	Defined Initialized Bytes	Reserve and fill each byte with a value

Table 3-4. Directives for data allocation and initialization

Example 3-1 shows how to declare an initialized string, initialized integer arrays, a zeroed memory region, and a few variables in different formats.

```
        AREA   myData, DATA, READWRITE
hello   DCB    "Hello World!",0   ; Allocate a string that is null-terminated
dollar  DCB    2,10,0,200         ; Allocate integers ranging from -128 to 255
scores  DCD    2,3.5,-0.8,4.0     ; Allocate 4 words containing decimal values
miles   DCW    100,200,50,0       ; Allocate integers between -32768 and 65535
p       SPACE  255                ; Allocate 255 bytes of zeroed memory space
f       FILL   20,0xFF,1          ; Allocate 20 bytes and set each byte to 0xFF
binary  DCB    2_01010101         ; Allocate a byte in binary
octal   DCB    8_73               ; Allocate a byte in octal
char    DCB    'A'                ; Allocate a byte initialized to ASCII of 'A'
```

Example 3-1. Data definition by using data allocation directive

(6) The EQU and RN directive

EQU and RN are to make an assembly program easier to understand. The EQU directive associates a symbolic name to a numeric constant. Like "#define" in a C program, EQU can be used to define a constant in an assembly code.

```
; Interrupt Number Definition (IRQn)
BusFault_IRQn    EQU    -11      ; Cortex-M Bus Fault Interrupt
SVCall_IRQn      EQU    -5       ; Cortex-M Supervisor Call (SVC) Interrupt
PendSV_IRQn      EQU    -2       ; Cortex-M Pend SVC Interrupt
SysTick_IRQn     EQU    -1       ; Cortex-M System Tick Interrupt
```

Example 3-2. EQU is equivalent to "define" in a C program.

The RN directive gives a symbolic name to a register.

```
Dividend         RN    6        ; Defines dividend for register 6
Divisor          RN    5        ; Defines divisor for register 5
```

Example 3-3. RN gives a special, meaningful name to a register.

(7) ALIGN

To improve performance, many processors require that the starting memory address of an instruction or a variable must be a multiple of 2^n. For example, an address aligned to a word boundary must be divisible by 4 (*i.e.*, 2^2). If instructions or data are not appropriately aligned in memory, some processors generate a misalignment fault signal and abort the memory access. Cortex-M processors allow unaligned memory accesses at the sacrifice of performance. Multiple memory accesses may be required to fetch a misaligned data item or instruction. Chapter 10.1 introduces alignment in detail.

The following shows an example usage of ALIGN and its layout of the data area.

```
      AREA myCode, CODE, ALIGN = 3   ; Memory address begins at a multiple of 8
      ADD r0, r1, r2                 ; Instructions start at a multiple of 8

      AREA myData, DATA, ALIGN = 2   ; Address begins at a multiple of 4
a     DCB 0xFF                       ; The first byte of a word (4 bytes)
      ALIGN 4, 3                     ; Align to the last byte of a word
b     DCB 0x33                       ; Set the fourth byte of a 4-byte word
c     DCB 0x44                       ; Add a byte to make next data misaligned
      ALIGN                          ; Force the next data to be aligned
d     DCD 0x12345                    ; Skip three bytes and store the word
```

Example 3-4. Data alignment in assembly language

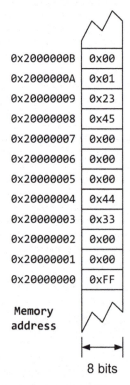

Memory address	
0x2000000B	0x00
0x2000000A	0x01
0x20000009	0x23
0x20000008	0x45
0x20000007	0x00
0x20000006	0x00
0x20000005	0x00
0x20000004	0x44
0x20000003	0x33
0x20000002	0x00
0x20000001	0x00
0x20000000	0xFF

8 bits

Figure 3-7. Data layout of Example 3-4. Assume the myData area starts at 0x20000000.

(8) EXPORT and IMPORT
EXPORT and IMPORT define and locate symbols externally defined in different source files. The EXPORT declares a symbol and makes this symbol visible to the linker. The IMPORT gives the assembler a symbol that is not defined locally in the current assembly file. The IMPORT is like the "extern" keyword in C.

(9) INCLUDE or GET
The INCLUDE or GET directive is to include an assembly source file within another source file. It is useful to include constant symbols defined by using EQU and stored in a separate source file. In Example 3-5, all constants are defined by using EQU directives and are stored in a separate assembly file called "*constants.s*". To include these constants, we can use a simple statement "INCLUDE constants.s".

```
        INCLUDE constants.s       ; Load Constant Definitions
        AREA myCode, CODE, READONLY
        EXPORT  __main
        ENTRY
__main  PROC
        ...
        ENDP
        END
```

Example 3-5. Using **INCLUDE** to load constants defined in a separate file

3.7 Exercises

1. Find five devices that use an ARM processor. Identify the instruction set they support (such as ARM32, Thumb, Thumb-2, or ARM64).

2. Identify two ARM Cortex-M processors and find what I/O peripherals are built into the processor chip.

3. Identify key differences between Cortex-M3 and Cortex-M4.

4. Compared with accumulator-based and stack-based instruction set, what are the advantages and disadvantages of the load-store instruction set?

5. The C language standard (C99 standard) specifies the minimum field width of each variable type. The actual size of a variable type varies by implementations. Find out the minimum size of the following variable types in terms of bytes.

      1) char
      2) short

```
3) signed short int
4) int
5) long
6) unsigned long int
7) long long
8) unsigned long long
9) float
10)double
```

6. An assembly program must have a subroutine named __main. Find why it must be named as __main. (Hints: Look at the assembly source code of the boot loader, which initializes the processor when the processor starts.)

7. What does "ALIGN 8, 5" mean? Draw the data memory layout if the data memory starts at 0x20000000.

```
        AREA   myData, Data
        ALIGN 4
a       DCB    1
b       DCB    2
c       DCB    3

        ALIGN 8,5
d       DCB    5
```

8. What are incorrect in the following assembly program?

```
            AREA myData, DATA, READWRITE
            String DCB "ABCDE"
            Array  DCD 1, 2, 3, 4, 5
            END

            AREA myCode, CODE, READONLY
            EXPORT   __main2
__main  PROC
            ...

sum         PROC
            ...
            ENDP

            ENDP
            END
```

9. How does an assembly program define a float or double variable? How is a float or double array defined?

Arithmetic and Logic

Data processing instructions can be classified into seven categories: arithmetic instructions, reorder instructions, extension instructions, bitwise logic instructions, shift instructions, comparison instructions, and data copy instructions. This chapter focuses on assembly instructions for arithmetic and logic operations.

4.1 Program Status Register

Cortex-M processors have five status flags: negative (**N**), zero (**Z**), overflow (**V**), carry (**C**), and saturation (**Q**).

- The negative flag (**N**) is set if the result of ALU is negative (*i.e.*, bit[31] is 1), and is cleared otherwise.
- The zero flag (**Z**) is set if the ALU result is zero, and is cleared otherwise.
- The carry flag (**C**) is set if a carry occurs in unsigned addition, and is cleared otherwise. For unsigned subtraction, it is set if no borrow has occurred, and is cleared otherwise.
- The overflow flag (**V**) is set if an overflow takes place when performing a signed addition or subtraction, and is cleared otherwise.
- The saturation flag (**Q**) is set if an SSAT or USAT instruction causes saturation, and is cleared otherwise.

Most data processing instructions of Cortex-M processors have an option to update these ALU status flags. These flags are stored in the program status register (PSR). The program status register is a combination of three special registers: the application program status register (APSR), the interrupt program status register (IPSR), and the execution program status register (EPSR).

Because APSR, IPSR, and EPSR have no overlap in bit fields, the processor combines them into one register PSR, or called xPSR, as shown in Figure 4-1, to allow convenient accesses.

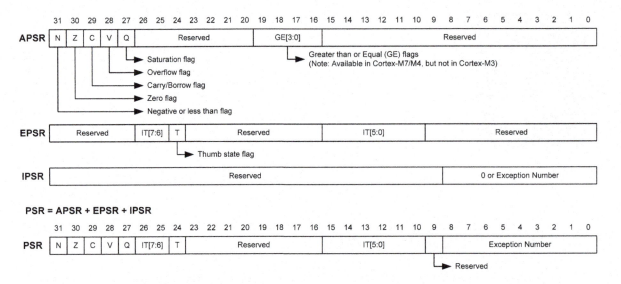

Figure 4-1. Program status register APSR, EPSR, and IPSR

In APSR, the GE flags indicate whether the corresponding results are greater than or equal to zero (see Chapter 24.7). The GE flags are only available on Cortex-M4 and M7.

In EPSR, the T flag indicates whether the processor is in Thumb state or ARM32 state. Since Cortex-M processors only support Thumb-2/Thumb instructions, the T flag has a fixed value of 1 in Cortex-M. Additionally, the IT bit fields (IT[7:6] and IT[5:0]) in EPSR hold the condition states associated with the current IF-THEN (IT) block. An IT block is a convenient approach to implementing conditionally executed instructions.

In IPSR, the least significant 9 bits are zero if the processor is in the thread mode, or the exception or interrupt number if the processor is in the handler mode. On reset, the processor is in the thread mode. Chapter 11 introduces the concept of interrupts.

These special registers can only be accessed by using two special instructions:

- MRS (move from a special register to a general register) and
- MSR (move from a general register to a special register).

Specifically, MRS reads these registers, and MSR writes to these registers. The following gives a few examples.

```
MRS r0, apsr          ; Read APSR
MRS r0, ipsr          ; Read IPSR
MRS r0, epsr          ; Read EPSR
MRS r0, xpsr          ; Read APSR, IPSR, and EPSR
MSR apsr_nzcvq, r0    ; Change N,Z,C,V,Q flags in APSR
MSR apsr_g, r0        ; Copy r0[19:16] to GE[3:0] in APSR (Not on Cortex-M3)
MSR apsr_nzcvqg, r0   ; Change N,Z,C,V,Q and GE flags (Not on Cortex-M3)
```

4.2 Updating Program Status Flags

It is an option for an arithmetic or logic instruction to set the processor status flags. If the S suffix is appended to an instruction mnemonic, the processor modifies the status flags based on the computation result. For example, the ADDS instruction changes the N, Z, C, and V flags when performing addition. On the contrary, ADD cannot change these flags. If an

ADD *vs* ADDS

instruction does not update these flags, the existing value of each flag, set by a previous instruction, is preserved.

Data comparison instructions (introduced in Chapter 4.9), such as CMP (compare), CMN (compare negative), TST (test), and TEQ (test equivalence), set these flags even though they do not have the S suffix.

Let us look at ADD instructions with and without the S suffix.

```
ADD  r1, r2, r3  ; r1 = r2 + r3, but won't update N, Z, C, and V flags
ADDS r2, r2, r3  ; r1 = r2 + r3, and update N, Z, C, and V flags
```

While the first instruction ADD does not change the N, Z, C, and V flags, the second instruction ADDS modifies the flags in the following ways:

(1) the overflow flag by assuming that r2 and r3 hold signed integers represented in two's complement,

(2) the carry flag by assuming that r2 and r3 hold unsigned integers,

(3) the zero flag by checking whether the result saved in the destination register r1 is zero or not, and

(4) the negative flag by checking the sign bit of r1 (the most significant bit of r1).

If the Barrel shifter is used, the source operand may update the program status flags. Chapter 4.5 introduces the Barrel shifter. For example, the bitwise logical ANDS instruction can update the N, Z, and C flags. In the following instruction, the N flag is set if the most significant bit of r1 is 1, and the Z flag is set if r1 equals 0.

```
ANDS r1, r2, r3              ; r1 = r2 AND r3
```

It is easy to understand that most logical instructions do not update the overflow flag. How does a logical instruction update the carry flag? The answer lies in the second operand of a logical instruction. If the second operand uses the Barrel shifter, then the processor updates the carry flag based on the shift or rotation result.

```
ANDS r1, r2, r3, LSL #3      ; r1 = r2 AND (r3 << 3)
```

When MOVS uses the Barrel shifter, the processor also updates the Z, N, and C flags.

```
MOVS r2, r1, LSR #3          ; r2 = r1 << 3
```

However, the Barrel shifter does not change the flags if it is employed in an arithmetic instruction. For example, in the following instruction, the flags depend on the result of addition, instead of logical shift left.

```
ADDS r1, r2, r3, LSL #3     ; r1 = r2 AND (r3 << 3)
```

If the program is written in assembly, it is the programmer's responsibility to interpret and use these flags correctly. For programs written in high-level languages, compilers automatically interpret these flags. As introduced in Chapter 2.4.3, if the ALU is to update the status flags when performing an arithmetic addition or subtraction, the processor updates both the carry flag and the overflow flag. It must be clear to programmers whether the numbers stored in the registers are signed or unsigned.

4.3 Shift and Rotate

As shown in Figure 4-2, the second ALU operand is equipped with a Barrel shifter, which is a special digital circuit for quick shift and rotation. Barrel shifters are usually not available on other processors such as PIC and AVR.

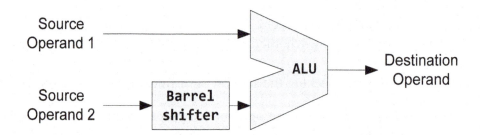

Figure 4-2. Barrel shifter is special hardware that performs quick shift and rotate operations on the second source operand.

There are five types of shift and rotate operations: LSL, LSR, ASR, ROR, and RRX, as shown in Figure 4-3.

- **LSL** (logical shift left) moves all bits of a register value left by n bits and zeros are shifted in at the right end. LSL is equivalent to multiplication by 2^n ("<<" operation in C).

- **LSR** (logical shift right) moves all bits of a register value right by n bits and zeros are shifted in at the left end. LSR is equivalent to unsigned division by 2^n (">>" operation on unsigned numbers in C).
- **ASR** (arithmetic shift right) moves all bits right by n bits and copies of the left most bit (the sign bit) are shifted in at the left end. ASR is equivalent to signed division by 2^n (">>" operation on signed numbers in C).
- **ROR** (rotate right) is the circular shift, in which all 32 bits are shifted right simultaneously as if the right end of the register is joined with its left end. The bit shifted out from the right end of the register is copied into the carry bit. The carry bit can be optionally used to update the carry flag of the processor status register.
- **RRX** (rotate right with extend) works similarly to ROR except that the carry bit joins the rotating circle, and RRX can rotate the data by only one bit.

Below gives a few examples of shift and rotate instructions.

```
LSL r1, r2        ; r1 = r1 << r2
LSL r1, #3        ; r1 = r1 << 3
LSL r1, r2, #3    ; r1 = r2 << 3
LSL r1, r2, r3    ; r1 = r2 << r3
ROR r1, r2        ; r1 = rotate r1 by r2 bits
RRX r1, r2        ; rotate r2 right by one bit (with extension)
```

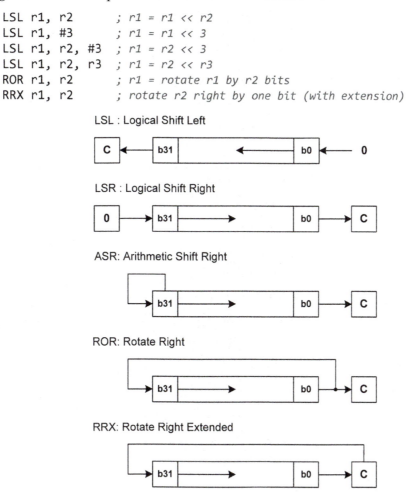

Figure 4-3. Shift and rotate operations. Note that the carry (C) is not APSR's carry flag.

The C language does not provide rotate operations (ROR and RRX). The compiler automatically uses a rotation instruction if it can improve the performance. Besides, ARM assembly language does not provide a rotate left assembly instruction. However, a rotate left by n bits can be replaced with a rotate right by $32 - n$ bits. For example, rotating left by 6 bits has the same result as rotating right by 26 bits.

Note the carry bit shown in Figure 4-3 is not the carry flag of the processor status register. Therefore, none of these shift and rotate instructions updates the status flags by default. If these flags need to be updated, a shift or rotate instruction must have the suffix S specified. What's more, these instructions cannot modify the overflow flags.

```
LSL  r1, #3        ; r1 = r1 << 3, but won't update the flags
LSLS r1, #3        ; r1 = r1 << 3, and update the N, Z, C flags
                   ; LSLS does not update the V flag
```

Programs often use the Barrel shifter to replace slow multiplication and division instructions to improve the speed, as shown below.

```
ADD r0, r2, r1, LSL #1    ; r0 = r2 + r1 << 1 = r2 + 2 × r1
ADD r1, r0, r0, LSR #3    ; r1 = r0 + r0 >> 3 = r0 + r0/8
```

The Barrel shifter used in a move (MOVS and MVNS), and logical/bitwise instruction with the S suffix (such as ANDS, ORRS, EORS, BICS) updates the carry flag. This chapter gives detailed discussions later.

4.4 Arithmetic Instructions

Table 4-1 lists arithmetic instructions that produce 32-bit results.

ADD {Rd,} Rn, Op2	Add. $Rd \leftarrow Rn + Op2$
ADC {Rd,} Rn, Op2	Add with carry. $Rd \leftarrow Rn + Op2 + Carry$
SUB {Rd,} Rn, Op2	Subtract. $Rd \leftarrow Rn - Op2$
SBC {Rd,} Rn, Op2	Subtract with carry. $Rd \leftarrow Rn - Op2 + Carry - 1$
RSB {Rd,} Rn, Op2	Reverse subtract. $Rd \leftarrow Op2 - Rn$
MUL {Rd,} Rn, Rm	Multiply. $Rd \leftarrow (Rn \times Rm)[31:0]$
MLA Rd, Rn, Rm, Ra	Multiply with accumulate. $Rd \leftarrow (Ra + (Rn \times Rm))[31:0]$
MLS Rd, Rn, Rm, Ra	Multiply and subtract. $Rd \leftarrow (Ra - (Rn \times Rm))[31:0]$
SDIV {Rd,} Rn, Rm	Signed divide. $Rd \leftarrow Rn / Rm$
UDIV {Rd,} Rn, Rm	Unsigned divide. $Rd \leftarrow Rn / Rm$
SSAT Rd,#n,Rm{,shift #s}	Signed saturate
USAT Rd,#n,Rm{,shift #s}	Unsigned saturate

Table 4-1. Arithmetic instructions with 32-bit results

4.4.1 Addition and Subtraction Instructions

Most of these instructions take two source operands, and the 32-bit result is saved in a destination register. While the first source operand is a register, the second source operand is flexible and can be a register, an immediate constant, or an inline Barrel shifter.

Examples of three register operands:

```
SUB r3, r2, r1      ; r3 = r2 - r1
SBC r3, r2, r1      ; r3 = r2 - r1 + Carry - 1
RSB r3, r2, r1      ; r3 = r1 - r2
```

Examples of an immediate number operand:

```
SUB r3, r2, #987    ; r3 = r2 - 987
RSB r3, r2, #987    ; r3 = 987 - r2
```

Examples of inline Barrel shifter:

```
RSB r0, r0, r0, LSL #5    ; r0 = r0 << 5 - r0 = 31 × r0
ADD r0, r0, r0, LSL #3    ; r0 = r0 + r0 << 3 = 9 × r0
```

The next section introduces the Barrel shifter in detail.

If an instruction has three operands, the second operand cannot be a constant number in most instructions (except SSAT and USAT). For example, the SUB instruction below has a syntax error.

```
SUB r0, #1, r3    ; Not allowed, causing a syntax error.
RSB r0, r3, #1    ; r0 = 1 - r3. RSB is for reverse subtraction.
```

Example 4-1 given below shows the implementation of subtracting two 96-bit integers by using SUB and SBC. A 96-bit integer is saved in three registers.

$$C(r8{:}r7{:}r6) = A(r2{:}r1{:}r0) - B(r5{:}r4{:}r3)$$

The program uses the LDR instruction (see Chapter 5.1). The LDR instruction sets a register to a constant value. A constant value is also called an immediate number.

```
; C = A - B
; Subtracting two 96-bit integers A (r2:r1:r0) and B (r5:r4:r3).
; Three registers to hold a 96-bit integer: upper word : middle word : lower word
; Result C (r8:r7:r6)
; A = 00001234,00000002,FFFFFFFF
; B = 12345678,00000004,00000001

LDR r0, =0xFFFFFFFF    ; A's lower 32 bits (See LDR in Chapter 5.1)
LDR r1, =0x00000002    ; A's middle 32 bits
LDR r2, =0x00001234    ; A's upper 32 bits
```

```
LDR r3, =0x00000001    ; B's lower 32 bits
LDR r4, =0x00000004    ; B's middle 32 bits
LDR r5, =0x12345678    ; B's upper 32 bits

; Subtract A from B
SUBS r6, r0, r3   ; C[31:0] = A[31:0] - B[31:0], update carry

; Carry flag is 1 if no borrow has occurred in the previous subtraction
SBCS r7, r1, r4   ; C[64:32] = A[64:32] - B[64:32] + carry - 1, update carry
SBC  r8, r2, r5   ; C[96:64] = A[96:64] - B[96:64] + carry - 1
```

Example 4-1. Subtracting two 96-bit integers. Each integer is stored in three registers.

4.4.2 Short Multiplication and Division Instructions

The result of a multiplication may have more than 32 bits. However, the destination register only holds the least significant 32 bits (LSB32) of the result.

```
MUL  r6, r4, r2        ; signed multiply, r6 = LSB32( r4 × r2 )
UMUL r6, r4, r2        ; unsigned multiply, r6 = LSB32( r4 × r2 )
MLA  r6, r4, r1, r0    ; r6 = LSB32( r4 × r1 ) + r0
MLS  r6, r4, r1, r0    ; r6 = LSB32( r4 × r1 ) - r0
SDIV r3, r2, r1        ; signed divide, r3 = r2/r1
UDIV r3, r2, r1        ; unsigned divide, r3 = r2/r1
```

4.4.3 Long Multiplication Instructions

Table 4-2 presents long multiplication instructions that produce 64-bit results.

UMULL RdLo,RdHi,Rn,Rm	Unsigned long multiply, *RdHi,RdLo ← unsigned(Rn × Rm)*
SMULL RdLo,RdHi,Rn,Rm	Signed long multiply, *RdHi,RdLo ← signed(Rn × Rm)*
UMLAL RdLo,RdHi,Rn,Rm	Unsigned multiply with accumulate, *RdHi,RdLo ← unsigned(RdHi,RdLo + Rn × Rm)*
SMLAL RdLo,RdHi,Rn,Rm	Signed multiply with accumulate, *RdHi,RdLo ← signed(RdHi,RdLo + Rn × Rm)*

Table 4-2. Long multiplication instructions

Two registers are used to store a 64-bit result, with the high register (RdHi) holding the most significant 32 bits, and the low register (RdLo) holding the least significant 32 bits.

UMULL and UMLAL assume that the operands Rn and Rm, and the 64-bit multiplication result is an unsigned integer. On the other hand, SMULL and SMLAL treat the operands as signed integers. UMLAL and SMLAL also perform accumulation.

```
UMULL r3, r4, r0, r1   ; r4:r3 = r0 × r1, r4 = MSB bits, r3 = LSB bits
SMULL r3, r4, r0, r1   ; r4:r3 = r0 × r1
UMLAL r3, r4, r0, r1   ; r4:r3 = r4:r3 + r0 × r1
SMLAL r3, r4, r0, r1   ; r4:r3 = r4:r3 + r0 × r1
```

4.4.4 Saturation Instructions

The saturation instructions limit a given input to a configurable signed or unsigned range. When the input value exceeds the specified range, its output is then set as the maximum or minimum value of the selected range. Otherwise, the output is equal to the input. The saturation instructions take one immediate source operand and one register source operand.

- SSAT saturates a signed integer x to the signed range $-2^{n-1} \le x \le 2^{n-1}-1$.

$$SSAT(x) = \begin{cases} 2^{n-1} - 1 & if\ x > 2^{n-1} - 1 \\ -2^{n-1} & if\ x < 2^{n-1} \\ x & otherwise \end{cases}$$

- USAT saturates a signed integer x to the unsigned range $0 \le x \le 2^n - 1$.

$$USAT(x) = \begin{cases} 2^n - 1 & if\ x > 2^n - 1 \\ x & otherwise \end{cases}$$

The following gives two examples in which n is 11. Note the second operand is an immediate number in SSAT and USAT.

```
SSAT   r2, #11, r1    ; output range: -2¹⁰ ≤ r2 ≤ 2¹⁰
USAT   r2, #11, r3    ; output range: 0 ≤ r2 ≤ 2¹¹
```

4.5 Barrel Shifter

The key advantage of Barrel shifters is that it can shift or rotate a register by a specified number of bits in one clock cycle. Typically, a Barrel shifter is implemented as a cascade of parallel 2-to-1 multiplexers. Figure 4-4 gives an example implementation of a four-bit Barrel shifter that performs rotate right. The S_1S_0 indicates the amount of rotation. The implementation of logic shift is similar, except that a zero bit is shifted in either from the right end or the left end.

As shown in Figure 4-2, the Barrel shifter is special hardware that can perform shift and rotation on the second ALU source operand. Therefore, not only can a shift and rotate instruction be used as a standalone assembly instruction, but it can also be utilized in other instructions to make changes to the second source operand.

S_1	S_0	Y_3	Y_2	Y_1	Y_0
0	0	D_3	D_2	D_1	D_0
0	1	D_0	D_3	D_2	D_1
1	0	D_1	D_0	D_3	D_2
1	1	D_2	D_1	D_0	D_3

Table 4-3. Truth table of rotation right

ASR and LSR differ on whether the sign is preserved. For example,

```
ADD r1, r0, r0, LSL #3    ; r1 = r0 + r0 << 3 = r0 + 8 × r0
ADD r1, r0, r0, LSR #3    ; r1 = r0 + r0 >> 3 = r0 + r0/8 (unsigned)
ADD r1, r0, r0, ASR #3    ; r1 = r0 + r0 >> 3 = r0 + r0/8 (signed)
```

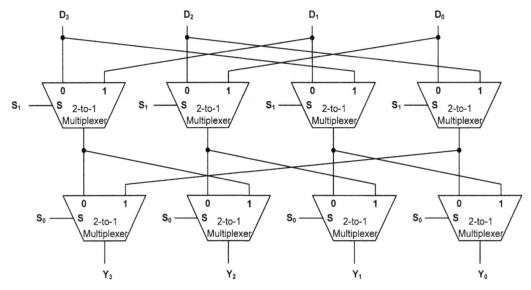

Figure 4-4. Example four-bit Barrel shifter that performs rotate right

We can leverage Barrel shifter to speed up the application.

- Without Barrel shifter, two separate instructions would be required to carry out each of the above instructions. This would not only increase the size of a binary program but also take more processor cycles to complete the same task.
- Barrel shifter can also replace slow multiplication instructions, as shown in the following example.

```
ADD r1, r0, r0, LSL #3    ⟺    MOV r2, #9        ; r2 = 9
                                MUL r1, r0, r2    ; r1 = r0 * 9
```

4.6 Bitwise Logic Operations

Bitwise operations treat input operands as a sequence of binary bits, rather than as integer numbers. The computation is carried out at the bit level. For example, we can reset a specific bit of a register to zero or set a specific bit a register to one, leaving the other bits unchanged.

There are four commonly used bitwise Boolean operators: AND, OR, Exclusive OR (⊕), and negation (NOT). The output of the Exclusive OR is true only when the input bits differ (*i.e.*, one is true, and the other is false). Table 4-4 shows their truth table.

a	b	a and b	a or b	$a \oplus b$	not a
0	0	0	0	0	1
0	1	0	1	1	1
1	0	0	1	1	0
1	1	1	1	0	0

Table 4-4. Truth table of logic operations

Table 4-5 shows the bitwise assembly instructions supported in Cortex-M.

`AND {Rd,} Rn, Op2`	Bitwise logic AND. $Rd \leftarrow Rn$ & $operand2$
`ORR {Rd,} Rn, Op2`	Bitwise logic OR. $Rd \leftarrow Rn \mid operand2$
`EOR {Rd,} Rn, Op2`	Bitwise logic exclusive OR. $Rd \leftarrow Rn \wedge operand2$
`ORN {Rd,} Rn, Op2`	Bitwise logic NOT OR. $Rd \leftarrow Rn \mid (NOT\ operand2)$
`BIC {Rd,} Rn, Op2`	Bit clear. $Rd \leftarrow Rn$ & $NOT\ operand2$
`BFC Rd, #lsb, #width`	Bit field clear. $Rd[(width+lsb-1):lsb] \leftarrow 0$
`BFI Rd, Rn, #lsb, #width`	Bit field insert. $Rd[(width+lsb-1):lsb] \leftarrow Rn[(width-1):0]$
`MVN Rd, Op2`	Logically negate all bits. $Rd \leftarrow 0xFFFFFFFF\ EOR\ Op2$

Table 4-5. Bitwise Logic Instructions

These instructions operate at the bit level. They perform logic operations for each pair of bits that are at the same position of inputs. For example, suppose r0 = 0xD5755755 and r1 = 0xAABAAAA9, the following shows the result of various bitwise logic operations.

```
AND r2, r0, r1    ; r2 = r0 bitwise AND r1 ⟹ r2 = 0x80300201

           r0   11010101011101010101011101010101
           r1   10101010101110101010101010101001
           r2   10000000001100000000000100000001


ORR r2, r0, r1    ; r2 = r0 bitwise OR r1 ⟹ r2 = 0xFFFFFFFD

           r0   11010101011101010101011101010101
           r1   10101010101110101010101010101001
           r2   11111111111111111111111111111101


EOR r2, r0, r1    ; r2 = r0 bitwise Exclusive OR r1 ⟹ r2 = 0x7FCFFDFC

           r0   11010101011101010101011101010101
           r1   10101010101110101010101010101001
           r2   01111111110011111111110111111100


ORN r2, r0, r1    ; r2 = r0 bitwise NOT OR r1 ⟹ r2 = 0xD5755757

           r0   11010101011101010101011101010101
           r1   10101010101110101010101010101001
       NOT r1   01010101010001010101010101010110
           r2   11010101011101010101011101010111
```

```
BIC r2, r0, r1    ; r2 = bit clear r0 according to r1 ⟹ r2 = 0x55455554

         r0    1 1 0 1 0 1 0 1 0 1 1 1 0 1 0 1 0 1 0 1 0 1 1 1 0 1 0 1 0 1 0 1
         r1    1 0 1 0 1 0 1 0 1 0 1 1 1 0 1 0 1 0 1 0 1 0 1 0 1 0 1 0 1 0 0 1
     NOT r1    0 1 0 1 0 1 0 1 0 1 0 0 0 1 0 1 0 1 0 1 0 1 0 1 0 1 0 1 0 1 1 0
         r2    0 1 0 1 0 1 0 1 0 1 0 0 0 1 0 1 0 1 0 1 0 1 0 1 0 1 0 1 0 1 0 0

MVN r2, r1        ; r2 = NOT r1 ⟹ r2 = 0x55455556

         r1    1 0 1 0 1 0 1 0 1 0 1 1 1 0 1 0 1 0 1 0 1 0 1 0 1 0 1 0 1 0 0 1
         r2    0 1 0 1 0 1 0 1 0 1 0 0 0 1 0 1 0 1 0 1 0 1 0 1 0 1 0 1 0 1 1 0
```

Bit mask

We often use bit masks to manipulate a particular subset of binary bits in a single bitwise operation conveniently. For an integer N, its bit mask is constructed as follows:

- The mask has the same number of bits in binary as the integer N.
- Bit mask(i) is set if bit $N(i)$ is to be operated; otherwise, mask(i) is 0.
- If $N(i)$ is 1, we say bit $N(i)$ is masked.

The mask can separate the binary bits of an integer into two parts. The part selected by the bit mask is examined or modified, and the other part is ignored. If a bit in the bit mask is 1, the corresponding bit in the target variable is chosen. For example, a mask of 0b00110100 (0x34) selects bits 2, 4, and 5 of the target variable. The following gives C and assembly example programs to set, clear, toggle and check bits in a variable.

- N = 0xA2 = 0b10100010
- Mask = 0x34 = 0b00110100

Bitwise Operators	Symbol	Example
AND	&	C = N & Mask; // C = 0b00100000 = 0x20
OR	|	C = N | Mask; // C = 0b10110110 = 0xB6
EXCLUSIVE-OR (EOR)	^	C = N ^ Mask; // C = 0b10010111 = 0x97
NOT	~	C = ~N; // C = 0b01011101 = 0x5D
SHIFT RIGHT	>>	C = N >> 2; // C = 0b00101000 = 0x28
SHIFT LEFT	<<	C = N << 2; // C = 0b10001000 = 0x88

Example 4-2. The mask selects bit 0, 2, 4, and 5.

Checking a bit via bitwise AND (&)

C Program	Assembly Program 1	Assembly Program 2

char a = 0x34;
char mask = 1<<5;
char b;
// Check bit 5
b = a & mask;
	LDR r0,#0x34 ; r0 = a
	LDR r1,#(1<<5) ; r1 = mask
	ANDS r2,r0,r1 ; r2 = b
		LDR r0,#0x34 ; r0 = a
		ANDS r2,r0,#(1<<5)

We can check whether a bit is 1 by performing bitwise AND operation with the corresponding mask. In this example, register r2, representing variable b, is non-zero only when bit 5 in register r0 is 1.

Setting a bit via bitwise OR (|)

C Program	Assembly Program 1	Assembly Program 2

char a = 0x34;
char mask = 1<<5;
// Set bit 5
a |= mask;
	LDR r0,#0x34 ; r0 = a
	LDR r1,#(1<<5) ; r1 = mask
	ORR r0,r0,r1
		LDR r0,#0x34 ; r0 = a
		ORR r0,r0,#(1<<5)

ORR a bit with 1 sets this bit. ORR a bit with 0 does not change it. Therefore, ORR a variable with the mask sets all bits marked by the mask, while keeping all the other bits unchanged.

Clearing a bit via bitwise AND (&)

C Program	Assembly Program 1	Assembly Program 2

char a = 0x34;
char mask = 1<<5;
// Reset bit 5
a &= ~mask;
	LDR r0,#0x34 ; r0 = a
	LDR r1,#(1<<5) ; r1 = mask
	MVN r1,r1 ; NOT
	EOR r0,r0,r1
		LDR r0,#0x34 ; r0 = a
		BIC r0,#(1<<5)

AND a bit with 0 clears this bit. AND a bit with 1 does not change it. Therefore, AND a variable with the negation of the mask clears all data bits marked by the mask.

Toggling a bit via bitwise EOR (^)

C Program	Assembly Program 1	Assembly Program 2

char a = 0x34;
char mask = 1<<5;
// Toggle bit 5
a ^= mask;
	LDR r0,#0x34 ; r0 = a
	LDR r1,#(1<<5) ; r1 = mask
	EOR r0,r0,r1
		LDR r0,#0x34 ; r0 = a
		EOR r0,r0,#(1<<5)

As illustrated by the truth table given in Table 4-6, exclusive OR (EOR) between 1 and a bit inverts this bit, and exclusive OR between 0 and a bit keeps the bit unchanged. Therefore, exclusive OR between a data and its mask toggles all data bits masked.

Data bit	Mask bit	Data bit $\oplus$ Mask bit
0	1	1
1	1	0
0	0	0
1	0	1

Table 4-6. Truth table of Exclusive OR. Use bitwise EOR with a 1 to toggle a bit.

In C, the Boolean operations are **A && B** (Boolean and), **A||B** (Boolean or), and **!B** (Boolean not), which are different from the above bitwise operations.

- The Boolean operators perform word-wide operations, not bitwise. For example, "`0x10 & 0x01`" equals `0x00`, but "`0x10 && 0x01`" equals `0x01`.
- The bitwise negation expression "`~0x01`" equals `0xFFFFFFFE`, but Boolean NOT expression "`! 0x01`" equals `0x00`.

Using EQU to define a mask in assembly

To make programs easier to read, we often give a name to a mask. For example, we define the bit masks for the clock enable and disable bits for GPIO ports.

```
RCC_AHB2ENR_GPIOAEN  EQU  (0x00000001)  ; GPIO port A clock enable
RCC_AHB2ENR_GPIOBEN  EQU  (0x00000002)  ; GPIO port B clock enable
RCC_AHB2ENR_GPIOCEN  EQU  (0x00000004)  ; GPIO port C clock enable

LDR r7, =RCC_BASE                    ; Address of reset and clock control (RCC)
LDR r1, [r7, #RCC_AHB2ENR]           ; Load AHB2ENR from memory into r1
ORR r1, r1, #RCC_AHB2ENR_GPIOAEN ; Enable clock of GPIO port A
ORR r1, r1, #RCC_AHB2ENR_GPIOBEN ; Enable clock of GPIO port B
ORR r1, r1, #RCC_AHB2ENR_GPIOCEN ; Enable clock of GPIO port C
STR r1, [r7, #RCC_AHB2ENR]           ; Save to RCC->AHB2ENR
```

By using EQU, the program defines three constants (such as `RCC_AHB2ENR_GPIOAEN`). These constants are bit masks, which make it easier to manipulate individual bits. It is not a good programming style to set or clear bits directly by using constants instead of a named mask, such as the following instruction.

```
ORR r1, r1, #0x7    ; Set bits 0, 1, and 2
```

Updating program status flags in assembly

The logic operations with S suffix, including ANDS, ORRS, EORS, ORNS, and MVNS update the N, Z, C flags in APSR. None of them affects the V flag. Neither BFC nor BFI updates these four flags.

It is understandable that a logical instruction with S suffix can update the negative and zero flags in APSR. You may wonder how a logic operation can change the carry flag. The carry flag is updated when the second source operand uses the Barrel shifter. For example,

```
ANDS r0, r1, r2, LSL #3    ; Update N, Z, C flags. (V is unchanged.)
```

The carry flag of the above ANDS operation is, in fact, the carry of the "LSLS r2, #3" operation.

4.7 Reversing the Order of Bits and Bytes

Instructions for reversing the bit or byte orders are useful, particularly when data exchanged between two systems have different formats. For example, the REV instruction is useful to convert data that are exchanged between different endian systems.

RBIT Rd, Rn	Reverse bit order in a word. *for (i = 0; i < 32; i++) Rd[i] ← RN[31– i]*
REV Rd, Rn	Reverse byte order in a word. *Rd[31:24] ← Rn[7:0], Rd[23:16] ← Rn[15:8],* *Rd[15:8] ← Rn[23:16], Rd[7:0] ← Rn[31:24]*
REV16 Rd, Rn	Reverse byte order in each halfword. *Rd[15:8] ← Rn[7:0], Rd[7:0] ← Rn[15:8],* *Rd[31:24] ← Rn[23:16], Rd[23:16] ← Rn[31:24]*
REVSH Rd, Rn	Reverse byte order in bottom halfword and sign extend. *Rd[15:8] ← Rn[7:0], Rd[7:0] ← Rn[15:8],* *Rd[31:16] ← Rn[7] & 0xFFFF*

Table 4-7. Instructions for changing the order of bits or bytes

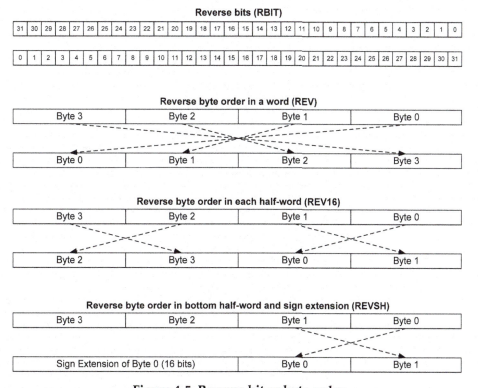

Figure 4-5. Reverse bit or byte order

The following gives a few examples of changing the bit or the byte order of a value stored in register r0.

```
LDR    r0, =0x12345678  ; r0 = 0x12345678
RBIT   r1, r0           ; Reverse bits, r1 = 0x1E6A2C48

LDR    r0, =0x12345678  ; r0 = 0x12345678
REV    r1, r0           ; Reverse byte order, r1 = 0x78563412
REV16  r2, r0           ; Reserve byte order in halfwords, r2 = 0x34127856

LDR    r0, =0x33448899  ; r0 = 0x33448899
REVSH  r1, r0           ; Reverse bytes in lower halfword and extend sign
                        ; r0 = 0xFFFF9988
```

Example 4-3. Assembly codes to change the order of bits or bytes.

4.8 Sign and Zero Extension

Most computers represent signed integers in two's complement. When a signed integer is converted to another signed integer with more bits, the sign bit (*i.e.*, the most significant bit or the leftmost bit) should be duplicated to maintain the integer's sign. Duplicating the sign bit is called *sign extension*.

When an unsigned integer is converted to another unsigned integer with more bits, *zero extension* is deployed to place zeros in the upper bits of the output.

In Example 4-4, when signed variable a and b are assigned to variable c, sign extension is performed. However, when unsigned d is assigned to e, zero-extension is performed.

- The int_8 (signed char), int_16 (signed short), and int_32 (signed integer) are standard integer data types defined in the header file *stdint.h*. They define 8-, 16- and 32-bit signed integers, respectively.
- The unsigned integer definition includes uint_8 (unsigned char), uint_16 (unsigned short), and uint32_t (unsigned integer).

```
int_8    a = -1;   // a signed 8-bit integer,   a = 0xFF
int_16   b = -2;   // a signed 16-bit integer,  b = 0xFFFE
int_32   c;        // a signed 32-bit integer
c = a;             // sign extension, c = 0xFFFFFFFF
c = b;             // sign extension, c = 0xFFFFFFFE

uint_8   d = 1;    // an unsigned 8-bit integer, d = 0x01
uint_32  e;        // an unsigned 32-bit integer
e = d;             // zero extension, e = 0x00000001
```

Example 4-4. Example of sign and zero extension performed in a C program

Table 4-8 shows assembly instructions that perform sign and zero extension.

SXTB {Rd,} Rm {,ROR #n}	Sign extend a byte. $Rd[31:0] \leftarrow Sign\ Extend((Rm\ ROR\ (8 \times n))[7:0])$
SXTH {Rd,} Rm {,ROR #n}	Sign extend a halfword. $Rd[31:0] \leftarrow Sign\ Extend((Rm\ ROR\ (8 \times n))[15:0])$
UXTB {Rd,} Rm {,ROR #n}	Zero extend a byte. $Rd[31:0] \leftarrow Zero\ Extend((Rm\ ROR\ (8 \times n))[7:0])$
UXTH {Rd,} Rm {,ROR #n}	Zero extend a halfword. $Rd[31:0] \leftarrow Zero\ Extend((Rm\ ROR\ (8 \times n))[15:0])$

Table 4-8. Instructions for zero and sign extension

The following program gives a few examples of sign and zero extension. Assume the value of register r0 is 0x11228091.

```
; r0 = 0x11228091
SXTB r1, r0   ; r1 = 0xFFFFFF91, sign extend a byte
SXTH r1, r0   ; r1 = 0xFFFF8091, sign extend a halfword
UXTB r1, r0   ; r1 = 0x00000091, zero extend a byte
UXTH r1, r0   ; r1 = 0x00008091, zero extend a halfword
```

Example 4-5. Example code of sign and zero extension

4.9 Data Comparison

There are four different data comparison instructions.

CMP Rn, Op2	Compare	Set NZCV flags on $Rn - Op2$
CMN Rn, Op2	Compare negative	Set NZCV flags on $Rn + Op2$
TST Rn, Op2	Test	Set NZCV flags on Rn AND $Op2$
TEQ Rn, Op2	Test equivalence	Set NZCV flags on Rn EOR $Op2$

Table 4-9. Data comparison instructions

- The CMP instruction subtracts the value of Op2 from the value in Rn. It is the same as a SUBS instruction, except that the processor discards the result. CMP updates the N, Z, C, and V flags per the subtraction result.
- The CMN instruction adds the value of Op2 to the value in Rn. "CMN Rn, Op2" is like "ADDS Rn, Op2" except that the result is discarded. CMN updates N, Z, C, and V.
- The instruction "TST Rn, Op2" performs a bitwise AND operation on Rn and Op2. Different from "ANDS Rn, Op2", the TST instruction discards the result. TST

updates the N and Z flags. If Op2 uses the Barrel shifter, TST also updates the C flag during the calculation of Op2. However, it does not affect the V flag.
- The TEQ instruction performs a bitwise exclusive OR operation on Rn and Op2. "TEQ Rn, Op2" is the same as "EOR Rn, Op2" except that the result is discarded. TEQ updates the N, Z, and C flags.

TEQ and TST have different usages.

- TEQ is to check whether two values are equal, and TST is to exam whether target bits set by the second operand are clear. After TEQ completes, the zero flag is set if two operands are equal; otherwise, the zero flag is clear.
- TST cannot check the equivalence of two operands. For example, when r0 = 0b1010 and r1 = 0b0101, the instruction "TST r0, r1" sets the zero flag because the result of AND is 0. However, these two operands are not equal.

	r0	r1	Action
TST r0, r1	0b1010	0b0101	Set flag Z
TEQ r0, r1	0b1010	0b0101	Clear flag Z
TST r0, r1	0b1010	0b1010	Clear flag Z
TEQ r0, r1	0b1010	0b1010	Set flag Z

The following gives a few examples of data comparison.

```
CMP r0, #3          ; Compare r0 with 3
CMN r0, #10         ; Compare r0 with -10
CMP r0, r1          ; Compare r0 and r1
TEQ r0, #'?'        ; Compare r0 with ASCII value of '?' (0x3F)

MOV r1, #(1<<31)    ; r1 = 0x80000000
TST r0, r1          ; check whether the sign bit is 1.
```

4.10 Data Movement between Registers

We can classify instructions for moving data between registers into two categories:

- Move data between two general-purpose registers (r0 – r12)
- Move data between a general-purpose register and a special-purpose register

MOV (move) and MVN (move not) are used to copy data between two general-purpose registers. MRS and MSR move content between special registers and general registers.

Special registers include APSR, IPSR, EPSR, IEPSR, IAPSR, EAPSR, PSR, MSP, PSP, PRIMASK, BASEPRI, BASEPRI_MAX, FAULTMASK, and CONTROL.

MOV	$Rd \leftarrow operand2$
MVN	$Rd \leftarrow$ NOT $operand2$
MRS Rd, spec_reg	Move from special register to general register
MSR spec_reg, Rm	Move from general register to special register

Table 4-10. Data copy instructions

MOV and MVN can also load an immediate number into a register, as introduced in Chapter 5.4.4. The following are a few examples of MOV and MVN.

```
MOV r4, r5          ; Copy r5 to r4
MVN r4, r5          ; r4 = bitwise logical NOT of r5
MOV r1, r2, LSL #3  ; r1 = r2 << 3
MOV r0, PC          ; Copy PC (r15) to r0
MOV r1, SP          ; Copy SP (r14) to r1
```

The following instructions copy a special-purpose register to a general-purpose register.

```
MRS r0, APSR  ; Read flag state into r0
MRS r0, IPSR  ; Read exception/interrupt state into r0
MRS r0, EPSR  ; Read execution state into r0
MRS r0, PSR   ; Copy combined CPSR, EPSR, and SPSR into r0
```

The following shows how to copy a general-purpose register to a special-purpose register.

```
MSR APSR, r0     ; Write flag state
MSR BASEPRI, r0  ; Write to base priority mask register; Disable
                 ; exceptions with same or lower priority level
```

4.11 Bit Field Extract

Table 4-11 shows two instructions that extract adjacent bits from one register.

- The #lsb parameter, ranging from 0 to 31, specifies the starting position.
- The #width parameter, ranging from 1 to (32 − #lsb), indicates the number of contiguous bits to be extracted.

SBFX Rd, Rn, #lsb, #width	Signed Bit Field Extract $Rd[(width-1):0] \leftarrow Rn[(width+lsb-1):lsb]$ $Rd[31:width] \leftarrow Replicate(Rn[width+lsb-1])$
UBFX Rd, Rn, #lsb, #width	Unsigned Bit Field Extract $Rd[(width-1):0] \leftarrow Rn[(width+lsb-1):lsb]$ $Rd[31:width] \leftarrow Replicate(0)$

Table 4-11. Bit field extract instructions

UBFX simply places zero in the upper bits, while SBFX duplicates the sign bit. The sign bit, in this case, is not the most significant bit; instead, it is the bit at the position of #width + #lsb - 1.

The following shows two examples of extracting 8 bits from register r3, starting at bit 4. One has no sign extension, and the other has sign extension.

```
; Assume r3 = 0x1234CDEF
UBFX r4, r3, #4, #8    ; r4 = 0x000000DE (zero extension)
SBFX r4, r3, #4, #8    ; r4 = 0xFFFFFFDE (sign extension)
```

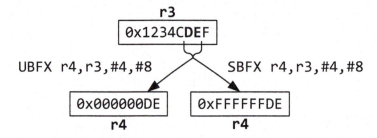

Figure 4-6. Extracting 8 bits starting at bit position 4, *i.e.*, r4 = r3[11:4]

4.12 Exercises

1. LSL (logic shift left) can speed up some special multiplication because it runs much faster than MUL. Use LSL to implement the following C statements.

   (1) $x = 31 * x$;
   (2) $x = 38 * x$;
   (3) $x = 17 * x$;

2. Suppose r0 = 0x0F0F0F0F, and r1 = 0xFEDCBA98, find the result of the following operations.

   ```
   (1) EOR r3, r1, r0
   (2) ORR r3, r1, r0
   (3) AND r3, r1, r0
   (4) BIC r3, r1, r0
   (5) BFI r3, r1, #4, #8
   (6) MVN r3, r1
   (7) MVN r3, r0
   (8) MVN r3, r0
       ADD r3, r1, r3
   ```

3. Suppose r0 = 0x56789ABC, find the result of the following operations. These operations run independently.

    ```
    (1) RBIT  r1, r0
    (2) REV   r1, r0
    (3) REV16 r1, r0
    (4) REVSH r1, r0
    ```

4. Translate the following C statement into an assembly program, assuming 16-bit signed integers x, y and z (*i.e.*, signed short) are stored in 32-bit register r0, r1, and r2, respectively.

$$x = x * y + z - x;$$

5. Translate the following C statement into an assembly program, assuming 16-bit unsigned integers x and y (*i.e.*, unsigned short) are stored in register r0, and r1, respectively.

$$x = x \% y;$$

6. Write an assembly program that calculates the value of the following given polynomial, assuming signed integers x and y are stored in register r0 and r1, respectively.

$$y = 3x^3 - 7x^2 + 10x - 11.$$

7. Write an assembly program that calculates the remainder of the division between two unsigned 32-bit integers.

8. Explain why Cortex-M processors do not provide any left rotation instructions. They only offer ROR (rotate right) and RRX (rotate right extended).

9. Explain the difference between the Barrel shifter's role in the following instructions:

    ```
    (1) ANDS r1, r2, r3, LSL #3
    (2) ADDS r1, r2, r3, LSL #3
    ```

10. Write an assembly program that reverses the byte order of a register without using the REV instruction.

11. Write an assembly program that swaps the upper halfword and the lower halfword of a register.

12. Implement the BIC (bitwise clear) instruction by using other assembly instructions.

13. Suppose Mask = 0x00000F0F and P = 0xABCDABCD. What are the results of the following bitwise operations?

```
(1) Q = P & Mask;
(2) Q = P | Mask;
(3) Q = P ^ Mask;
(4) Q = ~Mask;
(5) Q = P & ~Mask;
```

14. Suppose r0 = 0xFFFFFFFF, r1 = 0x00000001, and r2 = 0x00000000. Initially the N, Z, C, and V flags are zero. Find the value of the N, Z, C, and V flags of the following instructions. (Assume each instruction runs individually, *i.e.*, these instructions are not part of a program.)

```
(1) ADD  r3, r0, r2
(2) SUBS r3, r0, r0
(3) ADDS r3, r0, r2
(4) LSL  r3, r0, #1
(5) LSRS r3, r1, #1
(6) ANDS r3, r0, r2
```

15. Suppose we have a hypothetical processor, of which each register has only five bits. r0 = 0b11101 and r1 = 0b10110. What are the N, Z, C, and V flags of the following instructions? Assume initially N = 0, Z = 0, C = 1, V = 0, and these instructions are executed independently (*i.e.*, they are NOT part of a program)

```
(1) ADDS r3, r0, r1
(2) SUBS r3, r0, r1
(3) EOR  r3, r0, r1
(4) ANDS r3, r1, r1, LSL #3
```

16. What is the value in register r1? Assume r0 = 0x00001016

```
(1) USAT r1, #8, r0
(2) SSAT r1, #8, r0
(3) USAT r1, #9, r0
(4) SSAT r1, #9, r0
```

17. Write short assembly programs to complete the following tasks.

(1) Reset all even bits in register r0 to zero and keep all odd bits unchanged
(2) Set all odd bits in register r0 to one and keep all even bits unchanged
(3) Toggle all odd bits in register r0 and keep all even bits unchanged

CHAPTER 5

Load and Store

A load instruction sets a register to some value. The value might be a constant directly specified in the program or a value that is stored in memory. A store instruction saves the value held in a register to the memory.

5.1 Load Constant into Registers

Many assembly instructions use constant numbers, often called *immediate numbers*. One command usage is to set a register to a specific constant value.

MOV Rd, #<immed_8>	Move 8-bit immediate value (0-255) to the register
MVN Rd, #<immed_8>	Move the bitwise inverse of 8-bit immediate value (0-255) to the register
MOVT Rd, #<immed_16>	Move 16-bit immediate value to top halfword [31:16] of the register. Bottom halfword unaltered.
MOVW Rd, #<immed_16>	Move 16-bit immediate value to bottom halfword [15:0] of the register and clear top halfword [31:16]
LDR Rt, =#<immed_8>	Equivalent to MOV
LDR Rt, =#<immed_32>	A pseudo instruction

Table 5-1. Instructions for loading constants into a register.

5.1.1 Data Movement Instruction MOV and MVN

All immediate numbers start with a "#" sign. If the immediate number is less than 8 bits, we can use MOV to set the register value.

```
MOV r0, #0xFF          ; Set r0 to the hexadecimal value 0xFF
MOV r0, #0b10011100    ; Set r0 to the binary value 10011100
MOV r0, #54            ; Set r0 to the decimal value 54
MOV r0, #0d54          ; Set r0 to the decimal value 54
```

If the immediate number has 32 bits, we can use MOV to set the register value if the immediate number can be obtained by using the following format:

$$\#immed\_32 = \#immed\_8 \; ROR \; (2 \times \#immed\_4)$$

where ROR is the circular right rotate. For example, right rotating 0xAF by 24 bits can get 0x0000AF00.

$$0x0000AF00 = 0xAF \; ROR \; (2 \times 12)$$

Besides, these instructions can also use a few 32-bit values with some regular patterns, such as 0xABABABAB, 0x00AB00AB, and 0xAB00AB00.

5.1.2 Pseudo Instruction LDR and ADR

A *pseudo instruction* is an instruction that is available to use in an assembly program, but not directly supported by the microprocessor. Compilers translate it to one or multiple actual machine instructions when the assembler builds the program into an executable. Pseudo instructions are provided for the convenience of programmers.

As introduced later in this chapter, LDR loads data from the memory to a register. However, LDR can be a pseudo instruction that loads an immediate number into a register. A pseudo instruction is not a real machine instruction, but it provides convenience for programmers and improves the readability of programs. The assembler translates a pseudo instruction into one or multiple actual machine instructions.

```
LDR   r0, =array        ; Pseudo instruction
LDR   r1, [r0]          ; Not a pseudo instruction

LDR   r2, =0x12345678   ; Pseudo instruction
ADD   r1, r1, r2        ; r1 = r1 + r2
STR   r1, [r0]          ; Save r1 to memory

AREA myData, DATA       ; Directive: declare a data area
ALIGN                   ; Directive: align on a word boundary
                        ; Allocate padding bytes if necessary to make the
                        ; array to align properly
array DCW  1, 2, 3, 4, 5
```

Example 5-1. Using LDR pseudo instruction to load a memory address or an immediate number into a register.

Another widely used pseudo instruction in ARM assembly language is ADR (stands for address), which sets a register to a memory address within a certain range, as shown in Example 5-2. The syntax difference between LDR and ADR is that LDR needs an equal sign ("=") but ADR does not. The assembler translates an ADR instruction into an ADD or SUB instruction with one source operand as PC.

Also, the pseudo instruction LDR is different from the LDR instruction for accessing memory. For example, "LDR r1, =0x12345678" is a pseudo instruction, and "LDR r1, [r0]" is a real machine instruction that loads a word from memory. The assembler can distinguish them by checking the format of the operands specified in LDR.

```
loop ADD r1, r2, r3
     ADR r4, loop    ; A pseudo instruction, translated to "SUB r4, pc, #12"
```
Example 5-2. Using ADR pseudo instruction to load a memory address into a register

5.1.3 Comparison of LDR, ADR, and MOV

While ADR can only load a memory address label into a register, LDR is more versatile and can load an immediate number up to 32 bits. The real instructions translated from the LDR pseudo instruction depend on the immediate number.

LDR can load a 32-bit constant to a register.

MOV can only load a 12-bit constant into a register.

ADR can load a memory address.

- If the constant number can fit into the 12-bit immediate number format used by an MOV or MVN instruction, compilers translate the LDR pseudo instruction to MOV or MVN.
- Otherwise, compilers translate it into a regular LDR instruction that uses PC-relative memory address.

In the latter case, the immediate numbers are directly stored together with the instruction code in the machine executable. As introduced in Chapter 1.2, the executable is stored in the instruction memory.

Compilers replace the LDR pseudo instruction with an actual load instruction with a PC-relative memory address to load the immediate number from the instruction memory. Chapter 5.4.3 introduces PC-relative addressing in details.

```
LDR r1, =2            ; Translated to:  MOV r1, #2
LDR r2, =-2           ; Translated to:  MVN r0, #1
LDR r3, =0x12345678   ; Translated to:  LDR r2, [pc, #offset1]
LDR r4, =myAddress    ; Translated to:  LDR r2, [pc, #offset2]
                      ; LDR with a PC-relative address
```
Example 5-3. Pseudo-instruction LDR.

Note the syntax for specifying the constant number in MOV and LDR are different.

```
LDR r0, =0xFF         ; '=' before the constant
MOV r0, #0xFF         ; '#' before the constant
```

5.2 Big and Little Endian

Cortex-M processors support both big and little endian. The endian specifies the byte order if a data element has multiple bytes, as shown in Figure 5-1. We can use REV, which reserves the byte order, to convert the endian (See Chapter 4.7).

- Little endian means the low-order byte of the number is stored in memory at the lowest address, and the high-order byte at the highest address. (The little end comes first.)
- Big endian means the high-order byte of the number is stored at the lowest address, and the low-order byte at the highest address. (The big end comes first.)

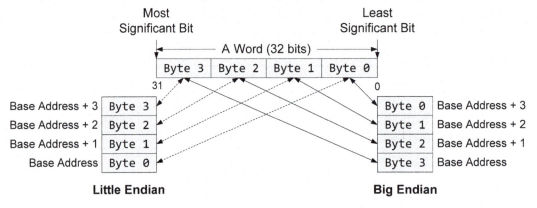

Figure 5-1. Comparison of little endian and big endian

In the example given in Figure 5-2, the assembly instruction "LDR r1, [r0]" loads a 32-bit value from the memory address 0x20008000 to register r1. Register r1 has different results, depending on whether the big or little endian is used.

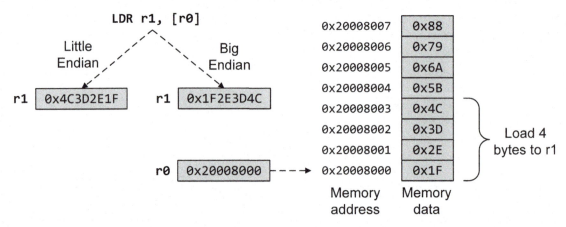

Figure 5-2. Register r1 is 0x4C3D2E1F under little endian, and 0x1F2E3D4C under big endian.

5.3 Accessing Data in Memory

A load instruction retrieves data stored at some memory address and saves the data in a specific register. A store instruction does the opposite. It saves the content of a register to the memory at a given memory address.

When an assembly program accesses data in memory, the memory address must be in a register. Example 5-4 assumes the memory address is in register r0. The program loads a 32-bit integer to register r1, increases it by 4, and saves the result in memory.

```
; Suppose r0 = 0x82000004
LDR r1, [r0]      ; r1 = a word (4 bytes) in memory starting at 0x82000004
ADD r1, r1, #4    ; r1 = r1 + 4
STR r1, [r0]      ; Save 4 bytes into memory starting at 0x82000004
```
Example 5-4. Loading a word from the memory

5.4 Memory Addressing

5.4.1 Pre-index, Post-index, and Pre-index with Update

Cortex-M processors support flexible memory addressing. They provide three memory address modes: pre-index, post-index, and pre-index with update, as shown in Table 5-2. Each mode has a base memory address (saved in a register) and a byte offset.

1. In the *pre-index* format, the target memory address is the base memory address plus the offset. The base memory address remains unchanged.
2. In the *pre-index with update* format, three steps are involved. First, it calculates the target memory address as the base plus the offset. Then, it accesses the data at the destination memory address. Finally, it updates the base memory.
3. In the *post-index* format, two steps are involved. First, it updates the base memory address as the sum of the base memory address and offset. Then it accesses the data by using the updated base memory address.

Memory Address Mode	Example	Equivalent
Pre-index	LDR r1, [r0, #4]	r1 ← memory[r0 + 4], r0 remains unchanged.
Pre-index with update	LDR r1, [r0, #4]!	r1 ← memory[r0 + 4] r0 ← r0 + 4
Post-index	LDR r1, [r0], #4	r1 ← memory[r0] r0 ← r0 + 4

Table 5-2. Three memory addressing formats

The following gives three examples to compare these three addressing modes. Suppose register r0 has an initial value of 0x20008000, and the processor uses little-endian.

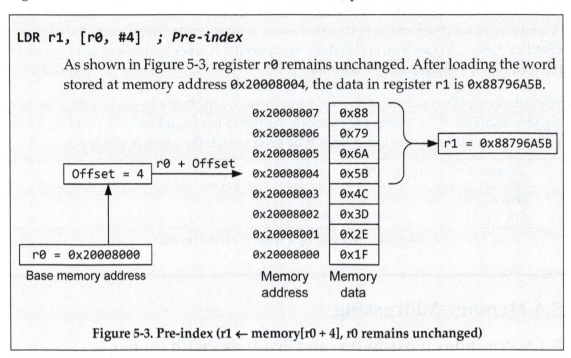

LDR r1, [r0, #4]   ; Pre-index

As shown in Figure 5-3, register r0 remains unchanged. After loading the word stored at memory address 0x20008004, the data in register r1 is 0x88796A5B.

Figure 5-3. Pre-index (r1 ← memory[r0 + 4], r0 remains unchanged)

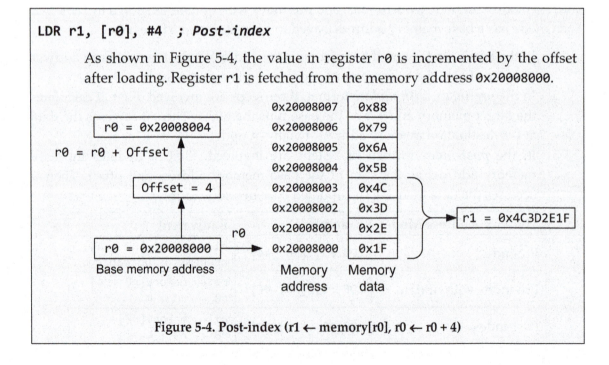

LDR r1, [r0], #4   ; Post-index

As shown in Figure 5-4, the value in register r0 is incremented by the offset after loading. Register r1 is fetched from the memory address 0x20008000.

Figure 5-4. Post-index (r1 ← memory[r0], r0 ← r0 + 4)

```
LDR r1, [r0, #4]!   ; Pre-index with update
```

As shown in Figure 5-5, the value in register r0 is incremented by the offset after loading. Both the post-index and the pre-index with update change the base memory address. However, different with the post-index, the pre-index with update retrieves the word from the memory address 0x20008004, instead of 0x20008000.

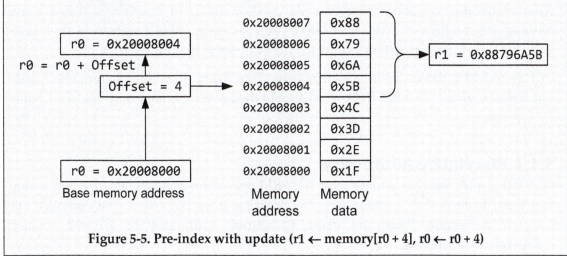

Figure 5-5. Pre-index with update (r1 ← memory[r0 + 4], r0 ← r0 + 4)

Table 5-3 summarizes the results of three addressing modes described above.

Instruction	Result of r0	Result of r1	Comment
LDR r1, [r0, #4]	0x20008000	0x88796A5B	Pre-index
LDR r1, [r0], #4	0x20008004	0x4C3D2E1F	Post-index
LDR r1, [r0, #4]!	0x20008004	0x88796A5B	Pre-index with update

Table 5-3. Example of three addressing modes

5.4.2 Load and Store Instructions

Table 5-4 and Table 5-5 list load and store instructions. Only the pre-index format is presented. However, load and store instructions with the other two formats are similar.

LDR Rt, [Rn, #offset]	Load word, $Rt \leftarrow mem[Rn + offset]$
LDRB Rt, [Rn, #offset]	Load byte, $Rt \leftarrow mem[Rn + offset]$
LDRH Rt, [Rn, #offset]	Load halfword, $Rt \leftarrow mem[Rn + offset]$
LDRSB Rt, [Rn, #offset]	Load signed byte, $Rt \leftarrow Sign\ Extend\ (mem[Rn + offset])$
LDRSH Rt, [Rn, #offset]	Load signed halfword, $Rt \leftarrow Sign\ Extend\ (mem[Rn + offset])$
LDM Rn, register_list	Load multiple words

Table 5-4. Load data of different sizes from memory to a register

STR Rt, [Rn, #offset]	Store word, *mem[Rn + offset] ← Rt*
STRB Rt, [Rn, #offset]	Store lower byte, *mem[Rn + offset] ← Rt*
STRH Rt, [Rn, #offset]	Store lower halfword, *mem[Rn + offset] ← Rt*
STM Rn, register_list	Store multiple words

Table 5-5. Store value of a register in memory

When a byte or halfword is loaded into a 32-bit register, we should draw attention to whether the memory data represents a signed or unsigned number. If it is a signed number, we should use LDRSB or LDRSH to preserve the number's sign and value. LDRSB and LDRSH perform sign extension, which duplicates the sign bit.

In LDM and STM, the order in which registers are listed does not matter. The lowest-numbered register is loaded from or written to the lowest memory address (see Chapter 5.5 for details).

5.4.3 PC-relative Addressing

PC-relative addressing is widely used by ARM processors to locate nearby instructions and data. Even if the original assembly program does not use it, the compiler may translate a memory index by using PC-relative addressing to achieve position-independent addressing.

The target memory address is as follows:

$$Target\ Memory\ Address = PC + 4 + Offset$$

The program counter (PC) always incremented by 4, pointing to the next 32-bit instruction or the next two 16-bit instructions. Even if a 16-bit Thumb assembly instruction reads PC, the value returned is the address of this instruction plus 4 bytes.

PC-relative addressing is often used to set a register to a complicated value. For example, the program needs to set register r1 to 0xF1234567. We cannot use the instruction "MOV r1, #0xF1234567" because the constant number is too large. As an alternative, we use the pseudo instruction "LDR r1, =0xF1234567".

The compiler translates the above LDR pseudo instruction into a PC-relative LDR instruction.

- Suppose the constant 0xF1234567 is stored at the memory location 0x08000144.
- The compiler uses the PC-relative addressing for the load word instruction. If the memory address of the load word (LDR) instruction is 0x0800012C, the difference between 0x08000144 and 0x0800012C is 24 in decimal.
- Thus, the memory address is [pc, #20]. The target address is pc + 4 + 20.

The following shows the translated PC-relative load instruction.

0x0800012C	LDR r1, [pc, #20] ; @0x08000144
...	...
0x08000144	DCW 0x4567 ; lower halfword
0x08000146	DCW 0xF123 ; upper halfword

Example 5-5. Using PC-relative addressing to load a large constant number into a register

5.4.4 Example of Accessing an Array

The following three examples iterates through an array of five 32-bit integers by using three different addressing modes. Suppose we want to load an array of five integers into registers r1, r2, r3, r4, and r5. The following uses three different address modes to access the array and calculate the sum of the array. Assume the array is defined as follows.

```
          AREA myData, DATA, READWRITE
array     DCD 1, 2, 3, 4, 5
```

(1) Iterate an array by using pre-index

```
    LDR r0, =array      ; Using LDR pseudo instruction, r0 = array address
    LDR r1, [r0]        ; r1 = array[0]. After loading, r0 = array
    LDR r2, [r0, #4]    ; r2 = array[1]. After loading, r0 = array + 4
    LDR r3, [r0, #8]    ; r3 = array[2]. After loading, r0 = array + 8
    LDR r4, [r0, #12]   ; r4 = array[3]. After loading, r0 = array + 12
    LDR r5, [r0, #16]   ; r5 = array[4]. After loading, r0 = array + 16
```

(2) Iterate an array by using post-index

```
    LDR r0, =array      ; Using LDR pseudo instruction, r0 = array address
    LDR r1, [r0], #4    ; r1 = array[0]. After loading, r0 = array + 4
    LDR r2, [r0], #4    ; r2 = array[1]. After loading, r0 = array + 8
    LDR r3, [r0], #4    ; r3 = array[2]. After loading, r0 = array + 12
    LDR r4, [r0], #4    ; r4 = array[3]. After loading, r0 = array + 16
    LDR r5, [r0], #4    ; r5 = array[4]. After loading, r0 = array + 20
```

(3) Iterate an array by using pre-index with update

```
    LDR r0, =array      ; Using LDR pseudo instruction, r0 = array address
    LDR r1, [r0]        ; r1 = array[0]. After loading, r0 = array
    LDR r2, [r0, #4]!   ; r2 = array[1]. After loading, r0 = array + 4
    LDR r3, [r0, #4]!   ; r3 = array[2]. After loading, r0 = array + 8
    LDR r4, [r0, #4]!   ; r4 = array[3]. After loading, r0 = array + 12
    LDR r5, [r0, #4]!   ; r5 = array[4]. After loading, r0 = array + 16
```

The above example codes only work well for a short array. If the length of the array is long, then the assembly program needs to use conditional branch instructions (see Chapter 6) to implement a loop to iterate the array.

5.5 Loading and Storing Multiple Registers

A sequence of registers can be stored in consecutive memory locations in one assembly instruction. Similarly, multiple words can be loaded from sequential memory locations to registers in one instruction too.

There are four different addressing modes for loading and storing multiple registers, as shown in Table 5-6.

Addressing Mode	Description	Instructions
IA	Increment After	STMIA, LDMIA
IB	Increment Before	STMIB, LDMIB
DA	Decrement After	STMDA, LDMDA
DB	Decrement Before	STMDB, LDMDB

Table 5-6. Four different addressing modes for STM and LDM

- IA: The memory address is incremented by 4 after a word is loaded or stored.
- IB: The memory address is incremented by 4 before a word is loaded or stored.
- DA: The memory address is decremented by 4 after a word is loaded or stored.
- DB: The memory address is decremented by 4 before a word is loaded or stored.

The assembly instruction format is as follows:

```
STMxx rn{!}, {register_list}
LDMxx rn{!}, {register_list}
```

where the base register rn holds the starting memory location and xx is one of the addressing modes (IA, IB, DA, or DB).

- The exclamation mark "!" is optional. If it is specified, the instruction writes a modified value back to register rn. If it is omitted, register rn is not updated.
- The order in which registers are listed in the register list does not matter at all. When multiple registers are stored or loaded, they are sorted by name, and the lowest-numbered register is saved to or read from the lowest memory address.

Figure 5-6 shows the result of "STMxx r0!, {r3,r1,r7,r2}" under four different address modes (where xx = IA, IB, DA, or DB). Note the order in which the four registers are listed does not matter. Register r1, the lowest numbered register, is always stored at the lowest memory address in all memory address modes. For STMIA and STMDA, the base register r0 points to an empty memory location at the end, while it points to a valid data item for STMIB and STMDB.

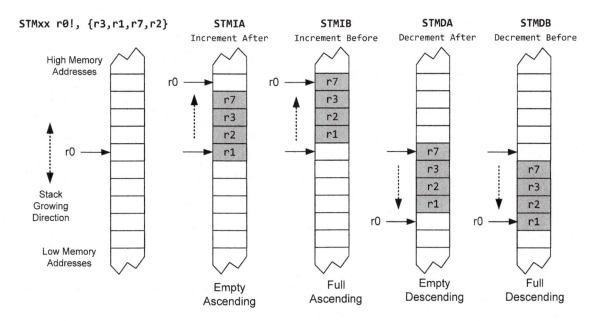

Figure 5-6. Example of four different memory addressing mode for STM.

Figure 5-7 shows the result of "LDMxx r0!, {r3,r1,r7,r2}" under four different address modes (where xx = IA, IB, DA, or DB). Like STM, the order in which registers are listed does not matter in an LDM instruction. The lowest-numbered register is loaded from the lowest memory address.

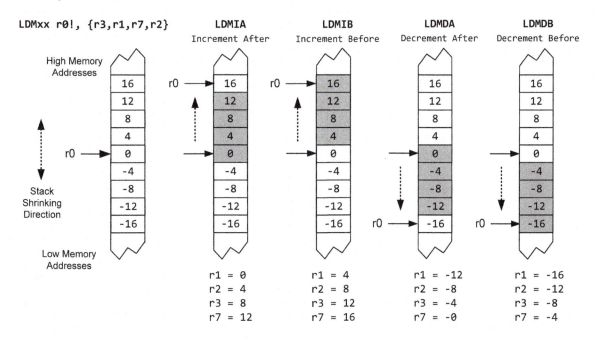

Figure 5-7. Example of four different memory address modes for LDM.

For Cortex-M processors, STM is STMIA, and LDM is LDMIA. The following are synonyms.

- STM = STMIA (Increment After) = STMEA (Empty Ascending)
- LDM = LDMIA (Increment After) = LDMFD (Full Descending)

Note that when loading or storing multiple values by using STM and LDM, the destination memory address must be word-aligned. Therefore, in the instruction "LDMxx rn{!}, {register_list}" or "STMxx rn{!}, {register_list}", the least significant two bits of register rn are ignored. If aligned checking is enabled, any unaligned access made by LDM or STM (*i.e.*, when bit[1:0] in register rn are not zero) generates a usage fault.

Chapter 8.3 explains how to implement a stack by using the STM and LDM instructions.

5.6 Exercises

1. Suppose r0 = 0x20008000, and the memory layout is as follows:

Address	Data
0x20008007	0x79
0x20008006	0xCD
0x20008005	0xA3
0x20008004	0xFD
0x20008003	0x0D
0x20008002	0xEB
0x20008001	0x2C
0x20008000	0x1A

a) What is the value of r1 after running LDR r1, [r0] if the system is little endian? What is the value if the system uses the big-endian?

b) Suppose the system is set as little endian. What are the values of r1 and r0 if the following instructions are executed separately?

- LDR r1, [r0, #4]
- LDR r1, [r0], #4
- LDR r1, [r0, #4]!

2. Write an assembly program that converts a 32-bit integer stored in memory from little endian to big endian, without using the REV instruction. Make sure that the result is saved back to the memory.

3. Suppose r0 = 0x20000000 and r1 = 0x12345678. All bytes in memory are initialized to 0x00. Suppose the following assembly program has run successfully. Draw a table to show the memory value if the processor uses little endian.

```
STR r1, [r0], #4
STR r1, [r0, #4]!
STR r1, [r0, #4]
```

4. What is the memory value of Question 3 if the processor uses big endian?

5. When an 8-bit or 16-bit data is loaded from the data memory into a 32-bit register, whether sign extension or zero extension is performed depends on the data's sign.

  • LDRSB (load register with signed byte) LDRSH loads a signed byte and LDRB (load register with byte) for an unsigned byte.
  • LDRSH (load register with signed halfword) and LDRH (load register with halfword) read load a 16-bit signed and unsigned number from memory into a register, respectively.

What is the value in register r1 in the following instructions if r0 = 0x20008000? Assume the system is little endian.

```
(1) LDRSB r1, [r0]
(2) LDRSH r1, [r0]
(3) LDRB  r1, [r0]
(4) LDRH  r1, [r0]
```

Memory address	Data
0x20008002	0xA1
0x20008001	0xB2
0x20008000	0xC3
0x20007FFF	0xD4
0x20007FFE	0xE5

6. Suppose r0 = 0x20008000. What address is register r7 loaded from in the following instructions? What is the value of r0 after executing each instruction? Assume each instruction runs separately, i.e., they are not part of a program.

```
(1) LDMIA r0, {r1, r3, r7, r6, r2}
(2) LDMIB r0, {r1, r3, r7, r6, r2}
(3) LDMDA r0, {r1, r3, r7, r6, r2}
(4) LDMDB r0, {r1, r3, r7, r6, r2}
```

7. Suppose r0 = 0x20008000. What address is register r7 stored at in the following instructions? What is the value of r0 after executing each instruction? Assume each instruction runs separately, *i.e.*, they are not part of a program.

    (1) STMIA r0!, {r3, r9, r7, r1, r2}
    (2) STMIB r0!, {r3, r9, r7, r1, r2}
    (3) STMDA r0!, {r3, r9, r7, r1, r2}
    (4) STMDB r0!, {r3, r9, r7, r1, r2}

8. Suppose r0 = 0x20008000. What is the value in register r0, r3, r5, r7, and r9 after running the following instructions? Assume each instruction runs separately, *i.e.*, they are not part of a program.

    (1) LDMDB r0, {r3, r7, r9, r5}
    (2) LDMIA r0, {r7, r3, r9, r5}
    (3) LDRIB r0, {r3, r9, r5, r7}
    (4) LDRDA r0, {r9, r5, r7, r3}

High Memory Addresses

Address	Value
0x20008010	16
0x2000800C	12
0x20008008	8
0x20008004	4
0x20008000	0
0x20007FFC	-4
0x20007FF8	-8
0x20007FF4	-12
0x20007FF0	-16

Low Memory Addresses

9. In the following load instruction based on PC-relative addressing, what is the address range in which the target data can be located? Assume the memory address of this instruction is 0x10004000. The PC-relative offset is a 12-bit signed integer.

    LDR r1, =label

CHAPTER 6

Branch and Conditional Execution

Normally instructions of an assembly program run in the same sequential order as they are listed in the program. When one instruction completes, the program counter is incremented by the control unit within the processor and ordinarily points to the next instruction. However, modifying the program counter at runtime can dynamically change the execution order. We call it changing the flow of control. There are four major approaches to alter the flow of control:

1. branch instructions,
2. conditional execution,
3. calling a subroutine, and
4. interrupts.

This chapter focuses on the first two approaches. Chapter 8 discusses subroutines, and Chapter 11 presents interrupt.

6.1 Condition Testing

Most assembly instructions can be selectively executed based on the N, Z, C, and V flags of the application program status register (APSR). Table 6-1 lists the condition flags for comparing signed and unsigned numbers.

Compare	Signed	Unsigned	Relationship Tested
==	EQ	EQ	Equal to
!=	NE	NE	Not equal to
>	GT	HI	Greater than
≥	GE	HS	Greater than or equal to
<	LT	LO	Less than
≤	LE	LS	Less than or equal to

Table 6-1. Summary of the comparison suffix for signed and unsigned numbers

These flags provide convenience for programmers and improve the code readability.

> For example, the following two assembly instructions calculate the absolute value of a signed integer stored in register r1. The second instruction RSB is executed if r1 is less than 0. The condition flag "LT" tests the negative flag, and the processor ignores the RSB instruction if the negative flag is 0.
>
> ```
> CMP    r1, #0        ; CMP updates N, Z, C, and V flags
> RSBLT  r1, r1, #0    ; Run r1 = 0 - r1 if r1 < 0. LT = signed Less Than.
> ```

Cortex-M processors have 15 condition flags, as summarized in Table 6-2. These condition flags check whether N, Z, C, and V meet specific requirements. When an instruction has no conditional flag, it defaults to "AL" and is always executed.

Suffix	Description	Flags tested	Logic Implementation
EQ	EQual	Z = 1	Z
NE	Not Equal	Z = 0	$\bar{Z}$
CS/HS	unsigned Higher or Same	C = 1	C
CC/LO	unsigned LOwer	C = 0	$\bar{C}$
MI	MInus (negative)	N = 1	N
PL	PLus (positive or zero)	N = 0	$\bar{N}$
VS	oVerflow Set	V = 1	V
VC	oVerflow Clear	V = 0	$\bar{V}$
HI	unsigned HIgher	C = 1 & Z = 0	$C\bar{Z}$
LS	unsigned Lower or Same	C = 0 or Z = 1	$\bar{C} + Z$
GE	signed Greater or Equal	N = V	$NV + \bar{N}\bar{V}$
LT	signed Less Than	N != V	$N\bar{V} + \bar{N}V$
GT	signed Greater Than	Z = 0 & N = V	$Z(NV + \bar{N}\bar{V})$
LE	signed Less than or Equal	Z = 1 or N != V	$Z + N\bar{V} + \bar{N}V$
AL	ALways		

Table 6-2. Summary of flag testing for various signed and unsigned comparisons

The CMP instruction "CMP r0, r1" is equivalent to the subtraction operation r0 - r1, except the result is discarded.

When two registers in the instruction "CMP r0, r1" represent unsigned integers,

- the carry flag is set if no borrow occurs during the subtraction (*i.e.*, r0 ≥ r1), and
- the carry flag is cleared if borrow does occur during the subtraction (*i.e.*, r0 < r1).

Therefore, the HS, LO, HI and LS suffix check the zero flag (if necessary) and the carry flag.

When two registers in the instruction "CMP r0, r1" represent signed numbers, Table 6-3 summarizes the meaning of all four possible combinations of the negative flag (N) and the overflow flag (V).

	N = 0	N = 1
V = 0	r0 ≥ r1	r0 < r1
V = 1	r0 < r1	r0 ≥ r1

Table 6-3. The meaning of the overflow and negative flags of "CMP r0, r1" if register r0 and r1 hold signed numbers.

Table 6-4 gives the detailed explanation of how to get the conclusions listed in Table 6-3.

- When two signed numbers are subtracted, there are two possible scenarios, in which overflow occurs: (1) the result of subtracting a positive number from a negative number is positive, or (2) the result of subtracting a negative number from a positive number is negative.
- When subtracting two numbers with the same sign, no overflow would occur.

In sum, if overflow occurs, the result is incorrect, and its sign indicated by the N flag is opposite to the sign of the actual result.

	N = 0	N = 1
V = 0	No overflow has occurred, implying the result is correct. The result is non-negative. Thus, r0 – r1 ≥ 0, *i.e.,* r0 ≥ r1.	No overflow has occurred, implying the result is correct. The result is negative. Thus, r0 – r1 < 0, *i.e.,* r0 < r1.
V = 1	Overflow has occurred, implying the result is incorrect. The result is mistakenly reported as non-negative, but it should be negative. Thus, r0 – r1 < 0 in reality, *i.e.,* r0 < r1.	Overflow has occurred, implying the result is incorrect. The result is mistakenly reported as negative, but it should be non-negative. Thus, r0 – r1 ≥ 0 in reality, *i.e.,* r0 ≥ r1.

Table 6-4. The signed greater or equal (GE) checks whether V equals N.

Table 6-4 leads to the following conclusions:

- If N = V, then r0 is signed greater than or equal to r1.
- If N ≠ V, then r0 is signed less than r1.

Therefore, the signed greater or equal suffix (GE) and the signed greater than suffix (GT) check whether the N flag is the same as the V flag.

6.2 Branch Instructions

A branch instruction is used to change the flow of program execution from a normal sequential order. It allows the microprocessor to begin execution a different set of instructions. There are two types of branch instructions: unconditional and conditional.

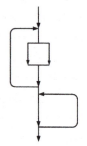

- An *unconditional* branch instruction always loads the memory address of the designated instruction into the program counter and starts to execute the new program flow. Assembly programs use a label to denote the designated instruction.

- A *conditional* branch instruction first checks whether a specific condition is satisfied or not. If the condition is satisfied, the processor then starts to execute the designated instruction, instead of the next sequential instruction. A conditional branch instruction is equivalent to "if the *condition* is true, then go to the *label*." When the program jumps away, we say the branch is taken. Otherwise, the branch is not taken.

We can append the condition suffix to the branch instruction "B" to form different conditional branch instructions, as summarized in Table 6-5. For example, "BEQ" compares two register values, and the branch is taken if the source operands are equal.

	Instruction	Description	Flags tested
Unconditional Branch	**B** *Label*	Branch to label	none
Conditional Branch	**BEQ** *Label*	Branch if **EQ**ual	Z = 1
	BNE *Label*	Branch if **N**ot Equal	Z = 0
	BCS/BHS *Label*	Branch if unsigned **H**igher or **S**ame	C = 1
	BCC/BLO *Label*	Branch if unsigned **LO**wer	C = 0
	BMI *Label*	Branch if **MI**nus (Negative)	N = 1
	BPL *Label*	Branch if **PL**us (Positive or Zero)	N = 0
	BVS *Label*	Branch if o**V**erflow **S**et	V = 1
	BVC *Label*	Branch if o**V**erflow **C**lear	V = 0
	BHI *Label*	Branch if unsigned **HI**gher	C = 1 & Z = 0
	BLS *Label*	Branch if unsigned **L**ower or **S**ame	C = 0 or Z = 1
	BGE *Label*	Branch if signed **G**reater or **E**qual	N = V
	BLT *Label*	Branch if signed **L**ess **T**han	N != V
	BGT *Label*	Branch if signed **G**reater **T**han	Z = 0 & N = V
	BLE *Label*	Branch if signed **L**ess than or **E**qual	Z = 1 or N = !V

Table 6-5. List of unconditional and conditional branch instructions

Note some ARM processors can directly support all branch instructions listed above. However, Cortex-M processors do not directly support these conditional branch instructions. Instead, compilers translate conditional branch instructions to if-then-else (IT) instructions. IT performs the same flag testing as presented in Table 6-5.

Program flow control structures such as *if-then*, *if-then-else*, *for* loop, and *while* loop use (1) CMP instructions followed by a branch instruction, (2) conditionally executed instructions (see Chapter 6.3), or (3) a combination of both. Table 6-6 summarizes conditional branch instructions for the comparison of signed and unsigned numbers.

Comparison	Signed	Unsigned
==	BEQ	BEQ
!=	BNE	BNE
>	BGT	BHI
≥	BGE	BHS
<	BLT	BLO
≤	BLE	BLS

Table 6-6. Comparison of branch instructions used for signed and unsigned comparison

Example: Go to the labeled instruction if two numbers are equal.

```
CMP r1, r2
BEQ Label
```

When comparing 0xFFFFFFFF or 0x00000001, which is greater? When they are unsigned integers, the first number is larger. However, if they are signed numbers, the second one is larger. When the program is written in assembly, it is the programmer's responsibility to tell the processor how to interpret data. If written in C, their corresponding variables are declared explicitly by programmers as signed or unsigned numbers.

When two numbers are unsigned integers, branch instructions should use an unsigned condition suffix.

C Program	Assembly Program

`unsigned int x, y, z;`
`x = 0x00000001;`
`y = 0xFFFFFFFF;`
 	
`if (x > y)`
`   z = 1;`
`else`
`   z = 0;`
	`        MOV r5, #0x00000001 ; r5 = x`
	`        MOV r6, #0xFFFFFFFF ; r6 = y`
	`        CMP r5, r6`
	`        BLS else      ; branch if ≤`
	`then    MOV r7, #1    ; z = 1`
	`        B   endif     ; skip next instruction`
	`else    MOV r7, #0    ; z = 0`
	`endif`

Example 6-1. Implementation of *if*-statement that compares two unsigned integers

When these two numbers are signed integers, branch instructions should use a signed condition suffix.

C Program	Assembly Program

`signed int x, y, z;`
 	
`x =  1;  // 0x00000001`
`y = -1;  // 0xFFFFFFFF`
 	
`if (x > y)`
`   z = 1;`
`else`
`   z = 0;`
	`         MOVS r5, #0x00000001 ; r5 = x`
	`         MOVS r6, #0xFFFFFFFF ; r6 = y`
	
	`         CMP  r5, r6`
	`         BLE  then      ; branch if signed ≤`
	`         MOVS r7, #1    ; z = 1`
	`         B    endif     ; skip next instruction`
	`then     MOVS r7, #0    ; z = 0`
	`endif`

Example 6-2. Implementation of *if*-statement that compares two signed integers

It is often that an assembly program compares against zero and checks whether the branch should be taken or not. Instructions CBZ (compare and branch on zero) and CBNZ (compare and branch on non-zero) are available to improve the performance of this common case by reducing one instruction.

One limitation is that CBZ and CBNZ can only branch forward, and the branch destination must be within 4 to 130 bytes after the instruction. The following shows example usages and their equivalent implement.

```
CBZ   r1, label    ⟹
```
```
CMP   r1, #0
BEQ   label   ; branch if equal
```

```
CBNZ r1, label     ⟹
```
```
CMP   r1, #0
BNE   label   ; branch if not equal
```

In addition to these standard branch instructions, the following are special branch instructions that call a subroutine. Chapter 8.1 gives detailed descriptions and examples.

- "BL label" instruction copies the memory address of the instruction immediately after the BL instruction into the link register (r14), and then branches to the instruction addressed by the label.
- "BX Rm" is like "BL label" except that the target instruction address is saved in register Rm.
- "BLX Rm" first places the address of the next instruction after the BLX instruction into the link register and then branches to the address held in Rm.

BL label	Branch with link. $LR = PC + 4$; $PC = label$
BLX Rm	Branch with link and exchange. $LR = PC + 4$; $PC = Rm$
BX Rm	Branch and exchange. $PC = Rm$

Table 6-7. Branch instructions that call a subroutine.

6.3 Conditional Execution

Besides four data comparison instructions (CMP, CMN, TEQ, and TST), most instructions can update the program status flags (N, Z, C, and V) if the suffix S is added. One of the salient features of ARM assembly language is that an instruction can be executed optionally based on the program status flags. This feature is often not available in other assembly languages.

The condition flags introduced in Chapter 6.1 can be a suffix of almost all instructions to implement conditional execution. The conditional branch instructions presented in the previous section are a special case of conditional execution.

We take the add instruction as an example to illustrate conditional execution. By default, the instruction "ADD r3, r2, r1" is always executed no matter what value the program status flags are. The conditional flag, such as EQ, can be appended to ADD to form a conditionally executed instruction ADDEQ, as shown in Table 6-8.

Add instruction	Condition	Flags tested
ADDEQ r3, r2, r1	Add if **EQ**ual	Add if Z = 1
ADDNE r3, r2, r1	Add if **N**ot **E**qual	Add if Z = 0
ADDHS r3, r2, r1	Add if Unsigned **H**igher or **S**ame	Add if C = 1
ADDLO r3, r2, r1	Add if Unsigned **LO**wer	Add if C = 0
ADDMI r3, r2, r1	Add if **M**inus (Negative)	Add if N = 1
ADDPL r3, r2, r1	Add if **PL**us (Positive or Zero)	Add if N = 0
ADDVS r3, r2, r1	Add if o**V**erflow **S**et	Add if V = 1
ADDVC r3, r2, r1	Add if o**V**erflow **C**lear	Add if V = 0
ADDHI r3, r2, r1	Add if Unsigned **HI**gher	Add if C = 1 & Z = 0
ADDLS r3, r2, r1	Add if Unsigned **L**ower or **S**ame	Add if C = 0 or Z = 1
ADDGE r3, r2, r1	Add if Signed **G**reater or **E**qual	Add if N = V
ADDLT r3, r2, r1	Add if Signed **L**ess **T**han	Add if N != V
ADDGT r3, r2, r1	Add if Signed **G**reater **T**han	Add if Z = 0 & N = V
ADDLE r3, r2, r1	Add if Signed **L**ess than or **E**qual	Add if Z = 1 or N = !V

Table 6-8. Conditionally executed ADD instruction

Conditionally executed instructions can help facilitate the implementation of the selection and loop control structures. The following gives an example.

```
CMP    r1, r0      ; Perform r1 - r0 but discard the subtraction result
ADDSPL r3, r3, #1   ; Increment r3 by 1 and update flags if r1 ≥ r0
```

6.4 If-then Statement

An *if-then* statement in C selectively executes a block of code based on whether a given Boolean condition is true or false.

- If the condition is true or non-zero, the block is executed.
- Otherwise, the block is skipped, and the control returns to the first statement after the if-then statement.

The following example calculates the absolute value of a signed integer *a* and increases the variable *x* by 1.

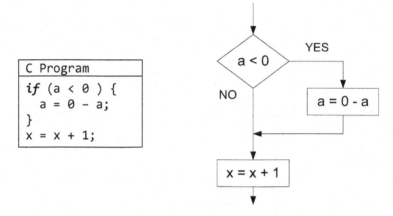

Assuming variable *a* and *x* are stored in register r1 and r2, respectively, the following gives two assembly implementations equivalent to the above C code.

An *if-then* statement can be implemented by using a conditional branch instruction (Example 6-3) or a conditionally executed instruction (Example 6-4).

```
        ; r1 = a, r2 = x
        CMP r1, #0          ; Compare a with 0
        BGE endif           ; Go to endif if a ≥ 0
then    RSB r1, r1, #0      ; a = - a
endif   ADD r2, r2, #1      ; x = x + 1
```

Example 6-3. An *if-then* statement can be implemented by using a conditional branch.

```
        ; r1 = a, r2 = x
        CMP   r1, #0        ; Compare a with 0
        RSBLT r1, r1, #0    ; a = 0 - a if a < 0
        ADD   r2, r2, #1    ; x = x + 1
```

Example 6-4. An *if-then* statement can be carried out by using conditional execution.

Compared with conditional branch instructions, conditionally executed instructions are concise and provide convenience for programmers. However, we should use conditionally executed instructions only when the if-statement body is short. What's more, in a nested-*if* statement, conditional branches are often preferred.

Compound Boolean expression

In mathematics, a Boolean (or logical) condition can be a compound expression combined with logical operators AND, OR, and NOT.

C language uses three special symbols as logical operators: && for Boolean AND, || for Boolean OR, and ! for Boolean NOT. In C, we write a Boolean condition like this:

$$x > 20\ \&\&\ x < 25$$
$$x == 20\ ||\ x == 25$$
$$!(x == 20\ ||\ x == 25)$$

The NOT operator (!) has higher precedence than the AND operator (&&), which has higher precedence than the OR operator (||).

If-then statement with a compound logical OR expression

A compound logical expression combined by logical OR can be implemented by multiple comparison instructions that test each simple logical expression. Example 6-5 shows how to implement an *if*-statement with a compound logic OR expression.

C Program	Assembly Program

`// x is a signed integer`
`if(x <= 20 || x >= 25){`
`    a = 1;`
`}`
	`        ; r0 = x, r1 = a`
	`        CMP   r0, #20    ; compare x and 20`
	`        BLE   then      ; go to then if x <= 20`
	`        CMP   r0, #25    ; compare x and 25`
	`        BLT   endif     ; go to endif if x < 25`
	`then    MOV   r1, #1     ; a = 1`
	`endif`

Example 6-5. A generic approach to implementing *if-then* with a compound logical OR

Example 6-6 gives a simplified assembly implementation that uses conditionally executed instructions.

C Program	Assembly Program

`// x is a signed integer`
`if(x <= 20 || x >= 25){`
`    a = 1;`
`}`
	`        ; r0 = x, r1 = a`
	`        CMP     r0, #20    ; compare x and 20`
	`        MOVLE r1, #1      ; a = 1 if x <= 20`
	`        CMP     r0, #25    ; compare x and 25`
	`        MOVGE r1, #1      ; a = 1 if x >= 25`

Example 6-6. Using Conditional execution to implement a compound logical OR.

Sometimes conditional comparison (such as CMPNE) and conditional execution can simplify the program, as shown below.

C Program	Assembly Program

`if(x == 20 || x == 25){`
    `a = 1;`
`}`
	`; r0 = x, r1 = a`
	`CMP    r0, #20  ; compare x and 20`
	`CMPNE r0, #25  ; CMP if r0 ≠ 25`
	`MOVEQ r1, #1    ; r1 = 1 if Z = 1`

Example 6-7. Conditional comparison (such as CMPNE) tests a compound expression

However, using conditional branch and execution can only implement an if-then statement in which the actions performed are simple. A generic approach to implementing an *if-then* structure with a compound logic OR expression is to use conditional branch instructions.

If-then statement with a compound logical AND expression

It is harder to test in assembly a compound logical expression combined by AND. De Morgan's laws are often used to break a logical AND compound expression into a logical OR expression.

$$\overline{A \ and \ B} = \overline{A} \ or \ \overline{B}$$

For example:

$$\overline{x > 20 \ and \ x < 25} = \overline{x > 20} \ or \ \overline{x < 25}$$
$$= x \leq 20 \ or \ x \geq 25$$

Therefore, when the condition of the if-statement is x > 20 && x < 25, in the assembly implementation given in Example 6-8, we test whether x ≤ 20 or x ≥ 25.

C Program	Assembly Program

`if(x > 20 && x < 25){`
    `a = 1;`
`}`
	`; Assume r0 = x, r1 = a`
	`CMP   r0, #20  ; compare x with 20`
	`BLE   endif    ; go to endif if x <= 20`
	`CMP   r0, #25  ; compare x with 25`
	`BGE   endif    ; go to endif if x >= 25`
	`MOVS r1, #1    ; a = 1`
	`endif`

Example 6-8. Using De Morgan's laws to convert a logical AND to a logical OR

If-then statement with a compound logical AND and OR expression

When a compound logical expression includes both AND and OR operators, the techniques introduced previously must be combined.

```
if ( x == 5 || (x > 20 && x < 25) )
        a = 1;
```

The following gives an example implementation.

```
; Assume r0 = x, r1 = a
CMP   r0, #5     ; compare x with 5
BEQ   then       ; if x == 5, go to then

CMP   r0, #20    ; compare x with 20
BLE   endif      ; go to endif if x ≤ 20

CMP   r0, #25    ; compare x with 25
BGE   endif      ; go to endif if x ≥ 25

then  MOVS r1, #1  ; a = 1
endif
```

Example 6-9. Assembly implementation of a logic expression with both AND and OR

6.5 If-then-else Statement

The *if-then-else* statement selects one of two alternative sets of statements to execute. It first evaluates the given Boolean condition.

- If the condition is true, the statements following the *if* statement are executed.
- Otherwise, the statements following the *else* statement are executed.

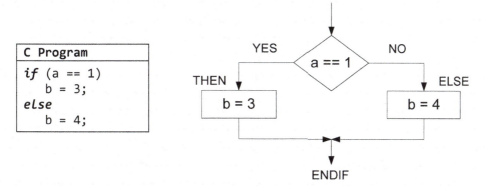

```
C Program

if (a == 1)
    b = 3;
else
    b = 4;
```

In the C program shown above, variable *b* is set to 3 if *a* is 1; otherwise, *b* is set to 4.

Assume the content of variable *a* is stored in register r1, and *b* in register r2, Example 6-10 gives two equivalent implementations of the above *if-else* C program. One implementation is based on branch instructions, and the other uses conditionally executed instructions.

To make assembly code easy to understand, we should give each label a meaningful name, such as "then", "else", and "endif".

Assembly Program 1	Assembly Program 2
``` ; r1 = a, r2 = b CMP r1, #1 ; compare a and 1 BNE else ; go to else if a ≠ 1 then MOV r2, #3 ; b = 3 B endif ; go to endif else MOV r2, #4 ; b = 4 endif ```	``` ; r1 = a, r2 = b CMP r1, #1 ; compare a and 1 MOVEQ r2, #3 ; b = 3 if a = 1 MOVNE r2, #4 ; b = 4 if a ≠ 1 ```

Example 6-10. Assembly implementation of *if-then-else* based on conditional branch and conditional execution

6.6 For Loop

The *for* loop repeatedly executes a block of codes if the specified condition is satisfied. A for loop contains three expressions, as shown below.

- The *initial expression* is executed only once often to initialize loop indices.
- The *condition expression* is tested before each iteration is executed. The loop body is executed if the condition expression is true. Note the loop body is skipped if the condition expression is false at the very first time it is evaluated.
- The *loop expression* is typically used to increment or decrement loop indices after each loop.

```
for (initial_expression; condition_expression; loop_experssion) {
    // loop body
    ...
}
```

The following C program calculates the sum of the first 10 non-negative integers.

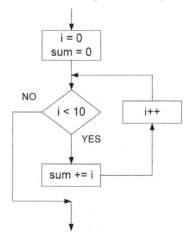

C Program
``` int i; int sum = 0; for(i = 0; i < 10; i++){   sum += i; } ```

Assume r0 = *i* and r2 = *sum*. Example 6-11 gives three different approaches to translating the above *for* loop into the assembly.

Assembly Program 1	Assembly Program 2	Assembly Program 3

```MOV r0, #0 ; i```
 ```MOV r1, #0 ; sum```
 	
 ```   B   check```
 ```loop ADD r1, r1, r0```
 ```   ADD r0, r0, #1```
 ```check CMP r0, #10```
 ```   BLT loop```
 ```endloop```
	```MOV r0, #0 ; i```
	 ```MOV r1, #0 ; sum```
	
	 ```loop CMP r0, #10```
	 ``` BGE endloop```
	 ``` ADD r1, r1, r0```
	 ``` ADD r0, r0, #1```
	 ``` B loop```
	 ```endloop```
		```MOV r0, #0 ; i```
		 ```MOV r1, #0 ; sum```
		
		 ```loop CMP r0, #10```
		 ``` ADDLT r1, r1, r0```
		 ``` ADDLT r0, r0, #1```
		 ``` BLT loop```
		 ```endloop```

Example 6-11. Assembly implementation of *for* loop based on conditional branch and conditional execution

6.7 While Loop

A *while* loop tests the condition expression before executing the loop body. If the condition expression is true, the loop body is then executed. Otherwise, the loop is terminated. Thus, the loop body may not be performed.

```
while (condition_expression) {
    // Loop body
    ...
}
```

The following C program uses a *while* loop to calculate the sum of the first 10 integers, starting with 0.

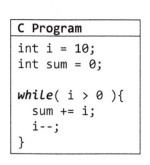

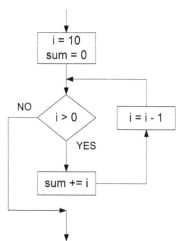

Assume the variable *i* is saved in register r0 and the variable *sum* is stored in r1, Example 6-12 gives three different assembly implementations of the above while loop.

Assembly Program 1	Assembly Program 2	Assembly Program 3

`        MOV   r0, #10 ; i`
`        MOV   r1, #0  ; sum`
 	
`        B     check`
`loop    ADD   r1, r1, r0`
`        SUB   r0, r0, #1`
`check   CMP   r0, #0`
`        BGT   loop`
`endloop`
	`        MOV   r0, #10 ; i`
	`        MOV   r1, #0  ; sum`
	
	`loop    CMP   r0, #0`
	`        BLE   endloop`
	`        ADD   r1, r1, r0`
	`        SUB   r0, r0, #1`
	`        B     loop`
	`endloop`
		`        MOV   r0, #10 ; i`
		`        MOV   r1, #0  ; sum`
		
		`loop    CMP     r0, #0`
		`        ADDGT   r1, r1, r0`
		`        SUBGT   r0, r0, #1`
		`        BGT     loop`
		`endloop`

Example 6-12. Assembly implementation of *while* loop

The first implementation checks the condition expression at the end of the loop. The second and third implementations check the conditional expression at the beginning of the loop. Since the loop body is not large, the last implementation uses conditionally executed instructions.

6.8 Do While Loop

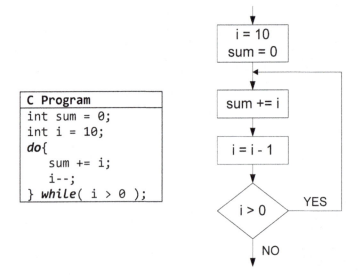

```
C Program
int sum = 0;
int i = 10;
do{
    sum += i;
    i--;
} while( i > 0 );
```

The *do-while* loop is like the *while* loop. The key difference is that the condition expression is evaluated before executing the loop body in the while loop, whereas the condition expression is assessed at the end of each iteration in the do-while loop.

Therefore, the *while* loop executes the loop body zero or more times sequentially, whereas the do-while loop executes the loop body at least once.

```
do {
    // Loop body
    ...
} while (condition_expression)
```

Again, we use the example of calculating the sum of the first 10 integers, starting with 0. Example 6-12 gives two equivalent assembly implementations (r0 = i, r1 = sum).

Assembly Program 1	Assembly Program 2

`        MOV r0, #10    ; i = 10`
`        MOV r1, #0     ; sum = 0`
 	
`loop    ADD r1, r1, r0  ; sum += i`
`        SUB r0, r0, #1  ; i--`
`        CMP r0, #0`
`        BGT loop`
`endloop`
	`        MOV  r0, #10    ; i = 0`
	`        MOV  r1, #0     ; sum = 0`
	
	`loop    ADD  r1, r1, r0 ; sum += i`
	`        SUBS r0, r0, #1 ; i--`
	`        BGT  loop`
	`endloop`

Example 6-13. Assembly implementation of *do-while* loop

The second implementation uses SUBS that performs subtraction and updates the N, Z, C, and V flags. Therefore, there is no need to use CMP before the BGT instruction.

6.9 Continue Statement

A *continue* statement in a loop is to skip the remaining statements in the current iteration and transfer the control to the next iteration of the loop. Example 6-14 calculates the sum of all integers between 0 and 9, excluding 5. The assembly program uses the condition code "NE" to skip the add instruction if r0 equals 5.

C Program	Assembly Program

`int i;`
`int sum = 0;`
 	
`for(i = 0; i < 10; i++) {`
`    if (i == 5) // skip 5`
`        continue;`
`    sum += i;`
`}`
	`        MOVS  r0, #0        ; i = 0`
	`        MOVS  r1, #0        ; sum = 0`
	
	`loop    CMP   r0, #10`
	`        BGE   endloop`
	`        CMP   r0, #5`
	`        ADDNE r1, r1, r0    ; sum += i`
	`        ADD   r0, r0, #1    ; i++`
	`        B     loop`
	`endloop`

Example 6-14. Assembly implementation of *continue* in a loop

6.10 Break Statement

A *break* statement is to exit the current loop, including for, while, and do-while. It is useful when the number of iterations in a loop cannot be predetermined. When there are nested loops, the break statement terminates the nearest enclosing loop. It is easy to confuse the break and continue statements.

The following two C programs illustrate the difference between break and continue.

Example code for break	Example code for continue

`for(int i = 0; i < 5; i++){`
`    if (i == 2) break;`
`    printf("%d, ", i)`
`}`
	`for(int i = 0; i < 5; i++){`
	`    if (i == 2) continue;`
	`    printf("%d, ", i)`
	`}`

Output: 0, 1,	Output: 0, 1, 3, 4,

Example 6-15. Comparing *break* and *continue*

The break statement is translated to a conditional or an unconditional branch statement in assembly. The following shows how the break statement is implemented by a combination of CBNZ and B instructions.

C Program	Assembly Program

`// Find string length`
`char str[] = "hello";`
`int len = 0;`
`char *p = str;`
` `
`for( ; ; ) {`
` `
`    if (*p == '\0')`
`        break;`
` `
`    p++;`
`    len++;`
`}`
	`        ; r0 = string memory address`
	`        ; r1 = string length`
	`        MOV  r1, #0        ; Len = 0`
	` `
	`loop    LDRB r2, [r0]`
	` `
	`        CBNZ r2, notZero`
	`        B    endloop`
	` `
	`notZero ADD  r0, r0, #1    ; p++`
	`        ADD  r1, r1, #1    ; Len++`
	` `
	`        B    loop`
	`endloop`

Example 6-16. Implementation of *break* in assembly

6.11 Switch Statement

A *switch* statement in C allows the program to make multiple choices based on a switch expression. If the value of the expression matches with one of the predetermined set of integer values defined in the program, the program branches accordingly. When there are many choices, the switch statement makes the program more structured and easier to read than a combination of *if-then* or *if-then-else* statements.

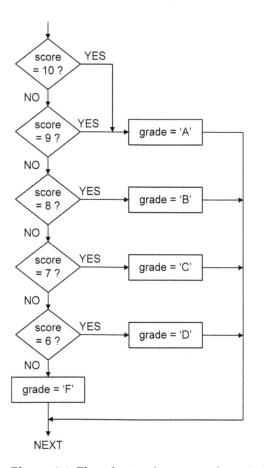

The body of a switch structure consists of an optional default label, a series of case labels and case expressions, and lists of statements for each instance.

- The switch expression must be evaluated to an integer or a character.
- If the switch expression does not match any of the case constants, the default label is then selected.
- A break statement in the switch structure is used to exit the switch.
- After exiting, the processor then executes the instruction immediately after the switch structure.

Example 6-17 gives the implementation in C to convert a numeric grade to its corresponding letter grade. Figure 6-1 gives the flowchart.

Figure 6-1. Flowcharts of an example *switch* program

The assembly code can use the table branch byte (TBB) instruction to implement the switch statement.

```
TBB [PC, r0]    ; PC = PC + 4 + 2 × BranchTable[r0]
```

TBB relies on the branch table defined immediately after the TBB instruction. In the branch table, each table item takes one byte, and it represents the offset in halfwords between the current PC and the memory address of the target instruction. The memory address of the instruction to which the program should branch is calculated as follows:

$$target = PC + 4 + 2 × BranchTable[r0]$$

Thus, the program counter (PC) is

$$PC = PC + 4 + 2 \times BranchTable[r0]$$

TBB [Rn, Rm]	Table branch byte
TBH [Rn, Rm, LSL #1]	Table branch halfword

Table 6-9. Table branch instructions

The table branch halfword (TBH) instruction is like TBB. However, each item in the branch table takes halfwords.

```
TBH [PC, r0]    ; PC = PC + 4 + 2 × BranchTable[r0]
```

We use a simple example to illustrate how to use TBB or TBH instruction to implement a switch statement in assembly.

The following assembly code uses TBB to implement a switch statement, which converts a numeric score to its corresponding letter grade.

C Program	Assembly Program

`unsigned int score;`
`char grade;`
 	
`switch (score){`
  `case 10:`
 	
  `case 9:`
    `grade = 'A';`
    `break;`
 	
  `case 8:`
    `grade = 'B';`
    `break;`
 	
  `case 7:`
    `grade = 'C';`
    `break;`
 	
  `case 6:`
    `grade = 'D';`
    `break;`
 	
  `default:`
    `grade = 'F';`
    `break;`
`}`
	`; r0 = numeric score ( 0 ≤ r0 ≤ 10 )`
	`; r1 = letter grade`
	
	`  SUBS r2, r0, #6    ; r2 is branch index`
	`  CMP  r2, #5`
	`  BHS  default       ; branch if unsigned r2 ≥ 5`
	
	`  ; r2 is the index;`
	`  ; pc = pc + 4 + 2 × BranchTable[r2]`
	`  TBB  [pc, r2]     ; Table Branch Byte`
	
	`BranchTable`
	`  DCB  (case_6 - BranchTable)/2    ; index = 0`
	`  DCB  (case_7 - BranchTable)/2    ; index = 1`
	`  DCB  (case_8 - BranchTable)/2    ; index = 2`
	`  DCB  (case_10_9 - BranchTable)/2 ; index = 3`
	`  DCB  (case_10_9 - BranchTable)/2 ; index = 4`
	
	`  ALIGN`
	
	`case_10_9`
	`  MOV  r1, #0x41     ; ASCII 'A' = 0x41`
	`  B    exit`
	
	`case_8`
	`  MOV  r1, #0x42     ; ASCII 'B' = 0x42`
	`  B    exit`

```
case_7
        MOV   r1, #0x43        ; ASCII 'C' = 0x43
        B     exit

case_6
        MOV   r1, #0x44        ; ASCII 'D' = 0x44
        B     exit

default
        MOV   r1, #0x46        ; ASCII 'F' = 0x46

exit
```

Example 6-17. Converting score to letter grade

6.12 Exercises

1. Translate the following code into a C program and explain what it does.

```
        MOV r2, #1
        MOV r1, #1

loop    CMP r1, r0
        BGT done
        MUL r2, r1, r2
        ADD r1, r1, #1
        B   loop

done    MOV r0, r2
```

2. We can use the REV instruction to perform conversion between 32-bit little endian and big endian numbers. Write an assembly program that uses bitwise operators, such as &, |, ^, <<, and >>, to implement the endian conversion. You cannot use REV in your program.

3. Define an array with 10 unsigned integers in assembly code, and write an assembly program that calculates the mean of these 10 integers (truncating the result to an integer).

4. Define an array with 10 unsigned integers a_i ($0 \le i \le 9$) in assembly code, and write an assembly program that calculates the sum of the cube of these 10 unsigned integers.

$$sum = \sum_{i=0}^{9} a_i^3$$

The following defines the array and its size in the data memory.

```
        AREA myData, DATA
array   DCD   2, 4, 7, 3, 1, 2, 10, 11, 5, 13
size    DCD   10
```

5. Write an assembly program that converts all lowercase letters to their corresponding upper cases.

6. Write an assembly program that calculates the kinetic energy (E), E = MC², where the mass (M) is 15 kg and is stored in r0. C is the speed of light (299,792,458 m/s) and is stored in r1. The result E has 32-bit and is stored in register r2.

7. Write an assembly program that calculates the value of the following integer expression:

$$7x^2 + 9xy + \frac{3x}{y} + 11x + 13y + 5$$

where unsigned integers $x = 4$ and $y = 2$.

8. Test for complex roots in solution to the following quadratic equation:

$$ax^2 + bx + c = 0$$

The solution has complex roots if $b^2 - 4ac$ is smaller than 0 and real roots otherwise. Suppose a, b, and c are signed integers and they are stored in register r0, r1, and r2. Write an assembly program that set register r3 to 1 if the solution has complex roots and 0 otherwise.

9. Write an assembly program that calculates the following function. Assume register r0 holds the signed integer x, and register r1 saves the result.

$$f(x) = \begin{cases} -1 & \text{if } x < 0 \\ 0 & \text{if } x = 0 \\ 1 & \text{if } x > 0 \end{cases}$$

10. Write an assembly program that calculates the following cost function. Assume the unsigned integer input x is stored in register r0 and the cost is in register r1.

$$cost(x) = \begin{cases} 9x & \text{if } x \leq 10 \\ 8x & \text{if } x > 10 \text{ and } x \leq 100 \\ 7x & \text{if } x > 100 \text{ and } x \leq 1000 \\ 6x & \text{if } x > 1000 \end{cases}$$

11. Translate the following C program into an assembly program. The C program finds the minimal value of three signed integers. Assume a, b, and c is stored in register r0, r1, and r3, respectively. The result min is saved in register r4.

```
if (a ≤ b && a < c) {
    min = a;
} else if (b < a && b < c) {
    min = b;
} else {
    min = c;
}
```

12. Assume two dates are stored in memory as follows. Write an assembly program to compare these two dates. If date1 comes before date2, set register r0 to 1; otherwise, set r0 to -1.

```
        AREA myData, DATA
date1   DCD 12, 31, 2014   ; month, day, year
date2   DCD 01, 20, 2013   ; month, day, year
```

13. Write an assembly program that calculates the sum as given below. Variable n is saved in register r0, and the sum is stored in register r1.

$$sum = \sum_{i=1}^{n} i^2 = 1^2 + 2^2 + \cdots + n^2$$

14. Write an assembly program that calculates the factorial of a non-negative integer n. Assume n is given in register r0, and the result is saved in register r1.

$$f(n) = \prod_{i=1}^{n} i = n \times (n-1) \times (n-2) \times \cdots \times 3 \times 2 \times 1$$

15. When a two-dimensional (2D) matrix is declared in a C program, the matrix, in fact, is stored as a one-dimensional array in memory. C program uses a row-major approach to convert a 2D matrix into a 1D array. The following gives an example of storing a 3-by-3 matrix in memory.

Index	(0, 0)	(0, 1)	(0, 2)	(1, 0)	(1, 1)	(1, 2)	(2, 0)	(2, 1)	(2, 2)
Content	1	2	3	4	5	6	7	8	9
Memory offset in bytes	0	4	8	12	16	20	24	28	32

1st Row   2nd Row   3rd Row

Translate the following C program to an assembly program. Your assembly program must consist of two nested loops.

```
int a[4][3] = {
    {11, 12, 13}, // first row
    {21, 22, 23}, // second row
    {31, 32, 33}, // third row
    {41, 42, 43}  // fourth row
};

void main(void) {
    int i, j;
    for(i = 0; i < 4; i++)
        for(j = 0; j < 3; j++)
            a[i][j] = 2*a[i][j];
    return;
}
```

16. Write an assembly program that transposes the matrix defined in the previous question. Your assembly program should have two nested loops. In linear algebra, the transpose of a matrix $[a_{ij}]_{m \times n}$ is $[a_{ji}]_{n \times m}$.

$$[a_{ij}]_{m \times n}^{T} = [a_{ji}]_{n \times m}$$

For example:

$$\begin{bmatrix} 11 & 12 & 13 \\ 21 & 22 & 23 \\ 31 & 32 & 33 \\ 41 & 42 & 43 \end{bmatrix}^{T} = \begin{bmatrix} 11 & 21 & 31 & 41 \\ 12 & 22 & 32 & 42 \\ 13 & 23 & 33 & 43 \end{bmatrix}$$

CHAPTER 7

Structured Programming

Structured programming has been widely supported in high-level programming languages, such as C. to provide the clarity, simplicity, and ease of maintenance of programs. Structured programming is a technique that utilizes a top-down hierarchical method to solve a problem. It only uses sequence, selection, and loop control structures to implement programs.

A *goto* statement, which was available, is prohibited in most modern high-level languages. Although assembly language is not a structured programming language intrinsically, we can still apply fundamental principles of structured programming to simplify the complexity and increase the ease of programming.

This chapter introduces the basic idea of the top-down design and gives example assembly programs to illustrate how to realize structured programming by using three basic control structures. We use program flowcharts, which are a useful tool to facilitate structured programming.

7.1 Basic Control Structures

A software program solves a problem by using an appropriate combination of three basic control structures: sequence, selection, and loop.

- A *sequence* is a set of instructions that are completed in a sequential order.
- A *selection* lets the computer choose two alternatives based on whether a logic condition is true or false.
- A *loop* executes a sequence of instructions repeatedly if a logic condition is satisfied.

One common characteristic of these control structures is that each has only one entry point and one exit point. A control structure can be nested or embedded in another structure to form a compound structure. It has been mathematically proven that any program can be written by using only these three control structures.

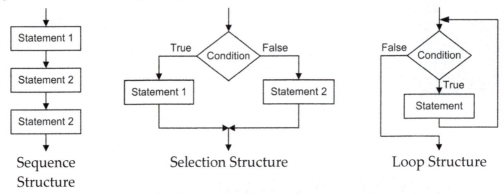

Sequence
Structure   Selection Structure   Loop Structure

Figure 7-1. Three basic control structures in structured programming

When we solve a large complex problem, the first step is to break down this massive problem into a set of simpler and more manageable sub-problems. This divide-and-conquer strategy effectively reduces the difficulty of problem-solving because each sub-problem is easier to solve, and the solution requires less time to develop, verify and maintain.

"Nothing is particularly hard if you divide it into small jobs."

Henry Ford,
Founder of Ford Motor

Our next step is to design a solution for each sub-problem. Usually, we make the solution to a sub-problem as a subroutine (or function). These subroutines communicate with each other by passing parameters (or arguments) and returning values. In this chapter, we focus on how to develop a simple program, and we will introduce how to build a subroutine in the next chapter.

The three control structures (sequence, selection, and loop) are implemented almost in every structured programming language.

- *Sequence*. All statements of a software program are assumed to run in a sequential order by default, even though on modern processors they might be executed out of order. Also, a function (or called subroutine) can be part of a sequence.
- *Selection*. The *if*, *if else* and *switch* statements are selection control structure. Although the *if* statement is sufficient to implement any selection structure, the *if else* and *switch* are provided for the convenience of programming.
- *Loop*. The loop in C includes *for*, *while* and *do while*. Two statements (*break* and *continue*) are available to change the regular control flow of a loop. The *break*

statement makes an immediate exit from the inner-most *for, switch, while,* and *do while* in which it appears. The *continue* makes the processor skip the remaining statements in the current loop body and begin the next iteration of the loop.

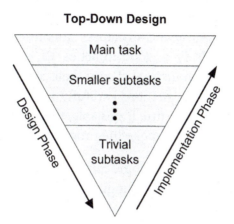

Figure 7-2. Top-down design (also called stepwise refinement)

Programming using hierarchical or nested control structures as well as subroutines in high-level languages is called **structured programming**.

The key process of structured programming is stepwise refinement, which is about solving a problem by making a series of design decisions. Each successive refinement logically decomposes a task into several subtasks. The stepwise process stops until all subtasks can be described successfully by using three basic control structures. Examples of the final subtask include "if P is true, then do X else do Y," or "while C is true, do Z." The final program code can be written naturally based on the result of the last decomposition.

However, *assembly language itself is not a structured programming language* because it does not directly support selection and loop structures. Assembly program uses conditional or unconditional branch instructions to implement the high-level selection and loop structure. A branch instruction in assembly is equivalent to a *goto* statement in a high-level language. Structured programming languages discourage the usage of goto statements. That is why some high-level languages have eliminated *goto* statements, and most textbooks do not cover it. Edsger Dijkstra, a famous computer scientist, published a letter titled "*Goto Considered Harmful*" in 1968.

In assembly languages, we must use branch instructions that are equivalent to goto. Despite this, we can still extend the principle of structured programming to assembly languages. We should still follow the stepwise refinement approach to solving a problem in assembly. While the basic control structures are not directly available, they can be readily implemented. Structured programming in assembly language involves two steps:

1. Top-down logical design. It performs stepwise refinement and constructs program flow by using high-level control structures.
2. Implementing the high-level structures identified in the previous step in assembly language. It is a good practice to give each instruction label a meaningful name to demonstrate clearly their corresponding control structures. We should use branch instructions carefully to ensure there are only one entry and one exit into each structure. If possible, the assembly instructions should be broken into subroutines that make the program more modularized.

These two steps separate the process of logic construction and low-level coding. In other words, we think in high-level structured language, but write code in low-level assembly language.

An indispensable tool that can help us use structured programming techniques in assembly language is program *flowcharts*. A program flowchart visually organizes the program logic flow and steps by using graphic symbols. A flowchart not only serves as valuable program documentation, but also more importantly as an aid to the top-down design and analysis during the problem-solving phase and an effective guideline during the software development phase. The following gives an example how to use flowcharts to aid programming.

Example: Find all Armstrong numbers less than 10,000.

Given a positive integer that has n digits, it is an Armstrong number if the sum of the nth powers of its digits equals the number itself. For example, 371 is an Armstrong number because we have $371 = 3^3 + 7^3 + 1^3$. We want to find all Armstrong numbers less than 10,000.

We can divide the task into 10,000 subtasks. Each subtask checks whether a given integer is an Armstrong number or not. Apparently, we need a loop structure to execute these 10,000 subtasks iteratively. The loop structure should have only one in and one out. We can further refine a subtask by using a selection structure. Specifically, a subtask prints the number if it is an Armstrong number.

The subtask of checking whether a number is Armstrong can be implemented as a subroutine that returns YES or NO for a given input integer. In general, using subroutines in a program helps decompose a complex task into smaller and simpler subtasks. Subroutines make program design, verification, and maintenance easier.

Figure 7-3 illustrates the top-down design process.

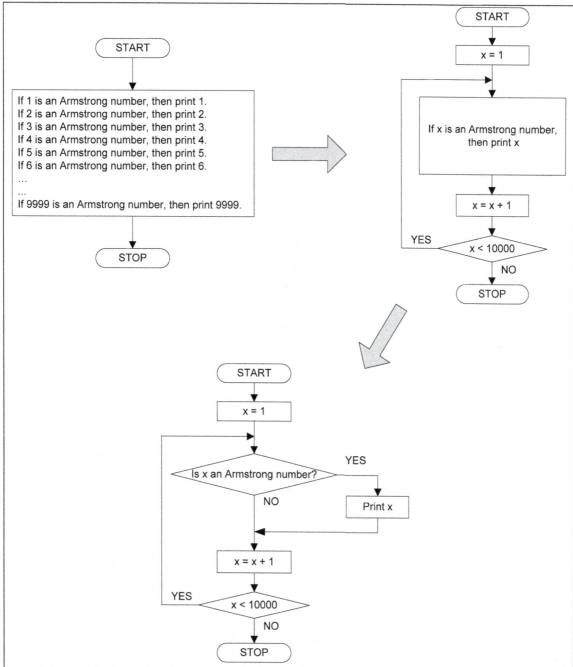

Figure 7-3. Example of top-down design to find Armstrong numbers less than 10,000

This subtask, however, is still complex. We can further decompose it into four smaller subtasks, as in Figure 7-4. The first three of them are still not straightforward, and we can implement them as subroutines. Within each subroutine, the above decomposition process repeats if necessary to break a subtask further into smaller subtasks. This process stops if we can express each subtask by using the three basic control structures. Chapter 7.6 shows the flowchart and program of identifying the number of digits in an integer, and Chapter 7.9 gives an implementation that checks whether an integer is an Armstrong number.

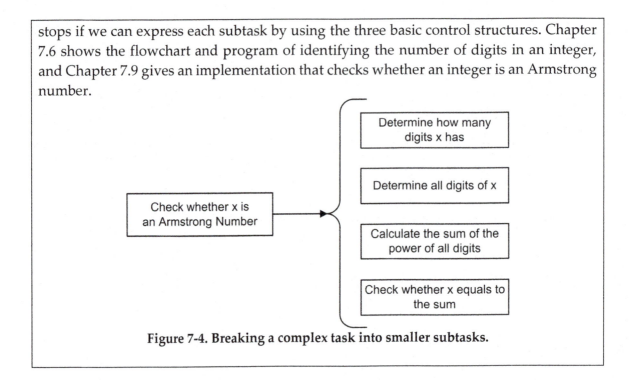

Figure 7-4. Breaking a complex task into smaller subtasks.

7.2 Register Reuse

There are always a limited number of physical registers available in a microprocessor. However, it is often that many variables are defined in a program. Therefore, we need to minimize the number of registers used for each chunk of codes to save registers for other chunks of codes.

If the program runs out of registers, we need to save the value of some registers back to memory to make registers free to use. When these variables are used later, we need to load their value back from memory again. Reducing the number of registers used by a piece of code can help eliminate some memory accesses, thus speeding up the application performance.

To minimize the footprint of registers, a program should reuse a register if possible. One simple strategy is that *a register can be reused outside its live range*. A live range of a register in a program is defined as the interval between the instruction that writes to the register and the last instruction that reads it before the register is written again.

The following example illustrates how this strategy works. Assuming global variables are allocated in the data memory starting at the address of 0x20000000. The assembly program needs to load variables B, C, and D from memory into registers first, then calculate the results and finally save the result in memory. A simple assembly implementation, as shown in Figure 7-5, uses eight registers.

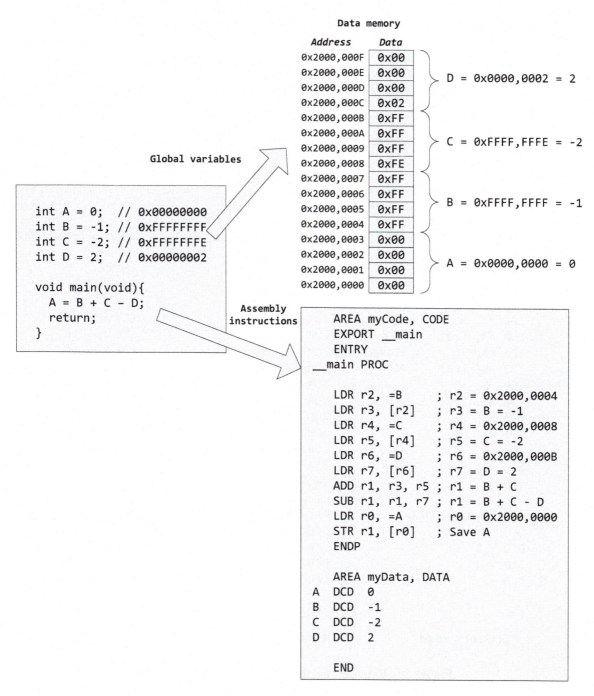

Figure 7-5. Simple assembly implementation and data memory layout

To reuse registers, first, we need to determine the live range of each register. A register may have multiple live ranges in a program. However, no live ranges of a register overlap with each other. A register can be reused outside its live range.

Figure 7-6 shows the process of renaming registers to reduce the number of registers used in the above program.

- During the first step, we can replace register r4, r6, and r0 by register r2, and replace r1 by r3. This reduces the total number of registers used by the program from eight to four.

- During the second step, we replace register r7 by r2, reducing the total number of registers to three.

- This process repeats if necessary.

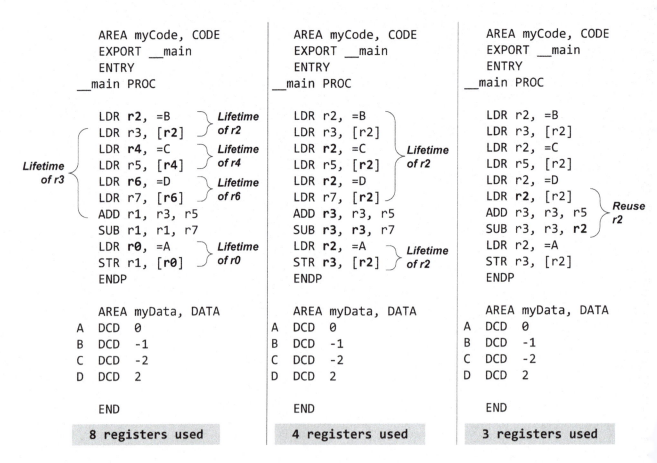

Figure 7-6. Reusing registers based on their live ranges

7.3 Example of Factorial Numbers

The factorial of a non-negative number n, denoted as $n!$, is the product of all positive integers less than or equal to n, as shown in the following math formula. There is one special case: $0! = 1$.

$$n! = \prod_{i=1}^{n} i = n \times (n-1) \times (n-2) \cdots \times 2 \times 1$$

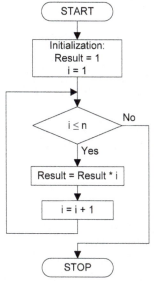

Figure 7-7. Flowchart of factorial program

This example illustrates implementing a *for* loop in assembly. The assembly needs to check the exit condition and update the loop index in each loop. There are different ways to implement the *for* loop. In this specific example:

- An unconditional branch instruction "B loop" is placed at the end of the loop body to implement a loop.
- At the beginning of the loop body, a *comparison* instruction (CMP) sets up the NZCV flags.
- A *conditional branch* (BGT in this example) exits the loop.

C Program	Assembly Program
	AREA factorial, CODE, READONLY EXPORT __main
int main(void) { int result, n, i;	ENTRY __main PROC
result = 1; n = 5;	MOV r0, #1 ; r0 = result MOV r1, #5 ; r1 = n

for (i = 1; i <= n; i++)
    result = result * i;
	MOV r2, #1 ; r2 = i = 1
	loop CMP r2, r1 ; compare i and n
	       BGT stop ; if i > n, stop
	       MULS r0, r2, r0 ; result *= i
	       ADD r2, r2, #1 ; i++
	       B loop

while(1);
}
	stop B stop
	       ENDP
	       END

7.4 Example of Counting Ones in a Word

In this example, we count the number of ones in a 32-bit word. One application of this code is to calculate the Hamming distance, which is defined as the number of different bits in two words. Given two words A and B, let $C = A \oplus B$, then the Hamming distance of A and B equals the number of ones in C. Hamming distance has a wide range of applications in information coding and cryptography.

The assembly implementation is given below. The assembly program checks two bits every time, and one of them is stored in the carry flag set by the "MOVS" instruction.

The C language cannot directly check the carry flag. This shows an advantage of assembly language over C language.

However, the C language cannot directly access the carry flag. To test whether a carry has occurred, we can use an *if*-statement that compares x and x << 1. If x is smaller than x << 1, then carry has occurred, implying the bit being shifted out has a value of 1; otherwise, the bit shifted out has a value of 0.

C Program	Assembly Program
| ```
// Count the number ones in x
// Result saved in counter

int main(void){

  unsigned int x = 0xAAAAAAAA;
  unsigned int y, z;

  unsigned int counter = 0;
  counter = x >> 31;

  while (x > 0) {
    y = x << 2;
    z = y >> 31;
    if (x<<1 > y) // check carry
      counter += z + 1;
    else
      counter += z;
    x = y;
  }
  while(1);
}
``` | ```
        AREA Count_Ones, CODE
        EXPORT __main
        ALIGN
        ENTRY
__main  PROC
        ; r0 = Input = x
        ; r1 = Number of ones = counter

        LDR   r0, =0xAAAAAAAA

        ; r1 = r0 >> 31
        MOV   r1, r0, LSR #31

        ; r0 = r0 << 2 and change Carry
loop    MOVS  r0, r0, LSL #2

        ; r1 = r1 + r0 >> 31 + Carry
        ADC   r1, r1, r0, LSR #31
        BNE   loop

stop    B     stop
        ENDP
        END
``` |

The following shows the initialization and the execution of the first loop. Note the ADC instruction does not update the carry flag. At the end of the first loop, we have r1 = bit[31] + bit[30] + bit[29].

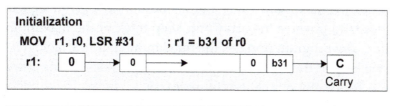

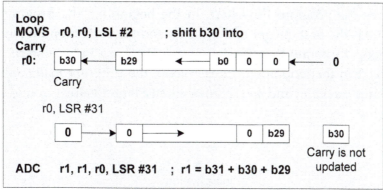

At the end of the first loop: r1 = b31 + b30 + b29

Figure 7-8. Result of the first loop. Register r0 holds the input. Register r1 holds the counting result.

The loop body runs 16 times, and each loop checks two bits. The following gives a detailed illustration of the above example to show the key idea.

1. Initially we have r0 = 0xAAAAAAAA. Note 0xA = 0b1010.
2. The counter r1 is initially set to r0>>31 (*i.e.,* r0 = 0x00000001).
3. During the first iteration of the loop:
   a) MOVS r0, r0, LSL #2   ⟹ Carry = 0 and r0 = 0xAAAAAAAC
   b) ADC   r1, r1, r0, LSR #31 ⟹ r1 = 1 + 0x00000000 + Carry = 1
   c) Since r0 does not equal zero, the loop runs again.
4. During the second iteration of the loop:
   a) MOVS r0, r0, LSL #2   ⟹ Carry = 0 and r0 = 0xAAAAAAA0
   b) ADC   r1, r1, r0, LSR #31 ⟹ r1 = 1 + 0x00000000 + Carry = 2
   c) Since r0 does not equal zero, the loop runs again.
5. During the third iteration of the loop:
   a) MOVS r0, r0, LSL #2   ⟹ Carry = 0 and r0 = 0xAAAAAAC0
   b) ADC   r1, r1, r0, LSR #31 ⟹ r1 = 1 + 0x00000000 + Carry = 3
   c) Since r0 does not equal zero, the loop runs again.
6. The loop repeats 16 times, and finally, we have r1 = 16.

7.5 Example of Finding the Maximum of an Array

This example finds the maximum value and its location in a given signed integer array. The program needs to traverse the array and keep track of the maximum value and its location or index. The program updates the maximum value variable if a larger value is found during the loop. If there are multiple maximum values in this array, only the first one is identified. This method is called *linear search*.

Figure 7-9 gives the program flowchart. In the beginning, the program assumes the maximum value is the first integer of this array, and the corresponding *maxLocation* is 0. It uses a *for* loop to iterate through the array. The loop index *i* starts with 0 and is incremented by 1 in the loop body. In each loop, the program loads an integer of this array and updates *maxValue* and *maxLocation* when a larger value is found when iterating through the array.

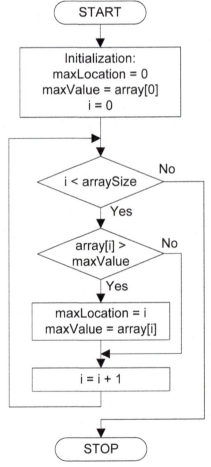

Figure 7-9. Flowchart of finding the maximum value of an integer array

The following shows the implementation of finding the highest value in C and assembly. Since array and size are declared as global variables with initial values in the C program, the corresponding assembly program places them in the initialized data area, defined by using the directive AREA. The assembly program starts to identify the array size and the memory address where the array is stored. Variables *i*, *maxLocation*, and *maxValue* are local variables and are stored in r2, r0, and r1, respectively. The assembly program initializes r0 to the first integer of the array and writes r1 to 0.

The memory address of the first integer of this array, which we also call the memory address of this array, is stored in register r4. The following statement loads *array[i]* into register r5. Because each integer takes 4 bytes in memory, the memory address of *array[i]* is r4 + r2 × 4.

```
LDR  r5, [r4, r2, LSL #2]
```

C Program	Assembly Program

`int array[10] = {-1, 5, 3, 8, 10,`
`23, 6, 5, 2, -10};`
 	
`int size = 10;`
	`       AREA myData, DATA`
	`       ALIGN`
	`array  DCD -1,5,3,8,10,23,6,5,2,-10`
	`size   DCD 10`

`int main(void) {`
`  int i, maxLocation, maxValue;`
	`       AREA findMax, CODE`
	`       EXPORT __main`
	`       ALIGN`
	`       ENTRY`
	`__main PROC`
	`       ; Identify the array size`
	`       LDR   r3, =size`
	`       LDR   r3, [r3]    ; array size`
	`       SUB   r3, r3, #1`

`  // Initialize max and location`
`  maxLocation = 0;`
`  maxValue = array[0];`
	`       ; Initialize max value and location`
	`       LDR   r4, =array`
	`       LDR   r0, [r4]    ; r0 = default max`
	`       MOV   r1, #0      ; r1 = max location`

`  // loop through the array`
`  for (i = 0; i < size; i++){`
`    if (array[i] > maxValue) {`
`      maxValue  = array[i];`
`      maxLocation = i;`
`    }`
`  }`
	`       ; Loop over the array`
	`       MOV   r2, #0          ; loop index i`
	`loop   CMP   r2, r3          ; compare i & size`
	`       BGE   stop            ; stop if i ≥ size`
	`       LDR   r5, [r4,r2,LSL #2]   ; array[i]`
	`       CMP   r5, r0          ; compare with max`
	`       MOVGT r0, r5          ; update max value`
	`       MOVGT r1, r2          ; update location`
	`       ADD   r2, r2, #1  ; update index i`
	`       B     loop`

`  while(1); // dead loop`
`}`
	`stop   B     stop        ; dead loop`
	`       ENDP`
	`       END`

7.6 Example of Counting Digits

Given a decimal integer, find how many decimal digits this number has. For example, the decimal number 9578 has four digits.

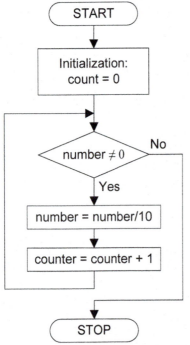

Figure 7-10. Flowcharts of counting decimal digits

The C program uses a simple while loop that repeatedly executes a block of code until a given Boolean condition becomes false.

The implementation of a *while* loop in assembly language is like a *for* loop. It often relies on a comparison instruction (CMP, CMN, TEQ, and TST) and a conditional branch instruction. However, CBZ (compare and branch if zero) and CBNZ (compare and branch if nonzero) is an effective combination instruction of two operations.

When integers are divided, any fractional part of the result is discarded. This rounding scheme is called *truncation toward zero*. For example, the result of 9/10 is zero. If the division result is negative, the SIDV and UDIV instructions truncate the result toward 0 rather than flooring. For example, the division of -8/3 is -2, not -3.

C Program	Assembly Program
	AREA countDigits, CODE, READONLY EXPORT __main ENTRY
int **main**(void){ int number, count;	__main PROC
number = 123456; count = 0;	LDR r0, =123456 ; *input integer number* MOV r1, #0 ; *number of digits*

while(number){
  number = number/10;
  count++;
}
	MOV r2, #10 ; *set r2 to 10*
	loop CBZ r0, stop ; *if r0 = 0, stop*
	      SDIV r0, r0, r2 ; *r0 = r0 / 10*
	      ADD r1, r1, #1 ; *count++*
	      B loop ; *loop again*

while(1);
}
	stop B stop
	      ENDP
	      END

7.7 Example of Parity Bit

The parity bit of a binary number indicates whether it contains an odd or even number of ones. Parity bits are widely used in communication and digital systems to detect data corruption when there are an odd number of bit errors.

There are two parity schemes: even parity and odd parity.

- In the *even parity*, the parity bit is set if there are an odd number of ones in the data; otherwise, it is cleared. Thus, the number of ones in the data and the parity bit is always even.
- On the other hand, the *odd parity* always keeps the total number of ones in the entire data set (including the parity) an odd number.

The exclusive OR of all bits in the whole data set including the parity bit should be 0 in the even parity scheme, and 1 in the odd parity scheme.

	Data bits	Parity bit	Total # of 1-bits (including parity)
Even Parity	10101010	0	4 (An even number of ones)
	10101011	1	6 (An even number of ones)
Odd Parity	10101010	1	5 (An odd number of ones)
	10101011	0	5 (An odd number of ones)

Table 7-1. Examples of even and odd parity

The following will implement a simple bit-counting algorithm that computes the odd parity. The key idea, proposed in reference [39], is to reset repetitively one of the 1-bits to 0 and invert the parity bit until all bits are 0. The reset operation is achieved by the bitwise logic AND operation between n and $n - 1$. The following gives two examples.

Example 1: n = 11 (0b1011)

	Step 1	Step 2	Step 3
n	1011	1010	1000
n-1	1010	1001	0111
n & (n-1)	1010	1000	0000
Parity	0	1	0

Example 2: n = 15 (0b1111)

	Step 1	Step 2	Step 3	Step 4
n	1111	1110	1100	1000
n-1	1110	1101	1011	0111
n & (n-1)	1110	1100	1000	0000
Parity	0	1	0	1

This algorithm is based on the observation that the *bitwise AND operation of* n & $(n-1)$ *always resets a 1-bit to zero*. The following gives a briefly proof. When we examine the least significant two bits, there are four possible scenarios. In each of the four scenarios, n & $(n-1)$ resets a 1-bit. The number of steps required to complete this algorithm does not depend on the total number of bits, but instead the number of ones in the tested data.

Cases	Bits[1:0]	n & $(n-1)$	Observation
1	11	10	A bit of 1 is reset.
2	10	00	A bit of 1 is reset.
3	01	00	A bit of 1 is reset.
4	00	Either the algorithm stops, or the last 1 on the rightmost is cleared.	A bit of 1 is reset.

The C program and assembly program for calculating the odd parity are shown below. In this example, we calculate the parity of a 32-bit integer, which is 0x11 in decimal, and 0b1011 in binary. The total number of 1-bits in this integer is an odd number; therefore, its parity bit, saved in register r1, is cleared.

C Program	Assembly Program
	``` AREA parity, CODE, READONLY EXPORT __main ENTRY ```
`int main(void){`	`__main PROC`
`  unsigned int n = 11;` `  int parity = 0;`	`        MOVS  r0, #11   ; number to be checked` `        MOVS  r1, #0    ; parity`

`  while (n) {`
`    parity = !parity;`
`    n = n & (n - 1);`
`  }`
	`loop    CBZ   r0, stop  ; branch to stop if zero`
	`        CMP   r1, #0    ; flip parity bit`
	`        MOVEQ r1, #1    ; if r1 = 0, set it`
	`        MOVNE r2, #0    ; if r1 ≠ 0, clear it`
	`        SUBS  r2, r0, #1 ; (n-1)`
	`        ANDS  r0, r0, r2 ; n = n & (n-1)`
	`        B     loop`

`  while(1);`
`}`
	`stop    B     stop`
	`        ENDP`
	`        END`

The CBZ (Compare and branch on zero) instruction can be replaced by the following two instructions.

```
CMP r0, #0     ; Compare register with 0
BEQ stop       ; Branch if equal
```

Another approach to implementing the C statement "parity = !parity;" is as follows:

```
MVN r1, r1      ; Negate all bits
AND r1, r1, #1  ; Clear all bits except bit[0]
```

7.8 Example of Perfect Numbers

If the sum of all proper divisors of a positive number equals the number itself, this number is a perfect number. For example, 6 is a perfect number because the sum of its proper divisors, including 1, 2, and 3, equals 6. Other examples are 28, 496, and 8128. This following presents a program to check whether a given positive number is perfect or not.

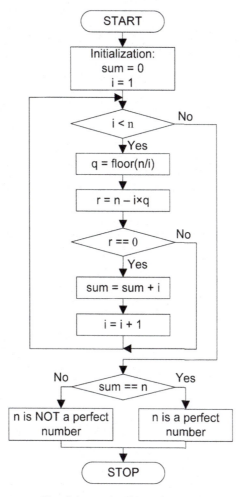

Figure 7-11. Checking whether n is a perfect number

For a given positive integer n, the program loops over the *loop* variable i from 1 to $n - 1$, then checks whether i is a divisor of n, and finally adds to *sum* if yes. After the loop completes, the program evaluates whether *sum* equals n. If yes, then n is a perfect number; Otherwise, n is not. To check whether i is a divisor of n, the program performs a modulo operation, which is simple in C (use % operator). However, this modulo operation takes several steps in assembly. First, it uses truncated division to find the quotient q, i.e., $q = \lfloor \frac{n}{i} \rfloor$, and then the remainder is calculated as $r = n - q \times i$. If the remainder is zero, then i is a divisor of n.

In the following program, the number to be checked is stored in variable *num*, which is assigned to register r1 in the assembly program. The flag indicating whether the integer is a perfect number or not is stored in register r0.

C Program	Assembly Program
	`        AREA perfectNumber, CODE` `        EXPORT __main`

`int main(void){`
`  unsigned int i, flag;`
`  unsigned int num, sum;`
	`        ALIGN`
	`        ENTRY`
	`__main PROC`

`  num = 28;` `  sum = 0;`	`        MOV   r1, #28      ; number to check` `        MOV   r2, #0       ; sum = 0`

`  for(i = 1; i < num; i++){`
`    if( num % i == 0)`
`      sum += i;`
`  }`
	`        MOV   r3, #1       ; i = 1`
	`loop    CMP   r3, r1       ; compare i & num`
	`        BHS   check        ; if i ≥ num, exit`
	`        UDIV  r4, r1, r3   ; r4 = num/i`
	`        MLS   r4, r3, r4, r1 ; r4 = num - i*r4`
	`        CMP   r4, #0       ; num % i`
	`        ADDEQ r2, r2, r3   ; sum += i`
	`        ADD   r3, r3, #1   ; i++`
	`        B     loop         ; Loop again`

`  if (sum == num)`
`    flag = 1;`
`  else`
`    flag = 0;`
	`check   CMP   r2, r1       ; compare sum & num`
	`yes     MOVEQ r0, #1       ; flag = 1`
	`no      MOVNE r0, #0       ; flag = 0`

`  while(1);`
`}`
	`stop    B     stop`
	`        ENDP`
	`        END`

"CMP r3, r1" updates the N, Z, C, and V flags based on the results of subtraction r3 – r1. The following BHS (Branch if unsigned higher or same) instruction checks the C flag. Also, BHS causes PC to branch away if the C flag is set, indicating that no borrowing has occurred during the subtraction.

"MLS r4, r3, r4, r1" performs the following operation: r4 = r3 – r4 × r1. If the product of r4 and r1 might have 64 bits, the most significant 32 bits are discarded.

The C statement "num % i" is translated into two assembly statements.

```
        UDIV  r4, r1, r3    ; r4 = num ÷ i
        MLS   r4, r3, r4, r1 ; r4 = num - i × r4
```

7.9 Example of Armstrong Numbers

An *n*-digit number is Armstrong if the sum of the nth powers of its digits equals the number itself. For example, the following are Armstrong numbers.

$$371 = 3^3 + 7^3 + 1^3$$

$$1634 = 1^4 + 6^4 + 3^4 + 4^4$$

$$54748 = 5^5 + 4^5 + 7^5 + 4^5 + 8^5$$

$$1741725 = 1^7 + 7^7 + 4^7 + 1^7 + 7^7 + 2^7 + 5^7$$

The following C and assembly programs check whether a given three-digit number is Armstrong. The program checks whether the sum of cubes of individual digits of this three-digit number is equal to the number itself.

C language provides a modulus operator (%) that calculates the remainder of an integer division. However, there are no modulus instructions in assembly. The following two assembly instructions implement the modulus operation (r2 = r1 % r3).

```
SDIV r6, r1, r3      ; r2 = remainder
MLS  r2, r3, r6, r1  ; r2 = r1 - r3 * r6
```

C Program	Assembly Program			
	AREA Armstrong, CODE, READONLY			
int **main**(void) {	EXPORT __main			
int number, sum, r;	ENTRY			
int flag, t;	__**main** PROC			
number = 371;		LDR	r0, =371	; number to be checked
sum = 0;		MOV	r4, #0	; sum = 0
t = number;		MOV	r1, r0	; save a copy, r1=number
while(t != 0) {		MOV	r3, #10	
r = t % 10;	loop	CBZ	r1, check	; if t = 0, exit Loop
sum = sum + r*r*r;		SDIV	r6, r1, r3	; r2 = remainder
t = t / 10;		MLS	r2, r3, r6, r1	; r2 = r1 - 10*r6
}		MUL	r3, r2, r2	; remainer^2
		MLA	r4, r3, r2, r4	; r4 = 10*r2 + r4
		MOVS	r3, #10	
		SDIV	r1, r1, r3	; t = t/10
		CBNZ	loop	
if (number == sum)	check	CMP	r0, r4	
flag = 1;	yes	MOVEQ r0, #1		; Armstrong
else	no	MOVNE r0, #0		; not Armstrong
flag = 0;				
while(1);	stop	B	stop	
}		ENDP		
		END		

7.10 Example of Palindrome String

A string is a palindrome if the string is read the same forward and backward. For example, "rats live on no evil star" is a palindrome. Write a program to check whether a given string is a palindrome.

The assembly program uses two memory pointers (r1 and r2), which are initially set to the memory address of the first letter and the last letter of the string to be checked. The program loads two characters pointed by r1 and r2, and compares them whether they are the same. If yes, the program updates the memory pointers and continues the comparison until r2 becomes larger or equal to r1.

The assembly program uses the post-index memory address mode, which automatically updates the memory pointer after loading data from memory. For example,

```
LDRB   r4, [r1], #-1
```

is equivalent to the following two instructions:

```
LDRB   r4, [r1]
SUB    r1, r1, #1
```

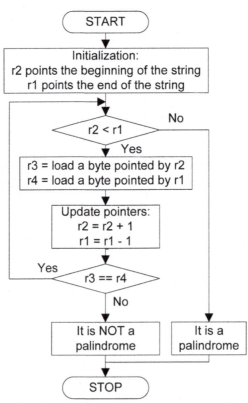

Figure 7-12. Check whether a given string is a palindrome.

A character string is an array of ASCII characters terminated with a null character ('0x00' in ASCII). Each character (including the NULL terminator) takes one byte in memory.

- In a C program, the compiler automatically adds a NULL character at the end of each string.
- In an assembly program, a string can be defined by using the DCB (define constant byte) directive. We should explicitly add "0" at the end of each string.

Note "LDR r6, =str" is a pseudo instruction, which is not a real instruction and is translated into a PC-relative load. It loads a 32-bit memory address, identified by the label *str*, into r6. The LDR pseudo instruction provides convenience for assembly programmers.

C Program	Assembly Program		
		AREA myData, DATA	
		ALIGN	
char str[26]="rats live on no evil star";	str	DCB "rats live on no evil star",0	
		AREA palindrome, CODE	
		EXPORT __main	
int **main**(void) {		ALIGN ENTRY	
int i = 0, j = 0;	__main	PROC	
int len = 0, flag = 1;		LDR r6, =str	
// find the string length		; find the string length	
while(str[i++]!='\0')		MOV r1, #0	; len
len++;		MOV r5, r6	; r5 = str
	strLen	LDRB r2, [r5], #1	; post-index
		CMP r2, #0	; check NULL
		ADDNE r1, r1, #1	; len++
		BNE strLen	; loop again
// if the string is not a		; check palindrome	
// palindrome, clear the flag		SUB r1, r1, #1	; len - 1
		ADD r1, r6, r1	; &str[len-1]
for(i=0,j=(len-1); i<j; i++,j--){		MOV r2, r6	; &str
if(str[j] != str[i]) {			
flag = 0;	cmpStr	LDRB r3, [r2], #1	; str[i]
break;		LDRB r4, [r1],#-1	; str[len-1-i]
}		CMP r3, r4	; compare
}		MOVNE r0, #0	; not Palindrome
}		BNE stop	; stop
		CMP r1, r2	; compare i & j
		BLT cmpStr	; loop again
		MOV r0, #1	; Palindrome
while(1);	stop	B stop	; dead loop
}		ENDP	
		END	

7.11 Example of Converting String to Integer (`atoi`)

A character takes one byte in memory, and it is represented by the corresponding ASCII value, shown in the following table. To convert the character "9" to its numeric value, the program subtracts `0x30` from the ASCII value of "9". The *atoi* function in C converts a numeric string to an integer.

Letter	0	1	2	3	4	5	6	7	8	9
ASCII	0x30	0x31	0x32	0x33	0x34	0x35	0x36	0x37	0x38	0x39

A simple way to implement the multiplication by 10 is to use the `MUL` instruction:

```
MOV r4, #10
MUL r3, r2, #10
ADD r2, r0, r3              ; r2 = 10*r2 + r0
```

However, the shift operations run faster than the `MUL` instruction.

```
ADD r3, r2, r2, LSL #2     ; r3 = r2 + r2*4 = 5*r2
ADD r2, r0, r3, LSL #1     ; r2 = 2*r3 + r0 = 10*r2 + r0
```

C Program	Assembly Program
	`        AREA myData, DATA` `        ALIGN`
`char str[] = "123456";`	`str     DCB    "123456",0`

	`        AREA atoi, CODE`
	`        EXPORT    __main`
	`        ALIGN`
	`        ENTRY`

`int main(){`
`  char *p = str;`
`  int value = 0;`
	`__main PROC`
	`        LDR   r1, =str`
	`        MOVS  r2, #0          ; r2 = value`

`  while( *p != '\0' ){`
`    // ASCII of '0' = 0x30`
`    // ASCII of '9' = 0x39`
`    if( *p<0x30 || *p>0x39)`
`      return 0;`
`    else`
`      value = \`
`        value*10 + (*p-0x30);`
 	
`    p++;`
`  }`
	`loop LDRB r0, [r1], #1  ; r0 = *p; p = p + 1`
	`      CBZ  r0, stop       ; check null terminator`
	`      CMP  r0, #0x30      ; 0x30 = '0'`
	`      BLT  stop           ; stop if < '0'`
	`      CMP  r0, #0x39      ; 0x39 = '9'`
	`      BGT  stop           ; stop if > '9'`
	`      SUBS r0, r0, #0x30 ; r0 = *p-48`
	`      ADD  r3, r2, r2, LSL #2   ; r3 = 5*r2`
	`      ADD  r2, r0, r3, LSL #1   ; r2 = 10*r2 + r0`
	`      B    loop`

`  while(1); //dead Loop`
`}`
	`stop B    stop`
	`      ENDP`
	`      END`

7.12 Example of Binary Search

If an array is already sorted in ascending order, we can use the binary search to locate a specific value in this array. It uses a divide-and-conquer approach, which divides the array in half and checks the middle point. If the middle is the target, the search completes successfully. If the middle is larger than the target, then it searches the first half of the array. Otherwise, it searches the second half. This search process repeats until the size of the remaining array is reduced to zero. The following gives the flowchart of binary search.

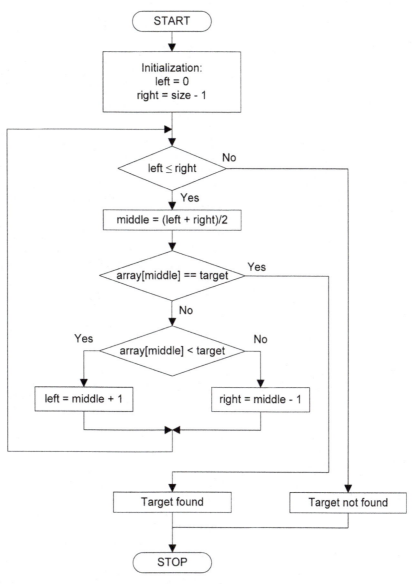

Figure 7-13. Flowchart of binary search over an array sorted ascendingly

For example, suppose the array consists of six integers, including 11, 12, 13, 14, 15, and 16 in order. The program searches for 12. The index of an array in C starts with 0.

- During the first round of the while loop, variable *left* is 0 and variable *right* is 5. Then, the *middle* is (*left* + *right*)/2 = (0 + 5)/2 = 2. Note C language uses truncation instead of rounding for integer arithmetic. Since array[*middle*], *i.e.*, array[2], is 13, which is larger than the target 12, we have *right* = *middle* – 1 = 2 – 1 = 1.

- During the second loop, *middle* = (*left* + *right*)/2 = (0 + 1)/2 = 0. Since array[0] is smaller than the target, we have *left* = *middle* + 1 = 0 + 1 = 1.

- During the third loop, the *middle* is (*left* + *right*)/2 = (1 + 1)/2 = 1. Because array[1] is equal to the target, the target has been found, and the while loop stops.

C Program	Assembly Program		

`int array[6] =`
`  {11, 12, 13, 14, 15, 16};`
`int size = 6;`
		`AREA myData, DATA`
		`ALIGN`
		`array  DCD  11,12,13,14,15,16`
		`size   DCD  6`	

`int main( void ) {`
 	
`  int left, right, middle;`
`  int target = 12;`
`  int targetLocation = -1;`
 	
`  left  = 0;`
`  right = size - 1;`
	`__main`	`AREA binarySearch, CODE`
		`EXPORT __main`
		`ALIGN`
		`ENTRY`
		`PROC`
		`MOVS r3, #12     ; search target`
		`MOVS r5, #-1     ; r5 = location`
		`LDR  r12, =array`
		`MOVS r1, #0      ; r1 = left`
		
		`LDR  r2, =size`
		`LDR  r2, [r2]`
		`SUB  r2, r2, #1  ; r2 = right`	

`  while( left <= right ){`
`    middle = (left + right)/2;`
`    if(array[middle]==target){`
`      targetLocation = middle;`
`      break;`
`    }`
`    if(array[middle] < target)`
`      left = middle + 1;`
`    else`
`      right = middle - 1;`
`  }`
	`loop`
	
	`found`
		`ADD  r0, r1, r2  ; r0 = left + right`
		`LSR  r0, r0, #1  ; middle = r0/2`
		`LDR  r4, [r12,r0,LSL #2] ; array[middle]`
		
		`CMP  r4, r3      ; compare with target`
		`SUBGT r2, r0, #1 ; right = middle - 1`
		`ADDLT r1, r0, #1 ; left = middle + 1`
		`BEQ  found`
		
		`CMP  r1, r2      ; compare left & right`
		`BLE  loop        ; loop if left ≤ right`
		`MOVEQ r5, r0`	

`  while(1); // dead loop`
`}`
	`stop`	`B    stop`
		`ENDP`
		`END`	

7.13 Example of Bubble Sort

Bubble sort is a straightforward and well-known sorting algorithm. It iterates through the unsorted portion of an array, repeatedly compares each pair of adjacent elements in this array, and swaps them if they are in reverse order. In each iteration, the largest element within the unsorted portion of the array sinks to the tail of this array for sorting in ascending order, and to the head of this array for sorting in descending order.

Assuming we want to sort an array of signed integers into ascending order. Figure 7-4 gives the flowchart.

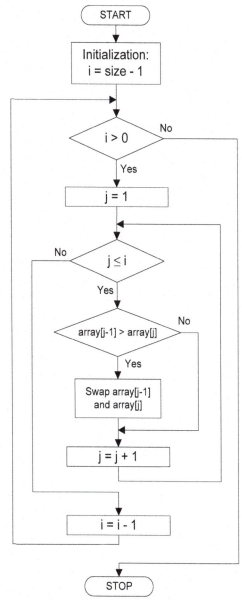

The program has a pair of nested loops. In the outer loop i, the ith largest number of the array is identified and moved toward the tail. The inner loop j iterates through the unsorted portion of the array and moves the greatest number in the unsorted portion to its proper place.

- In the first iteration of the outer loop (loop over i), we find the biggest number in this array and store it at array[$size$-1]. This is achieved by the following sequential steps. It first compares array[0] and array[1], then compares array[1] and array[2], ..., and finally compares array[$size$-2] and array[$size$-1]. If array[j-1] is larger than array[j], then they are swapped.

- In the second iteration of the outer loop, we find the greatest number in the subarray from array[0] to array[$size$-2], and store it into the position array[$size$-2].

- In each iteration, the size of the subarray to be sorted is reduced by one.

The above process repeats until the subarray size is reduced to zero. In the end, all numbers in this array are sorted in ascending order.

Figure 7-14. Flow chart of bubble sort

The following shows the implementation of bubble sort in C and assembly.

- In the assembly implementation, loop variable i is stored in register r1, and loop variable j is stored in register r0.
- The outer loop iterates n times, and the inner loop is always executed in each pass of the outer loop.
- During the first iteration of the outer loop, the inner loop iterates n times; during the second outer loop, the inner loop iterates $n - 1$ times, and so on.
- Therefore, the total number of comparisons when sorting an array of n integers, is $(n - 1) + (n - 2) + (n - 3) + \cdots + 1 = n(n + 1)/2$.

Note that the bubble sort algorithm is simple but inefficient. There are faster sorting algorithms, such as quick sort and heap sort.

C Program	Assembly Program

`int array[12] = {12, 11, 10, 9, 8, 7, 6, 5, 4, 3, 2, 1};`
 	
`int size = 12;`
	`        AREA myData, DATA`
	`        ALIGN`
	`array   DCD 12,11,10,9,8,7,6,5,4,3,2,1`
	`size    DCD 12`

`int main( void ) {`
`  int i, j, temp;`
	`        AREA bubbleSort, CODE`
	`        EXPORT __main`
	`        ALIGN`
	`        ENTRY`
	`__main  PROC`
	`        LDR r5, =array`
	`        LDR r6, =size`
	`        LDR r6, [r6]      ; array size`

`  for(i = size-1; i > 0; i--){`
 	
`    for(j = 1; j <= i; j++){`
 	
`      if(array[j-1]>array[j]){`
`      // swap them`
`        temp = array[j-1];`
`        array[j-1] = array[j];`
`        array[j] = temp;`
`      }`
`    }`
`  }`
	`        SUB r1, r6, #1   ; r1 = i = size -1`
	`loop_i  CMP r1, #0       ; check for i > 0`
	`        BLE stop         ; exit the loop i`
	`        MOV r0, #1       ; r0 = j = 1`
	`loop_j  CMP r0, r1       ; compare j and i`
	`        BGT exit_j       ; exit the loop j`
	`        SUB r2, r0, #1   ; r2 = j - 1`
	`        LDR r3, [r5,r2,LSL #2]   ; array[j-1]`
	`        LDR r4, [r5,r0,LSL #2]   ; array[j]`
	`        ; compare array[j-1] and array[j]`
	`        CMP r3, r4`
	`        STRGT r4, [r5,r2,LSL #2] ; array[j-1]`
	`        STRGT r3, [r5,r0,LSL #2] ; array[j]`
	`        ADD r0, r0, #1           ; j++`
	`        B    loop_j`
	`exit_j  SUB r1, r1, #1           ; i--`
	`        B    loop_i`

`  while(1);`
`}`
	`stop    B    stop`
	`        ENDP`
	`        END`

7.14 Exercises

1. Write an assembly program that converts all characters in a string to uppercase.

2. Write an assembly program that finds the least common multiple (LCM) of two integers. For example, LCM(4, 6) = 12.

3. Write an assembly program that calculates the result of x raised to the power of y, (*i.e.*, x^y), where x and y are two signed integers.

4. Write an assembly program that checks whether a given year is a leap year. A leap year is a year containing one additional day in February. A leap year meets one of the following requirements.

    - divisible by 400, or
    - only divisible by 4 but not by 100.

5. Write an assembly program that removes all vowel letters (a, e, i, o, u, A, E, I, O, U) from a string.

6. Let n be a positive integer. Integers a and b are congruent modulo n if they have the same remainder when divided by n. For example, 39 and 19 are congruent modulo 10. Write an assembly program that checks whether two unsigned integers, a and b, are congruent modulo n.

7. Write an assembly program that checks whether an unsigned number is a prime number or not.

8. Write an assembly program that reverses all bits of a 32-bit number without using the RBIT instruction.

9. Write an assembly program that checks whether an unsigned integer is a square of any unsigned integer. For example, $25 = 5^2$.

10. Write an assembly program that calculates the number of words in a string. The string is terminated with NULL, and words are separated by space.

11. Write an assembly program that finds the day of the week for a given date. Suppose the year is stored in r0, the month in r1, and the day of the month in r2. The day of the week is saved in r3 (0 = Sunday, 1 = Monday, *etc.*). Michael Keith and Tom Craver published the following method in 1990.

```
int day_of_week(int y, int m, int d) {
    static int t[] = {0, 3, 2, 5, 0, 3, 5, 1, 4, 6, 2, 4};
    y -= m < 3;
    return (y + y/4 - y/100 + y/400 + t[m-1] + d) % 7;
}
```

12. Write an assembly program that calculates the variance of an unsigned integer array, defined as follows:

$$\bar{x} = \frac{1}{n}\Sigma_i^n x_i \qquad var = \frac{1}{n}\Sigma_i^n (x_i - \bar{x})^2$$

13. Write an assembly program that calculates the sum of diagonal elements of an n-by-n integer matrix. The following gives an example matrix definition.

```
        AREA myData, DATA
size    DCD  4
matrix  DCD  1,2,3,4,5,6,7,8,9,10,11,12,13,14,15,16
```

14. Write an assembly program that calculates the dot product of two integer vectors of the equal number of elements. The dot product is defined as:

$$dot\ product = A \cdot B = \sum_{i=1}^{n}(a_i \times b_i) = a_1 b_1 + a_2 b_2 + \cdots + a_n b_n$$

```
         AREA myData, DATA
size     DCD  8
A_Array  DCD  1,2,3,4,5,6,7,8
B_Array  DCD  9,10,11,12,13,14,15,16
Product  DCD  0
```

15. Write an assembly program that performs matrix multiplication.

$$C_{(m \times n)} = A_{(m \times p)} \cdot B_{(p \times n)}$$

The (i, j) element of the product matrix, where $1 \le i \le m$ and $1 \le j \le n$ is:

$$c_{ij} = \sum_{k=1}^{p}(a_{ik} \times b_{kj}) = a_{i1} b_{1j} + a_{i2} b_{2j} + \cdots + a_{ip} b_{pj}$$

```
    AREA  myData, DATA
m   DCD    4   ; A has m rows
p   DCD    3   ; A has p columns
n   DCD    4   ; B has n columns

A   DCD    1,2,3,4,5,6,7,8,9,10,11,12   ; Matrix A
B   DCD    1,2,3,4,5,6,7,8,9,10,11,12   ; Matrix B
C   SPACE 64                            ; Reserve 16 words
```

CHAPTER 8

Subroutines

One key motivation of subroutines is to enable the reuse of a portion of the program code that carries out a specific task. Moreover, using subroutines can increase the quality and reliability of programs. A subroutine is also called a procedure, a function, or a routine.

One mistake which new software programmers often make is to duplicate code within a program by copy-and-paste. This programming style makes the program less modularized and difficult to read and debug. It increases the cost of developing and maintaining a large software project substantially.

Breaking the program codes into subroutines has two significant advantages.

> *"One of my most productive days was throwing away 1000 lines of code."*
>
> Ken Thompson, early developer of UNIX OS

- First, it decomposes a complex task into several simpler and more manageable subtasks, which makes the design, development, and debugging of each subtask much easier. We can develop and test each subtask separately, making it easier to find errors.
- Second, subtasks can be reused in a program or other subtasks repeatedly without duplicating any code, which saves time and effort by eliminating redundant development work.

A subroutine usually takes some input arguments and returns a result, when the subroutine exits. For example, when a subroutine finds the maximum of an array of elements, it may take two arguments: the memory address (a pointer in C language) of the array and the number of items in this array. It may also return the maximum value or the index (or the address of the maximum value). Using arguments makes a subroutine versatile and suitable for a variety of uses.

Implementing a subroutine using a high-level programming language such as Java, C, or C++ differs significantly from using an assembly language. Specifically, when a programmer develops a subroutine in assembly, we must consider two special issues.

1. Preserve and recover the caller's environment. The subroutine should be non-intrusive and avoid destroying the content of relevant registers, which are still meaningful for the caller. A subroutine takes two steps to preserve and to recover the caller's runtime environment.

   • First, the subroutine saves the environment by pushing registers to be used in the subroutine onto the stack at the beginning of the subroutine.

   • Second, the subroutine restores the environment by popping the content off the stack to registers at the end of the subroutine.

2. The standard of application binary interface specifies the protocol of passing input arguments to a subroutine and returning the result back to the caller. If subroutines developed in assembly follow the standard, a C program can call these subroutines. Following the standard also facilitates sharing code between different programmers.

8.1 Calling a Subroutine

An assembly program can use the branch and link (BL) instruction to call a subroutine. The BL instruction performs the following two operations:

1. Configure the link register (LR) as the memory address of the next instruction immediately after the BL instruction (PC + 4 in Cortex-M), and
2. Adjust the program counter (PC) as the memory address of the very first instruction of the subroutine.

Register LR stores the memory address of the instruction to be executed immediately after a subroutine exits. The address held in LR is also called **return address**. The return address is the memory address of the instruction immediately after the BL instruction in the caller program. Since a BL instruction takes 32 bits (*i.e.*, 4 bytes) in memory, the memory address of the instruction immediately after the BL instruction is PC + 4.

There are two different approaches to return from a subroutine.

   • The first one is to run the branch and exchange instruction "BX LR".

- The second one is to pop the LR value off the stack into PC, *i.e.,* "POP {PC}", if the subroutine has already pushed LR onto the stack.

Figure 8-1 shows an example in which the main program calls the subroutine *foo*, and the subroutine *foo* then calls the subroutine *bar*. Because each BL instruction takes 32 bits (*i.e.,* 4 bytes), the address of the next instruction immediately after a BL instruction is PC + 4.

- When the main program uses "BL foo" to call the subroutine *foo*, the processor carries out two operations: (1) set LR is set to $PC_1 + 4$, and (2) set PC to the memory address of the subroutine *foo*.

- When *foo* returns by executing "BX LR", the processor copies the content of LR to PC, making the next instruction after "BL foo" in the main program to start the execution.

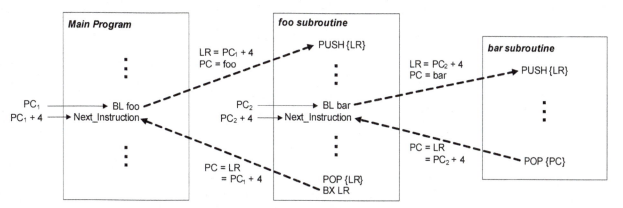

Figure 8-1. An example of calling subroutines. A subroutine should preserve the link register (LR) in the stack if this subroutine calls any subroutines.

When the subroutine *foo* calls another subroutine *bar*, the register *foo* should preserve LR in the stack at the beginning of the subroutine. In the example shown in Figure 8-1,

- When *foo* calls *bar*, "BL bar" sets LR to $PC_2 + 4$.

- When *bar* executes "POP {PC}", the processor sets LR to $PC_2 + 4$

Preserve Link Register (LR) in a subroutine if it calls another subroutine.

- If *foo* did not preserve and recover LR, *i.e.,* *foo* did not have "PUSH {LR}" and "POP {LR}" in the code, the "BX LR" instruction at the end of *foo* would not be able to return the control to the main program correctly. The processor would mistakenly set PC to $PC_2 + 4$, instead of $PC_1 + 4$ when *foo* exits.

- Therefore, *foo* should push LR onto the stack if it calls another subroutine or itself.

8.2 Stack

A stack is a last-in-first-out (LIFO) data structure, as shown in Figure 8-2. A stack has two fundamental operations: *push* and *pop*. The push operation adds an item to the top of the stack. The pop operation removes the item that was added last.

A stack also refers to a contiguous region in the data memory that software programs or processors use to hold a stack data structure. The stack pointer (SP) holds the memory address of the top of the stack. A program can utilize stacks to preserve and recovery the runtime environment when it calls a subroutine.

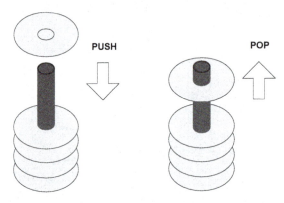

Figure 8-2. A stack is last-in-first-out (LIFO).

Per the direction in which the stack grows, a stack can be either descending or ascending, as shown in Figure 8-3.

- *Descending stack.* When the content of a register is pushed onto the stack, the stack pointer (SP) is decreased by 4 if it is a descending stack. The stack starts at a high memory address and grows downward, *i.e.*, in the direction toward lower memory addresses.

- *Ascending stack.* When a program pushes a register onto the stack, SP is increased by 4. The stack starts at a low memory address grows upward, *i.e.*, in the direction toward high memory addresses.

Also, a stack can be either a *full stack* or an *empty stack*.

- *Full stack.* If the memory location pointed by SP holds the last item that was pushed onto the stack, this stack is called a full stack.

- *Empty stack.* If the memory location pointed by SP is an empty spot and will store the next item to be pushed onto the stack, this stack is referred to as an empty stack.

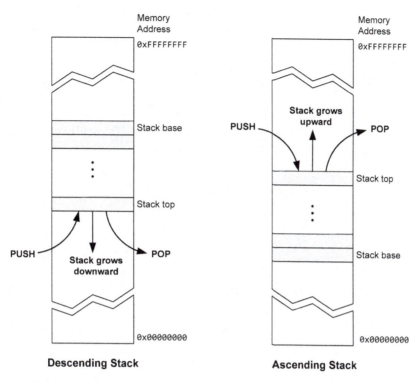

Figure 8-3. Comparing descending stack and ascending stack.

With a combination of the growth direction and the validness of the memory location pointed by the stack pointer, there are four types of stacks, including *full descending stack, full ascending stack, empty descending stack,* and *empty ascending stack.*

8.3 Implementation of Stack via STM and LDM

Table 8-1 shows the assembly instructions equivalent to the push and pop operations for these four types of stacks. For each push and pop operation, there are two implementations. Chapter 5.5 has explained these STM and LDM instructions.

Stack Name	Push		Pop	
	Equivalent	Alternative	Equivalent	Alternative
Full Descending(FD)	STMFD SP!,list	STMDB SP!,list	LDMFD SP!,list	LDMIA SP!,list
Empty Descending(ED)	STMED SP!,list	STMDA SP!,list	LDMED SP!,list	LDMIB SP!,list
Full Ascending(FA)	STMFA SP!,list	STMIB SP!,list	LDMFA SP!,list	LDMDA SP!,list
Empty Ascending(EA)	STMEA SP!,list	STMIA SP!,list	LDMEA SP!,list	LDMDB SP!,list

Table 8-1. Implementation of PUSH and POP by using STM and LDM instructions

ARM Cortex-M uses *full descending* stacks, as shown in Figure 8-4. For full-descending stacks, the push and pop operations are equivalent to STMDB and LDMIA, respectively.

Moreover, a Cortex-M processor supports two stacks: one main stack and one process stack. Therefore, there are two stack pointers: MSP and PSP. The stack pointer (SP) is a shadow of MSP or PSP. Chapter 23.1 discusses the usage of these two stacks. The initial value of these two stack pointers can be programmed. Typically, the system stack is placed in the top region of the system memory region.

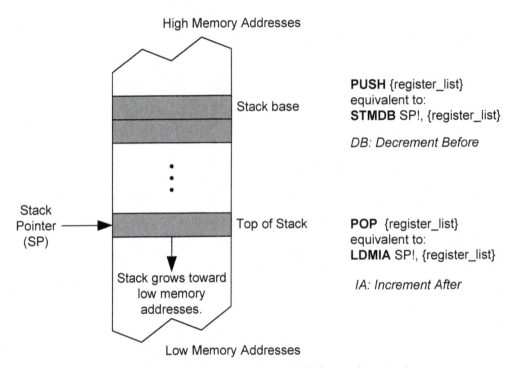

Figure 8-4. Cortex-M uses *full descending* stack

8.4 Preserving Runtime Environment via Stack

If a subroutine uses a register to hold some variable, the subroutine often must preserve the value of this register in the stack when the subroutine starts, and recover the register value from the stack when the subroutine exits. In this process, the callee preserves the caller's runtime environment.

Example 8-1 shows the motivation why a subroutine must preserve the runtime environment. The caller uses register r4 as a loop variable looping from 0 to 100. The loop body calls a subroutine named *foo*. However, the subroutine *foo* also uses register r4 as a local variable. If the subroutine does not preserve the content in register r4, r4 is mistakenly set to 10 after the subroutine completes. Thus, the loop in the caller does not perform as desired.

Caller Program	Subroutine/Callee

MOV r4, #100
 	
...
 	
BL foo
 	
...
 	
ADD r4, r4, #1   ; r4 = 101, not 11
	foo PROC
	...
	MOV r4, #10 ; foo changes r4
	...
	BX LR
	ENDP

Example 8-1. The loop in the caller program is not executed as desired.

To solve this issue, the subroutine stores the value of register r4 onto the stack before executing any other code, and then restores the content to r4 immediately before the subroutine returns. The stack push and pop operations preserve and recover the runtime environment, as illustrated below.

Caller Program	Subroutine/Callee

; main.s
 	
MOV r4, #100
 	
...
 	
BL foo
 	
...
 	
ADD r4, r4, #1   ; r4 = 101, not 11
	foo PROC
	
	PUSH {r4} ; preserve r4
	...
	MOV r4, #10 ; foo changes r4
	...
	POP {r4} ; Recover r4
	BX LR
	ENDP

Example 8-2. A subroutine preserves register values in the stack at the beginning and recovers register values from the stack before the subroutine exits.

The ARM embedded application binary interface (EABI) requires that a subroutine must preserve the content in registers r4 - r11 and r13 (SP) if this subroutine changes the value of these registers.

However, a subroutine is not required to preserve registers r0-r3, also called *scratch registers*. Thus, if the caller requires that the value in registers r0-r3 remains unchanged, the caller should push these registers onto the stack before it calls a subroutine.

Table 8-2 summarizes the register usage. Subroutines should meet the following requirements.

- Besides registers r0-r3, a subroutine also does not preserve the intra-procedure-call register r12 (IP) and the link register r14 (LR).

- Register r9 is platform dependent and has different purposes. For example, r9 can be a variable register to hold a local variable.
- Register IP allows a routine and any subroutine it calls to share an intermediate value. When the caller executes a BL instruction, the value of IP may be changed if the memory address of the destination instruction is beyond the range of the BL instruction. Therefore, software should not use register IP as a general-purpose register to hold important values.
- It is not required to preserve register LR. However, if a subroutine A() calls another subroutine B(), the subroutine A() should preserve LR in the stack (see Chapter 8.1).

Register	Usage	Subroutine Preserved	Notes
r0	Argument 1 and return value	No	If the 1st argument has 64 bits, r1:r0 hold it (r1 is upper word, r0 is bottom word).
r1	Argument 2	No	If the 2nd argument has 64 bits, r3:r2 hold it.
r2	Argument 3	No	If more than 4 arguments, use the stack.
r3	Argument 4	No	If the return has 64 bits, then r1:r0 hold it. If the return has 128 bits, then r0-r3 hold it.
r4	General-purpose V1	Yes	
r5	General-purpose V2	Yes	
r6	General-purpose V3	Yes	Variable registers for holding local variables.
r7	General-purpose V4	Yes	
r8	General-purpose V5	Yes	
r9	Platform specific/V6	No	Usage is platform-dependent.
r10	General-purpose V7	Yes	Variable registers for holding local variables
r11	General-purpose V8	Yes	
r12 (IP)	Intra-procedure-call register	No	It holds intermediate values between a procedure and the sub-procedure it calls.
r13 (SP)	Stack pointer	Yes	SP must be the same after a subroutine has completed.
r14 (LR)	Link register	No	LR does not have to contain the same value after a subroutine has completed.
r15 (PC)	Program counter	N/A	Do not directly change PC

Table 8-2. Standard of register usage of a subroutine

When using the push instruction to push multiple registers onto the stack, as shown in Example 8-3, the order in which the registers are listed in the bracket does not matter. These the registers are sorted in the descending order based on their numbers. The processor pushes the largest register first during the push, and pops the smallest register first during the pop.

Push and pop multiple registers	Equivalent assembly code

MOV r4, #4
MOV r5, #5
MOV r6, #6
	MOV r4, #4
	MOV r5, #5
	MOV r6, #6

PUSH {r4, r5, r6} ; The order in the bracket does not matter. ; The register list is sorted based on ; their names and the largest numbered ; register is pushed first.	; Equivalent code PUSH {r6} PUSH {r5} PUSH {r4}
POP {r6, r4, r5} ; The order in the bracket does not matter. ; The smallest numbered register is popped ; off the stack first.	; Equivalent code POP {r4} POP {r5} POP {r6}
; result: r4=4, r5=5, r6=6	; result: r4=4, r5=5, r6=6

Example 8-3. Push and pop operations of the stack

8.5 Passing Arguments to Subroutine via Registers

An assembly subroutine may be called by standard C programs or by assembly programs developed independently by different programmers. Therefore, all subroutines must follow the ARM EABI protocol in passing arguments and in returning a result.

The protocol of passing arguments is summarized below.

- When the caller passes up to four 32-bit arguments to a subroutine, the caller places these arguments in registers r0, r1, r2, and r3.

- When a subroutine takes two 64-bit arguments, such as "long long" and "double" in C, the caller puts the first 64-bit argument in registers r0 and r1, and the second 64-bit argument in registers r2 and r3. The most significant 32 bits are of these two arguments are in register r1 and r3, respectively.

- When the caller passes a 128-bit argument, the argument is contained in registers r0, r1, r2, and r3.

- When there are more than four 32-bit arguments, the first four arguments come in via registers r0 – r3, respectively, and the subroutine receives the rest arguments via the stack.

The protocol of returning a result is as follows.

- When a subroutine returns a 32-bit value, the return value is stored in register r0.

- If the result has 64 bits, it is stored in register r0 and r1.

- If the return has 128 bits, it is stored in registers r0, r1, r2, and r3.

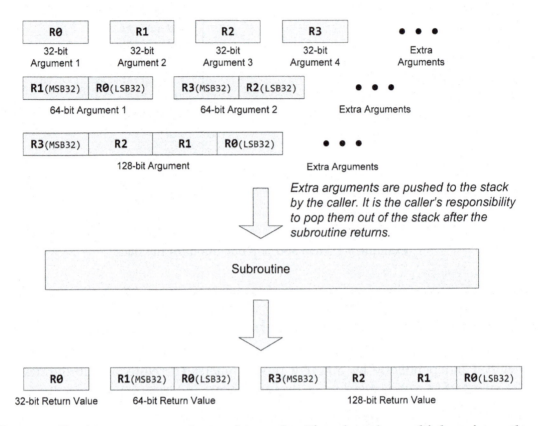

Figure 8-5. Passing arguments and returning a value. If a value takes multiple registers, the most significant 32 bits (MSB32) are stored in the highest numbered register.

8.5.1 Pass a Variable by Value and by Reference

Variables are stored in memory typically. A caller can pass variable arguments to a subroutine by value or by reference. In C, the arguments are always passed by value. However, C can use memory points to emulate passing a variable by reference. Figure 8-6 shows the comparison. If passed by value, the input argument remains unchanged.

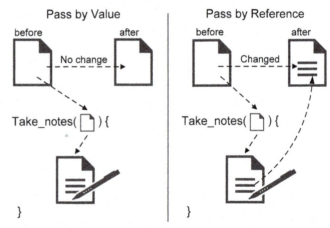

Figure 8-6. Comparison between pass by value and pass by reference.

- Passing a variable *by value* is to make a copy of the variable. After the callee returns, the caller's variable always remains unchanged.

- Passing a variable *by reference* is achieved by making a copy of the memory address of the caller's variable. The callee can change the value of the caller's variable because the callee knows the memory address of the caller's variable.

Example 8-4 shows a simple example that compares passing a variable to a subroutine by value and by reference. We can better understand their differences by looking at the assembly programs into which a C compiler translates them, as illustrated in Figure 8-7 and Figure 8-8.

Pass by Value	Pass by Reference
```c void fun(int n){ n = 1; // The value of n is passed // won't update caller's n } int main(void){ int n = 0; fun(n); // pass value of n printf("%d", n); } ```	```c void fun(int *n){ *n = 1; // The address of n // is passed. // dereference and // update memory } int main(void){ int n = 0; int *p = &n; fun(p); // pass pointer printf("%d", n); } ```
Program Output: 0	Program Output: 1

Example 8-4. Comparison of passing a variable by value and by reference in C

When compiling a C program, the compiler can assign a local variable to a register or store it in the heap region of the data memory, as discussed in Chapter 7.2. Suppose variable n in Example 8-4 is stored in the data memory. Figure 8-7 and Figure 8-8 compare the operations of passing a variable by value and by reference.

1. When a variable is *passed by value*, Figure 8-7 illustrates the key operations of the corresponding assembly code of Example 8-4.
   - The value of variable n is loaded from the memory to register r0.
   - While the subroutine changes the value of register r0, the value stored in memory remains unchanged.
   - Therefore, a subroutine cannot modify the in-memory variable if the variable is passed to the subroutine by value.

2. When a variable is *passed by reference*, Figure 8-8 shows the key operations of its assembly implementation of Example 8-4.

- The memory address of variable *n* is loaded into register r0 and is passed to the subroutine.
- Register r0 serves as a pointer to variable *n*.
- Since the memory address is sent to the subroutine, the subroutine can change the value of the variable by using the store instruction (STR).
- When the subroutine exits, the value of the caller's variable *n* in memory has been changed.

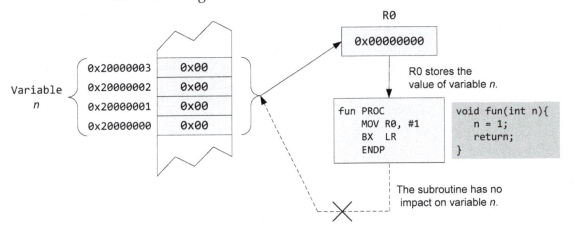

Figure 8-7. Example of passing a variable *by value*.
If variable n is passed to a subroutine by value, the subroutine cannot change the variable value stored in memory because the subroutine only knows the value but not the memory address of variable n. Therefore, after the fun subroutine exits, the value of n stored in memory is still 0, not 1.

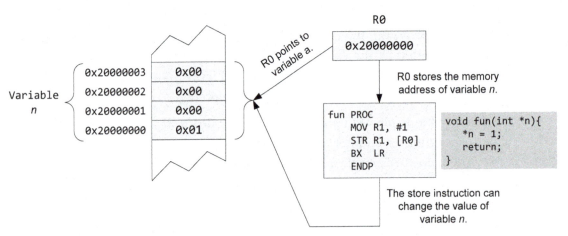

Figure 8-8. Example of passing a variable *by reference*.
If variable n is passed to a subroutine by reference, the memory address of variable n is passed. Therefore, the subroutine can change the value of variable n. After the subroutine exits, the value of n in memory is changed to 1.

8.5.2 Example of Passing by Value

In Example 8-5, two 32-bit integers are passed to the subroutine *sum2*. Per the application binary interface (ABI) protocol, the assembly program should meet the following requirements.

- The value of variable *a1* is received in register r0, and *a2* in register r1. An integer in C has 32 bits. Therefore, only one register is required to hold *a1*.

- The caller program assumes the subroutine saves the result *total* in register r0.

- Registers r0, r1, r2, and r3 are scratch registers, and the subroutine does not have to preserve them in the stack. If the caller wishes to safeguard the value of these registers, the caller must push them onto the stack before the subroutine is called, and pop them off stack after the subroutine completes.

- If a subroutine does not call any other subroutine, the subroutine is required to preserve the link register (LR) in the stack. Otherwise, the subroutine should preserve LR on entry and recover it on exit.

C Program	Assembly Program

`int t;`
`int sum2(int a1, int a2);`
	`        AREA sum, CODE`
	`        EXPORT __main`
	`        ALIGN`
	`        ENTRY`

`int main(){`
 	
`  t = sum2(1, 2);`
 	
`  while(1);`
`}`
	`__main PROC`
	`        MOV   r0, #1      ; 1st argument`
	`        MOV   r1, #2      ; 2nd argument`
	
	`        BL    sum2        ; result returned in r0`
	`                         ; LR points to LDR instr`
	`        LDR   r1, =t      ; memory address of t`
	`        STR   r0, [r1]    ; save the sum`
	`stop    B     stop`
	`        ENDP`

`int sum2(int a1, int a2){`
`  int total;`
 	
`  total = a1 + a2;`
 	
`  return total;`
`}`
	`sum2    PROC              ; name of procedure`
	`        ; r0 = 1st argument`
	`        ; r1 = 2nd argument`
	
	`        ADD   r0, r0, r1 ; r0 = r0 + r1`
	`        ; r0 = result to be returned`
	
	`        BX    lr          ; set PC to LR`
	`        ENDP              ; end of procedure`

	`        AREA myData, DATA`
	`t       DCD 0`
	`        END               ; end of program`

Example 8-5. Passing two arguments to a subroutine

In the following, we illustrate how to pass a 64-bit value to a subroutine. In C, a long long variable has 64 bits in memory. When a subroutine takes a long long variable, two registers, r0 and r1, are used to hold the value of this variable. Register r1 holds the most significant 32 bits, and register r0 contains the least significant 32 bits. For example, if the long long variable has a value of -2, then r0 is 0xFFFFFFFE and r1 is 0xFFFFFFFF.

The subroutine returns the 64-bit result in register r1 and r0. In the following example, the 64-bit sum should be 3. Thus, when the subroutine returns, r1 is 0x00000000 (the upper word), and r0 is 0x00000003 (the lower word). If the 64-bit result should be saved in the data memory, two STR instructions are used to store the upper and lower words, respectively.

C Program	Assembly Program

`long long t;`
 	
`long sum2(long long a1,`
`        long long a2);`
	`        AREA sum, CODE`
	`        EXPORT __main`
	`        ALIGN`
	`        ENTRY`

`int main(){`	`__main PROC`
	`        MOV   r0, #1    ; 1st 64-bit argument`
	`        MOV   r1, #0    ; r1:r0`
	`        MOV   r2, #2    ; 2nd 64-bit argument`
	`        MOV   r3, #0    ; r3:r2`

`  t = sum2(1, 2);`	`        BL    sum2     ; result in r1:r0`
	`                       ; LR points to LDR instr.`
	`        LDR   r3, =t    ; memory address of t`
	`        STR   r0, [r3]  ; save lower 32 bits`
	`        STR   r1, [r3, #4] ; save upper 32 bits`
	`                       ; r0 = 3, r1 = 0 in`
	`                       ; this example`

`  while(1);` `}`	`stop    B    stop` `        ENDP`

`long long sum2(long long a1,`
`long long a2){`
	`sum2    PROC           ; name of procedure`
	`        ; r1:r0 = 1st 64-bit argument`
	`        ; r3:r2 = 2nd 64-bit argument`

`  long long total;` `  total = a1 + a2;`	`        ADDS r0, r0, r2  ; add lower 32 bits` `        ADC  r1, r1, r3  ; add upper 32 bits`

`  return total;`
`}`
	`        ; r1:r0 = 64-bit return value`
	`        BX   lr          ; set PC to LR`
	`        ENDP             ; end of procedure`

	`        AREA myData, DATA`
	`t       DCQ 0             ; allocate 8 bytes`
	`        END               ; end of program`

Example 8-6. Passing two 64-bit arguments to a subroutine

8.5.3 Write a Subroutine in Different Files

Subroutines can be in separate source files. A compiler must compile these source files and then link them together to build an executable. Placing subroutines in multiple files improves the clarity and makes the code more manageable when the source code is large.

A subroutine should export its name of if it is called by codes in other source files. Exporting a subroutine allows other source files to reference it during the linking state. Similarly, a caller should import the subroutine name defined in a different source file.

Example 8-7 shows how an assembly program calls a subroutine implemented in a separate assembly source file.

- In the *sum2.s* file, "EXPORT sum2" is used to declare a symbol *sum2* that may be referred to in other source files. The directive "EXPORT" in assembly is like "EXTERN" in C.
- In the *main.s* file, "IMPORT sum2" is used to tell the assembler that the symbol *sum2* is defined in a different file.

Source file *sum2.s*	Source file *main.s*

<pre>   AREA sum, CODE
        EXPORT sum2
        ALIGN
 	
sum2   PROC
        ADD r0, r0, r1 ; return r0
        BX lr   ; set PC to LR
        ENDP
 	
        END</pre>
	<pre> AREA program, CODE
	        EXPORT __main
	        IMPORT sum2
	        ALIGN
	        ENTRY
	
	__main PROC
	        MOV r0, #1 ; 1st argument
	        MOV r1, #2 ; 2nd argument
	        BL sum2 ; return r0
	
	stop B stop
	        ENDP
	        END</pre>

Example 8-7. Implementing a subroutine stored in a separate file. The keywords IMPORT and EXPORT are used to call a subroutine stored in a separate source file.

A symbol can be the name of a subroutine or a data variable. A compiler resolves all symbols at the linking stage in which various pieces of code and data are combined into a single executable file. A linker performs the linking process.

- The EXPORT directive makes a symbol visible to all modular files during the linking stage. By default, the linker tries to locate a symbol locally within the current source file or included files.
- The IMPORT directive informs the linker that a symbol is defined or implemented in a different file.

8.5.4 Example of Passing by Reference

Pass-by-reference in C is a method that passes the memory address of a variable to the subroutine and thus allows the subroutine to change the variable value. A C program must declare an argument passed by reference as a pointer type. The following *swap* subroutine takes two arguments that are passed by reference.

C program	Assembly Program

```// swap two characters```
 ```void swap (char *x, char *y) {```
 ```   char t;```
 ```   t = *x;```
 ```   *x = *y;```
 ```   *y = t;```
 ```}```
	```; swap routine```
	 ```swap PROC```
	 ``` LDRB r2, [r0]```
	 ``` LDRB r3, [r1]```
	 ``` STRB r3, [r0] ; [r1] into [r0]```
	 ``` STRB r2, [r1] ; [r0] into [r1]```
	 ``` BX lr```
	 ``` ENDP```

Example 8-8. Implementation of passing by reference in assembly language

Example 8-9 shows a subroutine that swaps the first and the last character of a string. For example, the swap subroutine changes "abcde" to "ebcda".

```
char str[6] = "abcde";      // Include the NULL terminator into the length

int main(void){
    swap(str, str+4);       // The result is "ebcda".
}
```

Example 8-9. A C program calls a subroutine implemented in assembly language.

In contrast to passing by reference, another method is to *pass by value*. The key difference is whether the caller can see any changes made to an argument by a subroutine.

The arguments in Example 8-10 are passed by value. The callee receives a copy of the variables' values. These variables remain unchanged in the caller. Consequently, Example 8-10 fails to swap the characters in this string. The subroutine "swap(str[0], str[4])" does not affect the content of the string str at all.

C program (Incorrect code)	Assembly Program (Incorrect code)

```// failed to swap x and y```
 ```void swap (char x, char y) {```
 ```   char t;```
 ```   t = x;```
 ```   x = y;```
 ```   y = t;```
 ```}```
	```; swap routine```
	 ```swap PROC```
	 ``` MOVS r2, r0```
	 ``` MOVS r1, r0```
	 ``` MOVS r2, r1```
	 ``` BX lr```
	 ``` ENDP```

Example 8-10. A subroutine implemented in C and assembly language fails to swap two characters when arguments are passed by value.

8.5.5 Example of Greatest Common Divisor

This example gives a subroutine that calculates the greatest common divisor (GCD) of two positive integers. Figure 8-9 shows the flowchart of the *gcd* subroutine.

The subroutine uses Euclid's algorithm, *i.e.*, $gcd(a, b) = gcd(b, a \bmod b)$. The subroutine swaps *a* and *b* if *a* is smaller than *b*. It then repeatedly finds the GCD of the remainder (*a mod b*) and *b*. The remainder becomes smaller and smaller, and this process continues until the remainder becomes zero.

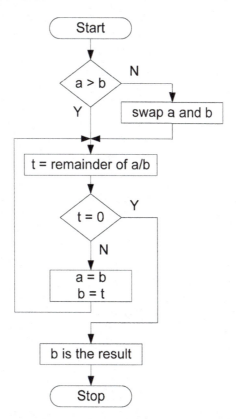

Figure 8-9. Flowchart of GCD subroutine

For illustration, suppose *a* = 2310 and *b* = 483. The program takes the following iterations:

1. *a* = 2310 and *b* = 483. Since 2310 = 4 × 483 + 378, the remainder of *a/b* is 378.
2. *a* = 483 and *b* = 378. Since 483 = 1 × 378 + 105, the remainder of *a/b* is 105.
3. *a* = 378 and *b* = 105. Since 378 = 3 × 105 + 63, the remainder of *a/b* is 63.
4. *a* = 105 and *b* = 63. Since 105 = 1 × 63 + 42, the remainder of *a/b* is 42.
5. *a* = 63 and *b* = 42. Since 63 = 1 × 42 + 21, the remainder of *a/b* is 21
6. *a* = 42 and *b* = 21. Since 42 = 2 × 21, the remainder of *a/b* is 0.
7. The program stops, and the GCD of 2310 and 483 is 21.

Per the ARM EABI protocol, the two arguments *a* and *b* are passed in register r0 and r1, respectively. The subroutine returns the result in register r0.

Since this *gcd* subroutine does not call any other subroutines, it does not have to preserve the link register (LR) in the stack. Also, the subroutine only uses registers r0, r1, r2, and r3. Thus, there is no need to push any registers onto the stack.

C Program	Assembly Program	

`int gcd(int a, int b);`
`int result;`
	`        AREA myData, DATA`
	`        ALIGN`
	`result  DCW 0`
		
		`; allocate four bytes`

`int main(void){`
`  result = gcd(21, 28);`
`  while(1);`
`}`
	`        AREA GCD, CODE`
	`        EXPORT __main`
	`        ALIGN`
	`        ENTRY`
	`__main PROC`
	`        MOV    r1, #21`
	`        MOV    r0, #28`
	`        BL     gcd`
	
	`        ; GCD is returned in r0`
	`        LDR    r2, =result`
	`        STR    r0, [r2]`
	`stop    B      stop`
	`        ENDP`
		
		`; 1ˢᵗ argument`
		`; 2ⁿᵈ argument`
		`; call subroutine`
		
		`; r2 = memory address`
		`; save result`

`int gcd(int a, int b) {`
`  int t; // temp variable`
 	
`  // swap a and b if a < b`
`  if( a < b ) {`
`    t = a;`
`    a = b;`
`    b = t;`
`  }`
 	
`  while( b != 0 ){`
`    t = a % b;`
`    a = b;`
`    b = t;`
`  }`
 	
`  return a;`
`}`
	`gcd     PROC`
	`        ; r0 = 1ˢᵗ argument = a`
	`        ; r1 = 2ⁿᵈ argument = b`
	
	`        CMP    r0, r1`
	`        MOVLT  r2, r0`
	`        MOVLT  r0, r1`
	`        MOVLT  r1, r2`
	
	`loop    CBZ    r1, exit`
	`        SDIV   r3, r0, r1`
	`        MLS    r2, r1, r3, r0`
	`        MOV    r0, r1`
	`        MOV    r1, r2`
	`        B      loop`
	
	`exit    BX     lr`
	
	`        ENDP`
	`        END`
		
		`; compare a & b`
		`; if a < b, swap a & b`
		
		`; if b = 0, exit`
		`; r3 = r0/r1`
		`; r2 = r1 - r3*r0`
		`; a = b`
		`; b = remainder`
		`; loop again`
		
		`; return in r0`

Example 8-11. Finding the greatest common divisor (GCD)

8.5.6 Example of Concatenating Two Strings

When a string is concatenated to another string, the destination string must have enough extra memory space to hold the resulting concatenated string. Otherwise, data stored after the target string in memory may be modified by mistake. Thus, in the data region, the statement "str1_ SPACE 20" reserves 20 bytes of memory space.

Each string ends with a NULL character. This example uses the post index memory addressing. The following instruction with post-index addressing

```
LDRB  r3, [r1], #1     ; post-index addressing
```

is equivalent to:

```
LDRB  r3, [r1]
ADD   r1, r1, #1
```

C Program	Assembly Program

`void strcat(char *s1, char *s2);`
 	
 `char s1[20] = "Shaking";`
 `char s2[10] = " hands";`
	<pre> AREA myData, DATA
	      ALIGN
	str1 DCB "Shaking",0
	str1_ SPACE 20 ; reserve space
	str2 DCB " hands",0</pre>

`int main(){`
  `strcat(s1, s2);`
  `while(1);`
 `}`
	<pre> AREA my_strcat, CODE
	      EXPORT __main
	      ALIGN
	      ENTRY
	__main PROC
	      LDR r0, =str1 ; 1st argument
	      LDR r1, =str2 ; 2nd argument
	      BL strcat ; call subroutine
	stop B stop
	      ENDP</pre>

`// Concatenate two strings`
 `void strcat(char *dst, char *src){`
 	
  `while(*dst != '\0')`
    `dst++;`
 	
  `while((*dst++ = *src++)!= '\0');`
 	
  `return;`
 `}`
	<pre>; Concatenate two strings
	strcat PROC
	loop LDRB r2, [r0] ; Load a byte
	      CBZ r2, copy ; null ending
	      ADD r0, r0, #1
	      B loop
	
	copy LDRB r3, [r1], #1 ; post-index
	      STRB r3, [r0], #1 ; post-index
	      CBNZ r3, copy
	
	      BX lr
	      ENDP
	      END</pre>

Example 8-12. Concatenating two strings in C and assembly

8.5.7 Example of Comparing Two Strings

The *strcmp* compares two null-terminated strings and returns a positive, zero, or a negative integer if the first string is greater than, equal to, or less than the second string, respectively.

The comparison starts with the first pair and continues with the next pair if the first pair is equal. When a pair is different from each other, the function *strcmp* returns the difference between this pair. The following gives a few examples.

- strcmp("their", "there") returns -9 because ASCII of "i" and "r" is 105 and 114, respectively.
- strcmp("their", "the") returns 105. A string must end with the NULL character. The ASCII value of "i" is 105 and the NULL terminator is 0.
- strcmp("the", "there") returns -114. ASCII of NULL and 'r' is 0 and 114.
- strcmp("their", "their") returns 0.

C Program	Assembly Program

```char str1[] = "dog";```
```char str2[] = "cat";```
```int   result;```
	``` AREA myData, DATA```
	```str1 DCB "dog",0 ; NULL terminated```
	```str2 DCB "cat",0 ; NULL terminated```
	```result DCW 0 ; allocate one word```

```int main(void){```
```   int result;```
 	
```   result = strcmp(str1, str2);```
 	
```   while(1);```
```}```
	``` AREA my_strcmp, CODE```
	``` EXPORT __main```
	``` ALIGN```
	``` ENTRY```
	```__main PROC```
	``` LDR r0, =str1 ; address of str1```
	``` LDR r1, =str2 ; address of str2```
	``` BL strcmp ; call subroutine```
	``` LDR r1, =result ; address of result```
	``` STR r0, [r1] ; save the result```
	```stop B stop ; dead loop```
	``` ENDP```

```// Compare two strings```
```int strcmp(char *s, char *t){```
 	
```   while(*s == *t){```
```   if (*s == '\0') return 0;```
```   s++;```
```   t++;```
```   }```
 	
```   return *s - *t;```
```}```
	```; Compare two strings```
	```strcmp PROC```
	``` ; r0 = s, r1 = t```
	```loop LDRB r2, [r0], #1 ; post-index```
	``` LDRB r3, [r1], #1 ; post-index```
	``` CBZ r2, exit ; NULL terminator```
	``` CMP r2, r3 ; if *s == *t```
	``` BEQ loop ; Compare again```
	```exit SUB r0, r2, r3 ; r0 = *s - *t```
	``` BX lr ; return r0```
	``` ENDP```
	``` END```

Example 8-13. Comparing two strings in C and assembly

8.5.8 Example of Inserting an Integer into a Sorted Array

The subroutine has three arguments,
passed in registers r0, r1, and r2. The
subroutine preserves registers r4 and
LR. In the end, it pops LR to PC, which
makes it return to the caller.

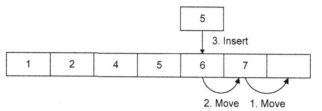

Suppose the array has been sorted in ascending order. The program starts with the last
element (*i.e.*, the largest one) of the array and compares the input integer with each array
element one by one. If the element is greater than the input, this element is moved to the
right by one; otherwise, the input is inserted at the current position.

C Program	Assembly Program

`int a[10] = {1, 2, 4, 5, 6, 7};`
 	
`void insert(int, int *, int);`
	`        AREA myData, DATA`
	`        ALIGN`
	`a       DCD 1,2,4,5,6,7`

`int main(void){`
`  insert(3, a, 5);`
`  while(1);`
`}`
	`        AREA insert_array, CODE`
	`        EXPORT __main`
	`        ALIGN`
	`        ENTRY`
	`__main PROC`
	`        MOV r0, #3   ; 1st argument, value`
	`        LDR r1, =a   ; 2nd argument, array`
	`        MOV r2, #5   ; 3rd argument, size`
	`        BL  insert   ; call subroutine`
	`stop    B   stop`
	`        ENDP`

`// input: value, pointer, size`
`void insert(int v, int *a, int s){`
`  int i;`
 	
`  for (i=s; i>0 && v<a[i-1]; i--){`
`    a[i] = a[i-1];`
`  }`
	`; r0 = value, r1 = array, r2 = size`
	`insert PROC`
	`        PUSH {r4, lr}`
	`loop    CMP r2, #0        ; check i > 0`
	`        BLE done          ; done if i ≤ 0`
	`        SUB r4, r2, #1    ; r4 = i - 1`
	`        LDR r4, [r1,r4,LSL #2]  ; a[i-1]`
	`        CMP r0, r4        ; compare v & a[i-1]`
	`        BGE done          ; done if v ≥ a[i-1]`
	`        STR r4, [r1,r2,LSL #2]  ; a[i]`
	`        SUB r2, r2, #1    ; i--`
	`        B   loop`

`  a[i] = v;`
`  return;`
`}`
	`done    STR r0, [r1,r2,LSL #2]  ; a[i] = v`
	`        POP {r4, pc}      ; exit`
	`        ENDP`
	`        END`

Example 8-14. Inserting an integer into a sorted array in C and assembly

8.5.9 Example of Converting Integer to String (itoa)

The C function *itoa* converts an integer to a string. To convert a digit d ($0 \le d \le 9$) to its ASCII value of the corresponding letter ch[1], we can

$$ch[0] = d + 0x30$$

or

$$ch[0] = d + '0'$$

Letter	0	1	2	3	4	5	6	7	8	9
ASCII	0x30	0x31	0x32	0x33	0x34	0x35	0x36	0x37	0x38	0x39

For a given unsigned integer, such as 12345, we extract the digits backward. We start with the least significant digit, which can be obtained by using modulo operation to find the remainder of the division of 12345 by 10, *i.e.*, mod(12345, 10). We append this digit to a string.

The modulo operation continues until we obtain all digits. In the end, we get a string of "54321". We need to reverse the string order and move the least significant digit from the first position to the end of the string.

Quotient/10	Quotient	Remainder	Reverse
12345/10 =	1234	5	
1234/10 =	123	4	
123/10 =	12	3	⇑
12/10 =	1	2	
1/10 =	0	1	
	If quotient is 0, stop	Result = "54321"	Result = "12345"

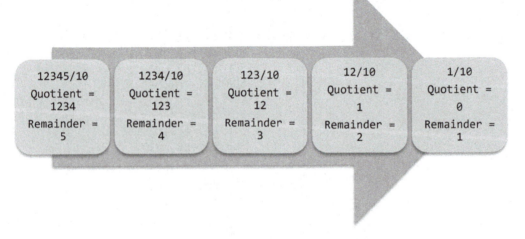

Figure 8-10. Basic steps of obtaining all digits of an integer

C Program	Assembly Program

`char str[20];`	`        AREA myData, DATA`
	`        ALIGN`
	`str     SPACE 20`

`void itoa(unsigned int, char *);`
 	
`int `**`main`**`(void){`
 	
`  itoa(12345, str);`
`  while(1);`
`}`
	`        AREA my_itoa, CODE`
	`        EXPORT__main`
	`        ALIGN`
	`        ENTRY`
	`__main  PROC`
	`        MOV  r0, #12345`
	`        LDR  r1, =str`
	`        `**`BL   itoa`**
	`stop    B    stop`
	`        ENDP`

`void `**`itoa`**`(unsigned int n,`
`char *s) {`
 	
`  char * p = s, temp;`
 	
`  // Build the string backward`
 	
`  for (; n != 0; n /= 10){`
`    *p = n % 10 + '0';`
`    p++;`
`  }`
 	
`  *p = '\0';`
 	
`  p--;  // skip NULL`
 	
`  // Reverse the string`
`  for(; p > s; s++, p--){`
`    temp = *p;`
`    *p = *s;`
`    *s = temp;`
`  }`
 	
`  return;`
`}`
	`itoa    PROC`
	`        PUSH {r4-r6, lr}`
	`        MOV  r2, r0          ; r2 = n`
	`        MOV  r3, r1          ; r3 = s`
	
	`        ; Build the string backward`
	`        MOV  r6, #10`
	`loop1   CBZ  r2, done        ; done if n = 0`
	`        UDIV r5, r2, r6      ; r5 = n/10`
	`        MLS  r4, r6, r5, r2  ; r4 = r2-10*r5`
	`        ADD  r4, r4, #0x30   ; n%10 + '0'`
	`        STRB r4, [r3], #1    ; *p = n%10+'0'`
	`        UDIV r2, r2, r6      ; n /= 10`
	`        B    loop1`
	
	`done    MOV  r4, #0`
	`        STRB r4, [r3]        ; *p = '\0';`
	`        SUB  r3, r3, #1      ; skip NULL`
	
	`        ; Reverse the string`
	`loop2   CMP  r3, r1          ; compare p & s`
	`        BLE  exit            ; exit if p ≤ s`
	`        LDRB r4, [r3]        ; swap`
	`        LDRB r5, [r1]`
	`        STRB r4, [r1]`
	`        STRB r5, [r3]`
	`        ADD  r1, r1, #1      ; s++`
	`        SUB  r3, r3, #1      ; p--`
	`        B    loop2`
	
	`exit    POP  {r4-r6, pc}`
	`        ENDP`
	`        END`

Example 8-15. Converting an integer to a string in C and assembly

8.5.10   Example of Matrix Transpose

In linear algebra, the transpose of a matrix $[a_{ij}]_{m \times n}$ is $[a_{ji}]_{n \times m}$. In C, a two-dimensional (2D) matrix in fact is stored as a one-dimensional array in memory. C uses a row-major approach to convert the 2D matrix into a 1D array, and it stores the matrix row by row contiguously in memory.

For example, a 3×3 matrix is stored as a simple 1D array in memory, as shown in Figure 8-11. We assume each element is an integer and takes four bytes. Because a memory address is always in terms of bytes, the memory offset is also expressed in bytes.

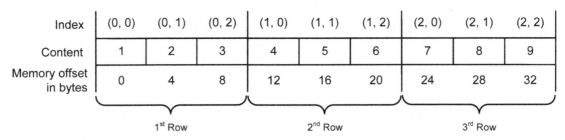

Figure 8-11. Linear layout of a two-dimensional matrix in memory

We can replace multiplication with shift operations to improve the speed. For example, the following instructions

```
MOV r1, #3
MUL r4, r0, r1
```

can be replaced by a single instruction "ADD r4, r0, r0, LSL #1", in which
$$r4 = r0 + r0 << 1 = 3 \times r0.$$
The shift and addition operations are faster than the multiplication instruction.

Figure 8-12 gives an example of matrix transpose. Note the items on the diagonal do not change. Therefore, the program only needs to swap elements in the upper right triangular matrix with the lower left triangle matrix.

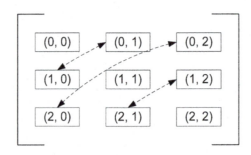

Figure 8-12. Demonstration of matrix transpose. None-diagonal elements are swapped.

C Program	Assembly Program
```int a[3][3] = { { 1, 2, 3 }, { 4, 5, 6 }, { 7, 8, 9} };```	``` AREA myData, DATA ALIGN matrix DCD 1, 2, 3, 4, 5, 6, 7, 8, 9```
```void transpose(int *p); int main(void){ int *p = &a[0][0]; transpose(p); while(1); }```	``` AREA Matrix_Transpose, CODE EXPORT __main ALIGN ENTRY __main PROC LDR r0, =matrix BL transpose stop B stop ENDP```
```void transpose(int *p){ int i, j, t; for(i=0; i<3; i++){ for (j=i+1; j<3; j++){ t = *(p + 3*i + j); *(p + 3*i + j) = *(p + 3*j + i); *(p + 3*j + i) = t; } } return; }```	```transpose PROC PUSH {r4-r7, lr} MOV r1, #0 ; r1 = i; loop_i CMP r1, #3 BGE exit_i ADD r2, r1, #1 ; j = i + 1 loop_j CMP r2, #3 BGE exit_j ; r4 = p + (3*i + j)*4 ADD r4,r1,r1,LSL #1 ; 3 * i ADD r4,r0,r4,LSL #2 ; 4 * r4 ADD r4,r2,LSL #2 ; r5 = p + (3*j + i)*4 ADD r4,r2,r2,LSL #1 ; 3 * j ADD r4,r0,r4,LSL #2 ; 4 * r4 ADD r4,r1,LSL #2 ; swap elements pointed by r4 and r5 LDR r6, [r4] LDR r7, [r5] STR r7, [r4] STR r6, [r5] ADD r2, r2, #1 B loop_j ; for loop j exit_j ADD r1, r1, #1 ; i++ B loop_i ; for loop i exit_i POP {r4-r7, lr} ENDP END```

Example 8-16. Transposing a matrix in C and assembly

8.5.11   Example of Removing a Character from a String

This example subroutine removes a specific character from a string. The subroutine starts to compare each character from the beginning and shift all following characters left one if this character is the same as the target characters. The subroutine adds a null terminator at the end of the string when it checks all characters.

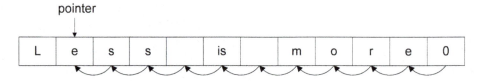

pointer

| L | e | s | s | | is | | m | o | r | e | 0 |

Figure 8-13. All following characters must be moved left when a character is removed.

C Program	Assembly Program
`char s[15] = "Less is more";` `void remove(char *s, char c);`	`        AREA myData, DATA` `str     DCB     "Less is more",0`

`int main(void){`
 	
`    // remove letter 'e' from s`
`    remove(s, 'e');`
`    while(1);`
`}`
	`        AREA removeChar, CODE`
	`        EXPORT__main`
	`        ALIGN`
	`        ENTRY`
	`__main  PROC`
	`        LDR     r0, =str   ; memory address`
	`        MOVS    r1, #'e'   ; ASCII of 'e'`
	`        ; r0 and r1 are arguments`
	`        BL      remove`
	`stop    B       stop       ; dead loop`
	`        ENDP`

`// Remove c from string s`
`void remove(char *s, char c){`
`    char *t = s;`
 	
`    for(; *s != '\0'; s++){`
 	
`        if (*s != c){`
`            *t = *s;`
`            t++;`
`        }`
 	
`    }`
 	
`    *t = '\0';`
`    return;`
`}`
	`remove  PROC`
	`        ; r0 = s, r1 = c`
	`        MOV     r2, r0     ; r2 = t = s`
	
	`loop    LDRB    r3, [r0]   ; r3 = *s`
	`        CBZ     r3, exit   ; null ending`
	
	`        CMP     r3, r1     ; compare *s & c`
	`        LDRBNE  r3, [r0]   ; get byte *s`
	`        STRBNE  r3, [r2]   ; store to *t`
	`        ADDNE   r2, r2, #1 ; t++`
	
	`        ADD     r0, r0, #1 ; s++`
	`        B       loop       ; do it again`
	
	`exit    STRB    r3, [r2]   ; *t = '\0';`
	`        BX      lr         ; return`
	`        ENDP`
	`        END`

Example 8-17. Implementation of removing a character from a string

8.5.12   Example of Finding Unique Numbers in an Array

This example removes any duplicate numbers in an array. It finds all unique members of an array. As shown in Figure 8-14, the program uses three loops over the array.

- The outer loop based on loop variable *i* selects a character to be compared with.
- The middle loop based on *j* compares each of all following characters with *array*[*i*].
- The inner loop based on loop variable *k* is used to shift all following characters to the left by one position if *array* [*j*] is equal to *array*[*i*].

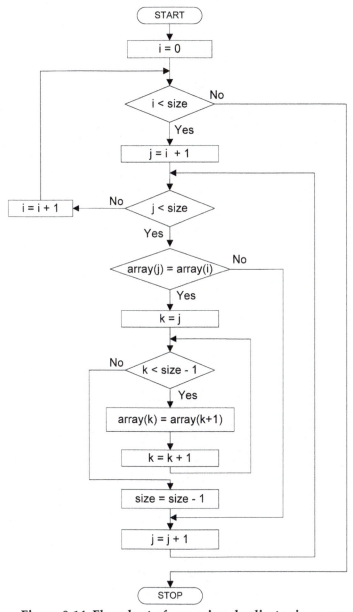

Figure 8-14. Flowchart of removing duplicates in an array

C Program	Assembly Program
| | ```
AREA myData, DATA
ALIGN
``` |
| ```
int array[50] = {
  7, 1, 7, 2, 1,
  3, 1, 2, 4, 5,
  2, 3, 2, 6, 7,
  2, 3, 2, 6, 7};
``` | ```
array DCD 7, 1, 7, 2, 1
      DCD 3, 1, 2, 4, 5
      DCD 2, 3, 2, 6, 7
      DCD 2, 3, 2, 6, 7
``` |
| `int size = 20;` | `size   DCD 20` |
| ```
int remove_dup(int *, int);

int main(){
 int i;




  size = remove_dup(array,
              size);

 for (i = size; i < 50; i++)
   array[i] = 0;



 while(1);
}
``` | ```
      AREA remove_duplications, CODE
      EXPORT __main
      ALIGN
      ENTRY
__main PROC
      LDR r0, =array
      LDR r1, =size
      LDR r1, [r1]
      BL  remove_dup

      MOV r4, r0     ; r0 = size returned
loop  CMP r4, #50
      BGE stop
      MOV r0, #0
      STR r0, [r1,r4,LSL #2] ; array[i]
      ADD r4, r4, #1
      B   loop
stop  B   stop
      ENDP
``` |
| ```
int remove_dup( int *array,
                int size) {
 int i, j, k;
 int *p;
 i = 0;
 while(i < size){
   j = i + 1;
   while(j < size) {
     if( *(p+i)==*(p+j) ){
       for(k=j; k<size-1; k++)
         *(p+k) = *(p+k+1);
       size--;
     } else
       j++;
   }
   i++;
 }
 return size;
}
``` | ```
remove_dup PROC
      ; r0 = array pointer
      ; r1 = size
      PUSH {r4-r8,lr}
      ; r5 = i, r6 = j, r7 = k
      MOV r5, #0     ; r5 = i
Li    CMP r5, r1     ; compare i and size
      BGE exit
      ADD r6, r5, #1 ; r6 = j, j = i + 1
Lj    CMP r6, r1     ; compare j and size
      BGE Ej
      LDR r8, [r0,r5,LSL #2]  ; r8 = *(p+i)
      LDR r4, [r0,r6,LSL #2]  ; r4 = *(p+j)
      CMP r8, r4     ; *(p+i) and *(p+j)
      BNE Ek2
      MOV r7, r6     ; r7 = k
      SUB r4, r1, #1 ; r4 = size - 1
Lk    CMP r7, r4     ; compare k and size-1
``` |
```

```
                         BGE Ek1
                         ADD r8, r0,r7,LSL #2
                         LDR r8, [r8, #4]        ; r8 = *(p+k+1)
                         STR r8, [r0,r7,LSL #2] ; *(p+k)

                         ADD r7, r7, #1          ; k++
                         B   Lk                  ; loop k

                 Ek1     SUB r1, r1, #1          ; size--
                         B   Lj                  ; loop j

                 Ek2     ADD r6, r6, #1          ; j++
                         B   Lj                  ; loop j

                 Ej      ADD r5, r5, #1          ; i++
                         B   Li                  ; loop i

                 exit    MOV r0, r1              ; return size

                         POP {r4-r8, pc}

                         ENDP
                         END
```

Example 8-18. Removing duplicates in an integer array in C and assembly

Figure 8-15 shows an example to illustrate the basic idea of using three nested loops to eliminate all duplicates in an array.

- The first loop indexed by *i* starts with the first element.
- The second loop indexed by *j* iterates through all items between (*i*+1) and the end of the array.
- When a duplicate is found, the third loop indexed by *k* is used to shift all numbers after the *j*th number left by 1. In this example, when the program finds the duplicate "7", all numbers after the "7" is moved left by one.

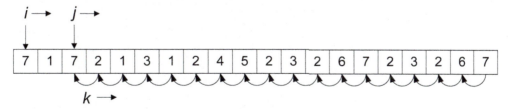

Figure 8-15. Variable *i*, *j*, and *k* are indices of three nested loops.
Loop *k* shifts numbers left after a duplicate is found.

8.6 Passing Arguments through Stack

A subroutine can receive up to four arguments via registers r0-r3. When a subroutine takes more than four arguments, additional parameters must be passed via the stack.

Example 8-19 shows a simple subroutine named *sum6* that takes six 32-bit integers and calculates their sum.

C Program	Assembly Program

`int sum6(int a1, int a2, int a3,`
`        int a4, int a5, int a6);`
	` AREA sum, CODE`
	` EXPORT __main`
	` ALIGN`
	` ENTRY`

`int main(){`
`  int t;`
 	
`  t = sum6(1, 2, 3, 4, 5, 6);`
`  while(1);`
`}`
	`__main PROC`
	`       MOV   r0, #5   ; 5th argument`
	`       MOV   r1, #6   ; 6th argument`
	`       MOV   r2, #3   ; 3rd argument`
	`       MOV   r3, #4   ; 4th argument`
	`       PUSH {r0, r1} ; push 5th and 6th`
	`       MOVS r1, #2    ; 1st argument`
	`       MOVS r0, #1    ; 2nd argument`
	`       BL    sum6`
	`stop   B     stop`
	`       ENDP`

`int sum6(int a1, int a2, int a3,`
`        int a4, int a5, int a6) {`
 	
`  int total;`
 	
`  total = a1 + a2 + a3 + a4 + a5 + a6;`
 	
`  return total;`
 	
`}`
	`sum6   PROC`
	`       PUSH {r4-r7, lr}`
	`       MOV   r4, r0`
	`       ; LDRD = Load double-word`
	`       LDRD r5, r6, [sp, #20]`
	`       ADD   r7, r4, r1  ; add a1 & a4`
	`       ADD   r7, r7, r2  ; add a2`
	`       ADD   r7, r7, r3  ; add a3`
	`       ADD   r7, r7, r5  ; add a5`
	`       ADD   r0, r7, r6  ; add a6`
	`       POP  {r4-r7, pc} ; return`
	`       ENDP`
	`       END`

Example 8-19. Passing six arguments in C and assembly

The caller puts the first four arguments in registers r0, r1, r2, and r3, and pushes the last two arguments onto the stack. When the subroutine starts, it first should preserve any non-scratch registers used in this subroutine. In this example, the subroutine pushes registers r4 - r7 and LR onto the stack.

The subroutine then uses a load double-word instruction (LDRD) to retrieve the additional two arguments by using SP-relative addressing.

```
LDRD r5, r6, [sp, #20]    ⟺    LDR r5, [sp, #20]
                                LDR r6, [sp, #24]
```

Note when a single push or pop instruction stores or loads multiple registers, the order in which these registers are listed in the instruction does not matter. The processor always pushes the largest register first, as introduced in Example 8-3. On the contrary, in a pop instruction, the value is popped to the register with the smallest register number first.

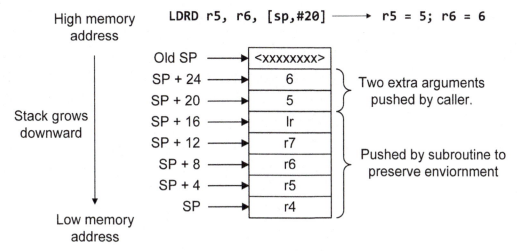

Figure 8-16. Memory layout after the subroutine preserves the environment

The LDRD instruction transfers two contiguous words starting at the memory address SP + 20 to two registers. The first destination register holds the word with a lower memory address. The LDRD instruction is equivalent to the following two LDR instructions:

```
LDR r5, [#sp, #20]    ; r5 = mem[sp + 20] = 5
LDR r6, [#sp, #24]    ; r6 = mem[sp + 24] = 6
```

The subroutine should not pop any arguments out from the stack. Per the application binary interface standard, the stack pointer (SP) must remain the same immediately before and after a subroutine is executed.

Example 8-20 gives a slightly more efficient implementation. The key idea is to reuse register r0 and, therefore, the subroutine does not need to push any registers onto the stack, reducing the number of memory accesses.

As well, because the subroutine *sum6()* does not call any other subroutines, it is not required to preserve the link register (LR) in the stack. Hence, it uses "BX LR" to return.

```
sum6 PROC
     ADD   r0, r0, r1    ; add 1st and 2nd arguments
     ADD   r0, r0, r2    ; add 3rd argument
     ADD   r0, r0, r3    ; add 4th argument
     LDRD  r2, r3, [sp]  ; Load 5th and 6th arguments
     ADD   r0, r0, r2    ; add 5th argument
     ADD   r0, r0, r3    ; add 6th argument
     BX    LR            ; return
     ENDP
```

Example 8-20. Improved implementation of the sum6 subroutine by reusing register r0

8.7 Recursive Functions

A *recursive function* is a function that calls itself directly or indirectly. If *foo*() calls *bar*(), and *bar*() calls *foo*(), then *foo*() calls itself indirectly. A recursive function solves a task by calling itself on smaller pieces of input data.

For example, *quick sort* is a recursive function. It randomly picks an element from an array and partitions the array into two subarrays, one with all elements smaller than the chosen element, and the other with all elements larger than the selected element. This process repeats on each subarray until there are only one or two items in each subarray. The result is a combination of these sorted subarrays.

A recursive function is an efficient divide-and-conquer tactic. It divides a large problem into smaller sub-problems of the same type, then solves those sub-problems, and finally combines the results to obtain the solution of the original problem.

Any problem solved by using a recursive function is also solvable by using a traditional iterative function based on loops. The advantages of recursive functions over iterative functions are twofold.

- A recursive function resembles the problem to be solved more naturally.
- Moreover, a recursive function is easier to program and debug in high-level languages such as C.

However, a recursive function usually is slower and requires more memory than its corresponding iterative function. Also, it is harder to debug a recursive function in assembly.

Example 8-21 shows recursive and iterative functions that calculate the factorial. Figure 8-7 shows the call graph of the recursive function when calculating *factorial*(5).

Recursive Function	Iterative Function
```int factorial(int n) { if(n==1) return 1; else return n * factorial(n-1); } int main(void){ int y; y = factorial(5); return 0; }```	```int factorial(int n) { result = 1; for (int i = 1; i < n; i++) result *= i; return result; } int main(void){ int y; y = factorial(5); return 0; }```

Example 8-21. Factorial function implemented by using recursive and iterative function

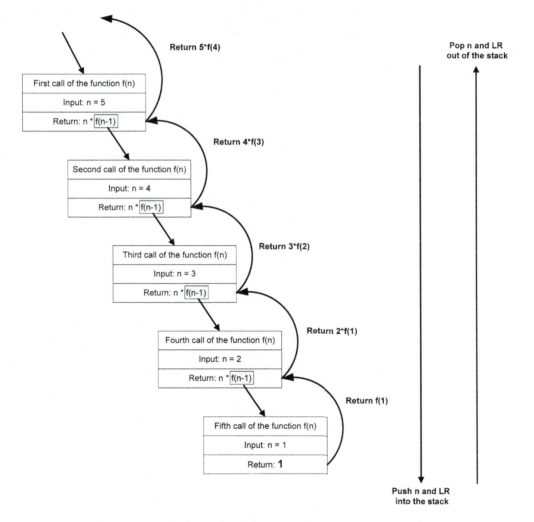

Figure 8-17. Call graph of the recursive factorial function

Each recursive function must have an *exit condition,* also known as a stopping case. The exit condition is to ensure that the recursive function does not go into an infinite loop. For example, the statement of "if (n == 1) return 1;" is the exit condition.

Figure 8-7 shows how the function *factorial*(5) runs step by step.

- *factorial*(5) calls *factorial*(4), and
- *factorial*(4) calls *factorial*(3), and
- *factorial*(2) calls *factorial*(1).
- After the exit condition is satisfied, *factorial*(1) returns the result backward to *factorial*(2) for calculating previously pending results.
- *factorial*(2) returns the result to *factorial*(3).
- *factorial*(3) returns the result to *factorial*(4).
- *factorial*(4) returns the result to *factorial*(5).
- *factorial*(5) completes and returns the final result.

Recursive functions utilize the stack to preserve the runtime environment and keep track of different call instances of the recursive functions. At least, a recursive function must preserve the link register (LR) in the stack. In the example of recursively calculating the factorial number, the subroutine must push LR and the input *n* onto the stack. The stack keeps growing as more data are pushed onto it during the recursive call. After the exit condition is satisfied, the stack begins to shrink as data are popped off the stack upon each function return.

In sum, when programming a recursive function in assembly, the function must manage the stack carefully to ensure the correctness and avoid infinite loop or stack overflow.

8.7.1 Example of Factorial Numbers

This section illustrates how the stack grows as a recursive function is called and how the stack shrinks when a recursive function is returned.

Suppose SP is 0x20000600, and r4 is 0 before the recursive factorial function starts. At the beginning of the subroutine, r4 and LR are pushed onto the stack. Recall that the BL instruction puts the memory address of the instruction immediately after the BL instruction into LR. The subroutine copies r0 to r4 because r0 is used to pass the argument when it calls itself.

Table 8-3 shows the stack content immediately after factorial(1) completes. The stack grows down toward the low memory address. Register r0 holds the input *n* passed to the subroutine. Because register r0 must hold the return result, the function copies r0 to r4. When the factorial function calls itself, LR points to the multiplication instruction "MUL r0, r4, r0", which multiples *n* and factorial(*n*-1).

Memory Address	Memory Content
0x20000600	
0x200005FC	0x08000134 (LR)
0x200005F8	0 (r4)
0x200005F4	0x08000148 (LR)
0x200005F0	5 (r4)
0x200005EC	0x08000148 (LR)
0x200005E8	4 (r4)
0x200005E4	0x08000148 (LR)
0x200005E0	3 (r4)
0x200005DC	0x08000148 (LR)
0x200005D8	2 (r4)
0x200005D4	0x08000148 (LR)
0x200005D0	

Table 8-3. Stack content immediately after factorial (1) completes.

C Program	Address	Assembly Program
int factorial(int n);		AREA main, CODE, READONLY EXPORT __main ENTRY

int **main**(void){
 	
  factorial(5);
  while(1);
}
	0x0800012E
	0x08000130
	0x08000134
		__main PROC
		     MOV r0, #5
		     BL factorial
		stop B stop
		     ENDP

int **factorial**(int n) {
  int f;
 	
  if(n==1)
 	
    f = 1;
 	
  else
    f = n***factorial**(n-1);
 	
  return f;
}
	0x08000136
	0x08000138
	0x0800013A
	0x0800013C
	0x0800013E
	0x08000140
	0x08000142
	0x08000144
	0x08000148
	0x0800014C
		factorial PROC
		     PUSH {r4, lr} ; *preserve*
		     MOV r4, r0 ; *r4 = n*
		     CMP r4, #1
		     BNE else ; *if n ≠ 1*
		     MOV r0, #1 ; *f = 1*
		loop POP {r4, pc} ; *return*
		else SUB r0, r4, #1 ; *n − 1*
		     BL factorial ; *r0 is input*
		     MUL r0, r4, r0 ; *n*f(n-1)*
		     B loop
		
		     ENDP
		     END

Example 8-22. Calculating factorial number in C and assembly

8.7.2 Example of Reversing a String

The reverse of "ABCD" is "DCBA". The following is a recursive reverse function. The key idea is to swap the first and last character, and reverse the substring excluding the first and the last characters. This process repeats for each substring.

C Program	Assembly Program

<pre>char str[20] = "Reverse me,
please!";</pre>
	<pre> AREA myData, DATA
	        ALIGN
	str DCB "Reverse me, please!",0</pre>

<pre>void swap (char *x, char *y);
void reverse(char *, int, int);
 	
int main() {
 	
  reverse(str, 0, 20);
  while(1);
}</pre>
	<pre> AREA reverse_string, CODE
	        EXPORT __main
	        ALIGN
	        ENTRY
	__main PROC
	        LDR r0, =str ; 1st argument
	        MOV r1, #0 ; 2nd argument
	        MOV r2, #20 ; 3rd argument
	        BL reverse ; Recursive call
	stop B stop
	        ENDP</pre>

<pre>// swap two characters in a string
void swap (char *x, char *y) {
    char temp;
    temp = *x;
    *x = *y;
    *y = temp;
}</pre>
	<pre>swap PROC ; Swap routine
	        LDRB r2, [r0] ; temp = *x
	        LDRB r3, [r1] ;
	        STRB r3, [r0] ; *x = y
	        STRB r2, [r1] ; *y = temp
	        BX lr
	        ENDP</pre>

<pre>// recursive function for reversion
void reverse(char *str,
            int start,
            int end) {
 	
  if (start == end)
    return;
 	
  swap (str + start, str + end);
  start++;
  end--;
 	
  reverse(str, start, end);
  return;
}</pre>
	<pre>reverse PROC
	        PUSH {r4-r6, lr}
	        MOV r6, r0 ; string pointer
	        MOV r4, r1 ; start position
	        MOV r5, r2 ; end position
	        CMP r4, r5 ; check start <= end
	exit POPEQ {r4-r6, pc} ; exit
	        ADD r0, r6, r4 ; [str + start]
	        ADD r1, r6, r5 ; [str + end]
	        BL swap
	        ADD r4, r4, #1 ; start++
	        SUB r5, r5, #1 ; end--
	        MOV r0, r6 ; 1st argument
	        MOV r1, r4 ; 2nd argument
	        MOV r2, r5 ; 3rd argument
	        BL reverse
	        POP {r4-r6, pc}
	        ENDP
	        END</pre>

Example 8-23. Reversing a string in C and assembly

8.7.3 Example of String Permutation

The following code finds all possible permutations of the characters in a string. For example, the permutation of "ABC" includes: "ABC", "ACB", "BAC", "BCA", "CAB", and "CBA". The program stores all permutations in a string named result, separated by space. The permute function uses two subroutines: *strcat* that concatenates two strings (given in Chapter 8.5.6) and *swap* that swaps two characters in a string (given in Chapter 8.7.2). As shown in Figure 8-18, the permutation of a string is found by recursively permuting all new substrings. New substrings are formed by swapping the first letter with all letters in the original string (excluding the first letter of each new string).

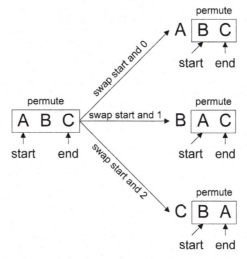

Figure 8-18. Permutation is achieved by swapping the first letter to every letter and permuting all substrings excluding the first letter of all new strings.

C Program	Assembly Program

```char str[4] = "ABC";```
```char result[200];```
```char sep[2] = " ";```
	``` AREA myData, DATA```
	``` ALIGN```
	```str DCB "ABC",0```
	```result SPACE 200```
	```sep DCB " ",0```

```void strcat(char *, char *);```
```void swap(char *, char *);```
```void permute(char *, int, int);```
 	
```int main() {```
 	
```   permute(str, 0, 2);```
```   while(1);```
```}```
	``` AREA permute, CODE```
	``` EXPORT __main```
	``` ALIGN```
	``` ENTRY```
	```__main PROC```
	``` LDR r0, =str```
	``` MOV r1, #0 ; start```
	``` MOV r2, #2 ; end```
	``` BL permute```
	```stop B stop```
	``` ENDP```

```// recursive permute function```	```; recursive permute function```

```c
// recursive permute function
void permute(char *str,
             int start,
             int end) {


  int i;


  if (start >= end){


    strcat(result, sep);


    strcat(result, str);



  } else {

    for (i=start; i<=end; i++){

      swap(str + start, str + i);




      permute(str, start+1, end);




      swap(str + start, str + i);



    }
  }
  return;

}
```

```asm
; recursive permute function
permute PROC

        PUSH {r4-r7, lr}

        MOV r4, r0      ; r0 = *str
        MOV r5, r1      ; r1 = start
        MOV r7, r2      ; r2 = end

        CMP r5, r7      ; start >= end
        BLT else        ; if less or equal

then    LDR r0, =result
        LDR r1, =sep
        BL  strcat      ; result + set

        LDR r0, =result
        MOV r1, r4      ; r1 = str
        BL  strcat      ; result + str

        B   exit

else    MOV r6, r5      ; r6 = variable i

loop    ADD r0, r4, r5  ; r0 = str + start
        ADD r1, r4, r6  ; r1 = str + i
        BL  swap

        MOV r0, r4      ; str
        ADD r1, r5, #1  ; start + 1
        MOV r2, r7      ; end
        BL  permute     ; recursive call

        ADD r0, r4, r5  ; str + start
        ADD r1, r4, r6  ; str + i
        BL  swap

        ADD r6, r6, #1  ; i++
check   CMP r6, r7      ; compare i & end
        BLE loop

exit    POP {r4-r7, pc}

        ENDP

        END
```

Example 8-24. String permutation in C and assembly

8.8 Exercises

1. Which of the following is equivalent to "PUSH {r7}"?

   (1) SP = SP – 4, and then memory[SP] = r7
   (2) SP = SP + 4, and then memory[SP] = r7
   (3) memory[SP] = r7, and then SP = SP – 4
   (4) memory[SP] = r7, and then SP = SP + 4

2. Which of the following instructions load five words from the stack into registers r1-r5? What are the value of registers r1-r5? (Assuming SP = 0x20008000, and these instructions are executed separately.)

   ```
   (1) LDMDA sp,  {r1-r5}
   (2) LDMDB sp,  {r1-r5}
   (3) LDMIA sp,  {r1-r5}
   (4) LDMIB sp,  {r1-r5}
   (5) LDMDA sp!, {r1-r5}
   (6) LDMDB sp!, {r1-r5}
   (7) LDMIA sp!, {r1-r5}
   (8) LDMIB sp!, {r1-r5}
   ```

Memory Address	Value
0x20008008	0x00000006
0x20008004	0x00000005
0x20008000	0x00000004
0x2000800C	0x00000003
0x20008008	0x00000002
0x20008004	0x00000001
0x20008000	0x00000000
0x20007FFC	0xFFFFFFFF
0x20007FF8	0xFFFFFFFE
0x20007FF4	0xFFFFFFFD
0x20007FF0	0xFFFFFFFC
0x20007FE8	0xFFFFFFFB
0x20007FE4	0xFFFFFFFA

3. What are the memory content after each of the following instruction completes? Assume register ri = i, i = 0, 1, 2, 3, and 5. (Assuming SP = 0x20008000 and these instructions runs independently).

   ```
   (1) STMDA sp,  {r1-r5}
   (2) STMDB sp,  {r1-r5}
   ```

```
(3) STMIA  sp,   {r1-r5}
(4) STMIB  sp,   {r1-r5}
(5) STMDA  sp!,  {r1-r5}
(6) STMDB  sp!,  {r1-r5}
(7) STMIA  sp!,  {r1-r5}
(8) STMIB  sp!,  {r1-r5}
```

Memory Address	a	b	c	d	a	b	c	d
0x20008008								
0x20008004								
0x20008000								
0x2000800C								
0x20008008								
0x20008004								
0x20008000								
0x20007FFC								
0x20007FF8								
0x20007FF4								
0x20007FF0								
0x20007FE8								
0x20007FE4								

4. How many bytes does the stack need to pass the arguments when each of the following function is called?

   (1) int32_t fun1(uint8_t a, uint16_t b, uint8_t c, int32_t d)

   (2) int32_t fun2(uint8_t a, uint16_t b, uint8_t c, int32_t d,
                    uint8_t e, int32_t f, uint8_t g)

   (3) int32_t fun3(uint8_t a, int32_t b, int64_t c,
                    uint8_t d, int32_t e)

   (4) int32_t fun4(uint8_t a, int64_t b, int64_t c,
                    uint8_t d, int32_t e)

5. Which register(s) holds the return value in the following functions?

   ```
   (1) int16_t    fun1()
   (2) int8_t   * fun2()
   (3) int32_t  * fun3()
   (4) int64_t    fun4()
   (5) int64_t  * fun5()
   ```

6. Why does a recursive assembly function have to preserve the link register?

7. Give two different assembly instructions to make a subroutine return.

8. Write a subroutine that checks whether a given number is a prime number. The subroutine takes one argument and returns true or false. Find all prime numbers between 100 and 200.

9. Write a subroutine that takes eight integer arguments and computes the product of these integers. The caller passes extra arguments to the subroutine via the stack.

10. Implement a subroutine of the Caesar shift encryption. It is a simple substitution encryption algorithm, in which each letter is replaced by another letter with a fixed number of offset down in the alphabet. For example, with a shift offset of 3, A becomes D, and B is substituted by E, and so on.

11. Write a subroutine called *MoviePrice* that calculates the movie ticket price based on the input argument called age. If the age is 12 or under, the price is $6. If the age is between 13 and 64, the price is $8. If the age is 65 or over, the price is $7.

12. Write a subroutine that calculates the value of the following expression based on two input arguments a and n.

$$S_n(a) = a + aa + aaa + \cdots + \overbrace{aa \ldots a}^{n}$$

For example, when $a = 3$ and $n = 5$, we have

$$S_5(3) = 3 + 33 + 333 + 3333 + 33333$$

13. Write a program that calculates $\sum_{n=0}^{10} n!$. The program should use two subroutines. One subroutine calculates the factorial $n!$, and the other subroutine calculates the sum of the factorials.

14. Write a program that uses a subroutine to find how many 1-bits exist in a 32-bit number.

15. Write a program that uses a subroutine to determine how many bits differ in two 32-bit numbers.

16. Mathematically, the cardinality of an array is defined as the number of unique elements in an array. Write a subroutine that calculates the cardinality of an integer array.

17. Write an assembly subroutine named f that calculates the following value

$$f(x, y) = ax^2 + bxy + c$$

where a, b, and c are constant integers, x and y are the input integers. Assuming a, b, and c are defined in the data memory, x and y are input arguments of this subroutine.

18. Write a recursive assembly subroutine that calculates the Fibonacci number.

$$F(n) = \begin{cases} 0 & \text{if } n = 0 \\ 1 & \text{if } n = 1 \\ F(n-1) + F(n-2) & \text{otherwise} \end{cases}$$

19. When PC is 0x08000100 in the following assembly program, the stack pointer (SP) is 0x20002000. Show the value of the link register (LR) and the whole stack content when PC = 0x08000120.

Memory Address	Instruction		
0x08000100		MOV	R0, #2
0x08000104		BL	QUAD
0x08000108		B	ENDL
0x0800010C	SQ1	PUSH	{LR}
0x08000110		MUL	R0, R0
0x08000114		BL	SQ2
0x08000118		POP	{PC}
0x0800011C	SQ2	PUSH	{LR}
0x08000120		MUL	R0, R0
0x08000124		POP	{PC}
0x08000128	QUAD	PUSH	{LR}
0x0800012C		BL	SQ1
0x08000130		POP	{LR}
0x08000134		BX	LR
0x08000138	ENDL	...	

20. Write a recursive assembly subroutine that checks whether a given string is a palindrome.

21. Write a recursive assembly subroutine that calculates the Kth power of 2 (i.e., 2^K).

22. Compared with iterative methods, what are the advantages and disadvantages of recursive methods?

CHAPTER 9

64-bit Data Processing

ARM Cortex-M is 32-bit processors, and the operands of assembly instructions cannot exceed 32 bits. There are a few exceptions, such as UMULL (unsigned multiply), UMLAL (unsigned multiply with accumulate), SMULL (signed multiply), and SMLAL (signed multiply with accumulate). We may need to perform arithmetic operations on integers that are greater than $2^{32} - 1$. One example is fixed-point arithmetic (see Chapter 12). This chapter focuses on how to implement 64-bit operations based on 32-bit instructions.

How to perform 64-bit operations on 32-bit processors?

9.1 64-bit Addition

Chapter 2.4.5.2 shows that an adder works in the same way for both unsigned and signed numbers when signed numbers are represented in two's complement. In other words, the same add assembly instruction works for both signed and unsigned integers.

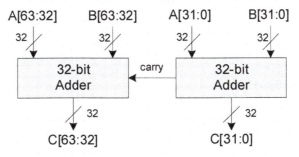

Figure 9-1. Adding two 64-bit integers

Suppose we are adding two 64-bit integers *A* and *B*, either signed or unsigned. A 64-bit number is stored in a pair of registers (r1:r0), with the most significant 32 bits stored in register r1, and the least significant bits stored in r0. Example 9-1 shows the codes.

```
; 64-bit addition: C (r5:r4) = A (r1:r0) + B (r3:r2)
; A = 0x00002222FFFFFFFF, B = 0x0000044400000001

LDR   r0, =0xFFFFFFFF    ; A's Lower 32 bits
LDR   r1, =0x00002222    ; A's upper 32 bits

LDR   r2, =0x00000001    ; B's Lower 32 bits
LDR   r3, =0x00000444    ; B's upper 32 bits

; Add two lower words
ADDS r4, r2, r0          ; C[31:0] = A[31:0] + B[31:0], update Carry

; Add two upper words and the carry from adding lower words
ADC  r5, r3, r1          ; C[64:32] = A[64:32] + B[64:32] + Carry
```

Example 9-1. Adding two 64-bit signed or unsigned integers

9.2 64-bit Subtraction

The following program performs 64-bit subtraction for both signed numbers and unsigned numbers. It is like the 64-bit addition, except the subtraction starts with the upper word. The carry flag is set if no borrow occurs on subtraction.

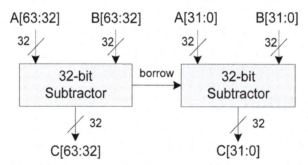

Figure 9-2. Subtracting two 64-bit integers

```
; 64-bit subtraction: C = r5:r4, A = r1:r0, B = r3:r2, C = A - B
; A = 0x00000002FFFFFFFF, B = 0x0000000400000001

LDR r0, =0xFFFFFFFF      ; A's Lower 32 bits
LDR r1, =0x00000002      ; A's upper 32 bits

LDR r2, =0x00000001      ; B's Lower 32 bits
LDR r3, =0x00000004      ; B's upper 32 bits

; Subtract two lower words
SUBS r4, r0, r2          ; C[31:0] = A[31:0] - B[31:0], update Carry

; Subtract two upper words and the borrow from subtracting lower words
SBC  r5, r1, r3          ; C[64:32] = A[64:32] - B[64:32] + Carry - 1
```

Example 9-2. Subtracting two 64-bit signed or unsigned integers

9.3 64-bit Counting Leading Zeros

Example 9-3 counts the number of leading zero bits before the first one in a 64-bit integer. The key instruction used is CLZ (Count Leading Zeros). It is useful to normalize an integer by removing all leading zeros and making the most significant bit a 1. When we count the number of leading zeros in a 64-bit number, there are two scenarios:

1. The upper word is not zero. Then the number of leading zeros in the 64-bit number equals the number of leading zeros of the upper word.
2. The upper word is zero. Then the number of leading zeros in the 64-bit number equals the number of leading zeros of the lower word plus 32.

```
; 64-bit input data = (r1:r0),
; r1 = upper word of 64-bit data,
; r0 = lower word of 64-bit data
; r2 = # of leading zero bits in the 64-bit data

; Counting # of leading zeros in upper word
CLZ    r2, r1          ; CLZ = Count leading zeros

; Counting # of leading zeros in lower word
CMP    r2, #32
CLZEQ  r3, r0          ; if r2 == 32, then count leading zero
                       ; bits of the lower word
ADDEQ  r2, r2, r3      ; if all bits of the upper word are zero,
                       ; add the leading zeros of the lower word
```

Example 9-3. Counting the number of leading zeros in a 64-bit number (r1:r0)

9.4 64-bit Sign Extension

When we extend a 32-bit signed integer to 64 bits, we must preserve the number's sign (either positive or negative) and value by duplicating the sign bit to the upper word. If the most significant bit (MSB) of the 32-bit signed integer is 1, the top word of the 64-bit number must be 0xFFFFFFFF.

```
; r0 = lower word of 64-bit data
; r1 = upper word of 64-bit data

TST    r0, 0x80000000    ; Check the sign bit
LDREQ  r1, =0xFFFFFFFF    ; If MSB is 1, duplicate 1 in upper word
LDRNE  r1, =0x00000000    ; If MSB is 0, duplicate 0 in upper word
```

Example 9-4. Extending a 32-bit signed integer (r0) to 64 bits (r1:r0)

9.5 64-bit Logic Shift Left

When a 64-bit number is shifted left, some of the bits in the lower word should be shifted into the upper word.

Figure 9-3. Logic shift left of a 64-bit number stored in two registers

The following gives an example of shifting a 64-bit number left by 3 bits. The most significant three bits of the lower word are shifted into the upper word. If the shift amount is larger than 32 bits, the lower word becomes zero.

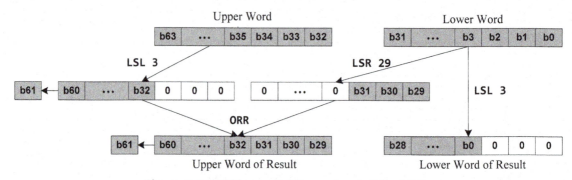

Figure 9-4. Shifting a 64-bit number left by 3 bits

```
; r0 = Lower word of 64-bit data, r1 = Upper word of 64-bit data
; r2 = Shift amount

MOV   r3, r0           ; Backup the lower word
MOV   r1, r1, LSL r2   ; Shift left the upper word
MOV   r0, r0, LSL r2   ; Shift left the lower word

; Shift bits of the lower word into the upper word
CMP   r2, #32

; if r2 < 32
RSBLO r5, r2, #32      ; r5 = 32 - r2
LSR   r4, r3, r5       ; r4 = r3 >> (32 - r2)
ORRLO r1, r1, r4       ; upper |= lower >> (32 - r2)

; if r2 ≥ 32
SUBHS r5, r2, #32      ; r5 = r2 - 32
LSLHS r1, r3, r5       ; upper = lower << (r2 - 32)
MOVHS r0, #0           ; lower = 0
```

Example 9-5. Shifting a 64-bit number (r1:r0) left by r2 bits

9.6 64-bit Logic Shift Right

When a 64-bit number is shifted right, the least significant bits of the upper word are shifted into the lower word, as shown in Figure 9-5.

Figure 9-5. Logic shift right of a 64-bit number stored in two registers

The following example shows logic shift right of a 64-bit number by 3 bits. The least significant three bits of the upper word are shifted into the lower word. If the shift amount is larger than 32 bits, the upper word becomes zero.

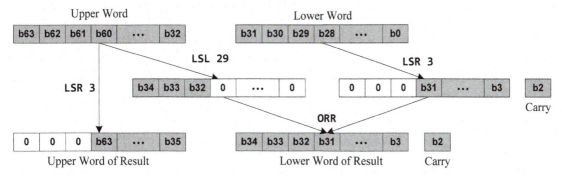

Figure 9-6. Shifting a 64-bit number right by 3 bits

```
; r0 = Lower word of 64-bit data, r1 = Upper word of 64-bit data
; r2 = Shift amount

MOV   r3, r1                 ; Backup the upper word

MOV   r1, r1, LSR r2         ; Shift right upper word
MOV   r0, r0, LSR r2         ; Shift right lower word

; Shift bits of the upper word into the lower word
CMP   r2, #32

; if r2 < 32
RSBLO  r5, r2, #32           ; r5 = 32 - r2
ORRLO  r0, r0, r3, LSL r5    ; lower |= upper << (32 - r2)

; if r2 ≥ 32
SUBHS  r5, r2, #32           ; r5 = r2 - 32
LSRHS  r0, r3, r5            ; lower = upper >> (r2 - 32)
MOVHS  r1, #0                ; upper = 0
```

Example 9-6. Shifting a 64-bit number (r1:r0) right by r2 bits

9.7 64-bit Multiplication

We can use long multiply instructions (32-bit by 32-bit, with a 64-bit result) and the multiply accumulate instruction (MLA) to multiply two 64-bit numbers. Example 9-7 multiplies two 64-bit signed integers or unsigned integers.

```
; product (r5:r4) = multiplier (r1:r0) × multiplicand (r3:r2)
; r5:r4 = r0 × r2 + 2³² × (r1 × r2 + r0 × r3) + 2⁶⁴ × r1 × r3
; The last item in the above equation exceeds 64 bits and thus it is ignored.

UMULL  r4, r5, r0, r2   ; r5:r4 = r0 * r2
MLA    r5, r1, r2, r5   ; r5 = r5 + r1 * r2
MLA    r5, r0, r3, r5   ; r5 = r5 + r0 * r3
```

Example 9-7. Multiplying two 64-bit unsigned or signed integers

Note that UMULL multiplies two 32-bit unsigned integers, and SMULL multiplies two 32-bit signed integers. However, Example 9-7 also works correctly for multiplying two 64-bit signed numbers. For example, when multiplying (-2) and (-3), the above code can obtain the correct result (*i.e.*, 6), as shown below.

```
; A (r1:r0) = -2 = FFFF,FFFF,FFFF,FFFE
; B (r3:r2) = -3 = FFFF,FFFF,FFFF,FFFD

UMULL  r4,r5,r0,r2   ; r5:r4 = FFFF,FFFE × FFFF,FFFD = FFFF,FFFB,0000,0006
MLA    r5,r1,r2,r5   ; r5 = FFFF,FFFB + FFFF,FFFF × FFFF,FFFD = FFFF,FFFE
MLA    r5,r0,r3,r5   ; r5 = FFFF,FFFE + FFFF,FFFE × FFFF,FFFF = 0000,0000
                     ; r5:r4 = 0000,0000,0000,0006
```

Example 9-8. Multiplying -2 and -3

The reason UMULL in Example 9-7 also works correctly for 64-bit signed numbers is simple. If a negative number A is represented in two's complement, the processor reads it as $2^{64} - |A|$ if the processor treats it as an unsigned number. Given two 64-bit negative numbers A and B, the multiplication is as follows if they are treated as unsigned numbers.

$$(2^{64} - |A|)(2^{64} - |B|) = 2^{128} - 2^{64} \times (|A| + |B|) + |A| \times |B|$$

The first two items are larger than 2^{64}, and thus they can be discarded. Thus, the following are equivalent under the modulo 2^{64}.

$$(2^{64} - |A|)(2^{64} - |B|) = |A| \times |B| \quad mod \ 2^{64}$$

Similarly, if A is a negative 64-bit number and B is a positive one,

$$(2^{64} - |A|) \times B = 2^{64} \times B - |A| \times B = (2^{64} - |A| \times B) \quad mod \ 2^{64}$$

If the unsigned number $2^{64} - |A| \times B$ is read as a two's complement, it is $-|A| \times B$.

9.8 64-bit Unsigned Division

Dividing two 64-bit numbers works differently for signed numbers and unsigned numbers. This section discusses the implementation of 64-bit unsigned division.

It takes two registers to hold a 64-bit integer. When we say a 64-bit integer is stored in registers (r1:r0), we mean the upper word is in r1, and the lower word is in r0.

Table 9-1 illustrates the key idea of 64-bit unsigned division a/b. It is assumed that dividend a and divisor b are stored in registers r0-r3. The program also has two 64-bit outputs: the 64-bit quotient in r1:r0 and the 64-bit remainder in r3:r2.

```
Unsigned 64-bit division: (r1:r0)/(r3:r2)
Input: a = r1:r0 = dividend, b = r3:r2 = divisor,
Return: quotient (r1:r0) and remainder (r3:r2) of (r1:r0)/(r3:r2)


1. Initialization
        (1) Quotient(r9:r8)  = 0;
        (2) Remainder(r1:r0) = Dividend(r1:r0)

2. Loop over the following steps if remainder (r1:r0) ≥ divisor (r3:r2)
        (1) a_64_bit = remove leading zeros of remainder(r1:r0),
                • x = number of leading zero bits removed
                • CLZ instruction counts the number of leading zero bits
        (2) b_64_bit = remove leading zeros of divisor(r3:r2),
                • y = number of leading zero bits removed
        (3) g_32_bit = MSB_32(a_64_bit) / MSB_16(b_64_bit)
                • MSB: most significant bits
                • UDIV: unsigned 32-bit division
        (4) r6:r11 = unsign_extend_to_64_bits(g_32_bit << (y - 16)) >> x;
        (5) Quotient(r9:r8)  = Quotient(r9:r8) + (r6:r11)
        (6) Remainder(r1:r0) = Remainder(r1:r0) - (r6:r11) * Divisor(r3:r2)
        (7) If the remainder (r1:r0) is smaller than zero,
                • g_32_bit = MSB_32(a_64_bit) / (MSB_16(b_64_bit) + 1), and
                  go to step c.

3. Copy the results to the return registers
        (1) Quotient(r1:r0) = Quotient(r9:r8)
        (2) Remainder(r3:r2) = Remainder(r1:r0)
```

Table 9-1. Basic steps of dividing two 64-bit unsigned integers (a = b*q + r)

In the loop, the program shifts left both the dividend and the divisor to remove their leading zeros. Then the program divides their top word of the dividend by the top halfword of the divisor. The program calculates the remainder and the partial quotient, adjusted by the previous shift left operations. We use a simple example to illustrate the basic idea of the above algorithm.

Example of 64-bit division

Assuming the dividend and the divisor are given as follows:

- Dividend(r1:r0) = 0x0000,FFFF,FFFF,FFFF
- Divisor(r3:r2) = 0x0000,0000,0000,0001

The algorithm starts to initialize the quotient and the remainder, shown as follows:

- Quotient(r9:r8) = 0;
- Remainder(r1:r0) = Dividend(r1:r0) = 0x0000,FFFF,FFFF,FFFF

```
Loop 1:
   •  a_64_bit = 0xFFFF,FFFF,FFFF,0000              x = 16
   •  b_64_bit = 0x8000,0000,0000,0000              y = 63
   •  g_32_bit = MSB_32(a_64_bit) / MSB_16(b_64_bit)
              = 0xFFFF,FFFF / 0x0000,8000,
              = 0xFFFF,FFFF / 2^15
              = 0x0001,FFFF
   •  r6:r11   = unsign_extend_to_64_bits(g_32_bit << (y - 16)) >> x
              = unsign_extend_to_64_bits(0x0001,FFFF << (63 - 16)) >> 16
              = unsign_extend_to_64_bits(0x0001,FFFF << 47) >> 16
              = 0x0001,FFFF << 31
              = 0x0000,FFFF,8000,0000
   •  Quotient(r9:r8)  = Quotient(r9:r8) + (r6:r11)
                      = 0 + 0x0000,FFFF,8000,0000
                      = 0x0000,FFFF,8000,0000
   •  Remainder(r1:r0) = Remainder(r1:r0) - (r6:r11) * Divisor(r3:r2)
                      = 0x0000,FFFF,FFFF,FFFF - 0x0000,FFFF,8000,0000 * 1
                      = 0x0000,0000,7FFF,FFFF
```

```
Loop 2:
   •  a_64_bit = 0xFFFF,FFFE,0000,0000              x = 33
   •  b_64_bit = 0x8000,0000,0000,0000              y = 63
   •  g_32_bit = MSB_32(a_64_bit) / MSB_16(b_64_bit)
              = 0xFFFF,FFFE / 0x0000,8000
              = 0x0001,FFFF
   •  r6:r11   = unsign_extend_to_64_bits(g_32_bit << (y - 16)) >> x
              = unsign_extend_to_64_bits(0x0001,FFFF << (63 - 16)) >> 33
              = unsign_extend_to_64_bits(0x0001,FFFF << 47) >> 33
              = 0x0000,0000,7FFF,C000
   •  Quotient(r9:r8)  = Quotient(r9:r8) + (r6:r11)
                      = 0x0000,FFFF,8000,0000 + 0x0000,0000,7FFF,C000
                      = 0x0000,FFFF,FFFF,C000
   •  Remainder(r1:r0) = Remainder(r1:r0) - (r6:r11) * Divisor(r3:r2)
                      = 0x0000,0000,7FFF,FFFF - 0x0000,0000,7FFF,C000 * 1
                      = 0x0000,0000,0000,3FFF
```

```
Loop 3:
    • a_64_bit = 0xFFFC,0000,0000,0000                          x = 50
    • b_64_bit = 0x8000,0000,0000,0000                          y = 63
    • g_32_bit = MSB_32(a_64_bit) / MSB_16(b_64_bit)
               = 0xFFFC,0000 / 0x0000,8000
               = 0x0001,FFF8
    • r6:r11   = unsign_extend_to_64_bits(g_32_bit << (y - 16)) >> x
               = unsign_extend_to_64_bits(0x0001,FFF8 << (63 - 16)) >> 50
               = unsign_extend_to_64_bits(0x0001,FFF8 << 47) >> 50
               = 0x0000,0000,0000,3FFF
    • Quotient(r9:r8)  = Quotient(r9:r8) + (r6:r11)
                       = 0x0000,FFFF,FFFF,C000 + 0x0000,0000,0000,3FFF
                       = 0x0000,FFFF,FFFF,FFFF
    • Remainder(r1:r0) = Remainder(r1:r0) - (r6:r11) * Divisor(r3:r2)
                       = 0x0000,0000,0000,3FFF - 0x0000,0000,0000,3FFF * 1
                       = 0x0000,0000,0000,0000
```

9.9 64-bit Signed Division

The following program shows the algorithm of 64-bit signed division. For each 64-bit held in registers (rm:rn), register rm contains the upper word, and register rn holds the lower word.

The program is divided into three major steps.

- The program first converts the dividend and divisor to positive 64-bit integers if they are negative.
- Then the program computes 64-bit unsigned division presented in Chapter 9.8.
- At the end, the program adjusts the quotient and remainder based on the sign of the dividend and divisor.

```
; Signed 64-bit division algorithm: (r1:r0)/(r3:r2)
;
;
; Inputs:
;       Dividend (64 bits): r1:r0
;       Divisor (64 bits): r3:r2
; Return:
;       Quotient (64 bits): r1:r0
;       Remainder (64 bits): r3:r2

signed_64_mul PROC
        EXPORT signed_64_mul

        PUSH {r4, lr}
```

```
        ASRS r4, r1, #1              ; if r1 >= 0, r4[31:30] = 00;
                                     ; otherwise r4[31:30] = 11


        EOR  r4, r4, r3, LSR #1      ; if r3 >= 0, shift result[31:30] = 00;
                                     ; otherwise shift result[31:30] = 01


        ; If r1 >= 0 and r3 >= 0, r4[31:30] = (00)^(00) = 00
        ; If r1 >= 0 and r3 < 0,  r4[31:30] = (00)^(01) = 01
        ; If r1 < 0 and r3 >= 0,  r4[31:30] = (11)^(00) = 11
        ; If r1 < 0 and r3 < 0,   r4[31:30] = (11)^(01) = 10
        ; Bit r4[31] represents whether dividend >= 0
        ; Bit r4[30] represents whether dividend and divisor
        ; are both positive or both negative

        ; Convert dividend (r1:r0) to a positive number if it is negative
        BPL    Test1                 ; check whether dividend >= 0,
        RSBS   r0, r0, #0            ; if dividend < 0, r0 = -r0
        RSB    r1, r1, #0            ; if dividend < 0, r1 = -r1
        SUBLO r1, r1, #1            ; check if borrow occurs, LO = Unsigned Lower

        ; Convert divisor(r3:r2) to a positive number if it is negative
Test1 TST    r3, r3                 ; check whether divisor >= 0; bitwise AND
        BPL    uldiv                 ; branch if positive or zero
        RSBS   r2, r2, #0            ; if divisor is negative, r2 = -r2
        RSB    r3, r3, #0            ; if divisor is negative, r3 = -r3
        SUBLO r3, r3, #1            ; check if borrow occurs

        ; Perform unsigned division (r1:r0)/(r3:r2)
        ; The algorithm is discussed in Chapter 9.8.
uldiv BL unsigned_division_64_bits

        ; If dividend and divisor are not both positive or both negative,
        ; then convert the quotient to a negative number
Test2 TST    r4, #0x40000000        ; check bit r4[30]
        BEQ    Test3                 ; branch if ZERO is set
                                     ; i.e., branch if dividend >=0
        RSBS   r0, r0, #0            ; r0 = -r0
        RSB    r1, r1, #0            ; r1 = -r1
        SUBLO r1, r1, #1            ; check if borrow occurs

        ; If dividend (r1:r0) < 0,
        ; then convert the remainder to a negative number
Test3 TST    r4, #0x80000000        ; check bit r4[31] (i.e., sign bit)
        BEQ    exit                  ; branch if ZERO is set
        RSBS   r2, r2, #0            ; r2 = -r2
        RSB    r3, r3, #0            ; r3 = -r3
        SUBLO r3, r3, #1            ; check if borrow occurs

exit  POP {r4, pc}
      ENDP
```

Example 9-9. Implementation of 64-bit unsigned integer division

9.10 Exercises

1. LDRD and STRD can load and store two registers from memory, respectively. They load or store 64-bit numbers conveniently and efficiently. They take only one memory cycle if the destination memory address is a multiple of 8.

LDRD Rt1, Rt2, [Rn, #offset]	Load registers with two words Rt1 ← mem[Rn + offset], Rt2 ← mem[Rn + offset + 4]
STRD Rt1, Rt2, [Rn, #offset]	Store registers with two words mem[Rn + offset] = Rt1 mem[Rn + offset + 4] = Rt2

Assume r0 = 0x20008000, find out the value in register r0, r3, and r4 in the following instructions. These instructions run independently, *i.e.*, they are not part of a program.

    (1) LDRD r3, r4, [r0], #8
    (2) LDRD r4, r3, [r0, #8]
    (3) LDRD r3, r4, [r0, #8]!

Memory Address	Memory Data
0x2000800C	0x44444444
0x20008008	0x33333333
0x20008004	0x22222222
0x20008000	0x11111111

2. Implement the following function in assembly, which returns $2a + 2b$.

$$\text{int64\_t doublesum(int64\_t a, int64\_t b)}$$

3. Write an assembly program that compares two 64-bit signed integers.

$$\text{int8\_t compare64(int64\_t a, int64\_t b)}$$

The return value of is as follows:

$$return\ value = \begin{cases} -1, & a < b \\ 0, & a = b \\ 1, & a > b \end{cases}$$

4. Write an assembly program that compares two 64-bit unsigned integers. The return value is the same as Question 3.

$$\text{int8\_t compare64(uint64\_t a, uint64\_t b)}$$

5. Write an assembly program that calculates the number of leading ones in a 64-bit integer.

6. Write an assembly program that performs 64-bit rotation right.

7. Write an assembly program that calculates the sum of an array of 64-bit integers.

8. Write an assembly program that multiplies a 32-bit unsigned integer and a 64-bit unsigned integer. The product is limited to 64 bits.

9. Write an assembly program that divides a 64-bit unsigned integer and a 32-bit unsigned integer. The quotient is restricted to 32 bits.

10. Write an assembly program that uses the subtraction-based Euclid's algorithm to compute the greatest common divisor of two 64-bit integers.

```
uint64_t gcd(uint64_t a, uint64_t b) {
    while (a != b) {
        if (a > b)
            a = a - b;
        else
            b = b - a;
    }
    return a;
}
```

11. Implement the following in assembly to add two 128-bit unsigned numbers.

```
void add_128( uint64_t *sum_upper64, uint64_t *sum_lower64,
              uint64_t  in1_upper64, uint64_t  in1_lower64,
              uint64_t  in2_upper64, uint64_t  in2_lower64)
```

12. Implement the following in assembly to subtract two 128-bit signed numbers.

```
void sub_128( int64_t *diff_upper64, int64_t *diff_lower64,
              int64_t  in1_upper64,  int64_t  in1_lower64,
              int64_t  in2_upper64,  int64_t  in2_lower64)
```

13. Implement the following in assembly to run logic shift left on a 128-bit integer.

```
void LSL_128( uint64_t *out_upper64, uint64_t *out_lower64,
              uint64_t   in_upper64, uint64_t   in_lower64,
              uint32_t shift)
```

14. Implement the following in assembly to run logic shift right on a 128-bit integer.

```
void LSR_128( uint64_t *out_upper64, uint64_t *out_lower64,
              uint64_t   in_upper64, uint64_t   in_lower64,
              uint32_t shift)
```

CHAPTER

10

Mixing C and Assembly

Occasionally it is required to write a program in both C and assembly language. There are several possible reasons.

- First, an experienced programmer might want to optimize a performance-critical function manually in assembly, instead of relying on compilers. Many profiling tools can identify the most time-consuming functions. However, compilers often have limited intelligence in optimizing these functions. A handcrafted assembly code can out-perform high-level languages, such as C.

- Second, writing a program in assembly allows a programmer to use processor-specific instructions. For example, a test-and-set atomic assembly instruction can implement locks and semaphores. Another example is that most C compilers do not use some operations available on Cortex-M processors, such as ROR (rotate right) and RRX (rotate right extended).

- Third, assembly programs can directly access hardware, which is especially useful for device drivers and processor booting code.

The embedded application binary interface (EABI) briefly introduced in Chapter 8.2 defines low-level standards of interfacing program modules that are compiled separately, no matter whether these modules are written in C or assembly. The EABI specifies (1) standards for data types, data alignments, and executable file formats, and (2) conventions for function calls, parameter passing, registers usage, and stack frame. If a program is written in C, compilers ensure that these standards are followed strictly. However, if a program is

> *"The good thing about standards is that there are so many to choose from."*
>
> Andrew Tanenbaum,
> famous computer scientist

developed in assembly, it is the programmer's responsibility to adhere to these standards. The standard allows programmers to mix C and assembly in the application.

10.1 Data Types and Access

While the size of a basic data type in the C language depends on the compilers and platforms, the following table lists the typical size of commonly used data types in the C language.

Data Type	Size (bits)	Alignment	Data Range
bool	8	byte	0 or 1. Bits 1 – 7 are ignored
char	8	byte	-128 to 127 (signed), or 0 to 255 (unsigned)
int	32	word	-2,147,483,648 to 2,147,483,647 (signed), or 0 to 4,294,967,296 (unsigned)
short int	16	halfword	-32,768 to 32,767 (signed), or 0 to 65,536 (unsigned)
long int	32	word	same as int
long long	64	word	-9,223,372,036,854,775,808 to 9,223,372,036,854,775,807 (signed), or 0 to 18,446,744,073,709,551,616 (unsigned)
float	32	word	+/- (1.4023×10^{-45} to $3.4028 \times 10^{+38}$), always signed
double	64	word	+/- (4.9406×10^{-324} to 1.7977×10^{308}), always signed
long double	96	word	Enormous range
pointer	32	word	0 to 4,294,967,296

Table 10-1. Data size and alignment of basic data types in C

10.1.1   Signed or Unsigned Integers

When programming in an assembly language, it is the programmer's responsibility to interpret whether a data item is signed or unsigned. For example, when loading an 8-bit data into a 32-bit register, the program should use LDRSB (load register with signed byte) to access a signed character and LDRB (load register with byte) to retrieve an unsigned character.

- LDRSB loads a byte from memory into a register and performs sign extension. The sign extension duplicates the sign bit of the 8-bit data to all bits at the most significant side of a register to preserve the positive or negative sign.
- LDRB loads a byte from memory into a register and simply pads the left of the register with zeros.

For example, when a program loads an 8-bit binary data 0x88 (+136 for unsigned or -120 for signed) from memory into a 32-bit register, should the register be 0xFFFFFF88 or

0x00000088? It depends on the programmer's intention. If these 8 bits represent a signed number, LDRSB should be used to preserve the sign. If they represent an unsigned number, LDRB should be utilized. Similarly, LDRSH (load register with signed halfword) and LDRH (load register with halfword) bring a 16-bit signed and unsigned number into a register, respectively. Table 10-2 summarizes these load instructions.

Variable	Instruction	Description	Sign Extension
unsigned char	LDRB	Load register with byte	No
unsigned short	LDRH	Load register with halfword	No
unsigned/signed int	LDR	Load register with word	No
char	LDRSB	Load register with signed byte	Yes
short	LDRSH	Load register with signed halfword	Yes

Table 10-2. ARM assembly instructions for accessing various basic integer data types

Correspondingly, STRB (store register byte) and STRH (store register halfword) store either a signed number or an unsigned number into the memory. Loading or storing a 32-bit integer does not need to take care of the sign because each register has the same number of bits as the integer.

A 64-bit integer takes two registers, and it can be loaded by using two separate LDR instructions or a single LDRD (load registers with double words).

C Program	Assembly Program

signed long long x = -1;	LDR r3, =x ; Load memory address of x
	LDRD r0, r1, [r3] ; r0 lower word, r1 higher word
	
	x DCW 0xFFFFFFFF, 0xFFFFFFFF ; allocate 8 bytes

Example 10-1. Loading a 64-bit integer from the memory

10.1.2   Data Alignment

Most computer systems have some alignment requirement on the starting memory address of a variable. The memory address of a C variable often must be aligned, as listed in Table 10-1. The smallest unit exchanged between the processor and the memory is a byte (8 bits), and thus the memory address is always in terms of bytes.

A variable is n-byte aligned in memory if its starting memory address is some multiple of n. Typically, n is a power of 2, such as 2 (halfword aligned), 4 (word aligned), and 8 (double word aligned). Suppose a 32-bit variable is word aligned. If the address of the next available byte in memory is 0x8001, the variable is then stored in a continuous span of 4 bytes from 0x8004 to 0x8007. The compiler or the program inserts three meaningless bytes at memory addresses 0x8001, 0x8002, and 0x8003. These three bytes are called *padding bytes*.

Enforcing data alignment is to improve the memory performance. A memory system consists of multiple storage units, and the processor typically distributes data among these units in a round-robin fashion. Because the number of pins available on a processor is limited, these memory units typically share some pins in the memory address bus. To allow these memory units to transfer data concurrently, the target data stored in all memory units needs to share a portion of their memory addresses. The data alignment ensures that all data of a variable stored in different memory units meet this requirement. When the processor reads a properly aligned variable, only one access is required to transfer the data out of these memory units. Otherwise, two separate memory accesses might be necessary, slowing down the processor performance.

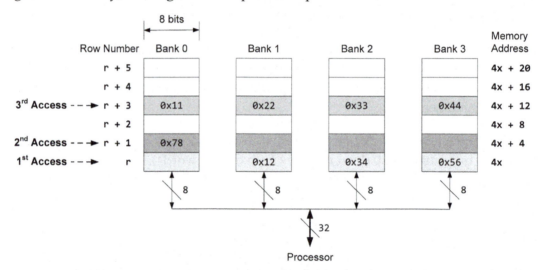

Figure 10-1. Loading unaligned data 0x78563412 takes two accesses even if the processor allows unaligned memory accesses. Loading aligned data 0x44332211 takes only one access.

As shown in Figure 10-1, the data memory is organized into four banks, and these banks can feed the 32-bit data bus. Four bytes in the same row of all banks can be loaded into the processor concurrently. In this example, data 0x78563412 is not aligned with word boundaries, and the processor takes two memory accesses to load the data 0x78563412 to a register. However, it takes only one memory access to load data 0x44332211.

As introduced in Chapter 3.6, the "ALIGN" directive gives data alignment requirements to compilers. The syntax is "ALIGN boundary, offset". The boundary is any power of 2. The default boundary is 4, making the next variable align to a word boundary. The offset specifies how many bytes the next variable should start from the word boundary. The default offset is 0.

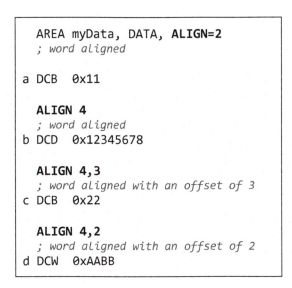

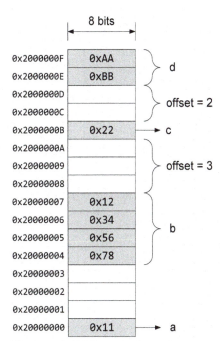

Figure 10-2. Memory layout

10.1.3   Data Structure Padding

A data structure defined in C language aggregates multiple basic variables into a single complex entity. By default, compilers ensure that all variables in a structure are aligned to their required memory boundaries. In a structure array, compilers also ensure that all variables in this array meet their alignment requirements. Therefore, compilers may place padding bytes between structure variables.

C language also supports *packed structures* in which variables are not aligned. Therefore, compilers do not add any padding bytes into a data structure. Packed structures are often used in communication protocols (such as USB) to save transmission time.

Figure 10-3 and Figure 10-4 compare the memory layout of an unpacked structure defined in Example 10-2.

Unpacked Structure	Packed Structure
```struct Position { char x; char y; char x; int time; short scale; } array[2];```	```__packed struct Position { char x; char y; char x; int time; short scale; } array[2];```

Example 10-2. Comparison of unpacked and packed structure in C

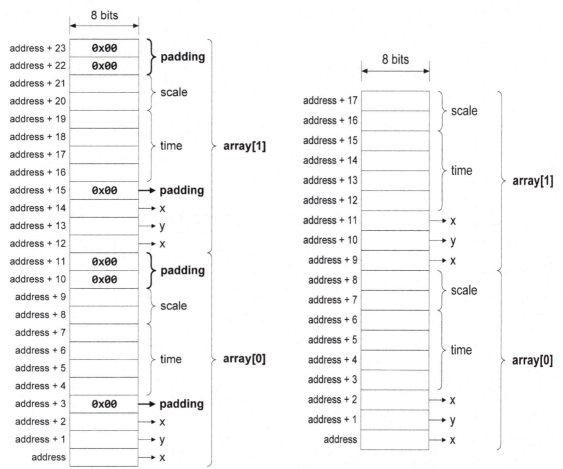

Figure 10-3. In an unpacked structure, variables are aligned. Specifically, the integer variable and the structure are aligned in words.

Figure 10-4. In a packed structure, variables are not aligned. Cortex-M processors support unaligned access in LDR/STR, LDRT/STRT, LDRH/STRH, and LDRHT/STRHT.

In Figure 10-3, the compiler inserts three padding bytes into the structure position.

- The first padding byte is added after variable *x* to make the next integer variable *time* aligned to some word boundary.
- In a structure array, the compiler also ensures that all variables in this array meet their alignment requirements. Therefore, two additional bytes are added at the end of the data structure, making the size of the *Position* structure a multiple of four. This padding also makes the variables in this array, particularly the time variable, align properly.

In fact, two structure definitions give below are equivalent. Compilers allocate proper padding bytes in an unpacked structure.

```
struct Position {                          struct Position {
    char x;                                    char x;
    char y;                                    char y;
    char x;                 Equivalent         char x;
    int time;                                  char padding_1;
    short scale;               ⟺               int time;
} array[2];                                    short scale;
                                               char padding_2[2];
                                           } array[2];
```

Example 10-3. Compiler inserts three padding bytes to an unpacked structure

In Figure 10-4, the *Position* structure uses the type modifier "__**packed**" to the compiler to produce an unaligned memory layout. Specifically, the integer variable *time* is not aligned to a word boundary, and the short variable *scale* is not aligned to a halfword boundary. Therefore, there is no padding between structure members or at the end of the structure. The __**unpack** modifier is often used to map a structure to a special data area in memory, such as a USB communication package received in a memory buffer.

Programs often do not use packed structures. No ARM processors released before ARM-V6 support unaligned memory accesses. The instruction "LDR r1, [r0]" would generate an alignment exception if the memory address stored in r0 were not a multiple of four. The Cortex-M processors do support unaligned memory accesses. However, unaligned accesses are still slower than aligned memory accesses, and thus it is recommended to avoid using unaligned accesses.

Packed structures and unpacked structures are not compatible with each other. We cannot assign or cast one to the other. The only way to assign a packed structure to an unpacked structure is to copy all structure members one by one.

Suppose we want to set *array[0].time* to 1234. Example 10-4 compares the assembly codes that update the *time* variable of the unpacked and packed structure respectively.

Unpacked Structure	Packed Structure

LDR r0, =array   ; *load base address*
 LDR r1, [r0, #4] ; *array[0].time*
 LDR r2, #1234   ; *pseudo instruction*
 STR r2, [r0, #4] ; *array[0].time*
	LDR r0, =array ; *load base address*
	 LDR r1, [r0, #3] ; *array[0].time*
	 LDR r2, #1234 ; *pseudo instruction*
	 STR r2, [r0, #3] ; *array[0].time*

Example 10-4. Accessing members of an unpacked and packed structure in assembly

In the unpacked structure, the access to *array[0].time* is aligned. However, in the packed structure, the access is misaligned. Even though the misaligned accesses "LDR r1, [r0, #3]" and "STR r2, [r0, #3]" are supported in Cortex-M, their access speed is slower than the aligned accesses "LDR r1, [r0, #4]" and "STR r2, [r0, #4]".

10.2 Special Variables

This section discusses two special types of variables in C: static variables and volatile variables.

10.2.1   Static Variables

> *A **static** variable is initialized only once. Its lifetime is across its entire program runtime.*

Different from local variables, a *static* C variable has a lifetime over the entire program runtime. A static variable declared within a C function is initialized only once at the compiling time no matter how many times this function is called. This static variable is visible only inside this function.

A static variable can be either global or local. A static local variable can only be visitable or available within the scope of the function in which this variable is declared. A static global variable can only be accessed within the source file in which it was declared, and other source files cannot access it.

A static variable is preferred to a global variable in C because a local or global static variable has a narrower access range. A program should avoid global variables whenever possible. A global variable is accessible to all source codes in all files. The biggest problem of using global variables is that they create hidden coupling between different software modules that is hard to identify

> *Always avoid **global** variables.*

and understand, thus increasing the risk of software bugs. Because of the implicit interference caused by global variables, a bug in one software module might cause the failure of another seemingly-unrelated module, making the debug process difficult.

One effective way to avoid global variables is to use static variables. As shown in Example 10-5, the counter is declared as a global static variable, instead of a global variable. Therefore, the counter can only be accessed within that source file. Codes in other source files cannot access the counter variable.

If a global variable is only accessed by one subroutine, the program may declare this variable as a local static variable within that subroutine. The access scope of a local static variable is the subroutine that declares it. When that subroutine is called successively, the value of the local static variable is retained.

```
static int counter = 0;

void increase(void){
    counter++;
}

void decrease(void){
    counter--;
}
```

Example 10-5. Example of using a global static variable

Example 10-6 and Example 10-7 compare how a local static variable and a local regular variable are accessed in assembly. All static variables are allocated in the data memory. However, a local variable is often stored in a register or the heap region of the data memory. A static variable is always loaded from memory first and then is stored back to the memory before exiting the subroutine. Therefore, if the subroutine is called again, the static variable keeps its previous value, instead of its initial value.

Example of a local non-static variable

C Program	Assembly Program

`int foo();`	`AREA static_demo, CODE`
	`EXPORT __main`
	`ALIGN`
	`ENTRY`

`int main(void) {`
    `int y;`
    `y = foo();  // y = 6`
    `y = foo();  // y = 6`
    `y = foo();  // y = 6`
    `while(1);`
`}`
	`__main PROC`
	`       BL foo   ; r0 = 6`
	`       BL foo   ; r0 = 6`
	`       BL foo   ; r0 = 6`
	`stop   B  stop`
	`       ENDP`

`int foo() {`
    `int x = 5;  // x is a local variable`
    `x = x + 1;`
    `return(x)`
`}`
	`foo    PROC`
	`       MOV r0, #5`
	`       ADD r0, r0, #1`
	`       BX  lr`
	`       ENDP`
	`       END`

Example 10-6. If x is not declared as static, *foo*() always returns the same value.

In the program given in Example 10-6, variable x is not declared as static. Thus, *foo* returns the same value each time it is called. From the assembly implementation, we can notice that the local variable x is always reinitialized when *foo* is called. Plus, in this example, x is stored in a register, and its value is lost (not saved in the data memory) after *foo* exits.

Example of a local static variable

C Program	Assembly Program

`int foo();`	`        AREA myData, DATA`
	`        ALIGN`
	`        // Reserve space for x`
	`x       DCD   5`
	
	`        AREA static_demo, CODE`
	`        EXPORT __main`
	`        ALIGN`
	`        ENTRY`

`int main(void) {`
`  int y;`
`  y = foo();  // y = 6`
`  y = foo();  // y = 7`
`  y = foo();  // y = 8`
`  while(1);`
`}`
	`__main PROC`
	`        BL foo    ; r0 = 6`
	`        BL foo    ; r0 = 7`
	`        BL foo    ; r0 = 8`
	`stop    B   stop`
	`        ENDP`

`int foo() {`
 	
`  // local static variable`
`  // x is initialized only once`
`  static int x = 5;`
 	
`  x = x + 1;`
`  return(x)`
`}`
	`foo     PROC`
	`        ; load address of x`
	`        LDR r1, =x`
	`        ; load value of x`
	`        LDR r0, [r1]`
	`        ADD r0, r0, #1`
	`        ; save value of x`
	`        STR r0, [r1]`
	`        BX  lr`
	`        ENDP`
	`        END`

Example 10-7. When x is declared as static, the *foo()* function returns different values.

In the program given in Example 10-7, variable x is declared as static locally within the *foo* function.

- The local static variable x is only initialized once. The initialization is carried out at compile time instead of at runtime. As you see from the assembly code, the variable is defined in the data region with an initial value of 5. No matter how many times *foo* runs, variable x is never re-initialized.

- When *foo* needs to increase the value of the local static variable x, the value of variable x is read from memory at the beginning of *foo* and is saved into the memory before *foo* exits. Therefore, *foo* returns a different result each time it runs. On the contrary, *foo* in Example 10-6, in which x is not static, always returns the same value.

Example 10-8 gives another example of using static variables. The program uses the static variable *sum* to check whether an integer number is a palindrome number. A palindrome number remains the same if all digits are reversed.

C Program	Assembly Program
`int isPal(int);`	<pre> AREA myData, DATA ALIGN sum DCD 0</pre>

<pre>int main(){
    int n;
    n = isPal(12321);
    while(1);
}</pre>
	<pre> AREA palindrome, CODE
	        EXPORT __main
	        ALIGN
	        ENTRY
	__main PROC
	        LDR r0, =12321
	        BL isPal
	stop B stop
	        ENDP</pre>

<pre>// Check palindrome number
int isPal(int n){
    static int sum = 0;
    int r;
    if(n!=0) {
 	
        r = n % 10;
 	
        sum = sum*10 + r;
 	
        isPal (n/10);
 	
    }
 	
    if (sum == n)
        return 1;
    else
        return 0;
}</pre>
	<pre>; Recursively check palindrome
	isPal PROC
	       PUSH {r4, lr}
	       MOV r4, r0
	       CBZ r4, done ; if n is 0, done
	       MOV r2, #10
	       SDIV r1, r4, r2 ; r1 = n/10
	       MLS r3, r1, r2, r4 ; r3 = n - r1 * 10;
	       LDR r1, =sum
	       LDR r1, [r1] ; r1 = sum
	       ADD r1, r1,r1,LSL #2 ; r1 = 5*sum
	       ADD r1, r3,r1,LSL #1 ; sum = sum*10+r;
	       LDR r2, =sum
	       STR r1, [r2] ; save sum
	       MOV r2, #10
	       SDIV r0, r4, r2 ; r0 = n/10
	
	       BL isPal ; recursive call
	done LDR r1, =sum
	       LDR r1, [r1]
	
	       CMP r1, r4
	       BNE no
	yes MOV r0, #1 ; if palindrome
	       B exit
	no MOV r0, #0 ; if not palindrome
	exit POP {r4, pc}
	       ENDP
	       END</pre>

Example 10-8. Using a local static variable *sum* in a function

10.2.2   Volatile Variables

When the compiler optimizes a C program, a hard-to-find hidden error is that the program mistakenly reuses the value of a variable stored in a register, instead of reloading it from memory each time. To avoid such compilation error, the program should declare the variable as volatile, such as:

> *A volatile variable is a variable that may be changed by an external input or an interrupt hander. Therefore, the processor should not use a register to cache this variable to avoid using stale data.*

```
volatile int variable;
```

The keyword volatile forces the compiler to generate an executable, which always loads the variable value from the memory whenever this variable is read, and always stores the variable in memory whenever it is written.

Example 10-10 gives a simple example to illustrate the necessity of declaring a variable counter, shared by two concurrently running tasks (*main* function and *SysTick_Handler*), as volatile. In this example, the main program uses the SysTick to implement a time delay. It sets up the SysTick timer and then waits until the SysTick interrupt service routine reduces the counter to 0. The SysTick decrements the counter by one when a system timer interrupt occurs. Chapter 11.7 gives the implementation of *SysTick_Init()*.

Main Program (*main.c*)	Interrupt Service Routine (*isr.s*)

`//volatile unsigned int counter;// correct`
`unsigned int counter;      // incorrect`
`extern void task();`
`extern void SysTick_Init();`
 	
`int main(void) {`
`   counter = 10;`
`   SysTick_Init();`
`   while(counter != 0);  // Delay`
`   // Continue the task`
`   while(1);`
`}`
	`   AREA ISR, CODE, READONLY`
	`   IMPORT counter`
	`   ENTRY`
	
	`SysTick_Handler PROC`
	`   EXPORT SysTick_Handler`
	`   LDR r1, =counter`
	`   LDR r0, [r1]    ; load counter`
	`   SUB r0, r0, #1  ; counter--`
	`   STR r0, [r1]    ; save counter`
	`   BX  LR          ; exit`
	`   ENDP`
	`   END`

Example 10-9. A C variable is not declared as *volatile* while it should be.

Compilers often attempt to optimize the program, but sometimes can cause troubles. The compiler observes that, after the counter is initialized to 10, the value of the counter variable is not modified directly by *main()* or indirectly by any subroutine called from *main()*. Loading data from memory is much slower than retrieving data from registers.

Therefore, the compiler may choose to reuse the value of the counter stored in a register, instead of fetching the counter value again from memory, when the counter is accessed in the while loop. Example 10-10 compares the assembly program generated by the compiler when the counter variable is declared as volatile or non-volatile.

- If the counter is not declared as volatile, the while loop is a dead loop. *SysTick_Handler* periodically decrements the counter and stores its value in memory. However, the main program repeatedly checks register r0, without reloading the latest value of the counter from memory.
- If the counter is declared as volatile, the dead loop problem is avoided.

If counter is not declared as volatile	If counter is declared as volatile

<pre>__main PROC
        LDR r1, =counter
        MOV r0, #10
        STR r0, [r1]
        BL SysTick_Init
 	
wait   CMP r0, #0 ; r0 does not hold
                   ; latest counter value
        BNE wait   ; Thus, a dead loop
stop   B   stop
        ENDP</pre>
	<pre>__main PROC
	        LDR r1, =counter
	        MOV r0, #10
	        STR r0, [r1]
	        BL SysTick_Init
	
	wait LDR r1, =counter
	        LDR r0, [r1]
	        CMP r0, #0
	        BNE wait
	stop B stop
	        ENDP</pre>

Example 10-10. Comparison of assembly instructions generated by the compiler when the counter variable is declared as volatile and non-volatile.

A C program should declare any variable that represents the data of a memory-mapped I/O register as volatile. Memory-mapped I/O has been widely used to access peripheral devices. Data and control registers of external devices are mapped to specific memory addresses, and a program can use memory pointers to access these hardware registers, such as the following C statement.

```
unsigned int *p = (unsigned int *) 0x60002400;
```

To prevent the compiler from optimizing out these memory pointers incorrectly, software must declare these pointers as volatile. The following example uses a memory pointer to access a 32-bit hardware register mapped to the memory address 0x60002400.

```
volatile unsigned int *p = (unsigned int *) 0x60002400;
```

> In sum, a variable should be declared as **volatile** to prevent the compiler from optimizing it away when (1) this variable is updated by external memory-mapped hardware, or (2) this variable is global and is changed by interrupt handlers or by multiple threads.

10.3 Inline Assembly

A block of assembly code, called *inline assembly*, can be directly embedded in a C program. It is convenient for programmers because it does not require different assemble and link processes. Another advantage of inline assembly is that it can flexibly access C variables without export and import operations, which would be needed if the assembly code were written as an assembly subroutine.

10.3.1   Assembly Functions in a C Program

When a C program declares a function with "__asm", the assembly code in this function has to preserve the environment.

When a block of assembly code is embedded within a function by using "__asm", the assembly code does not need to preserve the environment.

A C program can have inline assembly by using the "__asm" keyword. It has two different uses. The first is to specify a function that is implemented in assembly completely. The second is to specify multiple lines of assembly code within a C function.

When a function is declared with "__asm", the assembly implementation must preserve the runtime environment via the stack and recover the environment before exiting from the subroutine. The assembly code can directly access the registers and must follow the procedure call protocol. Example 10-11 and Example 10-12 use "__asm" to implement a C function in assembly.

```
__asm int sum4(int a, int b, int c, int d){
    ; arguments stored in r0, r1, r2, r3
    PUSH {r4, lr}        ; preserve environment in stack
    MOV r4, r0           ; r0 = 1st argument
    ADD r4, r4, r1       ; r1 = 2nd argument
    ADD r4, r4, r2       ; r2 = 3rd argument
    ADD r0, r4, r3       ; r3 = 4th argument, r0 = return
    POP {r4, pc}         ; recover environment from stack
}

int main(void){
    int s = sum4(1, 2, 3, 4);
    while(1);
}
```

Example 10-11. Using inline assembly to implement a subroutine that adds four integers.

```
char a[25] = "Hello!";
char b[25];

__asm void strcpy(char *src, char *dst){
loop    LDRB  r2, [r0], #1   ; 1st argument, r0 = src, post-index
        STRB  r2, [r1], #1   ; 2nd argument, r1 = dst, post-index
        CMP   r2, #0
        BNE   loop
        BX    lr
}

int main(void){
        strcpy(a, b);
        while(1);
}
```

Example 10-12. Using inline assembly to copy a string.

When a function is declared with "__asm", the compiler only creates the interface of this function and does not provide any actual implementation. Therefore, Example 10-11 uses PUSH and POP to preserve and recover the running environment of the caller.

10.3.2   Inline Assembly Instructions in a C Program

When "__asm" is used to declare a block of assembly instructions in a C function, the assembly code cannot access registers and does not need to preserve the runtime environment in the stack. The compiler automatically generates necessary code to preserve the environment.

Additionally, the assembly code treats each C variable as a register. These C variables are called *virtual registers,* and they can be accessed in assembly instructions. Compilers replace virtual registers with real registers.

Also, the comments of the assembly code should be in C style. Example 10-13 has a block of assembly instructions in a C function.

```
int sum4(int a, int b, int c, int d){
      int t;
      __asm {
          ADD t, a, b;   // t, a, and b are virtual registers
          ADD t, c;      // Cannot directly access r0 - r15
          ADD t, d;      // Must use comment style of C
      }
      return t;
}
int main(void){
      int s = sum4(1, 2, 3, 4);
      while(1);
}
```

Example 10-13. Using "__asm" to declare a block of assembly instructions in a C function.

10.4 Calling Assembly Subroutines from a C Program

A large software project often has its program code saved in multiple small source files, instead of a single monolithic file. This technique not only improves the software modularity and maintainability, but also reduces the compilation time. These files can be compiled separately so that unmodified files do not need to be recompiled.

This section shows how a C program calls assembly subroutines that are in separate source files.

- The assembly code must use the directive "EXPORT" or "GLOBAL" to make all variables or subroutines that are accessed in the C program as global. These directives make subroutine names visible outside this source code module. Consequently, the compiler can locate them when linking the object files generated from their source codes.
- The C program must declare these functions by using the keyword "extern".

10.4.1   Example of Calling an Assembly Subroutine

In the following example, the C program calls the assembly subroutine *strlen*, which calculates the length of a string. The C program and the assembly program are in two separate source files: *main.c* and *strlen.s*.

C Program (*main.c*)	Assembly Program (*strlen.s*)

`char str[25] = "Hello!";`
 	
`extern int strlen(char* s);`
 	
`int main(void){`
`    int i;`
`    i = strlen(str);`
`    while(1);`
`}`
	`        AREA stringLength, CODE`
	`        EXPORT strlen       ; make strlen visible`
	`        ALIGN`
	`strlen  PROC`
	`        PUSH {r4, lr}       ; preserve r4 and lr`
	`        MOV  r4, #0         ; initialize length`
	`loop    LDRB r1, [r0, r4]   ; r0 = string address`
	`        CBZ  r1, exit       ; branch if zero`
	`        ADD  r4, r4, #1     ; length++`
	`        B    loop           ; do it again`
	`exit    MOV  r0, r4         ; place result in r0`
	`        POP  {r4, pc}       ; exit`
	`        ENDP`

Example 10-14. A C program calls an assembly routine stored in a different file.

- The assembly subroutine follows the procedure call protocol defined in ARM embedded application binary interface (EABI) and assumes that argument *str* is passed in register r0. Furthermore, the caller expects that the assembly subroutine returns a 32-bit result in register r0 and a 64-bit result in registers r1:r0.

- The C program declares the assembly function to be called by using the keyword "extern" to inform the compiler that the implementation of this function is in another file.
- The assembly subroutine uses "EXPORT strlen" to make the symbol strlen visible to the linker. Note all symbols are case-sensitive.

10.4.2   Example of Accessing C Variables in Assembly

An assembly program can access global variables defined in a C program or a separate assembly source file. When an assembly program accesses a global variable defined elsewhere, it needs to import that variable name by using the directive "IMPORT". An imported variable name, or called a symbol, is resolved at link time. In the following example, the C program declares the global variable counter. The assembly code uses "IMPORT counter" to access this global variable.

C Program (*main.c*)	Assembly Program (*count.s*)
| ```c
int counter;

extern int getValue();
extern void setValue(int c);

void increment();

int main(void) {
    int c = 0;
    setValue(1);
    increment();
    c = getValue();
    while(1);
}

void increment(){
    counter += 1;
}
``` | ```
                AREA count, CODE
                IMPORT counter
                ALIGN

setValue    PROC
            EXPORT setValue
            LDR r1, =counter
            STR r0, [r1]
            BX   lr
            ENDP

getValue    PROC
            EXPORT getValue
            LDR r1, =counter
            LDR r0, [r1]
            BX   lr
            ENDP

increment   PROC
            EXPORT increment [WEAK]
            LDR r1, =counter
            LDR r0, [r1]
            ADD r0, r0, #1
            STR r0, [r1]
            BX   lr
            ENDP
            END
``` |

Example 10-15. Example of accessing a C variable in assembly routines

The assembly program exports the *increment* symbol with weak specified. By default, all exporting statements are strong. At the linking stage, a strongly exported symbol replaces a weakly-exported symbol of the same name. The linker reports a fatal error if there more than one strong instance of the same symbol name. Because the symbol *increment* is exported weakly and the one in the C program is exported strongly, the *increment* function defined in C overrides the one defined in the assembly. Thus, when the *increment* function is called, the *counter* variable is incremented by two, instead of one.

10.5 Calling C Functions from Assembly Programs

An assembly program can call functions implemented in C. The assembly program needs to follow the procedure call protocol defined in ARM embedded application binary interface (EABI).

- Specifically, the assembly program needs to place the input arguments of a C function in registers r0-r1 before it calls the function.
- The assembly program also expects that the result is returned in register r0 if the C function returns a value less than 32 bits.
- If the result has more than 32 bits, the result is returned in registers r0 – r4.

10.5.1   Example of Calling a C Function

In the following example, the assembly program calls the *strlen* function implemented in C. The C function returns the length of the string in register r0 to the assembly program. In the assembly code, the C function names must be imported to avoid linking errors.

Assembly Program (*main.s*)	C Program (*strlen.c*)

<pre>   AREA my_strlen, CODE
        EXPORT __main
        IMPORT strlen
        ALIGN
        ENTRY
 	
__main PROC
        LDR   r0, =str
        BL   strlen
stop   B   stop
        ENDP
 	
        AREA myData, DATA
        ALIGN
Str   DCB   "12345678",0
        END</pre>
	<pre>int strlen(char *s){
	    int i = 0;
	
	    while(s[i] != '\0')
	        i++;
	
	    return i;
	}</pre>

Example 10-16. Example of an assembly program that calls a C subroutine

If "WEAK" is specified in the import directive, the linker does not produce any error if the symbol is not defined externally. Instead, the linker then replaces the symbol with zero or some appropriate value. For example, if the label is not defined in the project, the linker then replaces it with the address of the next instruction after the branch.

```
IMPORT label [WEAK]
...
B label
...
```

Example 10-17. A symbol declared with weak prevents the linker from fatal linking error.

10.5.2   Example of Accessing Assembly Data in a C Program

To access variable *counter* defined in the assembly code, the C program has to use "extern int counter". This statement is to inform the compiler that this variable is defined outside this C program.

The assembly program allocates the memory space for the counter variable, and the C program only needs to indicate the existence of this variable without performing any memory allocation. Without the "extern" keyword, compilers would allocate space again for variable *counter* defined in the C program, thus producing an error of duplicated variables at the link stage.

Assembly Program	C Program
``` AREA main, CODE EXPORT __main IMPORT getValue IMPORT increment IMPORT setValue ALIGN ENTRY ```	``` extern int counter; int getValue() { return counter; } ```
``` __main MOVS r2, #0 MOVS r0, #1 BL setValue BL increment BL getValue MOV r2, r0 stop B stop ```	``` void increment() { counter++; } void setValue(int c) { counter = c; } ```
``` AREA myData, DATA EXPORT counter counter DCD 0 END ```	

Example 10-18. C functions access a variable defined in an assembly program.

10.6 Exercises

1. Translate the following C statement into the assembly.

$$x[1].c += 100;$$

The following gives the definition the structure array x[2]. Assume register r0 holds the starting address of this array.

```
__packed struct X {
    uint8_t a;
    int32_t b;
    int16_t c;
    int32_t d;
    uint8_t e;
} x[2];
```

2. Translate the following C statement into the assembly.

$$x[1].c += 100;$$

The structure array is defined below. Assume register r0 contains the starting address of this array.

```
struct Y {
    uint8_t a;
    int32_t b;
    int16_t c;
    int32_t d;
    uint8_t e;
} y[2];
```

3. Write a subroutine in the assembly that removes all occurrences of a given character in a string. The subroutine takes two parameters: the string pointer, and the character to be deleted. Write a C code that calls this subroutine. The string is defined as global in the C code.

4. Suppose we have the following *strcat* function written in C, which concatenates the second string to the first string. Write an assembly program that calls the *strcat* function. These two strings are defined in the data area in the assembly code.

```
void strcat (char * dst, char * src) {
    while(*dst++);
    while(*dst++ = *src++);
}
```

5. Write a subroutine *swap* in assembly that swaps two strings, and write a C program that calls the swap subroutine. These two strings are defined in the C program. (Hint: There is no need to swap all characters in the strings, and swapping the memory pointers in the assembly is sufficient.)

6. Write an assembly program that calls the following C function that returns the memory address of the last occurrence of a given character in a string.

```c
char * search (char * s, char c) {
    char *p = NULL;
    for(; *s; s++)
        if (*s == c)
            p = s;
    return p;
}
```

7. Suppose the following structure array is defined as global in a C program. Write an assembly program that iterates through the array and finds the total scores.

```c
struct Student_T {
    char c1;
    char c2;
    int score;
    char c3;
} students[10];
```

8. Write a subroutine *max4* in assembly to find the maximum value among four signed integers. These integers are passed to the subroutine via registers. Write a C program to test the *max4* subroutine.

9. Write an assembly subroutine that checks whether a given integer is a palindrome number. For example, 9, 11, 1234321, 141, 1221, and 120021 are palindrome numbers. Write a C program that calls the assembly subroutine. The input is an unsigned integer. The return is 1 if the number is a palindrome and 0 if not.

10. Identify and correct the errors in the following inline assembly program that calculates the sum of four integers.

```
__asm int sum4(int a, int b, int c, int d)
    // arguments stored in r0 - r3
    MOV r4, r0        ; r0 = 1st argument
    ADD r4, r4, r1    ; r1 = 2nd argument
    ADD r4, r4, r2    ; r2 = 3rd argument
    ADD r0, r4, r3    ; r3 = 4th argument, r0 = return
}
```

```
int main(void){
      int s = sum4(1, 2, 3, 4);
      while(1);
}
```

11. Identify and correct the errors in the following inline assembly code that calculates the sum of four integers.

```
int sum4(int a, int b, int c, int d){
      int t;
      __asm {
          ADD t, r0, r1;
          ADD t, r2;
          ADD t, r3;
      }
      return t;
}

int main(void){
      int s = sum4(1, 2, 3, 4);
      while(1);
}
```

12. Identify and correct the errors in the following two programs.

C Program (main.c)	Assembly Program (strcpy.s)

char src[9] = "Hello!";
char dst[9];
 	
int main(void){
    strcpy(dst, src);
    while(1);
}
	``
	        AREA stringCopy, CODE
	        ALIGN
	strcpy PROC
	loop LDRB r2, [r1] ; Load a byte, r1 = *src
	        STRB r2, [r0] ; Store a byte, r0 = *dst
	        ADD r1, #1 ; Increase memory pointer
	        ADD r0, #1 ; Increase memory pointer
	        CMP r2, #0 ; Zero terminator
	        BNE loop ; Loop if not null terminator
	        ENDP
	        END
	``

Interrupts

This chapter introduces the basic concepts of *interrupts* and *interrupt service routines*. We illustrate the programming of interrupts using the system timer (SysTick), external interrupts (EXTI), and software interrupts (SVC).

11.1 Introduction to Interrupts

An *interrupt* leverages a combination of software and hardware to force the processor to stop its current activity and begin to execute a particular piece of code called an **interrupt service routine** (ISR). An ISR responds to a specific event generated by either hardware or software. When an ISR completes, the processor automatically resumes the activity that had been halted. The halted process continues as if nothing had happened.

> *An interrupt is simply a hardware-invoked function call.*

Interrupts are widely used to respond to both internal and external hardware requests efficiently. For example, interrupts can inform a program of some timely external events (such as pushing a button and receiving a message in a communication port). Interrupts allow a processor to gracefully shutdown when there are critical errors (such as memory access violations, and detection of undefined instructions).

Interrupts also allow a processor to perform multiple tasks simultaneously. At any given time, the microcontroller is serving only one program activity. However, interrupts enable the processor to serve multiple computation tasks alternately in a multiplexing fashion. Multiple tasks can be handled in a preemptive or non-preemptive manner.

- In the *preemptive* scenario, if a new task is more urgent than the current task, this new task can stop the current one without requiring any cooperation. The new task will take over control of the processor. The processor resumes the old task after the new task completes.

- In the ***non-preemptive*** scenario, a new task cannot stop the current task until the current task voluntarily gives up control of the processor. A non-preemptive system often relies on the system timer, described in Chapter 23, to serve multiple tasks periodically in a round-robin fashion.

Interrupts enable a microcontroller to respond to human inputs or latency-sensitive events rapidly. An alternative to interrupts is busy-waiting or periodic ***polling***. In the polling scheme, the processor continually queries the I/O devices to check whether a specific event has happened, and handles the event. The latency of detecting the event is determined by the polling period. In the interrupt scheme, the processor provides a hardware mechanism that allows an internal or external device to generate a signal to immediately inform the processor of events that have occurred.

We use a telephone as an example to compare polling efficiency and interrupt efficiency. Suppose you are expecting a call. In the polling scheme, you pick up your telephone every 10 seconds to check whether there is anyone on the line calling you. In the interrupt scheme, you continue to perform whatever tasks you are supposed to complete while waiting for the telephone to ring. When the telephone finally rings (*i.e.*, you are interrupted), you can stop your current task and answer the phone. As you can see from this analogy, polling is much less efficient than using interrupts. With the polling scheme, you waste time that could be spent on other tasks picking up the telephone repeatedly without successfully receiving any calls.

11.2 Interrupt Numbers

Cortex-M processors support up to 256 types of interrupts. Each interrupt type, excluding the *reset* interrupt, is identified by a unique number, ranging from -15 to 240. Interrupt numbers are defined by ARM and chip manufacturers collectively. These numbers are fixed and software cannot re-define them. Interrupt numbers are divided into two groups.

- The first 16 interrupts are system interrupts, also called ***system exceptions***. Exceptions are the interrupts that come from the processor core. These interrupt numbers are defined by ARM. Specifically, the ARM CMSIS library defines all system exceptions by using negative values. CMSIS stands for Cortex Microcontroller Software Interface Standard.

- The remaining 240 interrupts are *peripheral interrupts*, also called non-system exceptions. The peripheral interrupt numbers start at 0. Peripheral interrupts are defined by chip manufacturers. The total number of peripheral interrupts supported varies among chips.

This numbering scheme allows software to distinguish system exceptions and peripheral interrupts easily. Table 11-1 shows the definition of all interrupt numbers for STM32L4. Although Cortex-M processors support 256 interrupts, not all interrupt numbers are used on STM32L4.

Cortex-M4 Processor Exceptions Numbers		STM32L4 specific Interrupt Numbers							
-14	Non-maskable interrupt	0	WWDG	16	DMA1_CH6	32	I2C1_ER	48	FMC	64	COMP	80	RNG
-13	Hard fault	1	PVD	17	DMA1_CH7	33	I2C2_EV	49	SDMMC1	65	LPTIM1	81	FPU
-12	Memory management	2	TAMPER_STAMP	18	ADC1_ADC2	34	I2C2_ER	50	TIM5	66	LPTIM2		
-11	Bus fault	3	RTC_WKUP	19	CAN1_TX	35	SPI1	51	SPI3	67	OTG_FS		
-10	Usage fault	4	FLASH	20	CAN1_RX0	36	SPI2	52	UART4	68	DMA2_Channel6		
-5	Supervisor call (SVCall)	5	RCC	21	CAN1_RX1	37	USART1	53	UART5	69	DMA2_Channel7		
-4	Debug monitor	6	EXTI0	22	CAN1_SCE	38	USART2	54	TIM6_DAC	70	LPUART1		
-2	PendSV	7	EXTI1	23	EXTI9_5	39	USART3	55	TIM7	71	QUADSPI		
-1	SysTick	8	EXTI2	24	TIM1_BRK	40	EXTI15_10	56	DMA2_Channel1	72	I2C3_EV		
		9	EXTI3	25	TIM1_UP	41	RTC_Alarm	57	DMA2_Channel2	73	I2C3_ER		
		10	EXTI4	26	TIM1_TRG	42	DFSDM3	58	DMA2_Channel3	74	SAI1		
		11	DMA1_CH1	27	TIM1_CC	43	TIM8_BRK	59	DMA2_Channel4	75	SAI2		
		12	DMA1_CH2	28	TIM2	44	TIM8_UP	60	DMA2_Channel5	76	SWPMI1		
		13	DMA1_CH3	29	TIM3	45	TIM8_TRG	61	DFSDM0	77	TSC		
		14	DMA1_CH4	30	TIM4	46	TIM8_CC	62	DFSDM1	78	LCD		
		15	DMA1_CH5	31	I2C1_EV	47	ADC3	63	DFSDM2	79			

Table 11-1. CMSIS Definition of interrupt numbers for STM32L4

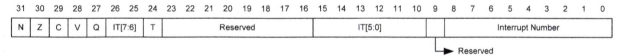

Figure 11-1. Program status register

When an interrupt is processed, the interrupt number is stored in the program status register (PSR), as shown in Figure 11-1. However, ARM Cortex-M does not store interrupt numbers in two's complement. Instead, the interrupt number in PSR adds a positive offset of 15 to the CMSIS interrupt number.

$$Interrupt\ number\ in\ PSR = CMSIS\ interrupt\ number + 15$$

In the rest of the book, unless specified otherwise, interrupt numbers are the ones defined by CMSIS. As will be introduced later, each interrupt number is used as an index into the interrupt vector table to search for the starting memory address of its corresponding interrupt service routine.

11.3 Interrupt Service Routines

An interrupt service routine (ISR), also called an *interrupt handler*, is a special subroutine that hardware invokes automatically in response to an interrupt. Each ISR has a default implementation in the system startup code (such as the assembly file startup_stm32xxxx.s). The default implementation of most ISRs is simply a dead loop, such as the interrupt handler for the system timer shown below.

```
SysTick_Handler  PROC
                 EXPORT  SysTick_Handler  [WEAK]
                 B       .            ; dead loop
                 ENDP
```

Example 11-1. Default implementation of interrupt handler for the system timer (SysTick)

All ISRs are declared as weak in the system startup code. The keyword weak means that another non-weak subroutine with the same name defined elsewhere can override this one. Example 11-2 gives two implementations in C and assembly, respectively. ISRs do not return any values because they are called by hardware (there is no software caller). Furthermore, ISRs (excluding *SVC_Handler*) do not take any input arguments.

C Code	Assembly Code

`void SysTick_Handler (void) {`
 	
  `...`
 	
`}`
	`SysTick_Handler  PROC`
	`        EXPORT  SysTick_Handler`
	
	  `...`
	
	`ENDP`

Example 11-2. User implementation of interrupt handler for the system timer (SysTick)

The *Reset_Handler* ISR, as shown below, is executed when the processor is reset or powered up. *Reset_Handler* eventually calls the *main* function. For a C program compiled in ARM Keil, *Reset_Handler* calls __main, which copies data segments from the instruction memory to the data memory, and then calls the user function *main*.

```
Reset_Handler PROC
              EXPORT  Reset_Handler   [WEAK]
              IMPORT  __main
              ; if your main program is written in assembly, make sure to
              ; to add code here to copy data segments to data memory
              LDR     R0, =__main
              BX      R0
              ENDP
```

Example 11-3. Default implementation of Reset_Handler

11.4 Interrupt Vector Table

There is an interrupt service routine (ISR) associated with each type of interrupt. Cortex-M stores the starting memory address of every ISR in a special array called the *interrupt vector table*. For a given interrupt number i defined in CMSIS, the memory address of its corresponding ISR is located at the (i + 16)th entry in the interrupt vector table. The interrupt vector table is stored at the memory address 0x00000004. Because each entry in the table represents a memory address, each entry takes four bytes in memory.

> *An interrupt number is used as an index into the interrupt vector table to locate the corresponding interrupt service routine.*

$$Address\ of\ ISR = InterruptVectorTable[i + 15]$$

For example, the interrupt number of SysTick is -1, the memory address of SysTick_Handler can be founding by reading the word stored at the following address.

$$Address\ of\ \text{SysTick\_Handler} = 0x00000004 + 4\times(-1 + 15) = 0x0000003C$$

The interrupt number of reset is -15. Thus, the memory address of Reset_Handler is

$$Address\ of\ \text{Reset\_Handler} = 0x00000004 + 4\times(-15 + 15) = 0x00000004$$

The following describes the booting process of Cortex-M. When an ARM Cortex processor is turned on or reset, the processor fetches two words located at 0x00000000 and 0x00000004 in memory. The processor uses the word located at 0x00000000 to initialize the main stack pointer (MSP), and the other one at 0x00000004 to set up the program counter (PC). The word stored at 0x00000004 is the memory address of the *reset_handler()* procedure, which is determined by the compiler and link script. Typically, the *reset_handler()* procedure calls the *main()* procedure, which is the user's application code. After PC is initialized, the program begins execution.

> **Booting process:**
>
> 1. **MSP = memory[0];**
> 2. **PC = memory[4];**

While the very first word in memory stores the memory address used to initialize MSP, the following words starting at 0x00000004 represent a vector table. This vector table stores the memory addresses of all interrupt and exception handling routines.

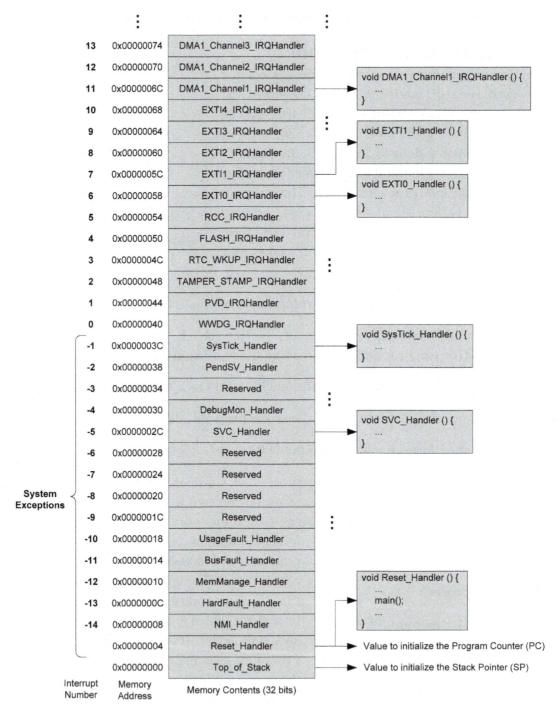

Figure 11-2. Interrupt vector table

Cortex-M processors use the ***nested vectored interrupt controller*** (NVIC) to manage interrupts. NVIC allows applications to enable specific interrupts and set their priority levels. The processor serves all interrupts based on their priority levels. The processor stops the currently running interrupt handler if a new interrupt with a higher priority occurs. The new interrupt task preempts the current lower-priority task, and the processor resumes the low-priority task when the handler of the new interrupt completes. *A higher value of the interrupt priority number represents a lower priority (or urgency).* The *reset_handler()* has top priority, and its priority number is -3.

Among all interrupts defined in the interrupt vector table, the first 15 interrupts (including reserved ones) deal with system abnormalities. These are called **system exceptions**. The remaining interrupts deal with the activities of peripherals. These are called **external interrupts**.

Examples of system exceptions include supervisor call interrupts, system timer interrupts, and fault-handling interrupts. Faults include bus faults for prefetch and memory accesses, memory management faults, instruction usage faults, and hard faults.

Examples of external interrupts include ADC interrupts, USB interrupts, and serial communication interrupts (SPI, I²C, and USART). These are used to inform the microcontroller of external events efficiently. Without these interrupts, the microcontroller then would have to resort to inefficient polling to check peripherals repeatedly, wasting precious computation cycles.

> *The interrupt vector table can be relocated to different regions (SRAM or FLASH). Thus, the processor can boot from different memory devices.*

The interrupt vector table is relocatable. While the interrupt vector table is located at the memory address `0x00000004`, this low memory address can be physically re-mapped to different regions, such as on-chip flash memory, on-chip RAM memory, or on-chip ROM memory. This allows the processor to boot from various memory regions. On STM32L4, the memory address `0x00000004` is an alias to `0x08000004` by default, which is in the address space assigned to the on-chip flash memory.

11.5 Interrupt Stacking and Unstacking

When serving an interrupt, the Cortex-M microcontroller performs automatic stacking and unstacking. Chapter 12.4.1.4 discusses automatic stacking and unstacking related to floating-point registers.

- **Interrupt Stacking.** Before executing the interrupt handler, the stacking process automatically pushes eight registers to preserve the running environment. These eight registers include the lowest four registers (r0, r1, r2, and r3) and four other registers (r12, LR, PSR, and PC).
- **Interrupt Unstacking.** After the interrupt handler completes, the unstacking process automatically pops the values of these eight registers off the stack. This recovers the environment that existed at the time instant immediately before the interrupt handler started to run. At the same time, the processor clears the corresponding active bits in the NVIC status registers.

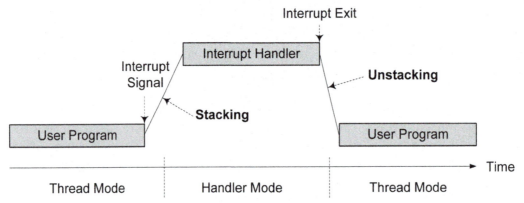

Figure 11-3. Automatic stacking and unstacking for interrupt handler

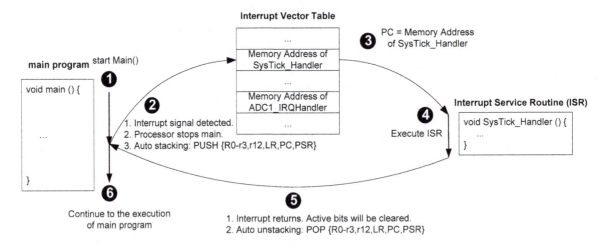

Figure 11-4. Steps of stacking and unstacking for interrupt handler

Since an interrupt may occur at any time, the program counter (PC) is preserved during interrupt stacking and then is recovered during interrupt unstacking. Thus, the processor can successfully continue executing the computation that had been interrupted.

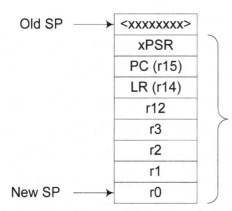

Old SP ────► | <xxxxxxxx> |
| xPSR |
| PC (r15) |
| LR (r14) |
| r12 |
| r3 |
| r2 |
| r1 |
New SP ────► | r0 |

- The processor automatically pushes these eight registers into the main stack before an interrupt handler starts.

- The processor automatically pops these eight registers out of the main stack when an interrupt hander exits.

Figure 11-5. Stacking and unstacking when an interrupt handler starts or exits (Assume there is no FPU. See Chapter 12.4.1.4 for stacking and unstacking of floating-point registers.)

The interrupt service routine exits by running "BX LR". Note that LR in an interrupt service routine has a meaning different from LR in a normal subroutine.

- LR in a regular subroutine represents the return address to the caller. When a regular subroutine is called, LR holds the memory address of the instruction to be processed after exiting the subroutine. The value of LR is copied to PC when a regular service routine exits.

- LR in an interrupt service routine indicates whether the processor uses the main stack or the process stack in the push and pop operations. Since the interrupt service routine preserves and recovers PC via stacking and unstacking, the LR register is not copied to set PC when an interrupt service routine exits. Instead, the LR register shall be fixed to a special value (see Chapter 23.1.2), to indicate whether the processor should unstack data out of the main stack (MSP) or the process stack (PSP). Chapter 23.1 gives a detailed explanation of LR for interrupts.

11.6 Nested Vectored Interrupt Controller (NVIC)

The nested vectored interrupt controller (NVIC) is built into Cortex-M cores to manage all interrupts. It offers three key functions:

1. Enable and disable interrupts
2. Configure the preemption priority and sub-priority of a specific interrupt
3. Set and clear the handing bit of a specific interrupt

The Cortex-M microcontroller supports up to 256 interrupts, in which the first 16 interrupts are system exceptions, and the rest 240 interrupts are peripheral interrupts.

The number of interrupts supported by a specific microcontroller, stored in ICTR (interrupt controller type register), differs among different manufacturers.

Each interrupt has six control bits, as listed in Table 11-2.

Interrupt control bit	Corresponding register (32 bits)
Enable bit	Interrupt set enable register (ISER)
Disable bit	Interrupt clear enable register (ICER)
Pending bit	Interrupt set pending register (ISPR)
Un-pending bit	Interrupt clear pending register (ICPR)
Active bit	Interrupt active bit register (IABR)
Software trigger bit	Software trigger interrupt register (STIR)

Table 11-2. Interrupt control bits

Each interrupt has an interrupt number, ranging from 0 to 256 for Cortex-M processors. A Cortex-M processor includes 16 system interrupts (0-15) defined by ARM. System interrupts are also called *system exceptions* or processor exceptions. The rest 240 interrupts are peripheral interrupts (also known as non-system interrupts), which are defined by chip manufacturers. Note that in the Cortex-M code library, the interrupt number of peripherals starts with 0.

Cortex-M defines eight registers for each control bit. For example, there are ISER0, ISER1, …, and ISER7, which can enable 256 interrupts.

1. *Enable and disable an interrupt*. Writing an enable bit to 1 can enable the corresponding interrupt. Writing an enable bit to 0 does not turn off the corresponding interrupt. Write a disable bit to 1 can disable the interrupt. Writing a disable bit to 0 has no impacts on the related interrupt. Separating enable bits and disable bits allows us to disable an interrupt conveniently without affecting the other interrupts.

2. *Pend and clear an interrupt*. If an interrupt occurs, the corresponding pending bit is set if the microcontroller cannot process this interrupt immediately. Writing the clear pending bit to 1 removes the corresponding interrupt from the pending list. When an interrupt is disabled but its pending bit has already been set, this interrupt instance remains active, and it is serviced before it is disabled.

3. *Trigger an interrupt*. Setting an active bit by software or hardware activates the related interrupt, and the microcontroller starts the corresponding interrupt handler. If software writes a trigger bit of the software trigger interrupt register (STIR) to 1, the related interrupt is also activated. Most system exceptions can only be activated by hardware.

11.6.1 Enable and Disable Peripheral Interrupts

Cortex-M has eight 32-bit Interrupt Set-Enable Registers (ISER), ISER0 – ISER7, and eight 32-bit Interrupt Clear-enable Register (ICER), ICER0 – ICER7. Writing a bit to 1 in ISER and ICER enables and disables the corresponding interrupt, respectively.

Figure 11-6 shows ISER0, ISER1 and ISER2 registers for enabling a peripheral interrupt for STM32L4 processors.

Interrupt Set Enable Register 0 (ISER0)

All Enable Bits = 0 (bits 31–0). Interrupt Number equals the bit position.

Bit / Interrupt Number	Interrupt Name
31	I2C1_EV
30	TIM4
29	TIM3
28	TIM2
27	TIM1_CC
26	TIM1_TRG
25	TIM1_UP
24	TIM1_BRK
23	EXTI9_5
22	CAN1_SCE
21	CAN1_RX1
20	CAN1_RX0
19	CAN1_TX
18	ADC1_ADC2
17	DMA1_CH7
16	DMA1_CH6
15	DMA1_CH5
14	DMA1_CH4
13	DMA1_CH3
12	DMA1_CH2
11	DMA1_CH1
10	EXTI4
9	EXTI3
8	EXTI2
7	EXTI1
6	EXTI0
5	RCC
4	FLASH
3	RTC_WKUP
2	TAMPER_STAMP
1	PVD
0	WWDG

Interrupt Set Enable Register 1 (ISER1)   Address of ISER1 = Address of ISER0 + 4

All Enable Bits = 0 (bits 31–0). Interrupt Numbers 63–32.

Interrupt Number	Interrupt Name
63	DFSDM2
62	DFSDM1
61	DFSDM0
60	DMA2_Channel5
59	DMA2_Channel4
58	DMA2_Channel3
57	DMA2_Channel2
56	DMA2_Channel1
55	TIM7
54	TIM6_DAC
53	UART5
52	UART4
51	SPI3
50	TIM5
49	SDMMC1
48	FMC
47	ADC3
46	TIM8_CC
45	TIM8_TRG_COM
44	TIM8_UP
43	TIM8_BRK
42	DFSDM3
41	RTC_Alarm
40	EXTI15_10
39	USART3
38	USART2
37	USART1
36	SPI2
35	SPI1
34	I2C2_ER
33	I2C2_EV
32	I2C1_ER

Interrupt Set Enable Register 2 (ISER2)   Address of ISER2 = Address of ISER0 + 8

All Enable Bits = 0 (bits 31–0). Interrupt Numbers 81–64.

Interrupt Number	Interrupt Name
81	FPU
80	RNG
78	LCD
77	TSC
76	SWPMI1
75	SAI2
74	SAI1
73	I2C3_ER
72	I2C3_EV
71	QUADSPI
70	LPUART1
69	DMA2_Channel7
68	DMA2_Channel6
67	OTG_FS
66	LPTIM2
65	LPTIM1
64	COMP

Figure 11-6. Interrupt Set Enable Registers for Peripheral Interrupts in STM32L

Each bit in an ISER register can enable one peripheral interrupt. The interrupt number of peripheral interrupts ranges from 0 to 240. Not all peripheral interrupts are used. For example, STM32L has only 45 peripheral interrupts. Note that all NVIC registers are little endian regardless of whether the processor deploys big endian or little endian.

The following C program can enable a peripheral interrupt whose interrupt number is IRQn. Bit j in register ISER i enables interrupt $IRQn = j + 32 \times i$.

```
WordOffset = IRQn >> 5;                        // Word Offset = IRQn/32
BitOffset = IRQn & 0x1F;                        // Bit Offset = IRQn mod 32
NVIC->ISER[WordOffset]  =  1 << BitOffset;      // Enable interrupt
```

Since each ISER register has 32 bits, the ISER register array index is obtained by shifting right the interrupt number IRQn by five bits. Note that the peripheral interrupt number starts with 0. For example, the interrupt number of Timer 5 is 50. Therefore, the following code can enable the Timer 5 interrupt:

```
NVIC->ISER[1] = 1 << 18;                        // Enable Timer 5 interrupt
```

Similarly, the following C program can disable the interrupt IRQn.

```
WordOffset = IRQn >> 5;                         // WordOffset = IRQn/32
BitOffset = IRQn & 0x1F;                         // BitOffset = IRQn mod 32
NVIC->ICER[WordOffset]  =  1 << BitOffset;       // Disable interrupt
```

```
; Input arguments:
;     r0: interrupt number of a peripheral interrupt
;     r1: 1 = Enable, 0 = Disable
Peripheral_Interrupt_Enable    PROC
    PUSH   {r4, lr}
    AND    r2, r0, #0x1F       ; Bit offset in a word
    MOV    r3, #1
    LSL    r3, r3, r2          ; r3 = 1 << (IRQn & 0x1F)
    LDR    r4, =NVIC_BASE

    CMP    r1, #0              ; Check whether enable or disable
    LDRNE  r1, =NVIC_ISER0     ; Enable register base address
    LDREQ  r1, =NVIC_ICER0     ; Disable register base address

    ADD    r1, r4, r1          ; r1 = addr. of NVIC->ISER0 or NVIC->ICER0
    LSR    r2, r0, #5          ; Memory offset (in words): IRQn >> 5
    LSL    r2, r2, #2          ; Calculate byte offset
    STR    r3, [r1, r2]        ; Enable/Disable interrupt
    POP    {r4, pc}
    ENDP
```

Example 11-4. Enabling/disabling a peripheral interrupt

Example 11-4 shows the assembly implementation of enabling or disabling a peripheral interrupt. The program takes two arguments: an interrupt number held in register r0 and a Boolean option of enabling and disabling stored in register r1.

The memory address [r1,r2] in the STR instruction is the memory address offset for NVIC->ISER[i] or NVIC->ICER[i], depending on whether the interrupt is to enabled or disabled. Because each ISER or ICER register controls 32 interrupts, the program uses the following two instructions to calculate the address:

```
LSR    r2, r0, #5     ; Memory offset in words = IRQn >> 5
LSL    r2, r2, #2     ; Offset in bytes = 4 × Offset in words
```

These two operations are equivalent to:

$$i = floor\left(\frac{Interrupt\ number}{32}\right)$$

$$Byte\ Offset = 4 \times i$$

For example, the program is to enable the interrupt numbered 77. The corresponding register is NVIC->ISER[2], which controls all interrupts from 64 to 95.

$$Byte\ Offset = floor\left(\frac{77}{32}\right) \times 4 = 2 \times 4 = 8$$

Thus, the memory address offset between the NVIC base address and NVIC->ISER[2] is 8. In most computer systems, memory is byte addressable, and thus the offset is in bytes. The registers NVIC->ISER[0] and NVIC->ISER[1] take 4 bytes each in memory. Accordingly, the offset of NVIC->ISER[2] from the NVIC base is 8 bytes.

11.6.2   Interrupt Priority

Priority determines the order of interrupts to be serviced. Each interrupt has an interrupt priority register (IP), which has a width of 8 bits. Each consists of two fields: the preemption priority number and the sub-priority number. *A lower value of a priority number represents a higher priority or a higher urgency.* Priority value 0 has the highest priority (or the highest urgency).

Lower priority value means higher urgency.

Usually, the peripheral interrupts have a positive interrupt level while a microcontroller core interrupt can have negative priority numbers, not changeable by software. When there are multiple pending interrupts, the interrupt that has the lowest interrupt number is serviced first by the processor.

Preemption is a widely-used technique that allows a time-sensitive and urgent computation task to take control of the processor from a relatively less urgent computation task. The preemption priority number defines the priority for preemption.

If the processor receives a new interrupt that has a lower preemption priority number than the preemption priority number of the current interrupt in progress, the current interrupt is stopped, and the processor starts to serve the new interrupt. The preempted interrupt is resumed after the new interrupt handler routine completes.

> *"Don't interrupt me while I'm interrupting."*
>
> Winston Churchill
> Former British Prime Minister

While Cortex-M processors use eight bits to store the priority number, STM32L processors only implement four bits. Thus, the STM32L microcontroller only supports 16 interrupt priority levels, ranging from 0 to 15. For a different Cortex-M processor, the interrupt priority byte might be different.

STM32L processors allow five different schemes to split the four-bit priority number. If we use n bits for the preempt priority number, then the sub-priority number has $4 - n$ bits, where $n = 0, 1, 2, 3,$ or 4. By default, two bits are used for the preempt priority number, and two bits are used for the sub-priority number, as shown in Figure 11-7.

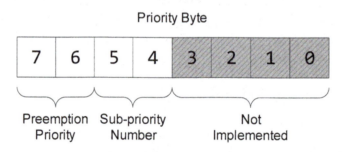

Figure 11-7. Interrupt Priority Byte of STM32L by default

For a system interrupt IRQn, its priority can be set as follows. Note that SHP (System Handler Priority) is defined as a byte array, instead of a word array.

```
typedef struct {
  ...
  volatile uint8_t SHP[12];   // System handler priority array
  ...
} SCB_Type;

// Set the priority of a system interrupt IRQn
SCB->SHP[((uint8_t)IRQn) & 0xF) - 4] = (priority << 4) & 0xFF;
```

SCB is the base memory address of the System Control Block (SCB). SHP is the base memory address of the System Handler Priority registers. Cortex-M has three SHP registers, as shown in Figure 11-8. For example, the interrupt number of SysTick is -1. The byte offset in the system handler priority array is as follows

```
((uint8_t)IRQn) & 0xF) - 4 = ((uint8_t)-1) & 0xF) - 4
                           = (0xFF & 0xF) - 4
                           = 11
```

Therefore, the following code sets the priority of SysTick to 1:

```
SCB->SHP[11] = (1UL << 4) & 0xFF;
```

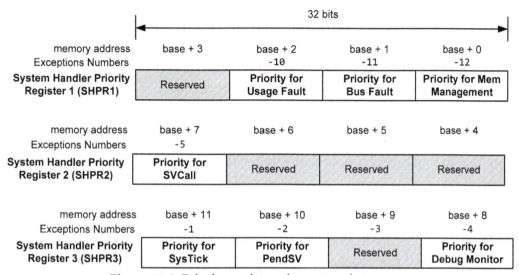

Figure 11-8. Priority registers for system interrupts

For a peripheral interrupt IRQn, its priority can be set as follows. Note that the interrupt priority (IP) array is defined as an array of bytes, not words.

```
typedef struct {
  ...
  volatile uint8_t  IP[240]; // Interrupt Priority Register
  ...
} NVIC_Type;

// Set the priority of a peripheral interrupt IRQn
NVIC->IP[IRQn] = (priority << 4) & 0xFF;
```

Figure 11-9 shows the memory layout of interrupt priority registers for the first 16 peripheral interrupt. For example, the following code sets the priority of EXTI Line 0, whose interrupt number is 6, to the lowest priority. Both the preemption priority and the sub-priority number are 0b11 (*i.e.*, 3).

```
// Set the priority for EXTI 0 (Interrupt number 6)
NVIC->IP[6] = 0xF0;
```

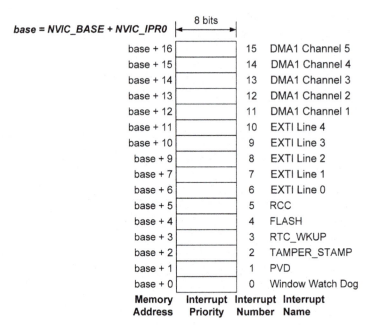

Figure 11-9. Example of interrupt priority (IP) registers for the first 16 peripheral interrupts.

Example 11-5 and Example 11-6 give two example assembly subroutines that set the priority of a system exception and a peripheral interrupt, respectively.

- Both functions use the STRB (store a byte) instruction, instead of STR (store a word). As discussed previously, the priority array is a byte array, instead of an integer array.
- Also, the subroutine shifts the priority left by four bits because the lower four bits of each priority register are not used in STM32L processors (see Figure 11-7).

```
; Input arguments:
;     r0: Interrupt Number IRQn
;     r1: Interrupt Priority

Set_System_Exception_Priority PROC

    PUSH {r4, lr}
    LSL  r2, r1, #4         ; r2 = priority << 4
    LDR  r3, =SCB_BASE      ; System control block base address
    LDR  r4, =SCB_HP_1_12   ; System handlers priority registers
    ADD  r3, r3, r4
    AND  r4, r0, #0x0F
    SUB  r4, r4, #4
    STRB r2, [r3, r4]       ; Save priority; Do not use STR
    POP  {r4, pc}

    ENDP
```

Example 11-5. Setting priority of system interrupts

```
; Input arguments:
;    r0: Interrupt Number IRQn
;    r1: Interrupt Priority

Set_Peripheral_Interrupt_Priority PROC

    PUSH {r4, lr}
    LSL  r2, r1, #4      ; r2 = priority << 4
    LDR  r3, =NVIC_BASE  ; NVIC base address
    LDR  r4, =NVIC_IPR0  ; Interrupt priority register
    ADD  r3, r3, r4
    STRB r2, [r3, r0]    ; Save priority; Don't use STR
    POP  {r4, pc}

    ENDP
```

Example 11-6. Setting priority of peripheral interrupts

11.6.3   Global Interrupt Enable and Disable

Besides using NVIC to configure individual interrupts, the Cortex-M processors also allow us to enable and disable a group of interrupts by using change processor state (CPS) instructions.

We use the priority mask register (PRIMASK) to enable or disable interrupts excluding hard faults and non-maskable interrupts (NMI). Also, we use the fault mask register (FAULTMASK) to enable or disable interrupts except for non-maskable interrupts (NMI).

Instruction	Action	Equivalent
CPSID i	Disable interrupts & configurable fault handlers	MOVS r0, #0 MSR PRIMASK, r0
CPSID f	Disable interrupts and all fault handlers	MOVS r0, #1 MSR FAULTMASK, r0
CPSIE i	Enable interrupts and configurable fault handlers	MOVS r0, #1 MSR PRIMASK, r0
CPSIE f	Enable interrupts and fault handlers	MOVS r0, #0 MSR FAULTMASK, r0
N/A	Disable interrupts with priority 0x05 - 0xFF	MOVS r0, #5 MSR BASEPRI, r0

Table 11-3. Instructions for enabling or disabling interrupts (excluding hard faults and NMI)

When the base priority mask register (BASEPRI) is non-zero, all interrupts with a priority value lower than or equal to BASEPRI are disabled. In this case, we also say that interrupts with a priority value lower than BASEPRI are unmasked (*i.e.,* enabled). A larger priority value represents lower priority (*i.e.,* lower urgency).

In the equivalent instructions given in Table 11-3, MSR transfers the content of a general-purpose register to a special-purpose register. Note that MOV or MOVS cannot access these special registers.

11.7 System Timer

The system tick timer (SysTick) is a simple 24-bit down counter to produce a small fixed time quantum. Software uses SysTick to create time delays or generate periodic interrupts to execute a task repeatedly.

- The timer counts down from N-1 to 0, and the processor generates a SysTick interrupt once the counter reaches zero.

- After reaching zero, the SysTick counter loads the value held in a special register named the SysTick Reload register and counts down again.

- The SysTick timer does not stop counting down when the processor is halted. The processor still generates SysTick interrupts during the process of debugging.

Another usage of SysTick timer is to create a useful hardware timer for the CPU scheduler in real-time operating systems (RTOS). When multiple tasks run concurrently, the processor allocates a time slot to each task according to some scheduling policy, such as the round robin. To achieve that, the processor utilizes a hardware timer to generate interrupts at regular time intervals. These interrupts inform the processor to stop the current task, save the context registers of the present task to the stack, and then select a new task in the job waiting queue to serve. Chapter 23 gives a detailed discussion. When SysTick timers are used as a system level function, processors often protect SysTick timers from being modified by software running in the unprivileged mode.

There are four 32-bit registers for configuring system timers. Their memory addresses are listed in Table 11-4. Chip manufacturers may have different names for these registers, but their memory addresses are the same for each ARM Cortex-M family.

```
SysTick_CTRL  EQU (0xE000E010)   ; SysTick control and status register
SysTick_LOAD  EQU (0xE000E014)   ; SysTick reload value register
SysTick_VAL   EQU (0xE000E018)   ; SysTick current value register
SysTick_CALIB EQU (0xE000E01C)   ; SysTick calibration register
```

Table 11-4. Memory address of control registers for SysTick timer

(1) SysTick control and status register (SysTick_CTRL)

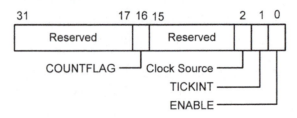

- **CLKSOURCE** indicates the clock source:

  0 = External clock. The frequency of SysTick clock is the frequency of the AHB clock divided by 8.

  1 = Processor clock

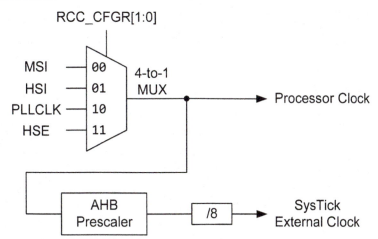

RCC_CFGR[1:0]

Figure 11-10. Two different clock sources for SysTick on STM32 processor. The default AHB prescaler is 1. RCC_CFGR register selects MSI, HSI, PLLCLK, or HSE.

Figure 11-10 shows the clock selection configured by the RCC_CFGR register. A different ARM Cortex processor might use a different clocking scheme.

- **TICKINT** enables SysTick interrupt request:

  0 = Counting down to zero does not assert the SysTick interrupt request

  1 = Counting down to zero asserts the SysTick interrupt request

- **ENABLE** enables the counter:

  0 = Counter disabled

  1 = Counter enabled

  To enable SysTick interrupt, the program needs to set up three bits:
  1. Set bit TICKINT in SysTick_CTRL to enable SysTick interrupt.
  2. Enable SysTick interrupt in the NVIC vector. Note that SysTick interrupt is enabled by default in the NVIC vector.
  3. Set bit ENABLE in SysTick_CTRL to enable the SysTick timer.

- **COUNTFLAG** indicates whether a special event has occurred.

  1 = Counter has transitioned from 1 to 0 since the last read of SysTick_CTRL

  0 = COUNTFLAG is cleared by reading SysTick_CTRL or by writing to SysTick_VAL.

(2) SysTick reload value register (SysTick_LOAD)

31   24 23   0
	RELOAD

As the SysTick counter wraps on zero, the SysTick_LOAD register provides the wrap-around value. After the counter counts down to zero, the counter restarts from the value in SysTick_LOAD.

If the SysTick interrupt is required once every N clock pulses, software should set SysTick_LOAD to $N − 1$. SysTick_LOAD supports any 24-bit values between 1 and 0x00FFFFFF or 16,777,215 in decimal. For example, if an application needs to generate a SysTick interrupt for each 100 clock pulses sent to the timer, SysTick_LOAD should be set to 99.

(3) SysTick current value register (SysTick_VAL)

31   24 23   0
	CURRENT

When SysTick is enabled, the 24-bit current counter value in the SysTick_VAL register is copied from the SysTick_LOAD register initially. However, this value in SysTick_VAL is arbitrary on reset.

The processor automatically decrements SysTick_VAL by one at each clock pulse sent to the timer. Writing any value to SysTick_VAL resets it to zero, making the counter restart from SysTick_LOAD on the next clock pulse. Reading SysTick_VAL returns the current timer value.

(4) SysTick calibration register (SysTick_CALIB)

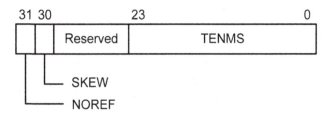

- The TENMS value in the calibration register (stored in the TENMS field) is the required preload value for generating a time interval of 10 *ms* (*i.e.*, a timer of 100 Hz). Software can use an external reference clock with high accuracy to calibrate the system timer. If TENMS is zero, we can calculate its value from the clock frequency that drives the timer's counter. The TENMS value provides a convenient way to generate a specific time interval. For example, to generate a SysTick interrupt every 1 *ms*, we can set SysTick_LOAD to TENMS/10.

- The SKEW indicates whether the 10 *ms* calibration is exact or inexact. If it is 0, the TENMS field cannot generate exactly 10 *ms* due to small variations in clock frequency.
- The NOREF indicates whether the processor chip has implemented a reference clock. If TENMS is 1, the reference clock has not been applied by the chip manufacturer.

Example of calculating the system timer interval

Figure 11-11 shows an example of how to calculate the time interval between two consecutive SysTick interrupts. In this example, SysTick_LOAD is 6. If the processor clock is 1 MHz and the SysTick counter takes it as the input clock, then we can calculate the SysTick interrupt period as follows:

$$SysTick\ Interrupt\ Period = (1 + SysTick\_LOAD) \times \frac{1}{SysTick\ Counter\ Clock\ Frequency}$$

$$= (1 + 6) \times \frac{1}{1MHz}$$

$$= 7\mu s$$

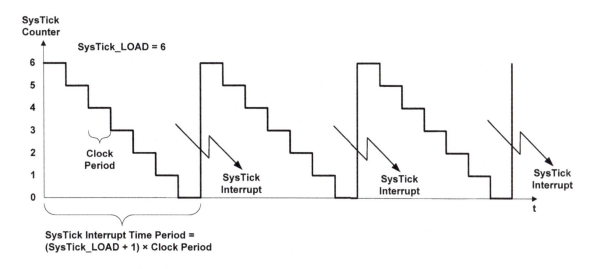

Figure 11-11. Example of SysTick interrupt when SysTick_LOAD is 6.

Figure 11-12 shows the flowchart of the SysTick initialization and an endless loop that use the delay function. The processor executes concurrently the SysTick interrupt handler (shown in Example 11-8) and the delay function (shown in Example 11-9).

The interrupt handler decrements the *ticks* variable by one whenever a SysTick interrupt is generated. The delay function uses polling to check constantly whether the SysTick handler decreases *ticks* to zero. The delay function exits when *ticks* reaches zero. To delay one second, the program should initialize *ticks* to 1000 if SysTick generates an interrupt every 1 *ms*. Note that *SysTick_Initialize()* function sets SysTick_LOAD to *ticks* - 1.

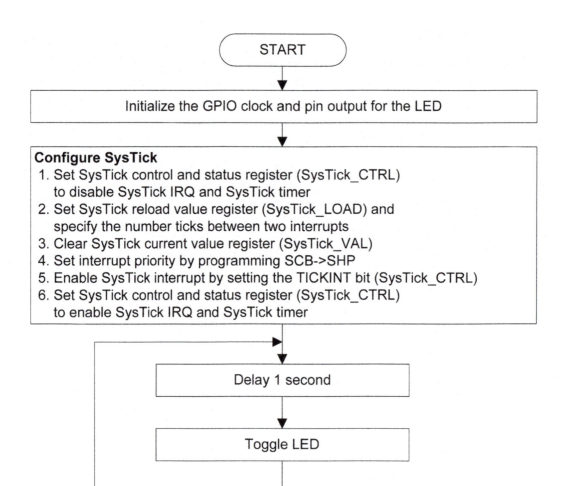

Figure 11-12 Flowchart of the main program to toggle an LED periodically

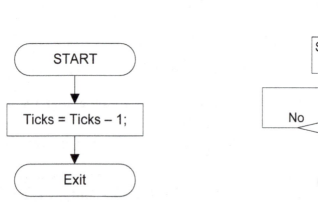

Figure 11-13. SysTick interrupt handler

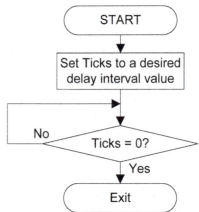

Figure 11-14. Delay function

To enable the SysTick interrupt request, we can use the following C statement to set bit 2 of SysTick_CTRL to 1 by using bitwise OR.

```
// Set bit 2 in SysTick_CTRL
*((volatile uint32_t *) 0xE000E010) |= 1UL<<2;
```

This statement first casts the memory address of SysTick_CTRL to a memory pointer, which points to a 32-bit unsigned integer. Then, it uses dereferencing to access the memory. Dereferencing a pointer mean, getting the value that is stored in the memory location pointed by the pointer.

However, directly dereferencing a numeric memory address is inconvenient to use in practice and its code is hard to read. To improve the code readability and create convenience in programming, we can cast a contiguous block of physical memory to a data structure.

Table 11-5 shows the key data structure of SysTick. The SysTick data structure includes four registers introduced previously. The memory address pre-defined is converted to a pointer variable pointing to the SysTick structure. Chapter 10.2.2 discusses the keyword "volatile".

```
// Permission definitions
#define __I    volatile const // defines as read only
#define __O    volatile       // defines as write only
#define __IO   volatile       // allows both read and write

// Memory mapping structure for SysTick
typedef struct {
  __IO uint32_t CTRL;         // SysTick control and status register
  __IO uint32_t LOAD;         // SysTick reload value register
  __IO uint32_t VAL;          // SysTick current value register
  __I  uint32_t CALIB;        // SysTick calibration register
} SysTick_Type;

// Memory address pre-defined by the chip manufacturer
#define SysTick_BASE   0xE000E010

// Cast a pointer to the SysTick struct
#define SysTick        ((SysTick_Type *) SysTick_BASE)
```

Table 11-5. Data structure of SysTick

The following gives a few example functions in C and assembly to show how to set up the SysTick timer and perform time delay. The *SysTick_Initialize()* function sets the SysTick to generate interrupts at a fixed-time interval. The input parameter *ticks* equals the time interval divided by the clock period.

```c
// Input:  ticks = number of ticks between two interrupts
void SysTick_Initialize (uint32_t ticks) {

  // Disable SysTick IRQ and SysTick counter
  SysTick->CTRL = 0;

  // Set reload register
  SysTick->LOAD = ticks - 1;

  // Set interrupt priority of SysTick
  // Make SysTick least urgent (i.e., highest priority number)
  // __NVIC_PRIO_BITS: number of bits for priority levels, defined in CMSIS
  NVIC_SetPriority (SysTick_IRQn, (1<<__NVIC_PRIO_BITS) - 1);

  // Reset the SysTick counter value
  SysTick->VAL = 0;

  // Select processor clock
  // 1 = processor clock;  0 = external clock
  SysTick->CTRL |= SysTick_CTRL_CLKSOURCE_Msk;

  // Enables SysTick exception request
  // 1 = counting down to zero asserts the SysTick exception request
  // 0 = counting down to zero does not assert the SysTick exception request
  SysTick->CTRL |= SysTick_CTRL_TICKINT_Msk;

  // Enable SysTick timer
  SysTick->CTRL |= SysTick_CTRL_ENABLE_Msk;
}
```

Example 11-7. Generating an interrupt periodically with a fixed-time interval in C

The SysTick interrupt handler decrements the *TimeDelay* variable, as shown below.

```c
void SysTick_Handler (void) { // SysTick interrupt service routine
  // TimeDelay is a global variable declared as volatile
  if (TimeDelay > 0)              // Prevent it from being negative
    TimeDelay--;                  // TimeDelay is a global volatile variable
}
```

Example 11-8. SysTick Interrupt Handler in C

The Delay function initializes the *TimeDelay* variable and waits until *TimeDelay* is decremented to zero by *SysTick_Handler()*.

```c
void Delay(uint32_t nTime) {
  // nTime: specifies the delay time length
  TimeDelay = nTime;         // TimeDelay must be declared as volatile
  while(TimeDelay != 0);     // Busy wait
}
```

Example 11-9. Delay function in C

The following shows the complete codes in assembly to initialize the system timer.

```
SysTick_Initialize PROC
  EXPORT SysTick_Initialize

  ; Set SysTick_CTRL to disable SysTick IRQ and SysTick timer
  LDR r0, =SysTick_BASE

  ; Disable SysTick IRQ and SysTick counter, select external clock
  MOV r1, #0
  STR r1, [r0, #SysTick_CTRL]

  ; Specify the number of clock cycles between two interrupts
  LDR r2, =262                  ; Change it based on interrupt interval
  STR r2, [r0, #SysTick_LOAD]   ; Save to SysTick reload register

  ; Clear SysTick current value register (SysTick_VAL)
  MOV r1, #0
  STR r1, [r0, #SysTick_VAL]    ; Write 0 to Systick value register

  ; Set interrupt priority for SysTick
  LDR   r2, =SCB_BASE
  ADD   r2, r2, #SCB_SHP
  MOV   r3, #1<<4               ; Set priority as 1, see Figure 11-7
  STRB  r3, [r2, #11]           ; SCB->SHP[11], see Figure 11-8

  ; Set SysTick_CTRL to enable SysTick timer and SysTick interrupt
  LDR r1, [r0, #SysTick_CTRL]
  ORR r1, r1, #3               ; Enable SysTick counter & interrupt
  STR r1, [r0, #SysTick_CTRL]

  BX  lr  ; Exit
  ENDP
```

Example 11-10. Configuring SysTick timer in assembly

We can implement *SysTick_Handler()* in assembly as follows. It decreases the *TimeDelay* variable (assume it is saved in register r10) by one when a SysTick interrupt is generated, *i.e.*, the SysTick counter counts down to zero.

```
SysTick_Handler   PROC
  EXPORT SysTick_Handler

  ; NVIC automatically stacks eight registers: r0 - r3, r12, LR, PSR and PC
  SUB r10, r10, #1    ; Decrement TimeDelay
  BX  lr              ; Exit and trigger auto-unstacking

  ENDP
```

Example 11-11. SysTick interrupt handler in assembly

The *delay* function given in Example 11-12. Register r0 is the input argument, representing the amount of delay in time units set by the *SysTick_Handler*. The function deploys a busy-waiting loop, which exits when the *TimeDelay* variable has been decreased to zero by the SysTick interrupt handler *SysTick_Handler()*.

```
delay  PROC
       EXPORT delay

       ; r0 is the TimeDelay input
       MOV  r10, r0      ; Make a copy of TimeDelay
loop   CMP  r10, #0      ; Wait for TimeDelay = 0
       BNE  loop         ; r10 is decreased periodically by SysTick_Handler
       BX   lr           ; Exit
       ENDP
```

Example 11-12. Delay subroutine in assembly

A common mistake in Example 11-11 and Example 11-12 is that a programmer might choose register r0, r1, r2, r3, or r12, instead of r10 to hold *TimeDelay*. The processor automatically pushes these registers onto the stack when SysTick_Handler starts, and then automatically pops them off the stack. Therefore, SysTick_Handler would fail to change *TimeDelay* if SysTick_Handler uses one of these registers to represent *TimeDelay*.

11.8 External Interrupt

External interrupts are interrupts triggered by peripherals or devices, external to the microprocessor core, such as push buttons and keypads. External interrupts are very useful because they allow the microcontroller to monitor external signals efficiently and promptly response to external events.

The external interrupt controller supports 16 external interrupts, named EXTI0, EXTI1, …, EXTI15. Each of these interrupts is only associated with one specific GPIO pin. However, a microcontroller has more than 16 GPIO pins. How does the microcontroller map GPIO pins to external interrupts?

The GPIO pins with the same pin number in all GPIO ports are assigned to the same external interrupt, as shown in Figure 11-15. In other words, only pins with the pin number k can be the source of external interrupt EXTI k. For example, the processor can map GPIO pin PA 0 to EXTI 0, PA 1 to EXTI 1, PA 2 to EXTI 2, and so on.

Also, there is only one external interrupt on all pins with the same number out of all GPIO ports. For example, if the pin PA 3 has an external interrupt on it, we cannot use the pins PB 3, PC 3, PD 3, or PE 3 as the external interrupt source.

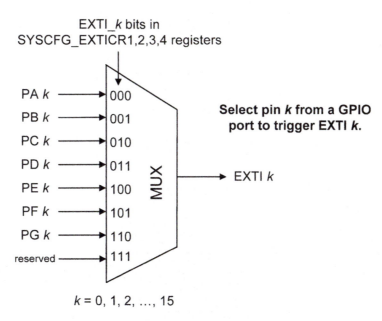

PA *k* 000
PB *k* 001
PC *k* 010
PD *k* 011
PE *k* 100
PF *k* 101
PG *k* 110
reserved 111

EXTI_*k* bits in
SYSCFG_EXTICR1,2,3,4 registers

Select pin *k* from a GPIO
port to trigger EXTI *k*.

EXTI *k*

k = 0, 1, 2, ..., 15

Figure 11-15. Mapping between external interrupt (EXTI) and GPIO pins. A multiplexer (MUX) is a circuit that selects one of its inputs and forwards the selected input to the output.

Figure 11-16 shows an example in which a button is connected to pin PA 3. When the button is pressed, the voltage on PA 3 goes high. Software should configure Pin PA 3 to be pulled down internally so that PA 3 remains low when the button is not pressed.

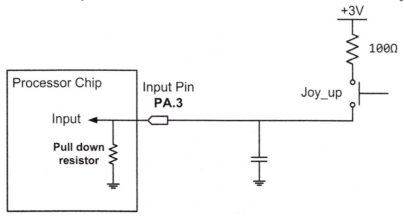

Figure 11-16. Interfacing an external button via external interrupt.

The external interrupt controller has a voltage monitor module that has a programmable edge detector. This hardware monitor module can monitor the voltage signal on GPIO pins. Software can select the rising edge, the falling edge, or both edges of the voltage signal on PA 3 to trigger an interrupt request named EXTI3. The EXTI3 interrupt request is then sent to the NVIC controller. Finally, the microcontroller responds to the interrupt request and executes the interrupt service routine *EXTI3_IRQHandler()*.

The following shows the software configuration to select GPIO pin k as the trigger source for external interrupt EXTI k.

1. Enable the clock of SYSCFG and corresponding GPIO port.
2. Configure the GPIO pin k as input.
3. Set up the SYSCFG external interrupt configuration register (SYSCFG_EXTICR) to map the GPIO pin k to the external interrupt input line k.
4. Select the active edge that can trigger EXTI k. The signal can be a rising edge, a falling edge or both. This is programmed via the rising edge trigger selection register (EXTI_RTSR1 or EXTI_RTSR2) and the falling edge trigger selection register (EXTI_FTSR1 or EXTI_FTSR2).
5. Enable EXTI k by setting the kth bit in EXTI interrupt mask register (EXTI_IMR1 or EXTI_IMR2). An interrupt can only be generated if the corresponding bit in the interrupt mask register is 1 (or called unmasked).
6. Enable interrupt EXTI k on NVIC controller via NVIC_EnableIRQ.
7. Write the interrupt handler for EXTI k. The EXTI pending register (EXTI_PR1 or EXTI_PR2) records the source of the interrupt. The function name of the interrupt handler is given by the startup assembly file *startup_stm32l476xx.s*. For example, the handler for EXTI 3 is called *EXTI3_IRQHandler()*.
8. In the interrupt handler, software needs to clear the corresponding pending bit to indicate the current request has been handled. Surprisingly, writing it to 1 clears a pending bit.

The following shows an example program that uses the external interrupt to light up the LED when the user push button is pressed. Example 11-13 illustrates the initialization for connecting EXTI 3 to pin 3 of GPIO port A.

```
void EXTI_Init(void) {

    // Enable SYSCFG clock
    RCC->APB2ENR |= RCC_APB2ENR_SYSCFGEN;

    // Select PA.3 as the trigger source of EXTI 3
    SYSCFG->EXTICR[0] &= ~SYSCFG_EXTICR1_EXTI3;
    SYSCFG->EXTICR[0] |=  SYSCFG_EXTICR1_EXTI3_PA;
    SYSCFG->EXTICR[0] &= ~(0x000F);

    // Enable rising edge trigger for EXTI 3
    // Rising trigger selection register (RSTR)
    // 0 = disabled, 1 = enabled
    EXTI->RTSR |= EXTI_RTSR_TR3;
```

```
    // Disable falling edge trigger for EXTI 3
    // Falling trigger selection register (FSTR)
    // 0 = disabled, 1 = enabled
    EXTI->FTSR &= ~EXTI_FTSR_TR3;

    // Enable EXTI 3 interrupt
    // Interrupt mask register: 0 = masked, 1 = unmasked
    // "Masked" means that processor ignores the corresponding interrupt.
    EXTI->IMR1 |= EXTI_IMR1_IM3;        // Enable EXTI line 3

    // Set EXTI 3 priority to 1
    NVIC_SetPriority(EXTI3_IRQn, 1);

    // Enable EXTI 3 interrupt
    NVIC_EnableIRQ(EXTI3_IRQn);
}
```

Example 11-13. Initialize and enable EXTI 3 for pin PA.3

Example 11-14 shows the code of the external interrupt handler of EXTI 3, which toggles an LED when PA 3 triggers an external interrupt.

One mistake that new programmers often make is that interrupt handlers do not clear interrupt pending flags. If the interrupt handler does not clear an interrupt pending flag after processing the interrupt, the microcontroller would mistakenly think another interrupt request has arrived and then repeatedly execute the interrupt handler.

```
void EXTI3_IRQHandler(void) {
    // Check for EXTI 3 interrupt flag
    if ((EXTI->PR1 & EXTI_PR1_PIF3) == EXTI_PR1_PIF3) {

        // Toggle LED
        GPIOB->ODR ^= 1<<8;             // Toggle PB.8 output

        // Clear interrupt pending request
        EXTI->PR1 |= EXTI_PR1_PIF3;   // Write 1 to clear
    }
}
```

Example 11-14. External interrupt handler for EXTI 3

External interrupts can not only monitor the external voltage applied to GPIO pins, but also monitor internal events, such as RTC alarm, COMP outputs, or internal wakeup events. Also, software can trigger EXTI interrupts by writing to the EXTI software interrupt event register (EXTI_SWIER).

11.9 Software Interrupt

Interrupt signals can be generated by hardware, such as hardware timers and peripheral hardware components. Software can also generate interrupt signals by setting the interrupt pending registers or by using special instructions. There are two major usages of software interrupt: exception handling and privileged hardware access.

Exception Handling: When exceptional conditions occur during execution, such as division by zero, illegal opcode, and invalid memory access, the processors should handle these abnormal situations to potentially correct software errors. The processor can capture two software faults, including division by error and unaligned memory access, if software enables these fault capture features. A software interrupt invoked by software faults is often referred to as a *trap*. Example 11-15 enables the trap of dividing by zero.

```
    LDR   r2, =SCB_Base        ; Base address of system control block (SCB)
    LDR   r3, [r2, #SCB_CCR]   ; Read Configuration and Control Register
    ORR   r3, r3, #16          ; Enable trap on dividing by 0
    STR   r3, [r2, #SCB_CCR]   ; Write Configuration and Control Register

    MOV   r0, #0
    MOV   r1, #1
    UDIV  r1, r1, r0           ; Invoke hard fault
```

Example 11-15. A trap that handles abnormal situations

If the software enables the dividing-by-zero trap and a division instruction (UDIV or SDIV) generates such a trap, the processor halts and invokes the hard fault handler shown in Example 11-16. The fault handler may print out the error message or reboot the processor.

```
HardFault_Handler PROC

    EXPORT HardFault_Handler

    ; Handle the error of division by 0
    ; For example, force the processor to reboot

    BL NVIC_SystemReset    ; Reboot the system using AIRCR register
    ENDP
```

Example 11-16. Hard fault interrupt handler

Privileged Hardware Access: When a user application runs in unprivileged mode and needs to access a hardware resource that is only accessible in privileged mode, a special instruction (supervisor call) generates a software interrupt and makes the processor switch from the unprivileged mode to the privilege mode. Chapter 23.2 introduces the supervisor call (SVC).

11.10   Exercises

1. Compare two methods of responding to external events: polling and interrupts. Discuss the advantages and disadvantages of each approach.

2. Give two example instructions that make an interrupt service routine exit.

3. The MSI (multi-speed internal) oscillator clock is selected as system clock source after startup from Reset, wakeup from Stop or Standby low power modes. The MSI clock has seven optional frequency ranges available: 100 KHz, 200 KHz, 400 KHz, 800 KHz, 1 MHz, 2 MHz, 4 MHz (default value), 8 MHz, 16 MHz, 24 MHz, 32 MHz, and 48 MHz. Write an assembly program that selects MSI 8 MHz as the system clock.

4. If the MSI 4.094 MHz clock is selected as the system clock and the SysTick selects it as the clock, what should the SysTick_LOAD register be to generate a SysTick interrupt every microsecond? What is the SysTick_LOAD value to produce a SysTick interrupt every millisecond?

5. Suppose software selects the default MSI (4 MHz) to drive the system timer (SysTick). Can you use this MSI to generate a SysTick interrupt every minute? If yes, show how do you set up the system timer registers. If not, give a solution to solve this problem.

6. Is it possible to use the SysTick Timer to generate an interrupt once every 12 seconds if there is only a clock of 2.097 MHz? If not, name two ways that you can solve this problem. If yes, how to set up the timer registers?

7. Suppose register i ($i \le 12$) is initialized to have a value of i (e.g. r0 = 0, r1= 1, r2 = 2, r3 = 3, etc.). Assume the main stack (MSP) is used. Also, in the interrupt handler, if LR = 0xFFFFFFF9, then the main stack (MSP) is used. If LR = 0xFFFFFFFD, then the process stack (PSP) is used. The program status register (PSR) = 0x00000020, PC = 0x08000020, and LR = 0x20008020, when the interrupt occurs.

   (1) Show the stack content immediately before the PUSH instruction runs. Suppose the stack pointer SP (*i.e.*, MSP in this case) was 0x20000600 immediately before the system timer interrupt occurs.

```
SysTick_Handler PROC
        PUSH {r4, r5, r6}
        ADD   r0, r0, #1
        ADD   r1, r1, #1
        ADD   r2, r2, #1
        ADD   r3, r3, #1
        ADD   r4, r4, #1
        ADD   r5, r5, #1
        ADD   r6, r6, #1
        ADD   r7, r7, #1
        ADD   r8, r8, #1
        ADD   r9, r9, #1
        ADD   r10, r10, #1
        ADD   r11, r11, #1
        ADD   r12, r12, #1
        POP   {r4, r5, r6}
        BX    LR
        ENDP
```

(2) What are the values of these registers (R0-R12, LR, SP, and PC) immediately after the interrupt exits?

8. Suppose the SysTick interrupt occurs when PC = 0x08000044, XPSR = 0x00000020, SP = 0x20000200, LR = 0x08001000, and register $R_i = i$, $i = 0, 1, 2, ..., 12$.

Memory Address	Instruction
	__main PROC
	...
0x08000044	MOV r3, #0
	...
	ENDP
	SysTick_Handler PROC
	EXPORT SysTick_Handler
0x0800001C	ADD r3, #1
0x0800001E	ADD r4, #1
0x08000020	BX lr
	ENDP

(1) Show the stack contents and the value of PC and SP when immediately entering the SysTick interrupt service routine.
(2) When executing the instruction "BX LR", how does the processor know whether it is exiting a standard subroutine or an interrupt service routine? What operations does the processor perform when a standard subroutine exits? What operations does the processor perform when an interrupt service routine exits?

Fixed-point and Floating-point Arithmetic

Let us review how real numbers work. In general, a real number can often be written in the following format:

$$\pm d_0.d_1 d_2 d_3 d_4 d_5 \cdots d_{n-1} \cdots \times b^e$$

where b is the base (or radix) and each d_i is a digit ($0 \le d_i < b$).

The decimal system, the most widely used number system in daily life, is based on powers of 10. Each digit represents a coefficient that multiplies the power of 10 represented by its position. For example,

$$654.321_{10} = 6 \times 10^2 + 5 \times 10^1 + 4 \times 10^0 + 3 \times 10^{-1} + 2 \times 10^{-2} + 1 \times 10^{-3}$$

All information is stored in the form of binary numbers in computers. A binary real number works in a similar way to a decimal real number.

$$101.011_2 = 1 \times 2^2 + 0 \times 2^1 + 1 \times 2^0 + 0 \times 2^{-1} + 1 \times 2^{-2} + 1 \times 2^{-3}$$

If we convert it to the decimal notation, we get

$$101.011_2 = 4 + 0 + 1 + 0 + 0.25 + 0.125 = 5.375$$

There are two common ways to represent an approximation of a real number: fixed-point format and floating-point format. It is an approximation because a finite number of digits cannot represent all real numbers. For example, the actual value of 1/3 is 0.333333..., which has an infinite number of digits.

As introduced previously, the fixed-point format has a fixed number of digits after the decimal point. In contrast, the floating-point format can have a various number of digits after the decimal point depending on the scale of the real number.

While fixed-point arithmetic has fixed resolution for a given representation range and simple math allowing easy and fast computation, floating-point arithmetic trades manufacturing cost and computation efficiency for better precision and a wider range of representation. The processor often includes a special component, called floating-point unit (FPU), to speed up floating-point processing.

In embedded systems, not all microcontrollers have FPU on the chip. In the absence of an FPU, fixed-point arithmetic is often preferred, because the software implementation of floating-point arithmetic is much more complex than the fixed-point arithmetic.

> *"There is no sense in being precise when you do not even know what you are talking about."*
>
> John von Neumann
> mathematician,
> computer scientist

Furthermore, if the dynamic range of an application's data set is small, the fixed-point format is preferred to improve the computational performance and accuracy. For example, video processing systems often use fixed-point arithmetic because pixel values have a fixed and regular format. On the contrary, audio systems often deploy floating-point arithmetic because the value of audio signals changes over a wide range.

While most desktops and servers use floating-point systems, the decision of using fixed-point or floating-point in an embedded system is sometimes difficult to make, as the cost of on-chip FPU has decreased sharply. For small applications running on limited computation capability or requiring long battery lifetime, fixed-point arithmetic is often preferred for simplified computation and improved energy efficiency. However, floating-point arithmetic can represent a wider dynamic range, and it is easier to develop a software program. The hardware has implemented complex floating-point functions, and the software can directly execute floating-point instructions supported by the hardware. Therefore, software programs do not need to worry about these functions.

12.1 Fixed-point Arithmetic

As its name suggests, a fixed-point number assumes there are a predefined number of binary bits to the right of the binary point. Assembly programs treat a fixed-point number as a normal integer and use integer arithmetic to handle these numbers. However, for programmers, there is a virtual decimal place at a fixed location of the binary representation. When two fixed-point numbers are added or subtracted, the bit strings can be treated as two integers and can be directly added or subtracted because their virtual decimal points are naturally aligned. However, when two fixed-point numbers are multiplied or divided, shift operations are required to fit the result into the same format as the operands.

12.1.1   Unsigned Fixed-point Representation

Unsigned fixed-point numbers often use the UQ$m.n$ notation, where m is the number of bits representing the integer portion, and n is the number of bits representing the fractional portion, as shown in Figure 12-1. When m is 0, the notation is simplified to UQn, such as UQ8.

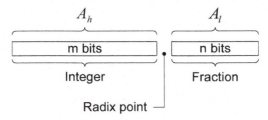

Figure 12-1. UQ$m.n$ representation of unsigned fixed-point numbers

In the UQ$m.n$ notation, the decimal value of an unsigned fixed-point number is calculated as follows:

$$f = A_h + A_l \times 2^{-n}$$

where A_h and A_l are the integer value of the integer portion and the fraction portion (h stands for high, l stands for low), respectively.

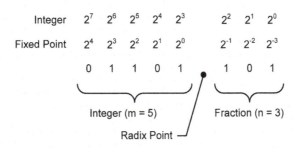

Figure 12-2. An example unsigned fixed-point number in UQ5.3 format.

In the example given in Figure 12-2, the integer portion $A_h = 01101_2 = 13$, and the fraction portion $A_l = 101_2 = 5$. Therefore, we have

$$01101.101_2 = A_h + A_l \times 2^{-3} = 13 + 5 \times 2^{-3} = 13.625$$

Suppose I_A and f are the integer value and the unsigned fixed-point value that a sequence of binary digits represents, respectively. Then we have

$$f = \frac{I_A}{2^n}$$

For example,

$$01101.101_2 = \frac{1\times2^6 + 1\times2^5 + 1\times2^3 + 1\times2^2 + 1\times2^0}{2^3} = \frac{109}{8} = 13.625$$

This concept is crucial because the computer usually implements fixed-point arithmetic by using integer operations. The key idea is that the computer processes these binary digits as if they were integers when in fact you, as the programmer, know that you are handling fixed-point numbers.

We can also use the radix or base to calculate the unsigned fixed-point value directly, as shown in the following example.

$$01101.101_2 = 1\times2^3 + 1\times2^2 + 1\times2^0 + 1\times2^{-1} + 1\times2^{-3} = 13.625$$

12.1.2   Signed Fixed-point Representation

Signed fixed-point numbers often use the $Qm.n$ notation. The total number of bits N is $m + n + 1$, with m bits for the integer portion, n bits utilized for the fractional portion, and 1 bit for the sign. In digital signal processing, m is often 0, such as Q0.7 and Q0.15 (simplified as Q7 and Q15).

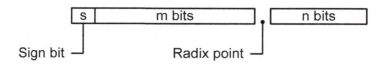

Figure 12-3. $Qm.n$ representation of fixed-point numbers ($m + n + 1$ bits totally)

Suppose binary digits $b_{N-1} \cdots b_2 b_1 b_0$ represent a signed fixed-point number in the $Qm.n$ format. The signed integer value that these binary digits represent in two's complement is

$$A = -1\times b_{N-1}\times2^{N-1} + \sum_{i=0}^{N-2}\left(b_i\times2^i\right)$$

where $N = m + n + 1$.

Then the signed fixed-point value is

$$f = \frac{A}{2^n}$$

> **Example**: Find the Q5.3 signed fixed-point value that 10010011 represents.
> $$10010.011_2 = \frac{-1\times2^7 + 1\times2^4 + 1\times2^1 + 1\times2^0}{2^3} = \frac{-109}{8} = -13.625$$

Like the unsigned fixed-point number, we often convert a signed fixed-point number f_A to an integer to facilitate the computation. In the above example, we have $I_A = 101010011_2 = -173$, because the binary integer is two's complement format.

12.1.3   Converting to Fixed-point Format

We can convert a real number to the fixed-point format $Qm.n$ or $UQm.n$ by multiplying it with 2^n and rounding the product towards nearest integer A.

In the signed fixed-point format $Qm.n$, the integer A is represented in two's complement.

$$A = round(f\times2^n)$$

> **Example 1**: Convert $f = 3.141593$ to unsigned fixed-point UQ4.12 format.
>
> (1) Calculate $f\times2^{12} = 12867.964928$
> (2) Round the result to an integer, $round(12867.964928) = 12868$
> (3) Convert the integer to binary: 12868 = 11_0010_0100_0100$_2$
> (4) Organize into UQ4.12: 0011.0010_0100_0100$_2$
> (5) Final result in Hex: 0x3244
> (6) Error: $\frac{12868}{2^{12}} - f = -8.5625\times10^{-6}$

> **Example 2**: Convert $f = -3.141593$ to signed fixed-point Q3.12 format.
>
> (1) Calculate $f\times2^{12} = -12867.964928$
> (2) Round the result to an integer, $round(-12867.964928) = -12868$
> (3) Convert the absolute value to binary: 12868 = 11_0010_0100_0100$_2$
>   Note that the integer is represented in two's complement.
> (4) Make the result into 16 bits: 0011_0010_0100_0100$_2$
> (5) Find the two's complement: 1100_1101_1011_1100$_2$
> (6) Final result in Hex: 0xCDBC
> (7) Error: $-\frac{12868}{2^{12}} - f = 8.5625\times10^{-6}$

It is interesting that the signed and unsigned fixed-point representation in the above two examples are two's complement to each other.

12.1.4   Fixed-point Range and Resolution Tradeoff

An unsigned fixed-point number UQ$m.n$ uses $m + n$ bits. For a signed fixed-point number Q$m.n$, an extra sign bit is used and thus a total of $m + n + 1$ bits are used. Since the total number of bits available is given, the fixed-point representation must play a tradeoff between the range and resolution, depending on the application's needs.

The *resolution* is defined as the smallest non-zero real number representable. It equals the gap between two consecutive numbers that are representable in fixed-point format. For UQ$m.n$ and Q$m.n$, the resolution of n is 2^{-n}. For example, the resolution of Q3.3 is 2^{-3} (*i.e.*, 0.125).

Note resolution differs from accuracy.

- *Accuracy* refers to the closeness of a numeric representation of a number to its true value. For example, when representing a real number, such as π, in UQ16.16, the error is the difference between the true value and the approximation in UQ16.16. Naturally, the maximum error is less than the resolution 2^{-n}.

- *Resolution* describes precision. It is the smallest change that is representable in the digital system. The precision or resolution does not measure how close a representation is from its true value; instead, it measures how close the values of different representations in the same format can be from each other.

We define the representable range as the maximal and minimal values that can be represented.

- *Range of unsigned fixed-point numbers*
  The range of unsigned integers represented by using $m + n$ bits is $[0, 2^{m+n} - 1]$. Therefore, the representable range of unsigned fixed-point numbers is $[0, 2^{m+n} - 1] \times 2^{-n}$, *i.e.*, $[0, 2^m - 2^{-n}]$.

- *Range of signed fixed-point numbers*
  The range of signed integers, represented in two's complement by using $m + n + 1$ bits, is $[-2^{m+n}, 2^{m+n} - 1]$. Therefore, the representable range of signed fixed-point numbers is $[-2^{m+n}, 2^{m+n} - 1] \times 2^{-n}$, *i.e.*, $[-2^m, 2^m - 2^{-n}]$.

Figure 12-4 and Figure 12-5 shows the range and resolution of UQ5 unsigned fixed-point numbers and Q4 signed fixed-point numbers, respectively.

The fixed-point representation plays a tradeoff between range and resolution. If n is too small, then we have a poor resolution, but a large representation range. On the other hand, if n is too large, then we have a good resolution, but a small representation range and high risk of overflow. For unsigned fixed-point numbers, we can choose to use

UQ16.16. However, if we need a larger range, we may use UQ20.12; if a higher resolution is needed, we may use UQ12.20.

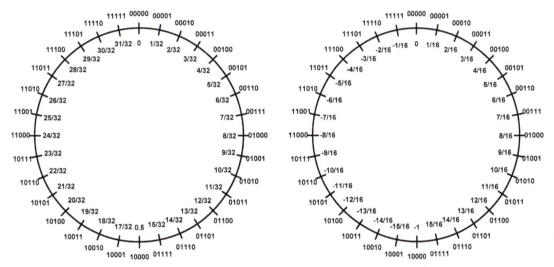

Figure 12-4. UQ5 unsigned fixed-point   Figure 12-5. Q4 signed fixed-point

If the dynamic range of application's data set does not fit in the representable range of a given Q$m.n$ format, we often use a predefined linear scaling and offsetting operation to transform the application's data set into the representation range. When the arithmetic operation completes, we perform a reverse scaling and shifting to recover the true data.

The linear scaling and offsetting are performed as follows. If the actual value of an application's data is V, and the represented approximation is $\tilde{V}$, then we have

$$\tilde{V} = V \times 2^{Scale} + offset$$

where $scale$ and $offset$ are two constants (can be positive or negative value) predefined by the application to ensure that $\tilde{V}$ falls in the available fixed-point range.

12.1.5   Fixed-point Addition and Subtraction

Suppose f_A, f_B and f_C are three unsigned fixed-point numbers in the UQ16.16 format, or three signed fixed-point numbers in the Q15.16 format. We define f_C as:

$$f_C = f_A + f_B$$

The following shows how to calculate f_C by using integer arithmetic.

If the radix point (or binary point) is ignored, the integer value that is represented by the bit string of f_A, f_B and f_C is I_A, I_B, and I_C, respectively. For signed fixed-point numbers, I_A, I_B and I_C may be negative because each bit string denotes an integer in two's complement.

The following equations show the conversion between f_A, f_B, f_C and I_A, I_B, I_C.

$$\begin{cases} I_A = f_A \times 2^{16} \\ I_B = f_B \times 2^{16} \\ I_C = f_C \times 2^{16} \end{cases} \Longleftrightarrow \begin{cases} f_A = I_A \times 2^{-16} \\ f_B = I_B \times 2^{-16} \\ f_C = I_C \times 2^{-16} \end{cases}$$

Thus, we can calculate the fixed-point addition $f_A + f_B$ as follows:

$$\begin{aligned} f_C &= f_A + f_B \\ &= I_A \times 2^{-16} + I_B \times 2^{-16} \\ &= (I_A + I_B) \times 2^{-16} \end{aligned}$$

Since

$$f_C = I_C \times 2^{-16}$$

Thus, we have the following equation:

$$I_C \times 2^{-16} = (I_A + I_B) \times 2^{-16}$$

We multiply 2^{16} on both sides of the above equation, and we have:

$$I_C = I_A + I_B$$

The above equation shows that f_C can be directly obtained by adding these two bit-strings that represent f_A and f_B. Adding two fixed-point numbers is performed in the same way as if these two bit-strings were representing two integers.

Similarly, for unsigned or signed fixed-point subtraction:

$$f_C = f_A - f_B$$

we have

$$I_C = I_A - I_B$$

Therefore, the binary result digits of fixed-point subtraction are the same as integer subtraction.

In sum, the addition and subtraction are simple. If bit strings represent fixed-point numbers, the program can treat them as integers during subtraction and addition. In other words, although they are fixed-point numbers, we can use integer "add" and "sub" instructions to calculate the addition and subtraction of two fixed-point numbers. The program tricks the processor into thinking adding or subtracting two integers while the program knows that fixed-point numbers are processed in fact.

```
; r0 = fixed-point number fa
; r1 = fixed-point number fb
; r2 = fixed-point number fc
  add   r2, r0, r1     ; fc = fa + fb
  sub   r2, r0, r1     ; fc = fa - fb
```

Example 12-1. Adding and subtracting two fixed-point numbers in UQ16.16 or Q15.16

12.1.6   Fixed-point Multiplication

This section shows how to calculate the fixed-point multiplication between f_A and f_B, i.e.

$$f_C = f_A \times f_B$$

where f_A, f_B and f_C are all unsigned fixed-point numbers in the UQ16.16 format or signed fixed-point numbers in the Q15.16 format. Mathematically, we have

$$
\begin{aligned}
f_C &= f_A \times f_B \\
&= (I_A \times 2^{-16}) \times (I_B \times 2^{-16}) \\
&= (I_A \times I_B) \times 2^{-32}
\end{aligned}
$$

We also know that

$$f_C = I_C \times 2^{-16}$$

Therefore, we get

$$I_C \times 2^{-16} = (I_A \times I_B) \times 2^{-32}$$

We can multiply 2^{16} on both sides of the above equation, and then we have

$$I_C = (I_A \times I_B) \times 2^{-16}$$

The above equation shows that we can treat fixed-point numbers f_A and f_B as integers first and calculate the product of these two integers. The result that we want is the middle 32 bits of the 64-bit product. Therefore, we need to shift the 64-bit product right by 16 bits, and the product is the least significant 32 bits of the shifted product.

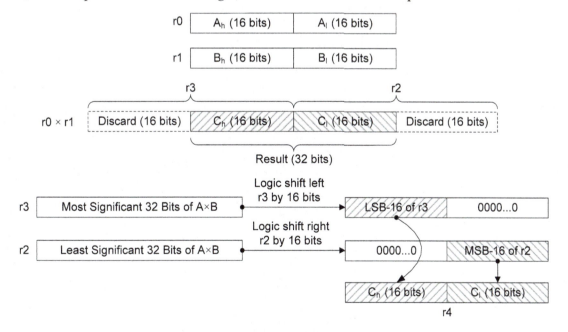

Figure 12-6. Multiplying two fixed-point numbers in UQ16.16 or Q15.16

Unsigned fixed-point format UQ16.16	Signed fixed-point format Q15.16

`; r0 = fixed-point number A`
`; r1 = fixed-point number B`
`; r4 = fixed-point product = A × B`
 	
`; Unsigned long multiply`
`; r2 = low word,  r3 = high word`
`UMULL  r2, r3, r0, r1`
 	
`; Shift left high word`
`LSLS   r3, r3, #16`
 	
`; Shift right low word`
`LSRS   r2, r2, #16`
 	
`; Pack two halfwords into a word`
`ORR    r4, r2, r3`
	`; r0 = fixed-point number A`
	`; r1 = fixed-point number B`
	`; r4 = fixed-point product = A × B`
	
	`; Signed long multiply`
	`; r2 = low word,  r3 = high word`
	`SMULL  r2, r3, r0, r1`
	
	`; Shift left high word`
	`LSLS   r3, r3, #16`
	
	`; Shift right low word`
	`LSRS   r2, r2, #16`
	
	`; Pack two halfwords into a word`
	`ORR    r4, r2, r3`

Example 12-2. Multiplying two fixed-point numbers in UQ16.16 or Q15.16

The multiplication should be unsigned for UQ16.16 and signed for Q15.16.

- Note that SMULL treats two source operands r0 and r1 as two's complement signed integers and produces a 64-bit product. If the exact product has 65 bits, we only keep the most significant 64 bits. SMULL places the least significant 32 bits of the 64-bit result into register r2 and the most significant 32 bits into register r3.
- For multiplying unsigned fixed-point numbers, we should use UMULL to multiply their corresponding integers.

12.1.7   Fixed-point Division

This section shows how to calculate the fixed-point division of f_A by f_B, i.e.

$$f_C = f_A \div f_B$$

where f_A, f_B and f_C are fixed-point numbers in UQ16.16 notation.

Mathematically we have,

$$\begin{aligned} f_C &= f_A \div f_B \\ &= (I_A \times 2^{-16}) \div (I_B \times 2^{-16}) \\ &= I_A \div I_B \end{aligned}$$

We also know that

$$f_C = I_C \times 2^{-16}$$

Therefore, we have

$$I_C = (I_A \div I_B) \times 2^{16} = (I_A \times 2^{16}) \div I_B$$

The above equation shows that we can treat fixed-point numbers f_A and f_B as integers first. Then we shift the dividend I_A left by 16 bits to make it a 64-bit number. After that, we divide this 64-bit number by the 32-bit divisor I_B. The 32-bit quotient is the result.

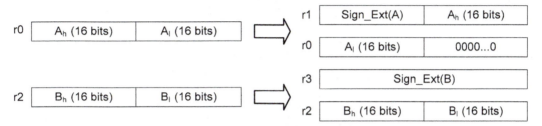

Figure 12-7. Dividing two fixed-point numbers in the format of UQ16.16 or Q15.16

```
; r0 = fixed-point number A
; r2 = fixed-point number B
; r4 = fixed-point quotient = A ÷ B

ASRS   r1, r0, #16        ; 16-bit sign in upper word
LSLS   r0, r0, #16        ; [r1:r0] stores sign extended A
ASRS   r3, r2, #31        ; [r3:r2] stores sign extended B
BL     division_64_bits   ; Take four input register (r0:r1, r3:r2)
MOV    r4, r0             ; division_64_bits places result in r0
```

Example 12-3. Dividing two fixed-point numbers in the format of UQ16.16 or Q15.16

ARM does not have any instructions that perform 64-bit integer division. Chapter 9.9 presents the implementation of 64-bit integer division.

12.2 Floating-point Arithmetic

The IEEE Standard for Floating-point Arithmetic (IEEE 754) is a *de facto* technical standard to store and operate real numbers in computers. It aims to provide portability across different platforms by defining a shared method of representing floating-point numbers and implementing floating-point operations. IEEE 754 has been widely supported by many processors with FPU and by many software libraries written for processors without FPU.

12.2.1   Floating-point Representation

The IEEE 754 standard uses a normalized notation, which includes three fields: the *sign* bit, the *fraction*, and the *true exponent*, as shown in Figure 12-7. We call it true exponent to differ from the biased exponent introduced later in this section.

The normalized notation implicitly assumes there is only one digit before the decimal point, and this digit must be 1. This bit is also called the *hidden bit* or the hidden 1 in IEEE 754.

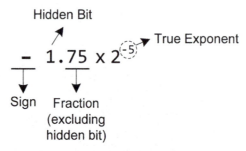

Figure 12-8. Normalized notation.

For example, the following numbers are not in normalized format: $10.746{\times}2^6$, $5.023{\times}2^3$, $-0.5{\times}2^{-7}$, and $0.05{\times}2^9$, because their integer part (all digits to the left of the decimal point) is not exactly 1. Additionally, $1.025{\times}10^3$ is not in the normalized format because the exponential part is based on 10, instead of 2.

We can convert $10.746{\times}2^6$ to the normalized format as follows:

$$10.746{\times}2^6 = \frac{10.746}{8}{\times}8{\times}2^6 = 1.34325{\times}2^9$$

Single-precision and double-precision, defined in IEEE 754, are two of the most commonly used formats. Half-precision is often used in digital signal processing applications. The half-precision, single-precision, and double-precision use 16, 32, and 64 bits to store a floating-point number, respectively. In C, the statement "float x" declares a single-precision variable, and "double y" declares a double-precision variable.

Half Precision (16 bits)

Single Precision (32 bits)

Double Precision (64 bits)

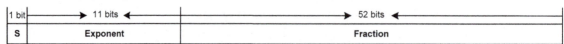

Figure 12-9. IEEE 754 single-precision and double-precision format

Compared with single precision, double precision has higher accuracy and can represent a much wider range of numbers. However, double-precision takes more memory space and bandwidth and is less computationally efficient. While most scientific applications running on desktops or servers use double precision, many embedded systems use single precision to reduce the hardware cost and improve the energy efficiency.

Each format has three fields. As shown in Figure 12-9, the *half-precision* has a sign bit, a 5-bit biased exponent, and a 10-bit fraction. The *single-precision* has a sign bit, an 8-bit biased exponent, and a 23-bit fraction. The *double-precision* has a sign bit, an 11-bit biased exponent, and a 52-bit fraction. The following discusses these three fields.

- The *sign bit* indicates whether the number is positive or negative. A value of 0 in the sign bit stands for a positive number, whereas a value of 1 denotes a negative number.
- The *biased exponent* is defined as the sum of the actual exponent and a bias constant. In other words, the true exponent equals the biased exponent minus the bias constant. The bias constant is 15 for half precision, 127 for single precision, and 1023 for double precision. For single precision, the actual exponent has a value falling between -127 and 128, and, therefore, the biased exponent is always non-negative, ranging from 0 to 255. You may wonder why the exponent field does not use two's complement of the true exponent, instead of the biased exponent. The key reason is that comparing two unsigned numbers can be executed much faster than comparing two signed numbers represented in two's complement. This can speed up floating point comparison.
- The *fraction* field consists of all bits to the right of the binary point. In the normalized format, as shown in Figure 12-7, the leading bit (the bit to the left of the decimal point) is always 1. This hidden bit is therefore not stored in the fraction field. When calculating the decimal value of a binary format, the hidden bit should be included. For example, if the fraction field is 0b0100101 in binary, the actual fraction is 1.0100101 in binary, which includes the fraction bits and the hidden leading bit with a value of 1.

We can calculate the floating-point number represented in IEEE 754 format by using the following formula (except a few special numbers discussed later):

$$f = (-1)^S \times (1 + Fraction) \times 2^{Exponent-Bias}$$

where

$$Bias = \begin{cases} 15, & \textit{Half Precision} \\ 127, & \textit{Single Precision} \\ 1023, & \textit{Double Precision} \end{cases}$$

The following gives two examples of converting floating-point numbers between different formats.

Example 1: Decoding `0xC1FF0000` into a floating-point number

We need to convert the hex value to a 32-bit binary bit string. These bits are divided into three groups: with bit 31 (the leftmost bit) being the sign bit, bits 30-23 (the next eight bits) being the exponent, and bits 22-0 (the rest) being the fraction.

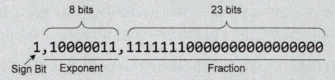

Figure 12-10. Partitioning bits of `0xC1FF0000` into three parts

1. The first step is to check the sign bit, which is the leading bit of the bit string. In this case, we have $S = 1$.

2. Convert the exponent `10000011` into a decimal integer.

$$10000011_2 = 131$$

3. Convert the fraction `11111110000000000000000` into a decimal real number.

$$
\begin{aligned}
0.1111111_2 &= 1 \times 2^{-1} + 1 \times 2^{-2} + 1 \times 2^{-3} + 1 \times 2^{-4} + 1 \times 2^{-5} + 1 \times 2^{-6} + 1 \times 2^{-7} \\
&= 0.5 + 0.25 + 0.125 + 0.0625 + 0.03125 + 0.015625 + 0.078125 \\
&= 0.9921875
\end{aligned}
$$

4. Calculate the represented real number as follows:

$$
\begin{aligned}
f &= (-1)^S \times (1 + Fraction) \times 2^{Exponent - 127} \\
&= (-1)^S \times (1 + 0.9921875) \times 2^{131 - 127} \\
&= -1 \times 1.9921875 \times 2^4 \\
&= -31.875
\end{aligned}
$$

Example 2: Encoding 14.5 into single-precision IEEE 754 format

The encoding involves the following five steps:
1. First, set up the sign bit. The sign bit S is cleared for a positive number and is set for a negative number. Therefore, $S = 1$ in this case.

2. Rewrite the floating number in the base-2 normalized format. Since 14.5 is larger than 2, we can repeatedly divide it by 2 until the quotient is smaller than 2 but greater than 1. Note, if the floating-point number to be converted is smaller than 1, we multiply it by 2, instead of dividing it by 2.

$$14.5 \div 2 = 7.25$$
$$7.25 \div 2 = 3.625$$
$$3.625 \div 2 = 1.8125$$

Therefore, we have

$$14.5 = 1.8125 \times 2^3$$
$$= (1 + 0.8125) \times 2^3$$

3. Calculate the exponent by adding the actual exponent and the bias. The bias is 127 for the single-precision.

$$Exponent = 3 + 127 = 130 = 1000010_2$$

4. Calculate the fraction by converting 0.8125 into binary. The conversion is achieved by repeatedly multiplying the fraction part (all digits to the right of the decimal point) of the product with 2 until the product becomes 1.

$$0.8125 \times 2 = 1.625 = 1 + 0.625$$

$$0.625 \times 2 = 1.25 = 1 + 0.25$$

$$0.25 \times 2 = 0.5 = 0 + 0.5$$

$$0.5 \times 2 = 1$$

Thus, the binary representation of 0.8125 is `0.1101`, which combines the leading digit of the products (the digit to the left of the decimal point) of the above multiplications. The following can help you understand why the above conversion process works.

$$0.8125 = \frac{1}{2} \times (1 + 0.625)$$

$$= \frac{1}{2} \times \left(1 + \frac{1}{2} \times (1 + 0.25)\right)$$

$$= \frac{1}{2} \times \left(1 + \frac{1}{2} \times \left(1 + \frac{1}{2} \times (0 + 0.5)\right)\right)$$

$$= \frac{1}{2} \times \left(1 + \frac{1}{2} \times \left(1 + \frac{1}{2} \times \left(0 + \frac{1}{2} \times 1\right)\right)\right)$$

$$= 1 \times \left(\frac{1}{2}\right)^{-1} + 1 \times \left(\frac{1}{2}\right)^{-2} + 0 \times \left(\frac{1}{2}\right)^{-3} + 1 \times \left(\frac{1}{2}\right)^{-4}$$

$$= 2^{-1} + 2^{-2} + 2^{-4}$$

$$= 0.1101_2$$

> Thus, the fraction is **11010000000000000000000**, which appends **0** to the result to make the length of the fraction bit string 23 bits.
>
> 5. The single-precision floating point format of 14.5 is
>   **01000001011010000000000000000000** in binary and **0x41680000** in hex.

12.2.2   Special Values

Figure 12-11 shows bit patterns representing special values including 0, $\pm\infty$, and NAN.

- We cannot represent zero in IEEE 754 format directly. Instead, we represent zero with a special pattern in which all bits of exponent and fraction are cleared. Because it is not required to clear the sign bit, there is a positive zero and negative zero, and hardware should treat them as equal.

- We denote the positive infinity and the negative infinity by a special pattern in which all exponent bits are one, and all fraction bits are zero.

- *NaN* (Not any Number) means that a floating-point arithmetic is invalid. We represent a NaN by any particular patterns in which all exponent bits are one, and the fraction is non-zero. For example, the following operations produce NaN: **0.0/0.0**, $-\infty + \infty$, $0 \times (\pm\infty)$, $\pm\infty/\pm\infty$, *sqrt*(**-1.0**), and *log*(**-10.0**). There are two types of NaN: *QNaN* (Quiet NaN) and *SNaN* (Signaling NaN). A *SNaN* generates a hardware exception signal to let the software handle the anomaly. A *QNaN* does not raise such a hardware signal.

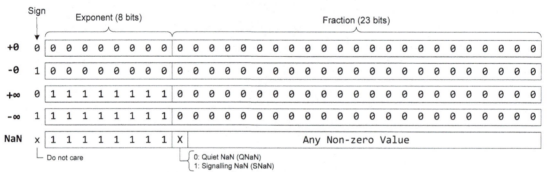

Figure 12-11. Special values in IEEE 754 single-precision

Floating operations normally use QNaN and let the NaN result propagate through most of all following arithmetic operations. For example, **0**×NaN = NaN, *sqrt*(NaN) = NaN, logic expressions "**0** < NaN", "**0** > NaN", and "**0** == NaN" are false, but "**0** != NaN" is true. Many processors, including ARM Cortex-M, are configurable so the same operation can produce either a *QNaN* or a *SNaN* to meet the application's need. In the default setting, *QNaN* is preferred over *SNaN*.

12.2.3   Overflow and Underflow

Now let us find the smallest and largest values that the single-precision format can represent.

- *Numbers closest to zero.* Since `0b00000000` is reserved in the exponent field, the minimal value of the exponent is `0b00000001`. The fraction can be as small as `0b000…00`. Thus, the numbers closest to zero are

$$(-1)^S \times (1 + 0) \times 2^{1-127} = \pm 2^{-126} \approx \pm 1.18 \times 10^{-38}$$

- *Numbers farthest from zero.* The maximum value of the exponent is `0b11111110` because `0b11111111` is reserved. The fraction can be as large as `0b111…111`. Thus, the biggest finite values are

$$(-1)^S \times (1 + (1 - 2^{-23})) \times 2^{254-127} = \pm(2^{128} - 2^{104}) \approx \pm 3.40 \times 10^{38}$$

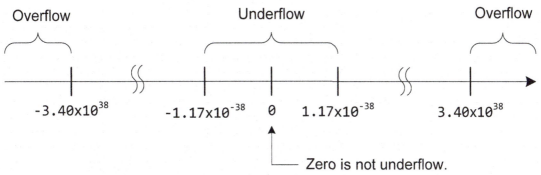

Figure 12-12. Representation range of IEEE 754 single-precision

Underflow and overflow can occur during computation.

- *Underflow.* If the exact result is non-zero and smaller than the smallest representable value, an *underflow* occurs, which may cause a loss of precision and create a significant computation error.
- *Overflow.* If the exact result is finite but exceeds the largest representable value, an *overflow* happens, which is another common cause of software failures.

When a processor detects an underflow or overflow, the hardware returns zero or the maximum number, respectively, and simultaneously generates an exception signal to provide an opportunity for the software to handle anomalies.

Overflow and underflow can cause strange and unexpected software failures that can be disastrous. On June 4, 1996, the Ariane 5 rocket veered off the designed course and destructed itself because an overflow occurred when assigning a floating-point number to an integer. That simple software failure caused an estimated loss of $370 million.

At the hardware level, overflow and underflow can be detected by checking whether the exponent of a floating-point arithmetic operation is too large or too small. The processor can generate a particular hardware signal upon overflow or underflow.

However, it is difficult for programmers to write software to handle the anomaly because the signal can be raised at any point in the program. For example, in the following simple C statement, if the subtraction causes an underflow, most processors automatically return zero as the result of the subtraction. Consequently, a divide-by-zero anomaly takes place, even though the *if*-statement aims to prevent it.

```
if (a != b)
    c = 1/(a - b);    // Divide-by-zero can still occur.
```

Example 12-4. An if-statement fails to prevent divide-by-zero error.

12.2.4   Subnormal Numbers

IEEE 754 standard also defines a subnormal format for a class of floating-point numbers filling between 0 and the minimum positive number that the normalized format can represent. Upon an underflow in the normalized presentation, the data can be "deformalized" to the subnormal format to trade the numeric range for accuracy. Formerly the subnormal format was called **denormal** format.

A bit string is a subnormal format if all bits of the exponent are zero, but at least one bit of the fraction is non-zero. Specifically, for single-precision, the decimal value it represents can be calculated as follows:

$$(-1)^S \times Fraction \times 2^{-126}$$

Note the subnormal format differs from the normalized format introduced previously in two major aspects:

1. The subnormal allows a leading zero in front of the decimal point in the fraction, while the normalized format assumes the fraction always has a leading hidden 1 to the left of the decimal point. Thus, when calculating the decimal values, the normalized format uses ($1 + Fraction$) while the subnormal uses $Fraction$ only.
2. All subnormal floating numbers have the same exponent, which is always 0.

The smallest positive number that the subnormal format in single-precision is

$$0,00000000,00000000000000000000001,$$

whose fraction value is 2^{-23}. Therefore, the smallest positive number is

$$2^{-23} \times 2^{-126} = 2^{-149} \approx 1.40 \times 10^{-45}$$

The largest positive number of single-precision subnormal format is

$$0,00000000,11111111111111111111111,$$

whose fraction value is $1 - 2^{-23}$.

Therefore, the largest positive subnormal number in the single-precision format is

$$(1 - 2^{-23}) \times 2^{-126} = 2^{-126} - 2^{-149}$$
$$\approx 1.175 \times 10^{-38}$$

12.2.5   Tradeoff between Numeric Range and Resolution

Compared with the fixed-point system, the floating-point system with the same number of bits can represent a larger numeric range at the cost of degraded resolution. Specifically, all floating-point numbers are not distributed uniformly across the represented range.

If the total number of bits is given, the fixed-point format must play a tradeoff between the representation range and the representation resolution. It has either a large range but inferior resolution, or a narrow range but superior resolution.

Let us consider a hypothetical floating-point system that is like the IEEE 754 standard. This system has only five bits: the sign bit, an exponent with two bits and a fraction with two bits. The bias for the normalized representation is 1. Therefore, the corresponding decimal value is as follows:

$$(-1)^S \times (1 + Fraction) \times 2^{Exponent-1}$$

For example, if the binary is 10110, its corresponding floating-point number is

$$(-1)^1 \times (1 + 0.10)_2 \times 2^{2-1} = -3/4$$

If the exponent is zero but the fraction is not zero, then it is in subnormal format, and its decimal value is

$$(-1)^S \times Fraction \times 2^0 = (-1)^S \times Fraction$$

For example, if the binary is 10010, the decimal is then

$$(-1)^1 \times (0.10)_2 = -1/2$$

We consider a fixed-point system in the format of Q3.2, with three bits set aside for the integer portion and two bits used for the fractional portion. The integer portion uses two's complement. For a fair comparison, we also require the fixed-point system uses the same bit patterns to denote special values, including $\pm\infty$, QNaN, and SNaN.

Table 12-1 lists the values represented by all possible bit strings in both fixed-point Q3.2 and 5-bit floating-point systems.

Binary	Floating-point	Notation for floating-point	Fixed-point
00000	0.0	Reserved	0.0
00001	¼	$(0.01)_2$	¼
00010	½	$(0.10)_2$	½
00011	¾	$(0.11)_2$	¾
00100	1.0	$(1+0.00)_2 \times 2^{1-1}$	1.0
00101	1¼	$(1+0.01)_2 \times 2^{1-1}$	1¼
00110	1½	$(1+0.10)_2 \times 2^{1-1}$	1½
00111	1¾	$(1+0.11)_2 \times 2^{1-1}$	1¾
01000	2.0	$(1+0.00)_2 \times 2^{2-1}$	2.0
01001	2½	$(1+0.01)_2 \times 2^{2-1}$	2¼
01010	3.0	$(1+0.10)_2 \times 2^{2-1}$	2½
01011	3½	$(1+0.11)_2 \times 2^{2-1}$	2¾
01100	+∞	Reserved	+∞
01101	QNaN	Reserved	QNaN
01110	SNaN	Reserved	SNaN
01111	SNaN	Reserved	SNaN
10000	-0.0	Reserved	-0.0
10001	-¼	$-(0.01)_2$	-¼
10010	-½	$-(0.10)_2$	-½
10011	-¾	$-(0.11)_2$	-¾
10100	-1.0	$-(1+0.00)_2 \times 2^{1-1}$	-1.0
10101	-1¼	$-(1+0.01)_2 \times 2^{1-1}$	-1¼
10110	-1½	$-(1+0.10)_2 \times 2^{1-1}$	-1½
10111	-1¾	$-(1+0.11)_2 \times 2^{1-1}$	-1¾
11000	-2.0	$-(1+0.00)_2 \times 2^{2-1}$	-2.0
11001	-2½	$-(1+0.01)_2 \times 2^{2-1}$	-2¼
11010	-3.0	$-(1+0.10)_2 \times 2^{2-1}$	-2½
11011	-3½	$-(1+0.11)_2 \times 2^{2-1}$	-2¾
11100	-∞	Reserved	-∞
11101	QNaN	Reserved	QNaN
11110	SNaN	Reserved	SNaN
11111	SNaN	Reserved	SNaN

Table 12-1. Resolution and range comparison of floating-point and fixed-point numbers

Figure 12-13 plots the representable floating-point and fixed-point numbers listed in the above table on the same axis.

1. The fixed-point system has a smaller range of representable real numbers than the floating-point system.

2. The fixed-point system uniformly distributes representable numbers across the representable range, with same gaps between any two consecutive numbers. Thus, its resolution remains fixed. The resolution means the closeness of two consecutive numbers. However, the difference between two consecutive floating-point numbers becomes larger as the exponent increases. Accordingly, the resolution of the floating-point system degrades gradually as the absolute value increases. When we consider subnormal numbers, the resolution of the floating-point system becomes reasonable.

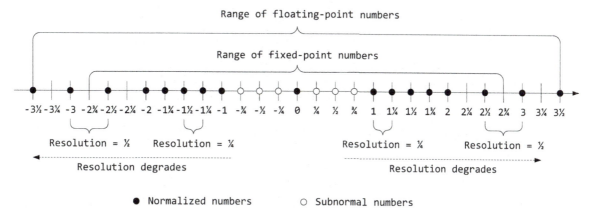

Figure 12-13. Comparing a floating-point and a fixed-point system with 5 bits. In the floating-point system, resolution degrades as the exponent increases. This is because the gap between two consecutive floating numbers increases. In this 5-bit example, overflow occurs if the absolute value is non-infinity but larger than 3 ½. Underflow takes place if the absolute value is non-zero but smaller than ¼.

12.2.6   Rounding Rules

A finite number of binary digits cannot represent all real numbers without any error. Therefore, we must find an approximate of each un-representable real number. The process of finding a representable approximation is called *rounding*.

IEEE 754 defines four different rounding rules:

- Round to the nearest value,
- Round toward zero (truncation),
- Round toward $+\infty$ (round-up), and
- Round toward $-\infty$ (round-down).

When a number is rounded to the nearest and the number is exactly halfway between its two nearest numbers, we break the tie by choosing the one whose least significant bit in the fraction field is zero.

We use decimal numbers to illustrate the four rounding rules. To simplify the presentation, we assume only 5 digits are allowed after the decimal point, and Table 12-2 gives the rounded result of four rounding modes.

Rounding Rule	Data	Rounded Result
Nearest	+0.123456	+0.12346
	-0.123456	-0.12346
Truncate	+0.123456	+0.12345
	-0.123456	-0.12345
Rounding up	+0.123456	+0.12346
	-0.123456	-0.12345
Rounding down	+0.123456	+0.12345
	-0.123456	-0.12346

Table 12-2. Four different rounding rules

Rounding to the nearest is often the default rounding rule. The other three rounding rules are statistically biased.

- For example, when we repeatedly add a set of randomly generated numbers, the rounded sums are statistically smaller than the true sums if rounded down, and are statistically larger if rounded up.
- For a set of negative numbers, the sums are statistically larger than the exact sum if truncated.

Rounding to the nearest is unbiased statistically. Its error is symmetrical and has an equal chance of being positive and negative. It uses both truncate and round up.

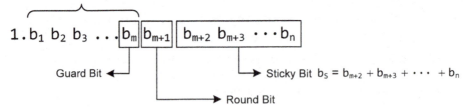

Figure 12-14. A binary number that is rounded to *m* bits after the point

Table 12-3 gives the algorithm of "rounding to nearest." It keeps *m* bits to the right of the point, as shown in Figure 12-14. It checks three bits:

1. the guard bit b_m
2. the round bit b_{m+1}
3. the sticky bit b_s, which is the bitwise logical OR of all bits to the right of the round bit.

1. Calculate sticky bit $b_s = b_{m+2} + b_{m+3} + \dots + b_n$
2. If round bit $b_{m+1} = 0$, directly truncate and remove bits $b_{m+1}b_{m+2}b_{m+2}\cdots b_n$
3. If round bit $b_{m+1} = 1$ and sticky bit $b_s = 1$, round up
4. If round bit $b_{m+1} = 1$ and sticky bit $b_s = 0$, round to even
   - If guard bit $b_m = 0$, directly truncate and remove $b_{m+1}b_{m+2}b_{m+2}\cdots b_n$
   - If guard bit $b_m = 1$, round up

Table 12-3. Algorithm of rounding to nearest with ties rounding to even

As shown in Table 12-3, there are three different scenarios when a number is rounded to the nearest. In the last scenario, when the round bit b_{m+1} is 1 and the sticky bit b_s is 0, this is a tie. The value has an equal distance to two nearest neighbor numbers. The tie is broken by using the "round to even" rule, *i.e.*, choose the one that has 0 as its guard bit.

Table 12-4 gives a few examples to illustrate the above nearest rounding algorithm. Suppose we want to keep two binary digits after the binary point (*i.e.*, $m = 2$).

Binary Real Number	Round bit b_{m+1}	Sticky Bit b_s	Rounded Result	Round to Nearest Method
0.000001	0	Do not care	0.00	Truncate
0.000011	0	Do not care	0.00	Truncate
0.000101	0	Do not care	0.00	Truncate
0.000111	0	Do not care	0.00	Truncate
0.011000	1	0	0.10	Round to Even (Round up)
0.001000	1	0	0.00	Round to Even (Truncate)
0.001011	1	1	0.01	Round up
0.001101	1	1	0.01	Round up
0.001111	1	1	0.01	Round up

Table 12-4. Examples of rounding to nearest ($m = 2$)

Tiebreaker: Round to Even

We use 0.011000 as an example to illustrate the "round to even" rule for breaking the tie. It has two nearest values, 0.01 and 0.10. It is precisely halfway between these two nearest values. We use round-to-even to break the tie, *i.e.*, we select the closest value as the one in which the trailing bit is zero.

Specifically, the round bit is 1, and the sticky bit is 0. Thus, we should use the round to even method, *i.e.*, the step 4 of the rounding algorithm listed in Table 12-3. Because the guard bit is 1, we select the round-up method, and the result is 0.10.

Similarly, when 0.001000 is rounded to the nearest, it uses truncate to break the tie.

12.3 Software-based Floating-point Operations

A floating-point unit (FPU) is a coprocessor that carries out floating-point arithmetic operations. FPU is not available on Cortex-M3/M0, but it is optional on Cortex-M4/M7.

Let us compare the assembly implementation of floating point multiplication on Cortex-M processors with and without FPU. The following is a simple C function that calculates the area of a rectangle.

```
float area_of_rectangle(float length, float width) {
    float area;
    area = length * width;
    return area;
}
```

Example 12-5 shows the assembly implementation of the above C function.

- Without any FPU coprocessor, the compiler makes the program call the software floating point library to perform multiplication. The library uses integer-based instructions to implement floating-point multiplication.

- If FPU is available, multiplication can be carried out by simply calling the assembly instruction VMUL.F32. Note s0 and s1 are two registers of the FPU coprocessor, and they are different from r0 and r1 of the processor core.

Chapter 12.4 gives detailed information about FPU programming. This section focuses on software-based floating-point operations.

Software-based Multiplication	Hardware-based Multiplication
; Inputs: ; r0 = length ; r1 = width ; Return: ; r0 = area	; Inputs: ; s0 = length ; s1 = width ; Return: ; s0 = area

area_of_rectangle PROC
    ; area = length * width
 	
    ; call software library
    BL __aeabi_fmul
 	
    BX lr   ; return area in r0
    ENDP
	area_of_rectangle PROC
	    ; area = length * width
	
	    ; Call FPU instructions
	    VMUL.F32 s0, s0, s1
	
	    BX lr ; return area in s0
	    ENDP

Example 12-5. Comparison of software- and hardware-based floating-point multiplication

12.3.1   Floating-point Addition

Assume two floating numbers have the same sign:

$$f_1 = (-1)^S \times (1 + F_1) \times 2^{E1}$$

and

$$f_2 = (-1)^S \times (1 + F_2) \times 2^{E2}$$

Without loss of generality, we also assume $E1 \geq E2$. Then mathematically, the addition is performed as follows:

$$
\begin{aligned}
f_1 + f_2 &= (-1)^S \times (1 + F_1) \times 2^{E1} + (-1)^S \times (1 + F_2) \times 2^{E2} \\
&= (-1)^S \times \left((1 + F_1) + (1 + F_2) \times 2^{E2-E1} \right) \times 2^{E1} \\
&= (-1)^S \times \left((1 + F_1) + \frac{1 + F_2}{2^{E1-E2}} \right) \times 2^{E1}
\end{aligned}
$$

We can implement the division operation in the above equation by using shift operations.

When the sign of two floating-point numbers differs, the adjusted fraction parts are subtracted, instead of added.

As shown in Figure 12-15, the core procedure of adding two floating-point numbers involves the following steps:

(1) shift the smaller fraction to match the larger one,
(2) add or subtract the fraction based on its sign bits,
(3) normalize the sum,
(4) round the sum to appropriate bits, and
(5) detect overflow and underflow.

The following illustrates the above algorithm by using a simple example. Suppose we are adding x and y, where

$$x = (1.1011011101)_2 \times 2^4$$

and

$$y = (1.1110101111)_2 \times 2^5$$

First, because the exponent of y is larger than x, we shift the fraction of x right by one bit to make the exponent match the larger one. Note we should not shift left the fraction of the operand with a larger exponent to match the lower exponent. The reason is that we may create a significant computational error if a larger operand causes an overflow when it is shifted.

$$x = (0.11011011101)_2 \times 2^5$$

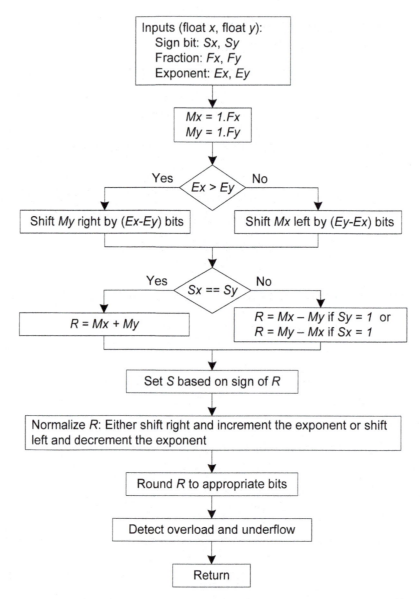

Figure 12-15. Flowchart of adding two floating numbers

Then we perform a simple addition. We do not need to worry about the alignment of the decimal points because both fraction bit strings have the same length.

```
    x =      0 . 1 1 0 1 1 0 1 1 1 0 1
    y =      1 . 1 1 1 0 1 0 1 1 1 1 0
x + y = 1 0 . 1 1 0 0 0 1 1 1 0 1 1
```

Thus, we get the sum:

$$x + y = (10.11000111011)_2 \times 2^5$$

The next step is to normalize the sum. In this case, we should shift the sum right by one bit because the integer part of the fraction of the sum has two bits. If the fraction of the sum has many leading zeros, including the integer part, then we should shift the fraction of sum left and reduce the exponent accordingly. The following is the sum after normalization.

$$x + y = (1.011000111011)_2 \times 2^6$$

During the normalization, the hardware can detect overflow or underflow by checking whether the result falls out of the representable data range.

While the implementation is complex because it needs to consider special inputs, such as $\pm\infty$ and NaN, the following shows a simplified implementation that ignore special inputs and does not detect overflow and underflow.

```
; Adding two floating-point numbers
; Input:  r0 = first operand, r1 = second operand
; Output: r0 = sum
;
; For each register,
;     bits[31] = sign (1 bit)
;     bits[30-23] = exponent (8 bits)
;     bits[22:0] = fraction (23 bits)

fadd PROC
    ; If inputs have different signs, flip the sign bit of the second operand
    ; and call the subtraction function.
    TEQ     r0, r1                  ; If r0 and r1 have the same sign, then N = 0
                                    ; Otherwise N = 1
    EORMI   r1, r1, #0x80000000     ; If N = 1, flip sign bit of second operand
    BMI     fsub                    ; call subtraction, return r0 - (-r1)


    ; r0 and r1 are guaranteed to have the same sign
    ; If r0 < r1 (unsigned comparison), swap them
    SUBS    r2, r0, r1              ; r2 = r0 - r1
    SUBSCC  r0, r0, r2              ; if r0 < r1, swap r0 and r1
    ADDSCC  r1, r1, r2              ; Guarantee r0 > r1


    ; Find the difference of exponents
    ; Now it has guaranteed that r0 > r1 (unsigned comparison)
    ; r3[8:0] = [sign:exponent] of r0 - [sign:exponent] of r1
    LSR     r2, r0, #23             ; r2[8:0] = [sign:exponent] of r0
    SUB     r3, r2, r1, LSR #23     ; r3 = difference of exponents


    ; Shift right the fraction of the smaller operand (r1) to make
    ; their exponents match and then add the fractions
    MOV     r12, #0x80000000        ; Set the leading hidden 1
```

```
ORR     r0, r12, r0, LSL #8   ; r0 = 1:fraction:0000,0000
ORR     r1, r12, r1, LSL #8   ; r1 = 1:fraction:0000,0000
LSR     r12, r1, r3           ; r12 = r1 >> difference between exponents
ADDS    r12, r0, r12          ; r12 = sum of both fractions
BCS     fraction_too_large    ; If fraction sum is 11.xxxx or 10.xxxx, skip

; Pact final result into r0
; The actual value of the fraction sum is 1.xxxxx
LSRS    r0, r12, #8           ; r0[22:0] = first 23 bits of fraction of sum
                              ; Guard bit is shifted into carry
ADC     r0, r0, r2, LSL #23   ; r0[31:23] = [sign:exponent] of sum,
                              ; also add guard bit into r0
BXCC    lr                    ; if guard bit is 0, return truncated result

fraction_too_large
; The actual value of the fraction sum is 11.xxxxx or 10.xxxxx
RRX     r0, r12, r1           ; Shift carry back into r0

; If guard bit is 1, perform rounding to even or round up
; and pack final result into r0
RSB     r3, r3, #32           ; r3 = 32 - r3, r3 = diff of exponents
LSLS    r1, r1, r3            ; r1 = all sticky bits
BICEQ   r0, r0, #1            ; Clear the round bit if all sticky bits
                              ; are zero (round to even)
LSRS    r0, r0, #8            ; r0[22:0] = first 23 bits of fraction of sum
                              ; Guard bit is shifted into carry
ADC     r0, r0, r2, LSL #23   ; r0[31:23] = [sign:exponent] of sum
                              ; also add guard bit into r0
BX      lr                    ; return
ENDP
```

Example 12-6. Simplified implementation of adding two floating-point numbers

The sum of adding two aligned fraction parts (including their leading hidden 1 bit) can have three possible results, 1.xxxxx, 10.xxxxx, or 11.xxxxx. When the integer part has two bits (10.xxxxx or 11.xxxxx), we need to shift the leading bit back to the fraction of the sum by running the instruction "RRX r0, r12, #1".

Furthermore, when the statement "ADC r0,r0,r2,LSL #23" packs the result into the single-precision format, the leading bit of the fraction sum is added to the exponent part because the leading bit is removed from the fraction sum before the packing operation. Therefore, if the fraction sum is 10.xxxxx or 11.xxxxx, then the "ADC" instruction automatically increases the exponent of the result by 1.

As the standard suggests, the default rounding should be the nearest rounding. When packing the results, "ADC" instead of "ADD" is used. The carry bit is added to the fractional part of the result to achieve the nearest rounding. In fact, the carry bit holds the guard bit. If the guard bit is 0, extra bits are truncated by the "LSRS r0, r0, #8" instruction. If all sticky bits are 0, then the round bit (the least significant bit of the fraction sum) is set to zero. If the sticky bits are not all zero, the guard bit is 1 and is added to the result.

12.3.2   Floating-point Multiplication

Suppose we multiply the following two floating-point numbers:

$$f_1 = (-1)^{S1} \times (1 + F_1) \times 2^{E1}$$
$$f_2 = (-1)^{S2} \times (1 + F_2) \times 2^{E2}$$

Mathematically, the product of two floating-point numbers

$$f_1 \times f_2 = ((-1)^{S1} \times (1 + F_1) \times 2^{E1}) \times ((-1)^{S1} \times (1 + F_1) \times 2^{E1})$$
$$= (-1)^{S1+S2} \times (1 + F_1) \times (1 + F_2) \times 2^{E1+E2}$$

As the above equation indicates, the multiplication involves the following four steps: (1) identify the sign of the product, (2) add the exponents together, (3) multiply the fractions, including the leading hidden one, and (4) normalize the result to the standard format.

The following gives a simplified implementation of multiplying two single-precision floating point numbers. The program does not handle special cases, such as overflow, underflow, and input of infinity and NaN.

The trick is to manage the multiplication of two fractions. Two fractions include their hidden leading 1. When a program multiplies two fractions of the same length, *i.e.*,

                    1.xx...x × 1.yy...y

where x and y are either 1 or 0, their product must be truncated to the same length. Suppose each fraction has n bits, their product has either $2n$ or $2n - 1$ bits because the leading bit of both fractions is 1.

We can use $n = 2$ as a simple example. In binary, we have three different scenarios:

                    1.1 × 1.1 = 10.11
                    1.1 × 1.0 = 01.10
                    1.0 × 1.0 = 01.10

In other words, the most significant two bits of the product of 1.xx...x and 1.yy...y can only be either 10 or 01.

- If the most significant bits are 01, we need to remove the leading zero bit.
- If the most significant bits are 10, we need to renormalize the result by shifting the fraction product right by one bit and then increasing the exponent by 1.

```
; Function of multiplying two single-precision floating-point numbers
; Input: r0 = first operand, r1 = second operand
; Output: r0 = product
; For each register,
;     bits[31] = sign (1 bit)
;     bits[30-23] = exponent (8 bits)
;     bits[22:0] = fraction (23 bits)

fmul PROC
  ; Add two exponents
  MOV   r12, #0x000000FF        ; mask
  ANDS  r2, r12, r0, LSR #23    ; r2[7:0] = exponent of r0
  ANDS  r3, r12, r1, LSR #23    ; r3[7:0] = exponent of r1
  ADD   r2, r2,r3               ; r2[7:0] = sum of both exponents

  ; If operands have different signs, set the product as negative
  TEQ   r0, r1                  ; check whether r0 and r1 have different signs
  ORRMI r2, r2, #0x100          ; i.e., check r2[8] = 1

  ; Multiply fractions
  MOV   r12, #0x80000000        ; Mask for leading hidden 1
  ORR   r0, r12, r0, LSL #8     ; r0 = 1:Fraction:00000000 (binary)
  ORR   r1, r12, r1, LSL #8     ; r1 = 1:Fraction:00000000 (binary)
  UMULL r1, r3, r0, r1          ; r1:r3 = 64-bit product of both fractions

  ; Perform rounding up and discard lower 32 bits of the fraction product
  CMP   r1, #0                  ; Are tailing 32 bits of the product
                               ; of two fractions are zero?
  ORRNE r3, r3, #1             ; if r1 ~= 0, round up, set r3[0] = 1

  ; Remove leading zero bit of fraction product
  ; Note there is at most one leading zero bit in the product
  LSLS  r3, r3, #1             ; r3 << 1, shift out leading bit
  RRXCS r3, r3, #1             ; If the leading bit was 1, recover it

  ; Pack final result into r0
  LSRS  r12, r3, #8           ; r12 = 0000,0000:24-bit fraction (binary)
                             ; Guard bit is shifted into carry
  ADC   r0, r12, r2, LSL #23  ; Pack result into r0
                             ; r2[8:0] = [sign:exponent] of product
                             ; Guard bit (carry bit) is added to fraction
  BXCC  lr                    ; If the guard bit is 0, return
  LSL   r12, r3, #24          ; r12 = [guard bit : all sticky bits]
  CMP   r12, #0x80000000      ; if guard bit is zero and sticky bits are
                             ; zero, clear the last bit of fraction
  BICEQ r0, r0, #1           ; round to even by setting r0[0] = 0;
  BX    lr                   ; return

  ENDP
```

Example 12-7. Simplified implementation of multiplying two floating-point numbers

12.4 Hardware-based Floating-point Operations

Cortex-M4 and Cortex-M7 can optionally have a floating-point Unit (FPU) coprocessor. An FPU coprocessor has its own data and control registers, and it supports single-precision arithmetic, accessing memory data, integer and precision conversion, and some double-precision arithmetic. This section introduces how to program FPU and handle exceptions in assembly.

12.4.1   FPU Registers

The FPU consists of 32 single-word general-purpose registers (S0, S2, …, S31) and four special-purpose registers (CPACR, FPCCR, FPCAR, and FPSCR), as shown in Figure 12-16.

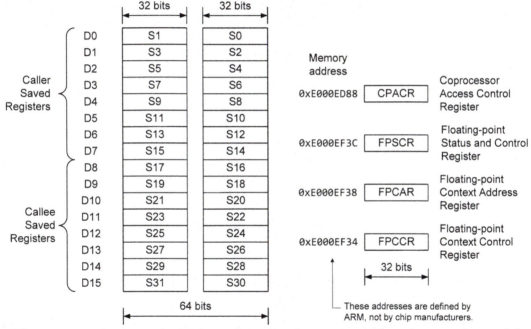

Figure 12-16. Floating-point registers (32 general-purpose 32-bit registers and 4 special registers). The processor remaps two 32-bit general-purpose registers to a 64-bit register. For example, S1 and S0 are remapped to D0. D0 uses the same hardware resources as S1 and S0. The callee subroutine must preserve registers D8-D15 or S16-S31 if it writes to them.

12.4.1.1 Floating-point General-purpose Registers (S0-S31, or D0-D15)

Each general-purpose floating-point register (S0, S2, …, S31) can hold one single-precision floating number. The prefix "S" stands for single-precision.

These 32 general-purpose floating-point registers can be mapped into 16 double-word registers (D0, D1, …, D15) for holding double-precision floating point numbers. The prefix

"D" stands for double-precision. For example, a double-precision register D0 consists of single-precision registers S1 and S0, with S1 holding the most significant word of D0, and S0 holding the least significant word of D0.

When a subroutine takes single- or double-precision floating point numbers as input arguments, registers S0-S15 or D0-D7 hold these input arguments.

- If the subroutine takes only single-precision numbers as input arguments, up to 16 arguments can be passed via registers. These arguments come in via registers S0-S15 in a sequential order. If more than 16 arguments are passed, the caller must push all additional arguments onto the stack.

- If only double-precision numbers are passed, up to 8 arguments can be passed via registers D1-D7. Extra arguments, if needed, should be passed via the stack.

- If a mixed of single-precision and double-precision numbers are passed, each number is assigned in turn to the next free register of the corresponding type.

Figure 12-17 shows an example that passes a mixed of float and double variables to a subroutine.

```
double fun(double a1, float a2, double a3, float a4, float a5, double a6, float a7, double a8)
```

64 bits

Double-precision View	D0		D1		D2		D3		D4		D5		D6		D7	
Single-precision View	S0	S1	S2	S3	S4	S5	S6	S7	S8	S9	S10	S11	S12	S13	S14	S15
Argument View	a1		a2	a4	a3		a5	a7	a6		a8					

Figure 12-17. Passing arguments to a subroutine via floating-point registers

If a subroutine returns a floating-point number, the return value is saved in register S0 for single-precision or D0 for double-precision. For other data types, such integers, the return value is in register r0-r4 (in Chapter 8).

When a subroutine takes as an input argument a pointer that points a single- or double-precision floating-point value, the pointer is not a floating-point value but a memory address, and thus it is passed via an integer register, instead of a floating-point register.

Example: passing float/double array pointers

```
float * fun(float * array1, double * array2, int array_size)
```

The variable array1 and array2 are array pointers, and they are passed via register r0 and r1, respectively. The array_size is passed in register r2. Additionally, this function returns a float pointer, which is saved in register r0.

12.4.1.2 Coprocessor Access Control Register (CPACR)

Cortex-M has two coprocessors: CP10 and CP11. They are vector floating point (VFP) coprocessors and carry out floating point arithmetic operations.

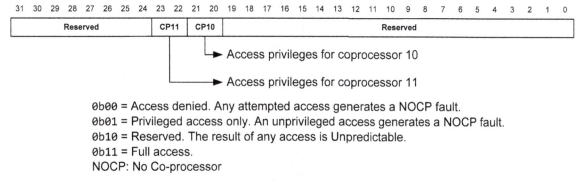

0b00 = Access denied. Any attempted access generates a NOCP fault.
0b01 = Privileged access only. An unprivileged access generates a NOCP fault.
0b10 = Reserved. The result of any access is Unpredictable.
0b11 = Full access.
NOCP: No Co-processor

Figure 12-18. Coprocessor Access Control Register (CPACR)

FPU is disabled by default. To use FPU, software must enable CP10 and CP11. The program should use the data synchronization barrier (DSB) to ensure the completion of all memory accesses. The instruction synchronization barrier (ISB) should also be used to flush the processor pipeline and ensure that all instructions are fetched from cache or memory again.

C Program	Assembly Program
| ```c
void FPU_Enable(void) {

  // Enable CP10 and CP11
  SCB->CPACR |= (0xF << 20);

  // Ensure the completion of
  // memory accesses
  __DSB();

  // Flush the processor pipeline
  // fetch buffers
  __ISB();

  return;
}
``` | ```
FPU_Enable PROC
    EXPORT FPU_Enable
    ; Load SCB base address (0xE000ED00)
    LDR r0, = SCB_BASE

    ; Read from SCB->CPACR
    LDR r1, [r0, #SCB_CPACR]

    ; Enable full access to CP10 and CP11
    ORR r1, r1, #(0xF << 20)

    ; Write to SCB->CPACR
    STR r1, [r0, #SCB_CPACR];

    DSB     ; Data Synchronization Barrier
    ISB     ; Instruction Syn. Barrier
    BX LR   ; Return
    ENDP
``` |

Example 12-8. Enabling VFP coprocessors

Similarly, to disable FPU, software must clear the enable bits of coprocessors 10 and 11 used by FPU: "SCB->CPACR &= ~(0xF << 20);".

Additionally, the processor must be in the privileged mode to enable or disable FPU. FPU must be enabled before any floating-point instruction is executed; otherwise, the processor generates a NOCP (No Coprocessor) usage fault. In most template projects provided in ARM Keil, we can enable FPU in the start-up assembly file (such as *startup_stm32f407xx.s*) before the instruction "BL __main". Chapter 23.1 introduces the processor modes.

12.4.1.3 Floating-point Status and Control Register (FPSCR)

The FPSCR register stores the FPU configuration, the condition flags and the exception flags. We only use VMRS to read FPSCR and VMSR to write to it.

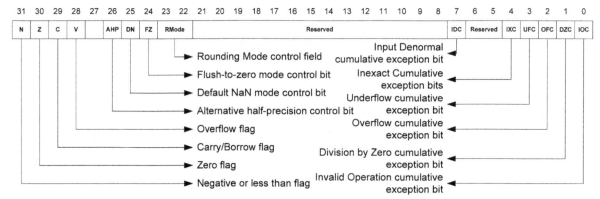

Figure 12-19. Floating-Point Status and Control Register (FPSCR)

N, Z, C, V Flags. The FPSCR register has the negative (N), zero (Z), carry (C), and overflow (V) flag bits. These bits are set by the single-precision comparison instructions VCMP.F32 and VCMPE.F32 (to be introduced later in this chapter).

The processor cannot directly use these flags to perform the conditional execution. Software program must use the VMRS instruction to transfer these flags to the processor's APSR for conditional execution, as shown below.

```
VMRS r4, FPSCR          ; Copy FPSCR to register r4
VMSR APSR_NZCV, FPSCR   ; Copy N, Z, C, V flags from FPSCR to APSR
```

APSR_nzcv includes a bit specifier to specify the APSR bits to be updated. The following gives a few examples of the bit specifier.

- APSR_NZCV is to access the N, Z, C, V bits in APSR.
- APSR_G is to access the GE[3:0] bits in APSR.
- APSR_NZCVQ is to access the N, Z, C, V, Q bits in APSR.
- APSR_NZCVQG is to access the N, Z, C, V, Q, GE[3:0] bits in APSR.

Rounding Modes. FPU carries out floating-point arithmetic with extra precision, and then rounds the result to fit into the destination precision. This internal extra precision ensures arithmetic results are as precise as the source operands. FPU supports four rounding modes, determined by two RMode control bits in FPSCR (*i.e.,* FPSCR[23:22]), as described below.

- 00: Round to nearest mode (default)
- 01: Round towards $+\infty$ mode
- 10: Round towards $-\infty$ mode
- 11: Round towards 0 mode

```
FPU->FPDSCR &= ~FPU_FPDSCR_RMode_Msk; // Clear rounding mode bits
FPU->FPDSCR |= 2 << 22;    // Select round toward positive infinity
```

Example 12-9. Selecting round to $+\infty$

The ARM FPU architecture provides three special modes, including the flushing-to-zero mode, the default NaN mode, and the alternative half-precision mode. These three modes are not compatible with the IEEE 754 standard.

- The *flush-to-zero mode* can be enabled by setting the FPSCR[24] bit. If this mode is enabled, all operands in the subnormal format are flushed to zero, except for instructions VABS, VNEG, and VMOV. Specifically, the input or the result of a single-precision arithmetic operation is treated as zero if its absolute value is larger than zero but smaller than 2^{-126}. If this mode is enabled, the FPU computation speed is improved at the expense of some accuracy.

- The *default NaN mode* can be enabled by setting the FPSCR[25] bit. NaN stands for not a number. As shown in Figure 12-11, there are many possible NaNs. In the IEEE 754 standard, two NaNs are different if they differ in any bit. IEEE 754 requires that any operation, which takes one or more quiet NaN operands, should return the input NaN as its result. If the default NaN mode is disable, FPU strictly follows IEEE 754 standard. However, if the default NaN mode is enabled, the result of any operation involving one or more NaNs is always the same pre-defined quiet NaN, which is 0x7FC00000.

- The *alternative half-precision mode* can be enabled by setting the FPSCR[26] bit. It selects either IEEE 754 half-precision floating point representation or ARM Cortex special 16-bit mode. The ARM alternative offers a larger range than IEEE 754 but does not support infinity and NaN.

Exceptions arise during abnormal events. Floating-point numbers are finite-precision approximation of real numbers. A floating-point operation may have range violation (overflow or underflow), rounding errors (inexact), invalid operation, or divide-by-zero. Cortex-M supports the following six exceptions. Once these exception flags are set, hardware does not automatically reset them.

- The *underflow exception* (UFC) and the overflow exception (OFC) are set respectively if the result has an absolute value greater than the largest floating-point number, or it is non-zero and smaller than the smallest non-zero floating-point number.

- The *inexact exception* flag (IXC) is set if the result of a single-precision float operation does not equal to the value that would be obtained if the operation were performed with unbounded precision and exponent range. This happens if the result lies between two floating-point numbers, leading to a rounding error.

- The *invalid operation* exception flag (IOC) is set if the result has no mathematical value or cannot be represented, such as $0 \times (\pm\infty)$, $\infty + (-\infty)$, $(\pm\infty)/(\pm\infty)$, and $sqrt(-1.0)$. The default output is either SNaN or QNaN.

- The *divide-by-zero* (DZC) exception flag is set if the divisor of a divide operation is zero, but its dividend is not zero.

- If a value is flushed to zero, the *input denormal cumulative* (IDC) exception flag bit of FPSCR is set.

12.4.1.4 Floating-point Context Address Register (FPCAR)

As introduced previously in Chapter 11, the processor performs automatic stacking when an interrupt/exception occurs. Without FPU support, the processor automatically pushes eight registers, including r0-r3, r12, LR, PC, and xPSR, onto the stack.

If FPU auto-stacking has been enabled (see the next section), the processor automatically pushes 17 additional registers, including s0-s15 and FPSCR onto the stack when interrupt takes place. The processor stores the stack location holding the value of register S0 to the floating-point context address register (FPCAR), as shown in Figure 12-20.

Additionally, the processor uses *lazy stacking* to reduce the interrupt latency. The lazy stacking allows the processor to skip the stacking of FPU registers, if not required, *i.e.,*

- if the interrupt handler does not use FPU, or
- if the interrupted program has not used FPU.

The processor reserves space in the stack for FPU registers. However, it only pushes FPU registers if FPU has been used and the interrupt handler will also FPU. Register FPCAR points to the unpopulated stack location reserved for FPU register S0 if stacking is deferred.

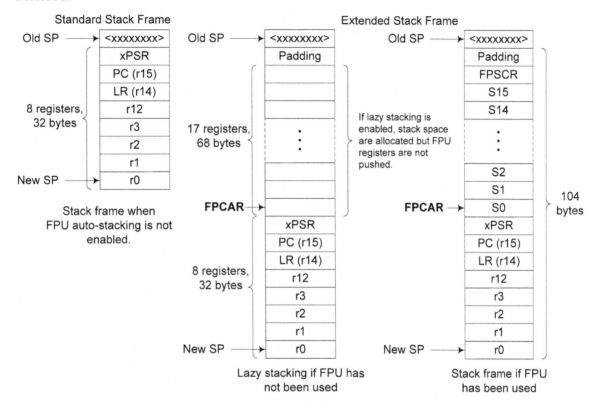

Figure 12-20. Lazy stacking on interrupt entry defers pushing FPU registers if FPU has not been used or the interrupt handler does not use FPU. FPCAR points to the memory location reserved for register S0. A 4-byte padding is added to make SP aligned to double words.

When the processor services an interrupt, it decides at runtime whether these FPU registers should be stored in the reserved stack space. The decision is made by checking the floating-point context active (FPCA) bit flag in the CONTROL register, which is a special register on Cortex-M processors.

- When the processor runs a floating-point instruction, it sets the FPCA bit flag in the CONTROL register automatically. The FPCA bit is automatically cleared when a new context, such as an interrupt service routine, is started.

- When the FPCA bit in the CONTROL register is 1 and the interrupt handler first uses any FPU instruction, the processor automatically pushes 17 additional registers onto stack and stores in the FPCAR register the memory address where the value of register s0 is in the stack.

The following example shows how to retrieve the previous FPSCR value from the stack, which is for the floating-point operations before the interrupt take places. The interrupt handler performs a dummy read to force the deferred FPU stacking in case that lazy stacking has been used.

```
void Example_IRQHandler(void) {

  uint32_t status, *fpscr;

  // Get the address where FPSCR is stored in the stack
  * fpscr = (uint32_t *)(FPU->FPCAR + 64);   // Full descending stack

  // Dummy access to populate the stack in case that lazy stack is active
  (void) __get_FPSCR();   // dummy read to FPSCR to force state preservation

  // Read FPSCR from stack
  status = *fpscr;

  // Check exception flag bits
  ...
}
```

Example 12-10. Retrieve FPSCR of previous FPU operations from the stack

12.4.1.5 Floating-point Context Control Register (FPCCR)

The Floating-point Context Control Register (FPCCR) controls the behavior of context saving and restoring during an interrupt. There are three different settings.

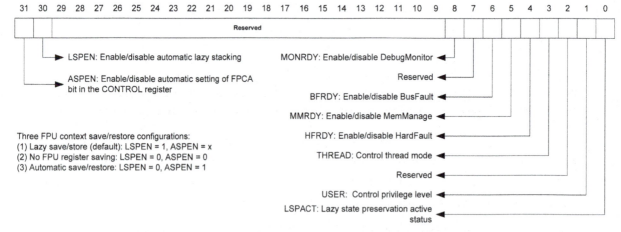

Figure 12-21. Floating-point Context Control Register (FPCCR)

- By default, the LSPEN (lazy state preservation enable) bit is 1, and it allows *lazy stacking* to reduce the exception or interrupt latency. When space has been allocated on the stack for FPU registers but pushing them onto the stack has been deferred, the lazy state preservation active status (LSPACT) flag is set.

- If both LSPEN and ASPEN (always state preservation enable) are 0, no floating-point registers are saved in the stack by the hardware when an interrupt occurs.
- If LSPEN is 0 and ASPEN is 1, floating-point registers are always automatically saved onto the stack by the hardware upon an interrupt.

Example 12-11 gives C functions that modify the stacking settings.

```c
void FPU_enableAutoStacking_disableLazyStacking(void) {
  // Disable lazy stacking
  FPU->FPCCR &= ~FPU_FPCCR_LSPEN_Msk;
  // Enable automatic stacking
  FPU->FPCCR |= FPU_FPCCR_ASPEN_Msk;
}

void FPU_enableStacking(void) {
  // Enable automatic and lazy stacking
  FPU->FPCCR |= FPU_FPCCR_ASPEN_Msk | FPU_FPCCR_LSPEN_Msk;
}

void FPU_disableStacking(void) {
  // Disable automatic and lazy stacking
  FPU->FPCCR &= ~(FPU_FPCCR_ASPEN_Msk | FPU_FPCCR_LSPEN_Msk);
}
```

Example 12-11. Enable and disable FPU automatic and lazy stacking

The FPCCR register also controls whether the processor can raise exceptions when it allocates the floating-point stack frame. These exceptions include the debug monitor exception, the bus fault, the memory management exception, and the hard fault.

When the floating-point stack frame is allocated, FPCCR also provides two flag bits, including USER and THREAD, to indicate whether the processor is in the user mode and the privileged mode, respectively.

If lazy stacking is enabled, the *lazy state preservation active* (LSPACT) bit in the FPCCR register indicates whether actual stacking of FPU registers has taken place. The processor sets LSPACT to 1 if stack space has been allocated but FPU stacking has been deferred on the entry of the interrupt handler. If LSPACT is 1, the processor stops the pipeline and starts to perform the deferred FPU stacking when the current interrupt handler runs a floating-point instruction. After FPU stacking completes, the processor clears the LSPACT flag to zero. Then, the processor continues the execution of the current interrupt handler.

12.4.2   Load and Store Floating-point Numbers

The following instructions access floating-point numbers stored in memory.

VLDR.F32 Sd, [Rn]	Load one single-precision float
VLDR.F64 Dd, [Rn]	Load one double-precision float
VSTR.32 Sd, [Rn]	Store one float registers
VSTR.64 Dd, [Rn]	Store one double register
VLDM.32 Rn{!}, list	Load multiple single-precision floats
VLDM.64 Rn{!}, list	Load multiple double-precision floats
VSTM.32 Rn{!}, list	Store multiple float registers
VSTM.64 Rn{!}, list	Store multiple double registers
VPOP.32 list	Pop float registers from stack
VPOP.64 list	Pop double registers from stack
VPUSH.32 list	Push float registers to stack
VPUSH.64 list	Push double registers to stack

The memory access instructions VLDR and VSTR support three addressing modes:

```
VLDR.F32 s0, [r0, #4]   ; Pre-index, s0 = mem[r0 + 4]
VLDR.F32 s0, [r0], #4   ; Post-index, s0 = mem[r0], r0 += 4
VLDR.F32 s0, [r0, #4]!  ; Pre-index with update, s0 = mem[r0 + 4], r0 += 4
```

Multiple floating-point numbers can be loaded or stored in one instruction:

```
VLDM.64 r0, {d0-d7}     ; Load 8 double precision numbers
VSTM.64 r0, {d0-d7}     ; Store 8 double precision numbers
```

Like LDM and STM introduced in Chapter 5.5, VSTM and VLDM can also have the suffix IA (Increment After) and DB (Decrement After), such as,

```
VSTMIA.64 r0, {d0-d7}
VSTMDB.64 r0, {d0-d7}
```

The push and pop operations are useful to save and restore registers via the stack.

```
VPUSH.32 {s16-s31}      ; Save floating point registers
VPOP.32  {s16-s31}      ; Restore floating point registers
```

For the convenience of the programmer, VLDR.F32 and VLDR.F64 can be used as a pseudo-instruction to load a constant into a floating-point system register.

```
VLDR.F32 s0, =2.71828
VLDR.F64 d2, =3.14159
```

The compiler translates the constant into IEEE 754 format, stores it in the instruction memory, and then uses PC-relative addressing to load the constant from memory. The compiler determines the offset relative to PC. When the processor calculates the target address, bit PC[1] is ignored to ensure that the target address is word-aligned.

```
VLDR.F32 s0, [pc, #0xA8]   ; load a float from PC + 4 + 0xA8
VLDR.F64 d2, [pc, #0xC4]   ; load a double from PC + 4 + 0xC4
```

12.4.3   Copy Floating-point Numbers

The following table lists instructions that copy floating-point numbers to a register.

`VMOV.F32 Sd, #imm`	Move an immediate float to float-register
`VMOV.F32 Sd, Sm`	Copy from single-precision register to single-precision register
`VMOV.F64 Dd, Dm`	Copy from double-precision register to double-precision register
`VMOV Sn, Rt`	Copy ARM core register to float register
`VMOV Sm1, Sm2, Rt1, Rt2`	Copy 2 ARM core registers to 2 float registers
`VMOV Dd[x], Rt`	Copy ARM core register to a half of a double-precision floating point register, where x is 0 or 1.
`VMOV Rt, Dn[x]`	Copy a half of a double-precision floating point register to ARM core register, where x is 0 or 1.

The `VMOV` instructions can be transfer content between ARM core registers and FPU coprocessor registers. For example,

```
VMOV s0, s1, r0, r1     ; s0 = r0, s1 = r1
VMOV r1, d0[1]          ; r1 = d0[1], i.e., r1 = s1
```

Note we can also use `VMOV` to initialize a single-precision register with a constant.

```
VMOV.F32 s1, #3.25      ; s1 = 3.25
```

12.4.4   Copy and Set the Status and Control Register

The `FPSCR` register holds the N, Z, C, and V flags, exception flags, and FPU configuration. VMRS and VMSR are special instructions to transfer contents between FPSCR and a general-purpose register.

`VMRS Rt, FPSCR`	Copy FPSCR to ARM core register or APSR
`VMSR FPSCR, Rt`	Copy to FPSCR from ARM Core register

The following shows example codes to set the rounding mode to round toward zero.

```
VMRS r0, FPSCR         ; Read current FPSCR
ORR  r0, r0, #(3<<22)  ; Set bits 22 and 23 to 1
VMSR FPSCR, r0         ; Save FPSCR
```

Note that conditional execution of floating-point arithmetic operations, such as `VMOVLT` and `VADDEQ.F32`, evaluate the N, Z, C, and V flags of APSR, not FPSCR.

The following instruction copies the N, Z, C, and V flags from FPSCR to APSR.

```
VMRS APSR_nzcv, FPSCR   ; Copy NZCV flags from FPSCR to APSR
```

12.4.5   Single-precision Arithmetic Operations

FPU in Cortex processors supports a limited number of single-precision floating point arithmetic operations, as listed below.

VADD.F32 {Sd,} Sn, Sm	Add floating points, Sd = Sn + Sm
VSUB.F32 {Sd,} Sn, Sm	Subtract float, Sd = Sn - Sm
VDIV.F32 {Sd,} Sn, Sm	Divide single-precision floats, Sd = Sn/Sm
VMUL.F32 {Sd,} Sn, Sm	Multiply float, Sd = Sn * Sm
VNMUL.F32 {Sd,} Sn, Sm	Negate and multiply float, Sd = -1 * Sn * Sm
VNEG.F32 Sd, Sm	Negate float, Sd = -1 * Sm
VABS.F32 Sd, Sm	Absolute value of floats, Sd = |Sm|
VSQRT.F32 Sd, Sm	Square-root of float

The following program shows a subroutine in C and assembly that calculates the area of a circle. The subroutine takes the input argument radius via the single-precision floating point register s0. The calculated area is also returned in register s0.

C Function	Assembly Function

`float area_of_circle(float radius){`
 	
`    float PI = 3.14;`
`    float area;`
`    area = PI * radius * radius;`
`    return area;`
`}`
	`area_of_circle PROC`
	`    EXPORT area_of_circle`
	`    VLDR.F32 s1,=3.14 ; Pseudo-instruction`
	`    VMUL.F32 s1,s1,s0 ; r0 = radius`
	`    VMUL.F32 s0,s1,s0 ; return area in s0`
	`    BX       LR`
	`    ENDP`

A C function can call an assembly floating-point function, as shown below.

Main Program	Assembly Function

`extern float sum(float *a,`
`                  int size);`
 	
`int main(void){`
`    float b = sum(a, 5);`
`    while(1);`
`}`
	`        AREA fun, CODE, READONLY, ALIGN=3`
	`        EXPORT sum      ; make sum visible`
	
	`sum     PROC`
	`        VLDR.F32  s0, =0.0    ; s = 0.0`
	`        MOVS      r3, #0     ; i = 0`
	`        B         check`
	
	`loop    VLDR      s1, [r0], #4 ; post-index`
	`        VADD.F32 s0, s0, s1   ; s += a[i]`
	`        ADDS      r3, r3, #1  ; i++`
	`check   CMP       r3, r1`
	`        BLT       loop`
	
	`        BX        lr           ; return`
	
	`        ENDP`
	`        END`

The multiply-accumulate (MAC) instructions compute expression $\pm a \pm b \times c$ efficiently in one instruction. The following table lists all MAC instructions.

VLMA.F32 {Sd,} Sn, Sm	Multiply float, then accumulate float, Sd = Sd + Sn*Sm
VLMS.F32 {Sd,} Sn, Sm	Multiply float, then subtract float, Sd = Sd - Sn*Sm
VNMLA.F32 Sd, Sn, Sm	Multiply float, then accumulate, then negate float, Sd = -1 * (Sd + Sn * Sm)
VNMLS.F32 Sd, Sn, Sm	Multiply float, then subtract, then negate float, Sd = -1 * (Sd - Sn * Sm)

The following table lists fused MAC instructions.

VFMA.F32 {Sd,} Sn, Sm	Multiply (fused) then accumulate float, Sd = Sd + Sn*Sm
VFMS.F32 {Sd,} Sn, Sm	Multiply (fused) then subtract float, Sd = Sd - Sn*Sm
VFNMA.F32 {Sd,} Sn, Sm	Multiply (fused) then accumulate then negate float, Sd = -1 * Sd + Sn * Sm
VFNMS.F32 {Sd,} Sn, Sm	Multiply (fused) then subtract then negate float, Sd = -1 * Sd - Sn * Sm

A fused operation performs no intermediate rounding. For example, the floating-point fused multiply-add instruction "VLMA.F32 Sd, Sn, Sm" calculates "Sd + Sn*Sm" as if with unlimited range and precision, and the rounding is only performed once at the end. A fused operation reduces rounding error but runs slower.

12.4.6 Single-precision comparisons

The comparison instructions, as shown below, compare two floating-point values and set the N, Z, C, and V bit flags of the Floating-point Status and Control Register (FPSCR). "MVRS APSR_nzcv FPSCR" copies the current N, Z, C, and V flag bits from the FPU's FPSCR register to the processor's APSR register.

VCMP.F32 Sd, <Sm | #0.0>	Compare two floating-point registers, or one floating-point register and zero
VCMPE.F32 Sd, <Sm | #0.0>	Compare two floating-point registers, or one floating-point register and zero, and raise exception for a signaling NaN

The following program shows a simple subroutine that returns the maximum of two floating-point values. Following the EABI standard, the floating-point input arguments come in via register s0 and s1, and the result comes out via register s0. The VCMPE instruction updates the NZCV flags in FPSCR. However, conditional execution does not check FPSCR. Therefore, we need to copy these flags to APSR.

C Program	Assembly Program

float **max**(float a, float b){
  if (a > b)
    return a;
  else
    return b;
}
	max PROC
	       EXPORT max
	       VCMPE.F32 s0, s1
	       ; *Copy NZCV flags to APSR*
	       VMRS **APSR_nzcv, FPSCR**
	       BGT **exit**
	       VMOV.F32 s0, s1
	exit BX lr
	       ENDP

Example 12-12. Selecting the max between two single-precision floating point numbers

The following gives two different assembly functions of finding the absolute value.

C Program	Assembly Program 1	Assembly Program 2

float **fabs**(float f) {
  if (f < 0)
    return -1.0*f;
  else
    return f;
}
	fabs PROC
	    VCMPE.F32 s0, #0.0
	
	    ; *Copy NZCV flags to APSR*
	    VMRS **APSR_nzcv, FPSCR**
	    BCS **exit**
	
	    VNEG.F32 s0, s0
	exit BX lr
	    ENDP
		fabs PROC
		
		    VABS.F32 s0, s0
		
		    BX lr
		
		    ENDP

Example 12-13. Calculating the absolute value of a single-precision floating point number

12.4.7   Precision Conversion

The following table lists all instructions that convert values to a different format. The option "R" forces the operation to use the rounding mode specified by FPSCR. Otherwise, rounding towards zero is used.

VCVT{R}.S32.F32 Sd, Sm	Convert from single-precision float to signed 32-bit (S32) or unsigned 32-bit (U32) integer.
VCVT{R}.U32.F32 Sd, Sm	
VCVT{R}.F32.S32 Sd, Sm	Convert to single-precision float from signed 32-bit (S32) or unsigned 32-bit (U32) integer.
VCVT{R}.F32.U32 Sd, Sm	
VCVT{R}.Td.F32 Sd, Sm, #n	Convert between single-precision and fixed-point. Td can be S16 (signed 16-bit), U16 (unsigned 16-bit), S32 (signed 32-bit), and U32 (unsigned 32-bit). #n is the number of fraction bits in the fixed-point number.
VCVT{R}.Td.F32 Sd, Sd, #n	
VCVT{R}.F32.Td Sd, Sm, #n	
VCVT{R}.F32.Td Sd, Sd, #n	
VCVT<B|T>.F32.F16 Sd, Sm	Converts half-precision float to single-precision (B = bottom half of Sm, T = top half of Sm)
VCVT<B|T>.F16.F32 Sd, Sm	Converts single-precision float to half-precision (B = bottom half of Sd, T = top half of Sd)

Example 12-14 illustrates the assembly implementation of converting an integer to a single-precision floating point format with and without FPU.

With FPU	Without FPU

VMOV.F32   s1,#3
VCVT.F32.S32 s0,s0
	``
	      MOV r0, #3
	      BL __aeabi_i2f
	
	__aeabi_i2f PROC
	      ANDS r1,r0,#0x80000000 ; r[31] = Sign
	      RSBSMI r0,r0,#0 ; If r0 < 0, r0 = 0 - r0
	      CLZ r3,r0 ; Count leading zeros
	
	      LSLS r2,r0,r3 ; Remove leading zeros
	      RSB r3,r3,#157 ; exp = 157 - # leading zeros
	                        ; Note that it is not 158,
	                        ; extra 1 is added later
	      BEQ exit ; if r2 is 0, return 0
	
	      ORRS r1,r1,r3,LSL #23 ; r1[30:23] = Exponent
	      ADD r0,r1,r2,LSR #8 ; r0[22:0] = Significand
	                             ; Exponent = Exponent + 1
	      ; Round to Nearest
	      LSLS r3,r2,#25 ; carry = round bit
	                        ; r3 holds sticky bits
	
	      BXCC lr ; round down if round bit is 0
	      ADD r0,r0,#1 ; round up since round bit is 1
	      BICEQ r0,r0,#1 ; if sticky bits are 0
	exit BX lr
	``

Example 12-14. Converting integer to single-precision float

We will give two examples to explain the basic procedures of converting an integer to a single-precision floating point number without using FPU.

Example 1: Converting 7 to single-precision float
1) Input: r0 = 00000000_00000000_00000000_00000111
2) Obtain sign: r1 = 00000000_00000000_00000000_00000000
3) Count the leading zeros of input: r3 = 29
4) Remove leading zeros: r2 = 11100000_00000000_00000000_00000000
5) Bias = 127
6) Obtain exponent_minus_1:
   r3 = 157 − 29 = 128 = 00000000_00000000_00000000_10000000
7) Place exponent: r1 = 00100000_00000000_00000000_00000000
8) Obtain significant: r2 LSR #8 = 00000000_11100000_00000000_00000000
9) Combine sign, exponent, and significant:
   r1 + r2 LSR #8 = 01000000_11100000_00000000_00000000

Example 2: Converting -3 to single-precision float

```
1)  Input: r0 = 11111111_11111111_11111111_11111101
2)  Obtain sign: r1 = 10000000_00000000_00000000_00000000
3)  Obtain absolute value: r0 = 00000000_00000000_00000000_00000011
4)  Count the leading zeros of input: r3 = 30
5)  Remove leading zeros: r2 = 11000000_00000000_00000000_00000000
6)  Bias = 127
7)  Obtain exponent_minus_1:
    r3 = 157 - 30 = 127 = 00000000_00000000_00000000_01111111
8)  Place exponent: r1 = 10111111_10000000_00000000_00000000
9)  Obtain significant: r2 LSR #8 = 00000000_11000000_00000000_00000000
10) Combine sign, exponent, and significant:
    r1 + r2 LSR #8 = 11100000_01000000_00000000_00000000
```

12.4.8   FPU Exception and Exception handling

As introduced previously, there are six floating-point exceptions, including input denormal (IDC), inexact (IXC), underflow (UFC), overflow (OFC), divide by zero (DZC), and invalid operation (IOC).

The following gives example instructions that set the exception flags in the FPSCR register.

```
VLDR.F32   s0, =0.0       ; Pseudo-instruction
VLDR.F32   s1, =-1.0      ; Pseudo-instruction
VDIV.F32   s2, s1, s0     ; s2 = -Infinity, Set DZC flag in FPSCR
VDIV.F32   s3, s0, s0     ; s3 = Quiet NaN (QNaN), Set IOC flag in FPSCR
VSQRT.F32  s4, s1         ; s4 = QNaN, Set IOC flag in FPSCR

VLDR.F32   s5, =2.12e30   ; A large constant, 2.12×10^30
VMUL.F32   s6, s5, s5     ; Set OFC and IXC flags in FPSCR

VLDR.F32   s5, =2.12e-30  ; A large constant, 2.12×10^-30
VMUL.F32   s6, s5, s5     ; Set UFC and IXC flags in FPSCR
```

By default, most processors do not handle these exceptions proactively. They do nothing more than setting exception flags to indicate an exception has occurred. This allows the computation to continue with a default output value specified by the IEEE 754 standard.

For example, the default output of the overflow, underflow, and invalid operator is infinity, zero, and NaN, respectively. Floating-point operations can propagate the infinity and NaN consistently throughout the computation. However, such default outputs may introduce devastating inaccuracies in some applications.

We can change the default output of floating-point exceptions. In general, a processor can handle an exception in two approaches: a *trap* or an *interrupt*.

- A *trap* handler returns an alternate result, instead of an exceptional result, and allows the program to resume execution.

- An *interrupt* handler takes over the control and performs alternate calculation when an exception occurs.

However, Cortex-M4 processors do not support traps. All floating-point exceptions are handled through via interrupts. As shown in Figure 12-22, five exceptions, including UFC, OFC, IDC, DZC, and IOC, are connected via a logical OR operator to generate FPU interrupts. Cortex-M4 processors do not allow the Inexact Exception (IXC) to produce FPU interrupts because rounding errors occur very frequently. Some processors allow the enabling and disabling the interrupt for each individual FPU exception.

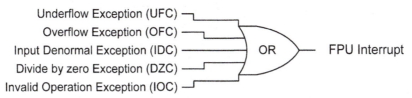

Underflow Exception (UFC)
Overflow Exception (OFC)
Input Denormal Exception (IDC)   OR   FPU Interrupt
Divide by zero Exception (DZC)
Invalid Operation Exception (IOC)

Figure 12-22. Cortex-M4 handles all floating-point exceptions via interrupts

The following assembly program shows how to process the overflow exception (OFC) in the FPU interrupt handler. Various methods are available to handle overflow. For example, the interrupt handler can convert the single-precision operation to a double-precision one to extend the range, or the handler can multiply the operands by a proper scaling factor to make the result within the current range. Software should enable FPU interrupts in NVIC by running "NVIC_EnableIRQ(FPU_IRQn);".

```
FPU_IRQHandler PROC
          EXPORT  FPU_IRQHandler

          VMRS r0, FPSCR      ; Read current FPSCR

          ; Overflow cumulative exception (OFC)
check_OFC ANDS r0, #(1<<2)
          BEQ  exit

          ; Handle OFC exception
          . . .

          ; Clear OFC flag
          . . .

exit      BX   LR
          ENDP
```

Clearing the FPU exception flags depends on the context save-and-restore behavior setting in the Floating-point Context Control Register (FPCCR) register. The following shows that example assembly code that clears all FPU exception flags.

1. Lazy save/store (default): LSPEN = 1, ASPEN = x

```
VMRS r0, FPSCR              ; Dummy access to force context saving
LDR  r1, =FPU_BASE          ; Load the base memory address of FPU
LDR  r0, [r1, #FPU_FPCAR]   ; r0 = FPU->FPCAR
LDR  r2, [r0, #64]          ; stacking 16 registers (s0-s15) and FPSCR
BIC  r2, r2, #0x8F          ; Clear all flags
STR  r2, [r0, #64]          ; Save into stack
                            ; When an interrupt exits, FPSCR is
                            ; updated during automatic unstacking
```

2. No FPU register saving: LSPEN = 0, ASPEN = 0

```
VMRS r0, FPSCR              ; Read FPSCR
BIC  r0, r0, #8F            ; Clear all flags
VMSR FPSCR, r0              ; Save FPSCR
```

3. Automatic save/restore: LSPEN = 0, ASPEN = 1

```
; Clear FPSCR flags by using a dummy read
VMRS  r1, FPSCR             ; Automatically cleared after read

; Clear exception flags saved in stack
TST   lr, #4
MRSEQ r0, msp               ; If LR = 0xFFFFFFF9, SP = MSP
MRSNE r0, psp               ; If LR = 0xFFFFFFFD, SP = PSP
LDR   r2, [r0, #96]         ; FPU stack = 16 registers(s0-s15) + FPSCR
BIC   r2, r2, #0x8F         ; Clear all flags
STR   r2, [r0, #96]         ; Save into stack
```

12.4.9   Example Assembly Programs

12.4.9.1 Look up a Float Array

Example 12-15 shows a simple subroutine that looks up a specific float number in a float array. The C subroutine takes three arguments, the array memory address, a target float number, and the array size. If the subroutine finds the target float in the array, it returns its location index; otherwise, it returns -1.

The subroutine takes three arguments, including the float array address, the target float, and the array size, in register r0, s0, and r1, respectively. Note that the float array address is a 32-bit integer, and thus it is passed via a core register instead of a floating-point register.

The VCMP.F32 instruction compares two float numbers and sets up the NZCV flags in the FPSCR register based on the comparison result. We need to copy these flags to the APSR register for the subsequent conditional branch or conditionally executed instructions.

C Function	Assembly Function

int32_t **lookup**(float *fArray,
        float f, uint32_t size){
	lookup PROC
	        EXPORT lookup ; *Make lookup visible*

int i;	MOV r2, r0 ; *r0 = array address*
	MOV r3, #0 ; *loop index i = 0*
	B check

for (i = 0; i < size; i++) {	loop ; *Find address of fArray[i]*
	        ADD r0, r2, r3, LSL #2
	        VLDR s1, [r0, #0] ; *s1 = fArray[i]*

if (fArray[i] == f) return i;	; *Compare f and fArray[i]* **VCMP.F32 s1, s0** **VMRS APSR_nzcv, FPSCR** ; *copy flags* ; *Return index i if equal* MOVEQ r0, r3 BXEQ lr

}
 	
    return -1;
}
	ADDS r3, r3, #1 ; *loop index ++*
	check CMP r3, r1 ; *r1 = array size*
	        BCC loop
	        MOV r0, #0xFFFFFFFF
	        BX LR ; *return -1 if failed*
	
	        ENDP

Example 12-15. Looking up a single-precision floating point array

12.4.9.2 Sine Function of Argument in Radians

Example 12-16 shows the C and assembly function that calculates the value of $\sin(x)$ based on the following *Taylor* expansion. The input x is in radians, not in degrees.

$$\sin(x) = \sum_{k=0}^{\infty} \frac{(-1)^k}{(2k+1)!} x^{k+1} \approx x - \frac{x^3}{3!} + \frac{x^5}{5!} - \frac{x^7}{7!} + \cdots$$

The computation loop repeats until the program achieves the desired maximum error. The input x is passed via register s0, and the result is returned also in register s0.

According to EABI, a subroutine must preserve in the stack any single-precision registers s16-s31 (double-precision registers d8-d15) that are written in the subroutine. It is not required to preserve registers s0-s15 (d0-d7) across subroutine calls. In this example, the instruction "VPUSH.32 {s16-s21}" is equivalent to "VPUSH.64 {d8-d10}". When multiple registers are pushed onto or popped off the stack, similar to PUSH and POP (see

Example 8-3), VPUSH pushes the largest numbered register first, and VPOP pops the smallest numbered register first. However, different from PUSH and POP, VPUSH and VPOP require that registers must be consecutive in their names.

C Function	Assembly Function

```float sine(float x) {```
 	
```   float ret = 0.0;```
```   float pow = x;```
```   float term = pow;```
```   float sign = 1.0;```
```   float fact = 1.0;```
```   int   k = 1;```
	```sine PROC```
	``` EXPORT sine```
	``` PUSH {r4, lr}```
	``` VPUSH.32 {s16-s21}```
	``` VMOV.F32 s16, s0 ; s16 = x```
	``` VLDR.F32 s18, =0 ; s18 = ret = 0.0```
	``` VMOV.F32 s17, s16 ; s17 = pow = x```
	``` VMOV.F32 s19, s16 ; s19 = term = x```
	``` VMOV.F32 s20, #1 ; s20 = sign = 1```
	``` VMOV.F32 s21, #1 ; s21 = fact = 1```
	``` MOVS r4, #1 ; r4 = k = 1```
	``` B check```

```while(fabs(term) >= 0.00001f){```
```   term = sign * pow/fact;```
 	
```   ret += term;```
 	
```   pow *= x * x;```
	```loop```
	``` VMUL.F32 s0,s20,s17 ; s0 = sign * power```
	``` VDIV.F32 s19,s0,s21 ; term = s0/fact```
	``` VADD.F32 s18,s18,s19 ; ret += term```
	``` VMUL.F32 s0,s16,s16 ; s0 = x*x```
	``` VMUL.F32 s17,s0,s17 ; pow *= x*x```
	
	``` LSLS r0, r4, #1 ; r0 = 2*k```
	``` ADDS r1, r0, #1 ; r1 = 2*k + 1```
	``` MULS r0, r1, r0 ; r0```
	
	``` VMOV s0, r0```

``` fact *= 2*k * (2*k+1);```	``` VCVT.F32.S32 s0, s0 ; convert to float``` ``` VMUL.F32 s21,s0,s21 ; fact *= 2k*(2k+1)```

```   sign = 0 - sign;```
```   k++;```
	``` VLDR.F32 s0, =0```
	``` VSUB.F32 s20,s0,s20 ; sign = 0 - sign```
	``` ADDS r4, r4, #1 ; k++```

```}```
 	
```   return ret;```
```}```
	```check```
	``` VABS.F32 s0, s19```
	``` VLDR.F32 s1, =0.00001```
	``` VCMPE.F32 s0, s1```
	``` VMRS APSR_nzcv, FPSCR ; copy NZCV flags```
	``` BGE loop```
	``` VMOV.F32 s0, s18 ; return ret in s0```
	``` VPOP.32 {s16-s21}```
	``` POP {r4, pc}```
	``` ENDP```

Example 12-16. Calculating *sine* value based on Taylor expansion

12.5 Exercises

1. Suppose two real numbers A and B are in the UQ16.16 format. Show the basic procedure to calculate the product C. $C = A \times B$. Note C is also in UQ16.16 format. List all key operations and write an assembly program to conduct the multiplication.

2. Convert 3.1415 to UQ8.8 format, and convert -3.1415 to Q7.8 format.

3. Convert the binary real number `1111.1101` to decimal.

4. Write an assembly program that calculates the sum of an array of UQ8.8 numbers.

5. Write an assembly program that calculates the sum of an array of UQ16.16 numbers.

6. Convert 3.1415 to IEEE 754 single-precision format.

7. Convert `0xC1F54000` to IEEE 754 single-precision decimal

8. Manually subtract the following two IEEE 754 single-precision numbers:

   `0xC1D15053 - 0xC3FD5053`

9. Manually add the two IEEE 754 single-precision numbers given in the previous question.

10. Manually multiply the following IEEE 754 single-precision numbers.

    `0xC0D40000 × 0x41C20000`

11. Manually divide the following IEEE 754 single-precision numbers.

    `0xC0D40000 ÷ 0x41C20000`

12. How many byte(s) boundary should a "float" type be aligned to in C?

13. Given the following C functions, what registers are used to pass these arguments? Which register holds the return value?

    (1) `float fun1(float a, float b, float c, uint8_t d, int32_t e);`
    (2) `double fun2(float f1, double f2, float f3, double f4);`
    (3) `uint16_t fun3(uint8_t a1, int32_t a2, float f1, float f2, float f3, double f4)`
    (4) `float * fun4(float *f1, float *f2, double *f3, float f4, double f5);`

14. How many bytes of the stack are needed to pass arguments when the following function is called?

```
(1) float fun1(float a, float b, float c, float d,
               float d, float e, float f);

(2) float fun2(uint8_t a1, float f1, uint16_t a2, uint8_t a3,
               float f2, int32_t a4, float f3, uint8_t a5,
               float f4, int32_t a6, uint8_t a7);

(3) float fun3(float f1,  float f2,  float f3,  float f4,
               float f5,  float f6,  float f7,  float f8,
               float f9,  float f10, float f11, float f12,
               float f13, float f14, float f15, float f16,
               float f17, float f18, float f19, float f20, float f21);

(4) double fun4(double d1, double d2, double d3, double d4, double d5,
                double d6, double d7, double d8, double d9, double d10);
```

15. Write an assembly function that finds the maximum value in a single-precision floating-point array.

```
float maxf(float *array, int array_size)
```

16. Write an assembly function that calculates the exponential value e^x.

```
float expf(float x)
```

The function should be based on the following Taylor expansion.

$$e^x = \sum_{k=0}^{\infty} \frac{x^k}{k!} \approx 1 + \frac{x}{1!} + \frac{x^2}{2!} + \frac{x^3}{3!} + \cdots$$

17. Write an assembly function that calculates the cosine value $\cos(x)$.

```
float cos(float x)
```

The function should be based on the following Taylor expansion.

$$\cos(x) = \sum_{k=0}^{\infty} (-1)^k \frac{x^{2k}}{(2k)!} \approx 1 - \frac{x^2}{2!} + \frac{x^4}{4!} - \frac{x^6}{6!} + \frac{x^8}{8!} - \cdots$$

18. When multiple registers are pushed onto or popped off the stack in one instruction, the register list is sorted. The largest numbered register is pushed first onto the stack, and the smallest numbered register is popped first. Assume stack pointer (sp) = 0x20006000, register Ri = i and Si = 1.0*i (r0 = 0, r1 = 1, ..., and s0 = 0.0,

s1 = 1.0, s2 = 2.0, …). Show the stack memory content in hex immediately after the processor executes the following two instructions.

```
push {r3-r5,r1,r9,r7} ; Registers do not have to be listed consecutively
vpush.32 {s16-s18}     ; Registers in the list must be consecutive
```

19. Translate the following assembly function into a C function. Explain what this function does and give the function a meaningful name.

```
myfun PROC
      EXPORT myfun
      VMUL.F32   s0, s0, s0
      VLMA.F32   s0, s1, s1
      VLMA.F32   s0, s2, s2
      VSQRT.F32  s0, s0
      BX lr
ENDP
```

20. Assume the main stack (MSP) is used.
    - Stack pointer (sp) = 0x20006000, Register Ri = i and Si = 1.0*i (r0 = 0, r1 = 1, …, and s0 = 0.0, s1 = 1.0, s2 = 2.0, …)
    - Additionally, the program status register (PSR) = 0x00000020, PC = 0x08000020, LR = 0x20008020, and FPCAR = 0x03000000.

    Show the stack memory content in hex immediate after an interrupt service routine is called in the following scenarios.
    (1) There is no FPU or FPU has not been used.
    (2) FPU has been used before the interrupt occurs, and the interrupt service routine will run floating-point instructions.

21. What is the value in register Si (i = 0, 1,…, 31) after the following SysTick interrupt handler has been executed once? Assume initially Si = 1.0*i (s0 = 0.0, s1 = 1.0, s2 = 2.0, …).

```
SysTick_Handler PROC
      VPUSH {s17-s19}
      VMOV.F32   s3,  #1
      VADD.F32   s0,  s3, s1
      VADD.F32   s4,  s3, s1
      VADD.F32   s13,  s3, s1
      VADD.F32   s15, s10, s1
      VADD.F32   s18, s15, s1
      VADD.F32   s20,  s7, s1
      VADD.F32   s31, s10, s12
      VPOP  {s17-s19}
      BX    LR
      ENDP
```

22. Suppose the SysTick interrupt occurs when
    - PC = 0x08000044, XPSR = 0x00000020,
    - SP = 0x20000200, LR = 0x08001000,
    - FPCAR = 0x03000000,
    - Processor's Register $R_i = i$, $i = 0, 1, 2, \ldots$, and
    - FPU Registers Si = 1.0*i (s0 = 0.0, s1 = 1.0, s2 = 2.0, …).

Memory Address	Instruction
	__main PROC
	. . .
0x08000044	VMOV.F32 s3, #2
	. . .
	ENDP
	SysTick_Handler PROC
	EXPORT SysTick_Handler
0x0800001C	VADD.F32 s15, s15, s11
0x08000020	VADD.F32 s17, s16, s10
0x08000024	BX lr
	ENDP

(1) Show the stack contents and the value of PC and SP when immediately entering the SysTick interrupt service routine.

(2) What is the value in register s15 and s17?

Instruction Encoding and Decoding

ARM has multiple instruction sets. The legacy ARM instruction set includes 32-bit instructions. All instructions in the Thumb instruction set have only 16 bits. The Thumb-2 consists of all 16-bit Thumb instructions as well as many 32-bit instructions, as shown in Figure 13-1.

The Cortex-M family has a series of processors that are backward compatible. The Cortex-M3 series extends Cortex-M0 series by adding more instructions for advanced data processing and bit field manipulations. Cortex-M4 extends the Cortex-M3 by adding digital signal processing and floating-point arithmetic instructions.

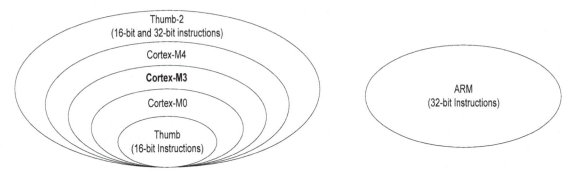

Figure 13-1. Comparison of Thumb, Thumb-2, and ARM instruction sets

13.1 Tradeoff between Code Density and Performance

These instruction sets play different tradeoff between code density and performance, as shown in Figure 13-2. Code density measures the size of a binary executable program. A high code density means that the binary program has a less number of bytes. A high code density is often preferred in embedded systems because less memory is required, thereby directly reducing cost and power consumption.

The 16-bit Thumb instructions decrease the size of the program code and accordingly reduce the memory capacity requirement. The 32-bit legacy ARM instructions increase the flexibility of encoding, such as directly encoding large immediate numbers and including more operands, thus improving the performance.

The Thumb-2 instruction set, consisting of a mix of 16-bit and 32-bit instructions, provides a good tradeoff between the code size and performance. Accordingly, the performance and code size ratio of Thumb-2 is the highest.

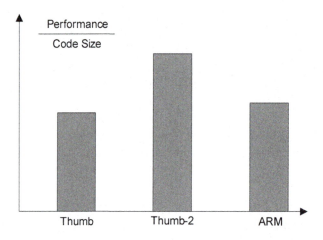

Figure 13-2. Thumb-2 plays a good tradeoff between the code density and performance.

13.2 Dividing Bit Streams into 16- or 32-bit Instructions

The processor always fetches four bytes (32 bits) from the instruction memory addressed by the program counter. Therefore, the program counter is always increased by four. These four bytes represents either one 32-bit instruction or two 16-bit instructions.

> "Looking at a program written in machine language is vaguely comparable to looking at a DNA molecule atom by atom."
>
> Douglas Hofstadter
> cognitive scientist

- If the most significant five bits are 11101, 11110, or 11111 in binary, this halfword is the least significant two bytes of a 32-bit instruction. The fetched four bytes represent one 32-bit instruction.

- Otherwise, these four bytes consist of two 16-bit instructions

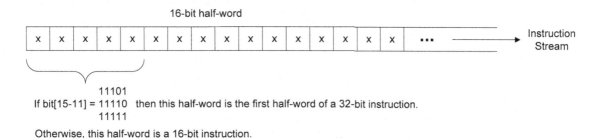

If bit[15-11] = 11101 / 11110 / 11111   then this half-word is the first half-word of a 32-bit instruction.

Otherwise, this half-word is a 16-bit instruction.

Figure 13-3. Identification of 16-bit and 32-bit Thumb instructions

Each machine instruction includes a binary operation code (opcode) and zero or more operands.

- The opcode specifies the operation that the processor carries out. The total number of bits in an opcode varies, depending on specific instructions. An opcode sometimes consists of two bit-fields: a major opcode that specifies the major category of this instruction, and a minor opcode that identifies a specific option within this category.

- If the operand is a register, generally four bits are required to represent a register because there are 16 registers. Most 16-bit instructions can only access the lower registers (r0 – r7) because only three bits are used to address a register operand in a 16-bit instruction.

- If the operand is an immediate number, 16-bit instructions usually limit it to 5 or 8 bits, and 32-bit instructions limit it to 8, 16, or 24 bits. It is interesting that 32-bit instructions can also encode some 32-bit immediate numbers with some special bit patterns.

The encoding of immediate numbers is complex in ARM. Let us look at the 12-bit immediate number. ARM uses a combination of a 4-bit rotation and an 8-bit immediate number to decode a 12-bit immediate number stored in the instruction. It is impossible to use the 4-bit rotation to place the 8-bit immediate number to all 32 possible positions in a word. The tradeoff is that the 8-bit immediate number can only be rotated to even positions because the exact rotation amount is twice as much as specified.

For example, if the 8-bit immediate number is 0b11001100, and the 4-bit rotation amount is 0b1001, the 32-bit immediate encoded is obtained as follows:

```
0b11001100 ROR 2 x 0b1001 = 0b00110011,00000000,00000000,00000000.
```

Note that not every immediate number can be directly encoded in an instruction.

13.3 Encoding 16-bit Thumb Instructions

The following table lists the major opcode of 16-bit Thumb instructions. Appendix F gives a detailed list of all 16-bit instructions.

15	14	13	12	11	10	9	8	7	6	5	4	3	2	1	0	
0	0	minor opcode														Shift, add, subtract, move, & compare
0	1	0	0	0	0	minor opcode			Rm/Rn			Rd/Rn				Data processing
0	1	0	0	0	1	minor opcode		Rm				Rd/Rn				Special data instructions & branch
0	1	0	0	1	x	minor opcode										Load from Literal Pool
0	1	0	1	x	x											Load/store single data item
0	1	1	x	x	x											Load/store single data item
1	0	0	x	x	x											Load/store single data item
1	0	1	0	0	Rd			imm8								Generate PC-relative address
1	0	1	0	1	Rd			imm8								Generate SP-relative address
1	0	1	1	minor opcode												Miscellaneous 16-bit instructions
1	1	0	0	0	Rd			register list								Store multiple registers
1	1	0	0	1	Rd			register list								Load multiple registers
1	1	0	1	minor opcode			offset-8									Conditional branch, & supervisor call
1	1	1	0	0	offset-11											Unconditional branch

The minor opcode of data processing instructions in which the destination operand is also one of the source operands has four bits (*i.e.*, bits[9-6]), as listed below.

Bit[9-8]	Bits [7-6]			
	00	01	10	11
00	AND	EOR	LSL	LSR
01	ASR	ADC	SBC	ROR
10	TST	RSB	CMP	CMN
11	ORR	MUL	BIC	MVN

For example, the minor opcode for the bitwise logic OR instruction is 1100 in binary, and thus the instruction of "ORR r1, r0" is encoded 0x4301, shown as follows. Note that register r1 is both the source operand and the destination operand. It is equivalent to "ORR r1, r1, r0".

15	14	13	12	11	10	9	8	7	6	5	4	3	2	1	0	
0	1	0	0	0	0	1	1	0	0	0	0	0	0	0	1	ORR r1, r0
		major opcode						minor opcode				Rn		Rd		

When there are three different register operands, a 32-bit instruction is required. For example, "ORR r2, r1, r0" cannot be encoded by a 16-bit instruction.

13.4 Encoding 32-bit Instructions

The decoding scheme of 32-bit instructions is summarized in a table given on the next page. Let's take data processing instructions with registers as operands as an example. These instructions share the same major opcode, which is `1110101`. However, the minor opcode and the bit fields are different, as defined in Table 13-1. Appendix G shows the format of all 32-bit instructions.

31 - 25	24 - 21	20	19-16	15	14-12	11-8	7	6	5	4	3-0	
major opcode	minor opcode	S	Rn	0	imm3	Rd	imm2				Rm	
1110101	0000	S	Rn	0	imm3	Rd	imm2	type			Rm	AND
1110101	0000	1	Rn	0	imm3	1111	imm2	type			Rm	TST
1110101	0001	S	Rn	0	imm3	Rd	imm2	type			Rm	BIC
1110101	0010	S	Rn	0	imm3	Rd	imm2	type			Rm	ORR
1110101	0011	S	Rn	0	imm3	Rd	imm2	type			Rm	ORN
1110101	0011	S	1111	0	imm3	Rd	imm2	type			Rm	MVN
1110101	0100	S	Rn	0	imm3	Rd	imm2	type			Rm	EOR
1110101	0110	S	Rn	0	imm3	Rd	imm2	tb	T		Rm	PKHBT, PKHTB
1110101	1000	S	Rn	0	imm3	Rd	imm2	type			Rm	ADD
1110101	1000	1	Rn	0	imm3	1111	imm2	type			Rm	CMN
1110101	1010	S	Rn	0	imm3	Rd	imm2	type			Rm	ADC
1110101	1011	S	Rn	0	imm3	Rd	imm2	type			Rm	SBC

Table 13-1. Major and minor opcode of commonly used 32-bit instructions

Example: Encoding "ORRS r3, r1, r0, LSL #2" into binary format

According to Table 13-1, we find that the minor opcode is `0010`. Following the instruction format in Appendix F, the 32-bit ORR instruction with three register operands has a format presented in Table 13-2. The S bit should be 1 because it is required to update the NZCV flags due to the "S" suffix. The shift type is `00`, representing logic shift left (LSL). The five-bit shift amount (imm3:imm2) is `00010`.

31 - 25	24 - 21	20	19 - 16	15	14 - 12	11 - 8	7	6	5	4	3 - 0
major opcode	minor opcode	S	Rn	0	imm3	Rd	imm2		type		Rm
1110101	0010	1	0001	0	000	0011	10		00		0000

Table 13-2. Instruction format of the 32-bit ORR instruction with three registers

Therefore, the binary encoding of "ORRS r3, r1, r0, LSL #2" is
`1110,1010,0101,0001,0000,0011,1000,0000`, which is `0xEA510380` in hex.

Encoding of 32-bit Thumb2 Instructions

31	30	29	28	27	26	25	24	23	22	21	20	19	18	17	16	15	14	13	12	11	10	9	8	7	6	5	4	3	2	1	0	
1	1	1	0	1	0	0	op		0	W	L	Rn				Register list																Load/store multiple
1	1	1	0	1	0	0	op1		1	op2		Rn																				Load/store dual or exclusive, table branch
1	1	1	0	1	0	1	op				S	Rn				0	imm3			Rd				imm2		op3		Rm				Data processing (shifted register)
1	1	1	0	1	1	op1										coproc								op								Coprocessor instructions
1	1	1	1	0	x	0	op				S	Rn				0	imm3			Rd				imm8								Data processing (modified immediate)
1	1	1	1	0	x	1	op					Rn				0	imm3			Rd				imm8								Data processing (plain binary immediate)
1	1	1	1	0	op							Rn				1	op1			op2												Branches and miscellaneous control
1	1	1	1	1	0	0	0	op1			0	Rn								op2												Store single data item
1	1	1	1	1	0	0	op1		0	0	1	Rn				Rt				op2												Load byte, memory hints
1	1	1	1	1	0	0	op1		0	1	1	Rn				Rt				op2												Load halfword, memory hints
1	1	1	1	1	0	0	op1		1	0	1	Rn								op2												Load word
1	1	1	1	1	0	0	x	x	1	1	1																					Undefined
1	1	1	1	1	0	1	0	op1				Rn				1	1	1	1					op2				Rm				Data processing (register)
1	1	1	1	1	0	1	1	0	op1			Rn				Ra								0	0	op2		Rm				Multiply, multiply accumulate, and absolute difference
1	1	1	1	1	0	1	1	1	op1			Rn												op2				Rm				Long multiply, long multiply accumulate, divide
1	1	1	1	1	1	op1										coproc								op								Coprocessor instructions

13.5 Calculating Target Memory Address

Cortex-M processors use PC-relative addresses for branch and load/store instructions. In PC-relative addressing, the processor calculates the target memory address as follows.

$$\text{Target address} = PC + 4 + \text{Offset}$$

where PC is the memory address of the current branch or load/store instruction. Note that Thumb instructions are always halfword aligned and thus the least significant bit of the PC is always 0.

PC-relative addressing has two advantages. First, it helps to achieve position-independent code, which allows the instructions to be placed in different memory regions. Second, it contributes to store immediate numbers in the instruction memory. Many immediate numbers, especially gigantic ones, cannot be directly encoded into a 16-bit or 32-bit instruction.

Example 1: Decoding **0100101000000110**

The above 16-bit instruction is decoded as "LDR Rt, [pc, #imm8<<2]", where #imm8 is 6 (00000110 in binary), according to 16-bit instruction format given in Appendix F. The offset is equal to #imm8 << 2 (*i.e.*, 24). Therefore, we can decode it as "LDR r2, [pc, #24]". If the memory address of this instruction is 0x080001CC, then the above instruction will load a word stored at the following target memory address:

Target address = $PC + 4 + \text{Offset} = 0x080001CC + 4 + 24 = 0x80001E8$

Example 2: Decoding **1101101111110111**

This 16-bit branch instruction is decoded as "B(cond) #imm8<<1", where the conditional code is 1011, representing "Less Than (LT)" (see Table 13-4), and #imm8 is 11110111. The offset is equal to 1111011<<1 = 111110110, representing -18 in two's complement.

Suppose the memory address of this branch instruction is 0x080001E2, then this branch instruction will jump to the instruction stored at the following target address if the comparison result is "Less Than."

Target address = $PC + 4 + \text{Offset} = 0x080001E2 + 4 + (-18) = 0x080001D4$

If we put a label, such as "loop", on the instruction stored at 0x080001D4, then we can translate this binary instruction to "BLT loop".

13.6 Instruction Decoding Example 1

We will show how to decode the following hex numbers into assembly instructions.

F04F, 0003, F04F, 0104, F04F, 0300, 2900
D003, 4403, F1A1, 0101, E7F9, 4618, E7FE

The first step is to divide all bits into instructions. If the most significant five bits of a halfword are 11101, 11110, or 11111, then this halfword starts a 32-bit instruction.

	15	14	13	12	11	10	9	8	7	6	5	4	3	2	1	0	16 or 32
0xF04F	1	1	1	1	0	0	0	0	0	1	0	0	1	1	1	1	32-bit
0x0003	0	0	0	0	0	0	0	0	0	0	0	0	0	0	1	1	instruction
0xF04F	1	1	1	1	0	0	0	0	0	1	0	0	1	1	1	1	32-bit
0x0104	0	0	0	0	0	0	0	1	0	0	0	0	0	1	0	0	instruction
0xF04F	1	1	1	1	0	0	0	0	0	1	0	0	1	1	1	1	32-bit
0x0300	0	0	0	0	0	0	1	1	0	0	0	0	0	0	0	0	instruction
0x2900	0	0	1	0	1	0	0	1	0	0	0	0	0	0	0	0	16-bit
0xD003	1	1	0	1	0	0	0	0	0	0	0	0	0	0	1	1	16-bit
0x4403	0	1	0	0	0	1	0	0	0	0	0	0	0	0	1	1	16-bit
0xF1A1	1	1	1	1	0	0	0	1	1	0	1	0	0	0	0	1	32-bit
0x0101	0	0	0	0	0	0	0	1	0	0	0	0	0	0	0	1	instruction
0xE7F9	1	1	1	0	0	1	1	1	1	1	1	1	1	0	0	1	16-bit
0x4618	0	1	0	0	0	1	1	0	0	0	0	1	1	0	0	0	16-bit
0xE7FE	1	1	1	0	0	1	1	1	1	1	1	1	1	1	1	0	16-bit

Table 13-3. Binary representation of the instructions

Decoding: 0xF04F, 0x0003 ⟹ MOV r0, #3

The five most significant bits of the first halfword is 11110, indicating that this halfword and the next halfword are parts of a 32-bit instruction. By looking up the opcode from the 32-bit decoding table (Appendix G), we know that this is an MOV instruction. According to the format of MOV instruction, we know that the destination register is 0000 (*i.e.*, r0), and the 11-bit immediate number is 00000000011 (*i.e.*, 3). Moreover, the S suffix is 0. Thus it is MOV, instead of MOVS. Therefore, this instruction is decoded as "MOV r0, #3".

	15	14	13	12	11	10	9	8	7	6	5	4	3	2	1	0
	1	1	1	op1		i	op2					S				
0xF04F	1	1	1	1	0	0	0	0	0	1	0	0	1	1	1	1

	15	14	13	12	11	10	9	8	7	6	5	4	3	2	1	0
	op	imm3			Rd				imm8							
0x0003	0	0	0	0	0	0	0	0	0	0	0	0	0	0	1	1

Decoding: 0xF04F, 0x0104 ⟹ MOV r1, #4

Similar to the previous instruction, we can decode this as "MOV r1, #4".

	15	14	13	12	11	10	9	8	7	6	5	4	3	2	1	0
	1	1	1	op1		i			op2			S				
0xF04F	1	1	1	1	0	0	0	0	0	1	0	0	1	1	1	1

	15	14	13	12	11	10	9	8	7	6	5	4	3	2	1	0
	op	imm3			Rd				imm8							
0x0104	0	0	0	0	0	0	0	1	0	0	0	0	0	1	0	0

Decoding: 0xF04F, 0x0300 ⟹ MOV r3, #0

Similar to the first instruction, we can decode this as "MOV r3, #0".

	15	14	13	12	11	10	9	8	7	6	5	4	3	2	1	0
	1	1	1	op1		i			op2			S				
0xF04F	1	1	1	1	0	0	0	0	0	1	0	0	1	1	1	1

	15	14	13	12	11	10	9	8	7	6	5	4	3	2	1	0
	op	imm3			Rd				imm8							
0x0300	0	0	0	0	0	0	1	1	0	0	0	0	0	0	0	0

Decoding: 0x2900 ⟹ CMP r1, #0

The most significant five bits is not 11101, 11110, nor 11111. Thus, it is a 16-bit instruction. The opcode is 001010, specifying it is a CMP instruction that compares a register with an 8-bit immediate number. The source operands include register r1 and an immediate number 0. Therefore, this instruction is decoded as "CMP r1, #0".

	15	14	13	12	11	10	9	8	7	6	5	4	3	2	1	0
	opcode						Rn			imm8						
0x2900	0	0	1	0	1	0	0	0	1	0	0	0	0	0	0	0

Decoding: 0xD003 ⟹ BEQ exit

Again, this is a 16-bit instruction. The condition code is listed as 0000, which represents EQ, according to Table 13-4.

	15	14	13	12	11	10	9	8	7	6	5	4	3	2	1	0
	1	1	0	1	cond				imm8							
0xD003	1	1	0	1	0	0	0	0	0	0	0	0	0	0	1	1

The 8-bit immediate number is 3. The immediate number is in two's complement format. Thus, the memory address offset can be negative, and the branch instruction can jump backward. The processor updates the program counter (PC) as follows if the branch is taken.

$$PC = PC + 4 + SignExtend\_to\_32Bits(imm8:'0')$$

In this example, we have $PC = PC + 4 + 3\times2 = PC + 10$, and the instruction that is branched to is 0x4618, to which we give a label "exit". Therefore, this instruction is decoded as "BEQ exit".

Condition Code	Suffix	Description
0000	EQ	EQual
0001	NE	Not Equal
0010	CS/HS	unsigned Higher or Same
0011	CC/LO	unsigned LOwer
0100	MI	MInus (Negative)
0101	PL	PLus (Positive or Zero)
0110	VS	oVerflow Set
0111	VC	oVerflow Clear
1000	HI	unsigned HIgher
1001	LS	unsigned Lower or Same
1010	GE	signed Greater or Equal
1011	LT	signed Less Than
1100	GT	signed Greater Than
1101	LE	signed Less than or Equal
1110	AL	ALways

Table 13-4. Condition code

Decoding: 0x4403 ⟹ ADD r3, r3, r0

This is a 16-bit instruction. The opcode shows it is "ADD". The destination register is DN:Rdn, *i.e.*, 0011 (r3). Register r3 is also a source operand. For this instruction, the S suffix is 0. Therefore, it is decoded as "ADD r3, r3, r0", or "ADD r3, r0".

	15	14	13	12	11	10	9	8	7	6	5	4	3	2	1	0
	opcode								DN	Rm				Rdn		
0x4403	0	1	0	0	0	1	0	0	0	0	0	0	0	0	1	1

Decoding: 0xF1A1, 0x0101 ⟹ SUB r1, r1, #1

This is a 32-bit instruction. The opcode indicates that it is SUB. The S suffix bit is 0, and thus it is not SUBS. The 12-bit immediate number (i:imm3:imm8) is 1. Thus, we have "SUB r1, r1, #1".

	15	14	13	12	11	10	9	8	7	6	5	4	3	2	1	0
	1	1	1	op1		op2							Rn			
						i	0	1	1	0	1	S				
0xF1A1	1	1	1	1	0	0	0	1	1	0	1	0	0	0	0	1

	15	14	13	12	11	10	9	8	7	6	5	4	3	2	1	0
	op	imm3			Rd				imm8							
0x0101	0	0	0	0	0	0	0	1	0	0	0	0	0	0	0	1

Decoding: 0xE7F9 ⟹ B loop

This 11-bit immediate number in this branch instruction is two's complement, representing -7. The program counter $PC = PC + 4 + (-7) \times 2 = PC - 10$, pointing to the instruction 0x2900, i.e., "CMP r1, #0". We labeled the CMP instruction as "loop", and this instruction is decoded as "B loop".

	15	14	13	12	11	10	9	8	7	6	5	4	3	2	1	0
	opcode					imm11										
0xE7F9	1	1	1	0	0	1	1	1	1	1	1	1	1	0	0	1

Decoding: 0x4618 ⟹ MOV r0, r3

The destination register of this 16-bit instruction is D:Rdn, i.e., 0000 (r0).

	15	14	13	12	11	10	9	8	7	6	5	4	3	2	1	0
	opcode						opcode2			Rm				Rdn		
									D							
0x4618	0	1	0	0	0	1	1	0	0	0	0	1	1	0	0	0

Decoding: 0xE7FE ⟹ B stop

This is a branch instruction, the program counter $PC = PC + 4 + (-2) \times 2 = PC$, which points to the instruction itself and creates a dead loop.

	15	14	13	12	11	10	9	8	7	6	5	4	3	2	1	0
	opcode					imm11										
0xE7FE	1	1	1	0	0	1	1	1	1	1	1	1	1	1	1	0

In summary, the following bit stream in hex format is decoded into 10 assembly instructions.

F04F,0003,F04F,0104,F04F,0300,2900,D003,4403,F1A1,0101,E7F9,4618,E7FE

Address Offset	Label	Binary Instruction	Decoded Instruction
0		F04F0003	MOV r0, #3
4		F04F0104	MOV r1, #4
8		F04F0300	MOV r3, #0
12	loop	2900	CMP r1, #0
14		D003	BEQ exit
16		4403	ADD r3, r3, r0
18		F1A10101	SUB r1, r1, #1
22		E7F9	B loop
24	exit	4618	MOV r0, r3
26	stop	E7FE	B stop

This program multiplies two integers, stored in register r0 and r1, respectively. The program saves the product in register r3 temporally during the execution and moves it to register r0 at the end. We can translate the above assembly program to a C program, which multiplies two integers via repeatedly adding the multiplicand to the product.

Assembly Program	C Program
``` MOV r0, #3 ; Multiplicand MOV r1, #4 ; Multiplier MOV r3, #0 ; Product loop CMP r1, #0 BEQ exit ADD r3, r3, r0 SUB r1, r1, #1 B loop exit MOV r0, r3 stop B stop ```	``` int a = 3; // Multiplicand int b = 4; // Multiplier int product = 0; for(int i = b; i > 0; i--) { product += a; } while(1); ```

13.7 Instruction Decoding Example 2

In this example, we will convert the following machine instructions into an assembly program. We examine the five most significant bits of each halfword to check whether it is a 16-bit instruction or part of a 32-bit instruction.

We find that two words, 0xF8511020 and 0xF84D1020, stored at the memory address 0x080001D6 and 0x080001DA respectively, are 32-bit instructions. The rest are 16-bit instructions.

Memory Address	HEX	Binary
0x080001C8	B08A	1011000010001010
0x080001CA	2100	0010000100000000
0x080001CC	4A06	0100101000000110
0x080001CE	6011	0110000000010001
0x080001D0	2000	0010000000000000
0x080001D2	E005	1110000000000101
0x080001D4	4905	0100100100000101
0x080001D6	**F851**	**1111100001010001**
0x080001D8	**1020**	**0001000000100000**
0x080001DA	**F84D**	**1111100001001101**
0x080001DC	**1020**	**0001000000100000**
0x080001DE	1C40	0001110001000000
0x080001E0	280A	0010100000001010
0x080001E2	DBF7	1101101111110111
0x080001E4	BF00	1011111100000000
0x080001E6	E7FE	1110011111111110
0x080001E8	0028	0000000000101000
0x080001EA	2000	0010000000000000
0x080001EC	0000	0000000000000000
0x080001EE	2000	0010000000000000

Table 13-5. Layout of instruction memory

The program also places two constants (0x20000028 and 0x20000000) in the binary instruction. They are the memory addresses of two variables in the data memory. The data memory layout is given as follows:

Memory Address	HEX
0x20000000	0
...	...
0x20000028	0x0001
0x2000002C	0x0002
0x20000030	0x0003
0x20000034	0x0004
0x20000038	0x0005
0x2000003C	0x0006
0x20000040	0x0007
0x20000044	0x0008
0x20000048	0x0009
0x2000004C	0x000A

Table 13-6. Layout of data memory

Following Appendix F and G, we can decode each binary instruction as follows.

Address	HEX	Binary and Decoded Instruction	Explanation
0x080001C8	B08A	1011_00001_0001010 **SUB SP, SP, #40**	SUB SP, SP, #imm7<<2 #imm7 = 0001010_2 #imm7 << 2 = 40

0x080001CA	2100	00100_001_00000000
		MOVS r1, #0
			MOV Rd, #imm8
			#imm8 = 00000000_2
			Rd = 001_2

0x080001CC	4A06	01001_010_00000110
		LDR r2, [pc, #24]
			LDR Rt, [pc, #imm8<<2]
			#imm8 = 00000110_2
			#imm8 << 2 = 11000_2 = 24
			Rt = 010_2
			
			Target address = pc + 4 + #imm8<<2
			= 0x080001CC + 4 + 24
			= 0x80001E8
			
			Load the memory address of the integer array. As results, r2 = 0x20000028

0x080001CE	6011	01100_00000_010_001
		STR r1, [r2, #0]
			STR Rt, [Rn, #imm5<<2]
			#imm5 = 00000_2
			Rt = 001_2
			Rn = 010_2

0x080001D0	2000	00100_000_00000000
		MOVS r0, #0
			MOV Rd, #imm8
			#imm8 = 00000000_2
			Rd = 000_2

0x080001D2	E005	11100_00000000101 **B check**	B #imm11<<1 #imm11 = 00000000101 #imm11<<1 = 10 Target pc = pc + 4 + 10 = 0x080001D2 + 14 = 0x080001E0

0x080001D4	4905	01001_001_00000101
		loop LDR r1, [pc, #20]
			LDR Rt, [pc, #imm8<<2]
			#imm8 = 00000101_2
			#imm8<<2 = 10100_2 = 20
			Rt = 001
			
			Target address = pc + 4 + #imm8<<2
			= 0x080001D4 + 4 + 20
			= 0x080001EC
			
			Load the memory address of the total variable. As results, r1 = 0x20000000

0x080001D6	F851	111110000101_0001	This halfword is part of a 32-bit instruction.

0x080001D8	1020	0001_000000_10_0000
		LDR r1, [r1,r0,LSL #2]
			LDR Rt, [Rn, Rm, LSL #imm2]
			#imm2 = 10_2
			Rt = 0001_2
			Rn = 0001_2
			Rm = 0000_2

0x080001DA	F84D	111110000100_1101	This halfword is part of a 32-bit instruction.

0x080001DC	1020	0001_000000_10_0000
		STR r1, [sp,r0,LSL #2]
			STR Rt, [Rn, Rm, LSL #imm2]
			#imm2 = 10_2
			Rt = 0001_2
			Rn = 1101_2
			Rm = 0000_2

0x080001DE	1C40	0001110_001_000_000
		ADDS r0, r0, #1
			ADD Rd, Rn, #imm3
			#imm3 = 001_2
			Rd = 000_2
			Rn = 000_2

0x080001E0	280A	00101_000_00001010
		check CMP r0, #10
			CMP Rn, #imm8
			#imm8 = 00001010_2 = 10
			Rn = 000_2

0x080001E2	DBF7	1101_1011_11110111
		BLT loop
			B(cond) #imm8<<1
			Cond = 1011_2 = Less Than
			#imm8 = 11110111_2
			#imm8<<1 = 111101110_2 = -18
			
			Target pc = pc + 4 − 18
			= 0x080001E2 − 14
			= 0x080001D4

0x080001E4	BF00	1011111100000000 **NOP**	
0x080001E6	E7FE	11100_11111111110 **self B self**	B #imm11<<1 #imm11 = 11111111110_2 #imm11<<1 = 111111111100_2 = -4 Target pc = pc + 4 + #imm11<<1 = pc + 4 − 4 = pc

The final decoded assembly program and its corresponding C program are given in the following table. The program uses PC-relative addressing to access the integer array *a* and the integer variable *total*. It is inferred from the binary code that the memory address of the array starts at 0x20000028, and the variable *total* is stored at 0x20000000.

Binary Program	Assembly Program	C Program

Refer to the data memory	`AREA myData, DATA`
	`total DCD 0`
	`a      DCD 1,2,3,4,5,6,7,8,9,10`
		`int total;`
		
		`int a[10] = {1, 2, 3, 4,`
		`5, 6, 7, 8, 9, 10};`

	`AREA myCode, CODE`
	`EXPORT __main`
	`__main PROC`
		`int main(void){`

B08A
2100
4A06
6011
2000
E005
	`      SUB  sp, sp, #0x28`
	`      MOVS r1, #0`
	`      LDR  r2, [pc, #24]`
	`      STR  r1, [r2, #0]`
	`      MOVS r0, #0`
	`      B check`
		`  int i;`
		`  int b[10];`
		
		`  total = 0;`

4905
F8511020
F84D1020
1C40
280A
DBF7
BF00
E7FE
	`loop  LDR  r1, [pc, #20]`
	`      LDR  r1, [r1,r0,LSL #2]`
	`      STR  r1, [sp,r0,LSL #2]`
	`      ADDS r0, r0, #1`
	`      CMP  r0, #10`
	`check BLT  loop`
	`      NOP`
	`self  B  self`
		`  for (i=0;i<10;i++){`
		
		`    b[i] = a[i];`
		
		`  }`
		
		`  while(1);`
		`}`

0028 ; *addr of a*
2000 ; *0x20000028*
0000 ; *addr of total*
2000 ; *0x20000000*
	`      DW 0x0028`
	`      DW 0x2000`
	`      DW 0x0000`
	`      DW 0x2000`	

	`      ENDP` `      END`	

13.8 Exercises

1. Translate the following 16-bit binary instructions into assembly instructions
    ```
    240A, 3430, 7004, 2A00,
    1E40, 1C49, 4288, BD30,
    468D, 0000, 6568, 6C20, 7A61
    ```

2. Translate the following 32-bit binary instructions into assembly instructions
    ```
    FB01F000, FBB2F5F4, FB042415,
    F2430039, F0210107, E8AC09C0,
    EA4F2030, EA804130, F04F0001,
    F0000301, EA4F0050
    ```

3. Translate the following binary program into an assembly program. What does the
    program perform? Translate the assembly program back to a C program.

0x080001FC	4601
0x080001FE	2941
0x08000200	DB04
0x08000202	295A
0x08000204	DC02
0x08000206	F1010020
0x0800020A	B2C1
0x0800020C	2961
0x0800020E	D007
0x08000210	2965
0x08000212	D005
0x08000214	2969
0x08000216	D003
0x08000218	296F
0x0800021A	D001
0x0800021C	2975
0x0800021E	D101
0x08000220	2001
0x08000222	4770
0x08000224	2000
0x08000226	E7FC
0x08000228	4A08
0x0800022A	4614
0x0800022C	E007
0x0800022E	7813
0x08000230	4618
0x08000232	F7FFFFE3
0x08000236	B908
0x08000238	7023
0x0800023A	1C64

0x0800023C	1C52
0x0800023E	7810
0x08000240	2800
0x08000242	D1F4
0x08000244	7020
0x08000246	BF00
0x08000248	E7FE
0x0800024A	0000
0x0800024C	0000
0x0800024E	2000
...	...
0x20000000	6854
0x20000002	2065
0x20000004	7571
0x20000006	6369
0x20000008	206B
0x2000000A	7262
0x2000000C	776F
0x2000000E	206E
0x20000010	6F66
0x20000012	2078
0x20000014	756A
0x20000016	706D
0x20000018	2073
0x2000001A	766F
0x2000001C	7065
0x2000001E	7420
0x20000020	6568
0x20000022	6C20
0x20000024	7A61
0x20000026	2079
0x20000028	6F64
0x2000002A	0067

4. Convert the binary search assembly program given in Chapter 7.12 to machine code manually.

General Purpose I/O (GPIO)

This chapter illustrates how a processor uses a GPIO pin as a digital input or digital output. Example applications presented include lighting an LED, interfacing a push button and scanning a keypad.

14.1 Introduction to General Purpose I/O (GPIO)

The number of pins available on a processor is usually limited. A processor pin that can be configured by software at runtime to perform various functions is called a general-purpose input/output (GPIO) pin. GPIO provides high flexibility of use and enormous convenience of system design. It enables a processor to meet the needs of a broad range of embedded system applications. However, the flexibility comes with a price tag. Software must perform a sophisticated initialization.

Software can program a GPIO pin as one of the following four different functions:

1. Digital input that detects whether an external voltage signal is higher or lower than a predetermined threshold

2. Digital output that controls the voltage on the pin

3. Analog functions that perform digital-to-analog or analog-to-digital conversion

4. Other complex functions such as PWM output, LCD driver, timer-based input capture, external interrupt, and interface of USART, SPI, I²C and USB communication

We call the last category of functions *alternate functions* (AF). The software can dynamically change the function of a GPIO pin at runtime. In this chapter, we focus on digital input and digital output, which are simply called input or output. Analog and other complex functions are introduced in the later chapters.

A GPIO port consists of a group of GPIO pins, typically 8 or 16, which share the same data and control registers.

- When a GPIO pin i is set as a *digital input*, the binary data read from this pin of this GPIO group is saved at bit i in the input data register (IDR). Each bit in IDR holds the digital input of the corresponding pin.

- When a GPIO pin i is configured as a *digital output*, bit i in the output data register (ODR) holds the output of this pin. Therefore, when changing the output of a GPIO pin, the programmer should only alter the value of the corresponding bit of ODR, without affecting the other bits in ODR. Chapter 4.6 introduces how to test, clear, set, and toggle a specific bit of a register in C and assembly.

- All GPIO pins in a GPIO port can be configured as input or output independently.

14.2 GPIO Input Modes: Pull Up and Pull Down

When a GPIO pin is used as digital input, the pin has three states: high voltage, low voltage, or high impedance (also called floating or tri-stated). Pull-up and pull-down are used to ensure the input pin has a valid high (logic 1) or a valid low (logic 0) when the external circuit does not drive the pin.

When software configures a pin as pull-up, the pin is internally connected to the power supply via a resistor, as shown in Figure 14-1. The pin is always read as high (logic 1) unless the external circuit drives this pin low.

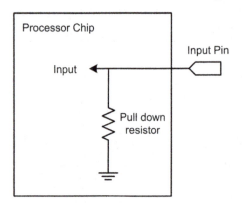

Figure 14-1. The GPIO pin is pulled up internally.

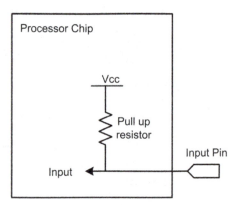

Figure 14-2. The GPIO pin is pulled down internally.

Similarly, when a pin is configured as pull-down, the pin is then internally connected to the ground via a resistor, as shown in Figure 14-2. The pin is always read as low (logic 0) unless the external circuit drives this pin high.

When a pin is neither pulled up nor pulled down internally, then the pin has high impedance, and the analog signal on the GPIO pin cannot reliably represent a logic value. Software can change the pull-up and pull-down setting of a GPIO pin dynamically at runtime.

When a pin is internally pulled up, but the external circuit drives the pin low, a pull-up current is generated and is drawn internally from the processor chip. Similarly, when a pin is pulled down within the chip, but the external circuit drives the pin to high, a pull-down current is drawn to the processor chip. To limit the pull-up/pull-down current, the internal resistors usually have a large impedance (> 10KΩ).

When an external circuit connected to a GPIO pin has a fair amount of capacitance, the process of pulling the pin voltage to the level of logic high or logic low takes a long time because the impedance of the pull-up and pull-down resistors is too large. We call pulling via large resistors *weak pull-up* or *weak pull-down*. The internal pulling often does not meet the speed requirement for fast communication protocols, such as I²C. To change the pin voltage rapidly, a

Strong vs Weak pull-up/pull-down

GPIO pin can be externally pulled up or down via a smaller resistor (several KΩs). Pulling via small resistors is often called **strong pull-up** or **strong pull-down**.

14.3 GPIO Input: Schmitt Trigger

Each GPIO input module usually includes a Schmitt trigger. A Schmitt trigger uses a voltage comparator to convert a noisy or slow signal edge into a clean edge with instantaneous transition.

In real systems, an input signal from external devices usually cannot change instantly. Such input signal tends to have a low slew rate (see definition in Chapter 14.5) because of inherent parasitic capacitance, resistance, or induction in the input data path. A processor chip usually has built-in Schmitt triggers to increase slew rate and enhance noise immunity for external input signals.

Figure 14-3 gives an example implementation of non-inverting Schmitt trigger with a reference voltage. The voltage comparator is an operational amplifier (op-amp) with positive feedback. The positive feedback is achieved by connecting the op-amp output to its non-inverting terminal (*i.e.*, the plus input lead).

The output voltage V_{out} responds rapidly to the difference between two input voltages V_+ and V_-. If V_+ is greater than V_-, V_{out} is quickly saturated to V_{SAT}; otherwise, V_{out} is zero in this example.

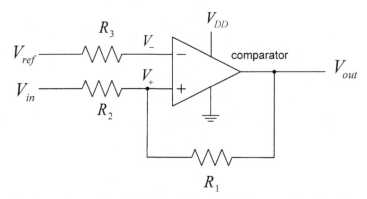

Figure 14-3. Circuit of non-inverting Schmitt trigger with hysteresis. Non-inverting means V_{in} is connected to the non-inverting terminal (*i.e.*, the plus input lead).

For an ideal op-amp, the current flowing through resistor R_3 is zero and thus we have

$$V_{ref} = V_-$$

The op-amp output V_{out} has two saturation values, as shown below

$$V_{out} = \begin{cases} V_{SAT} & if\ V_- < V_+ \\ 0 & if\ V_- > V_+ \end{cases}$$

However, V_+ depends on V_{out} and V_{in}. Therefore, V_{out} depends on both the input V_{in} and the recent history of V_{out}. Such an effect is called *hysteresis*.

Because the current flow into the positive input lead of the op-amp is assumed to be zero for an ideal op-amp, we can obtain the following equation by applying Kirchhoff's Current Law (KCL):

$$\frac{V_{in} - V_+}{R_2} = \frac{V_+ - V_{out}}{R_1}$$

Using the above equation, we can obtain the following expression:

$$V_+ = \frac{R_2}{R_1 + R_2} V_{out} + \frac{R_1}{R_1 + R_2} V_{in}$$

At the time instant when V_{out} transits from one saturation value to the other saturation value, we have

$$V_+ = V_{ref}$$

Thus

$$\frac{R_2}{R_1 + R_2}V_{out} + \frac{R_1}{R_1 + R_2}V_{in} = V_{ref}$$

Solving the above equation, we have

$$V_{in} = \left(1 + \frac{R_2}{R_1}\right)V_{ref} - \frac{R_2}{R_1}V_{out}$$

As discussed earlier, V_{out} has only two possible values. If $V_{out} = 0$ initially and V_{in} increases, we can obtain the trigger high threshold V_{TH} at which V_{out} transits to V_{SAT}:

$$V_{TH} = \left(1 + \frac{R_2}{R_1}\right)V_{ref} - \frac{R_2}{R_1}\times 0 = \left(1 + \frac{R_2}{R_1}\right)V_{ref}$$

On the other hand, if $V_{out} = V_{SAT}$ initially and V_{in} decreases, we can obtain the trigger low threshold V_{TL} at which V_{out} transits to 0:

$$V_{TL} = \left(1 + \frac{R_2}{R_1}\right)V_{ref} - \frac{R_2}{R_1}V_{SAT}$$

Therefore, V_{out} can be determined by comparing it with two thresholds V_{TH} and V_{TL}. Figure 14-4 shows the relationship of V_{out} and V_{in}. When V_{in} climbs through V_{TH}, V_{out} is rapidly switched to the upper limit V_{SAT}. Conversely, once V_{in} falls below V_{TL}, V_{out} makes a transition to the lower limit. Note that $V_{TH} > V_{TL}$, i.e., the threshold for switching to high is greater than the threshold of switching to low.

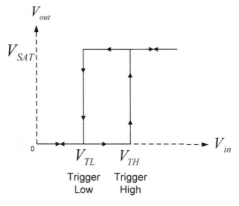

Figure 14-4. Relationship between V_{out} and V_{in} of inverting Schmitt trigger with reference voltage. V_{TL} and V_{TH} are the low and high switching thresholds.

Figure 14-5 compares the output voltage V_{out} of Schmitt trigger and a simple comparator when the input signal varies irregularly. Compared with a simple comparator, Schmitt trigger provides better noise rejection. The threshold of Schmitt trigger is larger than that of a simple comparator for switching high, and lower for switching low. If the input signal fluctuates slightly, the output of Schmitt trigger does not change. For this reason, Schmitt trigger is immune to undesired noise.

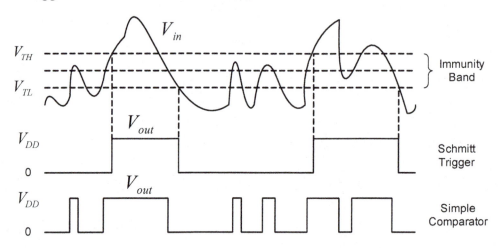

Figure 14-5. Comparing the voltage output of Schmitt trigger with a simple comparator. Schmitt trigger converts an irregular-shaped signal V_{in} into a square wave V_{out} based on two switching thresholds. The simple comparator uses a single threshold (the dotted line between V_{TL} and V_{TH}) to generate the output.

14.4 GPIO Output Modes: Push-Pull and Open-Drain

Software can configure a GPIO output pin as either push-pull or open-drain. Push-pull mode allows the pin to supply and absorb current. However, a GPIO pin in open-drain (also called collector) mode can only absorb current.

14.4.1   GPIO Push-Pull Output

A push-pull output consists of a pair of complementary transistors, as shown in Figure 14-6. Only one of them is turned on at any time.

- When logic 0 is outputted, the transistor connected to the ground is turned on to sink an electric current from the external circuit, as shown in Figure 14-7.

PUSH   PULL

- When the pin outputs logic 1, the transistor connected to the power supply is turned on, and it provides an electric current to the external circuit connected to the output pin, as shown in Figure 14-8.

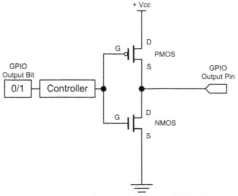

Figure 14-6. A push-pull GPIO digital output

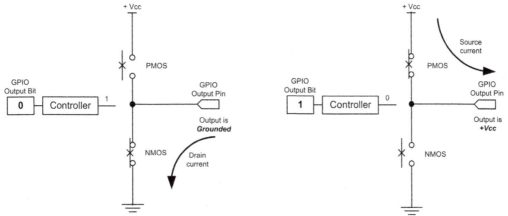

Figure 14-7. If the digital output is 0, then the GPIO output pin is pulled down to the ground in a push-pull setting.

Figure 14-8. If the digital output is 1, then the GPIO output pin is pulled up to the Vcc in a push-pull setting.

14.4.2   GPIO Open-Drain Output

An open-drain output consists of a pair of the same type of CMOS or transistors, as shown in Figure 14-9.

- When software outputs a logic 0, the open-drain circuit can sink an electric current from the external load connected to the GPIO pin.

OPEN   DRAIN

- However, when software outputs a logic 1, it cannot supply any electric current to the external load because the output pin is floating, connected to neither the power supply nor the ground.

An open-drain output has only two states: low voltage (logic 0), and high impedance (logic 1). It often has an external pull-up resistor.

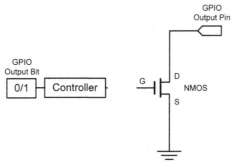

Figure 14-9. An open-drain GPIO digital output

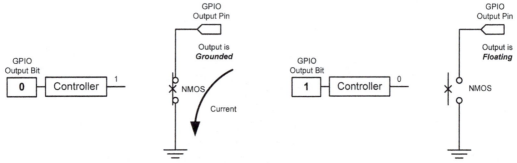

Figure 14-10. If the digital output is 0, then the output pin is pushed to the ground in an open-drain setting (the scenario of *drain*).

Figure 14-11. If the digital output is 1, then the output pin is floating in an open-drain setting (the scenario of *open*).

One important usage of open-drain outputs is to connect directly several outputs together and implement wired logic AND (active high) or OR (active low) circuit in an easy way. If multiple open-drain output pins are connected and are pulled up via a shared resistor, any output pin can drive the output voltage low. The pin voltage is high if and only if all pins output a high voltage level.

- If a high voltage level represents logic state 1 (*i.e.*, active high), it implements a wired-AND function. The final output is 1 (high) only if all outputs of connected pins are 1 (high).

- If a low voltage level represents logic state 1 (*i.e.*, active low), it implements a wired-OR function. The final output is 1 (low) if the output of any pins is 1 (low).

For example, the I2C communication protocol uses wired-OR to allow multiple master devices to operate on the same bus.

Figure 14-12 shows the implementation of wired-AND by using open drain and external pull-up when active high logic is used. The output C is determined by the following table.

Inputs				Output
Logic A	Logic B	Circuit A	Circuit B	
0	0	Drain	Drain	0
0	1	Drain	Open	0
1	0	Open	Drain	0
1	1	Open	Open	1

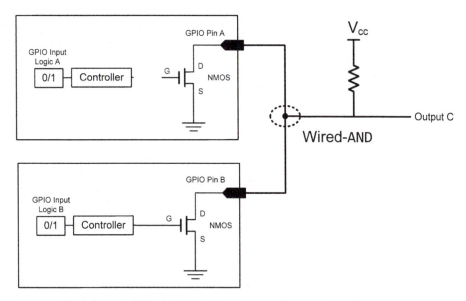

Figure 14-12. Implementation of Wired AND by using open drain and external pull up

Compared to open-drain, push-pull mode has the advantage of faster speed, because it can change the pin voltage faster if the external circuit has some capacitance. Another advantage is that it can supply current and simplify the circuit. For example, a push-pull output can directly control an external LED while an open-drain output cannot light up an LED without external voltage source.

However, the wired-OR characteristics can only be provided in open-drain outputs. Usually, push-pull output pins cannot be directly connected, because it might cause a potential short circuit. Additionally, open-drain output allows the pin to be pulled up to any voltage. This feature can be helpful when a GPIO pin is used as an input to another system that requires a higher level of input voltage.

14.5 GPIO Output Speed: Slew Rate

The slew rate of a GPIO pin is the speed of change of its output voltage per unit of time, as defined as follows.

$$Slew\ Rate = \frac{\Delta V}{\Delta t}$$

If the logic output of a GPIO pin changes from 0 to 1 and accordingly the voltage output of this pin rises from 0V to 3V in 3μs, then the slew rate is 1 volt per μs. Figure 14-13 shows an example of ΔV and Δt when the output voltage increases from low to high. The slew rate definition applies to both the rising edge and the falling edge of a voltage output.

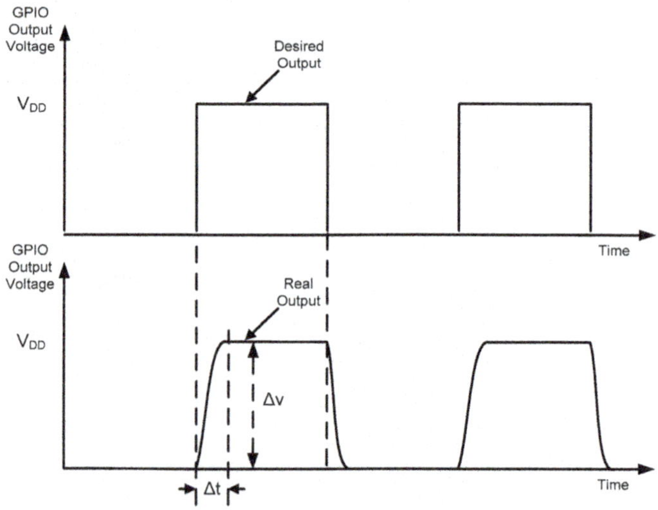

Figure 14-13. Comparing a desired square wave voltage output with the real GPIO output

The higher the slew rate, the shorter time the output voltage takes to rise or fall to desired values. Therefore, a higher slew rate allows faster speed at which the processor can toggle the logic level of a GPIO pin. Figure 14-13 also compares the desired square wave output and the real output when the logic output of a GPIO pin is toggled periodically. A shorter rise and fall time allows a GPIO pin to change its logic value more rapidly.

However, a large slew rate often causes high electromagnetic interference (EMI), also called radio frequency interference (RFI) to neighbor electronic circuits. A fast rising and falling signal has large-amplitude and high-frequency harmonics, which can transfer to a victim circuit via radiation, conduction, or induction, and may cause malfunctions. A slower valid slew rate is often preferred to minimize EMI disturbance.

The slew rate of the GPIO circuit is programmable by setting the GPIO output speed. For example, the digital output speed of a GPIO pin can be low speed (400 kHz), medium speed (2 MHz), fast speed (10 MHz), or high speed (40 MHz) in the STM32L processors.

14.6 Memory-mapped I/O

Typically, an on-chip peripheral device has a few registers, such as control registers, status registers, data input registers, and data output registers. A peripheral may also have data buffers, such as the display memory of the LCD controller. Input/output or I/O refers to data communication between the processor core and a peripheral device.

There are two complementary approaches to performing I/O operations: port-mapped I/O, and memory-mapped I/O.

- *Port-mapped I/O* uses special machine instructions, which are designed specifically for I/O operations. The memory address space and the I/O device address space are independent of each other. Each device is assigned one or more unique port numbers. For example, Intel x86 processors use IN and OUT instructions to read from or write to a port.

- *Memory-mapped I/O* does not need any special instructions. The memory and the I/O devices share the same address space. Each peripheral register or data buffer is assigned to a memory address in the memory address space of the microprocessor. Memory-mapped I/O is performed by the native load and store instructions of the processor. Therefore, memory-mapped I/O is a more convenient way to interface I/O devices. The most significant disadvantage is that memory-mapped I/O has a more complex address decoding unit than port-mapped I/O.

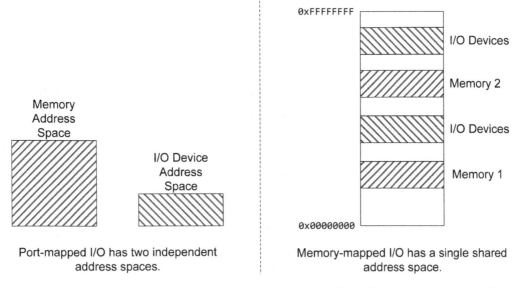

Port-mapped I/O has two independent address spaces.

Memory-mapped I/O has a single shared address space.

Figure 14-14. Comparison between port-mapped I/O and memory-mapped I/O

ARM Cortex-M processors use memory-mapped I/O to access peripheral registers. All peripheral registers on STM32L4 are mapped to a small memory region starting at 0x40000000. This region includes the memory addresses of all on-chip peripherals, such as GPIO, timers, UART, SPI, and ADC. The memory address of each peripheral register is determined by chip manufacturers, and usually cannot be changed by software.

A peripheral register usually takes four bytes in memory. For example, the output data register (ODR) of Port B on STM32L4 is mapped to memory addresses 0x48000414 to 0x48000417, with the upper halfword being reserved. Note that values stored in peripheral registers are in the format of little-endian (see Section 5.2).

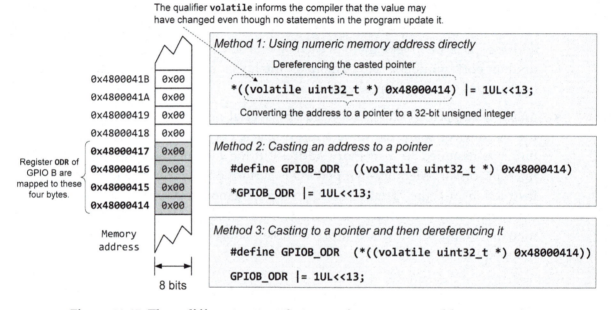

Figure 14-15. Three different approaches to casting a memory address to a pointer

To output high on pin i, $i = 0, 1, 2, ..., 15$, software needs to set bit i in ODR to 1. For example, to set the output of GPIO pin B 13 to high, software can use the following statement:

```
*((volatile uint32_t *) 0x48000414) |= 1UL<<13;
```

First, this C statement casts the numeric memory address to a pointer, which points to a volatile 32-bit unsigned variable. Note that we put a volatile qualifier on each register. When a variable is declared as volatile, the compiler is informed that even though no statements in the program appear to change it, the value might still change. Typically, compilers minimize the number of memory accesses, by temporally storing the memory value in a register, and then repeatedly using it without accessing the memory. The volatile qualifier on a variable prevents the compiler from making such optimization on this variable.

Then, it uses dereferencing to access the value stored in the memory location pointed to by the pointer. However, this C statement is difficult to read and maintain.

Figure 14-15 shows two better approaches (Methods 2 and 3), which use a macro to improve the code's readability. The macro in the second method represents type-casting. The macro in the third method represents both type-casting and dereferencing.

Nevertheless, these approaches are still inconvenient for two reasons.

- First, we must define many macros, one for each peripheral register, even though some peripherals share the same register layout.
- Second, if a function takes a peripheral as input, it is cumbersome to pass all registers of this peripheral as function arguments.

A better approach is to use structures and pointers. Typically, all registers of a peripheral, such as those of GPIO port B (shown in Figure 14-16), are mapped to a contiguous block of physical memory. Therefore, we can define a data structure whose memory layout matches the address assignment given by the chip manufacturer. In C, a struct encapsulates related variables into a single structure. All variables in a struct are stored contiguously in memory.

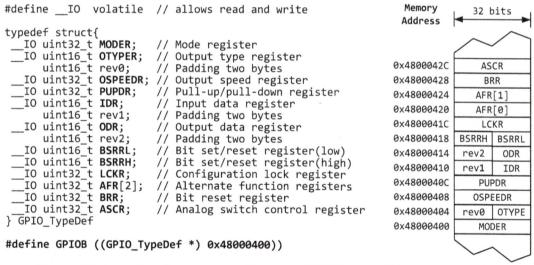

Figure 14-16. Casting the memory address of GPIO B to a GPIO structure pointer.

Let's take GPIO port B as an example. Each GPIO port has a set of registers, such as the mode register (MODER), the output data register (ODR), and the output speed register (OSPEEDR).

- The memory addresses of the registers are defined during the chip design stage. Software cannot change them.

- Each GPIO port has up to 16 pins, and each pin may take 1, 2, or 4 bits in a control register. For example, two bits are required to specify the mode of a GPIO pin. Therefore, the size of these control registers can be either 2, 4, or 8 bytes.
- Because the memory address of each register is word-aligned (*i.e.,* is a multiple of four, see Chapter 10.1.2), dummy bytes are padded in the data structure to correctly map the fixed physical memory layout to the data structure.

To conveniently access a set of registers which are contiguous in memory, we can cast the base memory address of a GPIO port to a pointer to a data structure, as shown below.

```
#define GPIOB ((GPIO_TypeDef *) 0x48000400))
```

In Figure 14-16, six bytes are padded in the GPIO_TypeDef structure, making its structure members align properly with their pre-defined memory addresses. Also, in the GPIO_TypeDef struct, we put a volatile qualifier on each register. This informs the compiler that the variable might change spontaneously by another task thread or by hardware.

If we want to set the output of GPIO port B pin 6 to high, we can use the following C statement. 1UL is an unsigned long integer with a value of 1. Note the pins are numbered 0 – 15, instead of 1 – 16.

```
GPIOB->ODR |= 1UL<<6;      // Set bit 6
```

Encapsulating all registers of a peripheral inside a structure provides several advantages.

1. It allows software to access registers in a very convenient way.
2. We can reuse the structure for all peripherals with the same sets of registers. For example, we can reuse the GPIO_TypeDef struct for all GPIO ports, as shown below.

```
#define GPIOA ((GPIO_TypeDef *) 0x48000000))
#define GPIOB ((GPIO_TypeDef *) 0x48000400))
#define GPIOC ((GPIO_TypeDef *) 0x40000800))
```

3. We can pass all registers of a peripheral to a function via a single struct pointer.

```
void GPIO_Init (GPIO_TypeDef * GPIO);

void main(void){
  GPIO_Init(GPIOA);
  GPIO_Init(GPIOB);

  ...
}
```

14.7 Lighting up an LED

The following shows the basic procedure for lighting up an LED. The software initialization involves two key steps. First, it enables the clock of the GPIO port B via the RCC module. Second, it configures pin 2 of GPIO port B as a general-purpose output pin, with the output type as push-pull. To light up the red LED, we need to output logic "1" to pin 2.

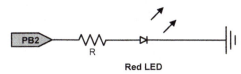

Red LED

Figure 14-17. Connection diagram between a processor pin and LED

In assembly, a load-modify-store sequence is required to change the register value stored in memory. Also, we can use "EQU" directive to create symbols for the GPIO B base address and ODR register offset, which make the assembly program more readable and self-documenting. The following is an example.

```
GPIOB_BASE EQU 0x48000400    ; Base memory address
GPIO_ODR   EQU 20            ; Byte offset of ODR from the base

LDR r7, =GPIOB_BASE          ; Load GPIO port B base address
LDR r1, [r7, #GPIO_ODR]      ; Read GPIOB->ODR
ORR r1, r1, #(1<<6)          ; Set bit 6
STR r1, [r7, #GPIO_ODR]      ; Write to GPIOB->ODR
```

Additionally, we also need to enable the clock of GPIO port B. To save energy, every peripheral's clock is turned off by default. We can enable the clock of a peripheral by setting the corresponding bit of the clock control register defined in the reset and clock control (RCC) structure, as shown below.

```
// Reset and clock control
typedef struct {
    __IO uint32_t CR;        // Clock control register
    __IO uint32_t ICSCR;     // Internal clock sources calibration register
    __IO uint32_t CFGR;      // Clock configuration register
    ...
    __IO uint32_t AHB1ENR;   // AHB1 peripheral clocks enable register
    __IO uint32_t AHB2ENR;   // AHB2 peripheral clocks enable register
    __IO uint32_t AHB3ENR;   // AHB3 peripheral clocks enable register
    ...
} RCC_TypeDef;

#define RCC ((RCC_TypeDef *) 0x40021000))
```

The following C statements enable the clock of GPIO port B.

```
#define RCC_AHB2ENR_GPIOBEN  (0x00000002)
RCC->AHB2ENR |= RCC_AHB2ENR_GPIOBEN;
```

Figure 14-18 shows the flowchart of initializing a GPIO pin as digital output with push-pull.

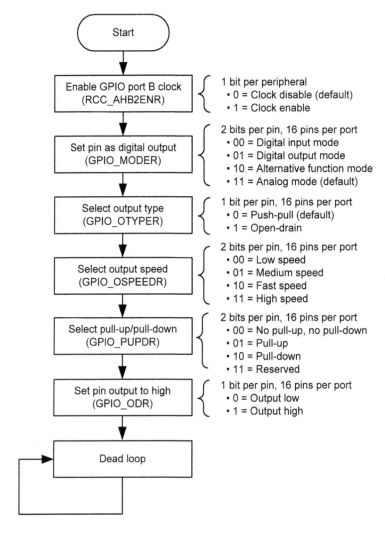

Figure 14-18. Flowchart of GPIO initialization

The following C program demonstrates how to set up a GPIO pin and light up an LED in detail. Suppose we use the GPIO pin PB 2 to drive a red LED.

- When we change the value of specific bits in a register, we need to preserve the value of the other bits in this register to avoid creating unexpected negative impacts. For example, if we want to set the least significant bit in register R, "R = 0x1;" is incorrect because it also clears all the other bits. Instead, we should use a bitwise logical OR operation "R |= 0x1;".

- When we change the value of multiple bits, it is a good practice to reset these bits before updating them. For example, if we want to set the least significant four bits $b_3b_2b_1b_0$ in register R to 1001, we need to clear these four bits first by running "R &= ~0xF; R |= 0x9;" If we do not clear these four bits first, we may fail to set the register correctly if their initial values are not 0. For example, if the value of $b_3b_2b_1b_0$ is 0111 initially, "R |= 0x9;" will lead a binary result of 1111.

Each GPIO port has a data output register (ODR) and a data input register (IDR).

- Each bit in ODR controls the output of a corresponding GPIO pin in this port. In a push-pull setting, if the bit value is 1, the output voltage on its corresponding GPIO pin is high; if the bit value is 0, the output voltage then is low.

- The IDR register records the input of all pins of a GPIO port.

```c
// Red LED is connected PB 2 (GPIO port B pin 2)
void GPIO_Clock_Enable(){
    // Enable the clock to GPIO port B
    RCC->AHB2ENR |= RCC_AHB2ENR_GPIOBEN;
}

void GPIO_Pin_Init(){
    // Set mode of pin 2 as digital output
    // 00 = digital input,          01 = digital output
    // 10 = alternate function,     11 = analog (default)
    GPIOB->MODER &= ~(3UL<<4);    // Clear mode bits
    GPIOB->MODER |= 1UL<<4;       // mode = 01, digital output

    // Set output type of pin 2 as push-pull
    // 0 = push-pull (default)
    // 1 = open-drain
    GPIOB->OTYPER &= ~(1<<2);

    // Set output speed of pin 2 as Low
    // 00 = Low speed,      01 = Medium speed
    // 10 = Fast speed,     11 = High speed
    GPIOB->OSPEEDR &= ~(3UL<<4);      // Clear speed bits

    // Set pin 2 as no pull-up, no pull-down
    // 00 = no pull-up, no pull-down  01 = pull-up
    // 10 = pull-down,                11 = reserved
    GPIOB->PUPDR &= ~(3UL<<4);        // no pull-up, no pull-down
}
```

```c
int main(void){
    GPIO_Clock_Enable();
    GPIO_Pin_Init();
    GPIOB->ODR |= 1UL<<6;   // Set bit 6 of output data register (ODR)
    while(1);               // Dead loop & program hangs here
}
```

Example 14-1. Lighting up an LED in C

The implementation in assembly is like the above C program. In the program,

- GPIOB_BASE and RCC_BASE are pre-defined memory addresses
- GPIO_MODER, GPIO_OTYPER, GPIO_OSPEEDR, GPIO_PUPDR, and GPIO_ODR are byte offset of its corresponding variable in the data structure GPIO_TypeDef defined previously.

It is a good practice to define a frequently used constant as some symbols associated with meaningful semantics. We can use the "EQU" directive to define symbols in assembly. This practice can effectively make a program easier to read and debug.

```
; Constants defined in file stm32l476xx_constants.s
;
; Memory addresses of GPIO port B and RCC (reset and clock control) data
; structure. These addresses are predefined by the chip manufacturer.
GPIOB_BASE          EQU     0x48000400
RCC_BASE            EQU     0x40021000

; Byte offset of each variable in the GPIO_TypeDef structure
GPIO_MODER          EQU     0x00
GPIO_OTYPER         EQU     0x04
GPIO_RESERVED0      EQU     0x06
GPIO_OSPEEDR        EQU     0x08
GPIO_PUPDR          EQU     0x0C
GPIO_IDR            EQU     0x10
GPIO_RESERVED1      EQU     0x12
GPIO_ODR            EQU     0x14
GPIO_RESERVED2      EQU     0x16
GPIO_BSRRL          EQU     0x18
GPIO_BSRRH          EQU     0x1A
GPIO_LCKR           EQU     0x1C
GPIO_AFR0           EQU     0x20  ;  AFR[0]
GPIO_AFR1           EQU     0x24  ;  AFR[1]
GPIO_AFRL           EQU     0x20
GPIO_AFRH           EQU     0x24

; Byte offset of variable AHB2ENR in the RCC_TypeDef structure
RCC_AHB2ENR         EQU     0x4C
```

The following shows the assembly program that sets pin B.2 output to high.

```
    INCLUDE stm321476xx_constants.s

    AREA    main, CODE, READONLY
    EXPORT      __main              ; make __main visible to linker
    ENTRY

__main PROC
    ; Enable the clock to GPIO port B
    ; Load address of reset and clock control (RCC)
    LDR r2, =RCC_BASE               ; Pseduo instruction
    LDR r1, [r2, #RCC_AHB2ENR]      ; r1 = RCC->AHB2ENR
    ORR r1, r1, #2                  ; Set bit 2 of AHB2ENR
    STR r1, [r2, #RCC_AHB2ENR]      ; GPIO port B clock enable

    ; Load GPIO port B base address
    LDR r3, =GPIOB_BASE             ; Pseduo instruction

    ; Set pin 2 I/O mode as general-purpose output
    LDR r1, [r3, #GPIO_MODER]       ; Read the mode register
    BIC r1, r1, #(3 << 4)           ; Direction mask pin 6, clear bits 5 and 4
    ORR r1, r1, #(1 << 4)           ; Set mode as digital output (mode = 01)
    STR r1, [r3, #GPIO_MODER]       ; Save to the mode register

    ; Set pin 2 the push-pull mode for the output type
    LDR r1, [r3, #GPIO_OTYPER]      ; Read the output type register
    BIC r1, r1, #(1<<2)             ; Push-pull(0), open-drain (1)
    STR r1, [r3, #GPIO_OTYPER]      ; Save to the output type register

    ; Set I/O output speed value as low
    LDR r1, [r3, #GPIO_OSPEEDR]     ; Read the output speed register
    BIC r1, r1, #(3<<4)             ; Low(00), Medium(01), Fast(01), High(11)
    STR r1, [r3, #GPIO_OSPEEDR]     ; Save to the output speed register

    ; Set I/O as no pull-up, no pull-down
    LDR r1, [r3, #GPIO_PUPDR]       ; r1 = GPIOB->PUPDR
    BIC r1, r1, #(3<<4)             ; No PUPD(00), PU(01), PD(10), Reserved(11)
    STR r1, [r3, #GPIO_PUPDR]       ; Save pull-up and pull-down setting

    ; Light up LED
    LDR r1, [r3, #GPIO_ODR]         ; Read the output data register
    ORR r1, r1, #(1<<2)             ; Set bit 2
    STR r1, [r3, #GPIO_ODR]         ; Save to the output data register

stop
    B  stop   ; dead loop & program hangs here
    ENDP
    END
```

Example 14-2. Lighting up an LED in an assembly program

14.8 Push Button

When a mechanical button is pressed, two metal contacts bang together and immediately rebound a couple of times before setting. These rebounds produce multiple signals within a few milliseconds due to the bounce effects. Figure 14-19 shows the voltage signal across a push button when it is pressed at the time instant 0. Because the processor runs at a fast speed, the processor can observe these falling and rising transitions and mistakenly thinks the push button has been pressed multiple times.

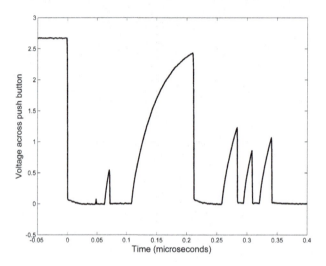

Figure 14-19. The voltage across a push button when there is no hardware debouncing

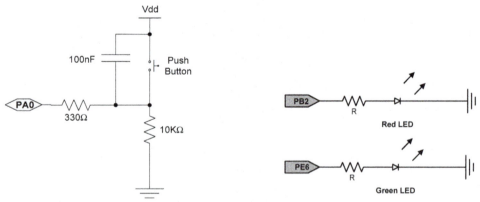

Figure 14-20. A push button with RC debouncer

Figure 14-21. Red and green LED

There are both hardware and software solutions to eliminate the bouncing effects. These solutions are called *debouncing*.

The *hardware debouncing* usually uses a simple RC circuit, which includes a capacitor connected in parallel with the pushbutton to filter out any high-frequency signals, as shown in Figure 14-20. When the switch is open, this capacitor is fully charged. Therefore, there is no current on these resistors, and the voltage on the processor pin is zero. As soon as the button is pressed, the capacitor is quickly discharged. If the button rebounds and the switch is open briefly, the capacitor cannot be recharged fast enough to pull the processor pin low. Figure 14-22 shows the voltage signals when the LED is lit up after the push button is pressed. It indicates that the voltage on the pin (PA 0) connected to the push button rises smoothly without generating any bouncing signals.

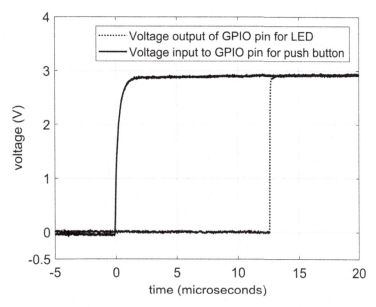

Figure 14-22. Voltage signals on the LED pin when the push button is pressed

The easiest *software debouncing* technique is *wait-and-see*, as shown in Example 14-3. When the program detects that a button is pressed, it re-examines the input signal after a short delay, typically between 20 and 50 *ms*. If the input signal still shows the button is pressed, the program then reports that the button has been pressed indeed.

```
bool is_button_pressed(){
    read button input;
    if (button is not pressed) return false;
    wait 50 ms;
    read button input again;
    if (button is not pressed) return false;
    return true;
}
```

Example 14-3. Pseudocode of *wait-and-see* software debouncing

However, the response time of the wait-and-see technique is significant and is not acceptable in many applications, such as gaming or mission-critical systems. A better software debouncing technique is *counter debouncer*. It polls the button input at regular intervals and requires a few consecutive positive readings to confirm the button has been pressed. In Example 14-4, the pin is polled every 5 *ms* during the debounce period 50 *ms*, and it requires 4 consecutive positive readings. If a button is pressed, this approach has less response time than the wait-and-see method.

```
bool is_button_pressed(){

   read button input;
   if (button is not pressed)
      return false;

   counter = 0;

   for(i = 0; i < 10; i++){
      wait 5 ms;
      read button input;
      if (button is not pressed) {
         counter = 0;              // bounce, reset counter
      } else {
         counter = counter + 1; // stable, increase counter
         if (counter >= 4)       // require 4 consecutive positive readings
            return true;
      }
   }
   return false;
}
```

Example 14-4. Pseudocode of *counter-debouncer* software debouncing

One issue in software debouncing methods is how to implement the time delay. Many new programmers use a large `for` or `while` loop to achieve the delay, as shown below.

```
void wait_ms(unsigned uint32_t ms){
   unsigned int i, j;
   for(i = 0; i < ms; i++)
      for(j = 0; j < 255; j++); // adjust 255 to achieve 1 ms delay
}
```

Example 14-5. Loop-based time delay

The loop-based time delay is not recommended for real-time embedded systems. First, these busy loops tie up the processor and prevent other tasks from running, wasting processor time and energy. Second, the timing may change dramatically based on compiler versions, compiler optimization levels, and processor speed.

A better implementation is to use timer interrupts, as shown in Example 14-6.

```
volatile uint8_t counter = 0;
volatile uint8_t pressed = 0;

// Set up timer 4 to generate an interrupt every 5 ms
...

void TIM4_IRQHandler(void) {
   ...
   if((GPIOA->IDR & 0x1) == 0x1){  // check input on pin PA.0
      counter++;              // button is pressed
      if (counter >= 4) {
         pressed = 1;      // set the flag
         counter = 0;      // reset counter
      } else {             // button is not pressed
         counter = 0;      // reset counter
      }
   }
}
```

Example 14-6. Using timer interrupts to implement counter debouncer

The following shows a polling I/O method (*busy waiting*) to constantly query the input of external devices. Software repeatedly checks whether the push button is pressed or not. Although the polling method is simple, it is inherently inefficient because the CPU wastes many cycles on querying or waiting for input. A method based on interrupts is more efficient than polling. See Chapter 11.8 external interrupts.

Suppose a push button is connected to the GPIO pin PA 0, and an LED is attached to the GPIO in PB 2, as shown in Figure 14-20 and Figure 14-21. Because hardware debouncing is used for the push button, software debouncing is not deployed in this example. All inputs of a GPIO port are stored in its input data register (IDR). Specifically, the input of pin 0 is saved at bit 0 in IDR. A low voltage input yields to a value of 0, and a high voltage generates a value of 1. Figure 14-23 gives the program flowchart.

```
// Enable the clock to GPIO port A and B
RCC->AHB2ENR |= RCC_AHB2ENR_GPIOAEN | RCC_AHB2ENR_GPIOBEN;

// Set mode of pin 0 as general-purpose input
// 00 = Digital input,        01 = Digital output
// 10 = Alternate function,   11 = Analog
GPIOA->MODER &= ~3UL;           // Set mode as input (00)

// Set I/O as no pull-up, no pull-down
// 00 = No pull-up/pull down, 01 = Pull-up
// 10 = Pull-down,            11 = Reserved
GPIOA->PUPDR &= ~3UL;           // Pull-up pull-down mask
```

```
// Set PB.2 as digital output with push-pull, no pull-up/pull-down
// See Example 14-1
...

while (1) {
  // Toggle red LED when button PA.0 is pushed
  if((GPIOA->IDR & 0x1) == 0x1){
    GPIOB->ODR ^= GPIO_ODR_ODR_2;        // Toggle pin PB.2
    while((GPIOA->IDR & 0x1) != 0x00); // Wait until button is released
  }
}
```

Example 14-7. Read pin PA.0, and toggle pin PB.2 if the input on PA.0 is 1. No software debouncing is used because pin PA.0 has been debounced by hardware.

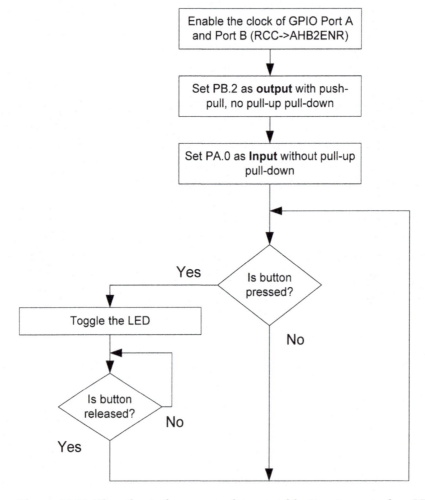

Figure 14-23. Flowchart of programming a pushbutton to control an LED

14.9 Keypad Scan

Suppose we have a keypad that has 12 keys, as shown in Figure 14-24. One simple way is to interface each key in the same approach as a push button, with each key having a dedicated pin to detect whether it is pressed or not. However, this would require 12 I/O pins, which is not desirable for many applications because the total number of pins available for use on a microcontroller is limited. To reduce the number of pins required, a keypad usually organizes its keys in a matrix, as shown in Figure 14-25. This matrix scheme decreases the number of I/O pins from 12 to 7 in this example.

On most processors, a GPIO pin provides only weak pull-up and weak pull-down internally. The internal pull-up and pull-down circuit consists of a 60KΩ resistor in series with a switchable PMOS/NMOS. The pull-up and pull-down configuration bits of a GPIO pin turn on or turn off the PMOS and NMOS.

When the load has a fair amount of capacitance, applications often require a strong pull-up or pull-down to shorten the rising or falling time of the voltage signal on a pin. In a strong pull-up or strong pull-down setting, the pin should be externally connected to the ground or high voltage via a resistor with a much lower resistance than the internal pull-up and pull-down resistors. In Figure 14-25, each pin connected to the input port (C1, C2, and C3) is pulled up to 3.3V via a 2.2KΩ resistor. Because these pins are externally pulled up, they should be configured as no pull-up and no pull-down internally.

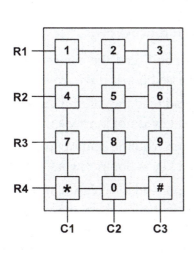

Figure 14-24. 3×4 keypad

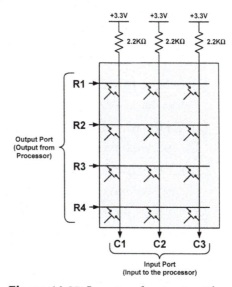

Figure 14-25. Input and output setting

Scanning algorithm is widely used to detect which key is pressed. The algorithm has two iterations of loops: looping over the row pins and then looping over the column pins. Suppose all row pins are set as output and all column pins are set as input. Each column pin is pulled up to a high-level voltage via a small resistor. The algorithm involves two steps.

1. Identify the column number of the pressed key. Set the output of all row pins as zero and read all column pins. If all columns are read as 1, then no key has been pressed. If one of them is zero, then at least one of the keys in that corresponding column is pushed down.

2. Identify the row number of the pressed key. Drive the output of the first row low (zero) while keeping the other rows at high (one). For example, suppose the input of column C2 is read as zero. If the input of C2 is still zero when the output of row R1 is high, then the pressed key is not located in row R1. Otherwise, row R1 is the row in which the pressed key is located. We repeat the process for all the other rows until the row is identified successfully.

The following gives a simple example how the scanning algorithm works when the key "0" is pressed.

1. Before key "0" is pressed, the row output port is set as low, *i.e.*, R1,R2,R3,R4 = 0000. If the input port is read now, C1, C2, and C3 are read as one, *i.e.*, C1,C2,C3 = 111.

2. When key "0" is pressed, the column C2 is connected to the ground via the R4 pin (because R4 is set to 0). Thus, we have C1,C2,C3 = 101 and we successfully identify that the pressed key is in the C2 column.

3. After the column is identified, we scan the output row by row.

    (1) Set the row output (R1,R2,R3,R4) as 0111, and read the column input. In this case, we have C1,C2,C3 = 111. The pressed key is not in row R1.

    (2) Set the row output (R1,R2,R3,R4) as 1011, and read the column input. In this case, we have C1,C2,C3 = 111. The pressed key is not in row R2.

    (3) Set the row output (R1,R2,R3,R4) as 1101, and read the column input. In this case, we have C1,C2,C3 = 111. The pressed key is not in row R3.

    (4) Set the row output (R1,R2,R3,R4) as 1110, and read the column input. In this case, we have C1,C2,C3 = 101. Because C2 is read as zero, the pressed key is in row R4.

4. After identifying that the pressed key is in column C2 and row R4, we can look up the pre-defined mapping table of the matrix keypad to find that key "0" has been pressed.

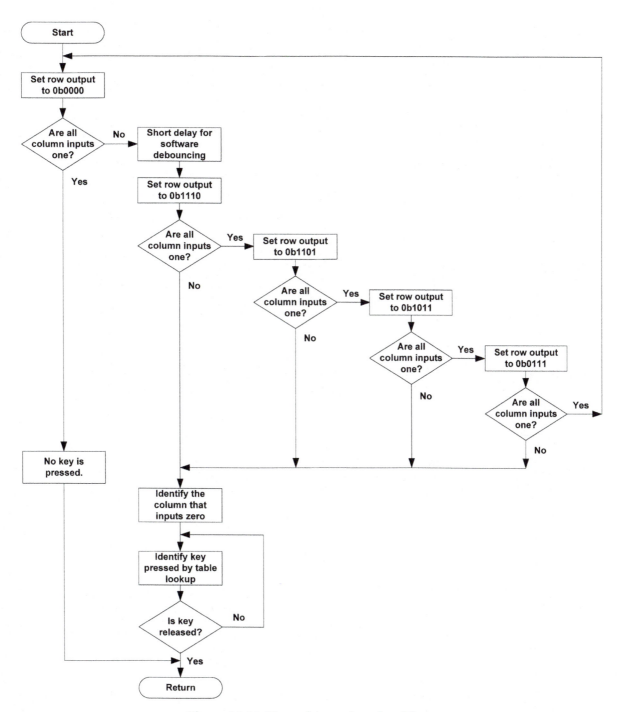

Figure 14-26. Keypad scanning algorithm.
All rows are set as output, and all columns are set as inputs.

Figure 14-26 gives the flowchart of the keypad scanning algorithm introduced previously.
In the following, we will show partial implementation scanning algorithm in C.

To facilitate the key lookup, we define a key-map array, which is used to convert the key position (row, column) to its corresponding logic number or letter.

```
unsigned char key_map [4][3] = {
    {'1','2','3'},  // 1st row
    {'4','5','6'},  // 2nd row
    {'7','8','9'},  // 3rd row
    {'*','0','#'},  // 4th row
};
```

The sketch of the scanning subroutine is given below. It identifies the row and column of the key pressed, and returns the ASCII value of the key pressed. When no key has been pressed, it returns 0xFF.

```
unsigned char keypad_scan(void) {

  unsigned char row, col;
  unsigned char key = 0xFF;

  // Check whether any key has been pressed
  //    1. Output zeros on all row pins
  //    2. Delay shortly, and read inputs of column pins
  //    3. If inputs are 1 for all columns, then no key has been pressed
  ...
  if ( ... )       // If no key pressed, return 0xFF
    return 0xFF;

  // If a key has been pressed, identify the row and column of key pressed
  for(row = 0; row < 4; row++) { // Row scan

    // Set up the row outputs
    ...

    // Read the column inputs
    ...

    for(col = 0; col < 3; col++) { // Column scan

      if ( ... )  // If the input from col pin is zero
        key = key_map[row][col];

    }
  }

  return key;
}
```

The main function repeatedly performs the scan operations, stores keys that have been pressed in a string array, and displays the string array on LCD. The keys '*' and '#' can be used to implement special functions. For example, we can use '*' to delete the last key pressed.

```
int main(void){

    unsigned char key;
    char str[50];
    unsigned char str_len = 0;

    // GPIO and clock configurations
    // LCD initializations
    // Configure row pins as open-drain to prevent potential
    // circuit shortage (see detailed explanation in the text below)
    ...

    while(1){

        key = keypad_scan();

        switch (mapped_key) {

            case '*':           // If * pressed
                ...
                break;
            case '#':           // If # pressed
                ...
                break;
            case 0xFF:          // No key pressed
                ...
                break;
            Default:            // Add key pressed to string
                str[str_len] = key;
                str[str_len + 1] = 0;   // NULL string terminator
                str_len++;
                if (str_len >= 48) str_len = 0;
        }

        LCD_DisplayString((uint8_t *)str);
    }
}
```

The algorithm presented in Figure 14-26 has one serious problem: it may cause a short circuit. During the second step, two row pins are shorted if multiple keys in the same column are pressed simultaneously. Specifically, the row pins that outputs 1 (*i.e.*, 3 V) is directly connected to the row pins that output 0 (*i.e.*, 0 V), thus potentially damaging the microcontroller. Figure 14-27 gives one example in which row pins R2 and R3 are connected if two keys marked are pressed simultaneously. When software scans row 2 or row 3, a short circuit is generated, causing potential hardware damage.

This circuit shortage issue can be resolved by either software or hardware.

- The hardware solution is to configure all output pins as open-drain, instead of push-pull. When a pin outputs one, the pin is then in HiZ state, and no circuit short can occur.

- The software solution is to switch the row pin from output to input when the rows are scanned. Specifically, when the output of a row pin is set to zero, software should change the mode of the other row pins from GPIO output to GPIO input. For example, when the third row is tested during the row locating process, row 3 is set to output zero, but row 1, 2, and 4 are set as input, instead of output, to avoid a circuit short.

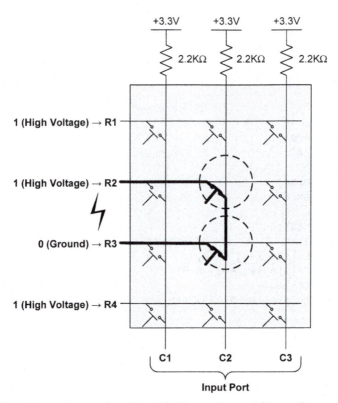

Figure 14-27. The GPIO pins connected to R2 and R3 are shorted if two keys marked by a circle are pressed simultaneously and the GPIO output is 1101.

Another method to avoid damage when multiple keys are pressed is to use reverse scanning algorithm. This approach changes the mode of the row port and the column port alternatively to GPIO input and GPIO output to detect the row and the column of a pressed key. This method requires both the row pins and the column pins to be pulled up by some small resistors. It involves two steps described below.

- During the first step, like the scanning algorithm described previously, it sets the row port as output and the column port as input and then reads the column input to identify the column.

- During the second step, it reverses the direction, sets the row port as input and the column port as output, and reads the row input to identify the row.

How does the microcontroller know when a keypad is pressed? There are two methods: polling or interrupt.

- The polling method scans the keypad periodically with a small time interval. This method is simple but causes a waste of time of microcontrollers. Additionally, because the microcontroller usually has multiple tasks, other tasks may potentially delay the scanning process, so the system is not responsive when a keypad is pressed.

- The interrupt method generates a signal to the processor when the keypad is pressed. This interrupt informs the processor to stop the current tasks and start to execute the scanning code. This method saves the microcontroller from periodically executing the scanning algorithm, thus saving the processor time. Also, the interrupt reduces the latency in responding when a keypad is pressed. However, the interrupt program is more complex to write and debug than polling.

14.10   Exercises

1. Write an assembly program that toggles an LED when the push button is pressed.

2. Write an assembly program that blinks an LED with a time interval of one second.

3. Write an assembly program that scans the keypad to verify a four-digit password. The password is set as 1234. If the user enters the correct password, the program turns the red LED on. Otherwise, the program turns the red LED on.

4. Write an assembly program to blink an LED to send out an SOS Morse code.
   - Blinking Morse code SOS (· · · — — — · · ·) DOT, DOT, DOT, DASH, DASH, DASH, DOT, DOT, DOT.
   - DOT is on for ¼ second and DASH is on for ½ second, with ¼ second between them.
   - At the end of SOS, the program has a delay of 2 seconds before repeating.

5. Write an assembly program to implement software debouncing for push buttons.

6. Use the logic analyzer to measure the time latency between pressing a button and lighting up an LED.

7. In STM Cortex processors, each GPIO port has one 32-bit set/reset register (GPIO_BSRR). We also view it as two 16-bit fields (GPIO_BSRRL and GPIO_BSRRH) as shown in Figure 14-16. When an assembly program sends a digital output to a GPIO pin, the program should perform a load-modify-store sequence to modify the output data register (GPIO_ODR). The BSRR register aims to speed up the GPIO output by removing the load and modify operations.

   • When writing 1 to bit BSRRH(i), bit ODR(i) is automatically set. Writing 0 to any bit of BSRRH has no effect on the corresponding ODR bit.

   • When writing 1 to bit BSRRL(i), bit ODR(i) is automatically cleared. Writing 0 to any bit of BSRRL has no effect on the corresponding ODR bit.

   Therefore, we can change ODR(i) by directly writing 1 to BSRRH(i) or BSRRL(i) without reading the ODR and BSRR registers. This set and clear mechanism not only improves the performance but also provides atomic updates to GPIO outputs.

   Write an assembly program that uses the BSRR register to toggle the LED.

CHAPTER 15

General-purpose Timers

Timers are special hardware components that provide accurate timestamps, time-interval measurements, and timer-related periodic events for both hardware and software. This chapter presents two example uses of timers: measuring the pulse lengths of input signals (input capture) or generating output waveforms (output compare and PWM).

15.1 Timer Organization and Counting Modes

A timer is a free-run hardware counter that increments or decrements once for every clock cycle. The counter runs continuously until the timer is disabled. The counting process restarts automatically when the counter reaches 0 during down-counting or some maximum value during up-counting. Software can select the frequency of the timer clock so that the free-run counter increments or decrements at some desired speed.

If a timer works as *output compare*, as shown in Figure 15-1, the comparator consistently compares the counter value with some given constant, and generates an output or an interrupt if they are equal. Software can program the constant value to control the timing of outputs or interrupts.

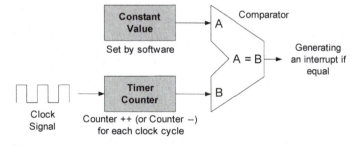

Figure 15-1. A timer is used as output compare. The timer counter is a hardware register, and it automatically increments or decrements by 1 for each clock cycle.

If the function of a timer is *input capture* (see Figure 15-2), the hardware automatically logs the counter value into a special register (called CCR) and generates an interrupt when the desired event occurs. Typically, the interrupt handler needs to copy register CCR to a user buffer to record the timing of past events. Then, software calculates the difference between two logged values and finds the time span of two events.

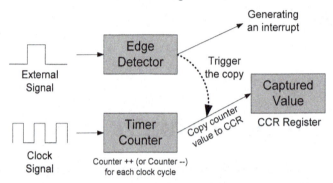

Figure 15-2. A timer is used as input capture. The edge detector triggers the hardware to copy timer counter to register CCR on rising or falling edges of monitored signal.

The hardware timer counter has three different counting modes: *up-counting*, *down-counting*, or *center-aligned counting*, as illustrated in Figure 15-3.

- In the *up-counting* mode, the counter starts from 0 to a constant and then restarts from 0. Software sets up the constant and stores it in a special register called the auto-reload register (ARR). For example, if ARR is 4, the counter value is 0, 1, 2, 3, 4, 0, 1, 2, 3, 4, and repeats until the timer is disabled.

- In the *down-counting* mode, the counter starts from the auto-reload value down to 0 and then restarts from the auto-reload value. For example, if ARR is 4, the counter value is 4, 3, 2, 1, 0, 4, 3, 2, 1, 0, and repeats until the timer is disabled.

- The third one is the *center-aligned counting* mode, which performs up-counting and down-counting alternatively. For example, if ARR is 4, the counter value is 0, 1, 2, 3, 4, 3, 2, 1, 0, and repeats until the timer is disabled.

The timer counter forms a periodical sawtooth or triangle wave. The period is controlled by both the clock frequency to the counter (f_{CLOCK_CNT}) and the value stored in the ARR register. For up-counting and down-counting, the counting period of the sawtooth waveform is

$$Counting\ Period\ of\ Sawtooth\ Waveform = (1 + ARR) \times \frac{1}{f_{CLOCK\_CNT}}$$

For center-aligned counting, the counting period of the triangle waveform is

$$Counting\ Period\ of\ Triangle\ Waveform = 2 \times ARR \times \frac{1}{f_{CLOCK\_CNT}}$$

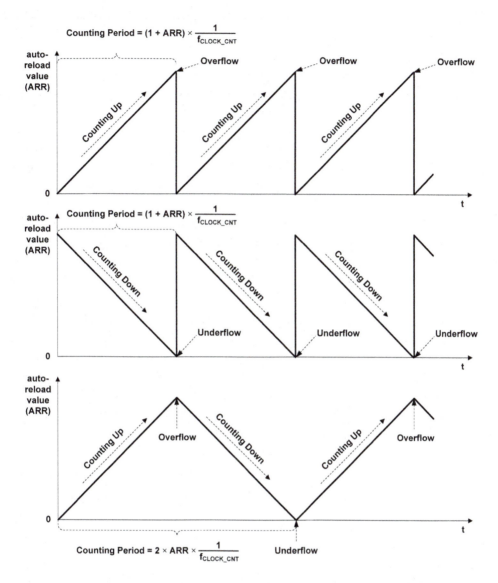

Figure 15-3. Three counting modes: up-counting, down-counting, and center-aligned counting

A timer counter has two update events: *overflow* and *underflow*, as shown in Figure 15-3. In the up-counting mode, overflow occurs when the counter is reset to 0. In the down-counting mode, underflow occurs when the counter is reset to ARR. In the center-aligned counting mode, underflow and overflow occur alternatively.

When using the timer to measure a large time span between the occurrences of two events, software must consider the overflow and underflow to avoid underestimating the time span. The timer interrupt handler can check appropriate flags in the timer's status register to count how many times overflow or underflow has occurred.

15.2 Compare Output

Figure 15-4 shows the basic diagram of the output compare of a timer. The timer counter (CNT) has 16 bits. The capture/compare register (CCR) holds the value that is compared with the timer counter.

In STM32L, four output channels share the same free-run timer counter. Therefore, the timer hardware compares the timer counter with four CCR registers simultaneously and generates four independent outputs based on the comparison results.

The clock to drive the timer counter ($CLOCK\_CNT$) can be slowed down by a constant factor called **prescaler** to generate output that spans over a long period.

$$f_{CLOCK\_CNT} = \frac{f_{CLOCK\_PSC}}{Prescaler + 1}$$

A large prescaler reduces the timer's resolution, but decreases the chance of overflow and underflow and improves the energy efficiency.

Different clocks can drive the timer. These clocks include built-in clocks within the processor chip, external crystal oscillators, or some internal trigger signal such as the output of another timer. External clocks are preferred over internal clocks because external clocks are more accurate than internal clocks.

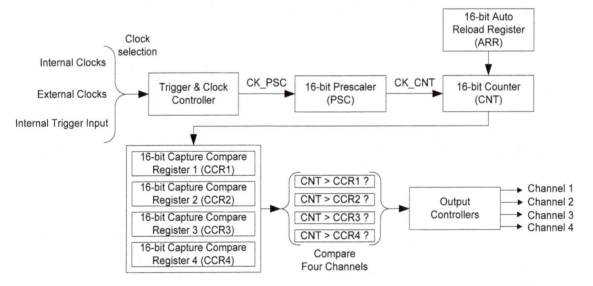

Figure 15-4. Output compare diagram of a timer with four channels. Some timers have more than four channels, with extra channels used internally, such as for triggering ADC.

15.2.1   Setting Output Mode

When the timer counter (CNT) equals the compare value (CCR), the output of a channel (OCREF) is programmable. The output can have different values, depending on the output compare mode (OCM), as shown in Table 15-1.

Output Compare Mode (OCM)	Timer Reference Output (OCREF)
Timing mode (0000)	Frozen
Active mode (0001)	Logic high if CNT = CCR
Inactive mode (0010)	Logic low if CNT = CCR
Toggle mode (0011)	Toggle if CNT = CCR
Forced inactive mode (0100)	Forced logic low (always low)
Forced active mode (0101)	Forced logic high (always high)

PWM output mode 1 (0110)	In up-counting:
	  Logic high if CNT < CCR, else logic low
	In down-counting:
	  Logic high if CNT ≤ CCR, else logic low

PWM output mode 2 (0111)	In up-counting:
	  Logic high if CNT ≥ CCR, else logic low
	In down-counting:
	  Logic high if CNT > CCR, else logic low

Table 15-1. Control of timer channel output

The active and inactive mode outputs a logic high and logic low, respectively, when the free-run counter CNT matches the capture and compare register (CCR). The toggle mode reverses the output whenever CNT and CCR match, making the output switch between logic high and logic low alternatively. The forced inactive and active mode makes the output stay low and high, respectively.

In digital circuits, there are two options to represent logic values: *active high* and *active low*, as shown in the table below. Software can change the logic representation for the output of each timer channel independently by programming the output polarity bit in the control register CCER. When the polarity bit is 0, active high is chosen to generate voltage outputs. Otherwise, active low is used.

	Active High Signals	Active Low Signals
Logic High (1)	High voltage	Low voltage
Logic Low (0)	Low voltage	High voltage

Figure 15-5 shows the channel reference output OCREF when the output mode is toggled, non-one-pulse high, and one-pulse high. In this example, the counter repeatedly counts up from 0 to ARR. Active high is always used for OCREF. However, depending on the polarity selection, the channel output is either OCREF or the negation of OCREF.

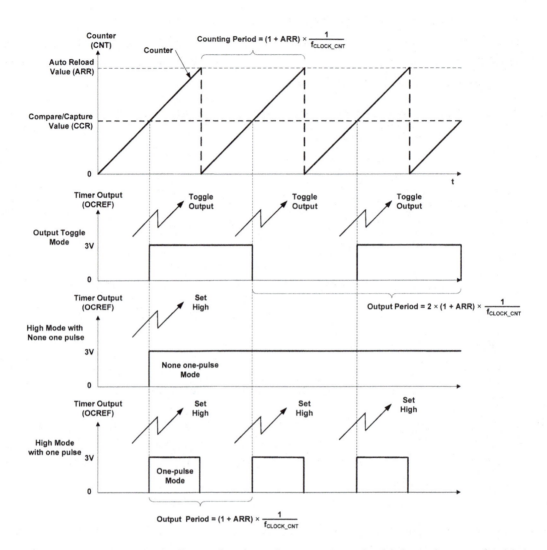

Figure 15-5. OCREF output in the mode of toggle, non-one-pulse high, and one-pulse high.

A timer channel may have two outputs: main output OC and complementary output OCN, which are the exclusive-OR between the channel reference output OCREF and its corresponding polarity bit in the CCER register, as shown below. The CCP and CCNP bits in the CCER register are the polarity bit of OC and OCN, respectively.

- If only OC or OCN is enabled:

$$OC = OCREF + Polarity\ bit\ for\ OC$$
$$OCN = OCREF + Polarity\ bit\ for\ OCN$$

- If both OC and OCN are enabled:

$$OC = OCREF + Polarity\ bit\ for\ OC$$
$$OCN = (not\ OCREF) + Polarity\ bit\ for\ OCN$$

Active high logic is always used for OCREF. However, OC and OCN can be either active high or active low, depending on their polarity bits. If the polarity bit is 0, the corresponding channel output is active high. Otherwise, it is active low.

If timer interrupt is enabled, an interrupt is generated if CNT matches CCR, or CNT has an overflow or underflow. The timer interrupt service routine must check the timer status register to find what event has occurred. The update interrupt flag (UIF) is set for an overflow or underflow, and the capture and compare interrupt flag (CCIF) is set when CNT matches CCR.

A separate DMA interrupt can also be generated to load a value stored in the data memory into ARR or CRR automatically. Chapter 19 introduces DMA operations.

15.2.2   Example of Toggling LED

This section uses the output compare mode of a timer to toggle a green LED attached GPIO pin PE6 every second, as shown below.

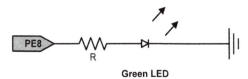

Green LED

Figure 15-6. The green LED is connected to pin PE 8 on STM32L4 Discovery Kit.

Each GPIO pin can perform multiple hardware functions. Functions that a pin supports vary among chips and manufacturers, but also differ between pins. Due to chip complexity and costs, it is impractical for a pin to support all functions. For STM32L4, the functions that pin PE8 supports are shown in Table 15-2. In this example, we use the alternative function 1 (timer 1, complementary output of channel 1) to toggle the LED.

PIN	**AF1**	AF6	AF12	AF13	AF15
PE8	**TIM1_CH1N**	DFSDM_CKIN2	FMC_D5	SAI1_SCK_B	EVENTOUT

Table 15-2. Available alternate functions for PE 8 on STM32L4

Suppose the system clock is 80 MHz and it is selected as the timer clock that drives the timer 1. driving the timer is 2.097 MHz. The following calculates the prescaler that slows down the clock of the timer counter to 2 KHz. Since we have

$$f_{CLOCK\_CNT} = \frac{f_{CLOCK\_PSC}}{Prescaler + 1}$$

We get

$$Prescaler = \frac{f_{CLOCK\_PSC}}{f_{CLOCK\_CNT}} - 1 = \frac{80MHz}{2KHz} - 1 = 40000 - 1 = 39999$$

To turn an LED on for 1 second and then off for 1 second repeatedly, the auto-reload register (ARR) should be 1999 because the clock frequency of the free-run counter is 2 KHz. The timer counts from 0 to 1999 repeatedly, taking 2000 cycles in each counting period. Register CCR can be set to any integer value between 0 and 1999.

The following is the C implementation. Software sets TIM1_CH1N (the complementary output of channel 1 of timer 1) as compare output and toggles the external LED connected to pin PE 8 every second.

```c
int main() {

  System_Clock_Init(); // Switch System Clock = 80 MHz

  RCC->AHB2ENR |= RCC_AHB2ENR_GPIOEEN; // Enable GPIOE clock

  // Set mode of pin 8 as alternate function
  // 00 = Input, 01 = Output, 10 = Alternate Function, 11 = Analog
  GPIOE->MODER  &= ~(3UL << 16);      // Clear bit 17 and bit 16
  GPIOE->MODER  |= 2UL << 16;         // Set mode as 10

  // Select alternate function 1 (TIM1_CH1N)
  GPIOE->AFR[1] &= ~(0xF); // ARF[0] for pin 0-7, ARF[1]: pin 8-15
  GPIOE->AFR[1] |= 1UL;    // TIM1_CH1N defined as 01

  // Set I/O output speed value as low
  // 00 = Low, 01 = Medium, 10 = Fast, 11 = High
  GPIOE->OSPEEDR &= ~(3UL<<16);

  // Set pin PE8 as no pull-up/pull-down
  // 00 = No PUPD, 01 = Pull up, 10 = Pull down, 11 = Reserved
  GPIOE->PUPDR &= ~(3UL<<16);

  // Enable timer 1 clock
  RCC->APB2ENR |= RCC_APB2ENR_TIM1EN;

  // Counting direction: 0 = up-counting, 1 = down-counting
  TIM1->CR1 &= ~TIM_CR1_DIR;

  // Clock prescaler (16 bits, up to 65,535)
  TIM1->PSC = 39999;

  // Auto-reload: up-counting (0-->ARR), down-counting (ARR-->0)
  TIM1->ARR = 2000-1;

  // Can be any value between 0 and 1999.
  TIM1->CCR1 = 500;

  // Main output enable (MOE): 0 = Disable, 1 = Enable
  TIM1->BDTR |= TIM_BDTR_MOE;

  // Clear output compare mode bits for channel 1
  TIM1->CCMR1 &= ~TIM_CCMR1_OC1M;
```

```
    // Select toggle mode (0011)
    TIM1->CCMR1 |= TIM_CCMR1_OC1M_0 | TIM_CCMR1_OC1M_1;

    // Select output polarity: 0 = active high, 1 = active low
    TIM1->CCMR1 &= ~TIM_CCER_CC1NP; // select active high

    // Enable output for channel 1 complementary output
    TIM1->CCER |= TIM_CCER_CC1NE;

    // Enable timer 1
    TIM1->CR1 |= TIM_CR1_CEN;

    while(1); // dead loop
}
```

Example 15-1. Lighting up an LED by using the compare-output function of a timer

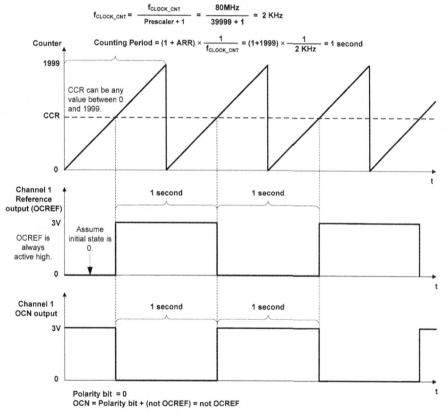

Figure 15-7. Voltage output signal on pin PE 8

Figure 15-7 shows the signals of the timer counter, the reference output (OCREF), and the complementary output (OCN) of channel 1. The initial state of OCREF is assumed to be 0 or low. If the initial state is critical, software can use the forced output mode to force OCREF to 1 (high) or 0 (low). Note that OCREF always uses active high logic.

15.2.3   Timer Update Events

An update event (UEV) is generated on each overflow in up-counting, on each underflow in down-counting, on both overflow and underflow in center-counting.

$$UEV\ Period = (1 + ARR) \times (1 + Prescaler) \times \frac{1}{f_{CK\_CNT}}$$

UEV events serve three purposes:

- Generate trigger output (TRGO) for other internal modules, such as timers, DMA, ADC, and DAC.
- Make updates of registers ARR, PSC, and CCR take effect immediately if the buffering (also called preload) mechanism is enabled. If the channel's preload enable bit (OCPE) in the CCMR1 register and the auto-reload preload enable bit (ARPE) in the CR1 register are set, the preload mechanism is enabled.
- Generate a timer interrupt request if the update interrupt flag bit (UIF) of the control register CR1 is set. Interrupt requests are sent to the interrupt controller (NVIC). In response, the processor executes the corresponding interrupt handler.

Software can disable UEV by setting the update disable bit (UDIS) in the CR1 register. If so, update events are not generated.

Software can also generate UEV events. If the update request selection bit (URS) in the CR1 register is set, setting the update generation bit (UG) in the event generation register (EGR) generates an UEV event.

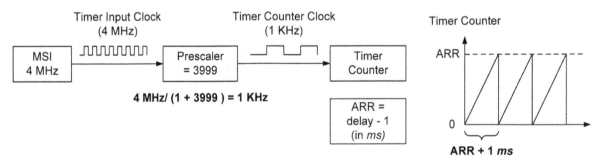

Figure 15-8. Implementation of hardware-precision delay

As shown in Example 15-2, software can use the timer update events to achieve hardware-precision delay. At 30 °C, MSI and HSI can reach an accuracy of ±0.6%. Assume MSI 4 MHz is selected to drive the timer, the prescaler is set to 3999, and the timer counters are in the up-counting mode, as shown in Figure 15-8. Thus, the timer counter is incremented by 1 every millisecond. Timer 7 is selected because it is a basic timer without advanced functions. We reserve advanced timers for complicate usage.

```
void delay(uint16_t ms) {

  if ( ms == 0 ) // Sanity check
    return;

  // Enable timer 7 clock
  RCC->APB1ENR1 |= RCC_APB1ENR1_TIM7EN;

  TIM7->CR1 &= ~TIM_CR1_CEN; // Disable timer 7
  TIM7->SR  = 0;             // Clear status register
  TIM7->CNT = 0;             // Clear counter
  TIM7->PSC = 3999;          // 4 MHz/(1 + 3999) = 1 KHz
  TIM7->ARR = ms - 1;        // ARR + 1 cycles
  TIM7->CR1 |= TIM_CR1_CEN;  // Enable timer 7

  // Loop until UIF is set
  while ( (TIM7->SR & TIM_SR_UIF) == 0 );
}
```

Example 15-2. Use timer updates to implement hardware-precision delay

Example 15-3 counts the number of overflows that have taken place on up-counting. If the UIF flag in the timer's status register (SR) is set, the timer interrupt handler increments the overflow counter and clears the flag bit UIF to 0 to prevent the interrupt handler from executing again.

```
volatile uint32_t overflow = 0;

int main(void) {

  // Initialization
  ...

  // Select counting direction
  // 0 = up-counting, 1 = down-counting
  TIM1->CR1 &= ~TIM_CR1_DIR;

  // Enable update interrupts
  TIM1->DIER |= TIM_DIER_UIE;

  // Enable TIM4 interrupt in NVIC
  NVIC_EnableIRQ(TIM1_IRQn);

  // Enable the counter
  TIM1->CR1 |= TIM_CR1_CEN;

  while(1);
}
```

```
void TIM1_IRQHandler(void) {

    // Check whether an overflow event has taken place
    if((TIM1->SR & TIM_SR_UIF) != 0) {

        // Increment the overflow counter
        overflow++;

        // Clear flag UIF to prevent reentrance
        TIM1->SR &= ~TIM_SR_UIF;
    }

    ...
}
```

Example 15-3. Counting the number of update events

In this example, the global variable `overflow` is declared as "`volatile`". This is to inform the compiler that no optimization should be made on this variable. While the compiler can observe that the interrupt handler changes the value of this variable, it is still possible that the compiler incorrectly reuses an old value if `overflow` was not volatile. The reason is that the compiler notices that the interrupt handler does not appear to be called in software and mistakenly assumes that the value of overflow would not change.

> *volatile: characterized by or subject to rapid or unexpected change*
>
> -- Merriam-Webster Dictionary

15.3 PWM Output

Pulse width modulation (PWM) is a simple digital technique to control the value of an analog variable. PWM uses a rectangular waveform to quickly switch a voltage source on and off to produce a desired average voltage output. Although the output is binary at any time instant, the average output over a time span can be any value between 0 and the maximum voltage.

Specifically, the percentage of time in the on state within one period is proportional to the mean value of the voltage output. Consequently, when software changes the duration of the on state, the output voltage is adjusted accordingly to emulate an analog signal.

PWM has been widely used in a variety of applications, such as motor speed and torque control, digital encoding in telecommunications, DC-to-DC power conversion, and audio amplification. This section uses PWM to control the brightness of an LED.

We should select the PWM switching frequency carefully to avoid serious negative impacts on applications. For example, the PWM switching frequency of an LED light must be at least 120 Hz to prevent the flickering effects that humans can see.

The average value of a simple PWM output based on a sawtooth carrier signal and a constant reference, as illustrated in Figure 15-9 and Figure 15-10, is linearly proportional to the *duty cycle*.

The duty cycle is defined as follows:

$$duty\ cycle = \frac{pulse\ on\ time\ (T_{on})}{pulse\ switching\ period\ (T_s)} \times 100\%$$

$$= \frac{T_{on}}{T_{on} + T_{off}} \times 100\%$$

where

$$pulse\ switching\ period = \frac{1}{PWM\ switching\ frequency}$$

By changing the duty cycle, software can control this average value. In the LED example, the brightness is determined by the PWM duty cycle. Figure 15-9 and Figure 15-10 give three examples in which the average output is 1/6 and 1/2, respectively.

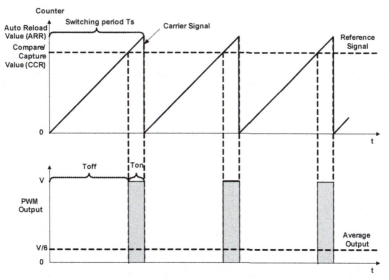

Figure 15-9. Example of simple PWM when duty cycle is 1/6

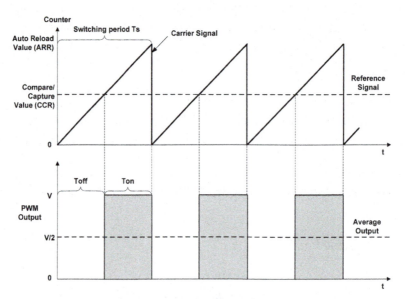

Figure 15-10. Example of simple PWM when duty cycle is 1/2

The PWM output signal is determined by three factors:

1. comparison between the timer counter (CNT) and the given reference valued stored in the compare and capture register (CCR),
2. the PWM output mode, and
3. the polarity bit.

As shown in Table 15-3, there are two PWM modes, which are opposite to each other.

- **PWM Mode 1:** If the counter is less than the reference signal, the timer reference output (OCREF) is then held at logic high; otherwise, it is held at logic low.

- **PWM Mode 2:** The timer reference output (OCREF) in mode 2 is the opposite of mode 1. If the counter is greater than the reference signal, OCREF is then held at active; otherwise, OCREF is held at inactive.

PWM Mode	Counting Mode	PWM Reference Output (OCREF)	
		Logic High	Logic Low
Mode 1	Up-counting	CNT < CCR	CNT ≥ CCR
	Down-counting	CNT ≤ CCR	CNT > CCR
Mode 2	Up-counting	CNT ≥ CCR	CNT < CCR
	Down-counting	CNT > CCR	CNT ≤ CCR

Table 15-3. Timer reference output (OCREF) of PWM mode 1 and mode 2

OCREF is an internal output, which always uses active high logic. However, the actual output (OC or OCN) can be *active high* or *active low*.

- In *active high*, a high voltage represents logic high (or called active), and a low voltage represents logic low (or called inactive).
- The output of *active low* is the opposite of active high.
- Selection of active high or active low is controlled by the polarity bit.

In sum, the actual PWM output (OC or OCN) is determined by both the PWM mode and the polarity bit.

Figure 15-11 shows an example of the timer reference output (OCREF) for center-counting.

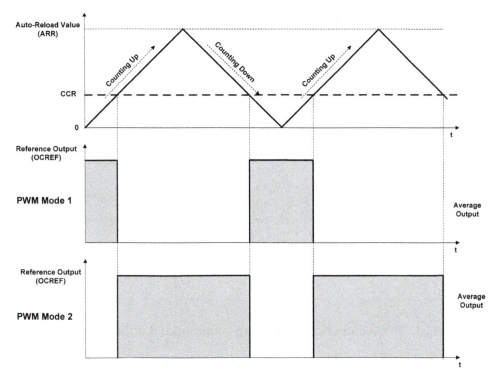

Figure 15-11. Reference output (OCREF) in PWM mode 1 and PWM mode 2

PWM Signal Period:

For up- or down-counting:

$$PWM\ Period\ = (1 + ARR) \times \frac{Clock\ Period\ of\ Timer}{1 + Prescaler}$$

For center-counting mode:

$$PWM\ Period\ = 2 \times ARR \times \frac{Clock\ Period\ of\ Timer}{1 + Prescaler}$$

PWM Duty Cycle:

Depending on the PWM mode and the polarity bit, the duty cycle of the main output OC or the complementary output OCN in up-counting or down-counting is

$$Duty\ Cycle\ = \begin{cases} \dfrac{CCR}{ARR+1} \\ 1 - \dfrac{CCR}{ARR+1} \end{cases}$$

Figure 15-12 gives an example of PWM mode 1 output on up-counting. The duty cycle of the main output (OC) is either 3/7 or 4/7, depending on polarity bit.

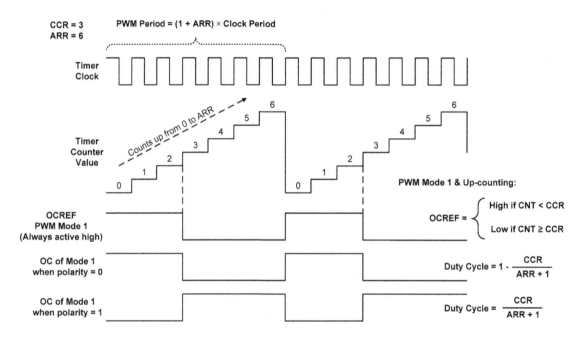

Figure 15-12. PWM outputs in Mode 1, up-counting, and different polarity bits

Similarly, as shown in Figure 15-13, depending on the PWM mode and the output polarity, the PWM duty cycle for center-counting is

$$Duty\ Cycle\ = \begin{cases} \dfrac{CCR}{ARR} \\ 1 - \dfrac{CCR}{ARR} \end{cases}$$

If the center-aligned counting mode, when register CCR is 0 or ARR, the timer reference output OCREF is 1 or 0, depending on the PWM mode.

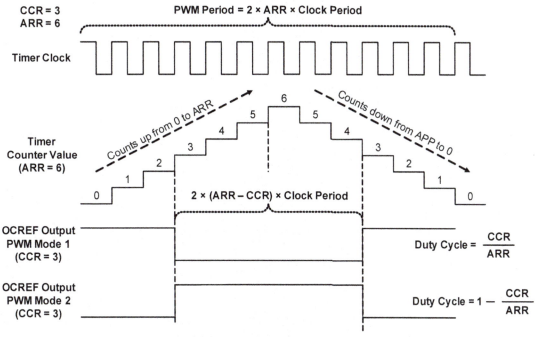

Figure 15-13. PWM outputs in center-aligned counting

15.3.1   PWM Alignment

A timer typically has multiple channels, as shown in Figure 15-4. Each channel can generate a PWM output signal. All channels share the timer counter and the ARR register. Thus, all PWM signals produced by the same timer have the same period. However, their duty cycle can be different because each channel has its own CCR register.

All PWM outputs of the same timer has the same period.

For a timer with up- or down-counting, its PWM signals are *edge-aligned*.

- In the example, given in Figure 15-14, all rising edges of the PWM signals are aligned with the overflow events of the timer counter. These PWM signals are also called **left-edge aligned** (or **rising-edge aligned,** or *leading-edge aligned*) because all pulses are turned on at the beginning of each PWM period.

- If the polarity bit is changed to 1, the PWM outputs of these three channels become **right-edge aligned**, or called **falling-edge aligned**, or *trailing-edge aligned* in which all pulses are turned off at the end of each PWM period.

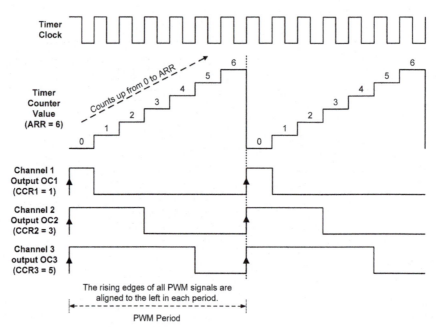

Figure 15-14. Rising edge aligned PWM outputs from multiple channels (up-counting, PWM mode 1, polarity bit = 0, Prescaler = 0).

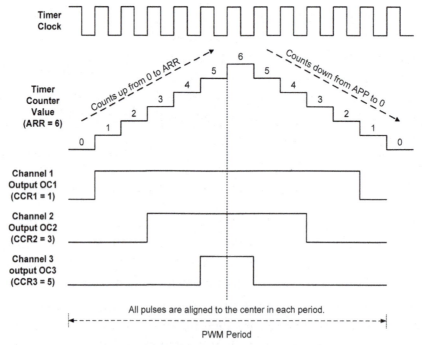

Figure 15-15. Center-aligned PWM outputs from multiple channels (center-counting, PWM mode 2, polarity bit = 0, Prescaler = 0)

For a timer with center-counting, the PWM signals of all associated channels are *center-aligned*, as shown in Figure 15-15. Both the rising edge and falling edge of each pulse are modulated. All pulses are centered in each PWM period. Center-aligned PWM signals are often preferred to edge-aligned in electronic circuits, such as motor control and power converters. Center-aligned PWM signals are symmetrical and thus have fewer harmonics, reducing noise interference and power consumption.

15.3.2   PWM Programming Flowchart

This section will show how software programs a timer to generate a PWM output signal to increase or decrease the brightness of an LED gradually. We will use the green LED on STM32L4 as an example (see Figure 15-20).

All alternate functions that pin PE 8 supports are listed in Table 15-2. Pin PE 8 will be the complementary output of channel 1 of timer 1 (TIM1_CH1N) if software sets its GPIO mode to alternate function (AF) and its AF value to 1. In sum, pin PE 8 is physically connected to the external LED, and software needs to make PE 8 function as TIM1_CH1N internally.

On STM32L4, the clock that drives the processor core and its peripherals, such as timers, has a frequency of 4 MHz by default. In this example, the prescaler factor is set as 63, thus the frequency at which the counter increments is

$$f_{CK\_CNT} = \frac{f_{CL\_PSC}}{Prescaler + 1} = \frac{4MHz}{39 + 1} = 100\ KHz$$

Suppose the refresh rate of the LED is 100 Hz. Putting it differently, the LED is turned off and then turned on in each cycle. There are 100 such cycles each second. Normally the human eye cannot detect flicker at a refresh rate higher than 100 Hz. Thus, we will see a steady and continuously source of light even though the LED is switched on and off 100 times per second.

For a given clock frequency, ARR determines the PWM period. Assume the counting mode is up-counting, and the LED refresh rate is 100 Hz. Thus, the PWM period should be

$$PWM\ Period = \frac{1}{LED\ Refresh\ Rate} = \frac{1}{100\ Hz} = 0.01\ second$$

At the same time, we have

$$PWM\ Period = (1 + ARR) \times \frac{1}{f_{CK\_CNT}}$$

Thus, we have

$$ARR = PWM\ Period \times f_{CK_{CNT}} - 1 = 0.01 \times 100 \times 10^3 - 1 = 999$$

When ARR is kept at a fixed value, CCR controls the duty cycle. Assume timer 1 uses PWM mode 1, in which the reference output (OCREF) is high for up-counting if the timer counter is less than CCR, and otherwise, OCREF is low.

Figure 15-16 shows that as CCR increases gradually, the duty cycle of OCREF also increases.

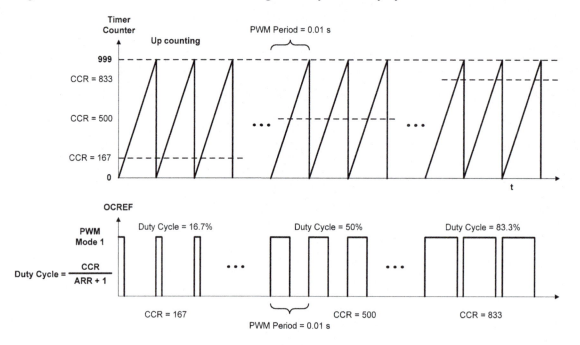

Figure 15-16. CCR controls the duty cycle of PWM output if ARR is fixed.

In this example, the complementary output of time 1 channel 1 (TIM1_CH1N) drives the LED. As discussed previously, the complementary output (OCN) of a channel is

$$OCN = OCREF + Polarity\ bit\ for\ OCN$$

If we use CCR to represent the LED brightness, we need to set the polarity bit (CCNP) for the complement output to 0. In other words, OCN waveform is the same as OCREF.

Figure 15-17 shows the program flow chart. The variable *direction* is either 1 or -1. The LED gets brighter and dimmer alternatively. A short delay is added between two consecutive updates to CCR to adjust the speed of brightness change.

In this example, software does not program the reset and clock controller (RCC). Accordingly, the processor uses the default clock settings. By default, the system clock is derived from the internal multi-speed internal RC oscillator (MSI). While MSI offers clocks signal with multiple clock frequencies ranging from 100 KHz to 49 MHz on STM32L4, its frequency is 4 MHz after reset.

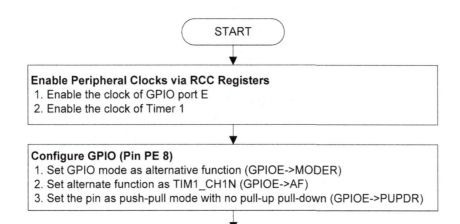

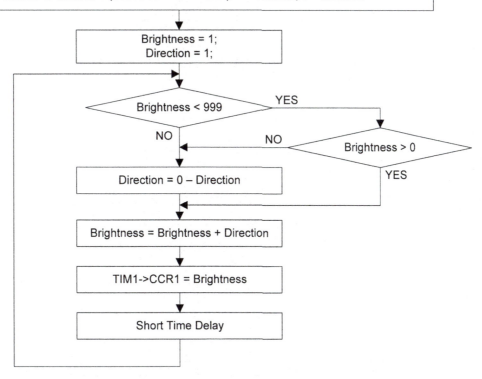

Figure 15-17. Flowchart for dimming an LED via PWM output of a timer

Example 15-4 initializes channel 1 of timer 1 to generate a PWM signal. The counting direction is up-counting. The PWM output is in mode 1.

- Each channel may have two outputs: the main output and the complementary output. Both can be enabled and disabled independently. Typically, these two outputs are connected to different GPIO pins on the processor chip.
- PE 8 is connected internally to the complementary output TIM1_CH1N, instead of the main output TIM1_CH1.

```c
void TIM1_Init() {

  // Enable TIMER 1 clock
  RCC->APB2ENR |= RCC_APB2ENR_TIM1EN;

  // Counting direction: 0 = Up-counting, 1 = Down-counting
  TIM1->CR1 &= ~TIM_CR1_DIR; // Select up-counting

  // Prescaler, slow down the input clock by a factor of (1 + prescaler)
  TIM1->PSC = 39;     // 4 MHz / (1 + 39) = 100 KHz

  // Auto-reload
  TIM1->ARR = 999;    // PWM period = (999 + 1) * 1/100KHz = 0.01s

  // Clear output compare mode bits for channel 1
  TIM1->CCMR1 &= ~TIM_CCMR1_OC1M;

  // Select PWM Mode 1 output on channel 1 (OC1M = 110)
  TIM1->CCMR1 |= TIM_CCMR1_OC1M_1 | TIM_CCMR1_OC1M_2;

  // Output 1 preload enable
  TIM1->CCMR1 |= TIM_CCMR1_OC1PE;

  // Select output polarity: 0 = Active high, 1 = Active low
  TIM1->CCMR1 &= ~TIM_CCER_CC1NP;   // OC1N = OCREF + CC1NP

  // Enable complementary output of channel 1 (CH1N)
  TIM1->CCER |= TIM_CCER_CC1NE;

  // Main output enable (MOE): 0 = Disable, 1 = Enable
  TIM1->BDTR |= TIM_BDTR_MOE;

  // Output Compare Register for channel 1
  TIM1->CCR1 = 500;     // Initial duty cycle 50%

  // Enable counter
  TIM1->CR1 |= TIM_CR1_CEN;
}
```

Example 15-4. Initialization of Timer 1 to generate PWM output in C

Example 15-5 changes the duty cycle of the PWM output. The code does not configure the system clock and thus the default MSI 4 MHz is selected. The GPIO initialization code is not given in the demo code. Within the endless loop, the compare and capture register for channel 1 (CCR1) is increased or decreased gradually after a short delay.

```c
void main(){

  int i;
  int brightness = 1;
  int stepSize = 1;

  // Pin PE.8 initialization:
  // AF mode, AF value = 1 (TIM1_CH1N), high-speed, push-pull
  ...

  while(1) {

    if ((brightness >= 999) || (brightness <= 0 ))
      stepSize = -stepSize;      // Reverse direction

    brightness += stepSize;      // Change brightness

    TIM1->CCR1 = brightness;     // Change duty cycle of channel 1 outputs

    for(i = 0; i < 1000; i++);   // Short delay
  }
}
```

Example 15-5. Example program to change the brightness.

15.4 Input Capture

As presented previously, a timer can be used for triggering an output at a specified time to general output signals (PWM output, comparator output). This section discusses the usage of timers as input capture.

Input capture is to find the time span between two rising or falling transitions in an internal or external signal. As shown in Figure 15-18, a capture occurs on (1) either rising or falling edges, (2) only falling edges, or (3) only rising edges.

When the desired transition is detected, the timer hardware automatically captures this time instant by copying the value of the free-run counter (CNT) to the compare and capture register (CCR). At the same time, the timer hardware generates an interrupt or DMA request and sets the CCIF flag in the status register (SR).

The difference between two consecutive transitions measures an elapsed time span, as shown in Figure 14-19.

- If the input signal is periodic, the difference of the counters captured at two consecutive rising edges or at two consecutive falling edges measures the period of the waveform.
- Similarly, the difference between a rising edge and a falling edge measures the pulse width.

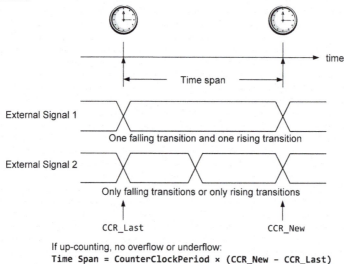

If up-counting, no overflow or underflow:
`Time Span = CounterClockPeriod × (CCR_New - CCR_Last)`

Figure 15-18. Input capture measures the time span between two events.

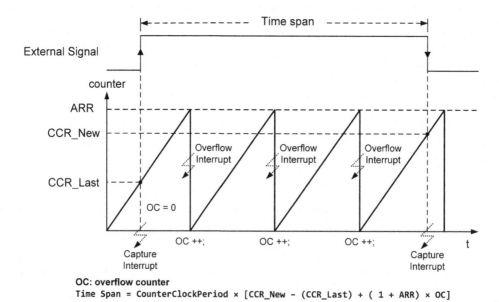

OC: overflow counter
`Time Span = CounterClockPeriod × [CCR_New - (CCR_Last) + ( 1 + ARR) × OC]`

Figure 15-19. Measuring the pulse width if the timer is up-counting. A variable OC (overflow counter) is used when measuring a long time span.

We can calculate the pulse width, the period, and the duty cycle of the input waveform by using two or three consecutive captures. As shown in Figure 15-19, when measuring a time span longer than the counting period, software must consider the overflow and underflow events of the free-running counter.

Each input channel has a configurable input source, a digital input filter, and an edge detector.

- The input source of the capture module has a few options. The capture signal can be an external signal applied to different timer channels (*i.e.*, on different GPIO pins) or an internal trigger signal made by other timers.
- The edge detector can be programmed to detect only falling edges, only rising edges or both.
- The filter specifies the number of events needed to validate a transition on the input. If we need to capture each valid transition, software should disable the external trigger filtering by setting the external trigger filter (ETF) to zero.

The digital input filter removes noise pulses in an input signal. For example, if the input signal of a push button takes 10 internal clock cycles to become stable, then we can make the filter duration last longer than 10 clock cycles. We can validate the transition by repeatedly sampling the inputs.

- If a sequence of consecutive samples remain unchanged and stay at the same level, then this level is considered as a stable input.
- If a noise spike occurs causing the input to change during any of the consecutive sampling points, the input is unstable and can be ignored, thus filtering out noisy transitions.

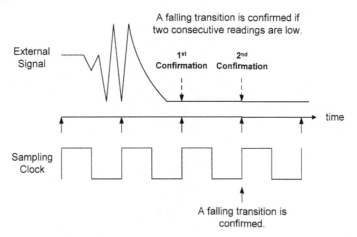

Figure 15-20. An example of filtering noise in the external signal. Two consistent readings are required to confirm a valid transition.

The sampling frequency of the filter is configurable. The number of consistent consecutive readings to validate a transition ranges from 0 to 8. If it is zero, then the noise filtering is disabled. Figure 15-20 shows an example in which the number of consistent readings is set to 2.

Software can select internal clocks, external clocks, or internal trigger input (such as another timer) as the clock of the 16-bit free-running counter. The clock frequency can be divided by a 16-bit clock prescaler (PSC) to reduce the clock frequency for the free-running counter.

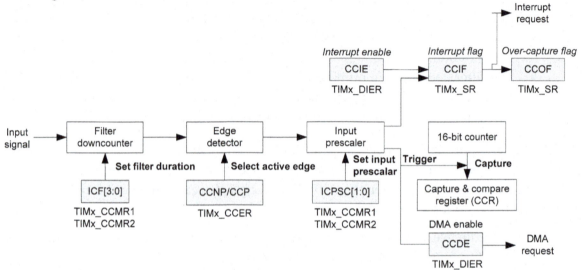

Figure 15-21. Diagram of input capture

Figure 15-21 shows the timer diagram for input capture. When the number of transitions on an input channel reaches the threshold defined by the *input capture prescaler* bits (ICPSC) in the capture/compare mode register (CCMR), a capture occurs, and the processor automatically performs the following operations.

- It latches the value of the free-running counter (CNT) to the capture/compare register (CCR) corresponding to that channel. There is a 16-bit capture/compare for each capture channel (CCR1 for channel 1, CCR2 for channel 2, CCR3 for channel 3, and CCR4 for channel 4).

- In the status register (SR), the capture/compare interrupt flag (CCIF) corresponding to that channel is set by hardware on a capture. If the CCIF flag has already been set, then hardware sets the corresponding capture/compare over-capture flag (CCOF) in the status register (SR). Software clears the CCIF flag by writing it to 0, or hardware automatically clears it if software reads the corresponding CCR register. Only software can clear the CCOF flag.

- If software enables the interrupt by setting the capture/compare interrupt enable bit (CCIE) in the DMA interrupt enable register (DIER), the timer hardware generates an interrupt.

- If software enables DMA by setting the capture/compare DMA request enable bit (CCDE) of the DIER register, the timer hardware generates a DMA request.

15.4.1   Configuring Input Capture

In the following, we use the channel 1 of timer 4 as an example to illustrate the basic procedure for capturing a rising edge transition of an external signal. Figure 15-23 shows the flowchart of setting the GPIO pin PB.6 as input capture.

1. *Select the active input.* Each timer supports four capture/compare channels in the STM32L processor, and software can configure each channel as a compare output or a capture input connected to one of the timer's external input or trigger sources. The CC1S[1:0] bits in the CCMR1 register configures the direction of channel 1 (input or output) and the input source of channel 1.

The usage of CC1S[1:0] bits are defined as follows:

- 00: Channel 1 is set as output.
- 01: Channel 1 is set as input, and it is mapped to timer input 1 (TI1).
- 10: Channel 1 is set as input, and it is mapped to timer input 2 (TI2).
- 11: Channel 1 is set as input, and it is mapped to TRC. The trigger output of another timer is used as the input.

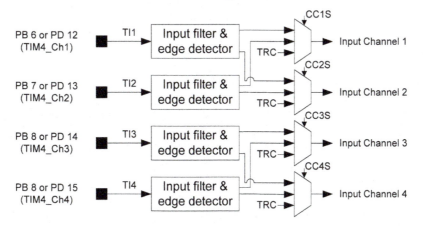

Figure 15-22. Selecting an input source for each capture channel

To link to the timer input 1 (TI1), we need to set CC1S bits to 01. Note, if CC1S bits are 00, then the channel is configured as a compare output. When a channel is set up as capture input, its corresponding CCR register becomes read-only.

2. **Set the input filter.** The IC1F bits in the CCMR1 register define the frequency used to sample TI1 and the length of digital filtering applied to TI1. The digital filtering is to check whether a number of consecutive readings of an input remain the same. If yes, the input is stable, and the input transition is valid. For example,

   - If IC1F is 0000, the digital filtering is disabled.
   - If IC1F is 0010, the sampling frequency is the counter frequency, and if four consecutive samplings remain the same, then the transition is valid.

3. **Set the active edge.** The CC1P bit and CC1NP bit in the CCER register collectively determine the edge of an active transition on the TI1 channel.

   - If CC1NP = 0 and CC1P = 0, then the edge detection is configured to capture only rising edges.
   - If CC1NP = 0 and CC1P = 1, only falling edges are captured.
   - If CC1NP = 1 and CC1P = 1, then both falling and rising edges are captured.

4. **Set the input prescaler.** If we want to capture the event each time an edge is detected in channel 1, the prescaler, defined by the IC1PSC bits in the CCMR1 register, should be reset to 0.

   > *Input filtering is to reduces noise.*
   >
   > *Input prescaler, also called frequency divider, is to reduce the frequency signal of input signals.*

   - When IC1PSC is 01, 10, and 11, the input capture is then performed once every 2, 4, and 8 events, respectively.
   - Depending on applications' needs, such as noise filtering, we might want to wait for multiple valid transitions before the counter is latched.

5. **Enable the input capture.** The input capture of channel 1 can be enabled by setting the CC1E bit in the CCER register.

6. **Enable interrupt and DMA if needed.** The related interrupt request is enabled by setting the CC1E bit in the DIER register.

   - The DMA request is enabled by setting the CC1DE bit in the DIER register.
   - The TIE bit enables trigger interrupt, and the UIE bit enables the update interrupt.

7. **Enable the timer counter.** Sets the counter enable bit (CEN) in the CR1 register.

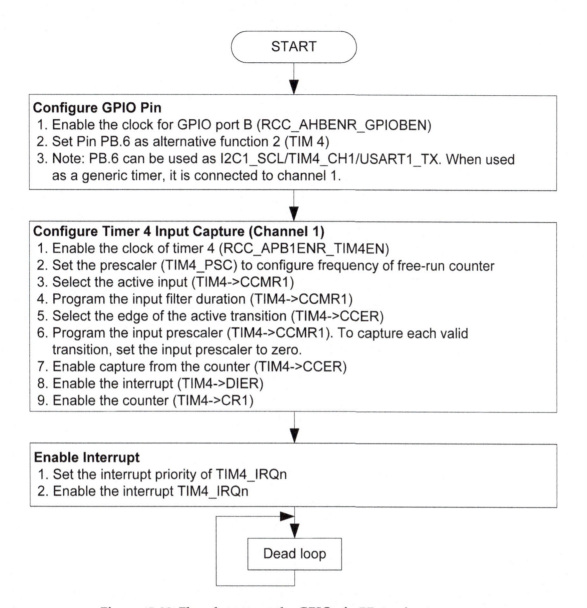

Figure 15-23. Flowchart to set the GPIO pin PB.6 as input capture

Example 15-6 shows the implementation of the timer interrupt service routine, which calculates the pulse width. It is assumed that the timer is up-counting and captures are made on both rising and falling edges. Assuming the input signal is low initially, it uses a global variable to track the signal polarity. The interrupt handler flips the signal polarity. The pulse duration is calculated only when the signal is low.

This example code does not take care of the counter overflow and, therefore, the time interval may be negative occasionally. A more robust code should check the update interrupt flag (TIM_SR_UIF) of the timer status register (TIM4->SR). If the update event occurs (*i.e.*, overflow during up-counting or underflow during down-counting), the time interval should be calculated differently.

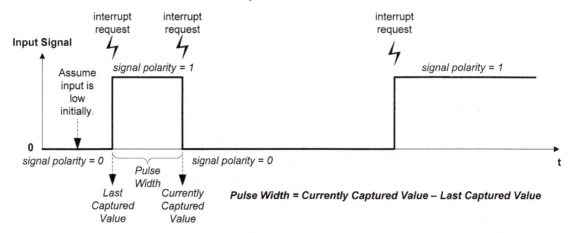

Figure 15-24. Calculating the pulse width by using input capture

```c
volatile uint32_t pulse_width = 0;
volatile uint32_t last_captured = 0;
volatile uint32_t signal_polarity= 0; // Assume input is low initially

void TIM4_IRQHandler() {

  uint32_t current_captured;

  if(TIM4->SR & TIM_SR_CC1IF != 0) { // Check interrupt flag is set

    // Reading CCR1 clears CC1IF interrupt flag
    current_captured = TIM4->CCR1;

    // Toggle the polarity flag;
    signal_polarity= 1 - signal_polarity;

    if (signal_polarity == 0){ // Calculate only when the current input is low
      pulse_width = current_captured - last_captured; // Assume up-counting
    }

    last_captured = current_captured;

  }

  if((TIM4->SR & TIM_SR_UIF) != 0) { // Check if overflow has taken place
    TIM4->SR &= ~TIM_SR_UIF; // Clear UIF flag to prevent re-entering
  }

}
```

Example 15-6. Timer interrupt handler in C. Assume the timer is up-counting.

Table 15-4 shows the configuration of pin PB 6 as timer function. The pin is set as no pull-up and no pull-down, and alternate function mode.

GPIO Pin	Connection	Mode	AF	Pull-up/Pull-down
Port B pin 6 (PB 6)	LED	AF	TIM4_CH1	No pull-up, No pull-down

Table 15-4. Connecting PB.6 to channel 1 of timer 4 internally

The following gives an example code of setting pin PB 6 (TIM4_CH1) as input capture. Register CCR stores the value of the counter after a transition detected. When a capture occurs, CCIF flag is set in the status register SR.

```c
#include <stdint.h>
#include "stm32l1xx.h"

int main(void) {
  // Enable GPIO Port B clock and configure GPIO port B pin 6 as
  // AF function 2 (i.e., TIM4_CH1) with no pull-up/pull-down
  ...


  // Enable the clock to timer 4
  RCC->APB1ENR |= RCC_APB1ENR_TIM4EN;

  // Set up an appropriate prescaler to slow down the timer's input clock
  TIM4->PSC = 127;

  // Set Auto-reload value to maximum value
  TIM4->ARR = 0xFFFF;    // Maximum 16-bit value

  // Set the direction of channel 1 as input, and select the active input
  TIM4->CCMR1 &= ~TIM_CCMR1_CC1S;   // Clear capture/compare 1 selection bits
  TIM4->CCMR1 |= TIM_CCMR1_CC1S_0; // CC1S[1:0] for channel 1:
                       //    00 = output
                       //    01 = input, CC1 is mapped on timer input 1
                       //    10 = input, CC1 is mapped on timer input 2
                       //    11 = input, CC1 is mapped on slave timer

  // Program the input filter duration: Disable digital filtering by clearing
  // IC1F[3:0] bits because we want to capture every event
  TIM4->CCMR1 &= ~TIM_CCMR1_IC1F;    // No filtering

  // Set the active transition as both rising and falling edges
  // CC1NP:CC1P bits: 00 = rising edge    01 = falling edge
  //                  10 = reserved       11 = both edges
  TIM4->CCER|=TIM_CCER_CC1P|TIM_CCER_CC1NP; // Both edges generate interrupts

  // Program the input prescaler: Clear prescaler to capture each transition
  TIM4->CCMR1 &= ~(TIM_CCMR1_IC1PSC);
```

```
    // Enable capture for channel 1
    // CC1E: 0 = disabled,  1 = enabled
    TIM4->CCER |= TIM_CCER_CC1E;

    // Allow channel 1 of timer 4 to generate interrupts
    TIM4->DIER |= TIM_DIER_CC1IE;

    // Allow channel 1 of timer 4 to generate DMA requests
    TIM4->DIER |= TIM_DIER_CC1DE; // Optional. Required if DMA is used

    // Enable the timer counter
    TIM4->CR1 |= TIM_CR1_CEN;

    // Set priority of timer 4 interrupt to 0 (highest urgency)
    NVIC_SetPriority(TIM4_IRQn, 0);

    // Enable timer 4 interrupt in the interrupt controller (NVIC)
    NVIC_EnableIRQ(TIM4_IRQn);

    while(1);
}
```

Example 15-7. Implementation of the initialization of a timer for input capture

15.4.2   Input Capture in Slave Mode with Reset

The interrupt handler in Example 15-6 can be simplified to the following if software sets timer 4 channel 1 as the slave mode with automatic reset.

```
volatile uint32_t pulse_width = 0;

void TIM4_IRQHandler(void) {

  if((TIM4->SR & TIM_SR_UIF) != 0)   // Check if overflow has taken place
    TIM4->SR &= ~TIM_SR_UIF;         // Clear UIF Flag to prevent re-entering

  if(TIM4->SR & TIM_SR_CC1IF != 0)   // Check interrupt flag is set
    pulse_width = TIM4->CCR1;        // Reading CCR1 clears CC1IF flag
}
```

Example 15-8. Interrupt handler if timer is in slave mode

Figure 15-25 illustrates the basic concepts. The timer uses each rising edge to reset the timer counter, and each falling edge to make a capture and generate a timer interrupt. For up-counting, the timer counter is re-initialized to zero upon a reset. Example 15-9 is the additional configuration that selects the slave mode with reset. This code should be added before the channel is enabled, *i.e.*, before software sets the CC1E bit in the CCER register. In this mode, a rising edge of the input signal reinitializes the counter, and a falling edge generates a timer interrupt. The pulse width is the CCR value captured.

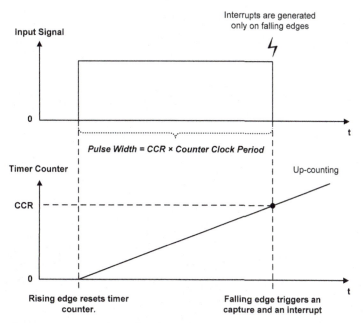

Figure 15-25. Input capture when the timer is set as slave mode with automatic reset

```
// Select falling edges as the active transition to generate interrupts
// CC1NP:CC1P bits: 00 = rising edge    01 = falling edge
//                  10 = reserved       11 = both edges
TIM4->CCER &= ~(TIM_CCER_CC1P | TIM_CCER_CC1NP); // Clear polarity bits
TIM4->CCER |= TIM_CCER_CC1P;   // Only falling edges generate interrupts


// Select the input trigger source
TIM4->SMCR &= ~TIM_SMCR_TS;    // Clear the trigger selection bits
TIM4->SMCR |= 4UL << 4;        // 100: TI1 Edge Detector (TI1F_ED)

// Select slave mode with reset
TIM4->SMCR &= ~TIM_SMCR_SMS;   // Clear slave mode bits
TIM4->SMCR |= 4;               // 0100 Slave mode with reset
```

Example 15-9. Setting Timer 1 as the slave mode with reset

Figure 15-26 shows the selection of the input signal to the slave mode controller and the capture signal to the capture module for channel 1.

- The input signal input (TGRI) to the slave mode controller can be selected from TI1F_ED, TI1FP1, TI2FP2, ETF, and various ITR from other timers. Depending on SMS bits in the SMCR register, the input signal can be used to trigger the reset of the timer counter (reset mode), stop and start the time counter based on polarity (gate mode) or start the counter on rising edges of TGRI (trigger mode). In Example 15-9, TGRI is used to reset the time counter. Specifically, it selects TI1F_ED as the trigger source. As a result, the counter is reset on both rising and falling edges of TI1F.

- The capture signal to the capture module can be TI1FP1, TI2FP2 or TRC. Example 15-9 selects TI1FP1 as the capture signal. Also, a capture is made on each falling edge of TI1F.

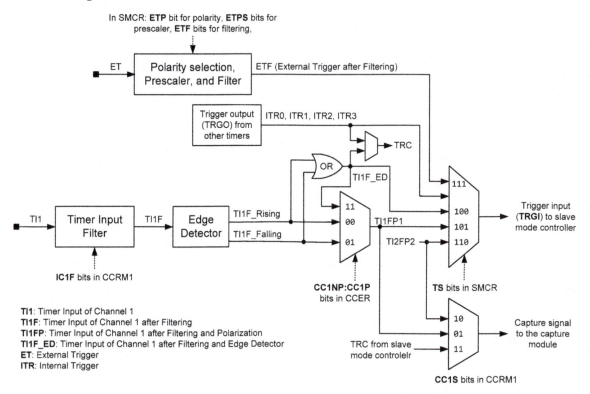

Figure 15-26. Internal trigger and capture signals for channel 1

Figure 15-17 shows an example time diagram of measuring the pulse width. It is assumed that no filtering has been applied to the input signal (TI1).

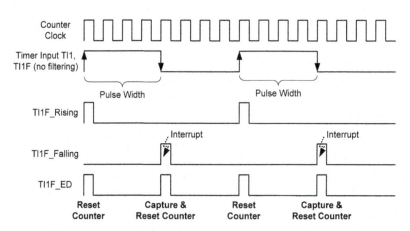

Figure 15-27. Counter reset events and capture events in slave mode with reset

15.4.3   Interfacing to Ultrasonic Distance Sensor

An ultrasonic distance sensor has one transmitter and one receiver. The transmitter generates short bursts of high-frequency ultrasonic waves. The receiver detects any wave reflected back from the target, as shown in Figure 15-28.

Without contacting with the target physically, it measures the difference in time between sending waves and receiving reflected waves. The distance is then calculated as follows:

$$Distance = \frac{Round\ Trip\ Time \times Speed\ of\ Sound}{2}$$

One example application is an automatic door opener, which opens a door when a person approaches. Compared with optical distance sensors, ultrasonic distance sensors are low cost but less accurate.

Figure 15-28. Ultrasonic distance sensor of HC-SR 04
(VCC = +5V, Trig = Trigger input to sensor, Echo = Echo time output of sensor)

To start a distance measurement, the processor should send a high pulse signal (≥3.2V) with a width of 10 μs to the trig pin. The ultrasonic transmitter then sends out 8 cycles of 40-KHz ultrasonic waves (*i.e.*, for 200 μs), which is greater than the upper limit of human hearing range (typically 20 KHz).

When the ultrasonic receiver detects any waves reflected within a predefined time window, it generates a high pulse (5V) on the echo pin. The pulse width is linearly proportional to the distance of the nearest objects.

Specifically, if the width of the pulse on the echo pin is in microseconds (μs), the distance, measured in centimeters, is calculated as follows:

$$Distance = \frac{Pulse\ Width\ (\mu s)}{58}\ cm$$

or

$$Distance = \frac{Pulse\ Width\ (\mu s)}{148}\ inch$$

The sensor can measure a distance between 2 *cm* and 400 *cm*, with a resolution of 0.3 *cm*, and the corresponding echo pulse width is between 150 *μs* and 25 *ms*. When the sensor detects no object, the echo pulse width is 38 *ms*.

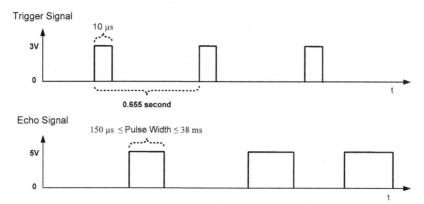

Figure 15-29. Trigger and echo signals

Suppose we want to measure the distance every 0.655 seconds, as shown in Figure 15-29 and Figure 15-30. We can use two timers to interface the ultrasonic distance sensor.

- The first timer, which is set as PWM output mode 1 and connected to the trigger pin of the sensor, generates a pulse signal with a width of 10 *μs*.

- The second timer, which is set as input capture and connected to the echo pin of the sensor, measures the pulse width of the echo signal. The second timer should be able to detect both the rising and falling edge of the echo signal.

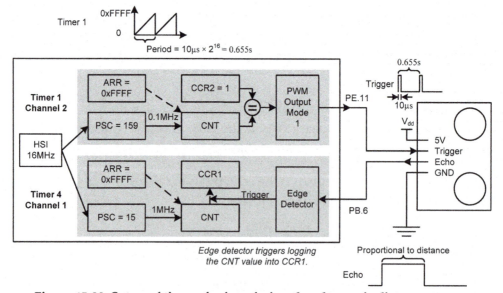

Figure 15-30. Setup of timers for interfacing the ultrasonic distance sensor.

As shown Figure 15-30, we use Timer 1 Channel 2 to drive the trigger pin. Suppose 16 MHz HSI is selected to drive the timers. The following shows the calculation of the period and pulse width of sensor trigger signal.

$$Timer\ 1\ Counter\ Clock = \frac{Timer\ 1\ Input\ Clock}{1 + Prescaler} = \frac{16\ MHz}{1 + 159} = 0.1\ MHz$$

$$PWM\ Period = (1 + ARR) \times Counter\ Clock\ Period = (1 + 0xFFFF)\frac{1}{0.1\ MHz} = 0.655\ s$$

$$PWM\ pulse\ width = CCR \times Counter\ Clock\ Period = 1 \times \frac{1}{0.1\ MHz} = 10\ \mu s$$

The distance measured is only in one direction with limited angular resolution. We can use multiple ultrasonic sensors to detect objects in several directions. Also, it is possible that an object reflects ultrasonic waves away if the target surface is oriented at unfavorable angles, resulting in the object being undetected. Additionally, objects with a soft or irregular surface might not reflect enough ultrasonic waves back, and accordingly, ultrasonic sensors fail to detect them. Moreover, sounds travel slower in colder air, and thus the program should perform some calibration to achieve better accuracy.

The following assembly code selects the 16MHz HSI clock as the system clock.

```
; Select HSI (16 MHz, 1% accuracy) as the system clock.
HSI_init   PROC
           EXPORT HSI_init

           ; Turn on HSI oscillator
           LDR   r0, =RCC_BASE
           LDR   r1, [r0, #RCC_CR]
           ORR   r1, r1, #RCC_CR_HSION
           STR   r1, [r0, #RCC_CR]

           ; Select HSI as system clock
           LDR   r1, [r0, #RCC_CFGR]
           BIC   r1, r1, #RCC_CFGR_SW
           ORR   r1, r1, #RCC_CFGR_SW_HSI
           STR   r1, [r0, #RCC_CFGR]

           ; Wait for HSI stable
WaitHSI    LDR   r1, [r0, #RCC_CR]
           AND   r1, r1, #RCC_CR_HSIRDY
           CMP   r1, #0
           BEQ   WaitHSI
           BX    LR
           ENDP
```

Example 15-10. Configuring high-speed internal clock (HSI)

Timer 4 uses the input capture to record the time instant when a rising or falling edge takes place in the echo signal, as shown in Figure 15-30. Software should set the update interrupt enable flag (UIE) and the capture event flag (CC1IE for channel 1) in the DMA/interrupt enable register (DIER) to allow these interrupts.

Timer 4 is set as counting upward. A counter overflow occurs when the 16-bit timer counter reaches 0xFFFF. Because the counter increments every 1μs, an overflow occurs every $2^{16} \times 1\ \mu s = 6.5\ ms$ in this example. When an overflow occurs, the timer generates an interrupt and sets up the UIF flag bit in the interrupt status register (SR).

Even though the duration of the echo signal from the sensor is limited to 38 ms, it is possible that the counter can overflow when measuring the pulse width of the echo signal, as shown in Figure 15-31.

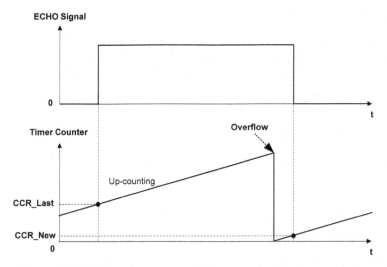

Figure 15-31. Overflow occurs between two capture events

Thus, we need a variable (named *overflow* in the following code) that counts the number of overflows within one pulse. The time span can be calculated as follows:

$$Time\ Span\ (\mu s) = (CCR_{New} - CCR_{Last}) + 65536 \times Overflows$$

in which is CCR_{New} is currently captured value and CCR_{Last} is the last captured value. The variable *Overflows* should be reinitialized to zero after the time span is calculated. After calculating the time span, the program should use the current counter value to update the last counter value to prepare the next calculation.

Example 15-11 shows the assembly implementation of the interrupt handler for timer 4 (TIM4_IRQHandler). The three variables *timespan, lastCounter,* and *overflow* should be defined in the data area.

```
; These three variables should be defined in the data area
timespan        DCD   0    ; Pulse width
lastCounter     DCD   0    ; Timer counter value of last capture event
overflow        DCD   0    ; Counter the number of overflows

; The following should be in the code area
TIM4_IRQHandler PROC
                EXPORT        TIM4_IRQHandler

                PUSH {r4, r6, r10, lr}

                LDR r0, =TIM4_BASE         ; Pseudo instruction
                LDR r2, [r0, #TIM_SR]      ; Read status register
                AND r3, r2, #TIM_SR_UIF   ; Check update event flag
                CBZ r3, check_CCFlag       ; Compare and branch on zero

                LDR r3, =overflow
                LDR r1, [r3]               ; Read overflow from memory
                ADD r1, r1, #1             ; Increment overflow counter
                STR r1, [r3]               ; Save overflow to memory

                BIC r2, r2, #TIM_SR_UIF   ; Clear update event flag
                STR r2, [r0, #TIM_SR]      ; Update status register

check_CCFlag    AND r2, r2, #TIM_SR_CC1IF ; Check capture event flag
                CBZ r2, exit               ; Compare and branch on zero

                LDR r0, =TIM4_BASE         ; Load base memory address
                LDR r1, [r0, #TIM_CCR1]    ; Read the new captured value

                LDR r2, =lastCounter
                LDR r0, [r2]               ; Load the last counter value
                STR r1, [r2]               ; Save the new counter value
                CBZ r0, clearOverflow      ; Compare and branch on zero

                LDR r3, =overflow
                LDR r4, [r3]               ; Load the overflow value
                LSL r4, r4, #16            ; Multiply by 2^16 (i.e., 65536)
                ADD r6, r1, r4
                SUB r10, r6, r0            ; r10 = timer counter difference
                LDR r2, =timespan
                STR r10, [r2]              ; Update timespan in memory

clearOverflow   MOV r0, #0
                LDR r3, =overflow
                STR r0, [r3]               ; clear overflow counter
exit            POP {r4, r6, r10, pc}
                ENDP
```

Example 15-11. Implementation of interrupt handler in assembly for measuring pulse width

In the above code, we use "LSL r4, r4, #16" instruction to replace multiplication with 65536 (*i.e.*, 2^{16}). A shift instruction runs much faster than a multiplication instruction. Additionally, the *lastCounter* variable is initialized to 0.

The code above calculates the time span between a rising edge and a falling edge. We can improve the code by only calculating the time span from a rising edge to a falling edge, and ignore the time span from a falling edge to a rising edge.

One common mistake is that the interrupt handler does not clear the update event flag in the interrupt status register (SR). In the above code, the hardware sets up interrupt flags in SR.

> *Interrupt handlers must clear interrupt flags in the status register to prevent the processor from re-entering the handler.*

- If the UIE bit in the DMA/interrupt enable register (DIER) is set, hardware sets the update flag when a counter overflow (or a counter underflow if the counter counts down) occurs.
- If the capture/compare interrupt enable (CCIE) bit is set in the DIER register, hardware sets the capture flag (CCIF) when a rising edge or a falling edge of an external signal is detected. Hardware also sets the over-capture flag (CCOF) if a new capture is made while the CCIF flag is set.

Hardware automatically clears the capture flag (CCIF) when software reads register (CCR). Therefore, TIM4_IRQHandler does not clear the CCIF flag explicitly.

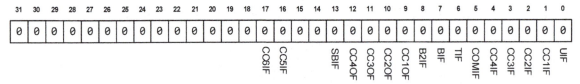

CCxIF: Interrupt flag on channel x
- For output on channel x, hardware sets this flag when the counter CNT matches register CCR.
- For input on channel x, hardware sets this flag when the counter CNT has been latched into register CCR.

CCxOF: Over-capture flag on channel x
- For input on channel x, hardware sets this flag when a new capture has been made while CCxIF was already set.

UIF: Update interrupt flag
- Hardware sets this flag when the counter CNT overflows during up-counting or the counter CNT under-flows during down-counting.

Figure 15-32. Timer status register (SR)

However, the interrupt handler must clear the update flag (UIF) in the status register (SR). If it were not cleared, the timer interrupt handler would repeatedly be called, which not only generates errors in calculating a time duration but also makes the processor have no time to run other codes with a lower priority.

15.5 Exercises

1. Suppose we want to use a timer to generate a PWM signal.

   - PWM has a duty cycle of 25%.
   - PWM has a fixed frequency of 320 Hz
   - The input clock to the timer is 32 MHz.
   - The timer uses PWM mode 2: the output is high if the counter is larger than or equal to the content of CCR.

   How would you design the prescaler (PSC), the auto-reload register (ARR), and the compare and capture (CCR)? Show your calculation.

2. Use an oscilloscope to measure duty cycles. Timer input clock has 2.097 MHz.
   a. What is the relationship between the timer input clock, the counter clock CK_CNT, the prescaler PSC, and the pulse period measured?

   b. We want to keep TIM4_ARR fixed, but set TIM4_CCR1 to three different values, as listed below. How would you set up the ARR, PSC, and CCR register values? Calculate the duty measured and verify the correctness.

   - Case 1: TIM4_CCR1 = 1/6 * (TIM4_ARR + 1)
   - Case 2: TIM4_CCR1 = 1/3 * (TIM4_ARR + 1)
   - Case 3: TIM4_CCR1 = 1/2 * (TIM4_ARR + 1)

3. Suppose the HSE (high-speed external clock) of 16 MHz is selected as the clock of the timer. To generate a 1Hz square wave with a duty cycle of 50%, how would you set up the timer? Indicate your counting mode and show the value of ARR, CCR, and PSC registers.

4. Write an assembly program that uses the output compare function of a timer to toggle an LED every second.

5. Write an assembly program that generates a PWM output signal to dim an LED periodically.

6. Write an assembly program that uses PWM to generate a square wave signal with a frequency of 440 Hz and a duty cycle of 50% (*i.e.*, musical tone A).

7. Write an assembly program that uses PWM to control a stepper motor via micro stepping.

8. Write an assembly program that uses the input capture function to measure the frequency of an external signal. Use a function generator to generate a 1HZ square

wave. Send the square wave to the STM32L board to verify the correctness of your assembly program.

9. Write an assembly program that uses the HC-SR04 ultrasonic distance sensor presented in Chapter 15.4.3 to measure the distance to an object.

10. In the timer interrupt handler, we need to increment the overflow counter if an overflow occurs. Register r3 holds the overflow counter. However, the main function cannot observe any changes in register r3 even though overflow events have occurred. Explain why.

```
; r3 = overflow counter

TIM4_IRQHandler PROC
    EXPORT TIM4_IRQHandler
    ...

    LDR   r0, =TIM4_BASE
    LDR   r1, [r0, #TIM_SR]     ; Read status register
    AND   r2, r1, #TIM_SR_UIF   ; Check update event flag
    CBZ   r2, check_CCIF        ; Compare and branch on zero

    ADDS r3, r3, #1             ; Increment the overflow counter

check_CCIF
    ...
    ENDP
```

CHAPTER
16

Stepper Motor Control

DC motors are often used in applications as diverse as robots, printers, machine tools, household appliances, medical equipment, automotive devices, and computer hard drives. DC motors can be classified into two broad categories: servo motors and stepper motors.

- A *servo motor* operates in a closed loop system because it needs continuous position feedback to control the motor to achieve some desired speed or position. Thus, servo motors are more expensive than stepper motors. We often use PWM signals to control a servo motor.

- A *stepper motor* rotates to a specific position in discrete steps. The control of a stepper motor can be an open loop system, which requires no position feedback.

Compared with stepper motors, servo motors are more suitable for applications that require high speed or high torque, or applications that have dramatic load changes. Stepper motors tend to have lower torque capacity at high speeds, lose steps if overloaded, and have a greater level of vibration due to the stepwise motion. However, stepper motors are less expensive due to the cost savings of the sensors and the controller and easier to interface with microprocessors. They are also suitable for applications that require low or medium accelerations or applications that have a constant load.

16.1 Bipolar and Unipolar Stepper Motor

Stepper motors are either *bipolar* or *unipolar*.

- A bipolar stepper motor often requires a power source with switchable polarities, such as a complicated H-bridge (see Figure 16-3). Such a power source can reverse the electric current and the electromagnetic polarity of each coil winding.

- A unipolar stepper motor requires only one power supply, and the electric current does not reverse its direction in each coil winding (see Figure 16-4). The unipolar motor uses half of its winding coil to generate the electromagnetic field while a bipolar motor uses a full winding coil. Therefore, a bipolar stepper motor usually has a higher torque capacity than a unipolar one of the same weight. However, a unipolar stepper motor has a simpler control circuit.

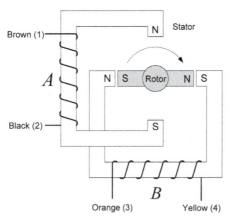

Figure 16-1. Bipolar stepper motor with two phases (A, B) on the stator, and two permanent magnetic poles on the rotor

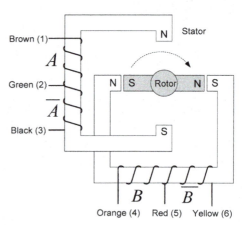

Figure 16-2. Unipolar stepper motor with two phases (A, B) on the stator, and two permanent magnetic poles on the rotor

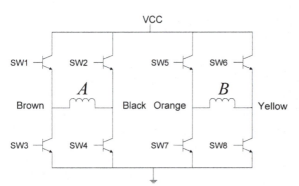

Figure 16-3. Circuit to drive a bipolar stepper motor. Each winding is fully utilized, but its electrical current reverses the direction alternatively.

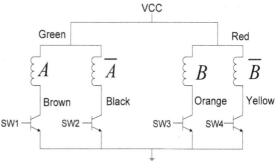

Figure 16-4. Circuit to drive a unipolar stepper motor. The electrical current always flows in one direction, but only half of each winding is utilized.

This chapter uses a *unipolar stepper motor* as an example to show how a processor controls stepper motors. The model is Mabuchi #PF35T, as shown in Figure 16-5. The motor has 2 phases and 48 steps per revolution (*i.e.*, 7.5 degrees per step). The rotor has 10 teeth.

Figure 16-5. A six-lead unipolar stepper motor

16.2 Step Angle

For each pulse, the shaft of a stepper motor rotates a fixed angle. Depending on the activation sequence of coil windings, the shaft can rotate a full step, a half step, or a specific fraction of a full step. The corresponding activation sequence is called full stepping, half stepping, and micro-stepping.

When the shaft rotates a full step, the angle it moves is referred to as **step angle**. We can calculate the step angle as follows:

$$Step\ Angle = \frac{360^{\circ}}{steps\ per\ revolution}$$

$$steps\ per\ revolution = P{\times}T$$

where P is the total number of phases on the stator, and T is the total number permanent-magnetic poles available on the rotor. In Figure 16-1 and Figure 16-2, there are only two poles on the rotor. In reality, there are more magnetic poles on the rotor to achieve a small step angle, as shown in Figure 16-6.

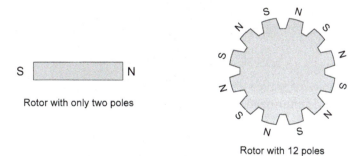

Figure 16-6. Number of magnetic poles on the rotor of a stepper motor

Usually, a stepper motor has two or three phases. A typical number of steps per revolution is 48, 72, 144, 180, and 200, resulting in a step angle of 7.5°, 5°, 2.5°, 2°, and 1.8°, correspondingly. The motor shown in Figure 16-5 has 2 phases on its stator and 24 poles on its rotor. Thus, its step angle is

$$Step\ Angle = \frac{360°}{2 \times 24} = 7.5°$$

For full stepping, a stepper motor rotates by one step angle for each input pulse. For half-stepping, it rotates half of a step angle. For micro stepping, the motor rotates a specific fraction of a step angle. Rotating a fixed angle for each pulse enables open loop position control. The number and the rate of the pulses control the position and the speed of the motor shaft, respectively.

16.3 Wave Stepping

As the simplest stepping method, wave stepping turns on one switch and energizes a single phase at a time. Figure 16-7 shows the control sequence of four switches of four winding coils (A, B, $\bar{A}$, and $\bar{B}$). For each switch, if its control signal is high, then the switch is turned on, and electric current flows through the corresponding winding coil. For example, when the signal of SW1 is high, the corresponding coil A is energized. Software turns on these switches alternatively in this control sequence.

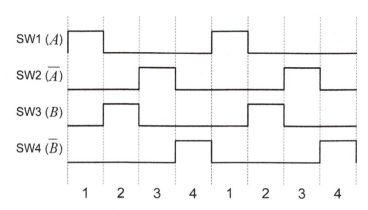

Figure 16-7. The sequence of wave stepping for two-phase unipolar stepper motors. The stator is energized in the sequence of A, B, $\bar{A}$, and $\bar{B}$.

To simplify the presentation, we assume the rotor has only two permanent magnetic poles, as shown in Figure 16-8. In reality, the rotor often has more poles to obtain a small step angle.

Therefore, the rotor rotates 90 degrees for each pulse in this simplified example. If the load on a stepper motor is not too large, the rotor is eventually locked at an angular position where the permanent-magnet rotor is aligned with the electromagnetic field of the activated coil winding. Figure 16-8 shows that the rotor is being pulled from the previously locked position when a new phase is energized.

This control sequence is called *wave stepping*. At any time, only one coil winding is energized, and thus it offers a relatively small torque. Therefore, wave stepping is not widely used in real systems.

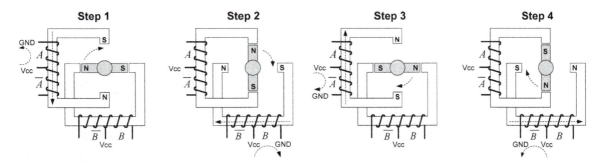

Figure 16-8. Wave stepping sequence of a simplified bipolar stepper motor with two phases on the stator and two poles on the rotor (90° stepping)

16.4 Full Stepping

While wave stepping activates one coil winding each time, *full stepping* energizes two coil windings alternatively.

- To turn the shaft clockwise, the coil activation sequence is $A\bar{B}$, AB, $\bar{A}B$, and $\bar{A}\bar{B}$, as shown in Figure 16-9.
- Reversing the activation sequence makes the shaft to rotate counterclockwise.

Both wave stepping and full stepping rotate the shaft a step angle each time and have the same number of steps in one revolution. However, the full stepping produces a higher torque than wave stepping because two coil windings push or pull the shaft simultaneously.

Figure 16-8 shows that the rotor starts to move from the angular position locked in the previous step. Reversing the control sequence supplied to the switches can change the rotation direction. For clockwise rotation, the coil activation sequence is $A\bar{B}$, AB, $\bar{A}B$, and $\bar{A}\bar{B}$. For counter-clockwise rotation, the coil activation sequence is $\bar{A}\bar{B}$, $\bar{A}B$, AB, and $A\bar{B}$.

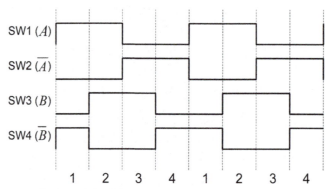

Figure 16-9. Sequence of full stepping for two-phase unipolar stepper motors

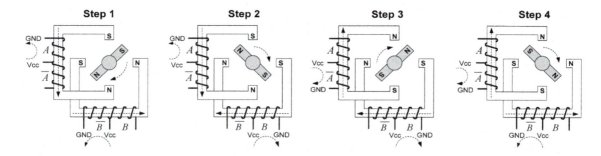

Figure 16-10. Full stepping sequence (90° stepping) on a simplified bipolar stepper motor

Example 16-1 and Example 16-2 show incomplete C programs that use full stepping to rotate a stepper motor 360 degrees clockwise and counter-clockwise, respectively.

```
// Full Step: 0b1001, 0b1010, 0b0110, 0b0101
// Each four-bit sequence represents the ON/OFF control of A, Ā, B, and B̄.

unsigned char FullStep[4] = {0x9, 0xA, 0x6, 0x5};

for(int j = 0; j < 48; j++){   // 48 steps ×7.5° per step = 360°
  for(int i = 0; i < 4; i++){
    for(int k = 0; k < 6000; k++) {;}  // A short delay
    // Winding A = (FullStep[i] & 0x8) >> 3
    // Winding Ā = (FullStep[i] & 0x4) >> 2
    // Winding B = (FullStep[i] & 0x2) >> 1
    // Winding B̄ = FullStep[i] & 0x1
    // Set the value of the GPIO output data register (ODR)

    ...

  }
}
```

Example 16-1. Incomplete C program rotating a stepper motor clockwise by full stepping

```
// Full Step: 0b1001, 0b1010, 0b0110, 0b0101
// Each four-bit sequence represents the ON/OFF control of A,Ā,B,and B̄.

unsigned char FullStep[4] = {0x9, 0xA, 0x6, 0x5};

for(int j = 0; j < 48; j++){   // 48 steps ×7.5° per step = 360°
  for(int i = 3; i >= 0; i--){
    for(int k = 0; k < 6000; k++){;}   // A short delay
    // Winding A = (FullStep[i] & 0x8) >> 3
    // Winding Ā = (FullStep[i] & 0x4) >> 2
    // Winding B = (FullStep[i] & 0x2) >> 1
    // Winding B̄ = FullStep[i] & 0x1
    // Set the value of the GPIO output data register (ODR)

    ...

  }
}
```

Example 16-2. Incomplete program rotating counter-clockwise by full stepping

16.5 Half Stepping

Figure 16-11 shows the activation sequence of half-stepping: $A\bar{B}$, A, AB, B, $\bar{A}B$, $\bar{A}$, $\bar{A}\bar{B}$, and $\bar{B}$. It energizes one winding coil and two winding coils alternatively. Half stepping provides less torque but twice as much rotation resolution as full stepping. Half stepping can rotate the shaft more smoothly than full stepping. However, it sometimes has only one half-coil winding activated and produces less torque than full stepping.

Figure 16-12 shows the rotation sequence of a simplified motor with only two poles on the rotor. It includes eight half-steps, and the shaft rotates 45° in each half-step.

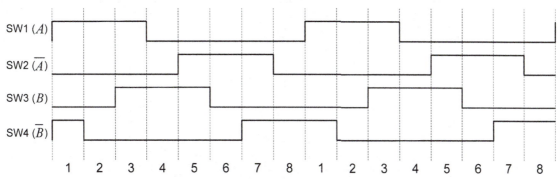

Figure 16-11. Sequence of half stepping for two-phase unipolar stepper motors

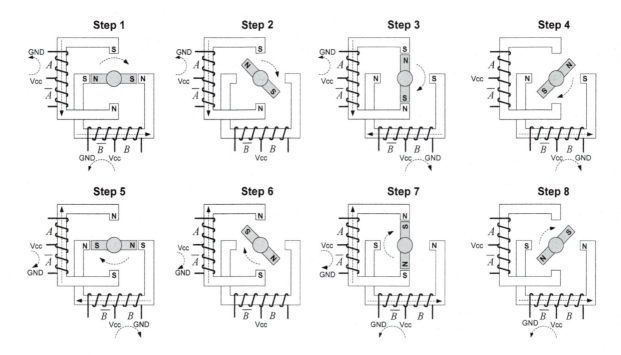

Figure 16-12. Half-stepping sequence for unipolar stepper motors (45° stepping)

Example 16-3 shows an incomplete C program that uses half-stepping to rotate a stepper motor 360 degrees clockwise.

```
// Half Step: 0b1001, 0b1000, 0b1010, 0b0010, 0b0110, 0b0100, 0b0101, 0b0001
// Each four-bit sequence represents the ON/OFF control of A, Ā, B, and B̄.

unsigned char HalfStep[8] = {0x9, 0x8, 0xa, 0x2, 0x6, 0x4, 0x5, 0x1};

for(int j = 0; j < 96; j++){   // 96 steps ×3.75° per step = 360°
  for(int i = 0; i < 8; i++){
    for(int k = 0; k < 6000; k++){;}  // A short delay
    // Winding A = (HalfStep[i] & 0x8) >> 3
    // Winding Ā = (HalfStep[i] & 0x4) >> 2
    // Winding B = (HalfStep[i] & 0x2) >> 1
    // Winding B̄ = HalfStep[i] & 0x1
    // Set the value of the GPIO output data register (ODR)

    ...

  }
}
```

Example 16-3. Incomplete C program that rotates a stepper motor clockwise by half stepping

16.6 Micro-stepping

As introduced previously, a microcontroller can use full stepping or half stepping to control a stepper motor. A stepper motor rotates exactly a full step angle or a half step angle in each excitation in full or half stepping, respectively, resulting in jerky and noisy movements of the motor.

In this section, we use the PWM to perform micro-stepping, which rotates a fraction of a full step angle in one excitation, such as 1/4, 1/8, 1/16, or 1/32 of a full step.

Micro-stepping divides a full step into multiple smaller steps. It moves the shaft in a smaller angle increment, provides a much smoother movement, and reduces the problems of movement noise and vibration.

The goal of micro-stepping is to adjust the electrical current dynamically in each winding to make the acceleration or deceleration of the shaft less noticeable. We can use PWM to generate a fast binary signal with an appropriately chosen duty cycle to adjust the amplitude of the voltage across each winding dynamically. Usually, the applied voltage on a winding is linearly proportional to the current generated.

Sine-cosine micro-stepping is a widely-used method to adjust the amplitude of the voltage on each winding. When two windings a and b are excited simultaneously, the overall static magnetic torque generated by both windings is

$$T = -ki_a \sin \theta + ki_b \cos \theta$$

where k is a constant, θ is the shaft mechanical angle from the last full-step position, and i_a and i_b are the electrical current in windings a and b.

When the shaft remains at a stable angle, the torque force is balanced, and thus we have $T = 0$. In sine-cosine micro-stepping, to make the overall torque force to be zero, we can set the electrical current in both windings as follows:

$$i_a = I_m \cos \theta$$

$$i_b = I_m \sin \theta$$

where I_m is a constant. Therefore, the overall static magnetic torque is

$$\begin{aligned} T &= -ki_a \sin \theta + ki_b \cos \theta \\ &= -kI_m \cos \theta \sin \theta + kI_m \sin \theta \cos \theta \\ &= 0 \end{aligned}$$

Microprocessors use discrete sine and cosine wave to drive both windings. Figure 16-13 shows the voltage signal of each phase of unipolar stepper motors if 1/4 micro-stepping is used. Figure 16-14 shows the voltage signal across each coil winding.

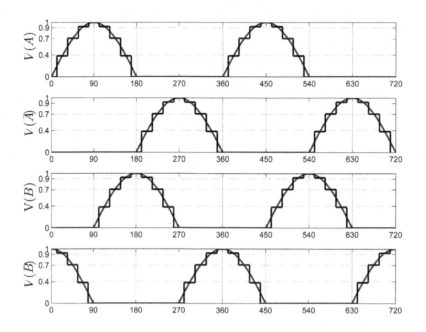

Figure 16-13. 1/4 sine-cosine micro-stepping for four-phase unipolar stepper motors

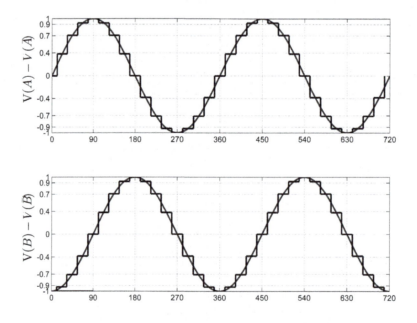

Figure 16-14. 1/4 sine-cosine micro-stepping for each coil winding of unipolar stepper motors

Suppose the auto-reload register (ARR) of a timer is $1000 - 1$ (*i.e.*, 999), software should set the compare and capture register (CCR) of the timer to the following sequence repeatedly for 1/4 micro-stepping.

```
uint16_t CCR_MicroStepping[] = {0, 383, 707, 924, 1000};
```

For 1/2 micro-stepping, the sequence of CCR should be

```
uint16_t CCR_MicroStepping [] = {0, 707, 1000};
```

For 1/8 micro-stepping, the sequence of CCR should be

```
uint16_t CCR_MicroStepping [] = {0, 195, 383, 556, 707, 832, 924, 981, 1000};
```

16.7 Driving Stepper Motor

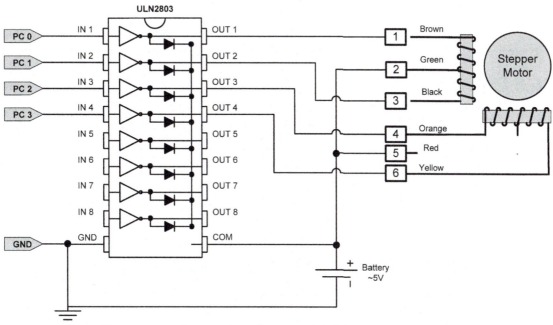

Figure 16-15. Connection diagram of driving a stepper motor

We cannot directly drive a stepper motor by using the GPIO pins of the microprocessor because the GPIO ports cannot provide sufficient electric current required by the stepper motor. The maximum electric current supplied by a GPIO pin is approximately 10 mA. The stepper motor used in this lab has only 20 Ωs, and it draws 3V/20Ω = 150 mA, which exceeds the maximum current that can be supplied by a GPIO pin. Software should configure the mode of these GPIO pins as digital output with push-pull.

Another important reason for not using GPIO pins to drive a motor directly is that the motor may cause a back electromotive force in the circuit while it is accelerating or decelerating. This generates a voltage that pushes against the current that induces it, which could potentially damage the microprocessor.

We can use the 8-channel Darlington driver (ULN2803) to drive the stepper motor, as shown in Figure 16-15. The ULN2803 is a high-voltage, high-current Darlington transistor array, which consists of eight NPN Darlington pairs. Each Darlington pair can collect currents up to 500 mA. The output pin can withstand at least 50V in the off state. Suppression diodes are included for inductive load driving. Outputs may be paralleled for high current capability.

For each Darlington pair, if a high positive voltage is applied to the input pin, then the corresponding output pin is grounded, and it can draw the electric current up to 500 mA. If the input pin has a low voltage supply, then the corresponding output pin cannot drain any current. An input pin takes ~1 mA current only.

16.8 Exercises

1. Write an assembly program that turns the stepper motor 360 degrees clockwise by using full stepping. What is the highest update frequency of the full-stepping control signals while the motor does not drop any steps? You might need to use an oscilloscope to find your update frequency.

2. Write an assembly program that turns the stepper motor 360 degrees counter-clockwise by using half-stepping. What is the highest update frequency of the half-stepping control signals while the motor does not drop any steps? You might need to use an oscilloscope to find your update frequency.

3. Write an assembly program that changes the rotation speed when the push button is pressed.

4. What would happen if the update frequency were higher than the maximum allowed in Question 1 and 2?

5. Write an assembly program that uses pulse-width modulated (PWM) to perform micro-stepping. Micro-stepping is a digital technique to turn a stepper motor smoothly.

Liquid-crystal Display (LCD)

An LCD is a cost-effective interface to display information to users in a friendly way. LCD modules are categorized into two groups:

- *External hardware driver.* These have an external LCD controller chip, such as the Hitachi HD44780, the Toshiba T6963, and the Seiko-Epson SED1330. They use standard protocols to exchange data and commands between the microprocessor and the LCD controller chip. The advantage of using an external hardware driver is that fewer processor pins are required, and the software to interface the LCD module is relatively easier.

- *Internal hardware driver.* These have a built-in hardware driver within the microprocessor chip. STM32L processors have a built-in LCD controller. The advantage of having an internal hardware LCD driver is that the system can be made smaller. However, it uses many processor pins and requires complex software to drive the LCD.

In this chapter, we first introduce the processors that already have an on-chip LCD hardware driver. Specifically, we focus on two important aspects. (1) How does the on-chip LCD hardware driver generate voltage signals to turn a display pixel on or off? (2) How does a software driver display a given character string on the LCD? The goal of the first aspect is to reduce the pin requirements, and the target of the second aspect is to provide a flexible and easy-to-use interface to application developers.

Additionally, this chapter also discusses how to interface off-chip (external) HD44780-compatible LCDs, which have been widely used in the industry. We explain the connection diagram, font encoding, sending data and commands, and generating and displaying customized characters on the LCD. The goal is to understand LCD communication protocols and signal timing.

17.1 Static Drive

When the voltage across a segment is greater than some threshold (V), the resulting electric field forces liquid crystals in this segment to align themselves to the electric field. Change of crystal orientation modifies light polarization and controls the amount of light that can pass through between two crossed polarizers. The crystals themselves do not emit any light, but those aligned crystals prevent light from passing through polarizers, causing the dark appearance. Applying the same voltage for a long period damages liquid crystals. Thus, the segment voltage is alternated. Usually, an LCD segment is driven by two square waveforms of the same frequency.

There are two types of LCD drivers: *static drive* and *multiplexed drive*. The static drive uses one dedicated pin to turn on or off an LCD segment (also called a pixel). Figure 17-1 shows an eight-segment display (including seven segments for the digit display and the dot). All segments share the same *com* signal. If the signals to drive the eight segment lines (SL i, i = 1 to 8) are set as in Figure 17-1, then the number 2 is displayed. The voltage across segment lines 1, 2, 4, 5, and 7 has an alternative voltage with amplitude larger than the threshold voltage. However, the voltage across segment 3 and 6 is a constant zero.

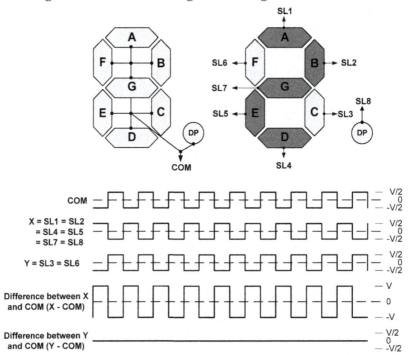

Figure 17-1. Static driving. There is only one common terminal in static driving. When a segment line has the same voltage waveform as the waveform of COM, this segment is turned off; otherwise, this segment line is turned on.

The static drive is simple but requires many pins. An LCD usually has many pixel segments. For example, the LCD on the STM32L kit can display up to six decimal numbers at once and has 96 pixel segments. If the processor uses one pin to drive each pixel segment, then 97 pins would be required. However, it is not desirable for a processor to use 97 pins for an LCD. This motivates the use of a multiplexed driver, introduced in the next section.

17.2 Multiplexed Drive

To reduce the number of pins required, LCD modules often use a special hardware technology, called a *multiplexed drive*. While all display segments in the static drive have a single shared terminal, a multiplexed drive shares two or more common terminal lines to reduce the number of pins.

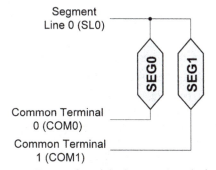

Figure 17-2. Example with duty ratio of 1/2. Each segment line drives two display segments.

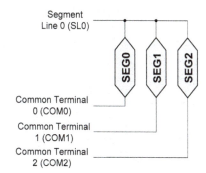

Figure 17-3. Example with duty ratio of 1/3. Each segment line drives three display segments.

Two of the key concepts of multiplexed LCD drives are *duty ratio* and *bias*.

$$Duty\ Ratio = \frac{1}{Number\ of\ Common\ Terminals}$$

$$Bias = \frac{1}{Number\ of\ Voltage\ Levels - 1}$$

Figure 17-2 and Figure 17-3 give two examples in which the duty ratio is 1/2 and 1/3, respectively. In these examples, there are two and three common terminals, respectively, and all segments are connected to one of these common terminals. In addition, two or three segments share the same segment line, respectively.

In the static drive given in Figure 17-1, nine pins are required, including one for the common terminal and eight for the display segments. If a multiplexed drive with a duty ratio of ½ is used to drive the same display, only six lines (or pins) are required, as shown in Figure 17-4. As discussed previously, the static drive would require 97 pins. A multiplexed drive with a duty ratio of ¼ can reduce the total pins needed to drive the LCD from 97 to 28, including 4 common terminals and 24 segment lines. In this setting, each segment line drives four display segments.

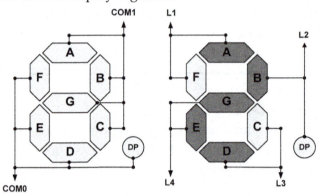

Figure 17-4. Multiplexed drive scheme of a segment digit display (Duty ratio = ½). It has two common terminal lines. Each segment line drives two display segments.

Compared with a static drive, a multiplexed drive reduces the total number of pins required at the cost of the brightness. The duty ratio represents the fraction of each time cycle that a segment is activated. In a multiplexed drive, each visible display segment is switched on and off with a frequency typically larger than 30 Hz. Human eyes usually cannot notice fast switching between on and off. If the duty cycle is ½, each visible display segment is on 50% of the time and off 50% of the time. By contrast, the static drive keeps each visible display segment on continuously.

Example 17-1 and Example 17-2 illustrate the basic concept of a multiplexed drive when the duty ratio is ½. These two segments share the same segment line signal. The following presents four different cases: (1) turning on both segments, (2) turning off both segments, (3) turning on only the first segment and (4) turning on only the second segment. The signals of two common terminals and the segment line are shown for each case. Note there are three voltage levels ($0, \pm V/2, \pm V$) for the voltage across each segment. Therefore, the bias is ½.

- When a segment is turned on, the magnitude of the voltage across this segment is either V/2 or V at any given time. If the activation threshold between V/2 and V, this segment is switched on or off quickly. The frequency of switching on and off is usually very fast so that the naked eyes cannot detect the flashing. However, the brightness is reduced by one half.
- When a segment is turned off, the magnitude of the voltage across the segment is either 0 or V/2 at any given time. These voltage levels are less than the activation threshold. Thus, the segment is constantly off.

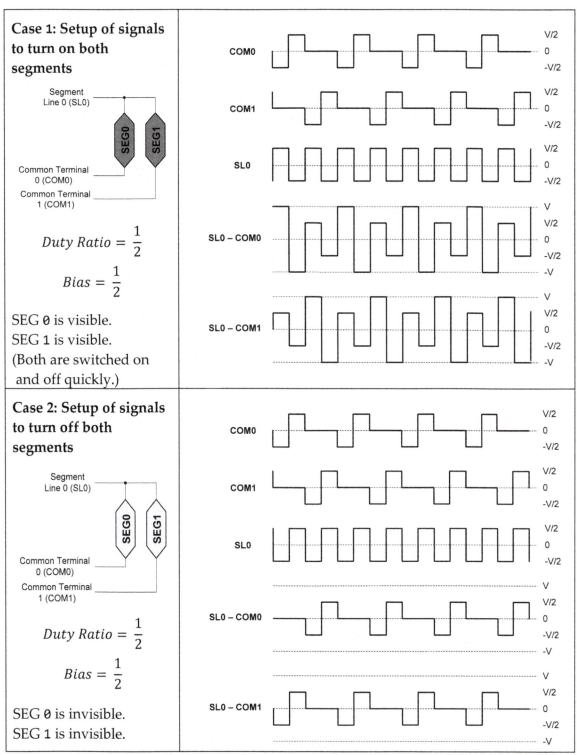

Case 1: Setup of signals to turn on both segments

$$Duty\ Ratio = \frac{1}{2}$$

$$Bias = \frac{1}{2}$$

SEG 0 is visible.
SEG 1 is visible.
(Both are switched on
and off quickly.)

Case 2: Setup of signals to turn off both segments

$$Duty\ Ratio = \frac{1}{2}$$

$$Bias = \frac{1}{2}$$

SEG 0 is invisible.
SEG 1 is invisible.

Example 17-1. Multiplexed drive with duty ratio of ½ (Case 1: both on, and Case 2: both off). COM0 and COM1 are the same for all cases. SL0 determines which segments are on.

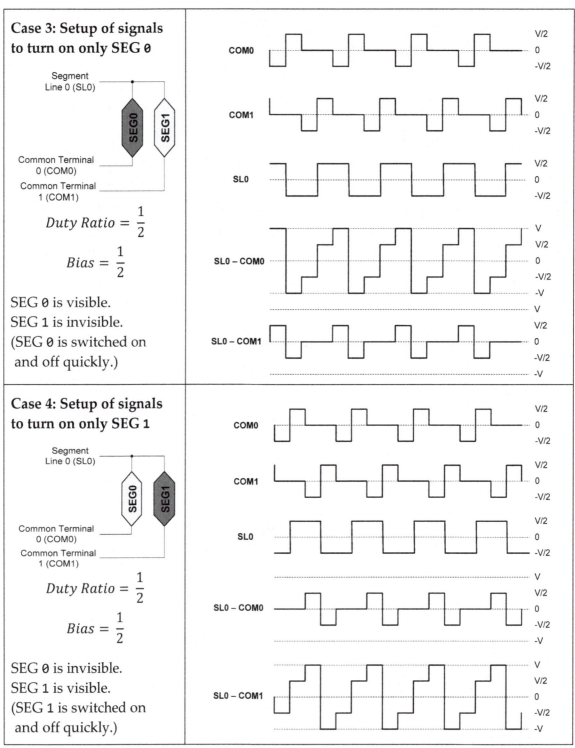

Example 17-2. Multiplexed drive with duty ratio of ½ (Case 3 & 4: one on and the other off).
COM0 and COM1 are the same for all cases. SL0 determines which segments are on.

17.3 STM32L Internal LCD Driver

17.3.1   Basic Introduction

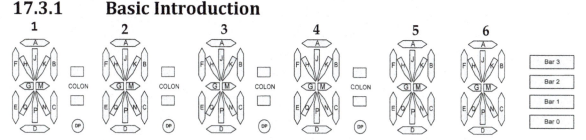

Figure 17-5 LCD on board with 6 digits and 4 bars

The LCD of the STM32L discovery kit has a total of 28 pins, including 24 segment lines (SEG0 - SEG23) and 4 common terminals (COM0 - COM3). The LCD can show six digits and four bars. There are 14 segments in each digit. There are 96 segments (pixels) in total. Each segment line drives four segments. Thus, the duty ratio is 1/4. Each GPIO pin that drives the LCD must be in alternate function (AF) mode.

Each segment/pixel can be turned on or off by setting or clearing the corresponding bit in the display memory. For example, to display the number "2" in the sixth character position, software needs to set six bits in the display memory, which are mapped to these six segments 6A, 6B, 6G, 6M, 6E, and 6D, respectively.

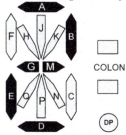

Figure 17-6. Displaying the number "2" by turning on segments 6A, 6B, 6G, 6M, 6E, and 6D.

In the following, we will explain the mapping relationship between bits in the display memory of the microcontroller and the segments of the external LCD module. For example, to display the number "2" at the 6th position on the LCD, which bits in the display memory should be set to 1?

- The mapping between LCD pins and LCD segments are fixed. It is determined by the LCD designers. Table 17-1 shows the mapping for the LCD module on the STM32L discovery kit.
- The mapping between display memory bits in the processor and processor pins is determined by the chip manufacturer. The display memory consists of 8 words,

as shown in Figure 17-7. There are 4 COM pins and 44 SEG pins, controlling a maximum of 176 pixels. All pixels controlled by a COM pin take two words in the display memory.

- Typically, a processor has more pins capable of driving an LCD than the number of pins on the LCD module. For a given board, software cannot choose which pins are used to drive the LCD module. It is up to circuit board designers to (1) select the subset of processor pins to drive the LCD module, and (2) determine the connection between the selected processor pins and the LCD pins. Table 17-1 shows the processor pins selected, and the connections between LCD pins (COM0 - COM3, SEG0 - SEG23, and VLCD) and the processor's GPIO pins.

Circuit Board Connection					
Subset of STM32L4 Pins Selected	Internal connection of LCD module				
	LCD Pin	COM3	COM2	COM1	COM0
PA7 (LCD_SEG4)	1 (SEG 0)	1N	1P	1D	1E
PC5 (LCD_SEG23)	2 (SEG 1)	1DP	1COLON	1C	1M
PB1 (LCD_SEG6)	3 (SEG 2)	2N	2P	2D	2E
PB13 (LCD_SEG13)	4 (SEG 3)	2DP	2COLON	2C	2M
PB15 (LCD_SEG15)	5 (SEG 4)	3N	3P	3D	3E
PD9 (LCD_SEG29)	6 (SEG 5)	3DP	3COLON	3C	3M
PD11 (LCD_SEG31)	7 (SEG 6)	4N	4P	4D	4E
PD13 (LCD_SEG33)	8 (SEG 7)	4DP	4COLON	4C	4M
PD15 (LCD_SEG35)	9 (SEG 8)	5N	5P	5D	5E
PC7 (LCD_SEG25)	10 (SEG 9)	BAR2	BAR3	5C	5M
PA15 (LCD_SEG17)	11 (SEG 10)	6N	6P	6D	6E
PB4 (LCD_SEG8)	12 (SEG 11)	BAR0	BAR1	6C	6M
PB9 (LCD_COM3)	13 (COM 3)	COM3			
PA10 (LCD_COM2)	14 (COM 2)		COM2		
PA9 (LCD_COM1)	15 (COM 1)			COM1	
PA8 (LCD_COM0)	16 (COM 0)				COM0
PB5 (LCD_SEG9)	17 (SEG 12)	6J	6K	6A	6B
PC8 (LCD_SEG26)	18 (SEG 13)	6H	6Q	6F	6G
PC6 (LCD_SEG24)	19 (SEG 14)	5J	5K	5A	5B
PD14 (LCD_SEG34)	20 (SEG 15)	5H	5Q	5F	5G
PD12 (LCD_SEG32)	21 (SEG 16)	4J	4K	4A	4B
PD10 (LCD_SEG30)	22 (SEG 17)	4H	4Q	4F	4G
PD8 (LCD_SEG28)	23 (SEG 18)	3J	3K	3A	3B
PB14 (LCD_SEG14)	24 (SEG 19)	3H	3Q	3F	3G
PB12 (LCD_SEG12)	25 (SEG 20)	2J	2K	2A	2B
PB0 (LCD_SEG5)	26 (SEG 21)	2H	2Q	2F	2G
PC4 (LCD_SEG22)	27 (SEG 22)	1J	1K	1A	1B
PA6 (LCD_SEG3)	28 (SEG 23)	1H	1Q	1F	1G

Table 17-1. Mapping between LCD pins and LCD segments

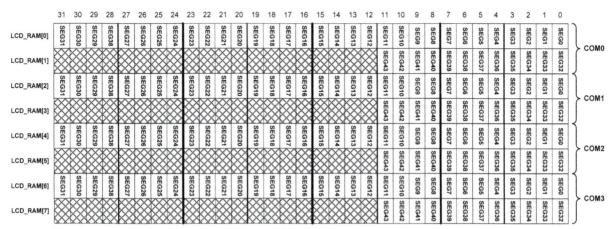

Figure 17-7. LCD display memory

Figure 17-8 shows the mapping between the display memory bits and LCD segments. The following uses segment 2D as an example to explain how this mapping is obtained.

> **Finding the mapping bit in the display memory for LCD segment 2D**:
> - The LCD internal connection in Table 17-1 indicates that segment 2D is controlled by LCD pin COM1 and pin SEG2.
> - The circuit board connection in Table 17-1 shows that the LCD's COM1 pin is connected to processor's PA9 (COM1) pin, and the LCD SEG2 pin is connected to processor's PB1 (LCD_SEG6) pin.
> - Thus, segment 2D is mapped to SEG6 of COM1. According to Figure 17-7, SEG6 of COM1 is bit 6 of LCD_RAM[2].
> - Therefore, LCD segment 2D is mapped to bit 6 of LCD_RAM[2] in the processor.

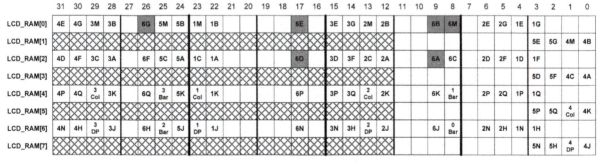

Figure 17-8. The mapping between display memory bits to LCD segments. Segments of "2" on the 6th position are shaded.

> **Displaying "2" in the 6th position on the screen**: Software needs to set six bits mapped to segments 6A, 6B, 6G, 6M, 6E, and 6D in the LCD data memory (LCD_RAM).
>
> ```
> LCD_RAM[0] |= 0x04020300;
> LCD_RAM[2] |= 0x00020200;
> ```

When software slowly generates display pixels or segments, the displaying process may take long enough for the human eye to notice. As a result, this may cause two problems: screen tearing and flickering.

- *Screen tearing* is a visual effect in which the LCD shows partial contents of multiple frames concurrently. Thus, the screen shows incoherent information.
- Usually, the display buffer needs to be cleared before the next frame is generated. Flickering refers to sudden brightness or contrast fluctuations. When buffer clearing becomes observable, pixels or segments intermittently appear and disappear, leading to the *flickering* problem.

One solution to this problem is *double buffering*, which is used on the LCD display controller on STM32 processors. As shown in Figure 17-9, it utilizes two buffers: an *off-screen buffer* (also called a back buffer) and an *on-screen buffer* (also known as a front buffer). The rationale behind double buffering is that copying to the on-screen buffer takes much less time than generating display data.

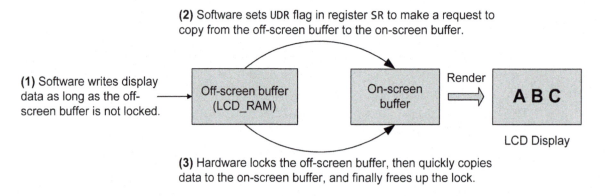

Figure 17-9. Double buffering technique to reduce flickers and ensure coherency

Software does not directly modify the display information in the on-screen buffer. Instead, all data are written to the off-screen buffer (LCD_RAM). After software writes a whole display frame to the off-screen buffer, the LCD controller takes three steps:

1. locks the off-screen buffer first to prevent any modification by clearing UDR flag in status register SR,
2. quickly copies data from the off-screen buffer to the on-screen buffer, and
3. finally frees up the lock to allow modification to the off-screen buffer.

The LCD software driver should follow the above double buffering protocol to ensure the coherency of the displayed information. Specifically, the following is the procedure to update the displayed information on the LCD.

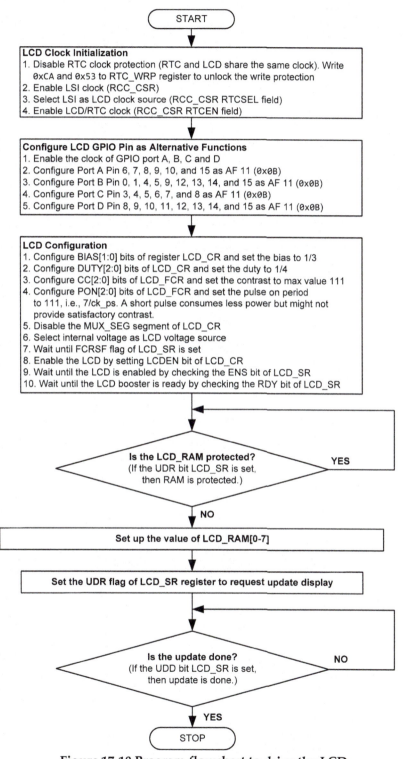

Figure 17-10 Program flowchart to drive the LCD

1. The LCD software driver should wait until the LCD controller clears the update display request (UDR) flag in the LCD status register (LCD_SR). The LCD controller sets UDR to 1 if the LCD controller has not copied the data stored in LCD_RAM to the display memory yet.

2. After the LCD controller clears the UDR flag, the driver starts to write the on/off setting (*i.e.*, 0 and 1) for each segment in the LCD_RAM.

3. The LCD software driver sets the UDR flag to inform the controller that the data are ready to be copied into the display memory. The UDR flag stays set until the end of the update, and during this period, the LCD_RAM is write-protected. The controller then generates the signals of common terminals (COM0 - COM3) and segment lines (SEG0 - SEG43) to drive the external LCD.

4. After setting the UDR flag, the software driver should wait until the controller sets the update display done (UDD) flag in the LCD status register (LCD_SR).

Figure 17-10 shows the flowchart for initializing the LCD controller. The LCD clock is the same clock as the real-time clock (RTC). Because the RTC clock domain is protected, the RTC domain needs to be unlocked first to configure the LCD clock source.

```
void LCD_RTC_Clock_Enable(void) {

    // Enable write access to the backup domain
    if ((RCC->APB1ENR1 & RCC_APB1ENR1_PWREN) == 0) {
        // Enable power interface clock
        RCC->APB1ENR1 |= RCC_APB1ENR1_PWREN;
        // Short delay after enabling an RCC peripheral clock
        (void) RCC->APB1ENR1;
    }

    // Select LSE as RTC clock source
    // RTC/LCD Clock: (1) LSE is in the backup domain (2) HSE and LSI are not
    if ((PWR->CR1 & PWR_CR1_DBP) == 0) {
        // Enable write access to RTC and registers in backup domain
        PWR->CR1 |= PWR_CR1_DBP;
        // Wait until the backup domain write protection has been disabled
        while((PWR->CR1 & PWR_CR1_DBP) == 0);
    }

    // Reset LSEON and LSEBYP bits before configuring LSE
    // BDCR = Backup Domain Control Register
    RCC->BDCR &= ~(RCC_BDCR_LSEON | RCC_BDCR_LSEBYP);

    // RTC Clock selection can be changed only if the backup domain is reset
    RCC->BDCR |=  RCC_BDCR_BDRST;
    RCC->BDCR &= ~RCC_BDCR_BDRST;
```

```
// Wait until LSE clock is ready
while((RCC->BDCR & RCC_BDCR_LSERDY) == 0) {
    RCC->BDCR |= RCC_BDCR_LSEON;  // Enable LSE oscillator
}

// Select LSE as RTC clock source
// RTCSEL[1:0]: 00 = No Clock, 01 = LSE, 10 = LSI, 11 = HSE
RCC->BDCR &= ~RCC_BDCR_RTCSEL;  // Clear RTCSEL bits
RCC->BDCR |= RCC_BDCR_RTCSEL_0; // Select LSE as RTC clock

// Disable power interface clock
RCC->APB1ENR1 &= ~RCC_APB1ENR1_PWREN;

// Enable LCD peripheral Clock
RCC->APB1ENR1 |= RCC_APB1ENR1_LCDEN;
}
```

Example 17-3. Program to enable the RTC clock and the LCD clock

17.3.2   Generic LCD Driver to Display Strings

In this section, we develop the key ideas needed to write a generic software function that can display a string. An LCD can usually show multiple alphanumeric characters. The on-chip driver maps each pixel of the LCD to a binary bit in the display memory.

The display memory is a special memory region used by the hardware driver to hold the on or off setting of each display pixel. If a bit in the display memory is set, the corresponding pixel should be visible. On the other hand, all string characters are stored as ASCII values (see Chapter 2.5) in the data memory.

Therefore, we need to create a function that sets up the display memory according to two key inputs:

1. the ASCII value of a given letter or number, and
2. the location where this letter or number should be displayed on the LCD.

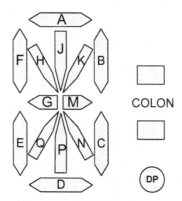

Figure 17-11. A display digit has 16 segments: 14 digit segments, 1 colon, and 1 decimal point.

Each digit consists of 16 display segments: 14 segments for the digit, 1 segment for the colon, and 1 segment for the decimal point, as shown in Figure 17-11. We use a 16-bit binary value to encode an alphanumeric character. When a segment is visible, the corresponding bit in its 16-bit code is set. If a segment is invisible, the corresponding bit is zero. For example, the letter "A" can be encoded as 0xFE00, because it turns on segments G, B, M, E, F, A, and C. Similarly, the number "2" can be encoded as 0xF500, making segments G, B, M, E, and A visible.

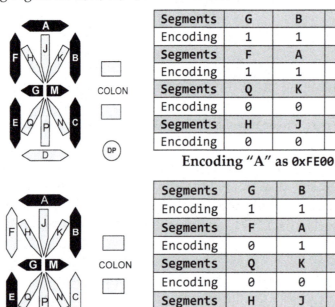

Segments	G	B	M	E	
Encoding	1	1	1	1	0xF
Segments	F	A	C	D	
Encoding	1	1	1	0	0xE
Segments	Q	K	Colon	P	
Encoding	0	0	0	0	0x0
Segments	H	J	DP	N	
Encoding	0	0	0	0	0x0

Encoding "A" as 0xFE00

Segments	G	B	M	E	
Encoding	1	1	1	1	0xF
Segments	F	A	C	D	
Encoding	0	1	0	1	0x5
Segments	Q	K	Colon	P	
Encoding	0	0	0	0	0x0
Segments	H	J	DP	N	
Encoding	0	0	0	0	0x0

Encoding "2" as 0xF500

Figure 17-12. Encoding "A" and "2"

Table 17-2 gives more examples of encoding five letters (A-Z) and five numbers (1-5).

	15	14	13	12	11	10	9	8	7	6	5	4	3	2	1	0	
	G	B	M	E	F	A	C	D	Q	K	Col	P	H	J	DP	N	Encoding
A	1	1	1	1	1	1	1	0	0	0	0	0	0	0	0	0	0xFE00
B	0	1	1	0	0	1	1	1	0	0	0	1	0	1	0	0	0x6714
C	0	0	0	1	1	1	0	1	0	0	0	0	0	0	0	0	0x1D00
D	0	1	0	0	0	1	1	1	0	0	0	1	0	1	0	0	0x4714
E	1	0	0	1	1	1	0	1	0	0	0	0	0	0	0	0	0x9D00
1	0	1	0	0	0	0	1	0	0	0	0	0	0	0	0	0	0x4200
2	1	1	1	1	0	1	0	1	0	0	0	0	0	0	0	0	0xF500
3	0	1	1	0	0	1	1	1	0	0	0	0	0	0	0	0	0x6700
4	1	1	1	0	1	0	1	0	0	0	0	0	0	0	0	0	0xEA00
5	1	0	1	0	1	1	1	1	0	0	0	0	0	0	0	0	0xAF00

Table 17-2. Encoding characters A, B, C, D and E, and numbers 1, 2, 3, 4 and 5

We use an array to encode all capital letters as follows.

```
uint16_t Letters[26] = {
    // A        B        C        D        E        F        G        H        I
    0xFE00, 0x6714, 0x1D00, 0x4714, 0x9D00, 0x9C00, 0x3F00, 0xFA00, 0x0014,

    // J        K        L        M        N        O        P        Q        R
    0x5300, 0x9841, 0x1900, 0x5A48, 0x5A09, 0x5F00, 0xFC00, 0x5F01, 0xFC01,

    // S        T        U        V        W        X        Y        Z
    0xAF00, 0x0414, 0x5B00, 0x18C0, 0x5A81, 0x00C9, 0x0058, 0x05C0
};
```

For any given capital letter, we can perform a simple array look-up to find its encoding. Chapter 2.5 gives functions to test for a lower-case or upper-case character in C, as well as the function to convert all alphabetic characters to their upper-case versions. For example, the ASCII values for 'A' and 'D' are 0x41 and 0x44, respectively. The encoding of 'D' is $Letters['D' - 'A']$, i.e., $Letters[3]$. The following C program is used to find the LCD encoding of a given alphabetic character. If the character is lower-case, the LCD displays its corresponding upper case.

```
// if c points to an upper-case letter
if ( (*c < 0x5B) && (*c > 0x40) ) { // ASCII 'A' = 0x41, 'Z' = 0x5A
    encoding = Letters[*c - 'A'];
}
// if c points to a lower-case letter, convert it to upper case
if ( (*c < 0x7B) && (*c > 0x60) ) { // ASCII 'a' = 0x61, 'z' = 0x7A
    encoding = Letters[*c - 'a'];
}
```

Similarly, the encoding of the digits 0-9 is stored in a separate array, as given below.

```
uint16_t Numbers[10] = {
    // 0        1        2        3        4
    0x5F00, 0x4200, 0xF500, 0x6700, 0xEA00,

    // 5        6        7        8        9
    0xAF00, 0xBF00, 0x4600, 0xFF00, 0xEF00
};
```

Suppose the variable c points to a numeric digit. Its LCD encoding can be found using the above *Numbers* array, with the array index equal to the difference between the ASCII value of this number and the ASCII value of '0'. Chapter 2.5 gives a function to test for a decimal digit (0 through 9).

```
encoding = Numbers [*c - 0x30];  // ASCII '0' = 0x30
```

We can clear the LCD screen by turning off all segments.

```
// Wait until the off-screen buffer has been unlocked
while ((LCD->SR & LCD_SR_UDR) != 0);

for (i = 0; i <= 8; i++)
    LCD->RAM[i] = 0;  // Clear the buffer

// Request to transfer data from off-screen buffer to on-screen buffer
LCD->SR |= LCD_SR_UDR;
```

We can convert the encoding of a number or a letter into a character array C[4] by using the following C program. For example, the encoding of "A" is 0xFE00. The character array C[4] will have the following content: C[0] = 0xF, C[1] = 0xE, C[2] = 0x0, and C[3] = 0x0.

```
uint8_t C[4];

for (offset = 12, i = 0; i < 4; offset -= 4, i++)
    C[i] = (encoding >> offset) & 0x0f;
```

The following program uses the 1st position as an example to illustrate how to decode and display a number or a letter. Following Figure 17-8, we can obtain the bits in LCD_RAM that are mapped to all segments at the 1st display position, as shown in Table 17-3.

Segments	1G	1B	1M	1E	
LCD_RAM[0]	Bit4	Bit 23	Bit 22	Bit 3	C[0]
Segments	1F	1A	1C	1D	
LCD_RAM[2]	Bit 4	Bit 23	Bit 22	Bit 3	C[1]
Segments	1Q	1K	1Colon	1P	
LCD_RAM[4]	Bit 4	Bit 23	Bit 22	Bit 3	C[2]
Segments	1H	1J	1DP	1N	
LCD_RAM[6]	Bit 4	Bit 23	Bit 22	Bit 3	C[3]

Table 17-3. Bits in LCD_RAM that are mapped to segments at the 1st position.

Based on the character array C[4], the following C program controls all segments at the 1st display position. The code that turns on or turns off segments at the other display positions is very similar.

```
// Clear corresponding bits in the off-screen buffer LCD->RAM

// 1E -> Bit 3, 1G -> Bit 4, 1M -> Bit 22, 1B -> Bit 23 in RAM[0]
LCD->RAM[0] &= ~( 1U << 3 | 1U << 4 | 1U << 22 | 1U << 23 );

// 1D -> Bit 3, 1F -> Bit 4, 1C -> Bit 22, 1A -> Bit 23 in RAM[2]
LCD->RAM[2] &= ~( 1U << 3 | 1U << 4 | 1U << 22 | 1U << 23 );
```

```
// 1P -> Bit 3, 1Q -> Bit 4, 1Col -> Bit 22, 1K -> Bit 23 in RAM[4]
LCD->RAM[4] &= ~( 1U << 3 | 1U << 4 | 1U << 22 | 1U << 23 );

// 1N -> Bit 3, 1H -> Bit 4, 1DP -> Bit 22, 1J -> Bit 23 in RAM[6]
LCD->RAM[6] &= ~( 1U << 3 | 1U << 4 | 1U << 22 | 1U << 23 );

// Segments: 1G 1B 1M 1E
LCD->RAM[0] |= ((C[0] & 0x1) << 4) | (((C[0] & 0x2) >> 1) << 23)
            | (((C[0] & 0x4) >> 2) << 22) | (((C[0] & 0x8) >> 3) << 3);

// Segments: 1F 1A 1C 1D
LCD->RAM[2] |= ((C[1] & 0x1) << 4) | (((C[1] & 0x2) >> 1) << 23)
            | (((C[1] & 0x4) >> 2) << 22) | (((C[1] & 0x8) >> 3) << 3);

// Segments: 1Q 1K 1Col 1P
LCD->RAM[4] |= ((C[2] & 0x1) << 4) | (((C[2] & 0x2) >> 1) << 23)
            | (((C[2] & 0x4) >> 2) << 22) | (((C[2] & 0x8) >> 3) << 3);

// Segments: 1H 1J 1DP 1N
LCD->RAM[6] |= ((C[3] & 0x1) << 4) | (((C[3] & 0x2) >> 1) << 23)
            | (((C[3] & 0x4) >> 2) << 22) | (((C[3] & 0x8) >> 3) << 3);
```

The following C code drives four bars shown in Figure 17-5.

```
void LCD_bar(uint32_t bar) {

  // Wait until the off-screen buffer has been unlocked
  while ((LCD->SR & LCD_SR_UDR) != 0);   // Wait for Update Display Request Bit

  // Bar 0: LCD (SEG11, COM3) -> Processor (SEG8,  COM3) -> Bit 8 of RAM[6]
  // Bar 1: LCD (SEG11, COM2) -> Processor (SEG8,  COM2) -> Bit 8 of RAM[4]
  // Bar 2: LCD (SEG9,  COM3) -> Processor (SEG25, COM3) -> Bit 25 of RAM[6]
  // Bar 3: LCD (SEG9,  COM2) -> Processor (SEG25, COM2) -> Bit 25 of RAM[4]

  LCD->RAM[6] &= ~(1U << 8 | 1U << 25);   // Turn off Bar 0 and Bar 2
  LCD->RAM[4] &= ~(1U << 8 | 1U << 25);   // Turn off Bar 1 and Bar 3

  if (bar & 0x1) LCD->RAM[6] |= 1U << 8;  // Bar 0
  if (bar & 0x2) LCD->RAM[4] |= 1U << 8;  // Bar 1
  if (bar & 0x4) LCD->RAM[6] |= 1U << 25; // Bar 2
  if (bar & 0x8) LCD->RAM[4] |= 1U << 25; // Bar 3

  // Request to transfer data from off-screen buffer to on-screen buffer
  LCD->SR |= LCD_SR_UDR;
}
```

We can also display some special characters as listed below. The percentage sign takes two spots on the screen to display. See Figure 17-12 for the encoding scheme.

?	*	-	%
0x6084	0xA0DD	0x00C0	0xEC00, 0xB300

17.4 Interfacing with External Character LCD Controllers

A character liquid crystal display (LCD) module often integrates an internal LCD controller. The HD44780-compatible interface is a de-facto industry controller for a broad range of character LCDs. Hitachi developed HD44780 controllers in the 1990s and nowadays a wide variety of LCD drivers, such as ST7066, KS0066U, and SED1278, are compatible to HD44780.

17.4.1   External Connection Diagram

A microprocessor can interface with the LCD module in two modes: 4- or 8-bit data bus mode, as shown in Figure 17-13 and Figure 17-14.

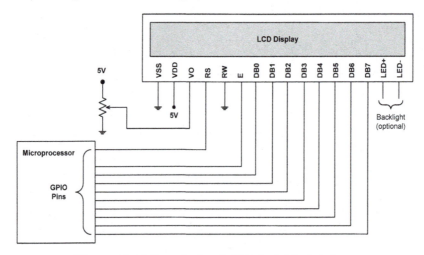

Figure 17-13. Interfacing LCD via 8-bit data bus

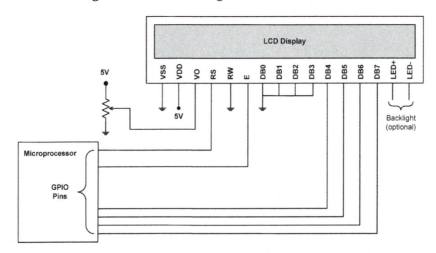

Figure 17-14. Interfacing LCD via 4-bit data bus (Pins DB3-0 are tied to the ground)

The 4-bit mode is more popular because it requires fewer pins from a microprocessor than the 8-bit mode. The microprocessor can write data to or read data from the LCD via the data bus (pins DB0 – DB7).

- Software can use the input VO to adjust the contrast.
- If the microprocessor does not need to read data from the LCD module, the RW pin can be set as write-only by connecting it to the ground.
- The LED+ and LED- pins provide 5V voltage to power on backlights if available.
- The E (Enable) pin provides a clock signal.
- The RS (Register Select) selects whether the command register or the data register should be the destination when writing data to the LCD controller.

The LCD module has two key registers: the data register and the command register. Both registers have 8 bits. The microprocessor sends a byte (such as an ASCII character) to the data register for display. The microprocessor initializes and controls the LCD by sending instructions to the command register via the data bus. Each instruction is a byte.

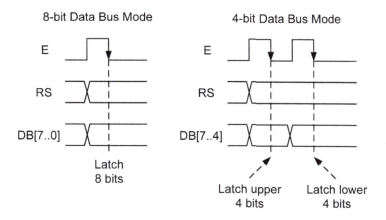

Figure 17-15. A falling signal on the E pin triggers the latch of data placed on the data bus.

Figure 17-15 shows example signal sequence of sending a byte to the LCD controller in 8- and 4-bit bus modes.

- If the RS (Register Select) pin is low, data bits placed on the data bus are stored in the command register; otherwise, the LCD controller saves data bits in the data register.
- When the voltage on the E (Enable) pin goes from high to low, the data on the bus are latched into the data or command register, depending on the RS signal.

In the 4-bit data bus mode, two falling signals are required to transfer the upper 4 bits followed by the lower 4 bits. In computing, a set of 4 bits or half a byte is a nibble. When sending a byte, the upper nibble is transmitted first. After the first falling edge of E, the microprocessor must place the lower nibble onto the data bus pins.

Assuming the data bus is configured to use only four bits, the following C program places the lower four bits of a byte on the data bus. Note that pins DB0, 1, 2, and 3 are not used.

```c
#define LCD_Port GPIOA    // GPIO Port A

#define LCD_RS   2    // RS (Register Select): 0 = command, 1 = data
#define LCD_EN   3    // Enable Pin

#define LCD_D4   4    // GPIO pin for DB 4
#define LCD_D5   5    // GPIO pin for DB 5
#define LCD_D6   6    // GPIO pin for DB 6
#define LCD_D7   7    // GPIO pin for DB 7

void LCD_PutNibble(uint8_t c) {

   if(c & 0x8)         // Place 4th bit on pin DB 7
      LCD_Port->ODR |= 1<<LCD_D7;
   else
      LCD_Port->ODR &= ~(1<<LCD_D7);

   if(c & 0x4)         // Place 3rd bit on pin DB 6
      LCD_Port->ODR |= 1<<LCD_D6;
   else
      LCD_Port->ODR &= ~(1<<LCD_D6);

   if(c & 0x2)         // Place 2nd bit on pin DB 5
      LCD_Port->ODR |= 1<<LCD_D5;
   else
      LCD_Port->ODR &= ~(1<<LCD_D5);

   if(c & 0x1)         // Place 1st bit on pin DB 4
      LCD_Port->ODR |= 1<<LCD_D4;
   else
      LCD_Port->ODR &= ~(1<<LCD_D4);
}
```

The following C program generates a falling edge on the E (Enable) pin.

```c
void LCD_Pulse(void) {

   LCD_Port->ODR |= 1<<LCD_EN;      // Set E high
   Delay(4);                         // Delay 40us
   LCD_Port->ODR &= ~(1<<LCD_EN);   // Set E Low
   Delay(4);                         // Delay 40us

}
```

17.4.2   Internal Font Encoding

An LCD display consists of k lines with n characters in each line (denoted as $n{\times}k$). Common sizes are 8×1, 16×1, 16×2, 20×2, 20×4, and 40×2. Typically, each character has 40 pixels (5 columns × 8 rows) or 50 pixels (5 columns × 10 rows), organized in a dot matrix format. The LCD can display standard ASCII printable characters, a few pre-defined symbols, as well as 8 user-programmable symbols. Note that an LCD with multiple displayable lines physically can be either one line or multiple lines logically from the programming point of view, depending on its manufacturer.

The image pattern of a character is encoded in binary, with one bit representing a dot pixel. If the pixel is visible, the corresponding bit is 1. The encoded binaries of a character are called a font. All fonts are stored as a simple linear table in the read-only memory (ROM) for fixed characters (ASCII letters and pre-defined symbols) and the RAM memory for programmable characters defined by applications. The RAM can hold the fonts of eight programmable characters.

Figure 17-16 shows the key data path of displaying the letter "R". The microprocessor sends the ASCII value (0x52) of letter "R" to the data register. The data register has 8 bits and can only hold one character. The LCD controller copies the data register into its internal display memory (DDRAM), which stores all characters to be displayed on the LCD. If the LCD size is 16×2, the display memory has at least 32 bytes.

For each character in the display memory, the LCD controller looks up the font table and obtains the binary pixel values of the target character. The controller then sends the binary font to the LCD driver to control the common terminal (COM) and segment lines to turn on or off individual pixels, based on the duty ratio introduced previously.

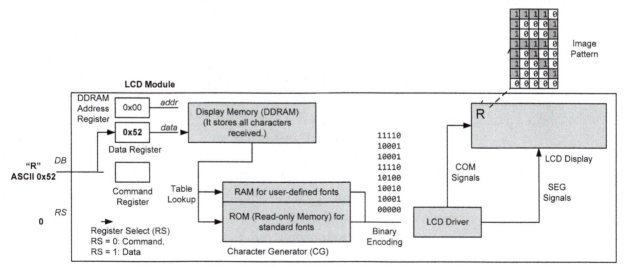

Figure 17-16. Key data path of displaying "R" on the LCD

An LCD may have multiple displayable lines physically. However, from the programming point of view, these physical lines may be organized by its manufacturer as one logical line with contiguous display memory (DDRAM) address across all lines.

Figure 17-17 compares the addressing scheme of one logic line and two logic lines.

- When two display lines are organized as one logic line, the DDRAM addresses for all characters are contiguous.
- When they are arranged as two separate logic lines, there is some gap between the address of the end of a line and the start of the next line.

DDRAM Address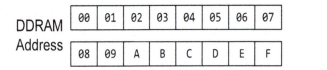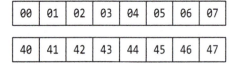

Figure 17-17. One logic line *vs.* two logic lines

17.4.3   Sending Commands and Data to LCD

Table 17-4 lists instructions for sending commands, and reading or writing data. Note that in Figure 17-14, the RW pin is tied to the ground because in the following demo the microprocessor does not need to read data from the LCD.

	RS	RW	DB7	DB6	DB5	DB4	DB3	DB2	DB1	DB0	
LCD Commands	0	0	0	0	0	0	0	0	0	1	Clear screen, and write DDRAM address to 0
	0	0	0	0	0	0	0	0	1	-	Return home (write DDRAM address to 0)
	0	0	0	0	0	0	0	1	I/D	S	Entry mode set
	0	0	0	0	0	0	1	D	C	B	Control display on/off, cursor, and blink
	0	0	0	0	0	1	SC	RL	-	-	Cursor/display shift
	0	0	0	0	0	DL	N	F	-	-	Set of data length, lines, and font type
	0	0	0	1	A5	A4	A3	A2	A1	A0	Set code generator CG-RAM address A5-A0
	0	0	1	A6	A5	A4	A3	A2	A1	A0	Set display memory DDRAM address A6-A0
	0	1	BF	A6	A5	A4	A3	A2	A1	A0	Ready busy flag (BF) and address A6-A0
	1	0	D7	D6	D5	D4	D3	D2	D1	D0	Write data D7-D0 to DDRAM or CG-RAM
	1	1	D7	D6	D5	D4	D3	D2	D1	D0	Read data D7-D0 from DDRAM or CG-RAM

Table 17-4. LCD instruction set

The following explains the parameters used in the above LCD commands.

- In the entry mode set command,
    - Increment/Decrement (I/D):
        0 = decrement mode, cursor/blink moves to left, and DDRAM address is decreased by one;

> 1 = increment mode, cursor/blink moves to right and DDRAM address is increased by one
- Shift (SH):   0 = entire shift off;
  > 1 = entire shift on, shift entire display per the I/D
- In the display control command,
  - Display (D):   0 = display off;   1 = display on
  - Cursor (C):   0 = cursor off;   1 = cursor on
  - Blink (B):   0 = blink off;   1 = blink on
- In the cursor/display shift command,
  - S/C: 0 = move cursor;   1 = shift display
  - Right or left (R/L): 0 = left;   1 = right
- In the function set command,
  - Data bus length (DL): 0 = 4 bits;   1 = 8 bits
  - Number of lines (N):   0 = 1 line;   1 = 2 lines
  - Font size (F):   0 = 5 × 8 dots; 1 = 5 × 11 dots

Figure 17-18 gives the flowchart of initializing the LCD into 8- or 4-bit data bus mode. The delay timing may differ for various LCD controllers.

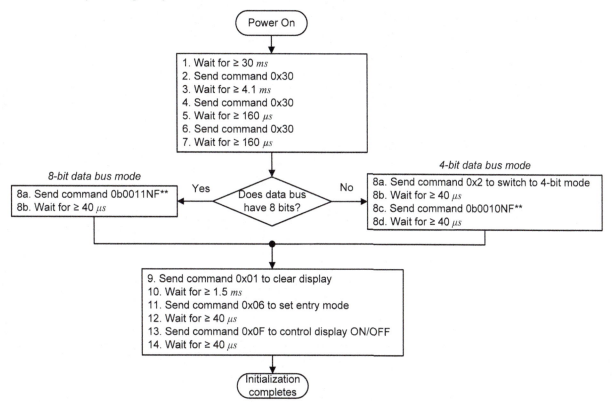

Figure 17-18. Flowchart of Initializing LCD controller

The following shows the implementation of C functions that send a command byte or a data byte to the LCD controller.

Sending Command to LCD	Sending Data to LCD
| ```c
void LCD_SendCmd(uint8_t c) {

  // RS: 0 = command, 1 = data
  LCD_Port->ODR &= ~(1<<LCD_RS);

  // Send Upper 4 bits
  LCD_PutNibble( c >> 4 );
  LCD_Pulse();

  // Send Lower 4 bits
  LCD_PutNibble( c & 0xF );
  LCD_Pulse();

  // Return to default
  LCD_Port->ODR |= 1<<LCD_RS;
}
``` | ```c
void LCD_SendData(uint8_t c) {

  // RS defaults to 1
  // No need to change RS

  // Send Upper 4 bits
  LCD_PutNibble( c >> 4 );
  LCD_Pulse();

  // Send Lower 4 bits
  LCD_PutNibble( c & 0xF );
  LCD_Pulse();

}
``` |

Figure 17-19 shows the microprocessor's output signals to display "hello" if the LCD uses the 4-bit bus mode. The RS is set to high to select the data register as the destination. The microprocessor generates two falling edges to send one ASCII byte. The upper nibble of each ASCII byte is sent first, followed by its lower nibble. The data bits are latched into the data register at the falling edge of the E signal.

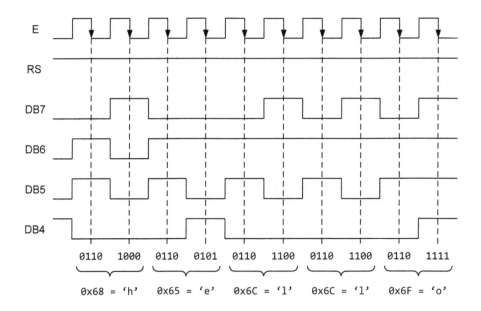

Figure 17-19. Pin signals of display "hello"

17.4.4   Programming Fonts

The LCD controller can display up to eight customized characters simultaneously. The microprocessor must store the font of special characters in the code generator (CG) RAM within the LCD controller.

The following gives an example of displaying a smiling face on the LCD with a font size of 5×8 dots. Figure 17-20 shows the font definition.

The font takes eight bytes. The least significant five bits of each byte specify the setting of on or off for each pixel in the corresponding row. The leading three bits of each byte are zero.

Software takes four steps to display the smiling face.

1. Software first uses `LCD_SendCmd()` to send a CG-RAM addressing command to ensure that data latched into the data register is to be saved into the CG-RAM, instead of the display memory (DDRAM).

2. Software uses `LCD_SendData()` to send eight bytes of the font definition to the CG-RAM.

3. After sending the fonts, software must send a DDRAM addressing command to ensure data sent later is copied to the DDRAM.

4. Software selects the font in DDRAM, making it displayed.

0	0	0	0	0	0b000 00000 = 0x00
0	1	0	1	0	0b000 01010 = 0x0A
0	1	0	1	0	0b000 01010 = 0x0A
0	1	0	1	0	0b000 01010 = 0x0A
0	0	0	0	0	0b000 00000 = 0x00
1	0	0	0	1	0b000 10001 = 0x11
0	1	1	1	0	0b000 01110 = 0x0E
0	0	0	0	0	0b000 00000 = 0x00

Figure 17-20. Bitmap of Smile Face

```
// Select CG-RAM and set address to 0x00
LCD_SendCmd(0x40 + 0x00);
Delay(4);                  // Wait > 39us

// Define smile face
LCD_SendData(0x00);   // 1st row byte
LCD_SendData(0x0A);   // 2nd row byte
LCD_SendData(0x0A);   // 3rd row byte
LCD_SendData(0x0A);   // 4th row byte
LCD_SendData(0x00);   // 5th row byte
LCD_SendData(0x11);   // 6th row byte
LCD_SendData(0x0E);   // 7th row byte
LCD_SendData(0x00);   // 8th row byte

// Select display RAM & set address to 0
LCD_SendCmd(0x80);    // 1st character
Delay(4);             // Wait > 39us

LCD_SendData(0x00);   // Display smile face
```

17.5 Exercises

1. Suppose the duty ratio of an LCD is ¼ and it has 100 display segments (pixels). How many pins are required to drive this LCD?

2. Write an assembly program that displays the animation of moving a ball from left to right.

3. Write an assembly program to display your last name on the LCD screen.

4. Write an assembly program to show any A-Z character at any position.

5. Write a generic assembly function that can display a string of characters.

6. Write a generic assembly function that can display any integer less than 999,999.

7. Write an assembly function that can display a floating-point number.

8. How is the data speed between an HD44780-compatible LCD and the processor adjusted?

9. How is an 8-bit data send to an HD44780-compatible LCD if the LCD is configured as 4-bit bus mode?

10. How does an HD44780-compatible LCD distinguish between data and LCD commands?

11. Write an assembly program that interfaces with the external HD44780-compatible LCD and display "ARM" on the LCD.

12. Write an assembly program that interfaces with the external HD44780-compatible LCD and displays special character "±" on the LCD.

CHAPTER 18

Real-time Clock (RTC)

A real-time clock (RTC) is a digital component that keeps track of calendar time and date. RTC modules are present in many appliances and electronic devices, such as washing machines, cameras, phones and medical devices. RTC can be used to  implement functions such as maintaining calendar time, periodically triggering the execution of a specific task, waking up the processor from sleep or low-power mode, providing a timestamp for sampled data, and calibrating internal hardware clocks.

RTC modules typically have very low power consumption. Many systems use a dedicated small battery or a supercapacitor to provide power for the RTC module. Consequently, even when the system is reset, put into sleep mode, or even turned off, the RTC does not stop. Thus, the microprocessor never loses track of time and date.

18.1 Epoch Time

The calendar time and date can be encoded in a single signed integer, which represents *epoch time* or UNIX time. If epoch time is positive, it is the number of seconds that have elapsed since `00:00:00` (midnight) on Thursday, January 1, 1970, UTC. If it is negative, it is the number of seconds before that time instant.

> *"The future is something which everyone reaches at the rate of 60 minutes an hour, whatever he does, whoever he is."*
>
> C. S. Lewis, novelist

If epoch time has 32 bits, the farthest representable time in the past is `20:45:52` UTC on December 13, 1901, when epoch time is -2^{31}. The farthest representable time in the future is `03:14:07` UTC on January 19, 2038, when epoch time is $2^{31} - 1$. If no action is taken, many systems will fail when the epoch time integer overflows, causing January 19, 2038 to wrap around to December 13, 1901. This is called the *year 2038 problem*.

Epoch time does not account for leap seconds. Due to the tidal drag of the moon, the Earth's spin slows at an average rate of 1.4 *ms* per century. To keep the time of day in phase with the rotation of the Earth, one second is added to UTC time approximately once per year. This second is called a *leap second*. The goal of leap seconds is to ensure the Sun,

> *Universal time is measured by the Earth's rotation with respect to the Sun.*

on average over a year, is directly overhead on the Greenwich meridian at noon. Between 1972 and 2017, 27 leap seconds have been added to UTC. Even though epoch time does not account for leap seconds, it meets the needs of many embedded applications, particularly those not related to astronomy, geodetics, and navigation.

Due to its simplicity, epoch time has been widely used in embedded systems for things such as clock synchronization between independent microcontrollers, and timestamping of events and data. However, the interface provided by the RTC module in many microprocessors is based on the human calendar, instead of epoch time.

For example, on an STM32L microprocessor, the time "08:30:45:09 AM, MON AUG 14 2017" is directly stored in the time register (TR), the date register (DR), and the subsecond register (TSSR). Software can read or modify each individual component of the date and time. Internally, the RTC maintains epoch time and its hardware automatically converts epoch time to the calendar date and time. This approach simplifies software, reduces memory space, and saves processor time, especially for real-time applications or resource-constrained systems.

Software can make conversions between human calendar and epoch time. The following example shows how to convert a calendar date and time to epoch time.

Example of converting 08:30:45 AM, AUG 14, 2017 (UTC) to epoch time

- There are 17,392 days between August 14, 2017, and January 1, 1970.
- Each day has 86,400 seconds (24×60×60 = 86400).

Epoch Time

$$= 17392 \ days \times \frac{86400 \ seconds}{day} + 8 \ hours \times \frac{3600 \ seconds}{hour}$$

$$+ \ 30 \ minutes \times \frac{60 \ seconds}{minute} + 45 \ seconds$$

$$= 1502699445 \ seconds$$

$$= 0x59915FB5$$

Example 18-1 converts epoch time to human calendar time. The process of getting the day, month and year is slightly more complex and is not shown in the code below. The complexity is due to the various number of days in a month, including 31, 30, 29, and 28 (leap year). The leap year can be checked by evaluating the following logic statement:

```
!((year) % 4) && (((year) % 100) || !((year) % 400)))
```

Details can be found in the `gmtime` function in the open-source GNU C Library.

```
int second, minute, hour, weekday;
int seconds_into_day, days_since_epoch;

// 24 * 60 * 60 = 86,400 seconds per day
seconds_into_day = (unsigned long) epoch_time % 86400;
days_since_epoch = (unsigned long) epoch_time / 86400;

second = seconds_into_day % 60;           // 0 <= second < 60
minute = (seconds_into_day % 3600) / 60;  // 0 <= minute < 60
hour = seconds_into_day / 3600;           // 3600 seconds per hour
weekday = (days_since_epoch + 4) % 7;     // January 1, 1970 is Thursday.
```

Example 18-1. Converting epoch time to calendar time

18.2 RTC Frequency Settings

The UNIX time number is incremented at a frequency of 1 Hz. Therefore, we must derive a 1-Hz clock from an input clock. The input clock is selected from among three sources: low-speed internal (LSI), low-speed external (LSE), or high-speed external (HSE) divided by 32, as shown in Figure 18-1.

External clocks are preferred over internal clocks for two important reasons: (1) internal clocks are less accurate, and (2) internal clocks are stopped if the system is powered down.

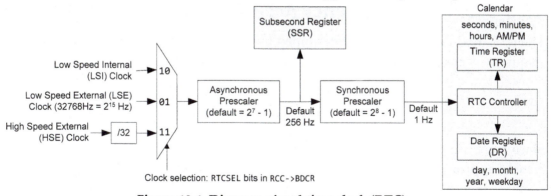

Figure 18-1. Diagram of real-time clock (RTC)

The RTC module uses two configurable prescaler registers (an asynchronous prescaler and a synchronous prescaler) to slow down the frequency of the input clock to 1 Hz, as shown below.

$$f_{1Hz} = \frac{f_{RTC}}{(Asynch\_Prescaler + 1) \times (Synch\_Prescaler + 1)} = 1\ Hz$$

The word *asynchronous* is used for the first prescaler because the RTC input clock is usually a clock that is not synchronized with the processor clock.

Low-speed external (LSE) crystal oscillators are highly recommended to drive RTC modules. A typical frequency is 32.768 kHz (2^{15} Hz, often called 32 kHz). This frequency has been widely used in quartz clocks and watches. These crystals are very inexpensive due to the massive volume production in the digital watch industry.

Typically, f_{RTC} is 32.768 kHz (*i.e.*, 2^{15} Hz), *Asynch_Prescaler* is 2^7-1 (*i.e.*, 127), and *Synch_Prescaler* is set as 2^8-1 (*i.e.*, 255). As shown below, this generates a 1-Hz clock.

$$f = \frac{f_{RTC}}{(Asynch\_Prescaler + 1) \times (Synch\_Prescaler + 1)}$$

$$= \frac{2^{15}}{(127 + 1) \times (255 + 1)} = \frac{2^{15}}{2^7 \times 2^8} = 1Hz$$

A battery usually powers the real-time clock module so that the processor does not lose any time or date information when the system is shut down. As such, the energy efficiency is critical to the real-time clock module. A larger *Asynch_Prescaler* value is preferred because it makes the real-time clock module more energy efficient.

18.3 Oscillator Frequency Accuracy

The RTC module's accuracy is determined by its oscillators. The error in the oscillation frequency is measured in **parts per million** (PPM).

$$PPM = \frac{Actual\ Frequency - Theoretical\ Frequency}{Theorectical\ Frequency} \times 10^6$$

Since there are 24×60×60 = 86400 seconds in a day, a PPM of 12 means a maximum error of approximately one second after one day has passed. 500 PPM implies the clock is off by up to 43 seconds per day.

The STM32L4 has three internal RC oscillators and two external oscillators. The internal oscillators are the 16-MHz HSI (high-speed internal), the MSI (multi-speed internal), and the 32.768 kHz LSI (low-speed internal).

The frequency of the oscillators drifts over time due to aging. It also decreases as the ambient temperature increases. Table 18-1 shows the frequency accuracy of the internal and external oscillators. With an accurate LSE (low-speed external clock), the STM32L4 can use built-in digital calibration circuitry to calibrate its internal oscillators automatically. The correction range is ± 480 ppm, and the correction resolution can be as small as ± 0.48 ppm. An accuracy close to ±20 ppm is common for LSE. An accuracy of ±20 ppm translates to ± 1.2 *ms* in a minute, ± 51.8 seconds in a month, or ± 10 minutes per year.

Parts per Million (PPM) = 10⁻⁶

	16MHz HSI	MSI	LSI	LSE
30°C	± 500 ppm	± 600 ppm	± 1500 ppm	Typically, ± 20 ppm

Table 18-1. Oscillator frequency accuracy at room temperature

18.4 Binary Coded Decimal (BCD) Encoding

The RTC module encodes time and date in Binary Coded Decimal (BCD) format, in which each digit (0 through 9) of a decimal number is represented by a fixed number of binary bits. Table 18-2 shows 4-bit BCD encoding.

Note that the BCD encoding is not the binary equivalent of a decimal. For example, the binary equivalent of 2018 is 0111_1110_0010, while the corresponding BCD code is 0010_0000_0001_1000, as shown in Figure 18-2.

Decimal Digit	BCD
0	0 0 0 0
1	0 0 0 1
2	0 0 1 0
3	0 0 1 1
4	0 1 0 0
5	0 1 0 1
6	0 1 1 0
7	0 1 1 1
8	1 0 0 0
9	1 0 0 1

Table 18-2. Binary coded decimal (BCD)

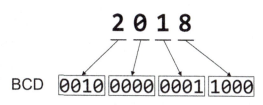

Figure 18-2. BCD encoding of 2018

In the RTC time and date registers, the unit's digit of the month, day, hour, minute, second, and last two digits of the year are encoded by two four-bit BCD codes. Some other digits are represented by only two or three bits. For example, the ten's digit for the second (ST) has a maximum value of 6, and thus only three bits are required. The date register does not record the first two digits of the year.

Figure 18-3 and Figure 18-4 shows how to set the time and date. The time can be in 12- or 24-hour format, with the PM bit indicating whether the time is in AM or PM. ST and SU stand for the second's ten's and unit's digit, respectively.

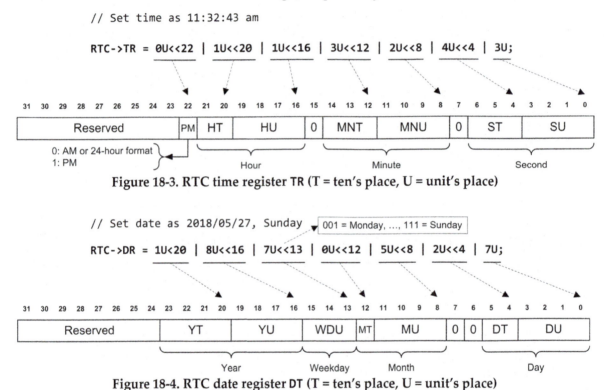

Figure 18-3. RTC time register TR (T = ten's place, U = unit's place)

Figure 18-4. RTC date register DT (T = ten's place, U = unit's place)

Although BCD requires more bits than the binary format to represent the time and date, the BCD format is more convenient for extracting and displaying the digits of the time and date. For example, if 8-bit BCD is used, software does not have to perform division or modular operations to get the ten's digit and the unit's digit of the minute.

It is easy to decode BCD into characters for display.

18.5 RTC Initialization

By default, the RTC registers are write-protected to prevent malicious or accidental modification. Software must perform the following actions to remove write-protection.

- First, the disable backup-domain protection bit (DBP) in the power controller control register (PWR->CR1) must be set to enable write accesses to the RTC registers, as shown in Example 17-3 in Chapter 17.
- Second, software must write the keys "0xCA" and "0x53" to the RTC write protection register (RTC->WPR).

```c
void RTC_Init(void) {

    // Enable RTC clock
    LCD_RTC_Clock_Enable (); // See Example 17-3

    // Disable write protection of RTC registers by writing disarm keys
    RTC->WPR = 0xCA;
    RTC->WPR = 0x53;

    // Enter initialization mode to program TR and DR registers
    RTC->ISR |= RTC_ISR_INIT;

    // Wait until INITF has been set
    while((RTC->ISR & RTC_ISR_INITF) == 0);

    // Hour format: 0 = 24 hour/day; 1 = AM/PM hour
    RTC->CR &= ~RTC_CR_FMT;

    // Generate a 1Hz clock for the RTC time counter
    // LSE = 32.768 kHz = 2^15 Hz
    RTC->PRER |= (2U<<7 - 1) << 16; // Asynch_Prescaler = 127
    RTC->PRER |= (2U<<8 - 1);       // Synch_Prescaler  = 255

    // Set time as 11:32:00 am
    RTC->TR = 0U<<22 | 1U<<20 | 1U<<16 | 3U<<12 | 2U<<8;

    // Set date as 2016/05/27
    RTC->DR = 1U<20 | 6U<<16 | 0U<<12 | 5U<<8 | 2U<<4 | 7U;

    // Exit initialization mode
    RTC->ISR &= ~RTC_ISR_INIT;

    // Enable write protection for RTC registers
    RTC->WPR = 0xFF;
}
```

Example 18-2. Initializing RTC in C

```
          AREA RTC_Demo CODE, READONLY
          EXPORT __main
          INCLUDE stm321476xx_constants.s
          ALIGN
          ENTRY

__main
          ; Power interface clock enable
          LDR    r0, =RCC_BASE
          LDR    r1, [r0, #RCC_APB1ENR]
          ORR    r1, r1, #RCC_APB1ENR_PWREN
          STR    r1, [r0, #RCC_APB1ENR]

          ; Disable backup domain write protection
          LDR    r0, =PWR_BASE
          LDR    r1, [r0, #PWR_CR]
          ORR    r1, r1, #PWR_CR_DBP
          STR    r1, [r0, #PWR_CR]

          ; Write '0xCA' and '0x53' to unlock the write protection
          LDR    r0, =RTC_BASE
          MOV    r1, #0xCA
          STR    r1, [r0,  #RTC_WPR]
          MOV    r1, #0x53
          STR    r1, [r0,  #RTC_WPR]

          ; Select and enable LSE Clock
          LDR    r0, =RCC_BASE
          LDR    r1, [r0, #RCC_CSR]
          ORR    r1, r1, #RCC_CSR_RTCSEL_LSE
          ORR    r1, r1, #RCC_CSR_RTCEN
          ORR    r1, r1, #RCC_CSR_LSEON
          STR    r1, [r0, #RCC_CSR]

          ; Wait until LSE clock ready
Wait      LDR    r0, =RCC_BASE
          LDR    r1, [r0, #RCC_CSR]
          AND    r1, r1, #RCC_CSR_LSERDY
          CMP    r1, #0
          BEQ    Wait

          ; Generate a 1-Hz clock for the calendar counter
          LDR    r0, =RTC_BASE
          LDR    r1, [r0, #RTC_PRER]
          ORR    r1, r1, #0xFF
          ORR    r1, r1, #0x7F0000
          STR    r1, [r0, #RTC_PRER]

          LDR    r0, =RTC_BASE
          LDR    r1, [r0, #RTC_ISR]
```

```
        ORR    r1, r1, #RTC_ISR_INIT
        STR    r1, [r0, #RTC_ISR]

        ; Wait until INITF flag is set
Wait2   LDR    r0, =RTC_BASE
        LDR    r1, [r0, #RTC_ISR]
        AND    r1, r1, #RTC_ISR_INITF
        CMP    r1, #0
        BEQ    Wait2

        ; Set time as 11:32:00 am
        LDR    r0, =RTC_BASE
        MOV    r2, #0
        MOV    r1, #1                    ; 1 = pm, 0 = am
        ORR    r2, r2, r1, LSL #22
        MOV    r1, #1                    ; hour's tens
        ORR    r2, r2, r1, LSL #21
        MOV    r1, #1                    ; hour's ones
        ORR    r2, r2, r1, LSL #16
        MOV    r1, #3                    ; min's tens
        ORR    r2, r2, r1, LSL #12
        MOV    r1, #2                    ; min's ones
        ORR    r2, r2, r1, LSL #8
        STR    r1, [r0, #RTC_TR]

        ; Exit initialization mode
        LDR    r0, =RTC_BASE
        LDR    r1, [r0, #RTC_ISR]
        BIC    r1, r1, #RTC_ISR_INIT
        STR    r1, [r0, #RTC_ISR]

        ; Enable the RTC protection
        LDR    r0, =PWR_BASE
        MOV    r1, #0xFF
        STR    r1, [r0, #PWR_CR]

stop    B stop
        END
```

Example 18-3. Initializing RTC in assembly

The assembly file stm321476xx_constants.s defines many constants, such as the base memory addresses:

```
RCC_BASE      EQU (AHB1PERIPH_BASE + 0x1000)
RTC_BASE      EQU (APB1PERIPH_BASE + 0x2800)
```

It also includes the byte offset from corresponding base memory addresses, such as

```
RCC_APB1ENR1 EQU 0x58
RTC_ISR       EQU 0x0C
```

18.6 RTC Alarm

The RTC module also provides alarm functions that allow the processor to execute a task at a scheduled time. For example, the RTC alarm can wake up the processor at a certain time after it has entered a low-power mode.

The STM32L RTC module has two programmable alarm units: alarm A and alarm B.

- The alarm time and date for alarm A are saved in the RTC_ALRMAR register, whereas for alarm B they are stored in the RTC_ALRMBR register. They can be written only if the ALRAWF flag is 1 in the RTC_ISR register.
- The alarm time and date are compared with the RTC date held in the RTC_DR register and the RTC time stored in the RTC_TR register.
- If enabled, the hardware module generates an RTC alarm interrupt if the time and date match.

The RTC module allows software to select the alarm time and date flexibly. The day of the week, the hour, the minute, and the second can be individually chosen by their mask bits to take part in the comparison. If a mask bit is 1, its corresponding time component is ignored during the alarm time comparison. These masks can be used to generate periodic alarms.

Suppose the alarm time register is set to 21:25:37 on Monday. Table 18-3 shows a few examples of various settings of the mask bits.

MSK 4 (day of week)	MSK 3 (hour)	MSK 2 (minute)	MSK 1 (Second)	When does the alarm occur?
0	0	0	0	At 21:25:37 on each Monday
1	0	0	0	At 21:25:37 every day
1	1	1	0	At the 37th second of every minute
0	0	0	1	At every second of 21:25 on each Monday
1	0	0	1	At every second of 21:25 every day
0	0	1	1	At every second of the 21st hour on each Monday
0	1	1	1	At every second on Monday

Table 18-3. Example of mask bit setting for various alarm time comparisons

The following program sets up alarm A, which occurs at the 30th second of each minute.

```
void RTC_Set_Alarm(void) {

  uint32_t AlarmTimeReg;

  // Disable alarm A
  RTC->CR &= ~RTC_CR_ALRAE;

  // Remove write-protection of RTC registers by writing "0xCA"
  // and then "0x53" into the WPR register
  RTC->WPR = 0xCA;                    // WPR: write protection register
  RTC->WPR = 0x53;

  // Disable alarm A and its interrupt
  RTC->CR &= ~RTC_CR_ALRAE;           // Clear alarm A enable bit
  RTC->CR &= ~RTC_CR_ALRAIE;          // Clear alarm A's interrupt enable bit
  // Wait until access to alarm registers is allowed
  // Write flag (ALRAWF) is set by hardware if alarm A can be changed.
  while((RTC->ISR & RTC_ISR_ALRAWF) == 0);

  // Set off alarm A if the second is 30
  // Bits[6:4] = Ten's digit for the second in BCD format
  // Bits[3:0] = Unit's digit for the second in BCD format
  AlarmTimeReg = 0x3 << 3;

  // Set alarm mask field to compare only the second
  AlarmTimeReg |= RTC_ALRMAR_MSK4;    // 1: Ignore day of week in comparison
  AlarmTimeReg |= RTC_ALRMAR_MSK3;    // 1: Ignore hour in comparison
  AlarmTimeReg |= RTC_ALRMAR_MSK2;    // 1: Ignore minute in alarm comparison
  AlarmTimeReg &= ~RTC_ALRMAR_MSK1;   // 0: Alarm sets off if the second match

  // RTC alarm A register (ALRMAR)
  RTC->ALRMAR = AlarmTimeReg;

  // Enable alarm A and its interrupt
  RTC->CR |= RTC_CR_ALRAE;            // Enable alarm A
  RTC->CR |= RTC_CR_ALRAIE;           // Enable alarm A interrupt

  // Enable write protection for RTC registers
  RTC->WPR = 0xFF;
}
```

Example 18-4. Initializing alarm A to generate an alarm on the 30th second of each minute

All RTC interrupts are connected to the EXTI controller. For example, the RTC alarm signal is linked to EXTI line 18 internally, and the RTC wakeup signal is connected to EXTI line 20. More details can be found in the STM32L4 reference manual. To enable the alarm interrupt, we must enable EXTI line 18, which is connected to the RTC alarm signals.

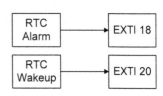

```
void RTC_Alarm_Enable(void){

  // Other initialization (see Example 18-2)
  ...

  // Configure EXTI 18
  // Select triggering edge
  EXTI->RTSR1 |= EXTI_RTSR1_RT18; // 1 = Trigger at rising edge

  // Interrupt mask register
  EXTI->IMR1 |= EXTI_IMR1_IM18;   // 1 = Enable EXTI 18 line

  // Event mask register
  EXTI->EMR1 |= EXTI_EMR1_EM18;   // 1 = Enable EXTI 18 line

  // Interrupt pending register
  EXTI->PR1  |= EXTI_PR1_PIF18;   // Write 1 to clear pending interrupt

  // Enable RTC interrupt
  NVIC->ISER[1] |= 1<<9;          // RTC_Alarm_IRQn = 41, See Chapter 11.6.1
  // It is equivalent to: NVIC_EnableIRQ(RTC_WKUP_IRQn);

  // Set interrupt priority as the most urgent
  NVIC_SetPriority(RTC_WKUP_IRQn, 0);

  ...

}
```

Example 18-5. Connecting RTC alarm interrupt to EXTI 18

In this example, when an RTC alarm interrupt takes place, we toggle the LED connected to GPIO pin PB 2. The RTC alarm interrupt handler must clear the interrupt pending flag of EXTI line 18 and the interrupt status flag of alarm A.

```
void RTC_Alarm_IRQHandler(void){

  // RTC initialization and status register (RTC_ISR)
  // Hardware sets the Alarm A flag (ALRAF) when the time/date registers
  // (RTC_TR and RTC_DR) match the alarm A register (RTC_ALRMAR), according
  // to the mask bits

  if(RTC->ISR & RTC_ISR_ALRAF){
    GPIOB->ODR ^= 1UL<<2;            // Toggle GPIO pin PB.2
    RTC->ISR &= ~(RTC_ISR_ALRAF);   // Clear the alarm A interrupt flag
  }

  // Clear the EXTI line 18
  EXTI->PR1 |= EXTI_PR1_PIF18;      // Write 1 to clear pending interrupt
}
```

Example 18-6. RTC Alarm interrupt handler

18.7 Using RTC to Wake Processors up from Sleep Mode

Power requirements are one of the most critical constraints in embedded systems, especially in mobile and portable systems. Cortex-M processors provide several operating modes, which offer various tradeoffs between energy efficiency and performance (*e.g.* processor speed and wake-up time). A mode that consumes less energy often requires a longer wake-up time.

The STM32L4 has eight power modes, as shown in Figure 18-5. After power-on or a system reset, the processor enters **run** mode. By changing on-chip peripherals to low-power modes or by turning off the clock to the peripherals and core, software can switch the processor to different power modes.

A typical approach is to use software to switch the processor to **sleep** or **standby** mode during idle periods, and wake the processor up when an interrupt or event occurs. In both modes, all clocks except LSI and LSE are stopped, and the processor core is turned off. Sleep and standby mode differ from each other in three major aspects.

- First, in standby mode, data in peripheral registers and SRAM are lost by default. However, data are retained in sleep mode.
- Second, peripherals are active in sleep mode but are turned off in standby mode.
- Third, when the processor exits from standby mode, a reset signal is generated internally, and the processor reboots. However, a reboot is not required when exiting from sleep mode. Therefore, the wake-up time for sleep mode is much shorter than it is for standby mode.

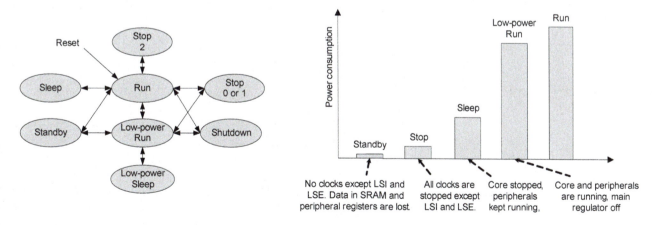

Figure 18-5. STM32L4 supports 8 power modes, which offer various performance levels and energy efficiencies.

Driven by LSI and LSE, the RTC module is an ultra-low power module which takes only a few *nA* of electric current. A small button battery can supply power to a RTC module for many years. Therefore, RTC keeps working even in standby or shutdown mode. Naturally, RTC is widely used to make the processor wake up from low-power modes periodically.

This section demonstrates how to switch the processor to sleep mode, and how to use the RTC to wake the processor up from sleep mode. Suppose we want to wake the processor up every five seconds. Software can program the RTC wakeup time by

Avoid waking-up too frequently

- selecting the clock (WUCKSEL bits in register CR), which drives the wakeup timer,
- setting the timer auto-reload value (register WUTR).

Example 18-7 shows a subroutine that programs the RTC wakeup timer to generate a wakeup event every 5 seconds. This subroutine can only be called after RTC write protection has been disabled (see Example 18-2).

```
void RTC_Wakeup_Configuration(void){
    // Wakeup initialization can only be performed when wakeup is disabled.
    RTC->CR &= ~RTC_CR_WUTE;     // Disable wakeup counter

    // WUTWF: Wakeup timer write flag
    // 0: Wakeup timer configuration update not allowed
    // 1: Wakeup timer configuration update allowed
    while( (RTC->ISR & RTC_ISR_WUTWF) == 0 );

    // WUCKSEL[2:0]: Wakeup clock selection
    // 10x: ck_spre (usually 1 Hz) clock is selected
    RTC->CR &= ~RTC_CR_WUCKSEL;
    RTC->CR |= RTC_CR_WUCKSEL_2;   // Select ck_spre (1Hz)

    // RTC wakeup timer register (Max = 0xFFFF)
    RTC->WUTR = 5;   // The counter decrements by 1 every pulse of
                     // the clock selected by WUCKSEL.

    // Enable wake up counter and wake up interrupt
    RTC->CR |= RTC_CR_WUTIE; // Enable wake up interrupt
    RTC->CR |= RTC_CR_WUTE;  // Enable wake up counter
}
```

Example 18-7. Programming RTC to generate a wake-up interrupt every 5 seconds

The processor enters sleep mode by executing "__WFI()" or "__WFE()", which run the assembly instruction "WFI" (*Wait For Interrupt*) and "WFE" (*Wait For Event*), respectively.

- If __WFI() is executed, the processor can be woken up by interrupt requests, system reset and debug operations.
- If __WFE() is executed, the processor can be woken up by events. Example events include interrupts, debug events, and events sent by the SEV (send event) instruction.

The behavior of the processor after being woken up depends on the Sleep-on-Exit bit in the System Control Register (SCR), as shown in Figure 18-6. When an interrupt request arrives, the processor is woken up from sleep mode and starts to execute the corresponding interrupt service routine.

- If the Sleep-on-Exit bit is 1, the function __WFI() does not return to its caller after the interrupt service routine completes. Instead, the processor will immediately enter sleep mode again if there are no new interrupt requests.
- If the Sleep-on-Exit bit is 0, the function __WFI() returns to its caller after the interrupt service routine completes. This allows the caller to resume the computation and execute the code after the __WFI() statement.

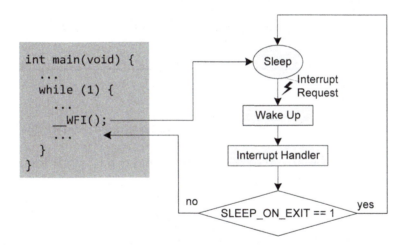

Figure 18-6. Continuous sleep if the Sleep-on-Exit bit is set

Example 18-8 shows the code that switches the processor to sleep mode. Depending on the application need, the Sleep-on-Exit bit can be either set or cleared. On STM32L4, the RTC wakeup interrupt is internally connected EXTI line 20. To enable RTC wakeup interrupts, we need to enable interrupts and events for EXTI line 20.

```
void Enter_SleepMode(void){

    // Cortex system control register
    SCB->SCR &= ~SCB_SCR_SLEEPDEEP_Msk;    // 0 = sleep, 1 = deep sleep
```

```
// SLEEPONEXIT: Indicates sleep-on-exit when returning from handler
// mode to thread mode:
//   0 = do not sleep when returning to thread mode.
//   1 = enter sleep, or deep sleep, on return from an ISR.
SCB->SCR &= ~SCB_SCR_SLEEPONEXIT_Msk;

// RTC wakeup interrupt is connected to EXTI line 20 internally.
// Enable EXTI20 interrupt
EXTI->IMR1 |= EXTI_IMR1_IM20;

// Enable EXTI20 event
EXTI->EMR1 |= EXTI_EMR1_EM20;

// Select rising-edge trigger
EXTI->RTSR1 |= EXTI_RTSR1_RT20;

NVIC_EnableIRQ(RTC_WKUP_IRQn);
NVIC_SetPriority(RTC_WKUP_IRQn, 0);

__DSB();   // Ensure that the last store takes effect
__WFI();   // Switch processor into the sleep mode
}
```

Example 18-8. Entering the sleep mode by using WFI

18.8 Exercises

1. Write a C program that converts the UNIX Epoch time to a calendar date and time.

2. Write a C program that converts a given calendar date and time to the UNIX Epoch time.

3. Write an assembly program that sets up the RTC date and displays the current date on an LCD.

4. Write an assembly program that sets up the RTC time and displays the current time on an LCD.

5. Implement an assembly program to allow users to change the date and time via the keypad.

6. Write an assembly program that utilizes the RTC alarm to toggle an LED every five seconds.

Direct Memory Access (DMA)

Direct memory access (DMA) is a useful technique for transferring data between peripherals and memory, or between memory and memory, without using many processor cycles. The processor needs to program the DMA controller and send a command to start the DMA transfer. However, during the transfer process, the processor is not involved and can execute other tasks. Therefore, DMA is a very efficient and widely-used approach to interface peripherals.

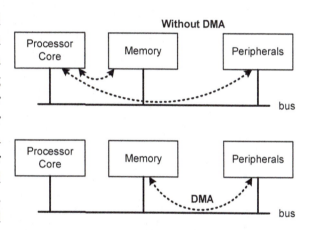

Figure 19-1. DMA runs on behalf of the processor

- For slow peripherals, DMA releases the processor from waiting for peripheral data and allows the CPU to serve other tasks.

- For fast peripherals, such as ADC and DAC, DMA improves the data transfer throughput because memory accesses take place without the involvement of the processor.

- For high-speed peripherals, DMA can help significantly reduce the rate at which interrupts are generated. Thus, DMA decreases the performance overhead from interrupts.

With DMA support, a peripheral does not need to have local memory to store data. Instead, data can be efficiently stored in data memory via DMA. This design not only reduces the cost but also improves the energy efficiency of embedded systems. This chapter presents the implementation of the bus matrix within the processor and gives an example of how to program a DMA controller.

19.1 Advanced Microcontroller Bus Architecture (AMBA)

The Advanced Microcontroller Bus Architecture (AMBA) is an open on-chip communication standard for embedded microcontrollers. Chip designers can use AMBA without paying royalties. AMBA was first introduced by ARM in 1996. AMBA 2.0, released in 1999, specifies the architecture and communication protocol of three bus standards, including the Advanced High-performance Bus (AHB), the Advanced System Bus (ASB), and the Advanced Peripheral Bus (APB). A bus is a set of physical connections that allows two or more components to communicate. Each bus architecture provides a set of separate communication paths to transfer data, instructions, and control signals. AMBA deploys a master/slave communication model in which only a master can control the bus and initiate data transfer.

- The AHB or ASB is the backbone bus that has high-performance and high clock frequency. It supports pipelined operation to achieve high bandwidth, burst transfers to reduce the latency of bus access arbitration, and multiple bus masters to allow several components to initiate data transfer. Bus arbitration refers to the process of deciding which bus master will be allowed to control the bus when there are multiple masters. AHB supports wider data transfer and has a higher bandwidth than ASB. AHB is used on ARM Cortex-M microprocessors.
- The APB is a simple, low-power, and low-bandwidth bus that is suitable for low-speed peripherals such as timers, USART, SPI, and LCD. These peripherals typically use memory-mapped registers to provide a simplified interface. Unlike AHB, communications in APB are not pipelined. All peripherals on the APB bus can only act in the role of a slave, which cannot initiate a transfer.

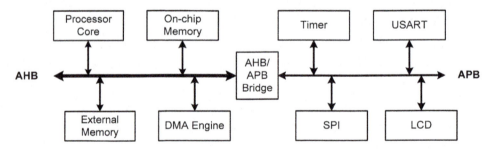

Figure 19-2. A simple system consisting of AHB, APB, and AHB/APB bridge

The AHB bus is connected to a bus matrix. The matrix uses a priority-based round-robin scheduling algorithm to ensure that no modules can block the data transmission of the other modules for a long time. The bus matrix also arbitrates any conflicts when multiple accesses are attempted simultaneously.

A bridge is required to connect the AHB and APB buses. The bridge allows a master on the AHB bus to communicate with a peripheral device on the APB bus, even though they use different communication protocols. The bridge acts as the only master on the APB bus and as a slave on the AHB bus. Due to the speed gap between AHB and APB, the bridge buffers addresses, controls and data from AHB to ensure that there is no data loss during the communications. The bridge also drives the APB peripherals and provides response signals to the AHB.

DMA controllers reside on the AHB bus. A DMA controller acts as a bus master and a bus slave. It has two ports. The slave port can accept data and commands from the processor when the processor sets up DMA transfers. The master port can initiate data transfer within the AHB bus or across the AHB/APB bridge. A DMA controller often manages multiple channels that can be programmed independently. While all channels of a DMA controller share the same interface to the AHB bus, each channel has its own dedicated interface to peripherals. Thus, multiple channels can perform DMA transfers simultaneously.

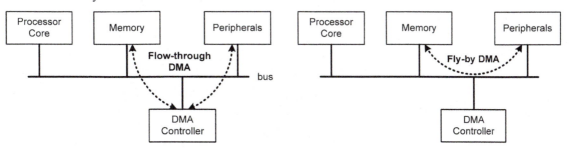

Figure 19-3. Flow-through *vs* fly-by DMA

DMA transfers can be either *flow-through* or *fly-by*, as shown in Figure 19-3.

- A *flow-through* (or fetch-and-deposit) DMA transfer involves two steps: (1) data are read one at a time from the source into a register in the DMA controller, and (2) data are written to the destination.
- A *fly-by* DMA transfer only requires one bus transfer. Data are directly transferred from the source to the destination without being read into the DMA controller.

Flow-through transfers are less efficient than fly-by transfers. However, flow-through transfers can be used for DMA operations between devices with different register sizes. For example, it can read twice from a 16-bit source and then write once to a 32-bit destination. Also, fly-by transfers cannot be used for memory-to-memory DMA in any embedded systems in which memory cannot be read and written in the same memory clock cycle. The DMA controllers on STM32L processors use flow-through transfers.

19.2 Interfacing a Peripheral without and with DMA

Figure 19-4 and Figure 19-5 compare operations when data is transferred from the serial port (USART) to RAM without and with DMA. STM32L4 divides on-chip peripherals into two groups, with one APB bus for each group (APB1 and APB2). There are two AHB-to-APB bridges that connect the AHB bus matrix to APB1 and APB2, respectively. STM32L4 provides two DMA controllers, offering 7 channels on each controller. Only one DMA controller is shown in Figure 19-4 and Figure 19-5.

Without DMA, the processor is fully occupied during the data transfer. It needs to perform two operations explicitly to read data from a peripheral. The first operation is a load instruction that copies a peripheral data register to a register in the processor core. The second operation is a store instruction that saves data to memory.

Similarly, the processor must perform a load and a store operation to write data to a peripheral. The processor reads the data from memory and writes the data to the peripheral.

Furthermore, without DMA, the processor uses either busy-waiting or interrupt methods to make sure that the peripheral's data register is ready to read or write. The busy-waiting method is simple but inefficient because it prevents the processor from performing other tasks. The interrupt approach is more efficient than busy-waiting. However, it is not suitable for high-speed peripherals because high-frequency interrupts can create a large performance overhead. Chapter 22.1.4 and Chapter 22.1.5 give a detailed implementation of sending and receiving data from a USART serial port by using busy-waiting (also known as polling) and interrupts.

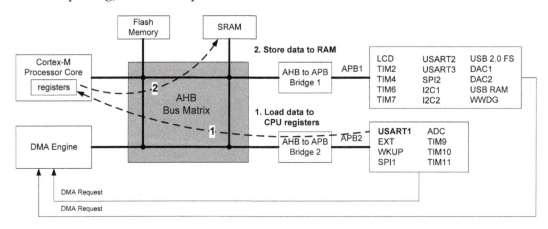

Figure 19-4. Receiving data from a USART serial port without DMA. The processor must execute load and store instructions to copy data from peripherals to the data memory.

On the contrary, if DMA is used, data exchange between memory and peripherals, or between two different memory regions, occurs without processor intervention. The processor only needs to set up the DMA transfers by programming the DMA controller and start the transfer by enabling the DMA channel. Once the transfer is in progress, the processor becomes available for other tasks.

For example, after the processor configures and initiates the DMA channel that responds to the USART1 *receive register not empty* (RXNE) events, the DMA engine copies data in the USART1 RX register to memory as soon as it is received.

- The "write to" and "read from" operations are offloaded from the processor core to the DMA controller.

- The DMA engine uses flow-through transfers. Each DMA transfer still takes two bus transfers to move data from USART1 to memory. Although DMA does not reduce the total latency of these two data transfers, this latency can be hidden from the processor.

- The DMA controller can generate an interrupt at the end of each DMA transfer sequence to inform the processor that data has been saved to memory and is ready to be processed.

In this way, DMA allows data computation and data transfer to take place in parallel, leading to performance improvement. DMA may stop the processor's access to the AHB bus for a short time if both are trying to access the same destination (memory or peripherals) at the same time.

Chapter 22.1.6 provides a detailed example of controlling USART 1 via DMA.

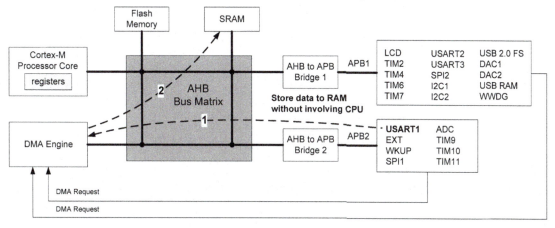

Figure 19-5. Receiving data from USART 1 by using DMA. The DMA engine reads data from the peripheral and then writes it to memory without the intervention of the processor. The DMA engine can inform the processor via interrupt upon completion.

19.3 DMA Channels

Let us take the STM32L4 as an example to illustrate the concept of a DMA channel. STM32L4 has two DMA controllers, with seven channels in each. Each channel can perform DMA transfers independently. Each channel has its own source, destination, transfer direction, transfer width, data amount, and trigger.

If a DMA channel is enabled, it performs a DMA transfer automatically for each trigger received. Figure 19-6 shows one DMA controller. Each channel can be programmed to be triggered by one event selected among eight events available to that channel. This is achieved by programming DMA controller's CSELR register. Software trigger is one of the eight trigger options on every channel.

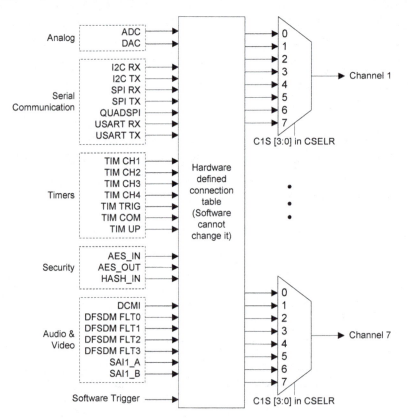

Figure 19-6. Selecting one trigger signal for each DMA channel

To reduce a chip's cost and complexity, each channel can only support up to eight trigger signals (also called requests) defined by the chip manufacturer. For a given DMA channel, software can only select one available trigger for that channel. In other words, not all triggers are available for a channel at the same time.

Table 19-1 and Table 19-2 show the possible triggers on each channel of DMA 1 and DMA 2. To avoid DMA conflicts, we need to consider the following questions when programming DMA: (1) Which DMA controller should we use? (2) Which channel should we use? (3) Which trigger should we select?

Trigger	Channel 1	Channel 2	Channel 3	Channel 4	Channel 5	Channel 6	Channel 7
0	ADC1	ADC2	ADC3	DFSDM1_FLT0	DFSDM1_FLT1	DFSDM1_FLT2	DFSDM1_FLT3
1	-	SPI1_RX	SPI1_TX	SPI2_RX	SPI2_TX	SAI2_A	SAI2_B
2	-	USART3_TX	USART3_RX	USART1_TX	USART1_RX	USART2_RX	USART2_TX
3	-	I2C3_TX	I2C3_RX	I2C2_TX	I2C2_RX	I2C1_TX	I2C1_RX
4	TIM2_CH3	TIM2_UP	TIM16_CH1 TIM16_UP	-	TIM2_CH1	TIM16_CH1 TIM16_UP	TIM2_CH2 TIM2_CH4
5	TIM17_CH1 TIM17_UP	TIM3_CH3	TIM3_CH4 TIM3_UP	TIM7_UP DAC2	QUADSPI	TIM3_CH1 TIM3_TRIG	TIM17_CH1 TIM17_UP
6	TIM4_CH1	-	TIM6_UP DAC1	TIM4_CH2	TIM4_CH3	-	TIM4_UP
7	-	TIM1_CH1	TIM1_CH2	TIM1_CH4 TIM1_TRIG TIM1_COM	TIM15_CH1 TIM15_UP TIM15_TRIG TIM15_COM	TIM1_UP	TIM1_CH3

Table 19-1. DMA triggers (requests) supported in each channel of DMA controller 1

Trigger	Channel 1	Channel 2	Channel 3	Channel 4	Channel 5	Channel 6	Channel 7
0	I2C4_RX	I2C4_TX	ADC1	ADC2	ADC3	DCMI	-
1	SAI1_A	SAI1_B	SAI2_A	SAI2_B	-	SAI1_A	SAI1_B
2	UART5_TX	UART5_RX	UART4_TX	-	UART4_RX	USART1_TX	USART1_RX
3	SPI3_RX	SPI3_TX	-	TIM6_UP DAC1	TIM7_UP DAC2		QUADSPI
4	SWPMI1_RX	SWPMI1_TX	SPI1_RX	SPI1_TX	DCMI	LPUART1_TX	LPUART1_RX
5	TIM5_CH4 TIM5_TRIG	TIM5_CH3 TIM5_UP	-	TIM5_CH2	TIM5_CH1	I2C1_RX	I2C1_TX
6	AES_IN	AES_OUT	AES_OUT	-	AES_IN	-	HASH_IN
7	TIM8_CH3 TIM8_UP	TIM8_CH4 TIM8_TRIG TIM8_COM	-	SDMMC1	SDMMC1	TIM8_CH1	TIM8_CH2

Table 19-2. DMA triggers (requests) supported in each channel of DMA controller 2

Each channel has a software priority and a hardware priority. When multiple channels are active, the DMA controller uses the priority level to determine the order of bus access when a bus resource conflict occurs. If two or more DMA channels have the same software priority level, the DMA controller uses the hardware priority to break the tie.

- *Software priority*. Programs can configure the software priority of each channel. When multiple channels are used, software should give a high priority to a channel that requires a high bandwidth, to achieve continuous data transfers and provide sustained data rates. There are four levels of priority, including very high (0b11), high (0b10), medium (0b01), and low (0b00).

- *Hardware priority*. On STM32L4 processors, channel 1 has the highest hardware priority, and channel 7 has the lowest. Users cannot change the hardware priority of DMA channels. When multiple channels have the same software priority, the DMA engine uses their hardware priority to arbitrate the bus accesses.

19.4 Programming DMA

Each DMA channel has four registers: the *channel memory address register* (CMAR), the *channel peripheral address register* (CPAR), the *channel number of data register* (CNDTR), and the *channel configuration register* (CCR). As shown in Figure 19-7, CMAR and CPAR specify the starting address of the data memory and the peripheral, respectively. The transfer between the memory and the peripheral can take place in either direction.

The CCR register specifies the data transfer direction, whether increment mode is used, whether circular mode is used, and the channel priority. The CCR register is also used to enable or disable *transfer error interrupts*, *half-transfer interrupts*, and *transfer-complete interrupts*. Software must specify the total number of data to transfer in the CNDTR register.

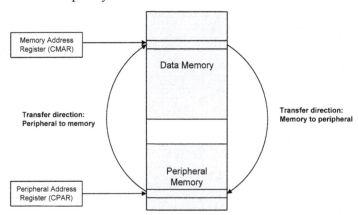

Figure 19-7. DMA transfer direction. On STM32L, memory-to-memory DMA is allowed, but peripheral-to-peripheral DMA is not.

Increment mode determines whether CPAR or CMAR increments after each DMA transfer, (see Figure 19-8). This mode can be programmed separately for CPAR and CMAR. For example, if increment mode for CMAR is enabled and MSIZE is four bytes, then the memory address stored in CMAR automatically increments by four after each DMA transfer.

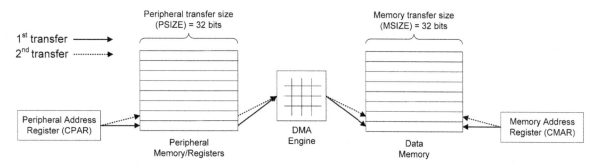

Figure 19-8. Example transfer from peripheral to data memory

Figure 19-9 configures the *receive buffer not empty* (RXNE) event of USART 1 as the trigger of DMA 2 channel 7 by programming the channel selection register (CSELR). All available triggers that can make DMA requests on channel 7 of DMA 2 are listed in Table 19-2. When USART receives a byte, hardware sets the RXNE flag. If the channel enable bit (EN) is set in the CCR register, each RXNE event triggers one DMA transfer request. Example 19-1 gives the implementation in C.

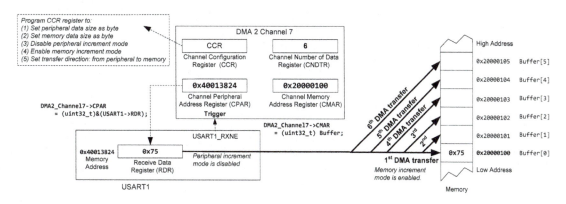

Figure 19-9. Configure DMA 2 channel 7 to receive 6 bytes from USART 1

```
RCC->AHB1ENR |= RCC_AHB1ENR_DMA2EN;       // Enable DMA clock
DMA2_Channel7->CCR &= ~DMA_CCR_EN;        // Disable DMA channel
DMA2_Channel7->CCR &= ~DMA_CCR_PSIZE;     // Peripheral data size 00 = 8 bits
DMA2_Channel7->CCR &= ~DMA_CCR_MSIZE;     // Memory data size: 00 = 8 bits
DMA2_Channel7->CCR &= ~DMA_CCR_PINC;      // Disable peripheral increment mode
DMA2_Channel7->CCR |=  DMA_CCR_MINC;      // Enable memory increment mode
DMA2_Channel7->CCR &= ~DMA_CCR_DIR;       // Transfer direction: to memory
DMA2_Channel7->CNDTR = 6;                 // Number of data to transfer
DMA2_Channel7->CPAR  = (uint32_t)&(USART1->RDR); // Peripheral address
DMA2_Channel7->CMAR  = (uint32_t) Buffer;        // Receive buffer address
DMA2_CSELR->CSELR &= ~DMA_CSELR_C6S;      // See Table 19-2
DMA2_CSELR->CSELR |= 2<<24;               // Map channel 7 to USART1_RX
DMA2_Channel7->CCR |= DMA_CCR_EN;         // Enable DMA channel 7
```

Example 19-1. Program DMA 2 Channel 7 to receive 6 bytes from USART 1

19.5 DMA Circular Mode

The DMA channel can run in *circular mode* or *normal mode*.

- If the CIRC bit in the CCR register is cleared, the DMA channel runs in **normal mode**. For each DMA transfer, hardware decrements the CNDTR register by 1. The DMA channel is disabled once CNDTR reaches 0. Once the DMA channel is enabled, software cannot modify CNDTR.
- If CIRC in CCR is set, the DMA channel runs in **circular mode**. Circular mode is often used for memory to implement a circular buffer. After CNDTR reaches 0, CPAR, CMAR, and CNDTR are automatically reset to the value originally programmed. Therefore, DMA can start the next round of DMA transfers. Circular mode is useful for DMA transfers for continuous data streams.

As shown in Figure 19-10, the CNDTR register of a DMA channel is set to 6. After the DMA completes 6 transfers, the buffer is automatically reused for subsequent DMA transfers.

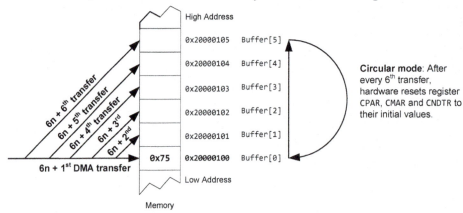

Figure 19-10. DMA in circular mode

Each DMA channel can generate three interrupts: transfer finished (TC), half-finished (HT), and transfer error (TE). The following code enables the TC interrupt of DMA 2 Channel 7.

```
// Enable the transfer complete interrupt
DMA2_Channel7->CCR |= DMA_CCR_TCIE;

// Disable the half transfer interrupt
DMA2_Channel7->CCR &= ~DMA_CCR_HTIE;

// Set the priority as the most urgent
NVIC_SetPriority(DMA2_Channel7_IRQn, 0);

// Enable NVIC interrupt
NVIC_EnableIRQ(DMA2_Channel7_IRQn);
```

Example 19-2. Enabling the TC interrupt for DMA 2 channel 7

19.6 DMA Interrupts

Software can identify the type of a DMA interrupt by checking the DMA interrupt status register (DMA_ISR), as shown in Example 19-3.

- Once half of the number of bytes (specified in the CNDTR register) are transferred, the half-transfer flag (HTIF) is set, and the DMA engine generates an interrupt if the half-transfer interrupt enable bit (HTIE) is set.
- At the end of the transfer, the transfer complete flag (TCIF) is set, and the DMA engine generates an interrupt if the transfer complete interrupt enable bit (TCIE) is set.
- If a DMA transfer accesses a restricted memory region, a DMA error takes place, and the hardware sets the transfer error flag (TEIF). The DMA controller automatically disables a faulty channel by clearing its EN bit, minimizing the performance impacts on the other active channels.
- If any of the transfer complete, half transfer and transfer error interrupts take place, hardware sets the global interrupt flag (GIF).
- Software clears these interrupt flags by writing 1 to the corresponding bit in the interrupt flag clear register (IFCR).

```
void DMA2_Channel7_IRQHandler(void) {

  if ( (DMA2->ISR & DMA_ISR_TCIF7) == DMA_ISR_TCIF7 ) {// transfer complete
    DMA2->IFCR |= DMA_IFCR_CTCIF7; // Clear flag TCIF by writing 1 to it
    ...
  }

  if ( (DMA2->ISR & DMA_ISR_HTIF7) == DMA_ISR_HTIF7 ) {// half transfer
    DMA2->IFCR |= DMA_IFCR_CHTIF7; // Clear flag IFCR by writing 1 to it
    ...
  }

  if ( (DMA2->ISR & DMA_ISR_GIF7) == DMA_ISR_GIF7 ) {// global interrupt
    DMA2->IFCR |= DMA_IFCR_CGIF7; // Clear flag HTIF by writing 1 to it
    ...
  }

  if ( (DMA2->ISR & DMA_ISR_TEIF7) == DMA_ISR_TEIF7 ) {// transfer error
    DMA2->IFCR |= DMA_IFCR_CTEIF7; // Clear flag CTEIF by writing 1 to it
    ...
  }
}
```

Example 19-3. Interrupt handler for DMA 2 channel 7

19.7 Exercises

1. How does the software know which specific event generates the interrupt when a DMA interrupt occurs?

2. Why is using DMA interrupt to retrieve data from a peripheral more efficient than repeatedly polling the peripheral?

3. Write an assembly program that uses DMA to copy 256 bytes of data from one memory region to another memory region.

4. Write an assembly program that uses DMA to perform analog-to-digital conversion (ADC). (Requires the background of Chapter 20).

5. Write an assembly program that uses DMA to perform digital-to-analog conversion (DAC). (Requires the background of Chapter 21)

CHAPTER 20

Analog-to-Digital Converter (ADC)

An analog-to-digital converter (ADC) produces a finite-precision signed or unsigned digital number to represent approximately the size of an analog voltage relative to a reference voltage. The reference voltage is a fixed voltage provided by the internal circuit of the microprocessor or by an external circuit connected to a pin of the microprocessor. It does not convert a voltage larger than the reference voltage.

Three key performance parameters of ADCs are *sampling rate, resolution,* **and** *power dissipation*.

- The *sampling rate* indicates how many conversions an ADC performs in a second. An ADC can perform up to several million or billion of samples per second.

- The number of bits in the ADC output is called *resolution*. While standard resolutions vary between 6 to 24 bits, the resolution has not been improved much in the past few years because a 12-bit or 24-bit resolution is often sufficient for most modern applications.

- The *power dissipation* measures the power efficiency of ADC converters. In many mobile embedded systems, it is the power budget, not the hardware speed, which limits the throughput of ADC converters.

20.1 ADC Architecture

There are three most popular ADC architectures: *sigma-delta* ADC for low-speed applications, *successive-approximation* (SAR) ADC for low-power applications, and *pipelined* ADC for high-speed applications.

- Sigma-delta ADCs are mostly used in applications requiring low sampling rates, but high resolution, typically less than 100 kilo samples per second and 12 to 24-

bit resolution, such as voice band and audio applications. They have been widely used in modern cell phones.

- SAR ADCs are suitable for applications with low-power data acquisitions and moderate sampling rates, typically less than 5 million samples per second (MSPS).

- Pipelined ADCs are widely used for high-speed applications, such as digital oscilloscopes, HDTV, and radar communication, requiring fast sampling rates greater than 5 MSPS and relatively low resolution less than 18 bits.

The ADC on STM32 microcontrollers is based on the *successive-approximation* (SAR) architecture, as shown in Figure 20-1. The architecture includes two major components: the sample-and-hold amplifier (SHA), and SAR digital quantization.

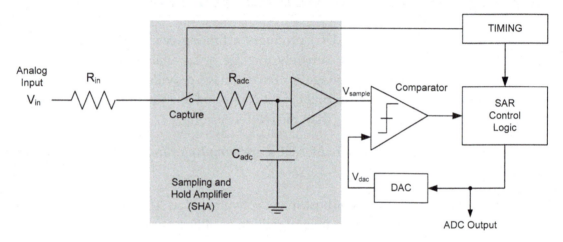

Figure 20-1. Basic architecture of successive-approximation (SAR) ADC

20.1.1   Digital Quantization

The digital quantization works as follows. The SAR control logic uses the binary search algorithm to find the digital number (ADC output) that represents the analog input most closely. The SAR control logic dynamically changes the ADC output so that the digital-to-analog converter (DAC) output V_{dac} gradually approaches the DAC input voltage V_{in}.

(1) The conversion starts with setting the internal DAC output V_{dac} to $\frac{1}{2}V_{REF}$ and then compares the DAC output V_{dac} with the ADC input V_{in}.

(2) If V_{in} is larger than $\frac{1}{2}V_{REF}$, the SAR logic controller sets the most significant bit (MSB) of the ADC result. Otherwise, the MSB of the ADC is cleared.

(3) Next, the DAC output V_{dac} is set to either $\frac{3}{4}V_{REF}$ or $\frac{1}{4}V_{REF}$, depending on the comparison result between V_{in} and V_{dac}.

(4) This process repeats until all bits of the ADC output have been determined.

If the ADC has a resolution of n bits, the successive-approximation conversion takes n steps to complete. It plays a tradeoff between the resolution and sampling rate. A higher resolution usually reduces the ADC conversion rate.

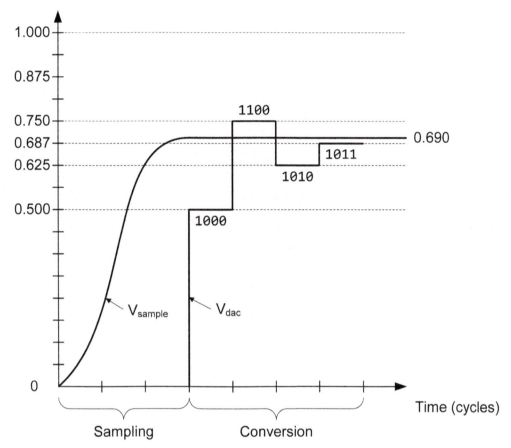

Figure 20-2. An example of four-bit successive-approximation (SAR) ADC. Suppose the input voltage is between 0 and 1 V.

Figure 20-2 shows an example of converting an input voltage of 0.690V into a 4-bit binary value by using SAR ADC. Suppose the range of the input voltage is between 0V and 1V.

(1) After the input voltage is sampled, the SAR control logic starts the conversion by setting V_{dac} as 0.5V (*i.e.*, the ADC output is 0b1000) and comparing it with V_{sample}.

(2) Since V_{sample} is larger than V_{dac}, the control logic then sets V_{dac} as 0.750V (*i.e.*, the ADC output is 0b1100).

(3) Because V_{sample} is smaller than V_{dac}, the control logic then sets V_{dac} as 0.625V.

(4) The above process repeats and the final output of the ADC is 0b1011. In this example, the conversion process takes four cycles.

20.1.2   Sampling and Hold

The sample-and-hold amplifier (SHA) includes a switched capacitor and one operational amplifier, which is used to sample the analog input voltage V_{in} and hold the value over a certain amount of time for subsequent ADC processing. The sampling and hold circuit is a simple resistor-capacitor circuit.

When the switch is closed, the voltage across the capacitor V_C increases exponentially, as shown in the following equation:

$$V_C(t) = V_{in} \times \left(1 - e^{-\frac{t}{T_c}}\right)$$

where $T_c = (R_{in} + R_{adc}) \times C_{adc}$. This shows that the input voltage V_{in} cannot be sampled instantly. For example, when the switch is closed for a time period of $3T_c$, the voltage across the capacitor V_C is only 95.02% of the input voltage V_{in}, as shown in Figure 20-3.

Thus, to achieve accurate analog-to-digital conversion, software should let the capture switch close for enough time. The amount of time that the capture switch remains closed is called *sampling time*.

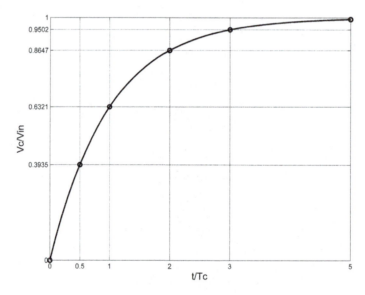

Figure 20-3. The change of the ratio of Vc to Vin over time

On STM32L processors, ADC uses the HSI as the default clock, no matter what clock the processor uses. ADC can use a clock divider to change the ADC clock speed. The divider is 1 for full speed (16 MHz), 2 for medium speed (8 MHz), and 4 for low speed (4 MHz). Each ADC channel can select its own sampling time, by setting the SMP[2:0] bits of the corresponding SMPRx registers (x=1, 2, or 3).

The total ADC conversion time is as follows. Note, if the ADC has a resolution of n bits, the conversion time of successive-approximation takes n cycles to complete.

$$T_{conversion} = Sampling\ Time + Channel\ Conversion\ Time$$

For 12-bit ADC conversion, if the sampling time is set to 4 cycles and the ADC clock is set to 16 MHz, then we have

$$T_{conversion} = 4 + 12 = 16\ cycles = 1\mu s$$

A larger sampling time is recommended if the ADC meets the application's speed requirement. As discussed earlier, to achieve accurate analog-to-digital conversion, the capture switch in the sample-and-hold component should be closed for a sufficient amount of time.

20.2 ADC Sampling Error

Suppose the ADC output has n bits, the ADC result of an input voltage V can be calculated as follows:

$$Digital\ Result = round\left(2^n \times \frac{V - V_{RL}}{V_{RH} - V_{RL}}\right)$$

where V_{RH} and V_{RL} are the high-reference voltage and the low-reference voltage, respectively. There are two conversion modes: the **single-end** mode and the **dual-end** mode. In the single-end mode, V_{RL} is 0 and the digital output is an unsigned number. Then we have

$$Digital\ Result = round\left(2^n \times \frac{V}{V_{RH}}\right)$$

In the dual-end mode, V_{RL} is equal to $-V_{RH}$ often and the digital output is a signed number represented in two's complement format.

$$Digital\ Result = round\left(2^n \times \frac{V + V_{RH}}{2V_{RH}}\right) = round\left(2^{n-1} \times \frac{V + V_{RH}}{V_{RH}}\right)$$

The ADC output approximates the analog input signal in time and amplitude. An analog signal is continuous in time and amplitude, and it has an infinite number of possible values. However, the ADC input is sampled with a fixed time interval, and the ADC result has only a limited number of possible values. Using a higher sampling frequency or using more bits to represent the digital output can reduce the error.

The difference between the actual analog value and the analog value represented by the quantized digital value is called **quantization error**. In the single-end mode, it is assumed that the input voltage is in the range $[0, V_{REF}]$. Figure 20-4 and Figure 20-5 show two different quantization methods in the single-end mode, in which V_{REF} is 5V. The digital ADC output in these examples has only three digits, which can only represent 8 possible values. Figure 20-4 uses the following quantization.

$$Digital\ Result\ =\ floor\left(2^3 \times \frac{V}{V_{REF}}\right)$$

Note the floor operation is to truncate the decimal part during the division, which is the default behavior of integer division in C.

Figure 20-5 uses the quantization method introduced previously.

$$Digital\ Result\ =\ round\left(2^3 \times \frac{V}{V_{REF}}\right) = floor\left(2^3 \times \frac{V}{V_{REF}} + \frac{1}{2}\right)$$

Apparently, the average quantization error in Figure 20-5 is half of the quantization of Figure 20-4. The quantization result based on the round function can be obtained from the result of the floor function by shifting the input voltage toward left by $0.5 \times \frac{V_{REF}}{8}$.

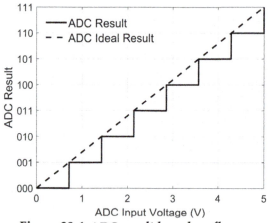

Figure 20-4. ADC result based on floor function in the single-end mode

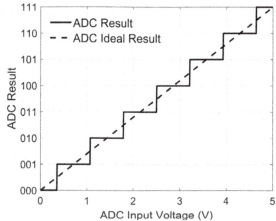

Figure 20-5. ADC result based on the round function in the single-end mode

In the single-end mode, if the ADC result has n bits, we can calculate the conversion result of an input voltage V as follows:

$$V = \frac{Digital\ Value}{2^n - 1} \times V_{REF}$$

20.3 ADC Diagram

STM32L4 has three ADC modules, named ADC1, ADC2, and ADC3. Software can set ADC1 and ADC2 to the dual mode, in which both ADC modules perform conversion simultaneously. The resolution can be 12, 10, 8 or 6 bits, depending on the application's need. By using a technique called oversampling, the resolution can increase to 16 bits.

The voltage input range of each channel is in $[V_{ref-}, V_{ref+}]$, where the V_{ref-} and V_{ref+} are two dedicated input pins on some processors and serve as external voltage references. Most processors also provide an internal reference voltage, which is measured individually at the manufacturing stage. For example, the internal reference voltage of STM32L is 3±0.01 V, and its corresponding converted value is stored in a protected memory area during the manufacturing process.

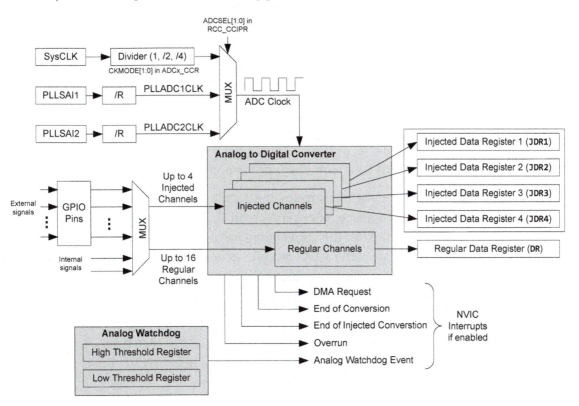

Figure 20-6. Analog-to-digital converter (ADC)

All ADC modules are driven by the same clock, which can be selected from three different clock sources, as shown in Figure 20-6. The ADC clock can be independent of the processor's clock. If the ADC clock runs at 80 MHz, one ADC module can achieve

5.33 million samples per second, with a resolution of 12 bits. If the resolution decreases, the ADC conversion rate can be even higher.

Each ADC module also has integrated analog watchdogs (AWD). Each watchdog has two programmable thresholds: an upper threshold and a lower threshold. AWD continuously monitors the ADC input voltage. If the ADC result is below the lower threshold or above the upper threshold, ADC can generate an interrupt or a signal named (AWD_OUT). The signal AWD_OUT is high if the threshold is violated. AWD_OUT can be selected as an external trigger (ETR) of a timer to start or stop a timer. An example usage of analog watchdogs is to monitor sensor data, such as internal temperature, and raise alarms and perform software actions if data is out of the target range. Without watchdogs, software would have to read and compare ADC results constantly. Thus, analog watchdogs can save processor's time and energy.

20.4 ADC Conversion Modes

The ADC module performs conversions on selected conversion channels in either the *single* conversion mode or the *continuous* conversion mode, as shown in Figure 20-7.

20.4.1   One Input Channel

Let's first consider single conversion on one input channel.

- For a channel in the regular group, the target channel is determined by the SQ1[4:0] bits in the SQR1 register. The 16-bit ADC data register (ADC_DR) holds the conversion result. After the conversion, the *end of regular conversion flag* (EOC) is set in the ISR register. The ADC module generates an interrupt request if the EOCIE bit is set in the interrupt enable register (IER).

- For a channel in the injected group, the JSQ1[4:0] bits in the JSQR register selects the conversion channel. The 16-bit register ADC_JDR1 holds the conversion result. After the conversion, the *end of injected conversion flag* (JEOC) is set in the ISR register. An ADC interrupt will be generated if the JEOCIE bit is set in the interrupt enable register (IER).

If the continuous conversion mode is used on one input channel, the ADC module automatically starts a new conversion immediately after it finishes one. The last conversion result is saved in the ADC_DR register for a regular channel and register ADC_JDR1 for an injected channel. The CONT bit in the CFGR register enables the continuous mode.

20.4.2   Multiple Input Channels

The ADC module can perform sampling and conversions on a set of pre-defined input channels in a round-robin fashion. This conversion scheme is called *scan* mode. For a regular group, this mode scans all channels defined in registers ADC_SQR1, ADC_SQR2, ADC_SQR3, and ADC_SQR4. For an injected group, the channels to be scanned are selected by the ADC_JSQR register. The ADC converts one channel of the group and then continues successively to convert the next channel of the group.

The conversion operation can be set up to perform only once or repeatedly, depending on bit CONT bit in the ADC_CFGR register. For the injected group, there is one data register for each injected channel. However, for a regular group, there is only one data register that is shared by all channels in this group. Therefore, after each conversion in a regular group, the software needs to read the data register between continuous sampling.

After each conversion, ADC result should be copied to a user buffer because ADC may overwrite the ADC data registers (DR, JDR1, JDR2, JDR3, and JDR4). An interrupt request or a DMA request can be triggered at the end of each conversion if enabled. Thus, to reduce the software overhead, we often use the ADC interrupt handler or the DAM controller to copy the ADC results to a user buffer.

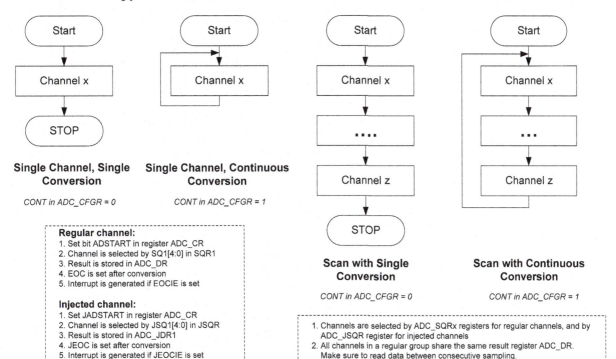

Figure 20-7 ADC conversion: single mode and continuous mode

20.5 ADC Data Alignment

Software can change the ADC resolution. The resolution can be either 12, 10, 8 or 6 bits, determined by the RES[1:0] bits in the ADC configuration register ADC_CFGR.

However, each ADC data register (DR, JDR1, JDR2, JDR3, and JDR4) has 16 bits. Because ADC results have fewer bits than ADC data registers, alignment must be considered when a data result is stored in a data register. Figure 20-8 shows different data alignment formats. ADC output data registers can be either right-aligned or left-aligned.

ADC results are signed when an offset is applied to a channel. If the OFFSET_EN bit flag is set in the ADC offset register (OFR), ADC results are subtracted by a constant defined in the OFR register before they are saved into ADC data register. If the OFFSET_EN bit is set in the OFR register, sign extension must be performed for both right and left alignment. A sign extension operation duplicates the left-most bit of a signed number (*i.e.*, the sign bit) to all bits to the left.

All output data except 6-bit ones are aligned based on halfwords, and their memory addresses are a multiple of 2. For 6-bit output, the alignment of the data portion is aligned to the byte boundary. Two zero bits are appended at the end of the 6-bit output for a regular channel, and one zero bit is added for an injected channel.

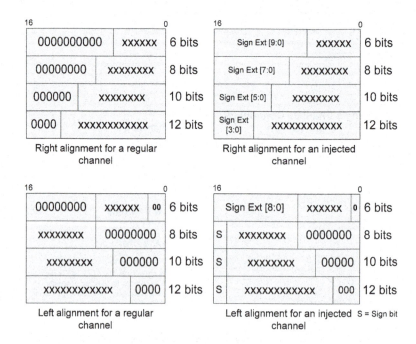

Figure 20-8 Data alignment of ADC data registers

20.6 ADC Input Channels

STM32L4 has three ADC modules (ADC1, ADC2, and ADC3) . Each module consists of a 12-bit successive-approximation (SAR) converter. Each converter has up to 19 channels. Table 20-1 shows the connection between ADC input channels and GPIO pins.

Analog Input Channel	Pin	Analog Input Channel	Pin
ADC123_IN 1	PC 0	ADC12_IN 13	PC 4
ADC123_IN 2	PC 1	ADC12_IN 14	PC 5
ADC123_IN 3	PC 2	ADC12_IN 15	PB 0
ADC123_IN 4	PC 3	ADC12_IN 16	PB 1
ADC12_IN 5	PA 0	ADC3_IN 6	PF 3
ADC12_IN 6	**PA 1**	ADC3_IN 7	PF 4
ADC12_IN 7	PA 2	ADC3_IN 8	PF 5
ADC12_IN 8	PA 3	ADC3_IN 9	PF 6
ADC12_IN 9	PA 4	ADC3_IN 10	PF 7
ADC12_IN 10	PA 5	ADC3_IN 11	PF 8
ADC12_IN 11	PA 6	ADC3_IN 12	PF 9
ADC12_IN 12	PA 7	ADC3_IN 13	PF 10

Table 20-1. Pin definition for analog input signal of STM32L4 processors

A GPIO pin can only be connected to a pre-defined input channel of an ADC module. For example, Pin PC 0 can be internally connected to the input channel 1 of all ADC modules (ADC123_IN1), including ADC1, ADC2, and ADC3. Pin PA 1 can be internally connected to the input channel 6 of ADC1 and ADC2 (ADC12_IN6). Some ADC input channels are connected to internal signals, such as internal temperature sensor, and battery monitor voltage. Detailed information can be found on the STM32L4 reference manual.

The program in Example 20-1 connects pin PA1 to the channel 6 of ADC1 and ADC2.

- The GPIO mode bits must be set to select the analog mode, which is the default GPIO mode when the processor is reset.
- In this example, pin PA 1 is configured as no pull-up and no pull-down internally. The pin will be floating, and the ADC result is random if the pin is temporarily not driven. Depending on the application's need, selecting pull-up or pull-down (either internally or externally) may be a better option to prevent the pin from floating.
- In addition, software sets a bit in the ASCR register to connect the corresponding pin and ADC.

```
// GPIO Mode:
//   00 = Digital input,        01 = Digital output,
//   10 = Alternate function,   11 = Analog(default)
GPIOA->MODER |= 3U<<2;   // Configure PA1 as analog mode

// GPIO Push-Pull:
//   00 = No pull-up/pull-down, 01 = Pull-up,
//   10 = Pull-down,            11 = Reserved
GPIOA->PUPDR &= ~(3U<<2); // No pull-up, no pull-down

// GPIO port analog switch control register (ASCR)
//   0 = Disconnect analog switch to the ADC input (reset state)
//   1 = Connect analog switch to the ADC input
GPIOA->ASCR |= 1U<<1;   // pin 1
```

Example 20-1. Configuring GPIO pin PA.1 as ADC input ADC12_IN6

Input channels of an ADC module care divided into two groups: injected group and regular group, as shown in Figure 20-6.

- A program can select up to four input channels to join the injected group. A channel in the injected group is referred to as an *injected channel*. Each injected channel has its own ADC data register.
- Software can also put input channels into a regular group. An input channel in the regular group is called a *regular channel*. All regular channels share an ADC data register.

Each channel can be single-ended input or differential input by configuring register DIFSEL. In the single-end mode, V_{REF-} is internally connected to the ground. In the differential mode, the ADC input is the difference between two external voltage inputs: ADC_IN i and ADC_IN i+1.

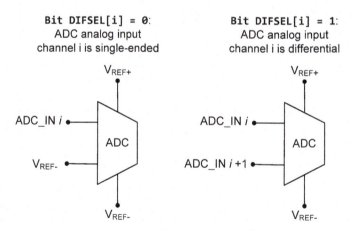

Figure 20-9. ADC input channels can be programmed to be single-ended or differential.

20.7 ADC Triggers

The ADC conversion can be triggered by using software or external signals.

- *Software trigger.* If EXTEN[1:0] bits in the CFGR register are zero, software trigger is selected. ADC conversion for the regular group starts immediately after software sets the ADSTART bit in the ADC_CR register. Similarly, if JEXTEN[1:0] bits are zero, setting the JADSTART bit starts the ADC conversion for the injected group immediately. Hardware automatically clears the ADSTART and JADSTART bits when (1) ADC is in the single conversion mode with software trigger, or (2) software sets the ADSTP or JADSTP bits to stop conversion. Therefore, if single-conversion with software trigger is used, software needs to set ADSTART or JADSTART again to make another ADC conversion.

- *External trigger.* Hardware signals can be used to trigger ADC conversions, leading to reduced CPU workload. External triggers can be selected from the outputs of a timer (channel outputs CC1, CC2, CC3, CC4, trigger output TRG0) and external processor pins.
  - *Trigger polarity.* The EXTEN[1:0] bits in the CFGR register and the JEXTEN[1:0] bits in the JSQR register select trigger edges for regular channels and injected channels, respectively. The trigger edge can be rising edges, falling edges, or both rising and falling edges.
  - *Trigger source.* The trigger source is selected by the JEXTSEL[3:0] bits in the CFGR register and the JEXTSEL[1:0] bits in the JSQR register select trigger source for regular channels and injected channels, respectively.

When ADC uses the software trigger, one common programming error is that the software does not set up the length of delay at the end of each regular conversion. Accordingly, the ADC conversion was only performed once, instead of continuously.

In defaulting setting, there is no delay before a new regular conversion can start. If the system clock is slow, there is no enough time for the processor to read the ADC data register (DR) before a new conversion completes. Therefore, it is a good practice to set the delay (DELS[2:0] bits in the ADC_CR2 register) as waiting until software has read the ADC_DR register or hardware has cleared the EOC flag (end of conversion) in the ADC_SR register. This delay setting is also called ADC *freeze mode.*

> *Tip: Insert some delay between conversions when the system clock is slow.*

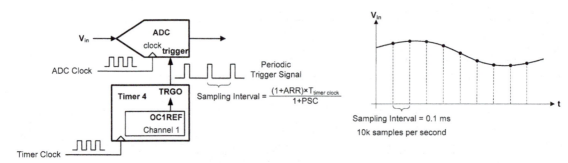

Figure 20-10. Selecting Timer 4's TRGO as ADC's trigger

The following C program sets the trigger output (TRGO) of timer 4 as the trigger signal of the ADC converter, as shown in Figure 20-10. Suppose the ADC sampling rate is 10 kHz. Therefore, timer 4 needs to generate 10,000 TRGO outputs per second. The *master mode selection bits* (MMS[2:0]) in the CR2 register select which timer's internal signal is used as the TRGO. This example selects the reference output of channel 1 (OC1REF) as TRGO.

```
void TIM4_Init(void){
  RCC->APB1ENR1 |= RCC_APB1ENR1_TIM4EN; // Enable clock of Timer 4
  TIM4->CR1 &= ~TIM_CR1_CMS;              // Clear edge-aligned mode bits
  TIM4->CR1 &= ~TIM_CR1_DIR;              // Counting direction: Up counting

  // Master mode selection
  // 000: UG bit from the EGR register is used as trigger output (TRGO).
  // 001: Enable - the Counter Enable signal is used as trigger output (TRGO).
  // 010: Update - The update event is selected as trigger output (TRGO).
  // 011: Compare Pulse - The trigger output send a positive pulse when the
  //      CC1IF flag is to be set (even if it was already high).
  // 100: Compare - OC1REF signal is used as trigger output (TRGO)
  // 101: Compare - OC2REF signal is used as trigger output (TRGO)
  // 110: Compare - OC3REF signal is used as trigger output (TRGO)
  // 111: Compare - OC4REF signal is used as trigger output (TRGO)
  TIM4->CR2 &= ~TIM_CR2_MMS;   // Clear master mode selection bits
  TIM4->CR2 |= TIM_CR2_MMS_2; // Select 100 = OC1REF as TRGO

  // OC1M: Output Compare 1 mode
  TIM4->CCMR1 &= ~TIM_CCMR1_OC1M;                        // Clear mode bits
  TIM4->CCMR1 |= TIM_CCMR1_OC1M_1 | TIM_CCMR1_OC1M_2;  // 0110 = PWM mode 1

  // Timer driving frequency = 80 MHz/(1 + PSC) = 80 MHz/(1+7) = 10MHz
  // Trigger frequency = 10MHz / (1 + ARR) = 10MHz/1000 = 10KHz
  TIM4->PSC  =   7;           // max 65535
  TIM4->ARR  = 999;           // max 65535
  TIM4->CCR1 = 500;           // Duty ration 50%

  TIM4->CCER |= TIM_CCER_CC1E; // OC1 signal is output
  TIM4->CR1  |= TIM_CR1_CEN;   // Enable timer
}
```

Example 20-2. Selecting channel 1's reference output (OC1REF) as the trigger output (TRGO)

The following C code selects ADC 1's trigger signal. These trigger signals are hardware signals generated by timers or external clock signal applied to a GPIO pin (EXTI 11). This example selects the external trigger 12 (EXT12), *i.e.*, the trigger output (TRGO) of timer 4, as the trigger signal for the regular group. For regular channels, if ADC has not been started, *i.e.*, ADSTART = 0, ADC ignores selected trigger signals. Similarly, the injected group also ignores hardware trigger signals if JADSTART = 0.

```
// ADC clock and GPIO initialization
...

// ADC External Triggers (EXT0 - EXT15)
//---------------------------------------------------------------
// Regular Channels              |  Injected Channels
//---------------------------------------------------------------
// EXT0  TIM1_CC1 event    0000  |  JEXT0  TIM1_TRGO event  0000
// EXT1  TIM1_CC2 event    0001  |  JEXT1  TIM1_CC4 event   0001
// EXT2  TIM1_CC3 event    0010  |  JEXT2  TIM2_TRGO event  0010
// EXT3  TIM2_CC2 event    0011  |  JEXT3  TIM2_CC1 event   0011
// EXT4  TIM3_TRGO event   0100  |  JEXT4  TIM3_CC4 event   0100
// EXT5  TIM4_CC4 event    0101  |  JEXT5  TIM4_TRGO event  0101
// EXT6  EXTI line 11      0110  |  JEXT6  EXTI line 15     0110
// EXT7  TIM8_TRGO event   0111  |  JEXT7  TIM8_CC4 event   0111
// EXT8  TIM8_TRGO2 event  1000  |  JEXT8  TIM1_TRGO2 event 1000
// EXT9  TIM1_TRGO event   1001  |  JEXT9  TIM8_TRGO event  1001
// EXT10 TIM1_TRGO2 event  1010  |  JEXT10 TIM8_TRGO2 event 1010
// EXT11 TIM2_TRGO event   1011  |  JEXT11 TIM3_CC3 event   1011
// EXT12 TIM4_TRGO event   1100  |  JEXT12 TIM3_TRGO event  1100
// EXT13 TIM6_TRGO event   1101  |  JEXT13 TIM3_CC1 event   1101
// EXT14 TIM15_TRGO event  1110  |  JEXT14 TIM6_TRGO event  1110
// EXT15 TIM3_CC4 event    1111  |  JEXT15 TIM15_TRGO event 1111
//---------------------------------------------------------------

// Select TIM4_TRGO event (1100) as external trigger for regular channels
ADC1->CFGR &= ~ADC_CFGR_EXTSEL;
ADC1->CFGR |=  ADC_CFGR_EXTSEL_3 | ADC_CFGR_EXTSEL_2;

// Select rising edges of hardware triggers
// 00: Software trigger
// 01: Hardware trigger detection on the rising edge
// 10: Hardware trigger detection on the falling edge
// 11: Hardware trigger detection on both the rising and falling edges
ADC1->CFGR &=~ ADC_CFGR_EXTEN;
ADC1->CFGR |=  ADC_CFGR_EXTEN_0;

// Trigger becomes immediately effective once software starts ADC.
ADC1->CR |= ADC_CR_ADSTART;

...
```

Example 20-3. Selecting rising edge of timer 4's TRGO as ADC1's triggers (regular channels)

20.8 Measuring the Input Voltage

A potentiometer, informally a pot, is a three-terminal variable resistor. It uses a sliding contact and works as an adjustable voltage divider. When two outer terminals are connected to Vcc and the ground respectively, the center terminal generates a voltage that varies from 0 to Vcc depending on the position of the sliding contact.

In the following sections, we use the internal voltage reference, which is 3V. In this example, we measure the input voltage adjusted by a potentiometer. If the input voltage V_{input} is larger than ½ of Vcc, then we turn on an LED. An interesting application is that we use the potentiometer to control the brightness of an LED dynamically if a PWM controls the LED. The V_{input} is used to adjust the duty cycle of the PWM output signal.

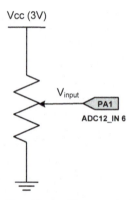

Figure 20-11. Measuring the voltage output of a potentiometer

Suppose the ADC result has 12 bits and ADC is configured as single-ended. Then, we have the following conversion result:

$$ADC\ Result = \frac{V_{input}}{V_{REF}} \times 4095$$

Therefore, we have

$$V_{input} = \frac{ADC\ Result}{4095} \times V_{REF}$$

20.9 ADC Configuration Flowchart

Figure 20-12 shows the flowchart of initializing the continuous ADC1 conversion for channel 6 (GPIO Port A Pin 1, *i.e.*, PA 1) with a software start of conversion. ADC generates an interrupt request at the end of each ADC conversion if the corresponding ADC interrupt is enabled.

- For a regular channel, hardware sets the end of conversion (EOC) flag at the end of each conversion, indicating that new ADC result has been stored in the ADC_DR register. Software must clear the EOC flag explicitly by writing 1 to it or implicitly by reading register ADC_DR.

- For an injected channel, hardware sets the injected end of conversion (JEOC) flag at the end of the conversion of each injected channel in the injected group. Only software can clear the JEOC flag.

- For a regular group, hardware sets the end of regular sequence (EOS) flag when ADC converts all channels in this group. Software clears EOS by writing 1 to it.

- Similarly, for an injected group, hardware sets the end of injected sequence (JEOS) flag when all channels in this group have been converted. Writing 1 to JEOS clears this flag.

At the beginning of the flowchart, the program turns on the HSI clock and waits until it is ready. The processor clock is independent of the ADC clock and can be higher or lower than the HSI clock.

By default, ADC modules are in the deep-power-down mode to improve energy efficiency. In this mode, ADC modules are disconnected from the internal power supply to reduce leakage currents. Example 20-4 shows the C function that wakes up the ADC 1.

```c
void ADC1_Wakeup (void) {

  int wait_time;

  // To start ADC operations, the following sequence should be applied
  // DEEPPWD = 0: ADC not in deep-power down
  // DEEPPWD = 1: ADC in deep-power-down (default reset state)
  if ((ADC1->CR & ADC_CR_DEEPPWD) == ADC_CR_DEEPPWD) {
    // Exit deep power down mode if still in that state
    ADC1->CR &= ~ADC_CR_DEEPPWD;
  }

  // Enable the ADC internal voltage regulator
  // Before performing any operation such as launching a calibration or
  // enabling the ADC, the ADC voltage regulator must first be enabled and
  // the software must wait for the regulator start-up time.
  ADC1->CR |= ADC_CR_ADVREGEN;

  // Wait for ADC voltage regulator start-up time. The software must wait for
  // the startup time of the ADC voltage regulator (T_ADCVREG_STUP, i.e., 20
```

```
   // us) before launching a calibration or enabling the ADC.
   wait_time = 20 * (80000000 / 1000000);
   while (wait_time != 0) {
     wait_time--;
   }
}
```

Example 20-4. Waking up ADC1

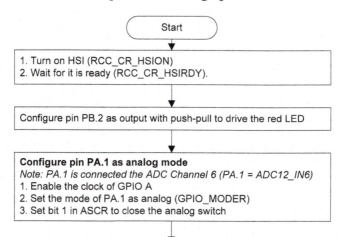

Start

1. Turn on HSI (RCC_CR_HSION)
2. Wait for it is ready (RCC_CR_HSIRDY).

Configure pin PB.2 as output with push-pull to drive the red LED

Configure pin PA.1 as analog mode
Note: PA.1 is connected the ADC Channel 6 (PA.1 = ADC12_IN6)
1. Enable the clock of GPIO A
2. Set the mode of PA.1 as analog (GPIO_MODER)
3. Set bit 1 in ASCR to close the analog switch

Initialization ADC 1
Note: HSI (16MHz) is always used for ADC on STM32L.
1. Enable ADC clock bit RCC_AHB2ENR_ADCEN in register RCC->AHB2ENR.
2. Disable ADC1 by clearing bit ADC_CR_ADEN in register ADC1->CR.
3. Enable I/O analog switches voltage booster (SYSCFG_CFGR1_BOOSTEN) in register ADC123_COMMON->CCR.
4. Set ADC_CCR_VREFEN bit in register ADC123_COMMON->CCR to enable the conversion of internal channels.
5. Configure the ADC prescaler to select the ADC clock frequency in ADC123_COMMON->CCR (select clock not divided).
6. Configure ADC_CCR_CKMODE bits in ADC123_COMMON->CCR to select synchronous clock mode (HCLK/1).
7. Configure all ADCs as independent (clear ADC_CCR_DUAL bits) in ADC123_COMMON->CCR
8. By default, the ADC is in deep-power-down mode where its supply is internally switched off to reduce the leakage currents.
   Therefore, software needs to wait up ADC. The ADC_Wakeup() function is provided in this chapter.
9. Configure RES bits in ADC1->CFGR to set the resolution as 12 bits.
10. Select right alignment in the ADC1->CFGR register.
11. Clear ADC_SQR1_L bits in ADC1->SQR1 to select 1 conversion in the regular channel conversion sequence.
12. Specify the channel number 6 as the 1st conversion in regular sequence (ADC1->SQR1)
13. Configure the channel 6 as single-ended (ADC1->DIFSEL).
14. Select ADC sample time in ADC1->SMPR1. The sampling time must be long enough for the input voltage source to charge the
    embedded capacitor to the input voltage level.
15. Select ADC as discontinuous mode by clearing the ADC_CFGR_CONT bits in ADC1->CFGR.
16. Clear ADC_CFGR_EXTEN bits in register ADC1->CFGR to select software trigger
17. Enable ADC1 by setting the ADC_CR_ADEN bit in register ADC1->CR
18. Wait until ADC1 is ready (i.e., wait until ADC_ISR_ADRDY bit in ADC1->ISR is set by hardware)

Using the software to trigger one ADC conversion:
1. Software can start one ADC conversion by setting the ADC_CR_ADSTART bit in the ADC1->CR register
2. Software has to wait the completion of ADC conversion by checking whether ADC_CSR_EOC_MST in the
   ADC123_COMMON->CSR register has been set by the hardware.
3. The conversion result is saved in register ADC1->DR.

Figure 20-12. Flowchart of configuring channel 6 of ADC1 (GPIO pin PA 1)

The following is an example C code of the ADC interrupt handler.

```c
void ADC1_2_IRQHandler (void) {
  if ((ADC1->ISR & ADC_ISR_EOC) == ADC_ISR_EOC) {
    // For a regular channel, check End of Conversion (EOC) flag
    // Reading ADC data register (DR) clears the EOC flag
    Result = ADC1->DR;

  } else if ((ADC1->ISR & ADC_ISR_JEOS) == ADC_ISR_JEOS) {
    // For injected channels, check End of Sequence (JEOS) flag
    // Reading injected data registers does not clear the JEOS flag
    // Each injected channel has a dedicated data register
    Result_1 = ADC1->JDR1;     // Injected channel 1
    Result_2 = ADC1->JDR2;     // Injected channel 2
    Result_3 = ADC1->JDR3;     // Injected channel 3
    Result_4 = ADC1->JDR4;     // Injected channel 4
    ADC1->ISR |= ADC_ISR_EOS;  // Clear the flab by writing 1 to it
  }
}
```

Example 20-5. Interrupt handler routine for ADC

The following shows how to select a conversion sequence in a regular group. Configuring the ADC regular sequence takes two steps. The first step is to set the total number of regular input channels. The second step is to place the target input channels in the regular sequence registers (SQR), starting from SQR1 to SQR5. The following shows the code for setting up an ADC sequence that includes only one regular channel.

```c
// ADC regular sequence register 1 (ADC_SQR1)
// 00000: 1 conversion in the regular channel conversion sequence
ADC1->SQR1 &= ~ADC_SQR1_L;

// Specify the channel number of the 1st conversion in regular sequence
ADC1->SQR1 &= ~ADC_SQR1_SQ1;
ADC1->SQR1 |= ( 6U << 6 );                  // PA1: ADC12_IN6
ADC1->DIFSEL &= ~ADC_DIFSEL_DIFSEL_6;   // Single-ended for PA1: ADC12_IN6
```

Example 20-6. Configuring ADC conversion sequence

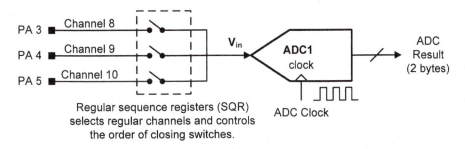

Figure 20-13. Setting the ADC sampling sequence for regular channels.

Suppose we want to perform a sequence of ADC conversion on three regular channels: channel 8 (PA 3), channel 9 (PA 4) and channel 10 (PA 5), as shown in Figure 20-13. We sample channel 9 first, channel 8, channel 10, and again channel 8. The following is the C program code.

```
// Set the sequence length: 00010 = 3 conversions in the regular sequence
ADC1->SQR1 &= ~0xF;        // Clear the sequence length
ADC1->SQR1 |= 3UL;         // 4 samples in this sequence

// 1st conversion in the regular sequence
ADC1->SQR1 |= 9U << 6;     // Select ADC12_IN9 as the 1st conversion

// 2nd conversion in the regular sequence
ADC1->SQR1 |= 8U << 12;    // Select ADC12_IN8 as the 2nd conversion

// 3rd conversion in the regular sequence
ADC1->SQR1 |= 10U << 18;   // Select ADC12_IN10 as the 3rd conversion

// 4th conversion in the regular sequence
ADC1->SQR1 |= 8U << 24;    // Select ADC12_IN8 as the 4th conversion
```

Example 20-7. Configuring an ADC conversion sequence: channel 9, 8, 10, and 8

All channels in a regular group share the data register (ADC->DR). Therefore, the interrupt handler needs to differentiate the results of these channels. We use a simple counter to indicate which channel is being sampled, *i.e.*, which channel the value in the data register (ADC->DR) belongs to.

```
volatile int counter = 0;
volatile uint16_t ADC_results[4];

// Following the ADC sequence defined in Example 20-7
//   ADC_results[0] = 1st conversion, ADC12_IN9
//   ADC_results[1] = 2nd conversion, ADC12_IN8
//   ADC_results[2] = 3rd conversion, ADC12_IN10
//   ADC_results[3] = 4th conversion, ADC12_IN8

void ADC1_2_IRQHandler (void) {
  // Check End of Conversion (EOC) Flag
  If ((ADC1->SR & ADC_SR_EOC) == ADC_SR_EOC) {
    if (counter % 4 == 0) {
      counter = 0;     // reset counter
    }
    ADC_results[counter] = ADC1->DR;
    counter++;
  }
}
```

Example 20-8. Saving ADC results of a regular conversion sequence

20.10   ADC with DMA

As presented in Chapter 19, direct memory access (DMA) is a hardware technology that provides efficient and fast data exchange between peripheral data registers and the main memory, without involving the processor. As presented in Table 19-1, ADC1 can be connected by the channel 1 of the DMA controller 1 on STM32L4.

Suppose the conversion sequence of a regular group is as follows: channel 9, 8, 10, and 8. Whenever the end of conversion flag (EOC) is a set, ADC generates a trigger signal and sends it to the DMA. Immediately after receiving the trigger signal, DMA automatically transfers the ADC result (stored in the AD's date register DR) to the memory buffer.

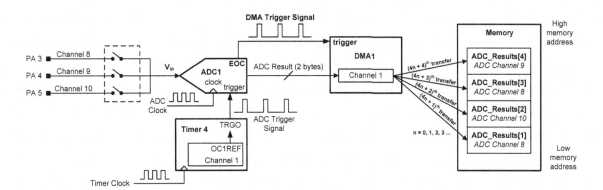

Figure 20-14. Configure DMA1 with circular mode

In the previous section, we give a short example code to set up a sequence of 4 conversions: channel 9, 8, 10, and 8. As shown in Figure 20-14, DMA automatically saves the results in the memory buffer ADC_Results. ADC_Results[0] holds the result of channel 9. ADC_Results[1] holds the result of channel 8. ADC_Results[2] holds the result of channel 10, and ADC_Results[3] holds the result of channel 8.

If the DMA channel 1 is in circular mode, the memory buffer ADC_Results is reused for the next round of ADC conversions. The circular mode allows the processor to reuse the result array ADC_Results repeatedly during each sequence of ADC conversions. At the end of the third ADC conversion, hardware automatically resets the destination memory address register (CMAR) to the address of ADC_Results[0], making the array continuously serve DMA requests.

The following programs DMA 1 channel 1 to transfer the results of ADC 1 to ADC_Results. Because all regular channels share the same data register (ADC1->DR), as shown in Figure 20-6, the address increment mode for the peripheral is turned off.

```
// Suppose ADC runs three regular channels
uint16_t  ADC_Results[4];          // buffer for four ADC results

// Initialization of ADC, GPIO, and clocks is not shown here
...

// Enable DMA1 Clock
RCC->AHB1ENR |= RCC_AHB1ENR_DMA1EN;

// DMA1 channel 1 configuration for ADC1
DMA1_Channel1->CCR &= ~DMA_CCR_MEM2MEM; // Disable memory to memory mode

// Channel priority level
// 00 = Low, 01 = Medium, 10 = High, 11 = Very high
DMA1_Channel1->CCR &= ~DMA_CCR_PL;
DMA1_Channel1->CCR |=  DMA_CCR_PL_1;     // High priority

// Peripheral size: 00 = 8-bits, 01 = 16-bits, 10 = 32-bits, 11 = Reserved
DMA1_Channel1->CCR &= ~DMA_CCR_PSIZE;
DMA1_Channel1->CCR |=  DMA_CCR_PSIZE_0; // data size = 16 bits

// Memory size: 00 = 8-bits, 01 = 16-bits, 10 = 32-bits, 11 = Reserved
DMA1_Channel1->CCR &= ~DMA_CCR_MSIZE;
DMA1_Channel1->CCR |=  DMA_CCR_MSIZE_0; // data size = 16 bits

// Peripheral increment mode (0 = disabled, 1 = enabled)
DMA1_Channel1->CCR &= ~DMA_CCR_PINC;     // peripheral in non-increment mode

// Memory increment mode (0 = disabled, 1 = enabled)
DMA1_Channel1->CCR |= DMA_CCR_MINC;      // memory in increment mode

// Circular mode (0 = disabled, 1 = enabled)
DMA1_Channel1->CCR |= DMA_CCR_CIRC;      // Circular mode

// Data transfer direction (0: Read from peripheral, 1: Read from memory)
DMA1_Channel1->CCR &= ~DMA_CCR_DIR;      // from peripheral to memory

// Number of data to transfer
DMA1_Channel1->CNDTR = 4;                // Length of ADC sequence = 4

// Peripheral address register
DMA1_Channel1->CPAR  = (uint32_t) &(ADC1->DR);

// Memory address register
DMA1_Channel1->CMAR  = (uint32_t) ADC_Results;

// DMA Channel Selection
// Map DMA channel 1 to ADC1
DMA1_CSELR->CSELR &= ~DMA_CSELR_C1S; // 0000: Channel 1 mapped on ADC1

// Enable DMA channel
DMA1_Channel1->CCR |= DMA_CCR_EN;
...
```

Example 20-9. Configuring DMA in circular mode to repeatedly transfer a sequence of four 16-bit ADC results

20.11   DMA with Ping-Pong Buffering

Ping-pong buffering, also called double buffering, is a software technique that uses two buffers to overlap data transfer and data processing, as shown in Figure 20-15. Software alternates between processing the ping buffer and the pong buffer. This scheme gives the processor more time to process data without pausing ADC conversion.

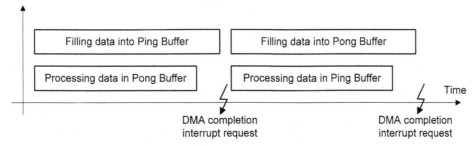

Figure 20-15. Using two buffers to overlap data transfer and data processing

While the DMA controller is filling the ping buffer with ADC data, the processor is processing the data stored in the pong buffer. Once the ping buffer is full, the processor starts to process the pong buffer while new data is being filled into the pong buffer. Therefore, data transfer and data processing are performed in parallel.

As shown in Figure 20-16, when DMA completes its data transfer, an interrupt request can be generated, and the DMA interrupt handler swaps the DMA source memory address between these buffers.

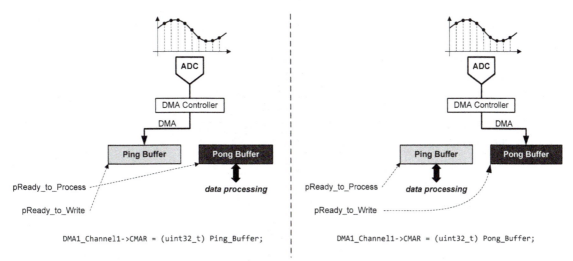

Figure 20-16. DMA controller fills these two buffers alternatively.

Example 20-10 shows the basic code that implements the ping-pong buffering.

```
uint32_t Buffer_Ping[SAMPLE_LENGTH];
uint32_t Buffer_Pong[SAMPLE_LENGTH];
uint32_t * pReady_to_Write = Buffer_Ping;
uint32_t * pReady_to_Process = Buffer_Pong;
volatile uint32_t ADC_DMA_Done = 0;

int main(void){
  ...
  while(1){
    while(ADC_DMA_Done == 0);   // Wait until DMA done
    // Processing data stored in pReady_to_Process
    ...
    ADC_DMA_Done = 0;
  }
}

void DMA1_Channel1_Initialization(void){
  ...
  DMA1_Channel1->CMAR = (uint32_t) pReady_to_Process;
  // Transfer complete interrupt enable
  DMA1_Channel1->CCR |= DMA_CCR_TCIE;
  // Enable DMA interrupt
  NVIC_EnableIRQ(DMA1_Channel1_IRQn);
  ...
}

void DMA1_Channel1_IRQHandler(void) {

  if ( (DMA1->ISR & DMA_ISR_TCIF1) == DMA_ISR_TCIF1 ) {

    DMA1->IFCR |= DMA_IFCR_CTCIF1; // Write 1 to clear TCIF flag

    if (pReady_to_Write == Buffer_Ping) {
      pReady_to_Write = Buffer_Pong;   // Fill the pong buffer
      pReady_to_Process = Buffer_Ping; // Process the ping buffer
    } else {
      pReady_to_Write = Buffer_Ping;   // Fill the ping buffer
      pReady_to_Process = Buffer_Pong; // Process the pong buffer
    }

    // DMA memory address register
    DMA1_Channel1->CMAR = (uint32_t) pReady_to_Write;
    ADC_DMA_Done = 1;
  }
  DMA1->IFCR |= (DMA_IFCR_CHTIF1 | DMA_IFCR_CGIF1 | DMA_IFCR_CTEIF1);
}
```

Example 20-10. Configuring DMA with ping-pong buffering

20.12   ADC Calibration

Calibration is a process that removes the offset error caused by process variation during manufacture. The offset error varies chip by chip.

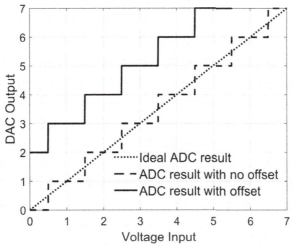

Figure 20-17. ADC output with offset error

On STM32L4, software can program ADC to calibrate itself automatically, as shown below. Calibration should be performed if the reference voltage changes more than 10% or the processor wakes up from a lower-power state.

```
void ADC_Calibration(void) {

    // Ensure ADC is off
    ADC1->CR &= ~ADC_CR_ADEN;

    // Wait until ADRDY is reset by hardware
    while((ADC1->ISR & ADC_ISR_ADRDY) == ADC_ISR_ADRDY);

    // Calibration for single ended input conversion
    // ADCALDIF: 0 = Single Ended, 1 = Differential Input
    ADC1->CR &= ~ADC_CR_ADCALDIF;

    // Each ADC provides an automatic calibration procedure which drives all
    // the calibration sequence including the power-on/off sequence of the ADC.
    // Calibration can only be initiated when the ADC is disabled (when ADEN=0).
    ADC1->CR |= ADC_CR_ADCAL; // Initiated the calibration

    // ADCAL bit stays at 1 during all the calibration sequence.
    // It is then cleared by hardware as soon the calibration completes.
    // Wait for calibration to complete
    while ((ADC1->CR & ADC_CR_ADCAL) == ADC_CR_ADCAL);
}
```

Example 20-11. ADC calibration

20.13   Exercises

1. Suppose V_{REF} = 1.5V, what is the minimum number of bits required to achieve a resolution of 1 mV?

2. Successive-approximate (SAR) ADC is widely used. Suppose the ADC has a resolution of 14 bits, and the time for sampling and hold is set as 6 clock cycles. How many clock cycles are required to complete one analog-to-digital conversion?

3. Write an assembly program that monitors an input voltage, as shown in Figure 20-11. When the voltage input is higher than Vcc/2, the LED is lit up. When the voltage is lower than Vcc/2, the LED is off. The input voltage can be controlled manually by using a potentiometer.

4. Write an assembly program that uses a potentiometer to control the brightness of an LED.

5. Write an assembly program that uses a potentiometer to control the rotation speed of a stepper motor.

6. Write an assembly program that uses a timer to trigger the ADC periodically.

7. Write an assembly program that uses the potentiometer to control the brightness of an LED.

8. Write an assembly program that shows the ADC measurement on an LCD.

9. Write an assembly program that uses the potentiometer to control the rotation speed of a stepper motor.

CHAPTER 21

Digital-to-Analog Converter (DAC)

A digital-to-analog converter (DAC) transforms a finite-precision digital number to an analog voltage. For example, music players use DAC to generate audio signals based on digital values encoded in a music file. This chapter introduces DAC architecture and programming, and presents an example application that uses DAC to synthesize music.

21.1 DAC Architecture

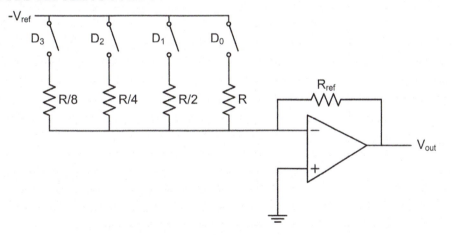

Figure 21-1. Basic architecture of a four-bit digital-to-analog converter (DAC). Note that we use the negative reference voltage $-V_{ref}$.

Figure 21-1 shows a simple implementation of a four-bit DAC. Suppose the digital value to be converted to an analog voltage has four bits in binary: $D_3 D_2\, D_1 D_0$, with D_3 being the most significant bit. D_i is either 0 or 1, for i = 0, 1, 2, and 3. If D_i is 0, the corresponding switch is open. Otherwise, the corresponding switch is closed.

Then the analog voltage output V_{out} can be calculated as follows:

$$V_{out} = V_{ref} \times \left(\frac{D_3}{R/8} + \frac{D_2}{R/4} + \frac{D_1}{R/2} + \frac{D_0}{R} \right) \times R_{ref}$$

We can rewrite the above equation as follows:

$$V_{out} = V_{ref} \times \frac{R_{ref}}{R} \times (D_3 \times 2^3 + D_2 \times 2^2 + D_1 \times 2 + D_0)$$

As we can see in the above equation, the voltage output is linearly proportional to the digital value to be converted. The output ranges between 0 and V_{ref}. For a 12-bit DAC, the conversion is performed as follows:

$$DAC_{output} = V_{ref} \times \frac{DOR}{4095}$$

DAC is often evaluated by its resolution, settling time, and glitches.

- **Resolution** is the smallest change that can occur in the analog output as the digital input varies. For an n-bit DAC, the total number of possible output levels is 2^n. If the output voltage range is between 0 and 5V, then the minimum change in the output of an 8-bit DAC is $5/2^8 = 0.0195V = 19.5mV$. For simplicity, we sometimes use the number of bits in the DAC input to represent its resolution.

- **Settling time** is the interval from an update of DAC's digital input to the instant when the DAC output becomes stable within a specified percentage (also called error band, such as 0.025% for 12-bit DAC, *i.e.*, 1 LSB). The slew rate of an amplifier output and the amount of swinging and signal overshoot can affect settling time.

- The **glitch** is the first peak transient that appears at the DAC output. Ideally, when the input changes, the DAC output should move monotonically to the new value. In practice, the output may have overshoot, undershoot, or both, due to capacitive coupling and switch timing skew. For example, some switches in Figure 21-1 operate faster than the others, resulting in a transient surge in current. The glitch is often measured by the glitch impulse area, which equals the area under the curve on a voltage-vs-time graph.

21.2 DAC on STM32L Processors

The STM32L processor has two independent DAC converters, with one channel in each converter. Both converters can be configured as a resolution of 8 bits or 12 bits. The two converters can update their output signals independently or synchronously. The synchronous mode can be useful for some applications. For example, a stereo audio player requires the DAC converter to synchronize the outputs of the left and right channels to avoid double-talk.

As shown in Figure 21-2, the DAC module includes the data holding registers (DHR), control logic, the data output register (DOR) and the DAC converter. The DAC converter needs the analog power supply (V_{DDA}) the analog ground (V_{SSA}) and the voltage reference (V_{REF}). The analog output range is from 0V to V_{REF}.

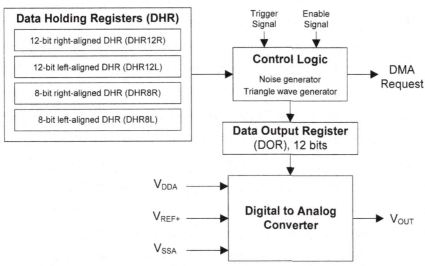

Figure 21-2. Digital to Analog Converter (DAC)

The control logic can add white noise and triangle wave to the output voltage V_{OUT}. White noise is a serially uncorrelated random disturbance with zero mean and constant and finite variance. White noise has many applications. It is often used in the production of electronic music to emulate instruments such as cymbals that have much noise in their frequency band. The triangle wave can be employed for device testing and digital music.

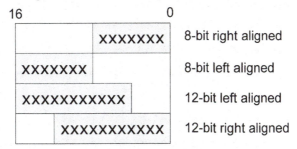

Figure 21-3 Data registers in single DAC channel mode

Each DAC channel has four data registers, listed below:

- 12-bit right-aligned data holding register (DAC_DHR12Rx)
- 12-bit left-aligned data holding register (DAC_DHR12Lx)

- 8-bit right-aligned data holding register (DAC_DHR8Rx)
- 8-bit left-aligned data holding register (DAC_DHR8Lx)

where x = 1 or 2. The data could be left- or right- aligned, as shown in Figure 21-3. When DAC uses dual channels, two values to be converted need to be stored in a shared dual-channel register. These registers include DAC_DHR8RD for 8-bit right alignment, DAC_DHR12LD for 12-bit left alignment, and DAC_DHR12RD for 12-bit right alignment.

21.3 Conversion Trigger

Software triggers, external timers, and internal timers can trigger DAC conversions. When a conversion is triggered, the data stored in one of the data holding registers (DAC_DHR12Rx, DAC_DHR12Lx, DAC_DHR8Rx, and DAC_DHR8Lx) is transferred to the DAC data output register (DAC_DORx, x = 1 or 2) to generate a corresponding analog output.

- When an internal timer is chosen as the trigger, the conversion starts after detecting a rising edge of the selected timer trigger output (TIMx_TRGO).

- When software is used as the trigger, the conversion starts after the trigger bit in the DAC_SWTRIGR register is set by software. The trigger bit is reset automatically by the hardware once the data content of DAC_DHR has been loaded into DAC_DOR.

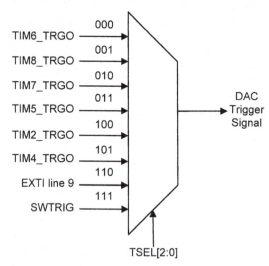

Figure 21-4. TSEL bits in the control register DAC_CR to select DAC trigger signal

The TSEL[2:0] bits in the control register DAC_CR selects the DAC trigger. When both DAC converters are triggered by the same source (*i.e.*, TSEL1 and TSEL2 choose the same trigger source), these two channels are synchronized, performing conversions at the same time.

21.4 Buffered Output

When the DAC output is used to drive some external load directly, such as earphones, the voltage output may be lower than the desired value due to loading effects, as shown in Figure 21-5. For example, when DOR (DAC data output register) is 0xFFF, the desired output should be 3V. The actual output voltage V_{OUT} is only 1.5V if the external load has exactly the same impedance as the DAC, *i.e.*, $R_{DAC} = R_{LOAD}$.

$$V_{OUT} = \frac{R_{LOAD}}{R_{DAC} + R_{LOAD}} \times V_{OUT}^{desired}$$

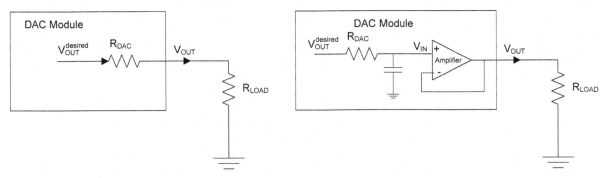

Figure 21-5. Load effects of DAC Module   **Figure 21-6. Buffered output to remove load effects.**

We can use an internal output buffer to avoid the load impedance problem. As shown in Figure 21-6, the voltage output buffer is implemented by using an amplifier.

- The amplifier has a high input impedance (close to infinity) so that the impact of R_{DAC} is diminished.
- The amplifier also has a low output impedance (close to zero) so that the effect of R_{LOAD} is removed.

Thus, V_{OUT} is kept close to the voltage desired.

$$V_{IN} = \frac{R_{IN,Amplifier}}{R_{DAC} + R_{IN,Amplifier}} \times V_{OUT}^{desired} \approx \frac{\infty}{R_{DAC} + \infty} \times V_{OUT}^{desired} = V_{OUT}^{desired}$$

$$V_{OUT} = \frac{R_{LOAD}}{R_{LOAD} + R_{OUT,Amplifier}} \times V_{IN} \approx \frac{R_{LOAD}}{R_{LOAD} + 0} \times V_{IN} = V_{IN} \approx V_{OUT}^{desired}$$

The output buffer can be enabled or disabled by the DAC_CR_BOFF bit in the control register DAC_CR.

21.5 Generating a Sinusoidal Wave via Table Lookup

Many microcontrollers do not have a floating-point unit (FPU) and rely on software that uses integer operations to implement a floating-point arithmetic function. While the software approach reduces the silicon cost, its main disadvantage is slow performance. While FPU takes two to ten clock cycles to complete a typical floating-point operation, a software library requires 50-100 or even more cycles.

If there is no FPU available on the processor, a popular software approach to improving the floating-point performance is to use a lookup table. The lookup table is an array that stores pre-calculated values of a floating-point operation under different inputs. To find the result of a given input, instead of performing expensive computations, we simply look up the table and find the proximate result. This method takes more memory and reduces the computation precision, but it improves the computation speed.

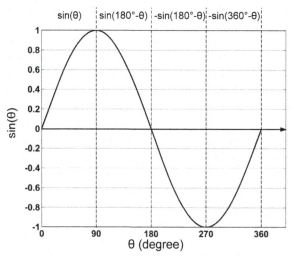

Figure 21-7. Converting θ into the range [0°, 90°]

We will use a lookup table to find the value of sin(x). Typically, we can use the following Taylor series to compute the value of sin(x).

$$\sin(x) = \sum_{n=0}^{\infty} \frac{(-1)^n}{(2n+1)!} x^{2n+1} \approx x - \frac{x^3}{6} + \frac{x^5}{120} - \frac{x^7}{5040}$$

Fortunately, the math C library has a function **sin** that can be directly used. The following program shows how to build a table if the result is limited to 12 bits (The data registers of DAC is limited to 12 bits). The program also offsets the output by 2048, because the DAC module cannot output a negative value.

$$TableValue\ (x) = \left(1 + \sin\left(\frac{x}{180}\pi\right)\right) \times 2^{11}$$

where the input x is in degrees. Because the value of the sine function is between [-1, 1], the table values are between [0, 4096]. When the sine function returns zero, the corresponding value in the table is 2048.

Additionally, 4096 has 13 bits in binary, and it is impossible to use 12 bits to represent 4096. Therefore, we use 4095 (*i.e.,* 0xFFF) to approximate 4096 in the table.

```c
#include <stdio.h>
#include <string.h>
#include <math.h>

int main(void){
   int i;
   signed int sine_table[91];
   float sf;

   // for 12-bit ADC, [0, 2047(0xFFF)];
   for (i = 0; i <= 90; i++){
      sf = sin(M_PI * i /180);
      sine_table[i] = (1 + sf) * 2048;
      if(sine_table[i] == 0x1000)
         sine_table[i] = 0xFFF; // sin(90) is out of range
   }
   printf("sine_table");
   for (i = 0; i < 90; i += 5){
      printf("\tDCD\t");
      printf("0x%03x,0x%03x,0x%03x,0x%03x,0x%03x\n", sine_table[i],
         sine_table[i+1], sine_table[i+2], sine_table[i+3], sine_table[i+4]);
   }
   printf("\tDCD\t0x%03x\n", sine_table[90]);
   return 0;
}
```

Example 21-1. C program to generate sine table

The following program shows how to use the pre-calculated table to find the value of sin(x), where x is in degrees. The DAC output voltage is between 0 and 3 V. It cannot output a negative voltage. The value found in the following program is used to set up the data register of the DAC module. When the data register is 0, the DAC analog output voltage is 0V. When the data register is 0xFFF, the DAC output voltage is 3V.

For the sine wave, we have the following setting:

- When sin(x) is -1, the DAC data register is 0;
- When sin(x) is 0, the DAC data register is 2048;

- When sin(x) is 1, the DAC data register is 4095.

```
unsigned int lookup_sine(int x){
    // x is the input in degrees
    x = mod(x, 360); // x might be larger than 360
    if (x < 90)  return sine_table[x];
    if (x < 180) return sine_table[180-x];
    if (x < 270) return 4096 - sine_table[x-180];
    return 4096 - sine_table[360-x];
}
```

Example 21-2. C program that uses the table lookup method to calculate the sine value

The following assembly program shows how to use the table lookup method to calculate the sine value in assembly. Note the assembly program follows the standard of embedded application binary interface (EABI), which takes the input argument in degrees in register r0 and returns the table lookup results in register r0 too. Note it is not required to preserve register r1.

```
; Input:
;      r0: x input argument in degrees
; Return:
;      r0: value of (1 + sin(x))*2^11
; Register used:
;      r1 = sine input argument (in degrees)
;      r4 = starting address of sine table
;      r6 = copy of the sine input argument (in degrees)

sine    PROC
        EXPORT sine
        PUSH   {r4,r6,lr}        ; preserve used registers in stack
        MOV    r6, r0            ; make a copy of x (in degrees)
        MOV    r1, r0            ; make a copy of x (in degrees)
        LDR    r4, =sine_table   ; load address of sine table
        CMP    r1, #90           ; determine quadrant
        BLS    retvalue          ; first quadrant (0 < x ≤ 90)
        CMP    r1, #180
        RSBLS  r1, r1, #180      ; second quadrant (90 < x ≤ 180)
        BLS    retvalue
        CMP    r1, #270
        SUBLE  r1, r1, #180      ; third quadrant (180 < x ≤ 270)
        BLS    retvalue
        RSB    r1, r1, #360      ; fourth quadrant (270 < x ≤ 360)
retvalue
        LDR    r0, [r4, r1, LSL #2]  ; get sin value from table
                                     ; memory address = sine_table + r1 * 4
        CMP    r6, #180          ; if 180 < x < 360
        RSBGT  r0, r0, #4096     ; 4096 - 2048*abs(sin(x))
        pop    {r4,r6,pc}        ; recovery environment
        ENDP
```

```
         ALIGN
sine_table    ; DAC has 12 bits. DCD = allocate words (4 bytes)
         DCD    0x800,0x823,0x847,0x86b,0x88e,0x8b2,0x8d6,0x8f9,0x91d,0x940
         DCD    0x963,0x986,0x9a9,0x9cc,0x9ef,0xa12,0xa34,0xa56,0xa78,0xa9a
         DCD    0xabc,0xadd,0xaff,0xb20,0xb40,0xb61,0xb81,0xba1,0xbc1,0xbe0
         DCD    0xc00,0xc1e,0xc3d,0xc5b,0xc79,0xc96,0xcb3,0xcd0,0xcec,0xd08
         DCD    0xd24,0xd3f,0xd5a,0xd74,0xd8e,0xda8,0xdc1,0xdd9,0xdf1,0xe09
         DCD    0xe20,0xe37,0xe4d,0xe63,0xe78,0xe8d,0xea1,0xeb5,0xec8,0xedb
         DCD    0xeed,0xeff,0xf10,0xf20,0xf30,0xf40,0xf4e,0xf5d,0xf6a,0xf77
         DCD    0xf84,0xf90,0xf9b,0xfa6,0xfb0,0xfba,0xfc3,0xfcb,0xfd3,0xfda
         DCD    0xfe0,0xfe6,0xfec,0xff0,0xff4,0xff8,0xffb,0xffd,0xffe,0xfff
         DCD    0xfff
         ; sin(90) = 1. However, 1 cannot be represented in Q12 notation
         ; thus we set sin(90) = 0xFFF
         END
```

Example 21-3. Generate sine wave output by using table lookup

21.6 DAC with Software Trigger

The DAC module on STM32L has two output channels: DAC1_OUT1 (Pin PA 4) and DAC1_OUT2 (Pin PA 5). Pin PA 4 is not directly accessible on STM32L4 Discovery Kit. If two DAC channels are needed, software can program the on-chip operational amplifier (OPAMP) and route DAC1_OUT1 to pin PA 3 (OPAMP1_VOUT).

```c
// DAC channel 2:   DAC_OUT2 = PA 5
void DAC_Channel2_Init(void){

  // Enable DAC Clock
  RCC->APB1ENR1 |= RCC_APB1ENR1_DAC1EN;

  // Disable DAC
  DAC->CR &= ~( DAC_CR_EN1 | DAC_CR_EN2 );

  // DAC mode control register (DAC_MCR)
  //--------------------------------------------------------------------------
  // DAC Channel 2 in normal Mode
  // 000: connected to external pin with buffer enabled
  // 001: connected to external pin and chip peripherals with buffer enabled
  // 010: connected to external pin with buffer disabled
  // 011: connected to on chip peripherals with Buffer disabled
  //--------------------------------------------------------------------------
  // DAC Channel 2 in sample & hold mode
  // 100: connected to external pin with buffer enabled
  // 101: connected to external pin and chip peripherals with buffer enabled
  // 110: connected to external pin and chip peripherals with buffer disabled
  // 111: connected to on chip peripherals with Buffer disabled
  //--------------------------------------------------------------------------
```

```
    DAC->MCR &= ~(7U<<16);    // mode = 000

    // Enable trigger for DAC channel 2
    DAC->CR |= DAC_CR_TEN2;

    // Select software trigger
    DAC->CR |= DAC_CR_TSEL2;

    // Enable DAC Channel 2
    DAC->CR |= DAC_CR_EN2;

    // Enable the clock of GPIO port A
    RCC->AHB2ENR |= RCC_AHB2ENR_GPIOAEN;

    // Set I/O mode as analog
    GPIOA->MODER |= 3U<<(2*5);      // Set the mode as analog (11)
}
```

Example 21-4. Configure DAC channel 2 with software trigger

The following program generates a sawtooth waveform on DAC channel 2 (pin PA 5).

```
// DAC channel 2:  DAC_OUT2 = PA 5
int main(void){

    unsigned int i, output = 0;

    DAC_Channel2_Init();

    while (1) {

        // Wait until DAC is not busy
        // Hardware sets BWST2 flag when software writes to DHR12R2.
        // Hardware clears BWST2 flag after hardware copies DHR12R2 to DOR.
        while ((DAC->SR & DAC_SR_BWST2) != 0);

        // Set DAC output
        DAC->DHR12R2 = output;          // Channel 2 12-bit right-aligned dat

        // Start software trigger.
        // Hardware clears SWTRIG2 once DHR12R2 has been copied to DOR
        DAC->SWTRIGR |= DAC_SWTRIGR_SWTRIG2;

        for(i = 0; i <= 10; i++);       // Short software delay

        output = (output + 1) & 0xFFF; // Increment output voltage
    }
}
```

Example 21-5. Using C program to generate a sawtooth analog output

21.7 Using Timer as a Trigger to DAC

In Example 20-2 given the previous chapter, timer 4 is configured to generate trigger output (TRGO). This trigger output can also be used to trigger DAC.

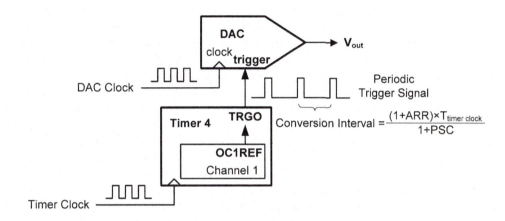

Figure 21-8. Using TIM4_TRGO to trigger DAC

The following C code selects TIM4_TRGO as DAC trigger.

```
...
// DAC Trigger selection
// 000: Timer 6 TRGO event
// 001: Timer 8 TRGO event
// 010: Timer 7 TRGO event
// 011: Timer 5 TRGO event
// 100: Timer 2 TRGO event
// 101: Timer 4 TRGO event
// 110: External Line9
// 111: Software trigger

// Clear trigger selection bits for channel 2
DAC->CR &= ~DAC_CR_TSEL2;

// Select TIM4_TRGO as the trigger of DAC channel 2 (101)
DAC->CR |= ( DAC_CR_TSEL2_0 | DAC_CR_TSEL2_2);
...
```

Example 21-6. Selecting TIM4_TRGO as the trigger signal to DAC channel 2

In the following, we will explain how to use DAC to play music. In digital audio, a common sampling frequency is 44,100 Hz (*i.e.*, 44.1 kHz). That means an analog audio signal is recorded as 44,100 digital values per second. Human ears can hear up to 20,000 Hz. The Nyquist–Shannon sampling theorem articulates that the sampling frequency must be at least twice the maximum frequency of signals audible to human ears. Most compact discs (CD) are recorded with this rate.

If DAC is used for music applications, timer 4 needs to generate an interrupt with a frequency of 44.1 kHz. If the 16MHz HSI is used, the prescaler (PSC) and the auto-reload register must meet the following requirement.

$$\frac{f_{HSI}}{(1 + PSC)(1 + ARR)} = f_{sampling} = 44.1 \, kHz$$

A large PSC is recommended to slow down the counter clock frequency. This reduces the energy consumption of the timer hardware.

For example, if we select PSC = 18, and ARR = 18, then DAC is performed at a rate of 44.3 kHz, which is only 0.5% off from 44.1 kHz.

$$\frac{f_{HSI}}{(1 + PSC)(1 + ARR)} = \frac{16MHz}{(1 + 18)(1 + 18)} = 44.3kHz$$

The timer interrupt handler increments the angle variable by a constant step size. Once the DAC conversion is fixed to 44.1 kHz, the frequency of the sine wave generated is determined by the step size of the angel variable during each time interrupt. To complete one cycle of the sinusoidal waveform, the input of the sine function should increase from 0° to 360°. The following illustrates how to calculate the step size.

If the frequency of a musical tone is f, the step size of the angular variable in the *TIM4_IRQHandler* can be calculated as follows:

$$Step \, Size = \frac{360°}{Number \, of \, DAC \, outputs \, in \, one \, sinusoidal \, cycle}$$

$$= 360° \div \frac{Period \, of \, Sine \, Wave}{Time \, Interval \, of \, DAC \, Outputs}$$

$$= 360° \div \left(\frac{1}{f} \div \frac{1}{44.3KHz}\right)$$

$$= 360° \div \frac{44.3KHz}{f}$$

For example, if f is 440 Hz (music tone A), we have

$$Step \, Size = 360° \div \frac{44.3KHz}{440Hz} \approx 3.576°$$

Cortex-M3 processors do not have an FPU, and they do not support floating-point instructions. Even though STM32L4 (Cortex-M4) has FPU, sometimes we still choose to use fixed-point format. Fixed-point arithmetic uses integer units of the processor core, thus saving power and resource.

In the following, we will use a fixed-point format. Example 11-7 gives a simplified C implementation. The key idea is that variable `StepSize` is multiplied by 1000. Variable `angle` is divided by 1000 when it is passed to the table lookup function.

```
int StepSize = 3576;     // Multiply by 1000
angle += StepSize;        // Increment angle
sine_value = sine_table_lookup(angle/1000);
```

Example 21-7. Using fixed-point format to represent the angle

The following is an example implementation of *TIM4_IRQHandler()*. You need to change the variable *degrees_desired* to generate the desired output sine-wave frequency.

```
void TIM4_IRQHandler() {

  if( (TIM4->SR & TIM_SR_ CC1IF) != 0 ) {

    // Data stored in the DAC_DHRx register are automatically transferred
    // to the DAC_DORx register after one APB1 clock cycle.

    // When using dual channels, the values stored in a shared register
    // DAC->DHR12RD = sin(v)<<16 | sin(v);

    // When not using dual channels, they are set separately
    // DAC->DHR12R1 = sin(v); // DAC channel-1 12-bit Right aligned data
    DAC->DHR12R2 = sin(v);     // DAC channel-2 12-bit Right aligned data

    // Adjust v appropriately for desired sine waveform frequency.
    v += degrees_desired;   // You need to calculate degrees_desired.
    if (v >= 360) v = 0;

    // Clear CC1IF flag to prevent mistakenly re-entering the interrupt.
    // CC1IF is cleared (1) by software or (2) by hardware if CCR1 is read.
    // The handler must clear CC1IF because CCR1 is not read.
    TIM4->SR &= ~TIM_SR_CC1IF;
  }

  if( (TIM4->SR & TIM_SR_ UIF) != 0 )
    TIM4->SR &= ~TIM_SR_UIF;

  return;

}
```

Example 21-8. The interrupt service handler of timer 4

21.8 Musical Synthesizing

A musical tone is a fundamental element of music. A tone is a periodic waveform, and its principal attributes include duration, pitch (frequency), loudness (amplitude), and timbre (spectrum and envelope). If a piano and a guitar play the same pitch at the same loudness with the same duration, they differ in timbre because they have different spectral content over time. An experienced listener can distinguish the instruments based on their timbres.

The sinusoidal waveform has been widely used to synthesize digital music due to its simplicity and flexibility. Instruments, such as the guitar, flute, and piano, are often mathematically modeled by sinusoids due to their fundamental physical characteristics and harmonics.

21.8.1   Musical Pitch

The pitch of a musical tone is determined by the frequency of the sinusoidal waveform. The musical note A above middle C, often noted as '$A4$' or '$A440$', has been standardized to 440 Hz. This note is often used as a reference in musical instrument tuning. The musical instrument digital interface (MIDI) standard assigns the A note as pitch 69. For a pitch p, we can calculate its frequency f as follows:

$$f = 440 \times 2^{(p-69)/12}$$

In other words, for a given frequency f, its pitch p is:

$$p = 69 + 12 \times \log_2 \left(\frac{f}{440}\right)$$

	0	1	2	3	4	5	6	7	8
C	16.352	32.703	65.406	130.813	261.626	523.251	1046.502	2093.005	4186.009
C#	17.324	34.648	69.296	138.591	277.183	554.365	1108.731	2217.461	4434.922
D	18.354	36.708	73.416	146.832	293.665	587.330	1174.659	2349.318	4698.636
D#	19.445	38.891	77.782	155.563	311.127	622.254	1244.508	2489.016	4978.032
E	20.602	41.203	82.407	164.814	329.628	659.255	1318.510	2637.020	5274.041
F	21.827	43.654	87.307	174.614	349.228	698.456	1396.913	2793.826	5587.652
F#	23.125	46.249	92.499	184.997	369.994	739.989	1479.978	2959.955	5919.911
G	24.500	48.999	97.999	195.998	391.995	783.991	1567.982	3135.963	6271.927
G#	25.957	51.913	103.826	207.652	415.305	830.609	1661.219	3322.438	6644.875
A	27.500	55.000	110.000	220.000	**440.000**	880.000	1760.000	3520.000	7040.000
A#	29.135	58.270	116.541	233.082	466.164	932.328	1864.655	3729.310	7458.620
B	30.868	61.735	123.471	246.942	493.883	987.767	1975.533	3951.066	7902.133

Table 21-1. Musical frequency (note pitch) table based on A4 = 440 Hz

Table 21-1 shows the frequency of different musical notes with consecutive pitches. When the pitch increases by 12, the frequency is doubled. In this table, each column, called an octave, has exactly 12 musical notes. The octave is numbered from 0 to 8. The note 'A4' denotes A in the fourth octave. The frequency of a musical note in the nth octave is the double of the corresponding note in the $(n\text{-}1)^{th}$ octave.

21.8.2   Musical Duration

The duration is the amount of time a musical tone takes, which determines the number of beats per minute (BPM) the song should be played. For example, a BPM of 60 provides a beat each second, and a BPM of 120 is twice as rapid. Typical BPM is between 40 and 200. A slow tempo (68-80 BPM) makes listeners relaxed, while a faster tempo (BMP 120-140) can energize listeners. In most songs, a standard 4-4 time signature is used. What this means is that there are four notes per measure, and a quarter note gets the beat.

Computer software can easily identify the time instants of each musical beat, and use it to synchronize other devices, such as LED light, drum machine, and audio effects to the audio source. The BPM is also an important criterion to identify the type of music a specific listener likes most.

21.8.3   Amplitude Modulation of Tones

The amplitude of a tone determines its loudness or volume. Most musical instruments do not generate tones with constant amplitude. They do not build up its volume to its maximum amplitude instantly nor fall to zero amplitude suddenly.

The attack, decay, sustain, and release (ADSR) envelope model has been widely used to modulate the amplitude of a tone over time to emulate how a tone is played on a musical instrument. It divides a tone into four different phases, as shown in Figure 21-10.

- *Attack*. The attack phase usually is fast, and a tone quickly reaches its peak intensity when a key is pressed on the real instrument. For most mechanical instruments, the duration of this phase is short.

- *Decay*. After reaching peak amplitude, the tone starts to fade gradually from the peak.

- *Sustain*. After the decay phase, the amplitude is maintained nearly at a constant level while a key is held, or a sustain pedal is pressed.

- *Release*. After the music key or pedal is released, the amplitude decreases from the sustained level to zero. While the duration of the release phase is typically short, it can last relatively long, such as eight seconds for a foghorn, and two seconds for a bell.

By changing the amplitude and duration of each phase, computers often use ADSR to emulate different musical instruments. For example, a guitar is the loudest immediately after a string is plucked, and it fades quickly after that. In contrast, when a key of a pipe organ is pressed, its corresponding tone has an almost constant amplitude.

The digital signal of a sinusoidal waveform with a frequency f, denoted as $S(n)$, can be generated based on the following formula:

$$S(n) = \sin\left(2\pi \frac{n \times f}{f_s}\right)$$

where f_s is the sampling frequency to this sinusoidal wave, and $n = 0,1,2,\cdots,f_s - 1$.

Thus, the modulated sinusoid signal $\tilde{S}(n)$ is the product of the generated sample value $S(n)$ and the ADSR modulated amplitude $ADSR(n)$.

$$\tilde{S}(n) = ADSR(n) \times S(n)$$

The ADSR modulated amplitude $ADSR(n)$ can be generated by using a simple digital filter,

$$ADSR(n) = g \times \overrightarrow{ADSR} + (1 - g) \times ADSR(n - 1)$$

where $\overrightarrow{ADSR}$ is the target modulated amplitude value, and g is the gain parameter. The filter gradually increases or decreases to the target value at a pace determined by the gain parameters.

ADSR has four different phases, and there are three parameters associated with each phase: the duration, the target amplitude value, and the gain parameter. For a given sampling frequency f_s, the duration of each phase is expressed by the number of samples in this phase. The total number of samples in all four phases should equal the total number of samples of the musical tone.

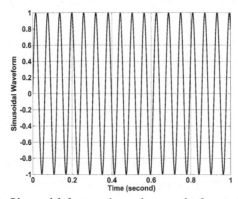

Figure 21-9. Sinusoidal waveform for musical note C0 (16.325Hz)

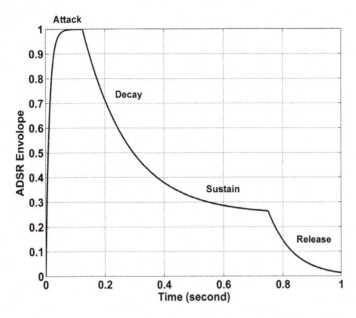

Figure 21-10. Attack, decay, sustain, and release (ADSR) envelope signal

Let us assume BPM is 60. Accordingly, each note is played for a duration of one second. Figure 21-9 shows the periodical waveform of the musical note C0, which has a frequency of 16.325Hz. Figure 21-9 shows the amplitude-modulating signal based on the ADSR envelope. Figure 20-12 presents the final modulated sinusoidal wave signal used to drive a speaker or headphones.

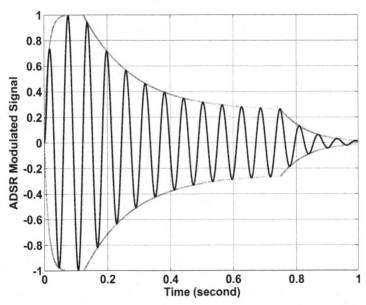

Figure 21-11. Modulated sinusoidal waveform for musical note C0 (16.325Hz)

As discussed earlier, a common sampling frequency in digital audio is 44,100Hz (*i.e.*, 44.1 kHz). If the music data is not compressed, the date rate of CD audio is as follows:

2 channels × 2 bytes/sample × 441,000 samples/channel/second = 176,400 bytes/second

A CD with 74 minutes of music has a total of 777 MB music data if it is uncompressed, as calculated below:

176,400 bytes/second × 60 seconds/minute × 74 minutes = 777 MB

Audio data are often stored in a compressed format to save memory or storage space.

The DAC voltage output is always positive on STM32L processors. A large capacitor is used to filter out the DC component. Additionally, a resistor is added to reduce the current to protect your earphone, as shown in Figure 21-12.

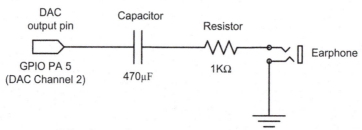

Figure 21-12. Filtering DC component of DAC output via a capacitor

We can use DAC to create a digital musical synthesis system. Suppose the frequency and time duration of music notes are predefined in the data area, as shown below in assembly.

```
        AREA myMusic, DATA
        ALIGN

        ; Size, frequency, time duration of "Twinkle Twinkle Little Star"
TT_S    DCD  42  ; Number of notes
TT_F    DCD 262, 262, 392, 392, 440, 440, 392  ; Twinkle twinkle little star
        DCD 349, 349, 330, 330, 294, 294, 262  ; How I wonder what you are
        DCD 392, 392, 349, 349, 330, 330, 294  ; Up above the world so high
        DCD 392, 392, 349, 349, 330, 330, 294  ; Like a diamond in the sky
        DCD 262, 262, 392, 392, 440, 440, 392  ; Twinkle twinkle little star
        DCD 349, 349, 330, 330, 294, 294, 262  ; How I wonder what you are!

        ; Set beats per minute (BMP) as 120
TT_T    DCD 1, 1, 1, 1, 1, 1, 2                 ; Twinkle twinkle little star
        DCD 1, 1, 1, 1, 1, 1, 2                 ; How I wonder what you are
        DCD 1, 1, 1, 1, 1, 1, 2                 ; Up above the world so high
```

```
        DCD 1, 1, 1, 1, 1, 1, 2              ; Like a diamond in the sky
        DCD 1, 1, 1, 1, 1, 1, 2              ; Twinkle twinkle little star
        DCD 1, 1, 1, 1, 1, 1, 2              ; How I wonder what you are!

        ; Size, frequency, time duration of "Happy Birthday"
HB_S    DCD  25   ; Number of notes
HB_F    DCD 392, 392, 440, 392, 523, 494       ; Happy Birthday to You
        DCD 392, 392, 440, 392, 523, 494       ; Happy Birthday to You
        DCD 392, 392, 784, 659, 523, 494, 440  ; Happy Birthday to Dear (name)
        DCD 349, 349, 330, 262, 294, 262       ; Happy Birthday to You

        ; Set beats per minute (BMP) as 240
HB_T    DCD 1, 1, 2, 2, 2, 4                 ; Happy Birthday to You
        DCD 1, 1, 2, 2, 2, 4                 ; Happy Birthday to You
        DCD 1, 1, 2, 2, 2, 2, 6             ; Happy Birthday to Dear (name)
        DCD 2, 2, 2, 2, 2, 4                 ; Happy Birthday to You
        END
```

Example 21-9. Note frequency and time duration of two simple songs

The following shows the key functions of implementing a music player in C. It uses a delay function to play the next note. The delay function can be implemented based on the SysTick timer. The interrupt handler calculates the step size based on the frequency.

```c
volatile uint32_t frequency, angle;

void play_Twinkle (void) {
  int i, duration;

  for (i = 0; i < TT_S; i++) {
    frequency = TT_F(i);
    duration  = TT_T(i);
    angle = 0;     // Restart the sine wave
    delay(duration);
  }
}

// Assume timer 4 generates 44300 interrupts per second
void TIM4_IRQHandler() {
  ...
  stepSize = 360 * 44300 * 1000 / frequency; // fixed-point format
  angle = (angle + stepSize) % 360000;
  DAC->DHR12R2 = sin(angle/1000);
  ...
}
```

Example 21-10. Basic implementation of playing music

21.9 Exercises

1. Assume an audio is recorded at a rate of 44,100 Hz, and the DAC is driven by the timer trigger output (TGRO). What is the time interval between two consecutive triggers? If the timer is driven by the HSI clock (16 MHz), how do you set the timer prescaler register (PSC) and the auto-reload register (ARR)? Show your calculations.

2. Assume we are required to generate a sinusoidal waveform of 293.665 Hz (music tone D), and the DAC converter is triggered by TIM4 TRGO with a frequency of 44,100Hz.

   a. How many DAC outputs should we produce during one cycle of the sinusoidal waveform?

   b. The angle of the sine function should increase from 0° to 360° to complete one cycle of the sinusoidal waveform. How many degrees should the angle variable be increased in timer interrupt handler each time?

   c. The processor only supports integer arithmetic. If the angle degree to be increased is not an integer, what can you do to get around this issue?

3. Write an assembly program that uses a table-lookup method to generate a sinusoidal wave. The built-in *logic analyzer* in MDK-Keil can only show the value stored in the data memory. The logic analyzer cannot analyze the value stored in a register. To solve this problem, we create a variable named "output" in the data area. In your main program, within the loop over different x values, make sure to store the lookup value into the memory address "output" so that the logic analyzer can display the value.

   ```
                AREA myData, DATA
                ALIGN
   output       DCD      0x000
   ```

   In the logic analyzer, you can click "Setup" and add a variable "(signed int) output" to observe. Make sure to adjust the data display range to show the curve. The logic analyzer can only monitor global variables. Thus, you need to add "EXPORT output" after the "EXPORT __main" to make the output as a global variable.

4. Write an assembly program that generates a sinusoidal waveform with a frequency of 440 Hz and use an oscilloscope to verify the frequency.

5. Write an assembly program to play the song of "Twinkle Twinkle Little Star."

CHAPTER 22

Serial Communication Protocols

This chapter introduces four important serial communication protocols, including universal asynchronous receiver and transmitter (UART), inter-integrated circuit (I²C), serial peripheral interface (SPI), universal serial bus (USB). Serial communication transfers a single bit each time and uses either a single wire for each communication direction or a shared wire for both directions. It differs from parallel communications, which use multiple communication wires and can transfer several bits at the same time. Compared with parallel communications, serial communications provide lower speed, but allow longer cable length and are less expensive.

22.1 Universal Asynchronous Receiver and Transmitter

One of the most common usages of universal asynchronous receiver and transmitter (UART) is for exchanging data between a microprocessor and a PC serial port to debug software or monitor systems. UART also has been widely used for various peripherals, such as printers, terminals, and modems. The keyword "universal" means the serial interface is programmable. UART is often configured to communicate synchronously, which is then called USART.

The asynchronous transmission allows bits to be transmitted in a serial fashion without requiring the sender to provide a clock signal to the receiver. However, both senders and receivers must agree on the data transmission rate before the communication starts. The sender and the receiver should use the same baud rate to set up the clock agreement. In digital systems, the baud rate is the bit rate, *i.e.,* the number of bits transmitted per second. Usually, the UART interface can tolerate a clock shift up to 10% during the transmission. In some analog systems, such as modems, the baud rate is larger than the corresponding bit rate when there are more than two voltage levels and a voltage signal transmitted can represent multiple bits.

Full-duplex   **Single-wire half-duplex**

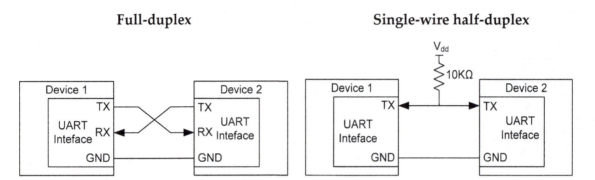

Figure 22-1. Connection between two UART devices in asynchronous mode

The transmission involves two communication lines (TX and RX), as shown in Figure 22-1.

- With full-duplex communication, data is always transmitted out bit by bit from the TX line and is received by the other device on its RX line. The receiver reassembles bits received into bytes.
- With the single-wire half-duplex communication, TX and RX are internally connected, and only one wire is used. TX is used for both sending and receiving data. In this mode, TX pins are pulled up externally because these two pins must be configured as open-drain.

For synchronous serial communication, the clock (CLK) pin of the devices must be connected. Also, the CTS (clear to send) line must connect with the RTS (request to send) line of the other device.

22.1.1   Communication Frame

UART divides data to be transmitted into frames. A frame is the smallest unit of communication. In a frame, the data length (7, 8, or 9 bits), the parity bit (even, odd, or no parity), the number of stop bits (0.5, 1, 1.5, or 2 bits), and the data order (MSB or LSB first) are configurable. Figure 22-2 shows one commonly used data frame: 8-P-1 (8 data bits, parity, 1 stop bit).

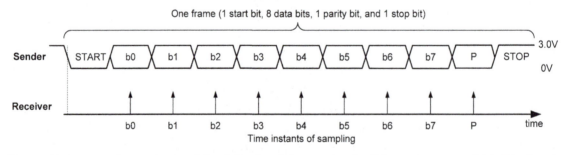

Figure 22-2. 8-P-1 frame (a start bit, eight data bits, one parity bit, and one stop bit). The least significant (LSB) of the data is sent out first in this example.

Each frame begins with a start bit, represented by a low-level voltage. After the start bit, the individual bits of each frame are shifted out of one UART interface and into another. Software can configure the data transmission order. Either the least significant bit (LSB) or the most significant bit (MSB) can be sent first. For example, suppose the LSB is sent first. When UART sends 0xE1, the bit stream 10001111 (read from left to right) is seen on the transmission line. The number of bits in the data can be programmed to be 7, 8 or 9.

When the sender sends a frame, the sender can optionally calculate the parity of this frame and send the parity bit to the receiver for error checking. The optional parity bit helps improve the data integrity. The parity bit uses a high-level voltage to represent a logic 0 and a low-level voltage to represent a logic 1. Software can configure logic 1 on the parity bit to represent either an odd or even number of ones in the transmitted data.

- *Even parity.* The combination of data bits and the parity bit contains an even number of 1s.
- *Odd parity.* The total number of 1s in the data bits and the parity bit is an odd number.

For example, if the data bits are 00010001 in binary, the parity bit will be 1 if odd parity is used, and 0 if even parity is used.

Each frame ends with a stop bit, represented by a high voltage. If no further data is transmitted, the voltage of the transmission line remains high. If the receiver does not obtain the stop bit, the current frame is considered corrupted and discarded. Additionally, the number of stop bit in each frame is usually one by default. However, it can be programmed to have 0.5, 1, 1.5, or 2 stop bits.

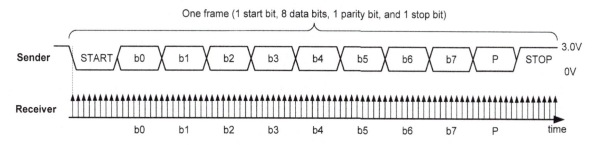

Figure 22-3. Receiver oversamples each bit 8 times

As the transmitter and receiver clocks are independent of each other, oversampling is an effective approach to mitigate the effects of clock deviation and avoid corruption by high-frequency noise. The most commonly used sampling rate is 8 or 16 times the baud rate (introduced in the next section). The receiver samples each bit 8 or 16 times and uses these values to estimate the middle of each bit pulse, resulting in a more reliable and robust transmission link.

22.1.2   Baud Rate

Historically the baud rate was used in telecommunications to represent the number of pulses or transitions physically transferred per second.

> **Baud Rate ≠ Bit Rate**

- By using phase shift and other technologies, a pulse on phone lines can represent multiple binary bits, resulting in a bit rate larger than the baud rate.
- In digital communication systems, because each pulse represents a single bit, the baud rate is the number of bits physically transferred per second, including the actual data content and the protocol overhead, leading to a bit rate lower than the baud rate.

For example, if the baud rate is 9600, and an 8-N-1 frame consists of a start bit, 8 data bits, a stop bit, and no parity bit, then the transmission rate of actual data is not 9600 bits per second/8 = 1200 bytes per second. Instead, it is 9600/(1 + 8 + 1) = 960 bytes per second. The start and stop bits are the protocol overhead.

On STM32L4, the baud rate is calculated as follows:

$$Baud\ Rate = \frac{(1 + OVER8) \times f_{PCLK}}{USARTDIV}$$

where f_{PCLK} is the clock frequency of the processor. The divider $USARTDIV$ is stored in the Baud Rate Register (BRR). The value of OVER8 is defined as follows.

$$OVER8 = \begin{cases} 0, & Signal\ is\ oversampled\ by\ 16 \\ 1, & Signal\ is\ oversampled\ by\ 8 \end{cases}$$

Also, the divider $USARTDIV$ can be calculated from BRR.

$$USARTDIV = \begin{cases} BRR, & Signal\ is\ oversampled\ by\ 16 \\ BRR[15:4] \times 16 + BRR[2:0] \times 2, & Signal\ is\ oversampled\ by\ 8 \end{cases}$$

Example 1: Oversampling by 16, processor core 80 MHz, baud rate = 9600. Find BRR.

$$OVER8 = 0$$

$$USARTDIV = \frac{(1 + OVER8) \times f_{PCLK}}{Baud\ Rate} = \frac{80000000}{9600} = 8333.33 \approx 8333$$

$$BRR = USARTDIV = 8333 = 0x208D$$

Example 2: Oversampling by 8, processor core 80 MHz, baud rate = 9600. Find *BRR*.

$$OVER8 = 1$$

$$USARTDIV = \frac{(1 + OVER8) \times f_{PCLK}}{Baud\ Rate} = \frac{2 \times 80000000}{9600} = 16666.67 \approx 16667$$

The hex equivalent of 1667 is `0x411B`.

$$BRR[3:0] = USARTDIV[3:0] \gg 1 = 0xB \gg 1 = 0x5$$

$$BRR[15:4] = USARTDIV[15:4] = 0x411$$

$$BRR = BRR[15:4]:BRR[3:0] = 0x4115$$

22.1.3   UART Standards

Voltage signals for UART are defined in different standards, such as RS-232, RS-422, and RS-485. The prefix RS stands for "recommended standard." Table 22-1 compares these three standards. While the voltage of the TX and RX line in RS-422 and RS-485 is differential, with two separate wires for each line, RS-232 uses a single-ended voltage with a shared ground.

Figure 22-4 compares *single-ended* and *differential signaling*. Besides the shared ground, single-ended signaling uses just one wire to transmit signals. Differential signaling uses two twisted wires with equal but opposite signals to transmit digital data. Electrical noise can be inducted into the signal wires or can be generated by the voltage difference between two ground references. Noise is coupled into both wires equally. Therefore, the noise can be canceled out at the receiver. Compared with single-ended signaling, differential signaling can transmit a higher frequency signal over a greater distance.

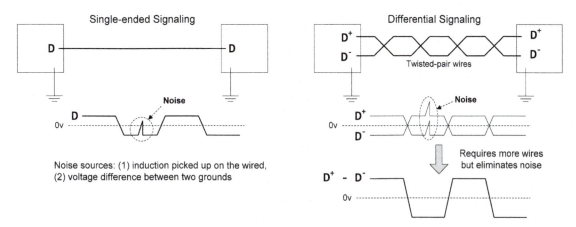

Figure 22-4. Comparison of single-ended and differential signaling

In RS-232, a voltage signal between +5V and +15V represents a logic one being transmitted, whereas a signal between -5V and -15V represents a logic zero. The receiver must interpret a voltage with +3V and +25V as a logic one, and a voltage with -3V to -25V as a logic zero. Any voltage signals between -3V and + 3V are invalid data. When the line is idle, the line must be driven to logic zero.

	RS-232	RS-422	RS-485
Voltage signal	Single-ended (logic 1: +5 to +15V, logic 0: -5 to -15 V)	Differential (-6V to +6V)	Differential (-7V to +12V)
Max distance	50 feet	4000 feet	4000 feet
Max speed	20 Kbit/s	10 Mbit/s	10 Mbit/s
Number of devices	1 master, 1 receiver	1 master, 10 receivers	32 masters, 32 receivers
Mode	Full duplex	Full duplex, half duplex	Full duplex, half duplex

Table 22-1. Comparing popular UART interfaces

Most modern computers only provide USB ports, not UART ports. Some old computers have RS-232 serial ports. However, we cannot directly connect an STM32 processor to the RS-232 port on a computer due to the voltage incompatibility. The STM32 processors can only tolerate voltage signals under 5V. Additionally, STM32 uses 0V to represent logic zero and 3V to represent logic one.

The FT232R chip converts a UART port to a standard USB interface, as shown below.

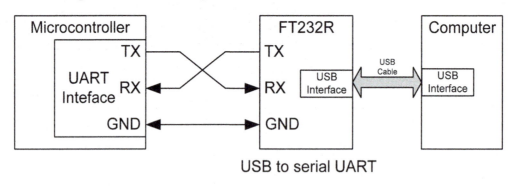

USB to serial UART

Figure 22-5. Serial communication via a USB-to-UART converter

The following diagram displays the voltage signal of the UART port when transmitting two data bytes, 0x32, and 0x3C. Each data frame includes one start bit, 8-bit data, and one stop bit. No parity bit is used in this example. After the start bit, the least significant bit of the data is transmitted first. For example, the binary value of `0x32` is `0b00110010`, and the bit sequence seen on the transmission (TX) line is `01001100`. The baud rate is set to 9,600, and thus each bit takes approximately 0.104ms. When the TX line is idle, the voltage on it is 3V. The start bit has 0V while the stop bit has 3V.

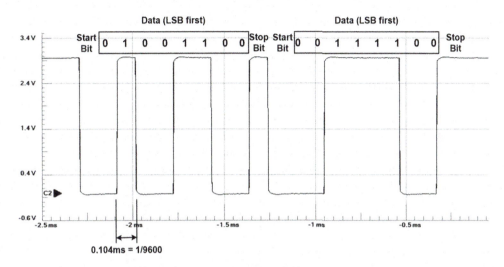

Figure 22-6. Voltage signal when transmitting 0x32 and 0x3C via UART
(1 start bit, 1 stop bit, 8 data bits, no parity, baud rate = 9,600)

22.1.4   UART Communication via Polling

The following sections introduce how to send or receive data via UART ports by using three different methods: polling, interrupt, and DMA. Polling is the simplest but most inefficient method. The interrupt approach is more efficient but not suitable for high data transfer rates. The DMA method is complex but the most effective.

Figure 22-7 shows the connection of two UART ports between two processors. The TX pin of one processor is connected to the RX pin of the other processor, and vice versa. Because the polling method blocks the processor from running other tasks, software cannot use polling to send and receive data simultaneously.

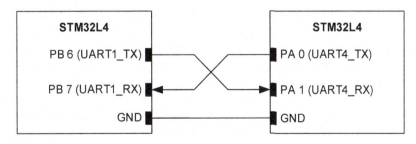

Figure 22-7. Connecting two UART ports

The code in Example 22-1 initializes a UART port in asynchronous mode (no hardware flow control) with oversampling by 16. Assume the UART clock is 80 MHz, and the baud rate is 9600. The data frame consists of 8 data bits, 1 start bit, 1 stop bit, and no parity bit. Software can initialize the UART ports using the following functions.

```
USART_Init(UART4);
USART_Init(USART1);
```

UART4 and USART1 are struct variables defined in the device header file (stm321476xx.h).

```
void USART_Init (USART_TypeDef * USARTx) {

  // Disable USART
  USARTx->CR1 &= ~USART_CR1_UE;

  // Set data length to 8 bits
  // 00 = 8 data bits, 01 = 9 data bits, 10 = 7 data bits
  USARTx->CR1 &= ~USART_CR1_M;

  // Select 1 stop bit
  // 00 = 1 Stop bit      01 = 0.5 Stop bit
  // 10 = 2 Stop bits     11 = 1.5 Stop bit
  USARTx->CR2 &= ~USART_CR2_STOP;

  // Set parity control as no parity
  // 0 = no parity,
  // 1 = parity enabled (then, program PS bit to select Even or Odd parity)
  USARTx->CR1 &= ~ USART_CR1_PCE;

  // Oversampling by 16
  // 0 = oversampling by 16, 1 = oversampling by 8
  USARTx->CR1 &= ~USART_CR1_OVER8;

  // Set Baud rate to 9600 using APB frequency (80 MHz)
  // See Example 1 in Section 22.1.2
  USARTx->BRR = 0x208D;

  // Enable transmission and reception
  USARTx->CR1 |= (USART_CR1_TE | USART_CR1_RE);

  // Enable USART
  USARTx->CR1 |= USART_CR1_UE;

  // Verify that USART is ready for transmission
  // TEACK: Transmit enable acknowledge flag. Hardware sets or resets it.
  while ((USARTx->ISR & USART_ISR_TEACK) == 0);

  // Verify that USART is ready for reception
  // REACK: Receive enable acknowledge flag. Hardware sets or resets it.
  while ((USARTx->ISR & USART_ISR_REACK) == 0);
}
```

Example 22-1. Initializing a UART port

Example 22-2 selects the system clock to drive USART1 and UART4.

```c
int main(void){

    // Enable GPIO clock and configure the Tx pin and the Rx pin as:
    // Alternate function, High Speed, Push-pull, Pull-up

    //------------------- GPIO Initialization for USART 1 -----------------
    // PB.6 = AF7 (USART1_TX), PB.7 = AF7 (USART1_RX)
    RCC->AHB2ENR |= RCC_AHB2ENR_GPIOBEN; // Enable GPIO port B clock

    // 00 = Input, 01 = Output, 10 = Alternate Function, 11 = Analog
    GPIOB->MODER   &= ~(0xF << (2*6)); // Clear mode bits for pin 6 and 7
    GPIOB->MODER   |=   0xA << (2*6);  // Select Alternate Function mode

    // Alternative function 7 = USART 1
    // Appendix I shows all alternate functions
    GPIOB->AFR[0]  |=   0x77 << (4*6); // Set pin 6 and 7 to AF 7

    // GPIO Speed: 00 = Low speed,   01 = Medium speed,
    //             10 = Fast speed,  11 = High speed
    GPIOB->OSPEEDR |=   0xF<<(2*6);

    // GPIO Push-Pull: 00 = No pull-up/pull-down, 01 = Pull-up (01)
    //                 10 = Pull-down, 11 = Reserved
    GPIOB->PUPDR   &= ~(0xF<<(2*6));
    GPIOB->PUPDR   |=   0x5<<(2*6); // Select pull-up

    // GPIO Output Type: 0 = push-pull, 1 = open drain
    GPIOB->OTYPER  &=  ~(0x3<<6);

    //------------------- GPIO Initialization for USART 4 -----------------
    // PA.0 = AF8 (UART4_TX),  PA.1 = AF8 (UART4_RX)
    // The code is very similar to the one given above.
    ...

    RCC->APB2ENR  |= RCC_APB2ENR_USART1EN;   // Enable UART 1 clock
    RCC->APB1ENR1 |= RCC_APB1ENR1_UART4EN;   // Enable UART 4 clock

    // Select system clock (SYSCLK) USART clock source of UART 1 and 4
    // 00 = PCLK,   01 = System clock (SYSCLK),
    // 10 = HSI16,  11 = LSE
    RCC->CCIPR &= ~ (RCC_CCIPR_USART1SEL | RCC_CCIPR_UART4SEL);
    RCC->CCIPR |= (RCC_CCIPR_USART1SEL_0 | RCC_CCIPR_UART4SEL_0);

    USART_Init(USART1);
    USART_Init(UART4);

    ...
}
```

Example 22-2. Enable and select the clock of UART ports

When UART receives a byte, hardware sets the receive register not empty flag (RXNE) in the status register (ISR). In the polling approach, software constantly checks the RXNE flag and reads the receive data register (RDR) once it is set. Reading register RDR clears the RXNE flag automatically.

Example 22-3 shows the implementation of receiving data by polling. This polling method is inefficient, and the while loop prevents the processor from running other tasks.

```
void USART_Read (USART_TypeDef *USARTx, uint8_t *buffer, uint32_t nBytes) {

  int i;

  for (i = 0; i < nBytes; i++) {
    while (!(USARTx->ISR & USART_ISR_RXNE)); // Wait until hardware sets RXNE
    buffer[i] = USARTx->RDR;                 // Reading RDR clears RXNE
  }
}
```

Example 22-3. Receive data from a UART port by using busy polling

When UART sends a byte, software must wait until the TxE (transmission data register empty) flag is set in the status register (ISR). Hardware sets the TxE flag when the content of the transmission data register (TDR) has been transferred into the shift register. Additionally, writing to the USART data register (DR) clears the TxE flag automatically. After exiting the *for* loop, software must wait for the transmission complete (TC) flag to ensure the last byte has been sent out.

Example 22-4 shows the implementation of sending data by polling. Again, the while loop prevents the processor from performing other tasks.

```
void USART_Write (USART_TypeDef *USARTx, uint8_t *buffer, uint32_t nBytes) {

  int i;

  for (i = 0; i < nBytes; i++) {
    while (!(USARTx->ISR & USART_ISR_TXE)); // Wait until hardware sets TXE
    USARTx->TDR = buffer[i] & 0xFF;          // Writing to TDR clears TXE flag
  }

  // Wait until TC bit is set. TC is set by hardware and cleared by software.
  while (!(USARTx->ISR & USART_ISR_TC));     // TC: Transmission complete flag

  // Writing 1 to the TCCF bit in ICR clears the TC bit in ISR
  USARTx->ICR |= USART_ICR_TCCF; // TCCF: Transmission complete clear flag
}
```

Example 22-4. Send data out via a UART port via busy polling

22.1.5   UART Communication via Interrupt

An USART interrupt can be generated upon the occurrence of several events, such as transmission data register empty (TxE), transmission complete (TC), received data register not empty (RXNE), overrun error detected (ORE), idle line detected (IDLE), and parity error (PE).

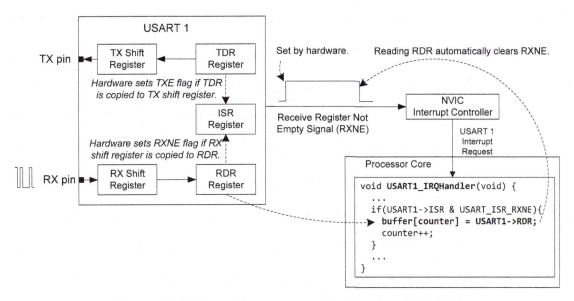

Figure 22-8. Using interrupt to receive data from USART 1

When UART receives a byte, an interrupt request is generated, and the processor responds to the request by executing the corresponding UART interrupt handler. The interrupt handler reads the receive data register (RDR) and copies it to the next empty buffer, as shown in Figure 22-8. Because several UART events can generate interrupts, the interrupt handler must check whether an RXNE event has taken place.

Software must enable UART interrupts to send or receive data, as shown in Example 22-5.

```
USART1->CR1 |= USART_CR1_RXNEIE;    // Receive register not empty interrupt
USART1->CR1 &= ~USART_CR1_TXEIE;    // Transmit register empty interrupt
NVIC_SetPriority(USART1_IRQn, 0);   // Set the highest urgency
NVIC_EnableIRQ(USART1_IRQn);        // Enable NVIC interrupt
```

Example 22-5. Enable UART sending and receiving interrupts

Example 22-6 shows the implementation of receiving data from UART by using interrupts. There are two global counter variables to record the number of bytes that have been received. The *receive()* function is generic, and is called by different UART interrupt handlers. Therefore, it takes three input arguments to differentiate UART ports, the receive buffers, and the byte counters.

```
#define BufferSize 32
uint8_t USART1_Buffer_Rx[BufferSize], USART4_Buffer_Rx[BufferSize];
volatile uint32_t Rx1_Counter = 0, Rx4_Counter = 0;

void USART1_IRQHandler(void) {
  receive(USART1, USART1_Buffer_Rx, &Rx1_Counter);
}

void UART4_IRQHandler(void) {
  receive(UART4, USART4_Buffer_Rx, &Rx4_Counter);
}

void receive(USART_TypeDef *USARTx, uint8_t *buffer, uint32_t *pCounter) {
  if(USARTx->ISR & USART_ISR_RXNE) {    // Check RXNE event
    buffer[*pCounter] = USARTx->RDR;    // Reading RDR clears the RXNE flag
    (*pCounter)++;                      // Dereference and update memory value
    if((*pCounter) >= BufferSize) {     // Check buffer overflow
      (*pCounter) = 0;                  // Circular buffer
    }
  }
}
```

Example 22-6. Receiving data from a UART port via interrupt

Example 22-7 gives a generic implementation to transmit data via a UART port by using interrupts. For example, software can send out the data by executing the following statement: UART_Send(USART1,buffer), which writes only the first byte to the transmit data register (TDR). This will start the transmission process. This function will immediately return to the caller after enabling TXE interrupt and write the first byte to the transmit data register (TDR). This allows the caller to continue to execute other tasks while the transmission is being performed in the background, as shown in Figure 22-9.

An interrupt will be generated after each byte has been sent. The interrupt handler writes the next byte to TDR to start the next transmission. This process repeats until a total of BufferSize bytes have been sent. The interrupt disables the interrupt for the TXE events.

```
volatile uint32_t Tx1_Counter = 0, Tx4_Counter = 0;

void UART_Send (USART_TypeDef *USARTx, uint8_t *buffer){
  USARTx->CR1 |= USART_CR1_TXEIE; // Enable TXE Interrupt
  // Write to Transmit Data Register (TDR) to start transmission
  // An interrupt will be initiated after data in TDR has been sent.
  USARTx->TDR = buffer[0];
}

void USART1_IRQHandler(void) {
  send(USART1, USART1_Buffer_Tx, &Tx1_Counter);
}
```

```
void UART4_IRQHandler(void) {
  send(UART4, USART4_Buffer_Rx, &Tx4_Counter);
}

void send(USART_TypeDef *USARTx, uint8_t *buffer, uint32_t *pCounter){
  if(USARTx->ISR & USART_ISR_TXE) {              // Check TXE flag
    (*pCounter)++;                               // Bytes that have been sent
    if( *pCounter <= BufferSize - 1) {           // Transmit the next byte
      USARTx->TDR = buffer[pCounter] & 0xFF;     // Writing to TDR clears TXE
    } else {                                     // Transmission completes
      (*pCounter) = 0;                           // Clear the counter
      USARTx->CR1 &= ~USART_CR1_TXEIE;           // Disable TXE interrupt
    }
  }
}
```

Example 22-7. Send data out via a UART port by using interrupt

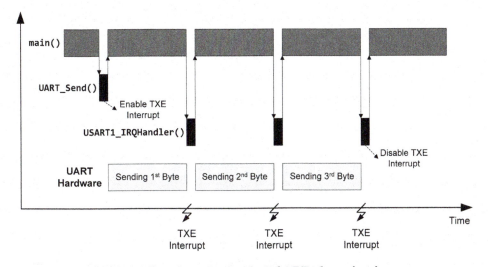

Figure 22-9. Sending three bytes via USART1 by using interrupts

Due to the non-blocking feature of interrupt, we can send and receive data simultaneously between two UART ports on the same processor, as shown in Figure 22-10.

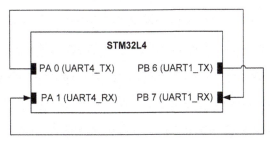

Figure 22-10. Communication between two ports on the same processor

22.1.6   UART Communication via DMA

Using a direct memory access (DMA) controller to move data between a buffer and UART data registers is the most efficient way to perform UART communication. Chapter 19 introduces DMA in detail.

Figure 22-11 shows the basic idea. As shown in Table 19-2, USART1_TX and USART1_RX can be connected to channels 6 and 7 of DMA controller 2, respectively. A TXE or RXNE event triggers a DMA request on channel 6 and channel 7, respectively.

- Whenever the TXE bit is set in the ISR register, DMA controller 2 transfers one byte via channel 6 from the memory buffer (pointed to by the CMAR register of DMA 2 channel 6) to the *transmit data register* TDR (pointed to by the CPAR register of DMA 2 channel 6).
- Similarly, whenever the RXNE bit is set in the ISR register, DMA controller 2 transfers one byte via channel 7 from the *receive data register* RDR to the buffer.

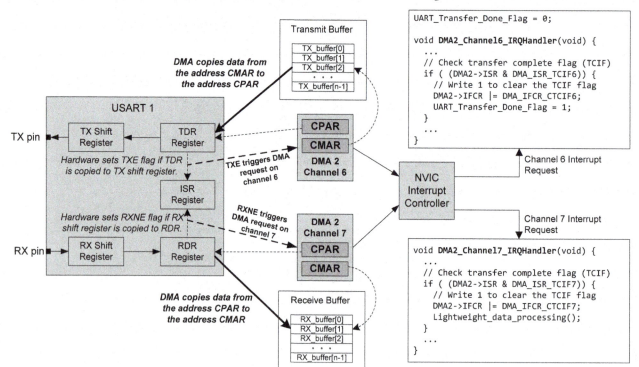

Figure 22-11. Using DMA to receive data from USART 1

To enable DMA for the transmission, software must set the DMAT bit in the CR3 register.

```
USART1->CR3 |= USART_CR3_DMAT;
```

To enable DMA for the reception, software must set the DMAR bit in the CR3 register.

```
USART1->CR3 |= USART_CR3_DMAR;
```

If DMA interrupts are enabled, the DMA controller can generate interrupt requests to execute the corresponding interrupt handler.

Example 22-8 and Example 22-9 give C code that configures channel 6 and 7 of DMA controller 2 to serve TX and RX of UART 1, respectively. Data transmission or reception takes place immediately when *UART1_DMA_Transmit* or *UART1_DMA_Receive* is called.

```c
void UART1_DMA_Transmit (uint8_t *pBuffer, uint32_t size) {
  RCC->AHB1ENR |= RCC_AHB1ENR_DMA2EN;     // Enable DMA2 clock
  DMA2_Channel16->CCR &= ~DMA_CCR_EN;      // Disable DMA channel
  DMA2_Channel16->CCR &= ~DMA_CCR_MEM2MEM; // Disable memory to memory mode
  DMA2_Channel16->CCR &= ~DMA_CCR_PL;      // Channel priority level
  DMA2_Channel16->CCR |=  DMA_CCR_PL_1;    // Set DMA priority to high
  DMA2_Channel16->CCR &= ~DMA_CCR_PSIZE;   // Peripheral data size 00 = 8 bits
  DMA2_Channel16->CCR &= ~DMA_CCR_MSIZE;   // Memory data size: 00 = 8 bits
  DMA2_Channel16->CCR &= ~DMA_CCR_PINC;    // Disable peripheral increment mode
  DMA2_Channel16->CCR |=  DMA_CCR_MINC;    // Enable memory increment mode
  DMA2_Channel16->CCR &= ~DMA_CCR_CIRC;    // Disable circular mode
  DMA2_Channel16->CCR |=  DMA_CCR_DIR;     // Transfer direction: to peripheral
  DMA2_Channel16->CCR |=  DMA_CCR_TCIE;    // Transfer complete interrupt enable
  DMA2_Channel16->CCR &= ~DMA_CCR_HTIE;    // Disable Half transfer interrupt
  DMA2_Channel16->CNDTR = size;            // Number of data to transfer
  DMA2_Channel16->CPAR  = (uint32_t)&(USART1->TDR);  // Peripheral address
  DMA2_Channel16->CMAR  = (uint32_t) pBuffer;        // Transmit buffer address
  DMA2_CSELR->CSELR &= ~DMA_CSELR_C6S;     // See Table 19-2
  DMA2_CSELR->CSELR |= 2<<20;              // Map channel 6 to USART1_TX
  DMA2_Channel16->CCR |= DMA_CCR_EN;       // Enable DMA channel
}
```

Example 22-8. Configure DMA 2 channel 6 for UART 1 transmit

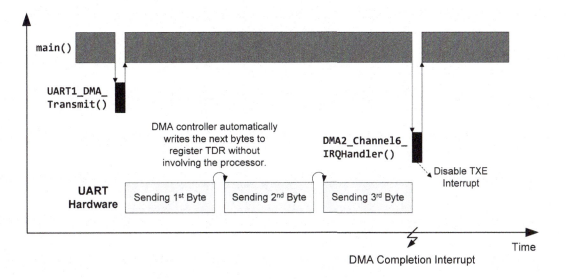

Figure 22-12. Sending three bytes via DMA.

```
void UART1_DMA_Receive (uint8_t *pBuffer, uint32_t size) {
  RCC->AHB1ENR |= RCC_AHB1ENR_DMA2EN;      // Enable DMA2 clock
  DMA2_Channel7->CCR &= ~DMA_CCR_EN;       // Disable DMA channel
  DMA2_Channel7->CCR &= ~DMA_CCR_MEM2MEM;// Disable memory to memory mode
  DMA2_Channel7->CCR &= ~DMA_CCR_PL;       // Channel priority level
  DMA2_Channel7->CCR |=  DMA_CCR_PL_1;     // Set DMA priority to high
  DMA2_Channel7->CCR &= ~DMA_CCR_PSIZE;    // Peripheral data size 00 = 8 bits
  DMA2_Channel7->CCR &= ~DMA_CCR_MSIZE;    // Memory data size: 00 = 8 bits
  DMA2_Channel7->CCR &= ~DMA_CCR_PINC;     // Disable peripheral increment mode
  DMA2_Channel7->CCR |=  DMA_CCR_MINC;     // Enable memory increment mode
  DMA2_Channel7->CCR &= ~DMA_CCR_CIRC;     // Disable circular mode
  DMA2_Channel7->CCR &= ~DMA_CCR_DIR;      // Transfer direction: to memory
  DMA2_Channel7->CCR |=  DMA_CCR_TCIE;     // Transfer complete interrupt enable
  DMA2_Channel7->CCR &= ~DMA_CCR_HTIE;     // Disable Half transfer interrupt
  DMA2_Channel7->CNDTR = size;             // Number of data to transfer
  DMA2_Channel7->CPAR  = (uint32_t)&(USART1->RDR);  // Peripheral address
  DMA2_Channel7->CMAR  = (uint32_t) pBuffer;        // Receive buffer address
  DMA2_CSELR->CSELR &= ~DMA_CSELR_C6S;     // See Table 19-2
  DMA2_CSELR->CSELR |= 2<<24;              // Map channel 7 to USART1_RX
  DMA2_Channel7->CCR |= DMA_CCR_EN;        // Enable DMA channel
}
```

Example 22-9. Configure DMA 2 channel 7 for UART 1 receive

Comparing Figure 22-9 and Figure 22-12, we can see that DMA is more efficient than the interrupt approach. When DMA completes, a DMA interrupt request will be generated. The DMA interrupt handler can change the completion flag, as shown below.

```
volatile uint8_t TransmissionCompleteFlag = 0;


void DMA2_Channel7_IRQHandler(void) { // USART1_RX

  if ( (DMA2->ISR & DMA_ISR_TCIF7) == DMA_ISR_TCIF7 ) {
    // Write 1 to clear the corresponding TCIF flag
    DMA2->IFCR |= DMA_IFCR_CTCIF7;
    TransmissionCompleteFlag = 1;
  }

  if ( (DMA2->ISR & DMA_ISR_HTIF7) == DMA_ISR_HTIF7 ) // half transfer
    DMA2->IFCR |= DMA_IFCR_CHTIF7;

  if ( (DMA2->ISR & DMA_ISR_GIF7) == DMA_ISR_GIF7 )   // global interrupt
    DMA2->IFCR |= DMA_IFCR_CGIF7;

  if ( (DMA2->ISR & DMA_ISR_TEIF7) == DMA_ISR_TEIF7 ) // transfer error
    DMA2->IFCR |= DMA_IFCR_CTEIF7;
}
```

Example 22-10. DMA interrupt handler

22.1.7   Serial Communication to Bluetooth Module

Bluetooth is a low-power, low-cost wireless communication protocol operating in the 2.4GHz band, which is a globally unlicensed radio frequency band for industry, science and medical (ISM) applications.

Bluetooth is based on a master-slave model. Up to seven active slave devices can be connected to the master to form a local network (called a *piconet*), while there may be other inactive slave devices in the piconet. The disadvantages of Bluetooth include that it has a short communication range (15-30 feet) and it is relatively insecure.

Bluetooth uses a technique of time division duplex (TDD) to coordinate the access to the physical channel. It divides the time into a fixed length interval (625 microseconds) called *slots*. Each second is divided into 1,600 slots. The master sets the ratio frequency and initiates a data communication.

- *Master sets the frequency hopping sequence.* Bluetooth divides the 2.4GHz band into 79 channels with their frequencies 1 MHz apart. To avoid interference on one specific channel, in each slot both the master and the slave device switch to a different channel. Such frequency hopping is performed 1,600 times per second, which allows a retransmission to occur soon on a different channel, hopefully on a clean one without any interference. We call this technique FHSS (frequency hopping spread spectrum). The master sets the frequency hopping sequence, and the slave devices follow the hopping sequence by using a special algorithm.

- *Master initiates communication.* The master transmits data to a slave in even numbered slots and receives data from a slave in odd numbered slots. A slave device is only allowed to transmit data in a slot if the master has polled it or sent a data packet to it in the preceding slot. The slave then responds to the master by sending a data packet or a NULL packet if the slave has nothing to send.

- Each Bluetooth device has a unique fixed 48-bit address, which is assigned at manufacture time. Two communicating devices need to know each other's address. Software programs can specify the address if programmers know it. The address can also be discovered during the device discovery process. The discovery process searches all devices nearby and identifies the one that matches a user-friendly name such as "Joe's Phone."

22.1.7.1 Bluetooth Transfer Protocols

There are many transfer protocols available between two Bluetooth devices. A standardized set of protocols designed for a particular type of device is termed as a Bluetooth device profile. The following gives a few examples.

- The radio frequency communication (RFCOMM) profile emulates the serial cable line and guarantees reliable delivery of every packet. It is used for devices such as PC, printers, and modems.

- The generic audio/video distribution profile (GAVDP) is used to stream video or audio data to devices such as stereo headphones and laptops.

- The audio/video remote control profile (AVRCP) provides a standard interface to control audio or video devices. Example devices include headphones, speakers, and TVs.

In this section, we focus on the RFCOMM profile designed for serial communication. There are inexpensive Bluetooth-UART modules such as the HC-05 (master or slave) and HC-06 (slave only) that support the RFCOMM profile. They include a UART interface for serial communication between the Bluetooth module and microprocessors, and a Bluetooth interface for wireless communication between two Bluetooth modules, as shown in Figure 22-13.

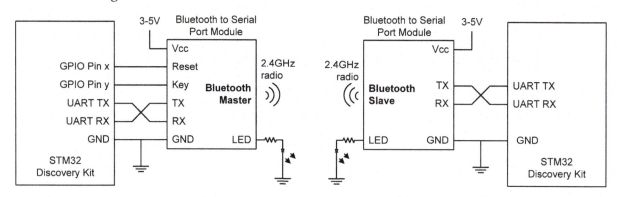

Figure 22-13. Serial port Bluetooth modules. Bluetooth modules communicate with each other in wireless. Each Bluetooth module transfers data to or from the processor via UART.

22.1.7.2 Pairing Bluetooth Modules

Two Bluetooth modules need to be paired and bound together before they can exchange data. The master device must know the 48-bit address of the slave device and the pairing password set by the slave device.

The microprocessor needs to send string commands via the serial interface to the Bluetooth master device to complete the pairing and binding process. These string commands start with "AT" (abbreviation for "attention") and end with a terminator "return", *i.e.*, with ASCII values of "0x0D,0x0A". Therefore, they also called "AT commands".

The following shows the procedure for configuring and pairing Bluetooth modules. It also lists frequently used AT commands that the microprocessor performs to set up the Bluetooth master module. In this example, we assume that the slave Bluetooth module has a MAC address of "0018,e4,0c680a" and a pairing password of "1234".

1. Pull the KEY pin high to put the Bluetooth master device in command mode

2. Pull the RESET pin low for a short time and then pull it high to reset the Bluetooth master module

3. Software sends the following commands via the UART interface to the Bluetooth master module. (The quote signs are not part of the command.)

    "AT+RESET\r\n"   ; add a return, i.e., "0x0D,0x0A", to the end
                              ; ASCII 0x0D = CR (carriage return)
                              ; ASCII 0x0A = NL (new line),

    "AT+UART=57600,0,0\r\n" ; Baud rate: 57,600 bits/s, 1 stop bit, no parity bit
                              ; 1st parameter: baud rate
                              ; 2nd parameter: 0 = 1 stop bit
                              ;   1 = 2 stop bits
                              ; 3rd parameter: 0 = no parity bit
                              ;   1 = parity bit

    "AT+ROLE=1\r\n"   ; A Bluetooth module can be either master or slave.
                              ; Set the module as a Bluetooth master.
                              ; 0 = Slave,
                              ; 1 = Master,
                              ; 2 = Slave Loop

    "AT+PSWD=1234\r\n"   ; Password code for pairing. The password is set by
                              ; the Bluetooth slave module.

    "AT+PAIR=0018,e4,0c680a\r\n" ; Paired with a 48-bit slave address

    "AT+BIND=0018,e4,0c680a\r\n" ; Bound with the target slave device

    "AT+CMODE=0\r\n"   ; 0 = Connect to the specified address
                              ; 1 = Connect to any address
                              ; 2 = Slave loop

4. Pull the KEY pin low to let the Bluetooth master device exit command mode and enter communication mode

5. Pull the RESET pin low for a short time and then pull it high to reset the Bluetooth master module

Table 22-2. Process of using AT commands to pair two Bluetooth devices

22.2 Inter-Integrated Circuit (I²C)

Inter-integrated circuit (I²C) is a standard bus protocol, originally developed by Philips in the late 1980s. It enables the communication between microprocessors and their peripheral devices by using two wires: a *serial data line* (SDA) and a *serial clock line* (SCL). The two-wire design reduces the number of physical pins, making it inexpensive and simple to interface. The data transfer rate of I²C can be up to 100 Kbit/s in standard mode, up to 400 Kbit/s in fast mode, and up to 3.4 Mbit/s in high-speed mode.

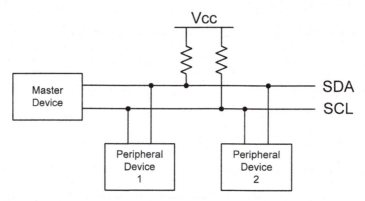

Figure 22-14. An example of I²C bus that connects one master and two peripheral devices. It uses two bidirectional open-drain wires: the serial data (SDA) line and the serial clock (SCL) line. Both wires are pulled up to a positive voltage supply. The combination of open-drain and external pull-up realizes a Boolean AND logic.

Each device, including master devices and peripheral devices, has a unique address, which typically has 7 bits, 10 bits, or 16 bits. Depending on the function, each device can serve as a transmitter, a receiver, or both. For example, a digital temperature sensor may operate only as a transmitter, an LCD driver may operate only as a receiver, and a memory device can be both a transmitter and a receiver.

The master device initializes a data transfer on the bus, and then generates the clock signals to permit that data transfer, and finally terminates the transfer after receiving all requested information. The device addressed by the master is called a *slave*. Multiple masters can co-exist on the same I²C bus. When multiple masters want to control the bus, an arbitration procedure is then performed. The bus capacitance limits the number of devices that can be connected to the bus.

22.2.1   I²C Pins

The pins of the master and peripheral devices connected to the SDA and SCL lines should be internally configured as *open-drain*, also known as *open collector* (see chapter 14.4.2).

An open-drain is a special type of output. The output pin connects to a positive voltage source if an active high (logic 1) is outputted. The output pin is in a high impedance state if a low (logic 0) is outputted. The high impedance is often achieved by keeping the output floated, *i.e.*, not connected to either the ground or the positive voltage source.

Software can configure the SDA and SCL pins of the processor as open-drained. However, the pull-up resistor within the processor is too large, often in the order of 100 kΩ. Such a large resistor provides pull-up power that is too weak for I²C. To reduce the rise time of the I²C lines, smaller resistors, such as 3 kΩ, are often used.

As shown in Figure 22-14, the SDA and SCL lines are connected to a positive supply voltage via two small pull-up resistors. The recommended resistance value is 4.7 kΩ for low speed, 3 kΩ for standard speed, and 1 kΩ for the fast speed.

22.2.2   I²C Protocol

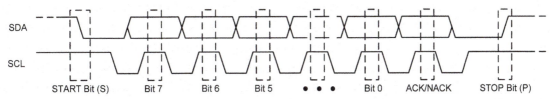

Figure 22-15. The timing diagram of sending N bits with the start bit (S) and the stop bit (P). The most significant bit (MSB) is sent out first. SDA can be updated when SCL is low. SDA must be held stable when SCL is high. The hexagonal shape on SDA line means SDA can be either high or low during that period.

The communication begins with a START bit (S) and terminates by a STOP bit (P).

- A START bit is defined as a high-to-low transition of SDA while SCL is high.
- A STOP bit is defined as a low-to-high transition of SDA while SCL is high.

The master generates both START and STOP bits. The I²C interfacing hardware of all peripheral devices is capable of detecting START and STOP. After the START bit, the master begins to send data byte by byte. For each byte, the most significant bit is transferred first. The slave sends an acknowledge bit to the master, informing the master that the slave has successfully received a byte.

After a byte is transferred, the receiver should answer the transmitter with either an acknowledge (ACK) bit or a not acknowledge (NACK) bit, as shown in Figure 22-16. The transmitter releases the SDA line during the acknowledge clock period (the ninth clock period) so that the receiver can pull SDA low. If the SDA line is low in the ninth clock period, an ACK takes place. If the SDA line is high in the ninth clock period, a scenario we call NACK occurs.

- When a master sends data to a slave, a NACK answered by the slave means that the communication has failed. The master needs to either generate a STOP to abort the current transfer or a START to restart the transfer.
- When a slave is transferring to a master, a NACK answered by the master means that the master sends a stop bit to terminate the communication after the current byte is transferred.

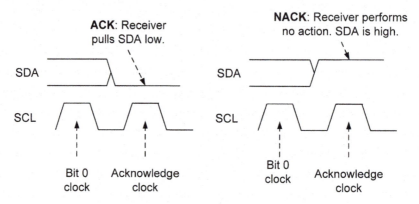

Figure 22-16. Comparison of ACK and NACK

Although the transfer clock signal is generated by the master, the slave can also control the transfer speed indirectly via *clock stretching*. If the slave is too busy to receive another byte, it holds the SCL line low to force the master to wait. Due to the wire AND logic, the master cannot drive SCL high if the slave holds SCL low. The master resumes data transfer after the slave releases SCL.

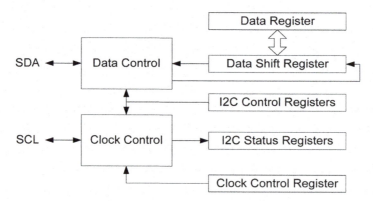

Figure 22-17. Simplified diagram of I²C

The STM32L processor has several I²C modules. Figure 22-17 shows the simplified data and clock control of one I²C module. The bytes stored in the data register are shifted in or out to the SDA line through an internal data shift register, with the most significant bit (MSB) in or out first.

- When the master is transmitting a byte to a slave, the master's I²C hardware automatically sets the TxE (transmitter buffer empty) flag in the status register if the master has received an acknowledge pulse (ACK) from the slave. A TxE event can inform software to send the next byte.

- On the other hand, if the master has received a byte successfully, the master's I²C hardware then automatically sets the RxNE (receiver buffer not empty) flag in the status register. A RxNE event can inform software to read the received byte.

If I²C interrupts are enabled, an I²C interrupt takes place under the following conditions.

- An I²C master generates an interrupt if a start bit is sent, a slave address is sent, hardware sets the TxE or RxNE flag, or the transfer of all data bytes completes.

- An I²C slave generates an interrupt if the address received matches its own address, a stop bit is received, or hardware sets the TxE or RxNE flag.

When there are multiple master devices on the I²C bus, clock synchronization and bus arbitration are required. During idle, both SCL and SDA have a high voltage level.

- *Clock synchronization.* The SCL interface of all devices performs a logic AND operation. When one master pulls SCL low, no other masters can pull it high.

- *Bus arbitration.* On the SCL rising edge, each master checks whether the SDA voltage level matches what it has sent. Whenever a master tries to transmit a high but detects a low on SDA, this master loses the arbitration. Each losing master immediately switches to slave receive mode because the winning master may be addressing it. A losing master will restart the transfer after it detects a STOP bit.

22.2.3   I²C Data Frame

Table 22-3 and Table 22-4 gives example message protocols between a master and a slave with a 7-bit and 10-bit address, respectively. If the address of a slave has 7 bits, the following lists the basic procedures.

1. The master begins by sending a start bit, the slave address, and a single bit ($R/\overline{W}$) representing the data transfer direction. The slave whose address matches the address sent by the master will answer with an ACK bit. The data transfer direction is represented by a single bit ($R/\overline{W}$). If the $R/\overline{W}$ bit is 1, then the master requests to receive data from the slave. If the $R/\overline{W}$ bit is 0, then the master requests to send data to the slave.

2. After the slave acknowledges the addressing successfully, data transfer takes place in the direction specified by the $R/\overline{W}$ bit. Data are transferred byte by byte. Each byte is followed by an ACK or NACK bit. Therefore, it takes 9 cycles to transfer one byte.

3. The master completes the communication by sending a STOP bit to the slave. The master may generate a START bit without sending a STOP bit first. This allows the master to communication with another slave or the same slave without releasing the bus. For example, a master may send a command to a slave and then immediately receive data from the slave.

S	Slave Address	R/$\overline{W}$	A	Data	A	Data	A	P
1 bit	7 bits	1 bit	1 bit	8 bits	1 bit	8 bits	1 bit	1 bit

Table 22-3. Example of reading two bytes from or writing two bytes to an I²C slave with a 7-bit address (S = Start, P = Stop, A = Acknowledge, R/$\overline{W}$ = 1 for reading and 0 for writing)

S	Slave Address (higher 2 bits)	R/$\overline{W}$	A1	Slave Address (lower 8 bits)	A2	Data	A	Data	A	P
1 bit	7 bits (11110xx)	1 bit (0)	1 bit	8 bits	1 bit	8 bits	1 bit	8 bits	1 bit	1 bit

Table 22-4. Example of writing two bytes to an I²C slave with a 10-bit address. The slave address is in the first two bytes after the start bit. (S = Start, P = Stop, A = Acknowledge)

S	Slave Address (higher 2 bits)	R/$\overline{W}$	A1	Slave Address (lower 8 bits)	A2	S	Slave Address (higher 2 bits)	R/$\overline{W}$	A3	Data	A	Data	A	P
1 bit	7 bits (11110xx)	1 bit (0)	1 bit	8 bits	1 bit	1 bit	7 bits (11110xx)	1 bit (0)	1 bit	8 bits	1 bit	8 bits	1 bit	1 bit

Table 22-5. Example of reading two bytes from an I²C slave with a 10-bit address. After sending two address bytes (R/$\overline{W}$ = 0), the master repeats the start bit and sends again the first address byte, with R/$\overline{W}$ being 1 to indicate reading.

If the address of a slave has 10 bits, the communication protocol differs slightly.

- After the start bit, the first byte sent out by the master consists of a five-bit constant (11110), two most significant bits of the slave address, and the R/$\overline{W}$ bit. The master then sends the next byte, which is the least significant eight bits of the slave address.

- After the master sends out the first byte, all slave devices compare it to their own address. It is possible that more than one device finds a match between the two leading bits of the 10-bit address. Therefore, multiple ACK bits might be generated during the A1 clock period.

- After the master sends out the lower 8 bits of the slave address, at most one device finds an address match, and thus no multiple ACK bits are generated during the A2 clock period.

- As shown in Table 24-4 and Table 24-5, reading from or writing to a slave have different communication sequences.

22.2.4   Interfacing Serial Digital Thermal Sensors via I²C

This section gives an example in which the microprocessor interacts with multiple simple digital sensors via the I²C bus. In this example, we use TC74 digital thermal sensors from Microchip© Technology, which provide low-power 8-bit temperature measurements, with a resolution of $\pm 1°C$ and a conversion rate of 8 samples per second. The sensor has five pins, as listed in Table 22-6, supporting an I²C interface.

Figure 22-18. TC74 temperature sensor

Pin No.	Symbol	Type	Description
1	NC	None	No internal connection
2	SDA	Bidirectional	I²C serial data line
3	GND	Ground	System ground
4	SCL	Input	I²C serial clock line
5	Vdd	Power	Power supply input

Table 22-6. Pin connection of TC74 digital temperature sensor

The slave address of a TC74 sensor has 7 bits. There are eight different binary addresses (from `1001000` to `1001111`), depending on the part number of the device. For example, the default address of TC74 A5 is `1001101`. Software can change the address to one of the eight allowed addresses. This programmable address is helpful particularly when there are multiple TC74 sensors connected on the same I²C bus.

7	6	5	4	3	2	1	0
Read/Write	Read-only						
1 = standby	1 = ready				Reserved		
0 = normal	0 = not ready						

Table 22-7. The configuration register of TC74 temperature sensor

TC74 internally has two 8-bit registers: (1) a temperature register with an address of `0x00`, and (2) a configuration register with an address of `0x01`.

- The temperature register holds the temperature measurement in units of degrees Celsius, represented in two's complement binary format. For example, a reading of `0x00` represents $0°C$ and a reading of `0xFF` represents $-1°C$. The representable temperature ranges from $-65°C$ to $127°C$.
- The configuration register is shown in Table 22-7. The most significant bit of the configuration register sets the sensor to either the standby state or the normal state. Bit 6 indicates whether the temperature data is ready or not. The tailing six bits are reserved.

The sensor provides two commands: (1) command code `0x00` to read the temperature register, and (2) command code `0x01` to read or write the configuration register. The following shows the communication sequence of reading and writing a byte from/to a TC74 temperature sensor.

Writing a Byte to TC74

S	Address	R/$\overline{W}$	ACK	Command	ACK	Data	ACK	P
1 bit	7 bits	1 bit	1 bit	8 bits	1 bit	8 bits	1 bit	1 bit

- The R/$\overline{W}$ bit is 0 for writing data to the configuration register of the sensor.
- The command byte selects which register the data is written to.
- The data byte specifies the data content to be written to the target register.
- The ACK bit is sent by the sensor to the microcontroller to acknowledge the receipt of each byte.

Assume the 7-bit slave address of TC74 is `1001101`. Figure 22-19 shows the I2C communication sequence that puts TC74 in standby mode.

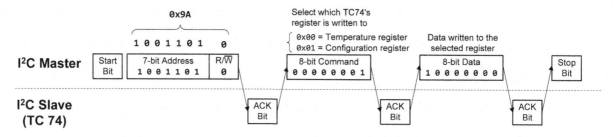

Figure 22-19. Putting TC74 with an address of `100110` (`0x4D`) in standby mode

Reading a Byte from TC74

Reading from TC74 involves two phases. Each phase has its own start bit, the address bits, and the R/$\overline{W}$ bit. The reason is that the second phase changes the transfer flow direction. This example shows that the master takes full control of all transfers. In the second phase, the master must re-initiate the transfer.

S	Address	R/$\overline{W}$	ACK	Command	ACK	S	Address	R/$\overline{W}$	ACK	Data	NACK	P
1 bit	7 bits	1 bit	1 bit	8 bits	1 bit	1 bit	7 bits	1 bit	1 bit	8 bits	1 bit	1 bit
	0x9A						0x9B					
1st phase: Select a register to read						2nd phase: Read the selected register						

- The first R/$\overline{W}$ bit is 0, indicating that the master will write an 8-bit command. The command selects which register is to be read. It is either `0x00` or `0x01`.
- The second R/$\overline{W}$ bit is 1, indicating that the master will read 8-bit data.
- The sensor sends the ACK bit to acknowledge the receipt of each byte.
- The master sends NACK to inform the slave to stop.

22.2.5   I²C Programmable Timings

Both I²C masters and slaves must meet the timing requirement of electrical signals defined in the I²C standard. Table 22-8 gives a few examples.

Timing Parameters	Standard		Fast		High-speed		Unit
	Min	Max	Min	Max	Min	Max	
SCL clock frequency	0	100	0	400	0	1000	kHz
Rise time of SDA & SCL	-	1000	20	300	-	120	µs
Fall time of SDA & SCL	-	300	20	300	-	120	µs
Low time of SCL	4.7	-	1.3	-	0.50	-	µs
High time of SCL	4.0	-	0.6	-	0.25	-	µs
Data hold time	5.0						µs
Data setup time	250	-	100	-	50	-	µs

Table 22-8. Example timing requirements of I²C electrical signals

Software can program the I²C's timing register (TIMINGR) to meet timing specifications. The timing register holds five parameters, including

- the clock prescaler (PRESC[3:0]),
- the clock SCL high period counter (SCLH[7:0]),
- the clock SCL low period counter (SCLL[7:0]),
- the data setup time counter (SCLDEL[3:0], also called SCL delay counter), and
- the data hold time counter (SDADEL[3:0], also called SDA delay counter).

22.2.5.1 Rise time and fall time

The *rise time* describes how long it takes for a voltage signal to increase from a low value to a high value. The 30-70 rise time is the amount of time taken by a voltage signal to increase from 30% of its final value to 70% of its final value. Similarly, the 30-70 *fall time* is the time taken by a signal to decrease from 70% of the final value to 30% of its final value. For the same circuit, the fall time is typically shorter than the rise time.

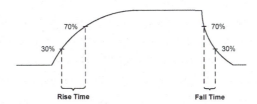

Figure 22-20. Definition of rise time and fall time

If two conductors are insulated and have a voltage potential between them, these two conductors form a capacitor. On circuit boards, the capacitance formed by copper traces, plates, wires, connections, and pins is called *parasitic capacitance*. Although parasitic capacitance is very small, its impacts on high-frequency signals cannot be ignored.

For the I²C bus, the rise time is determined by the value of pull-up resistor R and the bus capacitance C. The bus capacitance is the sum of the parasitic capacitances of the wires, connectors, and pins. The maximum bus capacitance allowed for I²C is 400pF, which limits the maximum number of I²C devices connected to the same bus. Figure 22-21 shows the equivalent circuit of an I²C bus.

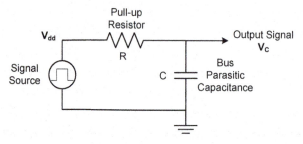

Figure 22-21. Equivalent circuit for I²C bus

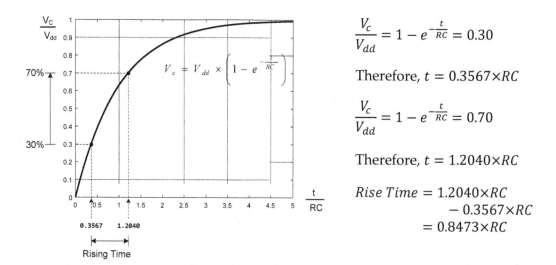

$$\frac{V_C}{V_{dd}} = 1 - e^{-\frac{t}{RC}} = 0.30$$

Therefore, $t = 0.3567 \times RC$

$$\frac{V_C}{V_{dd}} = 1 - e^{-\frac{t}{RC}} = 0.70$$

Therefore, $t = 1.2040 \times RC$

$$Rise\ Time = 1.2040 \times RC$$
$$- 0.3567 \times RC$$
$$= 0.8473 \times RC$$

Figure 22-22. Calculating the rise time

Figure 22-22 shows the calculation of the rise time. The pull-up resistors must be carefully chosen so that the rise time is smaller than the maximum allowed rise time, and the sink current is smaller than the maximum current allowed by an I²C pin.

$$\begin{cases} Rise\ Time = 0.8743 \times RC \leq RiseTime_{max} \\ \dfrac{V_{dd}}{R} \leq SinkCurrent_{max} \end{cases}$$

Therefore, we have

$$\frac{V_{dd}}{SinkCurrent_{max}} \leq R \leq \frac{RiseTime_{max}}{0.8743\ C}$$

22.2.5.2 Data hold time

When the falling edge of SCL is detected internally, a delay is inserted before data in the I2C TXDR register is sent out via the SDA line. The inserted delay t_{SDADEL} is programmed in the SDADEL field of register TIMINGR. The SDADEL counter starts to decrement automatically after the falling edge of SCL is detected internally. The delay completes when the SDADEL counter reaches zero.

All input signals are required to pass through analog and digital filters and slope detection, causing some delay. Suppose it takes t_{SYNC1} for the internal edge detector to detect a falling edge. As shown in Figure 22-23, the programmable SDA delay t_{SDADEL} is

$$t_{SDADEL} = [SDADEL \times (1 + PRESC) + 1] \times t_{I2C\_CLK}$$

As introduced earlier, the data line SDA is sampled periodically when the clock SCL is high, and SDA can change when SCL is low. The data hold time is defined as the amount of time after the falling edge of SCL during which SDA must remain at its current voltage level. Failing to do so may lead to SDA being improperly sampled when SCL transitions from high to low.

If t_r is the rise time, the **data hold time** is defined as follows:

$$Data\ Hold\ Time = t_{SYNC1} + t_{SDADEL} - t_r$$

The I²C standard specifies the minimum data hold time based on the speed mode. Because we have the following relationship:

$$Data\ Hold\ Time > t_{SDADEL}$$

we can program the SDADEL counter in the TIMINGR register such that

$$t_{SDADEL} > Minimum\ Data\ Hold\ Time\ Specified$$

Thus, the actual data hold time is guaranteed to be larger than the requirement specified.

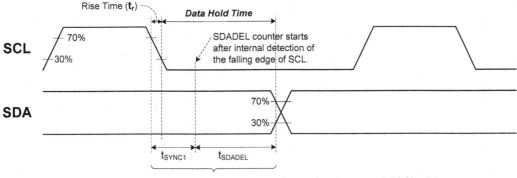

Figure 22-23. I²C data hold time.

22.2.5.3 Data setup time

When the clock line SCL is low, the data line SDA is updated either by the master or the slave, depending on the transfer direction. The data line is periodically sampled once the clock line SCL becomes high. Thus, SDA must remain its current voltage level before sampling starts, *i.e.*, before the rising edge of the clock takes place.

The *data setup time* is defined as the amount of time SCL is held low after a data bit has been placed on SDA.

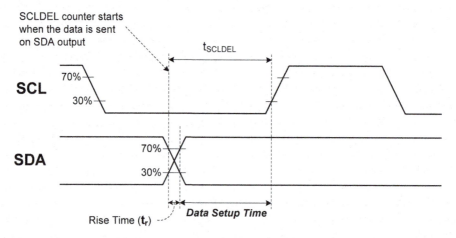

Figure 22-24. I²C data setup time

Software can configure the SCLDEL counter in the TIMINGR register such that the programmable SCL delay t_{SCLDEL} meets the following requirement:

$$t_{SCLDEL} > Minimum\ Data\ Setup\ Time\ Specified$$

The SCLDEL counter starts to decrement automatically after a data bit has been placed on SDA. In addition, we have

$$t_{SCLDEL} = (SCLDEL + 1) \times (1 + PRESC) \times t_{I2CCLK}$$

22.2.5.4 Master clock's minimum high and low time

The I²C clock timing is programmed by the SCLL and SCLH fields in the timing register. These two counters set the clock's low- and high-level durations, as well as the clock period, as shown below:

$$t_{low} = t_{SYNC1} + (SCLL + 1) \times (1 + PRESC) \times t_{I2CCLK}$$

$$t_{high} = t_{SYNC2} + (SCLH + 1) \times (1 + PRESC) \times t_{I2CCLK}$$

$$t_{period} = t_{low} + t_{high}$$

where t_{SYNC1} and t_{SYNC2} are the time it takes for the internal edge detector to detect a falling edge and a rising edge respectively. These delays include the delay caused by the analog filter, the digital filter, and the hardware edge detector.

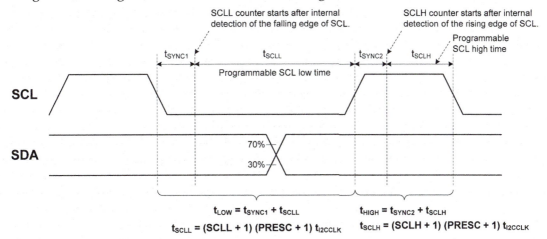

$$t_{LOW} = t_{SYNC1} + t_{SCLL}$$

$$t_{SCLL} = (SCLL + 1)\,(PRESC + 1)\,t_{I2CCLK}$$

$$t_{HIGH} = t_{SYNC2} + t_{SCLH}$$

$$t_{SCLH} = (SCLH + 1)\,(PRESC + 1)\,t_{I2CCLK}$$

Figure 22-25. I2C clock high and low durations

22.2.5.5 Example of setting the I²C timing

Table 22-9 lists key parameters of TC74 sensors.

Parameters	Value
Min high clock period	4.0 μs
Min low clock period	4.7 μs
Min data hold time	1250 ns
Min data setup time	1000 ns
Max rise time	1000 ns
Max fall time	300 ns
Input Capacitance SDA and SCL	5.0 pF
Maximum current on any pin	±50 mA

Table 22-9. Electrical parameters of TC74 temperature sensor

Rise time: if we use 1KΩ to pull up the SDA and SCL

$$t_{rise} = 0.8743 \times RC = 0.8742 \times 1000\Omega \times 5.0 \times 10^{-12}F = 4.4\ ns < 1000\ ns$$

Fall time: the fall time is the same as the rise time.

$$t_{fall} = t_{rise} = 4.4\ ns < 300\ ns$$

Electric Current:

$$Current = \frac{3V}{1000\Omega} = 0.3\ mA < 50\ mA$$

Let's use I2C1 in our example of setting up the timing register (TIMINGR) to meet the timing requirements. Suppose the system clock (SYSCLK) has been set to 80 MHz. Example 22-11 selects the SYSCLK as the source clock to drive I2C1.

```
RCC->APB1ENR1 |= RCC_APB1ENR1_I2C1EN;         // I2C1 clock enable

// 00 = PCLK, 01 = SYSCLK, 10 = HSI16, 11 = Reserved
RCC->CCIPR &= ~RCC_CCIPR_I2C1SEL;             // Clear bits
RCC->CCIPR |=  RCC_CCIPR_I2C1SEL_0;           // Select SYSCLK

RCC->APB1RSTR1 |=  RCC_APB1RSTR1_I2C1RST;     // 1 = Reset I2C1
RCC->APB1RSTR1 &= ~RCC_APB1RSTR1_I2C1RST;     // Complete the reset
```

Example 22-11. Selecting SYSCLK to the clock to drive I2C1

Suppose we choose the clock prescaler (PRESC) as 7. Then, the clock frequency of I2C1 is:

$$f_{I2CCLK} = \frac{f_{SYSCLK}}{1 + PRESC} = \frac{80\ MHz}{1 + 7} = 10\ MHz$$

Therefore,

$$t_{I2C\_PRESC} = \frac{1}{f_{I2CCLK}} = \frac{1}{10MHz} = 0.1\ \mu s$$

Data setup time: We select SCLDEL as 14.

$$t_{setup} > (1 + SCLDEL) \times t_{I2C\_PRESC} = (1 + 14) \times 0.1\ \mu s = 1.5\ \mu s > 1.0\ \mu s$$

Data hold time: Suppose we select SDADEL as 15.

$$t_{hold} > t_{SDADEL} > (1 + SDADEL) \times t_{I2C\_PRESC} = (1 + 15) \times 0.1\ \mu s = 1.6\ \mu s > 1.25\ \mu s$$

Low clock period: We select SCLL as 49.

$$t_{low} > (SCLL + 1) \times t_{I2C\_PRESC} = (1 + 49) \times 0.1\ \mu s = 5.0\ \mu s > 4.7\ \mu s$$

High clock period: We select SCLH as 49, too.

$$t_{high} > (SCLH + 1) \times t_{I2C\_PRESC} = (1 + 49) \times 0.1\ \mu s = 5.0\ \mu s > 4.0\ \mu s$$

31 30 29 28	27 26 25 24	23 22 21 20	19 18 17 16	15 14 13 12 11 10 9 8	7 6 5 4 3 2 1 0
PRESC[3:0]	Reserved	SCLDEL[3:0]	SDADEL[3:0]	SCLH[7:0]	SCLL[7:0]

In sum, software can program the timing register (TIMINGR) as follows:

```
I2C1->TIMINGR = 7U << 28 | 14U << 20 | 15U << 16 | 49U << 8 | 49U;
```

22.2.6   Sending Data to I²C Slave via Polling

During idle time, both SCL and SDA lines are pulled high. When the master wants to send data to a slave, the master first wait until the bus is ready by checking the BUSY flag in the ISR register, then sends a start bit by pulling SDA low, and places the clock signal on SCL. Then, the master sends the address frame, with the least significant bit being 0 to indicate that the master is the transmitter. After the address frame, the master starts to transfer data byte by byte. For each transfer, software must wait until the TXIS flag or the NACK flag is set. Hardware automatically sets the TXIS flag after it receives the acknowledgment bit from the slave, and clears the TXIS flag when the byte to be transferred has been written to the transmit data register (TXDR). The master stops the data transfer by terminating the clock on SCL and pulling SDA high. Software must wait until hardware sets the transfer complete flag (TC).

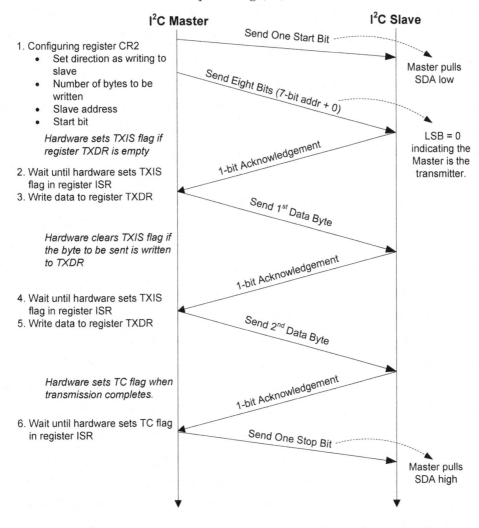

Figure 22-26. Time diagram when a master sends two bytes to a slave

22.2.7   Receiving Data from I²C Slave via Polling

After the master configures control register 2 (CR2), the master sends one start bit and the address byte on the SCL bus. The target slave responds with an acknowledgment bit (ACK) and then starts to transfer the data to the master byte by byte. When the master receives a byte, hardware sets the RXNE flag. Before software can read the receive data register (RXDR), software must wait until the RXNE flag is set. Hardware automatically clears the RXNE flag when software reads RXDR. If auto-end mode is used, the master will automatically send a NACK and a stop bit after the last byte has been transferred. Otherwise, software must send the stop bit explicitly. Additionally, software should wait until hardware sets the transfer complete flag (TC).

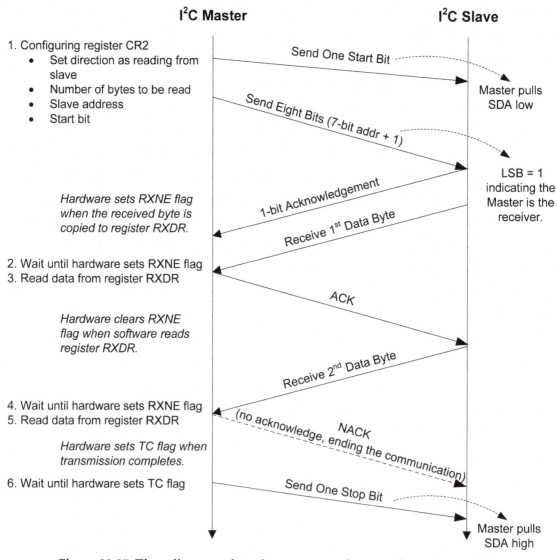

Figure 22-27. Time diagram when the master receives two bytes from a slave

22.2.8   Interfacing a Temperature Sensor via Polling

This section shows a C example program that interfaces with TC74 digital temperature sensors. Make sure that the VDD of the TC74 temperature sensor is 5V, as shown in Figure 22-28.

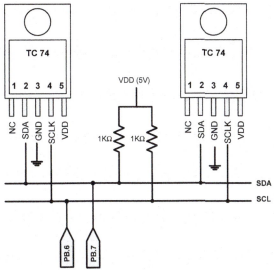

Figure 22-28. Connecting two TC74 digital temperature sensors via the I²C bus.

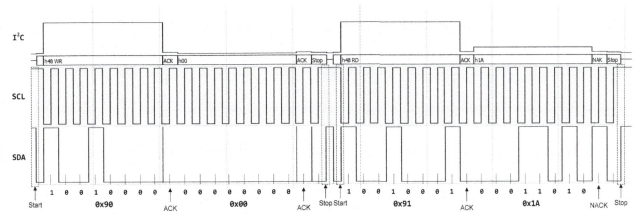

Figure 22-29. Signal capture on the SDA (the top signal) and SCL pin (the bottom signal).

There are two I²C modules on the STM32L processors. In this example, we use the first I²C module, which consists of the following two pins.

Pin	Connection	Mode	AF	Output Type	Pull-up/Pull-down	Clock
PB.6	I2C1_SCL	AF	I2C1	Open-drain	Pull-up	40 MHz
PB.7	I2C1_SDA	AF	I2C1	Open-drain	Pull-up	40 MHz

The following presents the initialization of the first I²C module.

```
void I2C_Init (I2C_TypeDef * I2Cx) {

  uint32_t OwnAddr = 0x52;

  // Enable the I2C clock & Select SYSCLK as the clock source
  // See Example 22-11
  ...

  // I2C CR1 Configuration
  // When the I2C is disabled (PE=0), the I2C performs a software reset.
  I2Cx->CR1 &= ~I2C_CR1_PE;          // Disable I2C
  I2Cx->CR1 &= ~I2C_CR1_ANFOFF;      // 0: Analog noise filter enabled
  I2Cx->CR1 &= ~I2C_CR1_DNF;         // 0000: Digital filter disabled
  I2Cx->CR1 |= I2C_CR1_ERRIE;        // Errors interrupt enable
  I2Cx->CR1 &= ~I2C_CR1_SMBUS;       // SMBus Mode: 0 = I2C mode;  1 = SMBus mode
  I2Cx->CR1 &= ~I2C_CR1_NOSTRETCH;   // Enable clock stretching

  // I2C TIMINGR Configuration (See Section 22.2.5.5)
  I2Cx->TIMINGR = 0;
  // SysTimer = 80 MHz, PRESC = 7, 80MHz/(1 + 7) = 10 MHz
  I2Cx->TIMINGR &= ~I2C_TIMINGR_PRESC; // Clear the prescaler
  I2Cx->TIMINGR |= 7U << 28;           // Set clock prescaler to 7
  I2Cx->TIMINGR |= 49U;                // SCLL: SCL low period (master mode) > 4.7 us
  I2Cx->TIMINGR |= 49U << 8;           // SCLH: SCL high period (master mode) > 4.0 us
  I2Cx->TIMINGR |= 14U << 20;          // SCLDEL: Data setup time > 1.0 us
  I2Cx->TIMINGR |= 15U << 16;          // SDADEL: Data hold time > 1.25 us

  // I2C Own address 1 register (I2C_OAR1)
  I2Cx->OAR1 &= ~I2C_OAR1_OA1EN;
  I2Cx->OAR1 = I2C_OAR1_OA1EN | OwnAddr; // 7-bit own address
  I2Cx->OAR1 &= ~I2C_OAR2_OA2EN;         // Disable own address 2

  // I2C CR2 Configuration
  I2Cx->CR2 &= ~I2C_CR2_ADD10;   // 0 = 7-bit mode, 1 = 10-bit mode
  I2Cx->CR2 |= I2C_CR2_AUTOEND;  // Enable the auto end
  I2Cx->CR2 |= I2C_CR2_NACK;     // For slave mode: set NACK
  I2Cx->CR1 |= I2C_CR1_PE;       // Enable I2C1
}
```

Example 22-12. Initializing I²C

The following subroutine *I2C_Start()* generates a start bit. This subroutine mainly programs the control register CR2. It selects the automatic end mode, in which a STOP bit is sent automatically when all bytes have been transferred. Hardware clears the STOP flag when a STOP bit has been sent successfully.

Similarly, the START bit is set by software and is cleared by hardware after the START bit followed by the slave address is sent. The input argument Direction selects the data transfer direction.

```
void I2C_Start(I2C_TypeDef * I2Cx, uint32_t DevAddress,
                       uint8_t Size, uint8_t Direction) {

  // Direction = 0: Master requests a write transfer
  // Direction = 1: Master requests a read transfer

  uint32_t tmpreg = I2Cx->CR2;
  tmpreg &= (uint32_t)~((uint32_t)(I2C_CR2_SADD    | I2C_CR2_NBYTES  |
                                   I2C_CR2_RELOAD  | I2C_CR2_AUTOEND |
                                   I2C_CR2_RD_WRN  | I2C_CR2_START   |
                                   I2C_CR2_STOP));

  if (Direction == READ_FROM_SLAVE)
    tmpreg |= I2C_CR2_RD_WRN;    // Read from Slave
  else
    tmpreg &= ~I2C_CR2_RD_WRN;   // Write to Slave

  tmpreg |= (uint32_t)(((uint32_t) DevAddress  & I2C_CR2_SADD) |
                      (((uint32_t) Size << 16) & I2C_CR2_NBYTES));

  tmpreg |= I2C_CR2_START;
  I2Cx->CR2 = tmpreg;
}
```

Example 22-13. Sending the start bit

The following subroutine generates a STOP bit. Hardware sets the STOPF flag after the STOP bit has been detected.

```
void I2C_Stop(I2C_TypeDef * I2Cx){

  // Master: Generate STOP bit after the current byte has been transferred
  I2Cx->CR2 |= I2C_CR2_STOP;

  // Wait until STOPF flag is reset
  while( (I2Cx->ISR & I2C_ISR_STOPF) == 0 );

  I2Cx->ICR |= I2C_ICR_STOPCF; // Write 1 to clear STOPF flag
}
```

Example 22-14. Generating a STOP bit

The bus busy flag in the ISR register indicates whether a data transfer is currently taking place. Hardware sets this flag once a START bit is detected. Hardware clears this flag when a STOP bit is detected.

```
void I2C_WaitLineIdle(I2C_TypeDef * I2Cx){
  // Wait until I2C bus is ready
  while( (I2Cx->ISR & I2C_ISR_BUSY) == I2C_ISR_BUSY ); // If busy, wait
}
```

Example 22-15. Waiting for the line idle

The *I2C_SendData()* sends multiple bytes to a target slave.

- It first waits until the SDA and SCL lines are idle (*i.e.*, the voltage of both lines are high). Then it sends a start bit and the slave address.
- Next, it begins to send out the data byte by byte. When the master successfully sends a byte to the target slave, the transmitter register empty (TXIS) flag is set by hardware. Before sending the next byte, normally the master should wait until TC is set. Writing to the data register (TXDR) clears the TXIS flag automatically.
- After all bytes have been sent, hardware sets the TC flag. Software waits until the TC flag is set. Hardware automatically clears the TC flag when the START bit or the STOP bit in the control register CR2 is set.
- At the end, the subroutine sends a stop bit and waits until the SDA and SCL lines are idle.

```
int8_t I2C_SendData(I2C_TypeDef * I2Cx, uint8_t SlaveAddress,
                    uint8_t *pData, uint8_t Size) {
  int i;
  if (Size <= 0 || pData == NULL) return -1;

  // Wait until the line is idle
  I2C_WaitLineIdle(I2Cx);

  // The last argument: 0 = Sending data to the slave
  I2C_Start(I2Cx, SlaveAddress, Size, 0);

  for (i = 0; i < Size; i++) {

    // TXIS bit is set by hardware when the TXDR register is empty and the
    // data to be transmitted must be written in the TXDR register. It is
    // cleared when the next data to be sent is written in the TXDR register.
    // The TXIS flag is not set when a NACK is received.
    while( (I2Cx->ISR & I2C_ISR_TXIS) == 0 );

    // TXIS is cleared by writing to the TXDR register
    I2Cx->TXDR = pData[i] & I2C_TXDR_TXDATA;
  }

  // Wait until TC flag is set
  while((I2Cx->ISR & I2C_ISR_TC) == 0 && (I2Cx->ISR & I2C_ISR_NACKF) == 0);

  if( (I2Cx->ISR & I2C_ISR_NACKF) != 0 )
    return -1;

  I2C_Stop(I2Cx);

  return 0;
}
```

Example 22-16. Transmitting data via I²C

The subroutine *I2C_ReceiveData*() receives data from an I²C slave. The program enables the acknowledgment in the subroutine *I2C_Start*(). Software waits until hardware sets the receive data register not empty flag (RXNE). Hardware sets the RXNE flag when the received data has been copied from the internal shift register into the receive data register (RXDR) and is ready to read. The RXNE flag is cleared when software reads register RXDR.

```c
int8_t I2C_ReceiveData(I2C_TypeDef * I2Cx, uint8_t SlaveAddress,
                       uint8_t *pData, uint8_t Size) {
  int i;

  if (Size <= 0 || pData == NULL) return -1;

  I2C_WaitLineIdle(I2Cx);

  I2C_Start(I2Cx, SlaveAddress, Size, 1);   // 1 = Receiving from the slave

  for (i = 0; i < Size; i++) {
    // Wait until RXNE flag is set
    while( (I2Cx->ISR & I2C_ISR_RXNE) == 0 );
    pData[i] = I2Cx->RXDR & I2C_RXDR_RXDATA;
  }

  while((I2Cx->ISR & I2C_ISR_TC) == 0); // Wait until TCR flag is set

  I2C_Stop(I2Cx);
  return 0;
}
```

Example 22-17. Receiving data via I²C

The following program shows the software that reads the temperature from the temperature sensor TC74.

```c
uint8_t Data_Receive[6];
uint8_t Data_Send[6];

System_Clock_Init();      // Set System Clock to 80 MHz
I2C_GPIO_init();
I2C_Initialization(I2C1);

while(1){
  SlaveAddress = 0x48<<1;   // A0 = 1001000 = 0x48
  Data_Send[0] = 0x00;      // 00 = command to read temperature register
  I2C_SendData(I2C1, SlaveAddress, Data_Send, 1);
  I2C_ReceiveData(I2C1, SlaveAddress, Data_Receive, 1);
  for(i = 0; i < 50000; i++); // Short software delay
}
```

Example 22-18. Interfacing TC74 Temperature sensor

22.2.9 Transferring Data via DMA on I²C Master

To enable DMA transfer, the *I2C_Init()* function given in Example 22-12 must add the following statements:

```
I2Cx->CR1 |= I2C_CR1_TXDMAEN;   // Enable DMA transmission requests
I2Cx->CR1 |= I2C_CR1_RXDMAEN;   // Enable DMA reception requests
```

In the following, we use I2C1 (PB6 and PB7) as an example to show DMA configuration on I2. As shown in Table 19-1, `I2C1_TX` and `I2C1_RX` can be connected to the channel 6 and 7 of the DMA controller 1, respectively. Example 22-19 and Example 22-20 show the DMA configuration. Note that the slave address cannot be transferred via DMA.

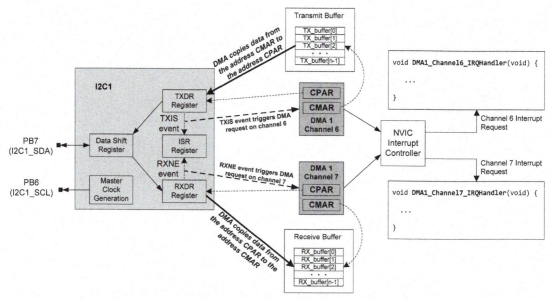

Figure 22-30. DMA Configuration for I2C1 on STM32L4

```
void DMA_Configure_I2C_TX (uint8_t *pTxBuffer, uint32_t size) {
  RCC->AHB1ENR |= RCC_AHB1ENR_DMA1EN;      // Enable DMA1 clock
  // Connect I2C1_TXDR to DMA 1 Channel 6
  DMA1_Channel6->CCR &= ~DMA_CCR_EN;       // Disable DMA channel
  DMA1_Channel6->CCR &= ~DMA_CCR_MEM2MEM;  // Disable memory to memory mode
  DMA1_Channel6->CCR &= ~DMA_CCR_PL;       // Channel priority level
  DMA1_Channel6->CCR |=  DMA_CCR_PL_1;     // Set DMA priority to high
  DMA1_Channel6->CCR &= ~DMA_CCR_PSIZE;    // Peripheral data size 00 = 8 bits
  DMA1_Channel6->CCR &= ~DMA_CCR_MSIZE;    // Memory data size: 00 = 8 bits
  DMA1_Channel6->CCR &= ~DMA_CCR_PINC;     // Disable peripheral increment mode
  DMA1_Channel6->CCR |=  DMA_CCR_MINC;     // Enable memory increment mode
  DMA1_Channel6->CCR &= ~DMA_CCR_CIRC;     // Disable circular mode
  DMA1_Channel6->CCR |=  DMA_CCR_DIR;      // Transfer direction: to peripheral
  DMA1_Channel6->CCR |=  DMA_CCR_TCIE;     // Transfer complete interrupt enable
  DMA1_Channel6->CCR &= ~DMA_CCR_HTIE;     // Disable Half transfer interrupt
  DMA1_Channel6->CNDTR = size;             // Number of data to transfer
```

```
  DMA1_Channel6->CPAR  = (uint32_t)&(I2C1->TXDR);   // Peripheral address
  DMA1_Channel6->CMAR  = (uint32_t) pTxBuffer;       // Transmit buffer address
  DMA1_CSELR->CSELR &= ~DMA_CSELR_C6S;      // See Table 19-1
  DMA1_CSELR->CSELR |= 3<<24;               // Map channel 6 to I2C1_TX
  DMA1_Channel6->CCR |= DMA_CCR_EN;         // Enable DMA channel
}
```

Example 22-19. Configuring DMA 1 channel 6 for I2C1 transmit

```
void DMA_Configure_I2C_RX (uint8_t *pRxBuffer, uint32_t size) {
  RCC->AHB1ENR |= RCC_AHB1ENR_DMA1EN;       // Enable DMA1 clock
  // Connect I2C1_RXDR to DMA 1 Channel 7
  DMA1_Channel7->CCR &= ~DMA_CCR_EN;        // Disable DMA channel
  DMA1_Channel7->CCR &= ~DMA_CCR_MEM2MEM;   // Disable memory to memory mode
  DMA1_Channel7->CCR &= ~DMA_CCR_PL;        // Channel priority level
  DMA1_Channel7->CCR |=   DMA_CCR_PL_1;     // Set DMA priority to high
  DMA1_Channel7->CCR &= ~DMA_CCR_PSIZE;     // Peripheral data size 00 = 8 bits
  DMA1_Channel7->CCR &= ~DMA_CCR_MSIZE;     // Memory data size: 00 = 8 bits
  DMA1_Channel7->CCR &= ~DMA_CCR_PINC;      // Disable peripheral increment mode
  DMA1_Channel7->CCR |=   DMA_CCR_MINC;     // Enable memory increment mode
  DMA1_Channel7->CCR &= ~DMA_CCR_CIRC;      // Disable circular mode
  DMA1_Channel7->CCR |=   DMA_CCR_DIR;      // Transfer direction: to peripheral
  DMA1_Channel7->CCR |=   DMA_CCR_TCIE;     // Transfer complete interrupt enable
  DMA1_Channel7->CCR &= ~DMA_CCR_HTIE;      // Disable Half transfer interrupt
  DMA1_Channel7->CNDTR = size;              // Number of data to transfer
  DMA1_Channel7->CPAR  = (uint32_t)&( I2C1->RXDR);  // Peripheral address
  DMA1_Channel7->CMAR  = (uint32_t) pRxBuffer;       // Transmit buffer address
  DMA1_CSELR->CSELR &= ~DMA_CSELR_C7S;      // See Table 19-1
  DMA1_CSELR->CSELR |= 3<<20;               // Map channel 6 to I2C1_RX
  DMA1_Channel7->CCR |= DMA_CCR_EN;         // Enable DMA channel
}
```

Example 22-20. Configuring DMA 1 channel 7 for I2C1 reception

The following examples illustrates how to send or receive data via DMA.

```
void I2C_SendData(uint8_t *pTxBuffer, uint32_t size, uint8_t SlaveAddress) {
  // DMA must be initialized before setting the START bit
  DMA_Configure_I2C_TX(pTxBuffer, size);   // Configure DMA 1 Channel 6
  I2C_WaitLineIdle(I2C1);                    // Wait until I2C is available
  I2C_Start(I2C1, SlaveAddress, Size, 0);  // 0 = Sending to the slave
}
```

Example 22-21. Sending data to an I²C slave via DMA

```
void I2C_ReceiveData(uint8_t *pRxBuffer, uint32_t size,uint8_t SlaveAddress) {
  // DMA must be initialized before setting the START bit
  DMA_Configure_I2C_TX(pRxBuffer, size);   // Configure DMA 1 channel 7
  I2C_WaitLineIdle(I2C1);                    // Wait until I2C is available
  I2C_Start(I2C1, SlaveAddress, Size, 1);  // 1 = Receiving from the slave
}
```

Example 22-22. Receiving data from an I²C slave via DMA

22.3 Serial Peripheral Interface Bus (SPI)

Serial peripheral interface (SPI) is a synchronous serial communication interface widely used to exchange data between a microprocessor and peripheral devices using four wires. For example, a digital camera often uses SPI to control its lens and save photos to a MMC or SD media.

SPI is simple, has low power requirements, and supports high throughput. Disadvantages of SPI include that it does not support multiple masters, and slaves cannot start the communication or control data transfer speed. The master initiates and controls all communications.

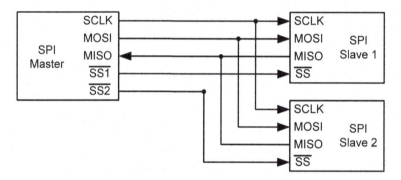

Figure 22-31. A SPI master device connecting to multiple SPI slave devices

A SPI interface consists of four lines: a master-in-slave-out data line (MISO), a master-out-slave-in data line (MOSI), a serial clock line (SCLK), and an active-low slave select line ($\overline{SS}$), as shown in Figure 22-31. SPI is also called four-wire serial interface.

SPI only supports a single master communicating with multiple slave devices. As shown in Figure 22-33, when the master wishes to exchange data with a slave, it pulls down the corresponding select line (SS$_N$). The master then generates clock pulses to coordinate the data transmission on the MOSI and MISO lines.

Data exchange can take place in both directions simultaneously, and this two-way serial channel is often called *full duplex*. Data bits are transmitted on both the MOSI line and the MISO line synchronously, with the flow directions opposite to each other. Note the SCLK line has only one direction, and only the master can generate the clock signal. The slave devices cannot control the clock line.

When there are multiple slave devices, the master decides which slave device it wants to communicate. There is a dedicated Slave Select (SS) line for each slave device. The master selects the target slave device by pulling the corresponding SS line to a low voltage prior to data transfer. The selected slave device then listens for the clock and MOSI signals. When there is only one slave device, the SS line can be directly connected to ground physically, or the program can make the slave continuously selected.

22.3.1   Data Exchange

SPI is a synchronous protocol, and the slave devices must send and receive data based on the clock provided by the master. It differs from an asynchronous protocol in which no clock signal is provided physically. SPI devices must exchange data at the same speed.

The master and a slave perform data exchange at synchronized time steps based on the clock signal generated by the master.

> *SPI master provides clock signal (SCLK) to SPI slaves.*

- When a bit is shifted out on the MISO line from the slave's data register during a clock period, a new data bit is shifted into this register from the MOSI line in the same clock period, as shown in Figure 22-32.
- When one device writes a bit to the data line at the rising or falling edge of the clock, the other device then reads the bit at the opposite edge of the same clock period.
- The data transfer size is usually a byte or halfword (16 bits).

Communication from the master to a slave and communication from a slave to the master are always taking place concurrently. In each communication link (either MISO or MOSI), each device sends out a data item and at the same time receives a new data item. No devices can just be a transmitter or a receiver.

Therefore, when a slave wants to send data to the master via the MISO line, the slave must wait for the clock signal. At the same time, the master must send some dummy data out via the MOSI line to generate the clock signal to initiate the data transfer, as shown in Figure 22-32.

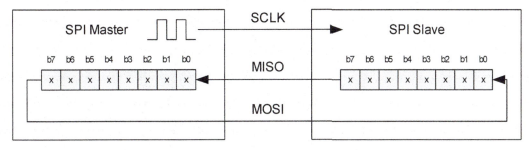

Figure 22-32. A byte is shifted out and in simultaneously via MOSI and MISO.

When a master exchanges data with slave n, the master must set $\overline{SS_n}$ low to select slave n, as shown in Figure 22-33. During the communication, the most significant bit of both data registers is sent out first.

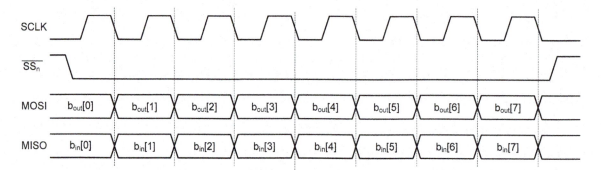

Figure 22-33. Communication signals between a master and slave n. In this example, the most significant bit is transferred first.

Figure 22-34 shows the signal of SCLK and MOSI when two bytes (0xAA and 0x3C) are sent out. In this example, the least significant bit (LSB) of each data is sent out first.

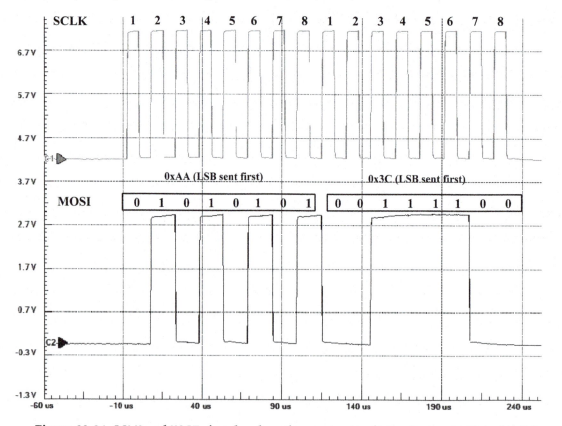

Figure 22-34. SCLK and MOSI signals when the master sends two bytes: 0xAA and 0x3C

22.3.2   Clock Configuration

The clock speed determines the data transfer rate. The data rate ranges from 1 to 20 megabits per second. The master can change the clock speed by programming the clock prescaler register. The clock frequency is usually between 100 KHz to 16 MHz.

For STM32L processors, the baud rate control factor is stored in the BR[2:0] bits of the SPI control register (CR1). The SCLK clock frequency is programmed by setting the baud rate control factor.

$$f_{SCLK} = \frac{f_{SYSCLK}}{2^{1+BR[2:0]}}$$

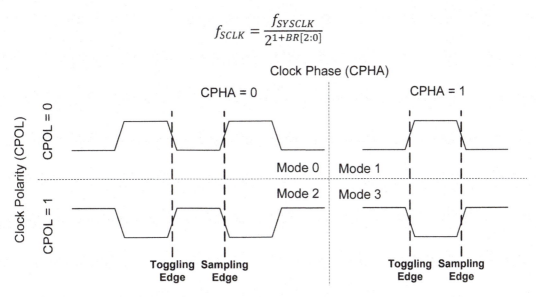

Figure 22-35. Configuration of clock phase and clock polarity

In addition to setting the clock frequency, four possible clock modes are available to program the clock edge used for data sampling and data toggling, as shown in Figure 22-35. The clock modes depend on two parameters: clock phase (CPHA) and clock polarity (CPOL).

- When CPOL is 0, the SCLK line is pulled low during idle time.
- When CPOL is 1, the SCLK line is pulled high during idle time.
- When CPHA is 0, the first clock transition (either rising or falling) is the first data capture edge.
- When CPHA is 1, the second clock transition is the first data capture edge.

The combination of CPOL and CPHA selects the clock edge for transmitting data and the clock edge for receiving data. For example, in mode 0 (CPOL = 0, CPHA = 0), the sender toggles the data on the falling edge of the clock, and the receiver samples the data on the rising edge of the clock. Note the reception of the first bit is delayed one-half cycle in Mode 0 and 2.

22.3.3   Using SPI to Interface a Gyroscope

This section shows how to interface the 3-axis gyro sensor L3GD20 which provides the angular velocity in three axes (yaw, pitch, and roll). The L3GD20 sensor supports two digital interfaces: I²C and SPI. When the voltage on the GYRO_CS pin is low, the SPI interface is selected. Otherwise, the I²C interface is selected.

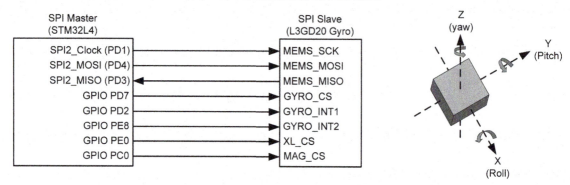

Figure 22-36. Connection between STM32L4 and L3GD20 gyroscope

The L3GD20 gyroscope internally has a set of 8-bit registers. The following program first reads the status register and checks whether angular velocity data are ready to read. If yes, the program reads 6 bytes of raw data and converts them into angular velocities.

```
#define L3GD20_STATUS_REG_ADDR        0x27  // Status register
#define L3GD20_OUT_X_L_ADDR           0x28  // Output Register
struct {
  float x;   // X axis rotation rate, degrees per second
  float y;   // Y axis rotation rate, degrees per second
  float z;   // Z axis rotation rate, degrees per second
} gyro;

int16_t gyro_x, gyro_y, gyro_z;
uint8_t gyr[6], status;

GYRO_IO_Read(&status, L3GD20_STATUS_REG_ADDR, 1); // Read status register
if ( (status & 0x08) == 0x08 ) {  // ZYXDA ready bit set
  // Read 6 bytes from gyro starting at L3GD20_OUT_X_L_ADDR
  GYRO_IO_Read(gyr, L3GD20_OUT_X_L_ADDR, 6);
  // Assume little endian (check the control register 4 of gyro)
  gyro_x = (int16_t) ((uint16_t) (gyr[1]<<8) + gyr[0]);
  gyro_y = (int16_t) ((uint16_t) (gyr[3]<<8) + gyr[2]);
  gyro_z = (int16_t) ((uint16_t) (gyr[5]<<8) + gyr[4]);
  // For +/-2000dps, 1 unit equals to 70 milli degrees per second
  gyro.x = (float) gyro_x * 0.070f;   // X angular velocity
  gyro.y = (float) gyro_y * 0.070f;   // Y angular velocity
  gyro.z = (float) gyro_z * 0.070f;   // Z angular velocity
}
```

Example 22-23. Reading x, y, and z rotation rates from the gyro sensor

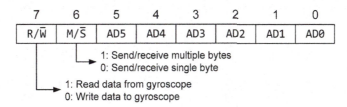

Figure 22-37. Command and address byte of internal registers in L3GD20 gyroscope

Example 22-24 and Example 22-25 show the procedure of writing data to and reading data from the gyro sensor by using the SPI interface. Figure 22-37 illustrates the bit definitions of the command and address byte. Bit 7 indicates the data transmission direction. Bit 6 shows whether a single or multiple bytes will be transmitted. When the $M/\bar{S}$ bar is set, the address will be automatically incremented by 1 after each byte is transmitted.

```
// PD7: GYRO_CS (High = I2C, Low = SPI)
#define L3GD20_CS_LOW      GPIOD->ODR &= ~(1U << 7);
#define L3GD20_CS_HIGH     GPIOD->ODR |=  (1U << 7);


void GYRO_IO_Write (uint8_t *pBuffer, uint8_t WriteAddr, uint8_t size) {

  uint8_t rxBuffer[32];

  if (NumByteToWrite > 0x01) {
    WriteAddr |= 1U << 6; // Select the mode of writing multiple-byte
  }

  // Set SPI interface
  L3GD20_CS_LOW;   // 0 = SPI, 1 = I2C
  Delay(10);       // Short delay

  // Send the address of the indexed register
  SPI_Write(SPI2, &WriteAddr, rxBuffer, 1);

  // Send the data that will be written into the device
  // Bit transfer order: Most significant bit first
  SPI_Write(SPI2, pBuffer, rxBuffer, size);

  // Set chip select High at the end of the transmission
  Delay(10);       // Short delay
  L3GD20_CS_HIGH; // 0 = SPI, 1 = I2C
}
```

Example 22-24. Writing data to the gyro sensor via the SPI interface

```
void GYRO_IO_Read (uint8_t *pBuffer, uint8_t ReadAddr, uint8_t size) {

  uint8_t rxBuffer[32];

  // Select read & multiple-byte mode
  uint8_t AddrByte = ReadAddr | 1U << 7 | 1U << 6;

  // Set chip select low at the start of the transmission
  L3GD20_CS_LOW; // 0 = SPI, 1 = I2C
  Delay(10);     // Short delay

  // Send the address of the indexed register
  SPI_Write(SPI2, &AddrByte, rxBuffer, 1);

  // Receive the data that will be read from the device (MSB First)
  SPI_Read(SPI2, pBuffer, size);

  // Set chip select High at the end of the transmission
  Delay(10);      // Short delay
  L3GD20_CS_HIGH; // 0 = SPI, 1 = I2C
}
```

Example 22-25. Receiving data from the gyro sensor via the SPI interface

The following shows the initialization of SPI, which sets SPI as the master.

```
void SPI_Init(SPI_TypeDef * SPIx){
  // Enable SPI clock
  if(SPIx == SPI1){
    RCC->APB2ENR   |= RCC_APB2ENR_SPI1EN;       // Enable SPI1 Clock
    RCC->APB2RSTR  |= RCC_APB2RSTR_SPI1RST;     // Reset SPI1
    RCC->APB2RSTR  &= ~RCC_APB2RSTR_SPI1RST;    // Clear the reset of SPI1
  } else if(SPIx == SPI2){
    RCC->APB1ENR1  |= RCC_APB1ENR1_SPI2EN;      // Enable SPI2 Clock
    RCC->APB1RSTR1 |= RCC_APB1RSTR1_SPI2RST;    // Reset SPI2
    RCC->APB1RSTR1 &= ~RCC_APB1RSTR1_SPI2RST;   // Clear the reset of SPI2
  } else if(SPIx == SPI3){
    RCC->APB1ENR1  |= RCC_APB1ENR1_SPI3EN;      // Enable SPI3 Clock
    RCC->APB1RSTR1 |= RCC_APB1RSTR1_SPI3RST;    // Reset SPI3
    RCC->APB1RSTR1 &= ~RCC_APB1RSTR1_SPI3RST;   // Clear the reset of SPI3
  }

  SPIx->CR1 &= ~SPI_CR1_SPE;   // Disable SPI

  // Configure duplex or receive-only
  // 0 = Full duplex (transmit and receive), 1 = Receive-only
  SPIx->CR1 &= ~SPI_CR1_RXONLY;
```

```
// Bidirectional data mode enable: This bit enables half-duplex
// communication using common single bidirectional data line.
// 0 = 2-line unidirectional data mode selected
// 1 = 1-line bidirectional data mode selected
SPIx->CR1 &= ~SPI_CR1_BIDIMODE;

// Output enable in bidirectional mode
// 0 = Output disabled (receive-only mode)
// 1 = Output enabled (transmit-only mode)
SPIx->CR1 &= ~SPI_CR1_BIDIOE;

// Data Frame Format
SPIx->CR2 &= ~SPI_CR2_DS;
SPIx->CR2  =  SPI_CR2_DS_0 | SPI_CR2_DS_1 | SPI_CR2_DS_2;   // 0111: 8-bit

// Bit order
// 0 = MSB transmitted/received first
// 1 = LSB transmitted/received first
SPIx->CR1 &= ~SPI_CR1_LSBFIRST;   // Most significant bit first

// Clock phase
// 0 = The first clock transition is the first data capture edge
// 1 = The second clock transition is the first data capture edge
SPIx->CR1 &= ~SPI_CR1_CPHA; // 1st edge

// Clock polarity
// 0 = Set CK to 0 when idle
// 1 = Set CK to 1 when idle
SPIx->CR1 &= ~SPI_CR1_CPOL; // Polarity low

// Baud rate control:
// 000 = f_PCLK/2    001 = f_PCLK/4    010 = f_PCLK/8    011 = f_PCLK/16
// 100 = f_PCLK/32   101 = f_PCLK/64   110 = f_PCLK/128  111 = f_PCLK/256
// SPI baudrate is set to 5 MHz
SPIx->CR1 |= 3U<<3;          // Set SPI clock to 80MHz/16 = 5 MHz

// CRC Polynomial
SPIx->CRCPR = 10;

// Hardware CRC calculation disabled
SPIx->CR1 &= ~SPI_CR1_CRCEN;

// Frame format: 0 = SPI Motorola mode, 1 = SPI TI mode
SPIx->CR2 &= ~SPI_CR2_FRF;

// NSSGPIO: The value of SSI is forced onto the NSS pin and the IO value
// of the NSS pin is ignored.
// 1 = Software slave management enabled
// 0 = Hardware NSS management enabled
SPIx->CR1 |= SPI_CR1_SSM;

// Set as Master: 0 = slave, 1 = master
```

```
     SPIx->CR1 |= SPI_CR1_MSTR;

     // Manage NSS (slave selection) by using Software
     SPIx->CR1 |= SPI_CR1_SSI;

     // Enable NSS pulse management
     SPIx->CR2 |= SPI_CR2_NSSP;

     // Receive buffer not empty (RXNE)
     // The RXNE flag is set depending on the FRXTH bit value in the SPIx_CR2 register:
     // (1) If FRXTH is set, RXNE goes high and stays high until the RXFIFO level is
     //     greater or equal to 1/4 (8-bit).
     // (2) If FRXTH is cleared, RXNE goes high and stays high until the RXFIFO level is
     //     higher than or equal to 1/2 (16-bit).
     SPIx->CR2 |= SPI_CR2_FRXTH;

     // SPI enable
     SPIx->CR1 |= SPI_CR1_SPE;
}
```

Example 22-26. Initializing SPI

The following subroutine is for the SPI master to send the data to an SPI slave.

- It checks the transmission buffer empty flag (TXE) and waits until hardware sets TXE. If TXE is set, the transmission register is ready to accept the next data to be transmitted.
- Writing to the SPI data register (DR) automatically clears the TXE flag.
- The subroutine also waits until the busy flag is cleared to ensure the last data has been successfully sent.

```
void SPI_Write(SPI_TypeDef * SPIx, uint8_t *txBuffer, uint8_t * rxBuffer, int
size) {
  int i = 0;

  for (i = 0; i < size; i++) {

    // Wait for TXE (Transmit buffer empty)
    while( (SPIx->SR & SPI_SR_TXE ) != SPI_SR_TXE );
    SPIx->DR = txBuffer[i];

    // Wait for RXNE (Receive buffer not empty)
    while( (SPIx->SR & SPI_SR_RXNE ) != SPI_SR_RXNE );
    rxBuffer[i] = SPIx->DR;

  }

  // Wait for BSY flag cleared
  while( (SPIx->SR & SPI_SR_BSY) == SPI_SR_BSY );
}
```

Example 22-27. Send data to an SPI slave by using polling

The following subroutine allows an SPI master to receive data from an SPI slave. Only the master can initiate the data transfer and controls the communication clock (SCLK). Therefore, the master must send a dummy byte data to the slave to start the clock.

```
void SPI_Read(SPI_TypeDef * SPIx, uint8_t *rxBuffer, int size) {
  int i = 0;
  for (i = 0; i < size; i++) {

    // Wait for TXE (Transmit buffer empty)
    while( (SPIx->SR & SPI_SR_TXE ) != SPI_SR_TXE );
    // The clock is controlled by master.
    // Thus, the master must send a byte
    SPIx->DR = 0xFF;  // A dummy byte

    // data to the slave to start the clock.
    while( (SPIx->SR & SPI_SR_RXNE ) != SPI_SR_RXNE );
    rxBuffer[i] = SPIx->DR;
  }

  // Wait for BSY flag cleared
  while( (SPIx->SR & SPI_SR_BSY) == SPI_SR_BSY );
}
```

Example 22-28. Receive data from an SPI slave by using polling

In Example 22-27 and Example 22-28, the SPI master uses a polling approach to send and receive data from an SPI slave. A more efficient approach is to use SPI interrupt or SPI DMA. Section 22.1.5 and 22.1.6 shows how to use interrupt and DMA for UART communication. Similarly, SPI can also use interrupt and DMA.

If enabled, a wide range of SPI events can generate interrupt requests. These events include:

1. transmit TXFIFO ready to accept new data,
2. data received in receive RXFIFO,
3. master mode fault when a bus conflict has been detected in multi-bus communication,
4. overrun error when RXFIFO is full and cannot accept new data,
5. TI frame format error when NSS signal does not follow the data format, and
6. CRC protocol error when the received CRC value does not match the CRC value calculated based on the received data.

SPI communication handled via DMA is the most efficient. Software can enable DMA by setting the RXDMAEN and TXDMAEN bit in the CR2 register. If enabled, hardware automatically generates a DMA request each time when the TXE or RXNE enable bit in the CR2 register is set. SPI also supports a special DMA mode in which hardware generates DMA requests when the receive or transmit FIFO reaches a pre-defined threshold.

22.4 Universal Serial Bus (USB)

Universal serial bus (USB) is a widely-used industry standard to connect multiple peripheral devices to a host (typically a computer). Compared to other serial or parallel communication standards, USB has the advantage of ease of use (such as plug and play, hot swapping without rebooting, and no power supply required), low cost, low power consumption, and fast data transfer.

USB 1.0, 2.0 and 3.0 specifications were officially released in 1996, 2000, and 2008, respectively. They are backward compatible. USB 2.0 also includes the USB OTG (on-the-go) protocol, which allows a USB device to perform both the master and slave roles. For example, a printer is a USB slave to a host PC, but it can also be a master when a USB flash drive is plugged in. In this chapter, we only cover the fundamental concepts of USB 1.0 and 2.0. This book does not cover USB OTG and USB 3.0.

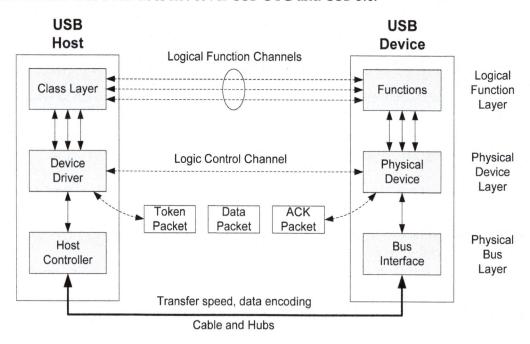

Figure 22-38. USB protocol stack

The USB protocol has three hierarchical layers.
- The bus layer takes care of wire connections, power supply to peripheral devices, transfer speed, and data signal encoding.
- The device layer establishes a logic control channel (endpoint 0) for the host to control and set up the device, detects errors in a packet, and breaks a high-level request into multiple packets.

- The logic function layer establishes multiple logical function channels between a host and a USB device. A USB device might have multiple functions. For example, a printer may have four functions: print, photocopy, scan, and fax. A logical channel allows the host to read data from or write data to a specific function of a USB device.

22.4.1   USB Bus Layer

USB supports four transmission speeds:

- low speed (1.5 Mbit/s = 187 KB/s)
- full speed (12 Mbit/s = 1.5 MB/s)
- high speed (480 Mbit/s = 60 MB/s)
- super speed (4.8 Gbit/s = 600 MB/s)

A standard USB cable has four shielded wires: ground, Vbus (5 volts), data plus (D+) and data minus (D-). The Vbus can provide power supply to USB devices. The D+ and D- wires are physically twisted to cancel out external electromagnetic interference. Voltage under 0.3V on a wire is considered low, and voltage over 2.8V is high.

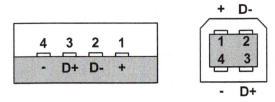

Figure 22-39. USB Connector type A plug (left) and type B plug (right)

Every high-speed USB device must support a data rate of 480Mb/s, with a clock accuracy of ±500 PPM (part per million). One PPM is 0.0001% or 1E-6. A PPM of 12 means a maximum error of approximately one second after one day has passed. 500 PPM implies the clock is off by up to 43 seconds per day. The internal clocks of a microprocessor often do not provide such high accuracy and, therefore, an external crystal oscillator is often deployed to drive the USB peripheral. For example, the internal clocks of the STM32L processor only provide an accuracy of ±600 PPM at room temperature, which implies the clocks can be up to 52 seconds off per day and up to 26 minutes off per month. An inexpensive external crystal oscillator is within ±20 PPM typically. STM32L4 can use a low-speed external clock to calibrate internal clocks.

Data are transmitted via the D+ and D- wires using differential signals. One of them must be high, and the other must be low. For example, for a full-speed connection, the wires are either in the "J" state (D+ = high and D- = low) or the "K" state (D+ = low and D- =

high). When no data is transferred (*i.e.*, idle state), the wires are in the J state. The states for low-speed are the opposite of the states for full-speed.

Non-return-to-zero inverted (NRZI) is used to encode a sequence of binary bits.

- Maintaining the current state denotes a binary 1.
- A binary 0 is represented by switching from the J state to the K state or from the K state to the J state (also called change-on-zero).

Figure 22-40 gives an example of encoding a binary bit string.

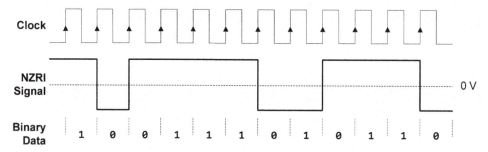

Figure 22-40. Example of NRZI data encoding for full speed

USB also uses the D+ and D- wires to transmit single-ended signals. We say the bus is in the SE0 (SE stands for single-ended) state when both are low, and in the SE1 state when both are high. SE0 is used when a transfer ends, or USB devices are disconnected or reset. SE1 is an illegal state except for battery charging.

Additionally, USB uses a technique called **bit stuffing** to ensure enough state transitions on D+ and D- for clock synchronization between the transmitter and the receiver. More specifically, an additional 0 bit is inserted into the bit streams after six consecutive ones.

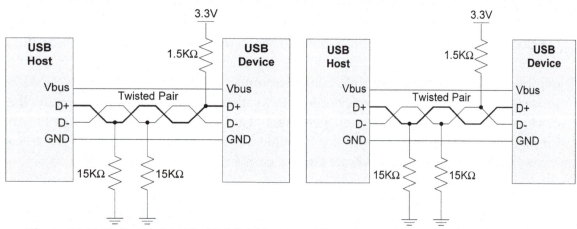

Figure 22-41. Full-speed mode (12 Mbit/s) identified by 1.5KΩ pull-up on D+

Figure 22-42. Low-speed mode (1.5 Mbit/s) identified by 1.5KΩ pull-up on D-

The USB speed is determined by pulling up the D+ or D- wire.

- When neither of them is pulled up, the host assumes no devices are connected.
- If the D+ wire is pulled up via a 1.5KΩ resistor to 3.3V, the host assumes a full-speed USB device is connected.
- The same pull-up on the D- wire indicates a low-speed device.
- A high-speed USB device is identified by initially pulling up the D+ wire. The host attempts to send or receive packets at high speed. If the communication is successful, the host assumes the device operates at high speed, and the device should remove the pull-up afterward. If the communication fails, the host assumes the device runs at full speed.

22.4.2   USB Device Layer

USB is a token-based data transfer protocol in which only a host can initiate the transfer. Each token has a target USB device address. The USB device with a matching address responds to the token packet issued by the host. The token packet also includes a target endpoint and the data transfer direction. A USB device might have multiple endpoints. Each endpoint is a predefined buffer in the USB device's memory.

The transfer direction can be either IN or OUT, from the perspective of the host.

- An IN token packet indicates that the host is requesting to read data from the target endpoint of the USB device.
- An OUT token packet indicates that the host is requesting to write data to the destination endpoint of the device.

A data transfer takes place between a host and the endpoint of a USB device. USB has four different types of data transfers: *control*, *bulk*, *interrupt*, and *isochronous*. The last three provide different tradeoffs between bandwidth, response time and reliability.

- The host uses *control transfers* to obtain basic information (called *descriptors*) of a USB device and to read or set the status and address of the device. All USB devices must support control transfers.
- *Bulk transfers* are designed to deliver relatively large but bursty data. It provides high bandwidth but requires the application to tolerate a long delay if the bus is busy. Printers, scanners, and mass storage devices use bulk transfers.
- For *interrupt transfers*, the host periodically queries a USB device for data. It provides less bandwidth than bulk transfers, but the maximum latency is limited to the query period. Mice and keyboards use interrupt transfer.
- *Isochronous transfers* provide guaranteed latency but are unreliable due to lack of error detection. Microphones and web cameras often use isochronous transfers.

At a lower level, a transfer consists of multiple packets. There are three packet formats: *token packets*, *data packets* and *acknowledge packets*. Figure 22-43 shows the packet structure of full/low speed. Each packet includes at least an SYNC byte, a PID byte, and EOP field.

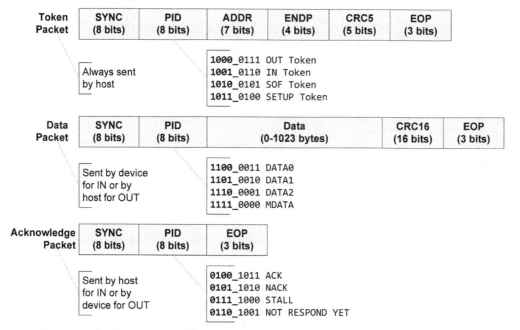

Figure 22-43. A transaction starts with a token packet sent by the host, then a data packet, and finally a handshake packet.

- **Synchronization field (SYNC)**. The SYNC byte is the first byte of a packet. It is used to ensure that the receiving clock is synchronized to the transmitting clock in a packet transfer. The value of the SYNC byte is 0b00000001. For full speed, since the idle state is the J state, the D+ and D- wires are in a sequence of "KJKJKJKK" when the SYNC byte is transmitted.

- **Packet identification field (PID)**. The PID byte identifies the type of packet being sent. The lower four bits of the PID bytes are the inverse of the upper four bits. This inversion is used for error checking. Also, the least-significant bit is sent out first. For example, if the PID field is 0b10000111, the actual PID code is 0b0001.

- **Address field (ADDR)**. An ADDR that has 7 bits can address 127 devices (address 0 is reserved). The host assigns the address. A device uses address 0 during the initial communication until the host assigns the device address.

- **Endpoint field (ENDP)**. It uses four bits to identify 16 endpoints within a USB device.

- **Data field**. The length of the data field varies from 0 to 1,023, depending on the transfer type and the USB speed. For example, the data field size is limited to typically

8 bytes in low-speed devices, and to 8, 16, 32 or 64 bytes for control transfers and 64 bytes for interrupt transfer in full-speed devices.

- **Cyclic redundancy check (CRC) field**. We use CRC to detect payload corruption arising from transmission errors.
  - Each token packet has a five-bit CRC, and each data packet has a 16-bit CRC. The basic idea of the CRC calculation involves three steps. First, the data bits to be protected are treated as a binary number. Second, we divide this binary number by another predefined binary number. Finally, we select the remainder of the division as the CRC code.
  - The receiver performs the same steps to compare the remainder calculated and the rest received (*i.e.*, CRC code). Typically, we use hardware circuits to calculate CRC for fast performance.
  - We call a contiguous sequence of erroneous data bits *burst errors*. An n-bit CRC can detect all single- and double-bit errors, and any single burst error that is shorter than or equal to n bits. It can also detect a fraction $1 - 2^{-n}$ of all longer burst errors.
- **End of packet field (EOP)**. EOP consists of SEC0 for two time units of a bit and a J-state for one time unit.

A transaction completes in three steps.

1. First, the host sends a token packet, indicating the recipient (specified in the ENDPOINT field) of the target USB device (ADDR field), and the transfer direction of the next data packet (packet ID).
2. Second, if the packet ID of the token packet is OUT or SETUP, the host sends a data packet to the specified endpoint of the target USB device, and the device must send an acknowledge packet back to the host. The acknowledge packet informs the host whether the device has successfully received the data.
3. If the token packet is an IN packet, the device sends the data packet, and the host replies with an acknowledge packet.

The USB host broadcasts a start-of-frame (SOF) packet every 1 *ms* for a full-speed bus and every 125µs for a high-speed bus. The host does not expect any USB devices to return any packet. The SOF packets provide time stamps for USB devices to schedule data transfers. For example, the host can use the SOF to inform a USB device to prepare for receiving or transmitting one data packet for an isochronous transfer.

START OF FRAME (SOF)	SYNC (8 bits)	Packet ID (8 bits)	Frame Number (11 bits)	CRC5 (5 bits)	EOP (3 bits)

Figure 22-44. Format of start-of-frame (SOF)

The USB hardware handles receiving a packet. The hardware automatically detects or generates the SYNC field, identifies the packets addressed to this USB device, performs CRC error checking, and detects or generates the end of the packet (EOP) field.

The USB hardware automatically generates interrupts for software to handle corresponding events. For example, when CRC checking fails or the device has not received any response from the host for a long time, the USB hardware generates an interrupt and sets the ERR bit of the USB interrupt status register.

22.4.3   USB Function Layer

A USB device may have multiple functions. For example, a web camera may have three functions: microphone, camera, and storage. A printer may have the functions of printing, scanning, and photocopying. Endpoints are the interface between a function of a USB device and the USB host. Data are transferred between the host and an endpoint. A USB device can have multiple endpoints. All USB devices must support endpoint 0, which is a special endpoint for the host to control USB devices.

A logic communication that takes place between the host and an endpoint is called a pipe or channel. An endpoint contains the endpoint number, the transfer type (control, isochronous, bulk, or interrupt), the transfer direction (IN or OUT), the maximum packet size, and the polling intervals in terms of the number of start-of-frames.

22.4.3.1 USB Descriptors

The properties of a USB device are defined in a hierarchy of descriptors. Figure 22-45 shows example descriptors of a USB device. Each device has one and only one device descriptor. Each device can have one or more configurations. Each configuration can have multiple interfaces.

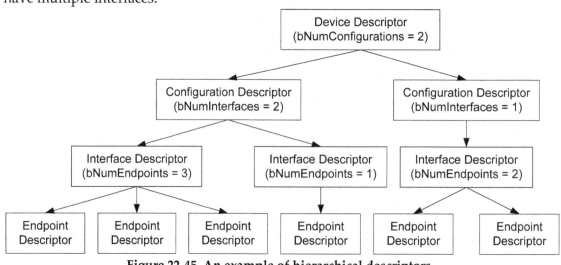

Figure 22-45. An example of hierarchical descriptors

- The device descriptor presents important information of the whole USB device, such as the vendor ID (signed by USB.org) and the product ID (assigned by the manufacturer), the total number of configurations, and the maximum packet size for endpoint 0.
- Although it is uncommon, a device might have multiple configuration descriptors. For example, a USB device might have a configuration for USB power supply and another configuration for battery power supply. When there are multiple configuration descriptors, the USB host must select one. A configuration descriptor contains information such as the total number of interfaces used for these settings and power requirements.
- An interface descriptor is associated with a function of the USB device. A configuration can include a set of interfaces. For example, a web camera can have one interface for its microphone and another interface for its camera. An interface descriptor describes information such as the number of endpoints for this interface, and the class and subclass codes (assigned by USB.org).

Figure 22-46 shows the format of each descriptor. All descriptors have three common fields:

(1) The *length* field specifies the number of bytes in the descriptor.
(2) The *bDescriptor* field indicates the type of descriptor (0x01 = Device, 0x02 = Configuration, 0x04 = Interface, 0x05 = Endpoint).
(3) The *bcdUSB* field states the highest USB version that the device supports in BCD code. For example, 0x0110 is USB 1.1, 0x0200 is USB 2.0, and 0x0300 is USB 3.0. Chapter 18.4 discusses the BCD code.

The *bDeviceClass*, *bDeviceSubClass*, and *bDeviceProtocols* are defined by USB.org. For example, a device class code of 0x09, 0xDC, and 0xFF specifies a USB hub, a diagnostic device, and a vendor specific device, respectively. When the device class code is 0x00, the interface class code determines the device class.

The *bInterfaceClass* is also predefined by USB.org. For example, the following are some example codes of interface class: audio (0x01), human interface device (0x03), physical interface device (0x05), image (0x06), printer (0x07), mass storage (0x08), smart card (0x0B), content security (0x0D), video (0x0E), personal healthcare (0x0F), and wireless controller (0xE0).

There is also a string descriptor, which defines an array of strings. The *iManufacturer*, *iProduct*, *iSerialNumber*, *iConfiguration*, *iFunction* and *iInterface* used in the above descriptors are the index to the string array.

Device Descriptor

Field Name	Size	Offset
bLength	1	0
bDescriptorType	1	1
bcdUSB	2	2
bDeviceClass	1	4
bDeviceSubClass	1	5
bDeviceProtocol	1	6
bMaxPacketSize	1	7
idVendor	2	8
idProduct	2	10
bcdDevice	2	12
iManufacturer	1	14
iProduct	1	15
iSerialNumber	1	16
bNumConfigurations	1	17

Interface Descriptor

Field Name	Size	Offset
bLength	1	0
bDescriptorType	1	1
bInterfaceNumber	1	2
bAlternateSetting	1	3
bNumEndpoints	1	4
bInterfaceClass	1	5
bInterfaceSubClass	1	6
bInterfaceProtocol	1	7
iInterface	1	8

Configuration Descriptor

Field Name	Size	Offset
bLength	1	0
bDescriptorType	1	1
wTotalLength	2	2
bNumInterfaces	1	4
bConfigurationValue	1	5
iConfiguration	1	6
bmAttributes	1	7
bMaxPower	1	8

Endpoint Descriptor

Field Name	Size	Offset
bLength	1	0
bDescriptorType	1	1
bEndpointAddress	1	2
bmAttributes	1	3
wMaxPacketSize	2	4
bInterval	1	6

String Descriptor

Field Name	Size	Offset
bLength	1	0
bDescriptorType	1	1
wLANGID[0]	2	2
wLANGID[1]	2	4
wLANGID[x]	2	6

Field Name	Size	Offset
bLength	1	0
bDescriptorType	1	1
bString	n	2

Figure 22-46. Format of device, configuration, interface and endpoint descriptor

22.4.3.2 Endpoint-Oriented Communication

Each transfer over USB is identified by a three-tuple: *device address, endpoint,* and *direction.* Every device must support endpoint 0, which is used for the host to control and set up the device. As shown in Figure 22-47, the web camera has four endpoints in the first configuration.

- Endpoint 0 is for the host to control the device.
- Endpoint 1 forms a channel to access the microphone.
- Endpoint 2 is to access the camera.
- Endpoint 3 is to access the storage.

To meet time constraints, isochronous transfers are preferred for transmitting audio and video signals from endpoint 1 and 2 to the host. Bulk transfers are selected for endpoint 3 IN and OUT to store and retrieve data. The web camera can have a second configuration, which includes another set of functions. The host decides which configuration is to be used for the web camera.

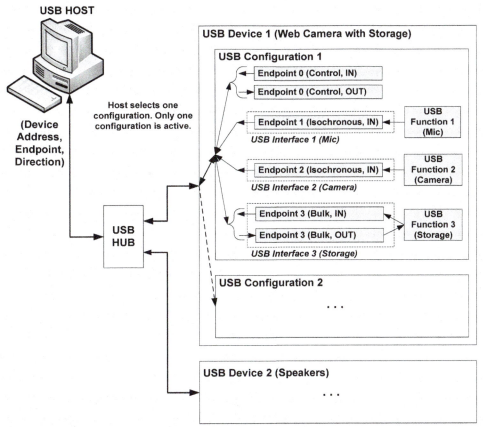

Figure 22-47. An USB configuration may have multiple functions (such as a microphone, camera, and storage device). All communications occur between the host and the endpoints of an USB configuration.

22.4.3.3 USB Enumeration

USB enumeration is the process of detecting and identifying a USB device. During a USB enumeration, the host performs the following steps:

1. Detect whether a device has been connected. When a USB device is plugged into a host, there is a change on the USB D+ or D- line because one of them is pulled up by the device.
2. Determine the USB speed. As introduced previously, pulling up the D- via 1.5KΩ pull-up to 3V indicates a low-speed device. The same pull-up on the D+ specifies a high-speed device.
3. Retrieve the device descriptor and identify what device is attached.
4. Retrieve all configuration descriptors. This process may take milliseconds to complete. The host selects one configuration.
5. Retrieve all interface descriptors.
6. Load the corresponding device driver. This is typically handled by operating systems on the host. The host uses *idVendor* and *idProduct* to match a driver.

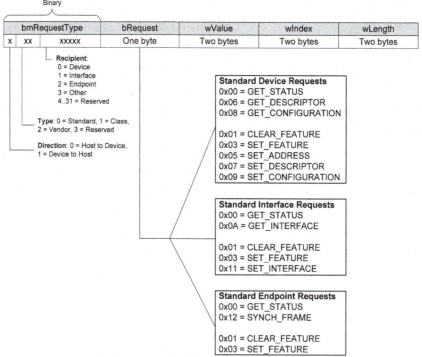

Figure 22-48. Format of setup request

The host sends a series of setup requests to complete the above enumeration process. The device responds to each setup request. Figure 22-48 shows the standardized format of a setup request. Figure 22-49 shows the procedures of retrieving the device description. Note the setup request is encapsulated into the data packet as its payload.

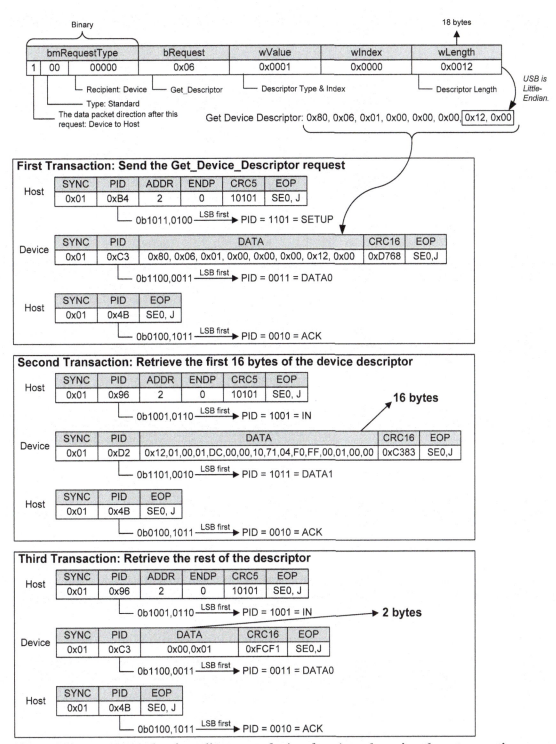

Figure 22-49. An example of sending a *get_device_descriptor* by using three transactions. Assume the maximum data size is 16 bytes. The request is sent as the payload of the first transaction.

After detecting a USB device is attached, the host waits for at least 100 *ms* to allow the completion of USB device plugging and then issues a reset request. The reset request sets the device into the default state. Initially, the default address of a USB device is 0. Each USB device should respond to all requests addressed to 0 before it is assigned a unique address.

It is the host's responsibility to assign a unique address to the USB device. The host sends an SET_ADDRESS request, which includes the assigned address, to the device, as shown in Figure 22-50. The device shall respond to all requests targeted to the assigned address.

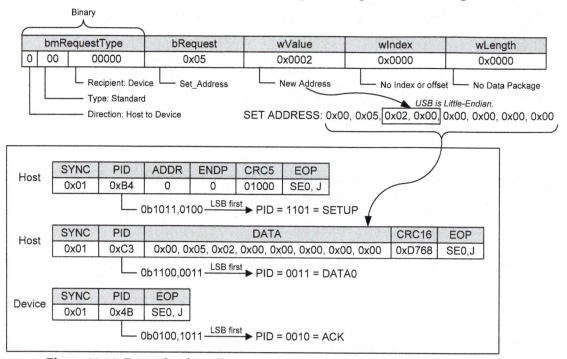

Figure 22-50. Example of sending a *set_address* request by using one transaction

Figure 22-51 shows the enumeration process in Windows operating systems.

- The host first uses a simple debouncing technique to wait for the USB device to plug in successfully and become stabilized.
- Then the host issues a reset request by using the default USB address 0. Because the host initially does not know the packet size supported by the control endpoint (*i.e.*, endpoint 0) of the USB device, the host issues two GET_DESCRIPTOR requests for the device descriptor. The first device descriptor request is to find the packet size supported by the device. Before issuing the second device descriptor request, the host sends another reset request to eliminate any confusion that the device may have. Some devices get confused if the host does not let the response to the first device descriptor request complete.

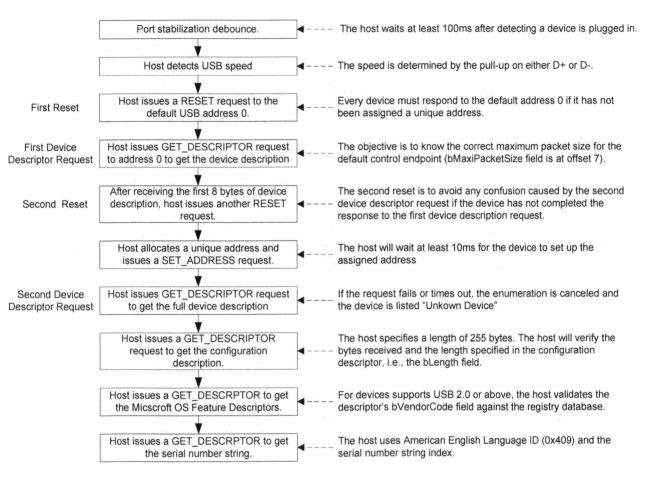

Figure 22-51. USB enumeration process in Windows

Windows operating systems (OS) also define proprietary descriptors for USB 2.0 and above, which allow the OS to install and configure the device automatically, making the process of plug and play smooth for users. The OS descriptors contain a variety of vendor-specific information, such as the identification code of a new type of device that incorporates new features of a standard USB device class or subclass. Figure 22-52 shows the format of the request that retrieves a vendor-specific OS descriptor.

bmRequestType			bRequest	wValue	wIndex	wLength
1	10	00000	**0x01**	Interface	Feature Index	Length

Binary

- Recipient: Device
- Type: Vendor
- The data packet direction after this request: Device to Host

GET_MS_DESCRIPTOR

- High Byte = 0
- Low Byte = InterfaceNumber

- 0x0001 = Genre:
- 0x0004 = Extended compat ID
- 0x0005 = Extended properties

Figure 22-52. Format of the request to retrieve an OS descriptor

22.4.4   USB Class Layer

As introduced previously, a USB device can perform multiple logical functions. The device layer allows a host to send a USB request to a given function via endpoints. Each function follows a predefined class protocol to handle USB requests. Examples of standardized USB class protocols include the human interface device (HID), the communications device class (CDC), the personal healthcare device class (PHDC), the mass storage class (MSC), the audio, and the video. Vendors can also customize the USB class protocols.

The HID class specifies the interactions to human interface devices such as keyboards, mice, and game controllers. We discuss HID in this chapter later.

The CDC class emulates a virtual UART to interconnect with a serial communication port, such as RS-232 COM port. As serial ports are being gradually eliminated on personal computers, more applications utilize the CDC function of USB to communicate devices such as modems, fax machines, and telephony devices.

The PHDC class specifies the standards to interact with personal health devices such as blood pressure monitors, glucose meter, cardiovascular fitness monitor, and weight scales. The protocols are grouped into three themes: health and wellness, disease management, and aging independently. Because low latency and high reliability are very critical in some applications, this class defines meta-data along with the message data so that the host can determine how to transfer data over USB to meet the latency and reliability requirements.

The MSC class is a protocol to access a USB storage device. Modern USB storage devices use bulk transfers to achieve high bandwidth. Another important specification is the boot ability, which allows a computer to boot from an external USB storage device, instead of an internal hard drive.

The audio class uses isochronous data transfers to stream audio data at a constant rate. For full-speed USB devices, a data frame spans 1 *ms*, and a device can transfer 0-1023 bytes per data frame, depending on the application's need. As introduced previously, isochronous transfers have no acknowledge packet and no error-checking ability. Thus, a transmission error may occur.

The video class provides the function of streaming video in real time like web cameras. Like the audio class, the video class also uses isochronous transfers. A video device shall complete a bandwidth negotiation process with the host. The video class allows the host to determine preferred stream parameters to the device. After the device reports to the host, the maximum bandwidth usage based on given parameters, the host uses the bandwidth information to identify alternate interfaces. An alternative interface is an interface that the device provides for replacing the default interface. For example, a video device with various resolutions provides different alternative interfaces that have different bandwidth requirements.

22.4.5   Human Interface Device (HID)

The HID class consists of devices that are used by humans to interact with a computer, such as a mouse, keyboard, touch screen, or game controller.

- One advantage of HID is that the host probably already has device drivers, and thus a programmer might not need to write any software for the host.
- One disadvantage of HID is that its bandwidth is relatively small because its maximum packet size for full speed is limited to 64 bytes. Because there is one data transfer per frame (1 *ms*), the bandwidth of HID is limited to 64KB/s.

HID is the interface descriptor, and it is not the device descriptor. HID specifies the class information.

- A class code of 0x03 in the interface descriptor indicates that the device is a HID device.
- ALL HID devices must have a control endpoint (endpoint 0), an interrupt IN endpoint, and an optional interrupt OUT endpoint.
- The device data, such letters pressed on a keyboard, are sent to the host via the interrupt IN endpoint.

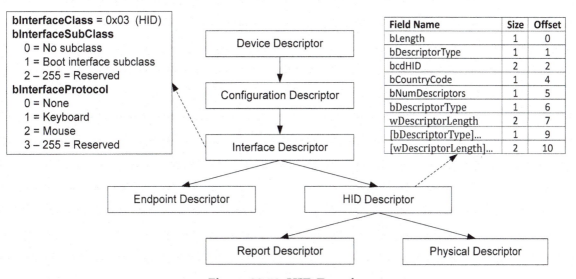

Figure 22-53. HID Descriptor

A special descriptor called **HID descriptor** defines the format of data exchanged between the host and the USB device.

- Example input data include the pressed key on a keyboard, and the X and Y data from a mouse.
- Example output data include LEDs indicating power status, caps lock or the number lock on a keyboard.

The host requests the HID descriptor during the USB enumeration process. A HID descriptor can include both report and physical descriptors.

- A report descriptor specifies the structure (data size, data type, and data meaning) of all data items that a device generates.
- A physical descriptor is optional and describes the part or parts of the human body used to activate the controls.

The objective of both descriptors is to help the USB host parse received data. This section gives two example HID descriptors (a keyboard and a mouse).

The following gives an example report descriptor of a keyboard. The ":" sign is to declare a bit-field in a structure. The LED structure includes three padding bits to extend the size of the structure to one byte.

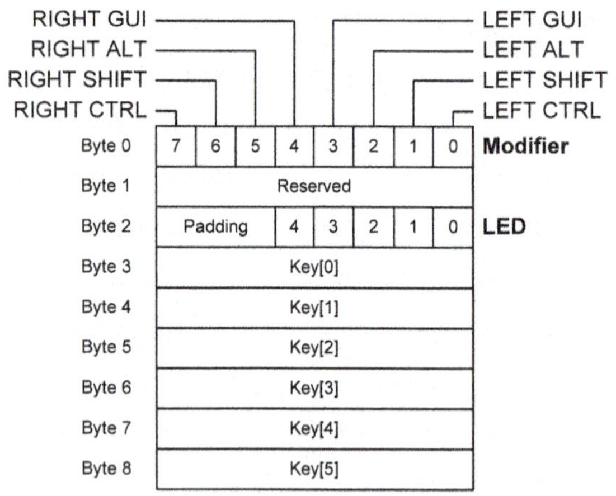

Figure 22-54. Report format of a keyboard

```
typedef struct _HID_KEYBOARD_REPORT{
    uint8_t modifier;
    // bit flags for
    // ALT, SHIFT, CTRL and GUI
    uint8_t reserved;
    struct {
        unsigned Num_Lock : 1;
        unsigned Caps_Lock : 1;
        unsigned Scroll_Lock : 1;
        unsigned Shift_Lock : 1;
        unsigned Power : 1
        unsigned Padding :3;
    } LED;
    uint8_t key[6];
} HID_KEYBOARD_REPORT;
```

HID class-specific requests are used during the enumeration. Supported class-specific requests for HID devices include GET_REPORT, SET_REPORT, GET_IDLE, SET_IDLE, GET_PROTOCOL, and SET_PROTOCOL. Figure 22-55 shows an example of GET_REPORT request to retrieve HID report descriptor.

Get HID Descriptor: 0x81, 0x06, 0x00, 0x22, 0x03, 0x00, 0x72, 0x00

Binary

bmRequestType			bRequest	wValue	wIndex	wLength
1	00	00001	0x06	0x2200	0x0003	0x0072

Recipient: Interface — Get_Descriptor — Descriptor Type & Index — Descriptor Length

Type: Standard

The data packet direction after this request: Device to Host

Figure 22-55. A *get_report* request to retrieve HID report descriptor

```
const uint8_t HID_Keyboard_ReportDescriptor[] = {
    0x05, 0x01,     // Usage page (generic desktop)
    0x09, 0x06,     // Usage (keyboard)
    0xA1, 0x01,     // Collection (application)
    0x75, 0x01,     //   Report size (1 bit)
    0x95, 0x08,     //   Report count (8): for 8 modifier bits
    0x05, 0x07,     //   Usage page (key codes)
    0x19, 0xE0,     //   Usage minimum (keyboard left control)
    0x29, 0xE7,     //   Usage maximum (keyboard right GUI)
    0x15, 0x00,     //   Logical minimum (0)
    0x25, 0x01,     //   Logical maximum (1)
    0x81, 0x02,     //   Input (data, variable, absolute)
    0x95, 0x01,     //   Report count (1): for reserved byte
    0x75, 0x08,     //   Report size (8 bits)
    0x81, 0x03,     //   Input (const, variable, absolute)
    0x95, 0x05,     //   Report count (5), for 5 LED outputs from the host
    0x75, 0x01,     //   Report size (1 bit)
    0x05, 0x08,     //   Usage page (LEDs)
    0x19, 0x01,     //   Usage minimum (number lock)
    0x29, 0x05,     //   Usage maximum (kana)
    0x91, 0x02,     //   Output (data, variable, absolute)
    0x95, 0x01,     //   Report count (1): LED report padding
    0x75, 0x03,     //   Report size (3 bits)
    0x91, 0x03,     //   Output (const, variable, absolute)
    0x95, 0x06,     //   Report count (6): Key arrays (6 bytes)
    0x75, 0x08,     //   Report size (8 bits)
    0x15, 0x00,     //   Logical minimum (0)
    0x26, 231, 0,   //   Logical maximum (231)
    0x05, 0x07,     //   Usage page (keyboard)
    0x19, 0x00,     //   Usage minimum (reserved)
    0x29, 231,      //   Usage maximum (keyboard application)
    0x81, 0x00,     //   Input (data, array, absolute)
    0xC0            // End collection
};
```

Table 22-10. HID keyboard report descriptor

Each row item in the HID descriptor includes a predefined type and value. For example, the second row in the HID keyboard report descriptor given in Table 22-10 has a type-value pair "0x09, 0x06",

- 0x09 represents the data type, and
- 0x06 represents the value.

The type 0x09 means the upper byte of the usage definition and the value 0x06 represents keyboard or keypad. The values are predefined, such as 0x02 for mouse, 0x0B for telephony devices, 0x0D for digitizers, and 0x80 for monitor devices.

The HID descriptor defines a report data structure with a total of eight bytes, as shown in Figure 22-54. The first byte of the data structure is a bitmap, which includes eight logical flags. The following two lines define the report size and the report count.

```
0x75, 0x01,    // Report size (1 bit)
0x95, 0x08,    // Report count (8)
```

The second byte is a reserved byte. The third byte defines five LED outputs from the USB host and three unused padding bits.

```
0x95, 0x05,    // Report count (5), for 5 LED outputs from the host
0x75, 0x01,    // Report size (1 bit)
...
0x95, 0x01,    // Report count (1): LED report padding
0x75, 0x03,    // Report size (3 bits)
```

Following the LED byte is a byte array, which is used to hold six key values. Note a keyboard does not send an ASCII value to the host when a key is pressed. Instead, it sends the HID key code, as shown in Appendix H.

Note it is often that two key inputs share the same key code. For example, the key code of "a" and "A" is 0x04. They are differentiated by the modifier byte shown in Figure 22-54. For example, when Key[0] = 0x04, it represents "A" if the LEFT SHIFT or the RIGHT SHIFT bit is set in the modifier. It represents "a" if none of these two bits is set.

The device needs to inform when a key is released. This can be done in two different forms.

- The first one is that the device sends a report in which all key values are zero.
- The second one is that the device sends a report in which different key values are stored, implying that previous keys have been released, and new keys are pressed.

The following gives an example report of a mouse with three buttons and a wheel. To create a mouse "click," two reports are needed. One is to report the button down (set the corresponding bit in the first byte), and the other is to report the button release (clear the corresponding bit in the first byte).

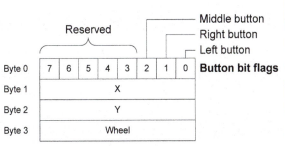

Figure 22-56. Report format of a mouse

```
typedef struct _HID_MOUSE_REPORT{
    struct {
        unsigned Left   : 1;
        unsigned Right  : 1;
        unsigned Middle : 1;
        unsigned Padding : 5;
    } Buttons;
    uint8_t X;
    uint8_t Y;
    uint8_t Wheel;
} HID_MOUSE_REPORT;
```

```
const uint8_t HID_ReportDescriptor[] = {
    0x05, 0x01, // Usage page (generic desktop)
    0x09, 0x02, // Usage (mouse)
    0xA1, 0x01, // Collection (application)
    0x09, 0x01, //   Usage (pointer)
    0xA1, 0x00, //   Collection (physical)
    0x05, 0x09, //     Usage page (buttons)
    0x19, 0x01, //     Usage minimum (button #1)
    0x29, 0x03, //     Usage maximum (button #3)
    0x15, 0x00, //     Logical minimum (0)
    0x25, 0x01, //     Logical maximum (1)
    0x95, 0x03, //     Report count (3), for middle, right and left buttons
    0x75, 0x01, //     Report size (1 bit)
    0x81, 0x02, //     Input (data, variable, absolute)
    0x95, 0x01, //     Report count (1)
    0x75, 0x05, //     Report size (5 bits), five padding bits
    0x81, 0x01, //     Input (const, variable, absolute)
    0x05, 0x01, //     Usage page (generic desktop)
    0x09, 0x30, //     Usage (X)
    0x09, 0x31, //     Usage (Y)
    0x09, 0x38, //     Usage (wheel)
    0x15, 0x81, //     Logical minimum (-127)
    0x25, 0x7F, //     Logical maximum (127)
    0x75, 0x08, //     Report size (8 bits)
    0x95, 0x02, //     Report count (3), for x, y, and wheel
    0x81, 0x06, //     Input (data, array, absolute)
    0xC0        //   End collection
    0xC0        // End collection
};
```

Table 22-11. HID mouse report descriptor

22.5 Exercises

1. Write an assembly program that periodically collects temperature readings from two TC74 digital temperature sensors. The sensors use I²C protocol.

2. Write an assembly program that periodically collects information from a Wii Nunchuk controller, which uses the I²C standard mode (100 Kbps). A Nunchuk has two push buttons (labeled as C and Z), an 8-bit 2-axis analog joystick (X, Y) and a 10-bit 3-axis accelerometer sensor (X, Y, and Z). It has two slave addresses, 0xA4 for writing and 0xA5 for reading. The data returned from a Nunchuk consists of 6 bytes. Note the communication is encrypted. One possible decoding is

   Data = (Received data XOR 0x17) + 0x17

Address	Data							
0x00	Joystick X							
0x01	Joystick Y							
0x02	Accelerometer X (bit 9 to bit 2)							
0x03	Accelerometer Y (bit 9 to bit 2)							
0x04	Accelerometer Z (bit 9 to bit 2)							
0x05	Accel. Z (bit 1)	Accel. Z (bit 0)	Accel. Y (bit 1)	Accel. Y (bit 0)	Accel. X (bit 1)	Accel. X (bit 0)	C button	Z button

   The initialization command has two bytes (0x40, 0x00), and a conversion command has only one byte (0x00). The conversion command is to ask the Nunchuk to collect the data from all its sensors and make the data ready to transfer. All commands should be sent to the slave address 0xA4. After the conversion command, the six-byte data can read out from the slave address 0xA5.

Joystick X	0x80 = Center, 0x00 = Full left, 0xFF = Full right
Joystick Y	0x80 = Center, 0x00 = Full up, 0xFF = Full down
Acceleration	0 – 1023.
Button	0 = pressed, 1 = released

3. Use the SPI protocol to interact with 3-axis gyroscope (Parallax L3G4200D). The gyroscope provides the rate of change in rotation on its X, Y and Z axes.

4. Use the SPI protocol to read an SD memory Card.

5. Implement a HID keyboard device. When the user button on the discovery kit board is pressed, the host PC automatically plays a YouTube video.

6. Implement a HID mouse device. The device automatically draws a picture on the host screen (such as drawing a circle in Paint in Windows).

Multitasking

23.1 Processor Mode and Privilege Level

Cortex-M processors have two execution modes: *handler mode* and *thread mode*, as shown in Figure 23-1. On reset, the processor enters thread mode by default. The processor enters handler mode when it starts to serve an interrupt request. The processor exits handler mode after the interrupt service routine completes.

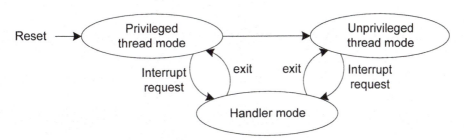

Figure 23-1. Thread mode and handler mode

In addition, Cortex-M provides two privilege levels: *privileged* or *unprivileged*.

- Thread mode execution can be privileged or unprivileged. While the privileged state allows software to access all resources in a processor, the unprivileged state prevents software from configuring or controlling some protected resources directly. When the processor is in the unprivileged state, software can indirectly access protected resources via supervisor calls (SVC).
- When the processor is reset, the processor enters the privileged thread mode by default. Software can change the thread mode from privileged to unprivileged, but not the other way around.
- When the processor is in handler mode, software is always executed at the privileged level.

Providing two privilege levels increases the security of the whole system. For example, at the unprivileged level, software cannot configure the system timer (SysTick), NVIC, or the system control block (SCB). Additionally, load/store instructions cannot access protected memory regions or peripherals.

23.1.1   Control Register

Cortex-M processors have a special-purpose register named CONTROL, as shown Figure 23-2. It has only three value bits: the floating-point context active flag (FPCA), the stack pointer selection bit (SPSEL) and the execution privilege in thread mode bit (nPRIV). The value of the CONTROL register is 0x00000000 on reset.

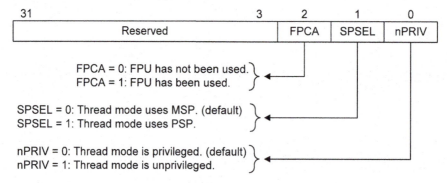

Figure 23-2. CONTROL register

- The nPRIV bit determines whether thread mode is privileged or unprivileged.
- The SPSEL bit controls whether MSP or PSP is the current stack. The stack pointer r14 (SP) shadows the main stack pointer register (MSP) or the process stack pointer register (PSP).
    o In handler mode, PUSH and POP stack operations use MSP. Additionally, the processor ignores any writes to the SPSEL bit.
    o In thread mode, PUSH and POP operations use either MSP or PSP.
    o On reset, MSP is the default active stack.
- The FPCA bit, as introduced in Chapter 12.4.1, indicates whether the processor has executed any floating-point instructions.

The following program shows how to read the CONTROL register, how to modify the CONTROL register to select the process stack (PSP) as the active stack, and how to switch to the unprivileged level.

```
__asm uint32_t get_CONTROL(void) {
    MRS r0, CONTROL    ; MRS: Move to register from status register
    BX  lr
}
```

Example 23-1. Reading the CONTROL register

```
__asm void select_PSP(void) {
  ; Assume PSP has already been initialized.
  MRS  r0, CONTROL  ; MRS: Move to register from status register
  ORRS r0, r0, #2   ; Set bit 2 to 1
  MSR  CONTROL, r0  ; MSR: Move to status register from register
  ISB               ; Ensure subsequent instructions use the new SP
  BX  lr
}
```

Example 23-2. Switching to the process stack (PSP)

```
__asm void select_Unprivileged(void) {
  ; Assume PSP has already been initialized.
  MRS  r0, CONTROL  ; MRS: Move to register from status register
  ORRS r0, r0, #1   ; Set bit 0 to 1
  MSR  CONTROL, r0  ; MSR: Move to status register from register
  ISB               ; Ensure subsequent instructions have the new privilege level
  BX  lr
}
```

Example 23-3. Switching to the unprivileged level

After programming the CONTROL register, the processor should execute the instruction synchronization barrier instruction (ISB) to flush the pipeline and re-fetch instructions. As ARM Cortex-M processors are pipelined, there are instructions that may have been fetched when the processor modifies the CONTROL register. To ensure all subsequent instructions use the updated privilege level or the new stack pointer, the processor should run ISB.

23.1.2   Exception Return Value (EXC_RETURN)

At the entry of an interrupt handler, the processor generates a special 32-bit value called *exception return value* (EXC_RETURN) and automatically stores this value in the link register (LR). When the interrupt handler executes the instruction "BX LR" to return to the interrupted program, the value of EXC_RETURN is copied to the program counter (PC), triggering the automatic interrupt unstacking.

At the entry of a subroutine, the link register stores the return address.

*At the entry of an interrupt handler, the link register holds **EXC_RETURN**.*

As shown in Figure 23-3, EXC_RETURN provides additional information regarding which mode the processor should return to after it handles an interrupt, and which registers should be unstacked. For ARM Cortex-M4F, EXC_RETURN offers three additional information bits, which inform the processor of the following:

- whether the processor should return to thread mode or handler mode,
- whether the processor should use MSP or PSP for interrupt unstacking, and
- whether the stack frame includes FPU registers (see Figure 12-20).

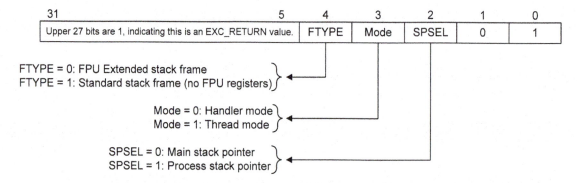

Figure 23-3. Definition of EXC_RETURN

For ARM Cortex-M processors without FPU, EXC_RETURN has three valid values: 0xFFFFFFF1, 0xFFFFFFF9, and 0xFFFFFFFD. For ARM Cortex-M processors with FPU, EXC_RETURN has three additional valid values: 0xFFFFFFE1, 0xFFFFFFE9, and 0xFFFFFFED.

23.1.3   Selection of MSP and PSP in Thread Mode

While the processor always uses MSP for PUSH and POP instructions executed in an interrupt service routine, there are two methods for choosing between MSP and PSP in thread mode.

- The first method is to modify the SPSEL bit in the CONTROL register. If SPSEL is 0, then MSP is used in thread mode. Otherwise, PSP is used.

- The second method is to modify the SPSEL bit of EXC_RETURN, which is stored in the link register (LR) when an interrupt service routine starts. If SPSEL of EXC_RETURN is 0, MSP will be the active stack after the interrupt handler completes; otherwise, PSP will be the active stack.

As shown in Figure 23-4, when the SPSEL bit in the CONTROL register is 0, MSP is used as the stack for both the user program and the interrupt handler. When entering the interrupt handler, hardware sets the SPSEL bit in LR to 0, indicating that the automatic unstacking should use MSP on interrupt exit.

However, when the SPSEL bit in the CONTROL register is 1, PSP is used in thread mode, and MSP is used in handler mode, as shown in Figure 23-5. The automatic stacking and unstacking for the interrupt handler are performed using PSP. If the interrupt handler uses PUSH or POP instructions, these instructions then use MSP. Hardware sets the SPSEL bit in LR is 1 when the interrupt handler starts, indicating that the automatic unstacking on interrupt exit should use PSP.

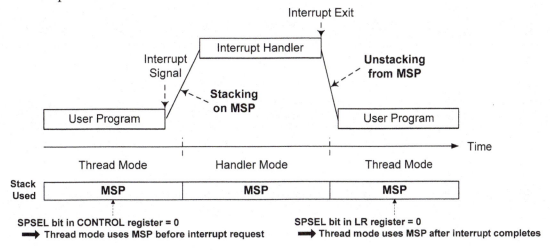

Figure 23-4. Selecting MSP in thread mode

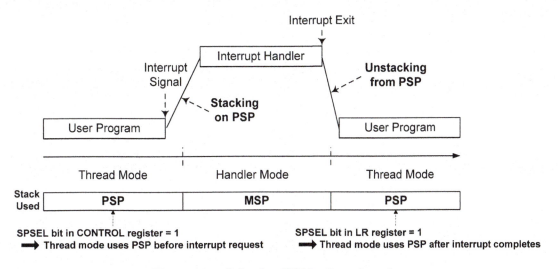

Figure 23-5. Selecting PSP in thread mode

23.2 Supervisor Call (SVC)

A software program can run in the privileged state or the user (unprivileged) state. When the processor is in the unprivileged state, the program cannot directly execute privileged instructions and has limited access to processor resources. For example, the program cannot change the processor state via the CPS instruction, cannot modify the system timer, and has restricted access to memory, peripherals, and processor status registers.

Supporting privileged and user states enhances the reliability and security of embedded systems. For example, certain areas of the memory address space and certain peripheral registers (such as RTC) can only be modified when the code runs at the privileged level. Furthermore, a user program running in the unprivileged state cannot change the processor to the privileged state. Thus, the aforementioned restrictions cannot be bypassed. However, a user program running in the unprivileged state may request some system level service that requires the processor to be in the privileged state. Software interrupts enable a user program to call for a privilege service without violating the restrictions.

The user program uses the supervisor call (SVC) instruction to execute privileged instructions. SVC can generate an exception, which immediately puts the processor into the privileged state. The user program can pass parameters to the SVC handler. One important parameter is the SVC number, which provides a convenient way to use the SVC handler to run different services. For example, the instruction "SVC #0x01" passes the immediate number 1 to the SVC handler.

Following the standard of stacking and unstacking, eight registers are pushed onto the stack before *SVC_Handler()* runs, and they are popped off the stack when the SVC handler exits, as shown below.

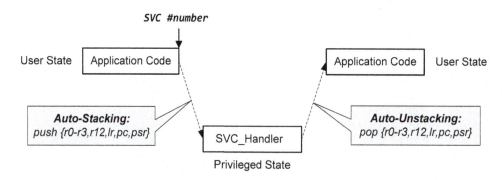

Figure 23-6. Process of stacking and unstacking when SVC interrupt handler is called

If the SVC interrupt performs critical operations, such as accessing some shared resources or data, all interrupts should be disabled when the processor is serving an SVC interrupt. This is to prevent the SVC interrupt handler from being temporally stopped by some interrupt with higher urgency. The SVC interrupt handler should run the pseudo instruction "CPSID I" first to disable all interrupts excluding hard faults and non-maskable interrupts. When the SVC handler exits, it runs the pseudo instruction "CPSIE I" to enable all interrupts. Chapter 11.6.3 introduces CPSID and CPSIE.

The SVC handler can retrieve the previous PC from the stack, which points to the instruction before the SVC handler starts. In this case, it is the SVC instruction. After retrieving PC, the SVC handler can retrieve the SVC instruction and obtain the 8-bit SVC number directly from the SVC instruction. Table 23-1 shows the SVC instruction format.

Instruction	15	14	13	12	11	10	9	8	7	6	5	4	3	2	1	0
SVC	1	1	0	1	1	1	1	1				imm8				

Table 23-1. Instruction format of SVC instruction

In the following example, the SVC handler selectively executes two different kernel functions based on the SVC number. Additionally, the user program can pass parameters to the kernel functions via registers (r0 - r3), following the standard protocol of a procedure call.

This example uses the process stack (PSP) for all assembly code running in the unprivileged mode. The instruction "MSR psp, r0" sets the content of PSP. The user program uses the instruction "MSR control, r0" to switch the processor to the unprivileged mode. Once the processor is in the unprivileged mode, a user application is not capable of changing the processor back to the privileged mode.

Note there is no corresponding statement in standard C language to call the SVC instruction. Inline assembly is used to make supervisor calls.

```
PSP_Stack_Size   EQU    0x00000400

        AREA   PSP_STACK, NOINIT, READWRITE, ALIGN=3

PSP_Stack_Mem SPACE    PSP_Stack_Size

        AREA   main, CODE, READONLY
        EXPORT __main
        ENTRY

__main PROC
        ; Initialize PSP
        LDR    r0, =PSP_Stack_Mem
        MSR    psp, r0

        ; Use PSP and set state as unprivileged
        MOV    r0, #0x3     ; bit 0: 0 = privileged, 1 = unprivileged
                            ; bit 1: 0 = MSP, 1 = PSP
        MSR    control, r0
```

```
            ; Prepare arguments for kernel functions
            MOV    r0, #1        ; First argument to kernel function
            MOV    r1, #2        ; Second argument to kernel function
            MOV    r2, #3        ; Third argument to kernel function
            MOV    r3, #4        ; Fourth argument to kernel function
            SVC    0x01          ; Call kernel function 1
            SVC    0x02          ; Call kernel function 2
stop        B      stop
            ENDP


SVC_Handler PROC
            EXPORT SVC_Handler
            ; Enter handler mode: MSP is used, processor is in privileged state
            CPSID I              ; Set PRIMASK to disable IRQ
            PUSH   {r4-r8,lr}    ; Those are pushed onto MSP

            ; Processor automatically pushes r0-r3, r12, LR, PC, and PSR
            ; onto the PSP stack. It is PSP because the processor was using PSP
            ; immediately before the interrupt.
            MRS    r7, psp
            LDR    r8, [r7, #24]  ; read saved PC from the stack
            LDRH   r8, [r8, #-2]  ; load halfword
            BIC    r8, r8, #0xFF00 ; Extract SVC number
                                 ; SVC instruction has 16 bits: 0xDF,#imm8
            CMP    r8, #0x01      ; if SVC number = 1, call kernel function 1
            BLEQ   kernel_func_1
            CMP    r8, #0x02      ; if SVC number = 2, call kernel function 2
            BLEQ   kernel_func_2
            POP    {r4-r8, lr}    ; Pop from MSP
            CPSIE I               ; Clear PRIMASK to enable IRQ
            BX     lr
            ENDP


kernel_func_1 PROC
            ; The processor is in the privileged state, and MSP is used.
            ; Run privileged instructions
            ...
            BX     lr              ; Exit the function
            ENDP


kernel_func_2 PROC
            ; The processor is in the privileged state, and MSP is used.
            ; Run privileged instructions
            ...
            BX     lr              ; Exit the function
            ENDP
            END
```

Example 23-4. Using inline assembly to make supervisor calls

23.3 CPU Scheduling

Many embedded systems use real-time operating systems (RTOS). One of the fundamental functions of RTOS is to schedule multiple computation tasks on the processor.

When two or more tasks are running at the same time, a scheduling algorithm is required to share the processor across multiple threads of execution. *Round Robin* is a simple and widely used scheduling algorithm in which the processor serves each task for a fixed period in circular order.

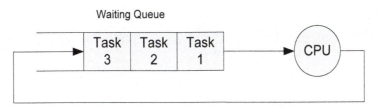

Figure 23-7. Basic concept of CPU scheduling

This section illustrates the implementation of a round-robin scheduling algorithm by using the system timer (SysTick), which generates interrupts at fixed time intervals. In the SysTick handler, the processor first stops the task running currently, and then starts to execute the next task.

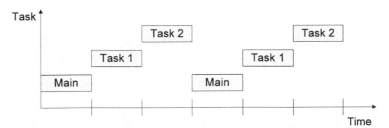

Figure 23-8. Time slices are assigned to tasks in circular order

The processor's time is divided into time slices (small time units with a fixed length). The operating system kernel assigns these time slices to each task in a circular order, as shown in Figure 23-8.

If the time slice is too small, frequent context switches lead to significant performance loss. On the other hand, if the time slice is too large, time-critical tasks might experience a long delay. A generic time slice has 10 to 100 *ms*. When a time slice ends, the processor switches to the next task.

The SysTick handler performs the following two operations during a context switch:

(1) The registers, such as the program counter and the stack pointer, used by the current task are stored onto the stack so that the task can be restarted from the same point later.

(2) The registers that belong to the new task are restored to recover the running environment for the new task. The SysTick handler should pop these registers off the stack.

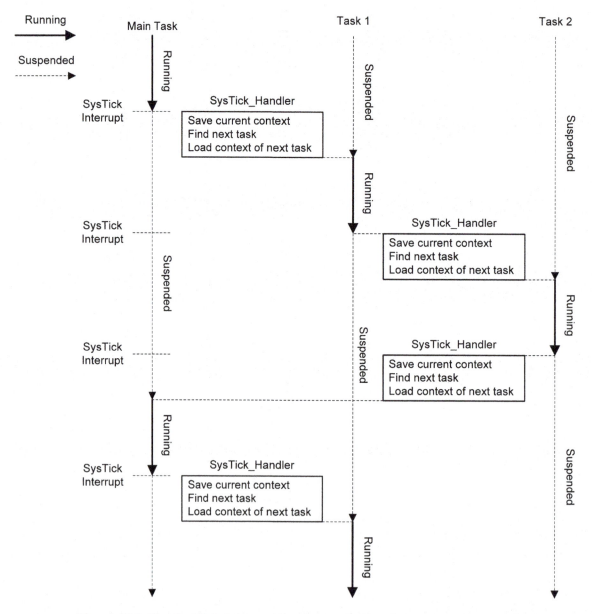

Figure 23-9. The SysTick interrupt service routine performs a context switch.

23.4 Example of Round Robin Scheduling

This section implements a simple *Round Robin* scheduling algorithm for three tasks. As shown below, each task increments a global counter in an infinite loop. Each task does not exit and never voluntarily gives up control of the processor to other tasks.

In most embedded systems, a task has an infinite loop and never exits. A task may constantly monitor inputs from external sensors, push buttons, or keyboards. A task may also repeatedly update outputs to the external display or to other systems via communication, or perform computation in response to sensed data or external events.

```c
// global counters
int counter_main = 0, counter_task1 = 0, counter_task2 = 0;

int main(void){
  int k;
  // Initialization code is not shown here
  ...

  while(1){
    counter_main++;                  // increase a global counter
    for(k = 0; k < 1000; k++);       // time delay
  }
}

void my_task_1(void *data){
  int i;
  while(1){
    counter_task1++;                 // increase a global counter
    for(i = 0; i < 1000; i++);       // time delay
  }
}

void my_task_2(void * data){
  int j;
  while(1){
    counter_task2++;                 // increase a global counter
    for(j = 0; j < 1000; j++);       // time delay
  }
}
```

This example has a mix of C and assembly languages. We must use assembly instructions because some necessary machine operations do not have corresponding C statements. This example shows the importance of assembly programming languages. Sometimes there are no equivalent C statements for some special assembly instructions. Thus, many OS kernel functions must be written in assembly.

To simplify the description, we assume the FPU is not used. When serving an interrupt request, the processor automatically pushes eight registers onto the stack: the lowest four registers (r0, r1, r2, and r3), and the highest four registers (r12, LR, PSR, and PC). When FPU is used, the stack frame is more complex (see Chapter 12.4.1.4 for details).

The processor also automatically pops them off the stack when exiting the interrupt handler. Thus, software only needs to preserve the remaining eight registers (r4 - r11) during a context switch. In the following, we assume software pushes eight registers (r4 - r11) onto the stack in descending order, with r11 being first and r4 last.

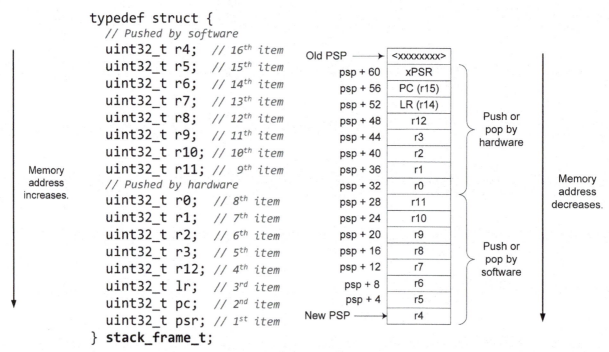

Figure 23-10. Memory layout of a stack frame (assuming the FPU is not used). Pay attention to the register definition order in the stack frame structure.

As shown in Figure 23-10, the structure *stack_frame_t* casts a stack frame pointer to a data structure pointer in the C language, for the convenience of accessing the content of each register pushed in the stack.

Note that the data structure and the stack grow in opposite directions. When a data item is pushed onto the stack, the stack pointer is decremented. However, when a data item is added to a data structure definition, the memory address offset increases. Because the program status register (PSR) is pushed first, the PSR content has the highest memory address, and thus it is the last item in the data structure.

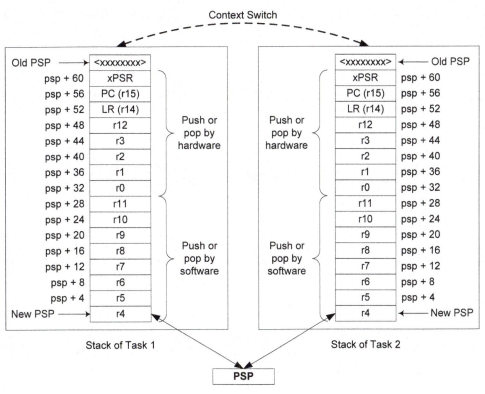

Figure 23-11. The process stack pointer (PSP) can switch between two stacks to perform a context switch.

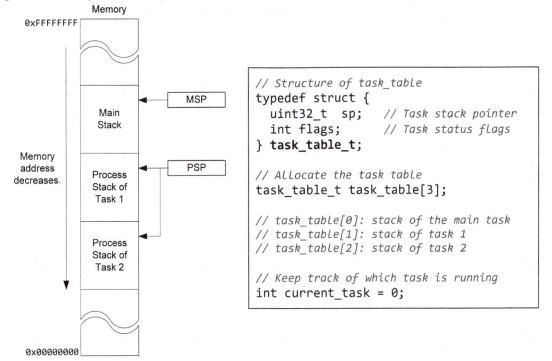

```
// Structure of task_table
typedef struct {
  uint32_t  sp;     // Task stack pointer
  int flags;        // Task status flags
} task_table_t;

// Allocate the task table
task_table_t task_table[3];

// task_table[0]: stack of the main task
// task_table[1]: stack of task 1
// task_table[2]: stack of task 2

// Keep track of which task is running
int current_task = 0;
```

Figure 23-12 Stack allocation

The program has a global task table, recording the stack pointer and status flags for each task, as shown above. Figure 23-12 shows the stack allocation of these three tasks. These three stacks are allocated in memory contiguously. It is assumed that *task_table*[0] is for the main task, *task_table*[1] is for task 1, and *task_table*[2] is for task 2. As introduced in Chapter 23.1, the processor has two stack pointers. We use the main stack (MSP) for the main task and the process stack (PSP) for task 1 and 2.

The following code shows how to cast the stack pointer to a stack frame pointer and access the content of a register stored in the stack directly.

```
stack_frame_t * frame;
frame = (stack_frame_t *)( task_table[i].sp - sizeof(stack_frame_t) );
frame->r0 = 0;
frame->pc = ((uint32_t)func);
task_table[i].sp =   (uint32_t) frame;
task_table[i].flags = TASK_FLAG_EXEC | TASK_FLAG_INIT;
```

One important procedure in the above code is to set the saved PC as the memory address of the task function. During the context switch, the SysTick interrupt service routine copies this PC value saved on the stack of this task to the PC register, which instructs the processor to start to execute this task function.

The following is the code for the main task. It initializes the stack and stack table for two tasks, sets up and enables the system timer, keeps incrementing a global variable (*counter_main*) in an infinite loop, and never exits.

```
int main(void){
   uint32_t k, var = 1;
   tasks_init();
   new_task(my_task_1, (uint32_t)&var);   // Initialize task 1 and one argument
   new_task(my_task_2, (uint32_t)&var);   // Initialize task 2 and one argument
   SysTick_Init();                        // See Chapter 11.7 for SysTick
   NVIC_EnableIRQ(SysTick_IRQn);          // Enable SysTick interrupt in NVIC
   while(1){
      counter_main++;                     // Increase the global counter
      for(k = 0; k < 1000; k++);          // Delay
   }
}
```

Because MOV cannot access special-purpose registers, the program must use MRS and MSR to read or write the PSP and MSP registers, as shown below.

```
__asm uint32_t  get_MSP(void){  // Read main stack pointer
   MRS r0, msp     ; copy msp to r0
   BX  lr          ; r0 holds result returned
}
```

```
__asm void set_MSP(uint32_t topStackPointer){  // Write main stack pointer
   MSR msp, r0      ; copy r0 to msp
   BX   lr          ; r0 holds result returned
}

__asm uint32_t  get_PSP(void){  // Read process stack pointer
   MRS r0, psp      ; copy psp to r0
   BX   lr          ; r0 holds result returned
}

__asm void set_PSP(uint32_t topStackPointer){  // Write process stack pointer
   MSR psp, r0      ; copy r0 to psp
   BX   lr          ; r0 holds result returned
}
```

The following shows the function for creating and initializing a new task. The task takes one input argument.

```
void new_task(void (*func)(void*), uint32_t args){
   // The first argument is a function pointer which points to the task function.
   // The second argument is the actual arguments passed to the task function.
   int i;
   stack_frame_t * frame;
   for(i=1; i < MAX_TASKS; i++){
     if( task_table[i].flags == 0 ){
       frame = (stack_frame_t *)( task_table[i].sp - sizeof(stack_frame_t) );
       frame->r4  = 0;
       frame->r5  = 0;
       frame->r6  = 0;
       frame->r7  = 0;
       frame->r8  = 0;
       frame->r9  = 0;
       frame->r10 = 0;
       frame->r11 = 0;
       frame->r0  = (uint32_t)args;
       frame->r1  = 0;
       frame->r2  = 0;
       frame->r3  = 0;
       frame->r12 = 0;
       frame->pc  = ((uint32_t)func);
       frame->lr  = 0;
       frame->psr = 0x21000000;      // Set default PSR value
       task_table[i].flags =  TASK_FLAG_EXEC | TASK_FLAG_INIT;
       task_table[i].sp     = (uint32_t) frame
       set_PSP(task_table[i].sp);
       break;
     }
   }
}
```

The system timer (SysTick) generates an interrupt after a fixed time interval. The key purpose of the SysTick interrupt handler is to perform a context switch, which allows all tasks to take over control of the processor in a circular order.

```
__asm void SysTick_Handler(void){
    IMPORT get_next_task
    IMPORT update_sp

    ; Before entering the handler, eight registers (r0-r3, r12, LR, PSR,
    ; and PC) have already been pushed automatically onto the main stack
    ; or the process stack.

    CPSID    I                ; Set PRIMASK to disable IRQ

    ; save the context of current task
    TST      lr, #0x04        ; LR=0xFFFFFFF9 => MSP; LR->0xFFFFFFFD => PSP
    MRSEQ    r0, msp          ; Get MSP if LR = 0xFFFFFFF9
    MRSNE    r0, psp          ; Get PSP if LR = 0xFFFFFFFD
    STMDB    r0!, {r4-r11}    ; Save partial context (r4-r11) onto the stack
    MSREQ    msp, r0          ; Update MSP if LR = 0xFFFFFFF9
    MSRNE    psp, r0          ; Update PSP if LR = 0xFFFFFFFD

    BL       update_sp
    BL       get_next_task    ; r0 = 0xFFFFFFF9 or 0xFFFFFFFD
    MOV      lr, r0           ; Set the link register

    ; load the context of new task
    TST      lr, #0x04        ; LR=0xFFFFFFF9 => MSP; LR->0xFFFFFFFD => PSP
    MRSEQ    r0, msp          ; Get MSP if LR = 0xFFFFFFF9
    MRSNE    r0, psp          ; Get PSP if LR = 0xFFFFFFFD
    LDMFD    r0!, {r4-r11}    ; Load partial context (r4-r11) from the stack
    MSREQ    msp, r0          ; Update MSP if LR = 0xFFFFFFF9
    MSRNE    psp, r0          ; Update PSP if LR = 0xFFFFFFFD
    CPSIE    I                ; Clear PRIMASK to enable IRQ
    BX       lr               ; Trigger unstacking (r0-r3, r12, LR, PSR, PC)
}
```

The handler first disables all interrupts to prevent interrupt overrun and then checks bit[2] of the link register to identify whether PSP or MSP should be used. After registers r4 to r11 have been pushed onto the stack, *update_sp()* is called to update the stack table. The subroutine *get_next_task()* uses the round-robin scheduling algorithm to identify the next task to be executed.

The context switch takes the following five steps:

1. Save the registers of the current task (r0 - r15, and psr). Registers from r4 to r11 are pushed onto the stack by the instruction "STMDB r0!, {r4-r11}". The processor automatically pushes the other eight registers, including r0 - r3, r12,

LR, PSR, and PC, onto the main stack (MSP) or the process stack (PSP) during the auto-stacking process. When an interrupt occurs, if SP is MSP, the processor pushes these eight registers onto the main stack. Otherwise, the processor pushes these eight registers onto the process stack.

2. Update the stack pointer and status flag of the stack table for the current task.

3. Search the task table, and identify the next task that is ready to run.

4. Set MSP or PSP to the stack pointer saved in the task table.

5. Recover the registers (r4 - r11) from the stack of the next task. The processor automatically recovers the other eight registers from the stack when the SysTick handler exits.

Either MSP (for the main task) or PSP (for task 1 and 2) is saved in the stack table.

```c
// Update the stack table
void update_sp(void) {
  //Save the current task's stack pointer
  if (current_task == 0) {
    task_table[current_task].sp = get_MSP();
  } else if ( (task_table[current_task].flags & TASK_FLAG_INIT) == 0 ) {
    task_table[current_task].sp = get_PSP();
  }
}
```

The following is the round-robin scheduler, which selects the next task in circular order. The return value is EXC_RETURN, which is used by the interrupt handler to set up the link register (LR). Hardware uses the EXC_RETURN to determine whether the main stack or the process stack should be used for automatic unstacking.

```c
// Identify the next task to be executed
uint32_t get_next_task(void) {
    current_task++;

    if (current_task == MAX_TASKS){

        current_task = 0;
        set_MSP( task_table[current_task].sp );
        return 0xFFFFFFF9;        // Exit interrupt by using the main stack

    } else if (task_table[current_task].flags & TASK_FLAG_EXEC){

        set_PSP(task_table[current_task].sp);
        if (task_table[current_task].flags & TASK_FLAG_INIT)
            task_table[current_task].flags &= ~TASK_FLAG_INIT;
        return 0xFFFFFFFD;        // Exit interrupt by using the process stack

    }
}
```

23.5 Exercises

1. Immediately after the instruction "SVN #0x01" is executed, draw a memory diagram that shows the stack contents.

2. Why does a software interrupt handler often disable interrupts when it starts?

3. If multiple concurrently running tasks increase the same counter variable, will the counter be incremented correctly? If not, how would you solve this issue?

4. When the processor starts to execute the interrupt handler, the processor automatically performs stacking. How does the processor identify whether MSP or PSP is used immediately before the interrupt handler is executed?

Digital Signal Processing (DSP)

Digital signal processing (DSP) is pervasive in modern technologies, ranging from multimedia to communication to various special devices such as automotive, robotics, and medical systems. Figure 24-1 shows a common DSP scheme that uses ADC to quantize an external analog input signal. A low pass analog filter is often used before ADC sampling to remove noises above the Nyquist frequency (one-half of the ADC sampling rate). In the same way, another low pass analog filter is often used after the DAC output to limit output frequencies.

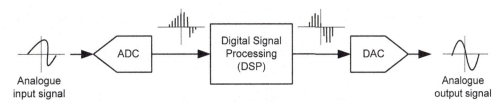

Figure 24-1. Common diagram of a DSP system

24.1 Fixed-point and Floating-point DSP

Based on the way numerical values are represented and operated, DSP systems are divided into two categories: *fixed-point* and *floating-point*. They strike different tradeoffs between accuracy, ease of use, cost, and power consumption.

- Floating-point DSP can express a very wide range of numbers more accurately than fixed-point DSP. For example, high-end audio applications often use floating-point DSP to achieve a high degree of accuracy because human ears are very sensitive.

- Floating-point DSP is easier to program and has a shorter time to market. Due to the nature of floating-point representation, numbers are automatically scaled. Fixed-point DSP often must use assembly instructions or compiler built-in functions. Also, it should take consideration of the data range to avoid overflow and underflow.

- To meet the speed requirement, floating-point DSP often uses high-performance FPU, which increases hardware cost and consumes more power. Fixed-point DSP only uses integer operations, which satisfy the cost and power constraints of many embedded systems.

Therefore, floating-point DSP is suitable for low-volume products, or applications in which software development cost is a serious concern or data range is very dynamic. Example applications are development prototyping, audio applications, medical devices, and military applications. On the contrary, fixed-point DSP is preferred in high-volume products, or applications in which cost and power are of great concern or data range is predictable. Example applications include video applications, speech recognition, and wireless communications.

Cortex-M4 and M7 provide SIMD (*Single-Instruction Multiple-Data*) instructions to accelerate fixed-point DSP performance cost-effectively. This chapter introduces these instructions in details.

24.2 Fixed-point Data Types in DSP

As discussed in Chapter 12, signed fixed-point numbers are denoted as Qn, where n is the number of fractional bits. A Qn number is a signed $(n + 1)$-bit two's complement integer, with the fixed-point value represented as that integer divided by 2^n.

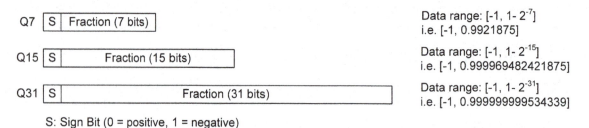

Q7 | S | Fraction (7 bits) | Data range: [-1, 1- 2^{-7}] i.e. [-1, 0.9921875]

Q15 | S | Fraction (15 bits) | Data range: [-1, 1- 2^{-15}] i.e. [-1, 0.999969482421875]

Q31 | S | Fraction (31 bits) | Data range: [-1, 1- 2^{-31}] i.e. [-1, 0.999999999534339]

S: Sign Bit (0 = positive, 1 = negative)

Figure 24-2. Signed fixed-point format Q7, Q15, and Q31

Fixed-point formats commonly used in DSP include Q7, Q15, and Q31, as shown in Figure 24-2. A value in Q7, Q15, and Q31 can be stored in a byte, halfword, and word, respectively. They can represent numbers between -1 and 1 (excluding 1). These formats align memory byte boundary, and thus it is efficient to load numbers from or store them in the data memory.

Software treats a signed fixed-point number as if it were a signed integer represented in two's complement. In C, we declare the data type of signed fixed-point variables as signed integers, as shown below.

```
// 8-bit fractional data type in Q7 format
int8_t  arrayA[1024];   // Q7  array

// 16-bit fractional data type in Q15 format
int16_t arrayB[1024];   // Q15 array

// 32-bit fractional data type in Q31 format
int32_t arrayC[1024];   // Q31 array
```

Example 24-1. Declaring signed fixed-point variables as signed integers in C

We can use shift operations to convert a value between Q7, Q15, and Q31 format, as shown in Figure 24-3. Because they are signed, ASR should be used to shift right.

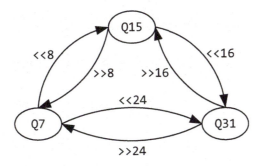

Figure 24-3. Conversion between Q7, Q15, and Q31

24.3 Saturation

Processors treat fixed-point numbers as integers with a fixed range.

- When a result of an arithmetic operation is larger than the maximum representable number, *overflow* occurs.
- When a result is smaller than the minimum representable number, *underflow* occurs. In ARM technical documents, underflow is often called as overflow.

When two's complement is used to represent signed fixed-point numbers, overflow and underflow result in a wrap-around phenomenon (see Figure 24-5). This generates significant errors, and the results can be catastrophic in DSP applications. Therefore, DSP processors often support arithmetic operations with saturation.

- Without saturation, overflow and underflow values are truncated, and only the least significant bits of the result are retained. Thus, overflow values are trimmed to very small values, and underflow values are wrapped around to very high values, leading to a wrap-around phenomenon (see Figure 24-5).
- When overflow or underflow occurs, saturation operation clamps the result to the maximum or minimum limit of the representable range (see Figure 24-6).

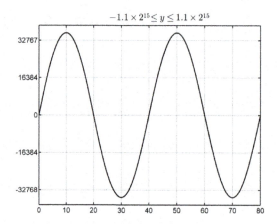

Figure 24-4. Equivalent integer values of a signal. Overflow and underflow occur if represented in Q15

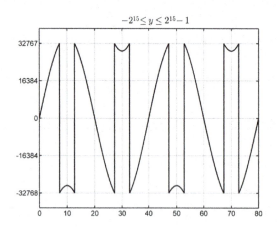

Figure 24-5. Wrapped-around output if there is no saturation

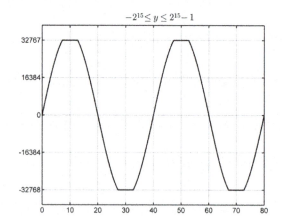

Figure 24-6. Saturated output

Chapter 4.4 introduces SSAT and USAT that saturate a 32-bit integer to a specific signed or unsigned range. The following are two instructions that saturate two halfwords of a register in parallel.

SSAT16 Rd,#imm4,Rm	Signed saturate two signed 16-bit values #imm4 =saturation bit position, $-2^{imm4 - 1} \leq x \leq 2^{imm4 - 1} -1$
USAT16 Rd,#imm4,Rm	Unsigned saturate two unsigned 16-bit values #imm4 = saturation bit position, $0 \leq x \leq 2^{imm4} - 1$

Table 24-1. Saturating two 16-bit values in parallel

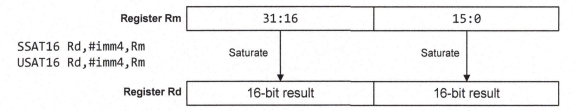

SSAT16 Rd,#imm4,Rm
USAT16 Rd,#imm4,Rm

Figure 24-7. Signed and unsigned saturation of two 16-bit operands

When overflow or underflow occurs, the Q bit flag in the application program status register (APSR) is set. Software can use the MRS instruction to read the Q flag and the MSR instruction to clear the Q flag. The Q flag is sticky in that once it has been set, it remains set until software explicitly clears it.

Read Q flag	Clear Q flag
MRS r0, APSR TST r0, #(1<<27) ; Z is 1 if Q is 0	MRS r0, APSR ; Read APSR BIC r0, r0, #(1<<27) ; Clear Q flag MSR APSR_nzcvq, r0 ; Write APSR

Example 24-2. Assembly code to read or clear Q flag.

24.4 Arithmetic Instructions

For DSP applications, Table 24-2 summarizes arithmetic instructions available in Cortex-M4 and M7. Note that only ADD, ADC, SUB, MUL, SDIV, UDIV, UMULL, SMULL, MLA, MLS, SMLAL, and UMULAL are available in Cortex-M.

Many of the instructions listed in Table 24-2 are SIMD (Single-Instruction Multiple-Data). SIMD instructions leverage data-level parallelism and simultaneously apply the same operation to each member of a set of data.

There exists much data-level parallelism in many applications such as multimedia, graphics, and encryption. For example, to increase the brightness, a constant value is added to the red, green, and blue values of each pixel in an image. This SIMD-based approach speeds up the computation cost-effectively.

Data Length & Operation	Instructions
8 ± 8 = 8	SADD8, QADD8, USADD8, UQADD8, SSUB8, QSUB8, USUB8, UQSUB8
(8 ± 8) ÷ two = 8	SHADD8, UHADD8, SHSUB8, UHSUB8
16 ± 16 = 16	SADD16, QADD16, USADD16, UQADD16, SSUB16, QSUB16, USUB16, UQSUB16, SASX, QASX, UASX, UQASX, SSAX, QSAX, USAX, UQSAX
(16 ± 16) ÷ two = 16	SHADD16, UHADD16, SHSUB16, UHSUB16, SHASX, UHASX, SHSAX, UHSAX
32 ± 32 = 32	QADD, QSUB, ADD, ADC, SUB, ADC
32 ± 32 x two = 32	QDADD, QDSUB
16 x 16 = 32	SMULBB, SMULBT, SMULTB, SMULTT
16 x 32 = 32	SMULWB, SMULWT,
32 x 32 = 32	SMMUL, SMMULR, MUL
32 x 32 = 64	UMULL, SMULL
32 ÷ 32 = 32	SDIV, UDIV
32 + 16 x 16 = 32	SMLABB, SMLABT, SMLATB, SMLATT
32 ± 16 x 32 = 32	SMLAWB, SMLAWT
32 ± 32 x 32 = 32	SMMLA, SMMLAR, SMMLS, SMMLSR, MLA, MLS
64 + 16 x 16 = 64	SMLALBB, SMLALBT, SMLALTB, SMLALTT
64 + 32 x 32 = 64	SMLAL, UMULAL
16 x 16 ± 16 x 16 = 32	SMUAD, SMUADX, SMUSD, SMUSDX
32 + 16 x 16 ± 16 x 16 = 32	SMLAD, SMLADX, SMLSD, SMLSDX
64 + 16 x 16 ± 16 x 16 = 64	SMLALD, SMLALDX, SMLSLD, SMLSLDX
16 x 16 + 32 + 32 = 64	UMAAL
$\sum_{i=1}^{4} absolute(8-8)_i$	USAD8
$32 + \sum_{i=1}^{4} absolute(8-8)_i$	USADA8

Table 24-2. Arithmetic instruction with different data sizes

Figure 24-8 shows an example SIMD instruction (SADD8) that adds four pairs of 8-bit signed integers in parallel. This approach has several advantages.

- First, parallel arithmetic operations accelerate the computation speed.
- Second, these concurrent operations amortize the overhead of instruction fetching, instruction decoding and data memory accessing.
- Last but not the least, a less number of branch instructions are required in a loop. Branch instructions are detrimental to performance. Modern microprocessors execute instructions in a pipeline fashion. When executing a branch instruction, a processor has to stall the execution pipeline if there is no branch prediction or flush the execution pipeline when a branch prediction turns out to be incorrect.

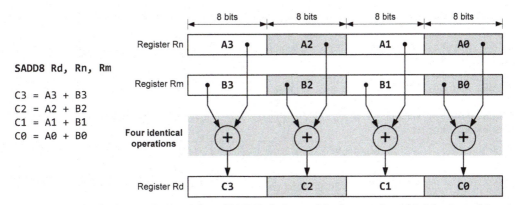

Figure 24-8. Example SIMD instruction (SADD8) that adds four pairs of 8-bit signed integers in parallel. The results are packed into one destination register (Rd).

Table 24-2 summarizes all SIMD addition and subtraction instructions. The following sections give a detailed explanation of these SIMD instructions.

Prefix/ Suffix	Signed (S)	Signed Saturating (Q)	Signed Halving (SH)	Unsigned (U)	Unsigned Saturating (UQ)	Unsigned Halving (UH)
ADD8	SADD8	QADD8	SHADD8	UADD8	UQADD8	UHADD8
SUB8	SSUB8	QSUB8	SHSUB8	USUB8	UQSUB8	UHSUB8
ADD16	SADD16	QADD16	SHADD16	UADD16	UQADD16	UHADD16
SUB16	SSUB16	QSUB16	SHSUB16	USUB16	UQSUB16	UHSUB16
ASX	SASX	QASX	SHASX	UASX	UQASX	UHASX
SAX	SSAX	QSAX	SHSAX	USAX	UQSAX	UHSAX

Table 24-3. Summary of 8- and 16-bit SIMD instructions for addition and subtraction

24.4.1   Parallel 8-bit Add and Subtract

As discussed previously, computers treat fixed-point numbers as if they were integers. The following lists instructions that add or subtract four pairs of 8-bit integers.

SADD8	Rd,Rn,Rm	Signed add 4 pairs of 8-bit integers
SSUB8	Rd,Rn,Rm	Signed subtract 4 pairs of 8-bit integers
UADD8	Rd,Rn,Rm	Unsigned add 4 pairs of 8-bit integers
USUB8	Rd,Rn,Rm	Unsigned subtract 4 pairs of 8-bit integers
QADD8	Rd,Rn,Rm	Saturating add 4 pairs of signed 8-bit integers
QSUB8	Rd,Rn,Rm	Signed saturating subtract 4 pairs of 8-bit integers
UQADD8	Rd,Rn,Rm	Unsigned saturating add 4 pairs of 8-bit integers
UQSUB8	Rd,Rn,Rm	Unsigned saturating subtract 4 pairs of 8-bit integers

Table 24-4. Parallel 8-bit add and subtract

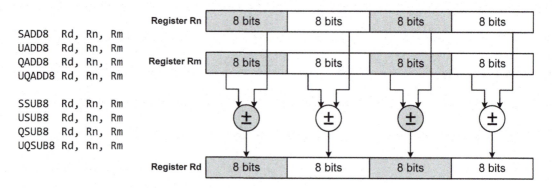

```
SADD8   Rd, Rn, Rm
UADD8   Rd, Rn, Rm
QADD8   Rd, Rn, Rm
UQADD8  Rd, Rn, Rm

SSUB8   Rd, Rn, Rm
USUB8   Rd, Rn, Rm
QSUB8   Rd, Rn, Rm
UQSUB8  Rd, Rn, Rm
```

Figure 24-9. Add or subtract 8-bit integers

Example 24-3 shows a simple C program, which adds the corresponding Q7 signed fixed-point numbers in two arrays. It executes the loops 1024 times.

```
int8_t A[1024], B[1024], C[1024];    // Q7 signed fixed-point
int i;

for (i = 0; i < 1024; i++){
    C[i] = A[i] + B[i];
}
```

Example 24-3. A C program that does not use SIMD

We can use SADD8 to speed up pairwise addition in the above C program. Example 24-4 shows the assembly implementation. This assembly program makes only 256 iterations, instead of 1024. It completes four add operations in each iteration.

```
     LDR    r3, =A          ; Address of array A
     LDR    r4, =B          ; Address of array B
     LDR    r5, =C          ; Address of array C

     MOV    r6, #256        ; Loop counter

loop LDR    r0, [r3], #4    ; Load four Q7 numbers, post-index: r3 = r3 + 4
     LDR    r1, [r4], #4    ; Load four Q7 numbers, post-index: r4 = r4 + 4
     SADD8  r2, r0, r1      ; Add four pairs of Q7 numbers
     STR    r2, [r5], #4    ; Store four Q7 numbers, post-index: r5 = r5 + 4
     SUBS   r6, r6, #1      ; Decrement loop counter
     BGT    loop
```

Example 24-4. An assembly program that uses SIMD

If the array size is not exactly divisible by four, a compensation loop is needed to handle the addition of remainder Q7 values after the main loop shown in Example 24-4. In the compensation loop, we can load each byte and add them up. To simplify the description of example codes, we assume the size of Q7 arrays is always a multiple of four and the size of Q15 arrays is always a multiple of two.

A C program can also call the compiler's built-in function (also called intrinsic function) __SADD8, as shown in Example 24-5, to utilize the SIMD capability of a microprocessor.

```c
int8_t A[1024], B[1024], C[1024];

uint32_t *pA, *pB, *pC, i;

pA = (uint32_t*) A;    // Pointer-to-pointer casting. It changes compiler's
pB = (uint32_t*) B;    // views on array A, B and C from signed 8-bit
pC = (uint32_t*) C;    // integers to unsigned 32-bit integers

for(i = 0; i < 256; i++) {
    *pC = __SADD8(*pA, *pB);   // Call compiler built-in function which
                               // calls the assembly SADD8 instruction
    pA++;          // Pointer is incremented by size of uint32_t (i.e., 4),
    pB++;          // because compiler views them as arrays of 32-bit
    pC++;          // unsigned integers

}
```

Example 24-5. A C program that uses SIMD

Example 24-6 gives the implementation of the __SADD8 function.

```c
uint32_t __SADD8(uint32_t op1, uint32_t op2){

  uint32_t result;

  __ASM {
      sadd8 result, op1, op2
  }

  return result;
}
```

Example 24-6. Implementation of the __SADD8 function

The results of parallel 8-bit add and subtract can be halved by using the following instructions, as shown in Figure 24-10.

SHADD8 Rd,Rn,Rm	Signed halving add 4 pairs of 8-bit integers
SHSUB8 Rd,Rn,Rm	Signed halving subtract 4 pairs of 8-bit integers
UHADD8 Rd,Rn,Rm	Unsigned halving add 4 pairs of 8-bit integers
UHSUB8 Rd,Rn,Rm	Unsigned halving subtract 4 pairs of 8-bit integers

Table 24-5. Parallel 8-bit instructions to add (or subtract) and division by two

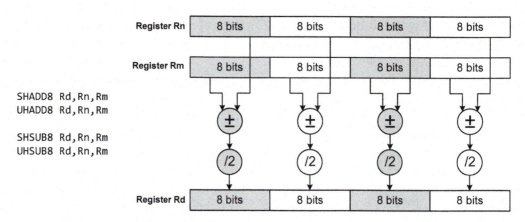

Figure 24-10. Add or subtract 8-bit values, and divide results in half

No 8-bit saturating addition and subtraction instructions change the Q flag in APSR when overflow occurs. Note that in ARM technical documents, underflow is distinguished from overflow, and underflow is referred to as overflow.

```
LDR    r0, =0x80808080
UQADD8 r2, r0, r0      ; r2 = 0xFFFFFFFF
                       ; unsigned saturating, 0x80 + 0x80 = 0xFF
                       ; Even though overflow occurs, Q flag is not changed

LDR    r0, =0x70707070
QADD8  r2, r0, r0      ; r2 = 0x7F7F7F7F,
                       ; signed saturating, 0x70 + 0x70 = 0x7F
                       ; Even though overflow occurs, Q flag is not changed

LDR    r0, =0x81818181
QADD8  r2, r0, r0      ; r2 = 0x80808080,
                       ; signed saturating, 0x81 + 0x81 = 0x80
                       ; Even though overflow occurs, Q flag is not changed

LDR    r1, =0x80808080
LDR    r2, =0x70707070

QSUB8  r3, r1, r2      ; r3 = 0x80808080,
                       ; signed saturating, 0x80 - 0x70 = 0x80
                       ; Even though overflow occurs, Q flag is not changed

QSUB8  r3, r2, r1      ; r3 = 0x7F7F7F7F,
                       ; signed saturating, 0x70 - 0x80 = 0x7F
                       ; Even though overflow occurs, Q flag is not changed

UQSUB8 r3, r2, r1      ; r3 = 0x00000000,
                       ; unsigned saturating, 0x70 - 0x80 = 0x00
                       ; Even though overflow occurs, Q flag is not changed
```

Example 24-7. Updating Q flags

24.4.2   Parallel 16-bit Add and Subtract

A 16-bit parallel add or subtract instruction carries out pairwise operations on halfwords, as shown in Figure 24-11.

SADD16 Rd,Rn,Rm	Signed add two pairs of 16-bit integers Rd[T] = truncate16(Rn[T] + Rm[T]) Rd[B] = truncate16(Rn[B] + Rm[B])
SSUB16 Rd,Rn,Rm	Signed subtract two pairs of 16-bit integers Rd[T] = truncate16(Rn[T] - Rm[T]) Rd[B] = truncate16(Rn[B] - Rm[B])
UADD16 Rd,Rn,Rm	Unsigned add two pairs of 16-bit integers Rd[T] = truncate16(Rn[T] + Rm[T]) Rd[B] = truncate16(Rn[B] + Rm[B])
USUB16 Rd,Rn,Rm	Unsigned subtract two pairs of 16-bit integers Rd[T] = truncate16(Rn[T] - Rm[T]) Rd[B] = truncate16(Rn[B] - Rm[B])
QADD16 Rd,Rn,Rm	Saturating add two pairs of signed 16-bit integers Rd[T] = signed_saturate16(Rn[T] + Rm[T]) Rd[B] = signed_saturate16(Rn[B] + Rm[B])
QSUB16 Rd,Rn,Rm	Signed saturating subtract 2 pairs of 16-bit integers Rd[T] = signed_saturate16(Rn[T] - Rm[T]) Rd[B] = signed_saturate16(Rn[B] - Rm[B])
UQADD16 Rd,Rn,Rm	Unsigned saturating add 2 pairs of 16-bit integers Rd[T] = unsigned_saturate16(Rn[T] + Rm[T]) Rd[B] = unsigned_saturate16(Rn[B] + Rm[B])
UQSUB16 Rd,Rn,Rm	Unsigned saturating subtract 2 pairs of 16-bit integers Rd[T] = unsigned_saturate16(Rn[T] - Rm[T]) Rd[B] = unsigned_saturate16(Rn[B] - Rm[B])

Table 24-6. Parallel 16-bit add and subtract

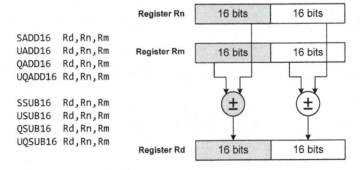

Figure 24-11. Add or subtract 16-bit values

The results can also be halved, as shown in Figure 24-12. Because saturation never occurs on add or subtract with dividing in half, there are no corresponding halving instructions for saturating add or subtract.

SHADD16 Rd,Rn,Rm	Signed halving add two pairs of 16-bit integers Rd[T] = (Rn[T] + Rm[T])/2 Rd[B] = (Rn[B] + Rm[B])/2
SHSUB16 Rd,Rn,Rm	Signed halving subtract two pairs of 16-bit integers Rd[T] = (Rn[T] - Rm[T])/2 Rd[B] = (Rn[B] - Rm[B])/2
UHADD16 Rd,Rn,Rm	Unsigned halving add two pairs of 16-bit integers Rd[T] = (Rn[T] + Rm[T])/2 Rd[B] = (Rn[B] + Rm[B])/2
UHSUB16 Rd,Rn,Rm	Unsigned halving subtract two pairs of 16-bit integers Rd[T] = (Rn[T] - Rm[T])/2 Rd[B] = (Rn[B] - Rm[B])/2

Table 24-7. Parallel 16-bit add (or subtract), and division by two

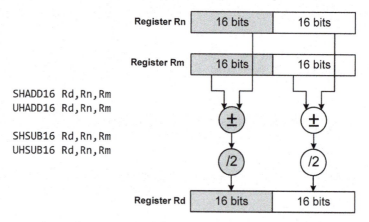

Figure 24-12. Add or subtract two pairs of halfwords, and divide results in half

All 16-bit saturating subtraction and addition instructions cannot set the Q flag in APSR.

```
LDR      r0,=0x80008000
UQADD16  r2,r0,r0      ; r2=0xFFFFFFFF,
                       ; unsigned saturating, 0x8000+0x8000=0xFFFF

LDR      r0,=0x70007000
QADD16   r2,r0,r0      ; r2=0xFFFFFFFF,
                       ; signed saturating, 0x7000+0x7000=0x7FFF

LDR      r1, =0x80008000
LDR      r2, =0x70007000

QSUB16   r3, r1, r2    ; r2=0x80008000,
                       ; signed saturating, 0x8000-0x7000=0x8000

QSUB16   r3, r2, r1    ; r2=0x7FFF7FFF,
                       ; signed saturating, 0x7000-0x8000=0x7FFF
```

24.4.3   32-bit Add and Subtract

Saturating add and subtract instructions (QADD and QSUB) for 32-bit integers is provided to eliminate the wrap-around phenomena. Note that they are not SIMD instructions because each of them processes only one pair of data elements. The Q flag is set if saturation occurs.

QADD Rd,Rn,Rm	Saturating add signed 32-bit integers Rd = saturate32(Rn + Rm)
QSUB Rd,Rn,Rm	Signed saturating subtract two 32-bit integers Rd = saturate32(Rn - Rm)

In the following example, the QADD and QSUB operations set the Q flag. Once the Q flag is set, it remains as 1 until software explicitly clears it.

```
LDR   r0, =0x70000000
ADD   r3, r0, r0        ; r3 = 0xE0000000, Q is unchanged
QADD  r4, r0, r0        ; r4 = 0x7FFFFFFF, Q = 1

; Q flag is sticky, and thus software has to clear it explicitly
MRS r0, APSR            ; Read flags
BIC r0, r0, #(1<<27)    ; Clear Q flag
MSR APSR_nzcvq, r0      ; Store flags

LDR   r1, =0x80000000
LDR   r2, =0x70000000
SUB   r3, r1, r2        ; r3 = 0x10000000
QSUB  r4, r1, r2        ; r4 = 0x80000000, Q = 1
```

With saturation, the second operand can also be doubled before it is added to or subtracted from the first operand. The saturation is applied to both doubling and addition/subtraction. The Q flag is set if saturation occurs on doubling or addition/subtraction.

QDADD Rd,Rn,Rm	Saturating double and add Rd = saturate32(Rn + saturate32(Rm * 2))
QDSUB Rd,Rn,Rm	Saturating double and subtract Rd = saturate32(Rn - saturate32(Rm * 2))

The double and add instruction (QDADD) is often used in a binary method to multiply a constant and a huge number such as a 256-bit number. Given a very large n-bit integer $K = \sum_{i=0}^{n}(k_i 2^i)$, where $k_i \in \{0, 1\}$, the product $K \times C$ can be written as

$$P = K \times C = \sum_{i=0}^{n-1} k_i \times (2 \times C)$$

The basic idea is that the program scans all bits of K starting from the most significant bit. Each individual bit of K determines the computation. If $k_i = 0$, the product is doubled; otherwise, a double and add operation is performed on the product if $k_i = 1$. Such multiplication method is called the binary double-and-add algorithm. Example 24-8 gives the pseudocode of its implementation.

```
P = 0;   // Initialization

for i from n-1 down to 0

   if(k(i) == 1) then
       P = 2*P + C
   else
       P = 2*P
   endif

endfor
```

Example 24-8. Pseudocode of double-and-add algorithm to multiply K and C

24.4.4   Sum of Absolute Difference

There are two special instructions, USAD8, and USADA8, which calculate the unsigned sum (or accumulated sum) of the absolute difference (SAD) between four pairs of 8-bit integers in parallel.

USAD8 Rd,Rn,Rm	Unsigned sum of absolute differences
USADA8 Rd,Rn,Rm,Ra	Unsigned sum of absolute differences and accumulate

The following equation defines the sum of absolute difference (SAD):

$$SAD = \sum_{i=1}^{4} absolute(a_i - b_i)$$

Computing the sum of absolute difference is often needed in block-based motion estimation in video compression. A video frame is divided into blocks of equal size. Motion estimation needs to calculate the similarity of blocks in two adjacent frames. The sum of absolute difference between a block in the current frame and a block in the last frame is often used to measure the similarity between these two blocks. In a video frame, each pixel typically has 24 bits, with 8 bits for each of red, green, and blue values.

Two instructions USAD8 and USADA8 can be used to calculate the absolute differences between four pairs of 8-bit unsigned values in parallel. USADA8 adds the sum of the absolute difference in a 32-bit unsigned accumulator.

By leveraging the data-level parallelism, we can use USADA8 to calculate the sum of absolute difference efficiently, as shown in Figure 24-8.

Compute the sum of absolute difference	C Function with inline assembly
``// Two 16-by-16 data blocks
uint8_t blk1[16][16];
uint8_t blk2[16][16];

uint32_t *a, *b;   // accessing 4 bytes

uint32_t sad = 0;

for(i = 0; i < 16; i++){
   for(j = 0; j < 4; j++){
      a = & blk1[i][4*j];
      b = & blk2[i][4*j];
      sad += __USADA8(*a, *b, sad);
   }
}``` | ```uint32_t __USADA8(uint32_t op1,
                   uint32_t op2,
                   uint32_t sad) {

   __ASM {
      USADA8 sad, op1, op2, sad
   }

   return sad;

}``` |

Example 24-9. Calculating the sum of absolute difference between two 16-by-16 blocks

24.4.5   Extension and Add

As introduced in Chapter 4.8, instructions SXTB, SXTH, UXTB, and UXTH perform signed or unsigned extension, which increases the bit width from a byte or halfword to a word.

- Signed extension fills in additional upper bits with 0 if the sign bit is 0, and fills those upper bits with 1 if the sign bit is 1, to preserve the sign and value.
- Unsigned extension, also called zero extension, pads the source operand with zeros from the left side to 32 bits.

When adding two numbers with different bit lengths, the extension and addition operations can be performed in one instruction, as shown below. Note that only ROR is allowed for the second source operand. The other shift operations, including LSL, LSR, ASR, and RRX, are not permitted in these instructions.

SXTAB Rd,Rn,Rm{,ROR #}	Rotate, signed-extend a byte to word, and add Rd = Rn + sign_extend((Rm, ROR #)[7:0])
UXTAB Rd,Rn,Rm{,ROR #}	Rotate, unsigned-extend a byte to word, and add Rd = Rn + zero_extend((Rm, ROR #)[7:0])
SXTAH Rd,Rn,Rm{,ROR #}	Rotate, signed-extend a halfword to word, and add Rd = Rn + sign_extend((Rm, ROR #)[15:0])
UXTAH Rd,Rn,Rm{,ROR #}	Rotate, unsigned extend halfword to word, and add Rd = Rn + zero_extend((Rm, ROR #)[15:0])

For example, we can add two 16-bit signed integers as follows:

```
LDR   r5, [r0]               ; Load two 16-bit values
SXTAH r3, r3, r5             ; sum += sign_extend(r5[B]), r3 = sum
SXTAH r3, r3, r5, ROR #16    ; sum += sign_extend(r5[T]), r3 = sum
```

For unsigned 16-bit integers, we should use UXTAH with zero extension:

```
LDR   r5, [r0]               ; Load two 16-bit values
UXTAH r3, r3, r5             ; sum += zero_extend(r5[B]), r3 = sum
UXTAH r3, r3, r5, ROR #16    ; sum += zero_extend(r5[T]), r3 = sum
```

Similarly, we can use UXTAB to add four 8-bit unsigned integers:

```
LDR   r5, [r0]               ; Load four 8-bit values
UXTAB r3, r3, r5             ; sum += zero_extend(r5[7:0]),   r3 = sum
UXTAB r3, r3, r5, ROR #8     ; sum += zero_extend(r5[15:8]),  r3 = sum
UXTAB r3, r3, r5, ROR #16    ; sum += zero_extend(r5[23:16]), r3 = sum
UXTAB r3, r3, r5, ROR #24    ; sum += zero_extend(r5[31:24]), r3 = sum
```

As shown in Figure 24-13, Cortex-M4 and M7 provide special SIMD instructions that first extract two bytes from the second operand, then extend them to halfwords, and finally add them to the corresponding halfwords in the first operand.

SXTAB16 Rd,Rn,Rm{,ROR #}	Rotate, dual extend 8 bits to 16 bits, and add Rd[T] = Rn[T] + sign_extend((Rm, ROR #)[23:16]) Rd[B] = Rn[B] + sign_extend((Rm, ROR #)[7:0])
UXTAB16 Rd,Rn,Rm{,ROR #}	Rotate, dual extend 8 bits to 16 bits, and add Rd[T] = Rn[T] + zero_extend((Rn, ROR #)[23:16]) Rd[B] = Rn[B] + zero_extend((Rn, ROR #)[7:0])

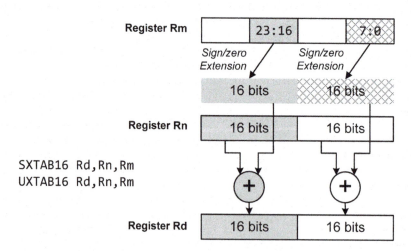

Figure 24-13. Dual extension from bytes to halfwords, and dual addition

In the following program, we can add the lower two 8-bit signed integers. At the same time, the upper two 8-bit signed integers are also added up. The sums are saved in the upper and lower halfword of the destination register.

```
LDR      r5, [r0]             ; Load four 8-bit values
SXTAB16 r3, r3, r5            ; sum[B] += sum[B] + sign_extend(r5[7:0])
                             ; sum[T] += sum[T] + sign_extend(r5[23:16])
SXTAB16 r3, r3, r5, ROR #8    ; sum[B] += sum[B] + sign_extend(r5[15:8])
                             ; sum[T] += sum[T] + sign_extend(r5[31:24])
```

24.4.6   Add and Subtract Halfwords with Exchange

In many DSP algorithms, such as Fast Fourier Transform (FFT), the sum and the difference of numbers are needed for subsequent processing. In the traditional approach, an addition and subtraction are executed in a serial fashion, which limits the throughput. To accelerate the computation, Cortex-M4 and M7 provide SIMD instructions that can perform one addition and one subtraction simultaneously, as listed in Table 24-8, Table 24-9, and Table 24-10.

- The prefix S, U, and Q stand for signed, unsigned, and saturating, respectively.
- In the instruction, A stands for add, S for subtracting, H for halving, and X for exchange.
- For unsigned saturation instructions, including UQASX and UQSAX, the results are saturated in the range $[-2^{15}, 2^{15}-1]$. For signed saturation instructions, including QASX and QSAX, the results are saturated in the range $[0, 2^{16}-1]$. However, these instructions do not change the Q flag even if saturation has occurred.

SASX Rd,Rn,Rm	Signed add and subtract with exchange Rd[T] = truncate16(Rn[T] + Rm[B]) Rd[B] = truncate16(Rn[B] - Rm[T])
UASX Rd,Rn,Rm	Unsigned add and subtract with exchange Rd[T] = truncate16(Rn[T] + Rm[B]) Rd[B] = truncate16(Rn[B] - Rm[T])
QASX Rd,Rn,Rm	Saturating add and subtract with exchange Rd[T] = saturate16(Rn[T] + Rm[B]) Rd[B] = saturate16(Rn[B] - Rm[T])
UQASX Rd,Rn,Rm	Unsigned saturating add and subtract with exchange Rd[T] = saturate16(Rn[T] + Rm[B]) Rd[B] = saturate16(Rn[B] - Rm[T])

Table 24-8. Exchange halfwords of 2nd operand, add together top halfwords, and subtract between bottom halfwords

SSAX Rd,Rn,Rm	Signed subtract and add with exchange Rd[T] = truncate16(Rn[T] - Rm[B]) Rd[B] = truncate16(Rn[B] + Rm[T])
USAX Rd,Rn,Rm	Unsigned subtract and add with exchange Rd[T] = truncate16(Rn[T] - Rm[B]) Rd[B] = truncate16(Rn[B] + Rm[T])
QSAX Rd,Rn,Rm	Saturating subtract and add with exchange Rd[T] = saturate16(Rn[T] - Rm[B]) Rd[B] = saturate16(Rn[B] + Rm[T])
UQSAX Rd,Rn,Rm	Unsigned saturating subtract and add with exchange Rd[T] = saturate16(Rn[T] – Rm[B]) Rd[B] = saturate16(Rn[B] + Rm[T])

Table 24-9. Exchange halfwords of 2nd operand, subtract between top halfwords and add together bottom halfwords

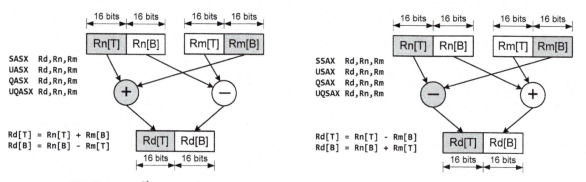

Figure 24-14. Add and subtract with exchange (ASX), and Subtract and add with exchange (SAX)

The results can also be halved in parallel, as shown in Figure 24-15.

SHASX Rd,Rn,Rm	Signed halving add and subtract with exchange Rd[T] = (Rn[T] + Rm[B])/2 Rd[B] = (Rn[B] - Rm[T])/2
UHASX Rd,Rn,Rm	Unsigned halving add and subtract with exchange Rd[T] = (Rn[T] + Rm[B])/2 Rd[B] = (Rn[B] - Rm[T])/2
SHSAX Rd,Rn,Rm	Signed halving subtract and add with exchange Rd[T] = (Rn[T] - Rm[B])/2 Rd[B] = (Rn[B] + Rm[T])/2
UHSAX Rd,Rn,Rm	Unsigned halving subtract and add with exchange Rd[T] = (Rn[T] - Rm[B])/2 Rd[B] = (Rn[B] + Rm[T])/2

Table 24-10. Exchange, add/subtract (or subtract/add), and halving

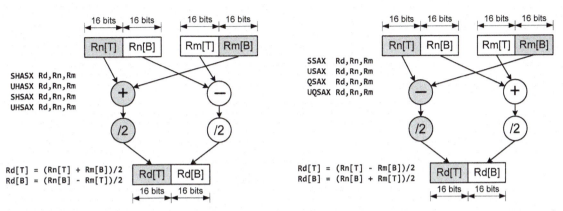

HASX: Exchange 2nd operand, halving add, and then halving subtract   HSAX: Exchange 2nd operand, halving subtract and then halving add

Figure 24-15. Exchange, add and subtract, and halving (ASXH), and Exchange, subtract and add, and halving (SAXH)

24.4.7   16-bit and 32-bit Multiplication

We can multiply two signed halfword integers selected from either the top or the bottom of two source operand registers. In these instructions, "T" specifies the top halfword of the corresponding operand, and "B" denotes the bottom halfword. The following lists instructions for signed halfword multiplication.

SMULBB Rd,Rn,Rm	Signed multiply bottom halfwords Rd = Rn[B]*Rm[B]
SMULBT Rd,Rn,Rm	Signed multiply bottom and top halfwords Rd = Rn[B]*Rm[T]
SMULTB Rd,Rn,Rm	Signed multiply top and bottom halfwords Rd = Rn[T]*Rm[B]
SMULTT Rd,Rn,Rm	Signed multiply top halfwords Rd = Rn[T]*Rm[T]

Table 24-11. Signed halfword multiplication

We can also multiply a 32-bit signed integer with a 16-bit signed integer selected from the top or bottom halfword of the second operand, as shown in Table 24-12. The actual product has 48 bits, but only the most significant 32 bits are kept.

SMULWB Rd,Rn,Rm	Signed multiply word by bottom halfword Rd = (Rn*Rm[B])>>16
SMULWT Rd,Rn,Rm	Signed multiply word by top halfword Rd = (Rn*Rm[T])>>16

Table 24-12. Signed multiplication between halfword and word

The SMULWB and SMULWT instructions can be used to implement conveniently signed fixed-point multiplication between Q15 and Q31, with the product kept in Q31 format.

We can also multiply two 32-bit signed integers, with the least significant 32 bits of the product truncated or rounded, as shown in Table 24-13. These two instructions multiply two Q31 fixed-point numbers, with the product remained in Q31 format. When the 64-bit exact product is reduced to 32 bits, the product can be either truncated or rounded to the nearest. The operation of rounding to the nearest is described in Chapter 12.2.6.

SMMUL Rd,Rn,Rm	Signed most significant word multiply with truncating Rd = (Rn*Rm)>>32
SMMULR Rd,Rn,Rm	Signed most significant word multiply with rounding to the nearest, Rd = (Rn*Rm)>>32

Table 24-13. Signed word multiplication

We can also multiply two pairs of 16-bit signed integers in parallel, calculate the sum or the difference of the 32-bit products, and store the result in the destination register, as shown in Figure 24-14. If there is a suffix X in the instruction mnemonic, the upper and lower halfword of the second source operand register is swapped before the multiplication operations are carried out. In other words, if the suffix X exists, the multiplication operations are $top{\times}bottom$ and $bottom{\times}top$; otherwise, they are $top{\times}top$ and $bottom{\times}bottom$.

SMUAD Rd,Rn,Rm	Signed dual multiply, then add products Rd = Rn[B]*Rm[B] + Rn[T]*Rm[T]
SMUADX Rd,Rn,Rm	Signed dual multiply with exchange, then add products Rd = Rn[T]*Rm[B] + Rn[B]*Rm[T]
SMUSD Rd,Rn,Rm	Signed dual multiply, then subtract products Rd = Rn[B]*Rm[B] - Rn[T]*Rm[T]
SMUSDX Rd,Rn,Rm	Signed dual multiply with exchange, then subtract products, Rd = Rn[B]*Rm[T] - Rn[T]*Rm[B]

Table 24-14. Dual 16-bit signed multiply with addition (or subtraction) of products

For Cortex-M3/M0, we can use the following C code to implement SMUAD instruction:

$$(((x >> 16) * (y >> 16)) + (((x << 16) >> 16) * ((y << 16) >> 16)))$$

where x and y are signed 32-bit integer variables, holding two Q15 values.

Although 16-bit multiplication does not generate overflow, the addition of two 32-bit products may overflow. SMUAD and SMUADX set the Q flag if the addition overflows.

```
LDR    r0, = 0x7FFF7FFF
SMUAD  r3, r0, r0      ; r3=(2^15-1)×(2^15-1)+(2^15-1)×(2^15-1)=0x7FFE0002, no overflow

LDR    r1, =0x80008000
SMUAD  r3, r1, r1      ; r3 = (-2^15)×(-2^15)+(-2^15)×(-2^15) = 2^31 = 0x80000000, overflow
SMUAD  r3, r0, r1      ; r3 = (-2^15)×( 2^15-1)+(-2^15)×(2^15-1) = 0x80010000, overflow
```

SMUSD and SMUSDX do not affect the Q flag because no overflow can occur.

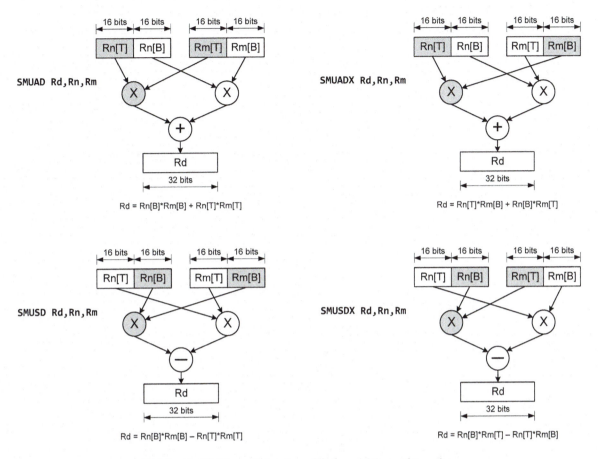

Table 24-15. Signed dual multiply add (or subtract)

One simple example is that we can use these instructions to calculate the sum or difference between two signed halfwords of a register.

```
MOV     r0, 0x00010001 ; top halfword = 1, bottom halfword = 1
SMUAD   r2, r1, r0     ; r2 = r1[T] + r1[B]
SMUSD   r2, r1, r0     ; r2 = r1[B] - r1[T]
SMUSDX  r2, r1, r0     ; r2 = r1[T] - r1[B]
```

These instructions are very helpful to implement digital filtering in DSP. The current output $y(t)$ of a linear digital filter consists of a linear combination of previous M filter outputs, including $y(t-1)$, $y(t-2)$, ..., and $y(t-M)$, and N filter inputs including $x(t)$, $x(t-1)$, ..., and $y(t-N+1)$, as shown in the following equation:

$$y(t) = \sum_{i=0}^{N-1} a_i \cdot x(t-i) - \sum_{j=1}^{M} b_j \cdot y(t-j)$$

where a_i and b_j are coefficient constants, and N and M are pre-defined integers. N is referred to as the feed forward filter order, and M is known as the feedback filter order.

When all inputs are expressed in the Q15 format, these dual-multiplication instructions can be used to speed up the multiplication. If inputs are in the Q8 format, we need to extend the inputs to 16-bit signed numbers. Chapter 24.6 introduces parallel sign extension instructions.

24.4.8   16-bit Multiply and Accumulate with 64-bit Result

Multiply and Accumulate (MAC) is one of the key operations in DSP algorithms. For example, the output of a finite impulse response (FIR) filter, which removes all previous output items from the general form presented previously:

$$y(t) = \sum_{i=0}^{N-1} a_i \cdot x(t-i)$$

where N is the filter window length (or called the filter order), a_i is the filter's coefficients, and x is the sequence of input signal. This process slides over a fixed-length window of signal samples to compute a sequence of outputs $y(t)$.

In C, the finite impulse response (FIR) uses a loop to sum up the products repeatedly. Note that one MAC operation is performed in each loop.

```
while(1) {
  y[t] = 0;  // Initialization
  for (i = 0, i < N; i++)
    y[t] = y[t] + a[i]*x[t-i];    // Multiply and accumulate
  t = t + 1;
}
```

To speed up the performance, microprocessors often have built-in hardware components to compute multiply and accumulate operations directly. Cortex-M4 and M7 provide MAC instructions with 16- or 32-bit input operands and 32- or 64-bit accumulator.

Figure 24-16, Figure 24-17, and Figure 24-18 present assembly instructions for signed 16-bit multiplication with a 64-bit accumulator. These instructions do not change the N, Z, C, V and Q flags in APSR.

SMLALD RdLo,RdHi,Rn,Rm	Dual signed multiply, accumulate long RdHi:RdLo = RdHi:RdLo + Rn[T]*Rm[T] + Rn[B]*Rm[B]
SMLSLD RdLo,RdHi,Rn,Rm	Dual signed multiply, subtract long RdHi:RdLo = RdHi:RdLo + Rn[T]* Rm[T] - Rn[B]*Rm[B]

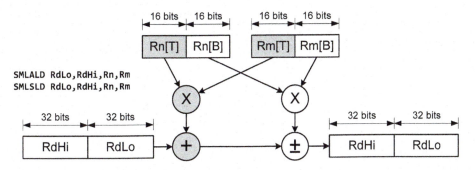

$$RdHi:RdLo = RdHi:RdLo + Rn[T]×Rm[T] ± Rn[B]×Rm[B]$$

Figure 24-16. Dual 16-bit signed multiply, addition (or subtraction), and 64-bit accumulate.

The following shows a program that uses SMLALD to calculate the sum of squares. Given two arrays *A* and *B*, each of them has 1024 signed fixed-point numbers in Q15 format. We want to calculate the sum of squares defined as follows:

$$S = \sum_{i=0}^{1023} (a_i - b_i)^2$$

The following gives the assembly implementation. Because each fixed-point number has 16 bits, a load operation retrieves two Q15 values from the data memory and stores them in one register. After QSUB16 calculates the difference between two pairs of Q15 values, SMLALD performs the multiply and accumulate operations based on the difference obtained.

```
     ; The result is stored in registers r6:r5
     LDR    r0, =A         ; Memory address of array A
     LDR    r1, =B         ; Memory address of array B
     MOV    r7, #256       ; Loop counter
     MOV    r6, #0         ; Initialize upper word of sum
     MOV    r5, #0         ; Initialize lower word of sum

loop LDR    r2, [r0], #4   ; Loads two halfwords from A, post-index
     LDR    r3, [r1], #4   ; Loads two halfwords from B, post-index
     QSUB16 r4, r2, r3      ; Two 16-bit subtractions in parallel
     SMLALD r5, r6, r4, r4  ; r6:r5 += r4[T]^2 + r4[B]^2
     SUBS   r7, r7, #1     ; Decrement loop counter
     BGT    loop
```

Example 24-10. Sum of squares

The following are dual 16-bit signed multiplication and 64-bit accumulation, with the halfwords of the second operand swapped before the multiplication.

SMLALDX RdLo,RdHi,Rn,Rm	Signed multiply accumulate long dual with exchange RdHi:RdLo = RdHi:RdLo + Rn[T]*Rm[B] + Rn[B]*Rm[T]
SMLSLDX RdLo,RdHi,Rn,Rm	Signed multiply subtract long dual with exchange RdHi:RdLo = RdHi:RdLo + Rn[B]* Rm[T] - Rn[T]*Rm[B]

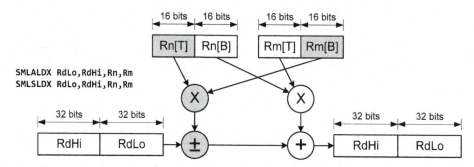

Figure 24-17. Exchange, dual signed multiply, addition/subtraction, and 64-bit accumulate.

The following shows single 16-bit signed multiplication and 64-bit accumulation.

SMLALBB RdLo,RdHi,Rn,Rm	RdHi:RdLo = RdHi:RdLo + Rn[B]*Rm[B]
SMLALBT RdLo,RdHi,Rn,Rm	RdHi:RdLo = RdHi:RdLo + Rn[B]*Rm[T]
SMLATTB RdLo,RdHi,Rn,Rm	RdHi:RdLo = RdHi:RdLo + Rn[T]*Rm[B]
SMLALTT RdLo,RdHi,Rn,Rm	RdHi:RdLo = RdHi:RdLo + Rn[T]*Rm[T]

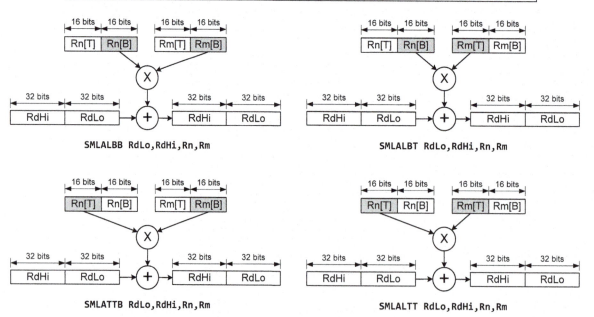

Figure 24-18. 16-bit signed multiply with 64-bit accumulate

24.4.9   16-bit Multiply and Accumulate with 32-bit Result

The accumulator can also be 32 bits in the MAC instructions discussed previously. Figure 24-19, Figure 24-20, and Figure 24-21 shows detailed operations. No overflow can occur during the 16-bit multiplication. However, overflow may occur during the accumulation. SMLAD and SMLSD set the Q flag in APSR if overflow occurs.

SMLAD Rd,Rn,Rm,Ra	Signed multiply accumulate dual Rd = Ra + Rn[T]*Rm[T] + Rn[B]*Rm[B]
SMLSD Rd,Rn,Rm,Ra	Signed multiply subtract dual Rd = Ra + Rn[B]*Rm[B] - Rn[T]* Rm[T]

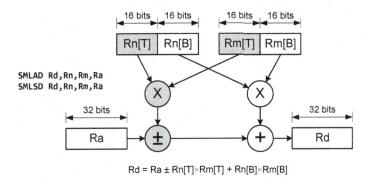

Figure 24-19. Dual 16-bit signed multiply with 32-bit accumulate (or subtract)

The top and bottom halfwords of the second source operand can be swapped before the multiplication if the suffix X is appended. The multiplication is then *top×bottom* and *bottom×top*. The Q flag is set if the addition overflows.

SMLADX Rd,Rn,Rm,Ra	Signed multiply accumulate dual with exchange Rd = Ra + Rn[T]*Rm[B] + Rn[B]*Rm[T]
SMLSDX Rd,Rn,Rm,Ra	Signed multiply subtract dual with exchange Rd = Ra + Rn[B]*Rm[T] - Rn[T]* Rm[B]

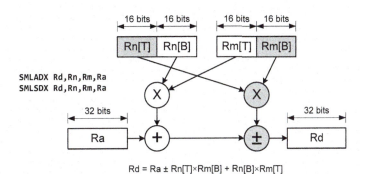

Figure 24-20. Exchange, dual 16-bit multiply, and 32-bit accumulate (or subtract)

We can also multiply two specific 16-bit signed values, either from the top or bottom halfword from two registers, and add the 32-bit signed product to an accumulator register. The Q flag is set if the accumulation overflows.

SMLABB Rd,Rn,Rm,Ra	Signed multiply bottom, accumulate long Rd = Ra + Rn[B]*Rm[B]
SMLABT Rd,Rn,Rm,Ra	Signed multiply bottom and top, accumulate long Rd = Ra + Rn[B]*Rm[T]
SMLATB Rd,Rn,Rm,Ra	Signed multiply top and bottom, accumulate long Rd = Ra + Rn[T]*Rm[B]
SMLATT Rd,Rn,Rm,Ra	Signed multiply top, accumulate long Rd = Ra + Rn[T]*Rm[T]

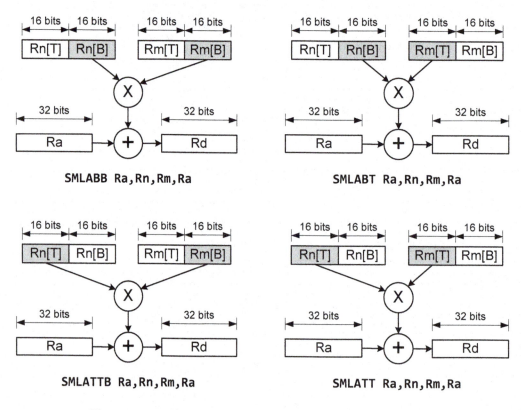

Figure 24-21. Single 16-bit multiply with 32-bit accumulate

The following assembly code can be used in a loop to calculate $\sum_{i=0}^{n} a_i \cdot x_i$, in which a_i and x_i are 16-bit signed values, such as Q15.

```
LDR     r4, [r1], #4    ; load a[i], a[i+1], r1 points to a[i+2] after loading
LDR     r3, [r0], #4    ; load x[i], x[i+1], r0 points to x[i+2] after loading
SMLABB  r5, r3, r4, r5  ; sum = x[i]*a[i], r5 = sum
SMLATT  r5, r3, r4, r5  ; sum = x[i+1]*a[i+1], r5 = sum
```

24.4.10   16×32 Multiply and Accumulate with 32-bit Result

We can also multiply the bottom or top halfword of one register with another register, with the product accumulated. If overflow occurs upon accumulating the product, the Q flag bit in APSR is set. The multiplication in SMLAWB and SMLAWT cannot cause overflow.

SMLAWB Rd,Rn,Rm,Ra	Signed multiply word by bottom halfword, accumulate Rd = Ra + (Rn*Rm[B])>>16
SMLAWT Rd,Rn,Rm,Ra	Signed multiply word by top halfword, accumulate Rd = Ra + (Rn*Rm[T])>>16

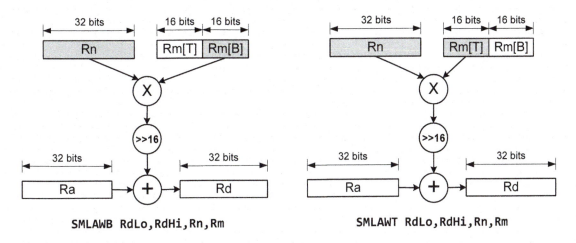

Figure 24-22. Single 16×32 multiply with 32-bit accumulate

24.4.11   32×32 Multiply and Accumulate with 32-bit Result

SMLAL and UMLAL are two instructions that first multiply two words and then accumulate the product to a 64-bit sum, as introduced in Chapter 4.4.

Cortex-M4 and M7 also support 32-bit accumulation with different rounding schemes. If R is specified, it uses rounding to nearest; otherwise, it uses rounding towards zero (*i.e.*, truncation).

SMMLA Rd,Rn,Rm,Ra	Signed most significant word multiply accumulate, Rd = Ra + (Rn*Rm)>>32, Truncate
SMMLAR Rd,Rn,Rm,Ra	Signed most significant word multiply accumulate, Rd = Ra + (Rn*Rm)>>32, Round to nearest
SMMLS Rd,Rn,Rm,Ra	Signed most significant word multiply subtract, Rd = Ra − (Rn*Rm)>>32, Truncate
SMMLSR Rd,Rn,Rm,Ra	Signed most significant word multiply subtract, Rd = Ra − (Rn*Rm)>>32, Round to nearest

24.4.12   Unsigned Long Multiply with Accumulate Accumulate

A special instruction UMAAL is implemented in hardware. It can be used to speed up the Separated Operand Scanning (SOS) algorithm (see reference [92] and [93]). The SOS algorithm multiplies two very large unsigned integers, such as 256 bits by 256 bits. UMAAL performs accumulation twice after the multiplication. It adds the upper word and the lower word of the 64-bit accumulator to the accumulator.

UMAAL RdLo,RdHi,Rn,Rm	Unsigned multiply accumulate accumulate long RdHi:RdLo = Rn*Rm + RdHi + RdLo

Suppose we want to multiply two large unsigned numbers A and B. Each of them has m words, i.e., $A = A_{m-1} \cdots A_2 A_1 A_0$ and $B = B_{m-1} \cdots B_2 B_1 B_0$. Both A_i and B_i have 32 bits ($0 \leq i \leq m - 1$), and A_0 and B_0 are the least significant word.

Let $P = A \times B$ and P has a total of $2m$ words. The SOS algorithm works similarly to standard pencil-and-paper multiplication. Figure 24-23 shows the procedure of multiplying two double-word integers A and B. Differing from standard multiplication, SOS uses block-based multiplications.

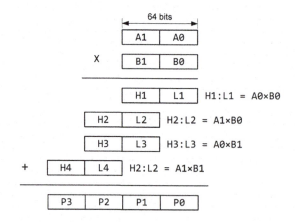

Figure 24-23. Multiplying two unsigned 64-bit integers

```
for i = 0 to 2m-1
    P[i] ← 0;            // Initialization

for i = 0 to m-1
    C ← 0
    for j = 0 to m-1
        C:S ← A[j]*B[i] + C + P[i+j]
        P[i+j] ← S
    P[i+m] ← C
```

Example 24-11. Pseudocode for Separated Operand Scanning (SOS) algorithm

The SOS algorithm, with pseudocode given in Example 24-11, performs two accumulation operations after the multiplication. The multiplication result consists of $2m$ words, including $P[0], P[1], \cdots, P[2m-1]$, with the least significant word in $P[0]$. The inner loop performs multiply-accumulate-accumulate operations in the following form:

$$C:S = a \times b + C + S$$

where the size of a, b, C and S is a word. The UMAAL instruction performs such operation.

SOS calculates the product P starting from the least significant word. The inner loop computes and accumulates partial product. It reuses the results stored in the 64-bit accumulator (C:S) for the next partial product.

During the computation process, we need to change the value of the upper or lower word of the accumulator before executing UMAAL. Therefore, the lower word (S) should be saved to the memory within the inner loop and the upper word (C) should be saved to the memory within the outer loop.

Figure 24-24 shows the basic steps of multiplying two 64-bit unsigned integers. The final product consists of 128 bits: $P[3] = C4$, $P[2] = S4$, $P[1] = S3$, and $P[0] = S1$. This example executes UMAAL four times. The second UMAAL execution does not directly produce any full result. However, it produces partial results, $C2$ and $S4$, which are used when calculating $P[2]$ and $P[1]$.

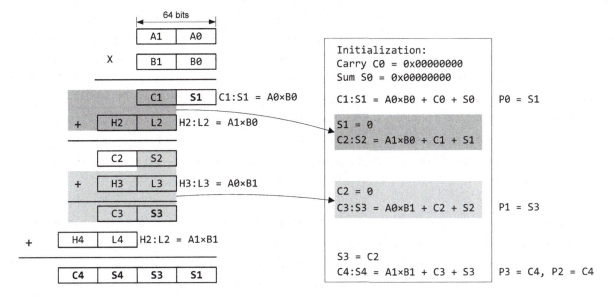

Figure 24-24. Accelerating SOS by using UMAAL

24.5 Packing Halfwords into a Word

We can pack two halfwords from two different registers into another register, as shown
in Figure 24-25.

PKHBT Rd,Rn,Rm{,Op2}	Pack halfword. Rd = Rn[B]:(Rm,Op2)[T] Op2 = LSL #n, n ≠ 0
PKHTB Rd,Rn,Rm{,Op2}	Pack halfword. Rd = Rn[T]:(Rm,Op2)[B] Op2 = ASR #n, n ≠ 0

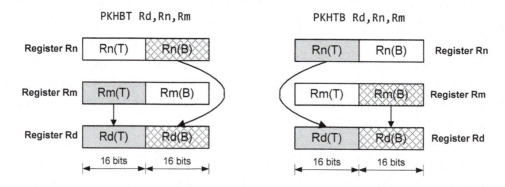

Figure 24-25. Packing two halfwords into a word (Bottom + Top, or Top + Bottom)

The following table gives the assembly instructions of four possible halfword packing
operations. When packing two top halfwords, the second source operand must be shifted
right by 16 bits. When packing two bottom halfwords, the second source operand should
be shifted left by 16 bits. This is because ASR is not permitted for the second source
operand in PKHBT, and LSL is not allowed in PKHTB.

	Top halfword of r1	Bottom halfword of r1
Top halfword of r0	PKHTB r3, r0, r1, ASR #16	PKHTB r3, r0, r1
Bottom halfword of r0	PKHBT r3, r0, r1	PKHBT r3, r0, r1, LSL #16

Example 24-12. Packing halfwords from two different registers into a word

To facilitate 16-bit SIMD instructions, we often need to place a constant number into both
halfwords of a register. The following example code adds a constant 0x1234 to both the
upper and lower halfword in the r4 register.

```
MOV    r3, #0x1234          ; r3 = 0x1234
PKHBT  r5, r3, r3, LSL #16  ; r5 = 0x12341234
SADD16 r4, r4, r5           ; add 0x1234 to both halfwords of r4
```

24.6 Signed and Unsigned Extension

As introduced in Chapter 4.8, SXTB, UXTB, SXTH, UXTH can extend a signed or unsigned byte or halfword to a word.

Cortex-M4 and M7 add two SIMD instructions, SXTB16 and UXTB16, which extend two bytes to two halfwords in parallel, as shown in Figure 24-26.

SXTB16 Rd,Rm {,ROR #n}	Signed extend byte to 16-bit value Rd[T] = sign_extend ((Rm, ROR #)[23:16]) Rd[B] = sign_extend ((Rm, ROR #)[7:0])
UXTB16 Rd,Rm {,ROR #n}	Unsigned extend byte to 16-bit value Rd[T] = zero_extend ((Rm, ROR #)[23:16]) Rd[B] = zero_extend ((Rm, ROR #)[7:0])

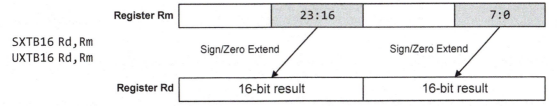

Figure 24-26. Signed and unsigned parallel extension of two bytes to two halfwords

Cortex-M4 and M7 also provide instructions for signed/unsigned extension and then addition, as listed below. The operations can be applied to a byte or halfword, or simultaneously to two bytes or halfwords.

SXTAB Rd,Rn,Rm{,ROR #}	Signed extend byte to word, and add Rd = Rn + sign_extend ((Rm, ROR #)[7:0])
UXTAB Rd,Rn,Rm{,ROR #}	Unsigned extend byte to word, and add Rd = Rn + zero_extend ((Rm, ROR #)[7:0])
SXTAH Rd,Rn,Rm{,ROR #}	Signed extend halfword to word, and add Rd = Rn + sign_extend ((Rm, ROR #)[15:0])
UXTAH Rd,Rn,Rm{,ROR #}	Unsigned extend halfword to word, and add Rd = Rn + zero_extend ((Rm, ROR #)[15:0])
SXTAB16 Rd,Rn,Rm{,ROR #}	Signed extend 2 bytes to 2 halfwords, and add Rd[T] = Rn[T] + sign_extend ((Rm, ROR #)[23:16]) Rd[B] = Rn[B] + sign_extend ((Rm, ROR #)[7:0])
UXTAB16 Rd,Rn,Rm{,ROR #}	Unsigned extend 2 bytes to 2 halfwords, and add Rd[T] = Rn[T] + zero_extend ((Rm, ROR #)[23:16]) Rd[B] = Rn[B] + zero_extend ((Rm, ROR #)[7:0])

Table 24-16. Instructions for extension and add

24.7 GE Flags

Most SIMD instructions do not change the N, Z, C, V and Q flags of the Application Program Status Register (APSR). However, there are SIMD instructions, as listed in Table 24-17, which can change the GE (Greater than or Equal) flags in APSR.

Table 24-17 summarizes the setting of GE flags for SIMD instructions. None of them is saturating instructions.

	GE = 1	GE = 0
SADD8, SADD16 SSUB8, SSUB16 SASX, SSAX	The corresponding result is greater than or equal to zero.	The corresponding result is smaller than zero.
UADD8 UADD16	The corresponding result did overflow, generating a carry.	The corresponding result did not overflow.
USUB8 USUB16	The corresponding result is greater than or equal to zero, meaning borrow did not occur.	The corresponding result is smaller than zero, meaning borrow did occur.
UASX USAX	1. "A" (Add) sets GE flags in the same way as ADDS sets the C flag. If overflow occurs, the corresponding GE flags are set. 2. "S" (Subtract) sets GE flags in the same way as SUBS sets the C flag. If borrow occurs, the corresponding GE flags are cleared.	

Table 24-17. Instructions that affect the GE flags in APSR

The GE flags are mostly used by the SEL instruction for selecting data from either the first or the second source operand register, as introduced in the next section.

- For signed arithmetic operations, including SADD8, SADD16, SSUB8, SSUB16, SASX, and SSAX, the GE flag is set if the corresponding result is greater than or equal to zero.
- For unsigned arithmetic operations, including UADD8, UADD16, USUB8, USUB16, UASX, and USAX, the GE flag is set if overflow occurs on unsigned addition or if no borrow occurs on unsigned subtraction.

The GE flags have four bits, one flag bit for each 8-bit parallel add or subtract, or two flag bits for each 16-bit parallel add or subtract.

For parallel 8-bit arithmetic operations listed in Table 24-17,

- flag GE[0] is for bits[7:0] of the result,
- flag GE[1] is for bits[15:8] of the result,
- flag GE[2] is for bits[23:16] of the result, and
- flag GE[3] is for bits[31:24] of the result.

For parallel 16-bit arithmetic operations listed above,

- flags GE[1:0] are for bits[15:0] of the result, and
- flags GE[3:2] are for bits[31:16] of the result.

For example, both GE[1] and GE[0] are set if the lower halfword result of SADD16 is greater than or equal to zero.

24.8 Byte Selection Instruction

In Chapter 4.11, we have introduced the instructions UBFX and SBFX to extract bits from a word. Cortex-M4 and M7 provide instruction SEL, which selects bytes or halfwords from two source operand registers depending on the GE flags in APSR, as shown in Figure 24-27.

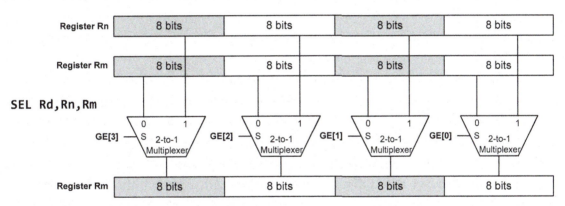

Figure 24-27. Select bytes from Rn or Rm based on GE flag bits in APSR

For example, we can use the SEL instructions to find the pairwise max and min between four pairs of Q7 values.

```
SSUB8 r3, r0, r1     ; If borrow does not occur, corresponding GE flag is 1
                     ; i.e., if result ≥ 0, GE = 1

; Select the larger Q7 of each pair
SEL    r4, r0, r1    ; if GE is 1, select byte from r0; otherwise from r1

; Select the smaller Q7 of each pair
SEL    r5, r1, r0    ; if GE is 1, select byte from r1; otherwise from r0
```

Example 24-13. Select the max and min of the corresponding signed bytes of r0 and r1

For parallel halfword arithmetic operations, two GE bits are set for each pair of halfword operation. Two bit flags GE[1:0] are for the lower halfword operation, and GE[2:0] are for the upper halfword operation. A halfword operation sets its both flag bits to the same value. Therefore, SEL instruction can also use the GE flags to select halfwords.

```
SSUB16  r3, r0, r1    ; If result ≥ 0, corresponding GE flag is 1
SEL     r4, r0, r1    ; Select the larger Q15 of each pair
SEL     r5, r1, r0    ; Select the smaller Q15 of each pair
```

Example 24-14. Choose the max and min of the corresponding signed halfword of r0 and r1

24.9 Basic DSP Functions

In this section, we focus on Q7 and Q15 basic vector-based operations, including

- Vector negate
- Vector absolute value
- Vector offset
- Vector shift left
- Vector mean
- Vector multiplication
- Vector dot product
- Vector min and max

To simplify assembly programs, we assume that the number of values is a multiple of four if the input arrays hold Q7 numbers and a multiple of two if the input arrays hold Q15 numbers.

24.9.1   Vector Negate

The following assembly program reverses the sign of all numbers in a Q7 array. It takes three arguments, including a pointer to the source array, a pointer to the destination array, and the total number of Q7 values in the source array. The program uses SIMD instruction QSUB8 to negate four Q7 values in parallel by subtracting them from zero.

```
vector_negate_Q7 PROC
      EXPORT  vector_negate_Q7

      ; r0 = pSrc, pointer to source Q7 array
      ; r1 = pDst, pointer to destination Q7 array
      ; r2 = # of Q7 values in source array

      PUSH    {r4,r5,lr}
      MOV     r3, #0
```

```
        MOV     r4, #0          ; Initialize loop counter

        B       check

loop    LDR     r5, [r0], #4    ; Load four Q7 values, post-index
        QSUB8   r5, r3, r5      ; Negate four Q7 values in parallel
        STR     r5, [r1], #4    ; Store results to destination array, post-index
        ADDS    r4, r4, #4      ; Processed four Q7 values in each loop
check   CMP     r4, r2
        BLT     loop

        POP     {r4,r5,pc}

        ENDP
```

Example 24-15. Negate an array of Q7 numbers

The following program uses QSUB16 instructions to reverse the sign of two Q16 numbers in parallel.

```
vector_negate_Q15 PROC
        EXPORT vector_negate_Q15

        ; r0 = pSrc, pointer to source Q15 array
        ; r1 = pDst, pointer to destination Q15 array
        ; r2 = # of Q15 values in source array

        PUSH    {r4,r5,lr}
        MOV     r3, #0
        MOV     r4, #0          ; Initialize loop counter
        B       check

loop    LDR     r5, [r0], #4    ; Load two Q15 values, post-index
        QSUB16  r5, r3, r5      ; Negate two Q15 values in parallel
        STR     r5, [r1], #4    ; Store two Q15 values, post-index
        ADDS    r4, r4, #2      ; Increase loop counter
check   CMP     r4, r2          ; Compare with array size
        BLT     loop

        POP     {r4,r5,pc}

        ENDP
```

Example 24-16. Negate an array of Q15 numbers

24.9.2   Vector Absolution Value

We can use SSUB8 and SEL to find the absolute values of all Q7 numbers in an array. The program processes four Q7 numbers in each loop. It first finds all positive values, then negates original numbers and finds positive ones again, and finally merges all positive values into the destination register.

```
vector_abs_Q7 PROC
        EXPORT    vector_abs_Q7

        ; r0 = pSrc, pointer to source Q7 array
        ; r1 = pDst, pointer to destination Q7 array
        ; r2 = # of Q7 values in source array

        PUSH   {r4-r8, LR}        ; Preserve registers
        MOV    r6, #0
        MOV    r3, #0             ; Initialize loop counter
        B      check

loop    LDR    r4, [r0], #4       ; Load four Q7 values

        SSUB8  r5, r4, r6         ; Set four GE bit flags, r6 = 0
        SEL    r7, r5, r6         ; Select all positive Q7 based on GE flags

        SSUB8  r5, r6, r4         ; Negate r4, and set four GE flags
        SEL    r8, r5, r6         ; Select all positive Q7 based on GE flags

        ORR    r5, r7, r8         ; Merge two selections
        STR    r5, [r1], #4       ; Store results

        ADDS   r3, r3, #4         ; Increase loop counter
check   CMP    r3, r2             ; Compare with array size
        BLT    loop

        POP    {r4-r8, pc}

        ENDP
```

Example 24-17. Find the absolution values of a Q7 array

Similar operations can also be performed for Q15 values. The following program stores the absolute value of a Q15 array to the destination array. Within each loop, two Q15 numbers are processed in parallel.

```
vector_abs_Q15 PROC
        EXPORT    vector_abs_Q15

        ; r0 = pSrc, pointer to source Q15 array
        ; r1 = pDst, pointer to destination Q15 array
        ; r2 = # of Q15 values in source array

        PUSH   {r4-r8, LR}        ; Preserve registers
        MOV    r6, #0
```

```
        MOV     r3, #0              ; Initialize loop counter
        B       check

loop    LDR     r4, [r0], #4        ; Load two Q15 values

        SSUB16  r5, r4, r6          ; Set GE flags
        SEL     r7, r5, r6          ; Select all positive Q15 based on GE flags

        SSUB16  r5, r6, r4          ; Negate r4, and set GE flags
        SEL     r8, r5, r6          ; Select all positive Q15 based on GE flags

        ORR     r5, r7, r8          ; Merge two selections
        STR     r5, [r1], #4        ; Store results

        ADDS    r3, r3, #2          ; Increase loop counter
check   CMP     r3, r2              ; Compare with array size
        BLT     loop

        POP     {r4-r8, pc}

        ENDP
```

Example 24-18. Find the absolution values of a Q15 array

24.9.3   Vector Offset with Saturation

The following assembly program shows how to add a constant Q7 offset to all Q7 numbers in an array. The program packs the 8-bit input *offset* into the 32-bit format *offset:offset:offset:offset*, and then uses QADD8 to add simultaneously four pairs of 8-bit Q7 numbers with saturation.

The program uses UXTB to zero extend the 8-bit *offset* input to 32 bits (*i.e.*, making the most significant 24 bits as zero). This is a preventive operation in case the input *offset* has been sign-extended to 32 bits when it is passed to this function via register r3.

```
vector_offset_Q7 PROC
        EXPORT vector_offset_Q7

        ; r0 = pSrc, pointer to source Q7 array
        ; r1 = pDst, pointer to destination Q7 array
        ; r2 = # of Q7 values in source array
        ; r3 = Offset constant in Q7 format

        PUSH    {r4-r6, lr}

        ; Pack 8-bit offset to 32 bit to use SIMD addition
        MOV     r5, #0xFF00
        UXTB    r6, r3                  ; r6 = zero extend offset to 32 bits
        AND     r5, r5, r3, LSL #8      ; r5 = 00:00:offset:00
```

```
        ORR     r6, r6, r5              ; r6 = 00:00:offset:offset
        MOV     r5, #0xFF0000
        AND     r5, r5, r3, LSL #16     ; r5 = 00:offset:00:00
        ORR     r6, r6, r5              ; r6 = 00:offset:offset:offset
        ORR     r6, r6, r3, LSL #24     ; r6 = offset:offset:offset:offset

        MOV     r4, #0                  ; Initialize loop counter

        B       check

loop    LDR     r5, [r0], #4            ; Load four Q7 values, post-index
        QADD8   r5, r5, r6              ; Add four pairs of Q7 values
        STR     r5, [r1], #4            ; Store four Q7 values, post-index
        ADDS    r4, r4, #4              ; Increase loop counter
check   CMP     r4, r2                  ; Compare with array size
        BLT     loop

        POP     {r4-r6, pc}
        ENDP
```

Example 24-19. Adding a constant offset to a Q7 array

The following example adds an offset to all values in a Q15 array. The program runs the PKHBT instruction to pack the 16-bit input *offset* into the format *offset:offset* to use QADD16.

```
vector_offset_Q15 PROC
        EXPORT vector_offset_Q15

        ; r0 = pSrc, pointer to source Q15 array
        ; r1 = pDst, pointer to destination Q15 array
        ; r2 = # of Q15 values in source array
        ; r3 = offset in Q15 format

        PUSH    {r4-r6, lr}
        PKHBT   r5, r3, r3, LSL #16     ; r5 = offset:offset
        MOV     r4, #0                  ; Initialize loop counter

        B       check

loop    LDR     r6, [r0], #4            ; Load two Q15 values, post-index
        QADD16  r6, r6, r5              ; Add two pairs of Q15 values
        STR     r6, [r1], #4            ; Store two Q15 values, post-index
        ADDS    r4, r4, #2              ; Increase loop counter
check   CMP     r4, r2                  ; Compare with array size
        BLT     loop

        POP     {r4-r6, pc}
        ENDP
```

Example 24-20. Adding a constant offset to a Q15 array

24.9.4   Vector Shift Left with Saturation

The following program shifts left Q7 numbers with saturation. For example, with saturation, `0x66 << 1 = 0x7F`.

```
vector_shift_left_Q7 PROC
        EXPORT vector_shift_left_Q7

        ; r0 = pSrc, pointer to source Q7 array
        ; r1 = pDst, pointer to destination Q7 array
        ; r2 = # of Q7 values in source array
        ; r3 = # of bits to be shifted

        PUSH    {r4-r10, lr}
        MOV     r5, #0xFF00
        MOV     r6, #0xFF0000
        MOV     r4, #0                    ; Initialize loop counter
        B       check

loop    LDRSB   r7,  [r0], #1             ; Load 1st Q7, sign extend to a word
        LDRSB   r8,  [r0], #1             ; Load 2nd Q7, sign extend to a word
        LDRSB   r9,  [r0], #1             ; Load 3rd Q7, sign extend to a word
        LDRSB   r10, [r0], #1             ; Load 4th Q7, sign extend to a word

        LSL     r7, r7, r3                ; Logic shift left 1st Q7 by r3 bits
        SSAT    r7, #8, r7                ; Saturate as 8-bit value
        AND     r7, r7, #0xFF             ; Keep only lowest 8 bits

        LSL     r8, r8, r3                ; Logic shift left 2nd Q7 by r3 bits
        SSAT    r8, #8, r8                ; Saturated as 8-bit value
        AND     r8, r5, r8, LSL #8        ; Shift result to position [15:8]
        ORR     r7, r7, r8                ; Combine the result of 1st and 2nd Q7

        LSL     r8, r9, r3                ; Logic shift left 3rd Q7 by r3 bits
        SSAT    r8, #8, r8                ; Saturate as 8-bit value
        AND     r8, r6, r8, LSL #16       ; Shift result to position [23:16]
        ORR     r7, r7, r8                ; Combine the result of 3rd Q7

        LSL     r8, r10, r3               ; Logic shift left 4th Q7 by r3 bits
        SSAT    r8, #8, r8                ; Saturate as 8-bit value
        ORR     r7, r7, r8, LSL #24       ; Combine the result of 4th Q7

        STR     r7, [r1], #4              ; Store result to destination array

        ADDS    r4, r4, #4                ; Increase loop counter
check   CMP     r4, r2                    ; Compare with array size
        BLT     loop
        POP     {r4-r10, pc}
        ENDP
```

Example 24-21. Shifting left all values of a Q15 array

The following program shifts left Q15 numbers with saturation.

```
vector_shift_left_Q15 PROC
      EXPORT vector_shift_left_Q15

      ; r0 = pSrc, pointer to source Q15 array
      ; r1 = pDst, pointer to destination Q15 array
      ; r2 = # of Q15 values in source array
      ; r3 = # of bits to be shifted

      PUSH   {r5-r6, lr}
      MOV    r4, #0              ; Initialize loop counter
      B      check

loop  LDRSH  r6, [r0], #2        ; Load 1st Q15, sign extend to a word
      LSLS   r6, r6, r3          ; Logic shift left 1st Q15 by r3 bits
      SSAT   r6, #16, r6         ; Saturated as 16-bit value

      LDRSH  r5, [r0], #2        ; Load 2nd Q15, sign extend to a word
      LSLS   r5, r5, r3          ; Logic shift left 2nd Q15 by r3 bits
      SSAT   r5, #16, r5         ; Saturated as 16-bit value
      PKHBT  r5, r6, r5, LSL #16 ; r5 = r6[15:0]:r5[15:0]
      STR    r5, [r1], #4        ; Store result to destination array

      ADDS   r4, r4, #2          ; Increase loop counter
check CMP    r4, r2              ; Compare with array size
      BLT    loop
      POP    {r5-r6, pc}

      ENDP
```

Example 24-22. Shifting left all values of a Q15 array

24.9.5   Vector Mean

The following program calculates the arithmetic mean of an array of Q7 values, defined by the formula below:

$$\bar{a} = \frac{1}{n} \sum_{i=0}^{n-1} a_i$$

The program extracts individual bytes and adds them up. SXTAB extracts the least significant byte of a register, and extends the byte to 32-bit signed number, and adds the 32-bit integer with another register.

```
vector_mean_Q7 PROC
      EXPORT vector_mean_Q7
      ; r0 = pSrc, pointer to source Q7 array
      ; r1 = # of Q7 values in source array
```

```
        PUSH   {r4-r6, lr}
        MOV    r3, #0                  ; sum = 0
        MOV    r4, #0                  ; Initialize loop counter
        B      check

loop    LDR    r5, [r0], #4            ; Load four Q7 values, post-index
        SXTAB  r3, r3, r5             ; sum += in[7:0]
        SBFX   r6, r5, #8, #8          ; r6 = in[15:8]
        ADD    r3, r3, r6             ; sum += in[15:8]
        SBFX   r6, r5, #16, #8         ; r6 = in[23:16]
        ADD    r3, r3, r6             ; sum += in[23:16]
        ADD    r3, r3, r5, ASR #24    ; sum += in[31:24]
        ADDS   r4, r4, #4             ; Increase loop counter
check   CMP    r4, r1                  ; Compare with array size
        BLT    loop

        SDIV   r3, r3, r1
        MOV    r0, r3                  ; sum returned in r0
        POP    {r4-r6, pc}
        ENDP
```

Example 24-23. Calculating the arithmetic mean of a Q7 array

The following program uses the MAC instruction SMLAD to speed up the calculation of the arithmetic mean.

```
vector_mean_Q15 PROC
        EXPORT vector_mean_Q15
        ; r0 = pSrc, pointer to source Q15 array
        ; r1 = # of Q15 values in source array

        PUSH   {r4-r6, lr}
        MOV    r3, #0                  ; sum = 0
        MOV    r6, #0x00010001         ; r3[T] = 1, r3[B] = 1
        MOV    r4, #0                  ; Initialize loop counter

        B      check

loop    LDR    r5, [r0], #4            ; Load four Q15 values, post-index
        SMLAD  r3, r5, r6, r3          ; r3 = 1*r5[T] + 1*r5[B]
        ADDS   r4, r4, #2             ; Increase loop counter
check   CMP    r4, r1                  ; Compare with array size
        BLT    loop

        SDIV   r3, r3, r1
        MOV    r0, r3                  ; sum returned in r0
        POP    {r4-r6, pc}
        ENDP
```

Example 24-24. Calculating the arithmetic mean of a Q15 array

24.9.6   Vector Pairwise Multiplication

Given two arrays, a_i and b_i ($0 \le i \le n-1$), the following programs calculate the pairwise product for Q7 and Q15 inputs:

$$c_i = a_i \times b_i$$

As introduced in Chapter 12.1.6, the product of multiplying two Q$m.n$ numbers can be obtained by multiplying two integers corresponding to these two fixed-point numbers, and then shift the product right by n bits.

Therefore, when multiplying two Q7 numbers, the product of corresponding 8-bit signed integers should be arithmetically shifted right by 7 bits.

```
vector_mult_Q7 PROC
      EXPORT vector_mult_Q7

      ; r0 = pSrcA, pointer to source Q7 array A
      ; r1 = pSrcB, pointer to source Q7 array B
      ; r2 = pDst, pointer to destination Q7 array
      ; r3 = # of Q7 values in source array

      PUSH    {r4-r8, lr}
      MOV     r4, #0                  ; Initialize loop counter

      B       check

loop  LDRSB   r5, [r0], #1            ; 1st Q7 of A
      LDRSB   r6, [r1], #1            ; 1st Q7 of B

      SMULBB  r5, r5, r6              ; r5 = r5[B]*r6[B]

      ; Shift product right by 7 bits and saturate result to 8 bits
      SSAT    r5, #8, r5, ASR #7
      STRB    r5, [r2], #1            ; Store results to destination array

      ADDS    r4, r4, #1             ; Increase loop counter
check CMP     r4, r3                 ; Compare with array size
      BLT     loop

      POP     {r4-r8, PC}            ; Recover registers and return

      ENDP
```

Example 24-25. Multiplying the corresponding values in two Q7 arrays

Example 24-25 shows the assembly program of pairwise multiplication between two Q7 arrays. In each loop, the program loads one byte from each array, multiply them, and store the product byte back to the data memory.

This example cannot leverage SIMD instructions to perform multiple pairs of Q7 values in parallel. The reason is that all SIMD parallel multiplication instructions supported in Cortex-M4 and M7 also perform accumulations simultaneously. Nevertheless, no accumulation is required in this example.

Similarly, when two Q15 numbers are multiplied, the product of their corresponding sized 16-bit integers should be right shifted right by 15 bits.

In the following sample program, we multiply two pairs of Q15 numbers in each loop.

```
vector_mult_Q15 PROC
        EXPORT vector_mult_Q15

        ; r0 = pSrcA, pointer to source Q15 array A
        ; r1 = pSrcB, pointer to source Q15 array B
        ; r2 = pDst, pointer to destination Q15 array
        ; r3 = # of Q15 values in source array

        PUSH    {r4-r9, LR}             ; Preserve registers
        MOV     r4, #0                  ; Initialize loop counter

        B       check

loop    LDR     r5, [r0], #4            ; Load two Q15 values from A
        LDR     r6, [r1], #4            ; Load two Q15 values from B

        SMULTT  r7, r5, r6              ; Multiply one pair
        SMULBB  r5, r5, r6              ; Multiply the second pair

        SSAT    r8, #16, r7, ASR #15    ; Saturate result to 16 bit
        SSAT    r7, #16, r5, ASR #15    ; Saturate result to 16 bit
        PKHBT   r9, r7, r8, LSL #16     ; Pack two Q15 result into a word
        STR     r9, [r2], #4            ; Store results

        ADDS    r4, r4, #2              ; Increase loop counter

check   CMP     r4, r3                  ; Compare with array size
        BLT     loop

        POP     {r4-r9, PC}             ; Recover registers and return

        ENDP
```

Example 24-26. Multiplying corresponding values in two Q15 arrays

24.9.7   Vector Dot Product

The following defines the dot product of two vectors.

$$P = A \cdot B = \sum_{i=0}^{n-1} A_i B_i = A_0 B_0 + A_0 B_0 + \cdots + A_{-1} B_{n-1}$$

To increase the precision, the product is in Q31 format even though inputs are in Q7. The product is Q63 if inputs are Q15.

The following program calculates the dot product of two Q7 arrays.

```
vector_dot_prod_Q7 PROC
      EXPORT vector_dot_prod_Q7

      ; r0 = pSrcA, pointer to source Q7 array A
      ; r1 = pSrcB, pointer to source Q7 array B
      ; r2 = # of Q7 values in source array

      PUSH    {r4-r9, LR}         ; Preserve registers
      MOV     r9, #0              ; Initialize accumulator
      MOV     r4, #0              ; Initialize loop counter

      B       check

loop  LDR     r5, [r0], #4        ; r0 = pSrcA, load four Q7 values from A

      SXTB16  r7, r5, ROR #8      ; Extract two Q7 values and make them Q15
      SXTB16  r8, r5              ; Extract the remaining two values

      LDR     r6, [r1], #4        ; r1 = pSrcB, load four Q7 values from B

      SXTB16  r5, r6, ROR #8      ; Extract two Q7 values and make them Q15
      SXTB16  r6, r6              ; Extract the remaining two values

      SMLAD   r9, r7, r5, r9      ; r9 = r9 + r7[T]*r5[T] + r7[B]*r5[B]
      SMLAD   r9, r8, r6, r9      ; r9 = r9 + r8[T]*r6[T] + r8[B]*r6[B]

      ADDS    r4, r4, #4          ; Increase loop counter
check CMP     r4, r2              ; r2 is the array size
      BLT     loop

      MOV     r0, r9              ; Return result in r0
      POP     {r4-r9, PC}         ; Recover registers and return

      ENDP
```

Example 24-27. Dot product of two Q7 arrays

Computing the dot product of two Q15 arrays is given below.

```
vector_dot_prod_Q15 PROC
      EXPORT vector_dot_prod_Q15

      ; r0 = pSrcA, pointer to source Q15 array A
      ; r1 = pSrcB, pointer to source Q15 array B
      ; r2 = # of Q15 values in source array

      PUSH    {r4-r8, LR}      ; Preserve registers
      MOV     r7, #0           ; Lower word of accumulator
      MOV     r8, #0           ; Upper word of accumulator
      MOV     r4, #0           ; Initialize loop counter

      B       check

loop  LDR     r5, [r0], #4     ; r0 = pSrcA, load two Q15 values
      LDR     r6, [r1], #4     ; r1 = pSrcB, load two Q15 values

      SMLALD  r7, r8, r5, r6   ; r8:r7 = r8:r7 + r5[T]*r6[T] + r5[B]*r6[B]

      ADDS    r4, r4, #2       ; Increase loop counter
check CMP     r4, r2           ; Compare with array size
      BLT     loop

      MOV     r0, r7           ; Return result in r1:r0
      MOV     r1, r8
      POP     {r4-r8, PC}      ; Recover registers and return

      ENDP
```

Example 24-28. Dot product of two Q15 arrays

24.9.8   Vector Min and Max

The following program finds both the global min and max of a Q7 array. The result is returned in register r0, with the max stored at the upper halfword and the min at the lower halfword.

```
vector_minmax_q15 PROC
      EXPORT vector_minmax_q15

      ; r0 = pSrc, pointer to source Q15 array
      ; r1 = # of Q15 values in source array

      PUSH    {r4-r6,lr}

      LDR     r2, [r0]         ; Initialize min
      LDR     r3, [r0]         ; Initialize max
```

```
        MOV     r4, #0          ; Initialize loop counter
        B       check

loop    LDR     r5, [r0], #4    ; Load two Q15 values, post-index
        SSUB16  r6, r3, r5      ; Compare current values with max
        SEL     r3, r3, r5      ; Select new max values
        SSUB16  r6, r5, r2      ; Compare current values with min
        SEL     r2, r2, r5      ; Select new min values
        ADDS    r4, r4, #2      ; Increase loop counter
check   CMP     r4, r1          ; Compare with array size
        BLT     loop

        ; Find the max of two halfwords of r3
        LSR     r6, r3, #16
        MOV     r5, #0xFFFF
        AND     r3, r3, r5
        SSUB16  r5, r3, r6
        SEL     r3, r3, r6

        ; Find the min of two halfwords of r2
        LSR     r6, r2, #16
        MOV     r5, #0xFFFF
        AND     r2, r2, r5
        SSUB16  r5, r6, r2
        SEL     r2, r2, r6

        ; Pack max to upper halfword and min to low halfword
        PKHBT   r0, r2, r3, LSL #16
        POP     {r4-r6,pc}
        ENDP
```

Example 24-29. Find the min and max in a Q15 array

24.10   Exercises

1. Find out the value of register r1.

	USAT16 r1, #1, r0	SSAT16 r1, #1, r0
r0 = 0x00000000	r1 =	r1 =
r0 = 0x000F000F	r1 =	r1 =
r0 = 0x00010001	r1 =	r1 =
r0 = 0x00020002	r1 =	r1 =
r0 = 0x00100010	r1 =	r1 =
r0 = 0xFFFFFFFF	r1 =	r1 =

2. Assume the value in register r1 and r0 is 0xF880FF7F. What is the value in register r2 after running each of the following instruction? What are the APSR.GE bit flags?

    (1) SADD8   r2, r1, r0
    (2) UADD8   r2, r1, r0
    (3) QADD8   r2, r1, r0
    (4) UQADD8 r2, r1, r0
    (5) SHADD8 r2, r1, r0
    (6) UHADD8 r2, r1, r0

3. Assume r1 = 0x7FFF1000 and r0 = 0xFFFF7FFF, what is the value in register r2 after running each of the following instructions?

    (1) SSUB16   r2, r1, r0
    (2) USUB16   r2, r1, r0
    (3) QSUB16   r2, r1, r0
    (4) UQSUB16 r2, r1, r0
    (5) UHSUB16 r2, r1, r0
    (6) SHSUB16 r2, r1, r0

4. Assume r1 = 0x0001FFFF and r0 = 0xFFFF0001, what is the value in register r2 after running each of the following instructions?

    (1) SMULBB r2, r1, r0
    (2) SMULBT r2, r1, r0
    (3) SMULTB r2, r1, r0
    (4) SMULTT r2, r1, r0
    (5) SMUAD   r2, r1, r0
    (6) SMUADX r2, r1, r0
    (7) SMUSD   r2, r1, r0
    (8) SMUSDX r2, r1, r0

5. Assume r1 = 0x22221111 and r0 = 0x44443333, what is the value in register r2 after running each of the following instructions?

    (1) PKHTB r2, r1, r0
    (2) PKHBT r2, r1, r0
    (3) PKHTB r2, r1, r0, ASR #16
    (4) PKHBT r2, r1, r0, LSL #16

6. Write an assembly program that uses SEL and packing instructions to achieve the following: pack the max of the upper halfwords of registers r1 and r0 and the min of the lower halfwords of registers r1 and r0 into register r3.

    • r3[31:16] = max(r1[31:16], r0[31:16])
    • r3[15:0] = min(r1[15:0], r0[15:0])

7. Convert a color image to a grayscale image. Suppose each pixel in the image has three 8-bit byte values: red (R), green (G), and blue (B). The image has 1024 pixels. All red values are stored in an array starting at the memory address 0x20000000, all green values starting at 0x20004000, and all blue values starting at 0x20008000. Write an assembly program that calculates the grayscale value of each pixel by using the following formula.

$$Greyscale = (R{\times}77 + G{\times}151 + B{\times}28)/256$$

8. Loop unrolling is a commonly used compiler technique to speed up the application performance. The basic idea is to duplicate the original loop body multiple times and reduce the number of loops. The following example illustrates the key idea of loop unrolling. The unrolled loop runs faster because fewer branch instructions are executed, and a larger loop body gives compilers more opportunity to optimize the performance.

Normal loop	Loop unrolling by four times

`int sum = 0;`
`for (i = 0; i < 100; i++)`
`    sum += a[i];`
	`int sum = 0;`
	`for (i = 0; i < 25; i++) {`
	`    sum += a[4*i];`
	`    sum += a[4*i + 1];`
	`    sum += a[4*i + 2];`
	`    sum += a[4*i + 3];`
	`}`

Rewrite subroutine `vector_dot_prod_Q15` given in Example 24-28 and unroll the loop twice. Assume the number of Q16 numbers in each array is a multiple of four.

9. Unroll the loop of `vector_mean_Q15` given in Example 24-24 four times. Assume the number of Q16 values in the input array is a multiple of eight.

10. Implement the following assembly subroutine that multiplies each element of a Q15 array with a Q15 constant. The results should be in the Q15 format.

```
vector_Q15_scale PROC

    ; r0 = memory address of Q15 array
    ; r1 = array size
    ; r2 = Q15 constant

ENDP
```

Appendix A: GNU Compiler

A-1. Introduction

The GNU Compiler Collection (GCC) consists of a suite of free, open-source, and widely used programming and debugging tools for many types of processors, such as x86/x64, ARM, MIPS, and AVR. The following lists a few important tools.

- The GNU C *compiler* (gcc) translates a C source file to an assembly file or to an object file (machine code).
- The *assembler* (as) converts an assembly program to an object file.
- The *linker* (ld) links object files and pre-compiled libraries into an executable file in a format such as ELF (Executable and Linkable Format).
- To program microprocessors, flash programmers often require us to convert the ELF format to a specific binary format that can be directly written to flash or ROM. We can use objcopy to achieve the conversion.
- The *debugger* (gdb) allows us to debug a program step by step.

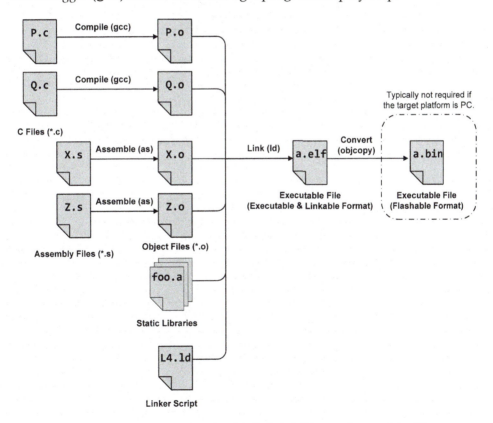

Figure A-1. A simple project that includes C files and assembly files.

To generate the executable a.elf and its corresponding flashable image a.bin from the project given in Figure A-1, we can use commands shown in Example A-1 below. The "-c" option flag instructs gcc to compile the source file without linking. The "-g" option generates debug tables for debugging. In the link command, the "-T" flag identifies the file "L4.ld" as the linker script, and the "-l" flag specifies that the static library "foo.a" should also be linked during the linking process.

```
gcc -c -g -o P.o P.c
gcc -c -g -o Q.o Q.c
as  -g -o X.o X.s
as  -g -o Z.o Z.s
ld -TL4.ld -lfoo -o a.elf P.o Q.o X.o Q.o
objcopy -O binary a.elf a.bin
```

Example A-1. Commands to build the project given in Figure A-1.

GCC tools are cross-platform. For example, we use a Linux PC to compile an application for a different target platform. To build the project for ARM Cortex-M microprocessors, we need to pass more option flags to the commands above. These options are shown in Table A-1 below. The "-mthumb" option forces the target code to use the Thumb and Thumb-2 instruction sets. The "-mcpu" option specifies the processor core.

If a FPU is available, the "-mfloat-abi" option can be either softfp or hard. Both generate hardware floating-point instructions. However, they differ in two aspects: (1) how they pass floating-point arguments to a subroutine, and (2) how they return a floating-point value at the end of a subroutine. softfp uses integer registers and/or the stack, and hard uses floating-point registers. The "fpv4-sp-d16" option means that the floating-point hardware is Vector Floating-point Architecture version 4, single-precision, and has 16 double-precision registers.

Architecture	Core	FPU	GNU Flags
ARMV6-M	Cortex-M0	N/A	-mthumb -mcpu=cortex-m0
	Cortex-M0+	N/A	-mthumb -mcpu=cortex-m0plus
	Cortex-M1	N/A	-mthumb -mcpu=cortex-m1
ARMV7-M	Cortex-M3	N/A	-mthumb -mcpu=cortex-m3
ARMV7E-M	Cortex-M4	No	-mthumb -mcpu=cortex-m4 -mfloat-abi=soft
		Yes	-mthumb -mcpu=cortex-m4 -mfloat-abi=hard (or softfp) -mfpu=fpv4-sp-d16
	Cortex-M7	No	-mthumb -mcpu=cortex-m7 -mfloat-abi=soft
		Yes	-mthumb -mcpu=cortex-m7 -mfloat-abi=hard (or softfp) -mfpu=fpv5-sp-d16

Table A-1. GNU command options for ARM Cortex-M processors

For ARM microprocessors, the names of GNU commands have a prefix of the form: [architecture][-os]-eabi. The eabi stands for Embedded Application Binary Interface. For ARM, the GNU assembler is arm-none-eabi-as, in which none means that the target has no operating system. Example A-2 shows a simple Makefile that compiles hello.s and builds hello.bin.

```
all: hello.bin

hello.o: hello.s
    arm-none-eabi-as -mthumb -mcpu=cortex-m4 -g -o hello.o hello.s

hello.elf: hello.o
    arm-none-eabi-ld -TSTM32L4.ld -o hello.elf hello.o

hello.bin: hello.elf
    arm-none-eabi-objcopy -O binary hello.elf hello.bin
```

Example A-2. Makefile to build a flashable file. The linker script is STM32L4.ld. The linker script varies depending on specific processor chips and applications.

A-2. GNU and ARM Assembly Syntax Comparison

The syntax for assembly language in GNU assembler and ARM's own assembler are slightly different from each other. While their main differences are described later in this appendix, this section gives simple ARM and GNU assembly programs that find the length of a string. Their syntax differences are highlighted.

ARM Assembly Program	GNU Assembly Program

`AREA myCode, DATA, ALIGN=4`
`EXPORT slen`
	`.syntax unified` @ for Thumb-2
	`.thumb` @ same as .code 16
	`.text` @ code section
	`.global slen` @ visible outside
	`.balign 4` @ aligned to words
	`.thumb_func`
	`.type slen, %function`

`slen PROC`
`     MOV    r1,#0      ; Len`
`loop LDRB   r2,[r0],#1 ; post-index`
`     CMP    r2,#0      ; check NULL`
`     ADDNE  r1,r1,#1   ; Len++`
`     BNE    loop       ; Loop again`
`     MOV    r0, r1`
`     BX     lr`
`     ENDP`
	`slen: MOV    r1,#0       @ Len`
	`loop: LDRB   r2,[r0],#1  @ post-index`
	`      CMP    r2,#0       @ check NULL`
	`      IT NE`
	`      ADDNE  r1,r1,#1    @ Len++`
	`      BNE    loop        @ Loop again`
	`      MOV    r0, r1`
	`      BX     lr`

`     AREA myCode, DATA`
`str  DCB "Hello World",0`
`     END`
	`      .data          @ data section`
	`str:  .asciz "Hello World"`
	`      .end`

Example A-3. Simple assembly program that calculates the length of a string.

1. Labels

In GNU assembly, each label ends with a colon (:). A label represents the memory address of an instruction or a data item. Labels allow us to conveniently refer to an assembly instruction or a data item from another part of the assembly program.

A label can contain alphanumeric characters and two special characters: underscore (_) and dollar ($). All labels are case-sensitive. The first character of a label cannot be a number. When a label is defined, the label must appear at the beginning of a line, without any leading whitespace.

2. Comments

There are three different methods for commenting in an assembly program.

1. A comment can be enclosed between two sets of forward slash/asterisk combinations: /* and */, in the same way as C comments.
2. If the source code is in a file whose name ends with a suffix .S or .s, a single-line comment can be placed after a double-slash (//).
3. A comment can be placed after an "*at*" character (@).

3. Directives

All directives in GNU assembly are prefixed by a "." (dot).

As introduced in Chapter 3, ARM microprocessors have two major instruction sets: (1) the 32-bit ARM instruction set, and (2) the Thumb-2 instruction set consisting of 16- and 32-bit instructions. We need to use .arm and .thumb to inform the GNU assembler which instruction set should be used to interpret following assembly code.

Also, the Unified Assembly Language (UAL) allows ARM and Thumb instruction set to share the same assembly syntax. If UAL is used, the same assembly program can be assembled to run on a variety of ARM processors. For the GNU assembler, support for UAL is provided by the statement ".syntax unified".

The following shows how to define a function in ARM and GNU assembly. While GNU syntax provides ".func" and ".endfunc", the GNU assembler for ARM does not support these two directives.

ARM Assembler	GNU Assembler

`myFunc PROC`
`    ; function body`
`    ENDP`
	`        .thumb_func`
	`        .type myFunc, %function`
	`myFunc:`
	`        /* function body */`

Table A-2. Defining a function in GNU and ARM

The following table shows frequently used directives in both the GNU and ARM assembler. Not every GNU directive has an equivalent ARM directive.

	GNU Assembly Syntax	ARM Assembly Syntax	Comments
Sections and Functions	`.data`	`AREA myData, DATA`	
	`.text`	`AREA myCode, CODE`	
	`.end`	`END`	
	`.type myFunc, %function` `.func myFunc`	`myFunc PROC`	
	`.endfunc`	`ENDP`	
	`.include "hardware.s"`	`INCLUDE "hardware.s"`	
	`.global or .globl myFunc`	`EXPORT myFunc`	
	`.global myFunc`	`IMPORT myFunc`	
	`.weak EXTI0_IRQHandler`	`EXPORT EXTI0_IRQHandler [WEAK]`	
Allocating Space and Alignment	`.byte 1, 0x1B`	`DCB 1, 0x1B`	8-bit
	`.hword or .short 1, 2`	`DCW 1, 0x1B`	16-bit
	`.word, .long or .int 98`	`DCD 98`	32-bit
	`.quad 1, 0x1B`	`DCQ 1, 0x1B`	64-bit
	`.ascii "string", 0`	`DCB "string", 0`	
	`.asciz "string"`	`DCB "string", 0`	
	`.float or .single 3.14`	`DCFS 3.14`	32-bit
	`.double 3.14`	`DCFD 3.14`	64-bit
	`.fill 20, 1, 0xFF`	`FILL 20, 0xFF, 1`	20 bytes
	`.space or .skip 255`	`SPACE 255`	
	`.balgin n`	`ALIGN n`	
Setting Symbols	`.equ (or .set) size, 4` `.equiv x, y+1`	`size EQU 4`	#define in C
		`area SETA 2`	Numeric
		`flag SETL {FALSE}`	Logic
		`name SETS "hello"`	String
	`weight .req r8`	`weight RN r8`	Register alias

Table A-3. Frequently used assembly directives

The directive `.equiv` works in the same way as `.equ` and `.set` except that the assembler reports an error if the target symbol is already defined. The directive `.equ` and `.set` can define the same symbol multiple times.

4. Conditional Instructions

The ARM assembler provides better support for conditional instructions. It automatically translates "ADDNE r3,r2,r1" to two instructions "IT NE; ADDNE r3,r2,r1". ARM assembler automatically adds an "IT" instruction. "IT" stands for If-Then. However, in GNU assembly, we have to add the "IT" instruction manually. The usage of the IT instruction is as follows:

$$IT\{x\{y\{z\}\}\}\ \{cond\}$$

where x, y, and z are optional and can be either T (for Then) or E (for Else). We can put up to four conditionally executed instructions after an IT instruction.

ARM Syntax	GNU Syntax
ADDNE r3,r2,r1	IT NE
	ADDNE r3,r2,r1 ; *Then*
ADDNE r3,r2,r1	ITE NE
SUBEQ r3,r4,r5	ADDNE r3,r2,r1 ; *Then*
	SUBEQ r3,r4,r5 ; *Else*
ADDGT r3,r2,r1	ITE GT
SUBLE r3,r4,r5	ADDGT r3,r2,r1 ; *Then*
	SUBLE r3,r4,r5 ; *Else*
SUBLE r3,r4,r5	ITE LE
ADDGT r3,r2,r1	SUBLE r3,r4,r5 ; *Then*
	ADDGT r3,r2,r1 ; *Else*
ADDNE r3,r2,r1	ITT NE
SUBNE r2,r4,r5	ADDNE r3,r2,r1 ; *Then*
	SUBNE r2,r4,r5 ; *Then*
ADDNE r0,r0,r1	ITTEE NE
SUBNE r2,r3,#1	ADDNE r0,r0,r1 ; *Then*
MOVEQ r3,r0	SUBNE r2,r3,#1 ; *Then*
MOVEQ r4,r1	MOVEQ r3,r0 ; *Else*
	MOVEQ r4,r1 ; *Else*

Table A-4. Usage of IT instructions

The IT instruction has 16 bits and Figure A-2 shows its encoding format. It consists of a 4-bit test condition code and a 4-bit if-then bit mask.

- The test condition code is defined for each conditional to be tested, as shown in Table A-5.
- The if-then mask indicates whether the condition or the inverse condition should be tested for the conditional instructions after the IT instruction, depending on the values of <x>, <y>, <z> (see *ARM v7-M Architecture Reference Manual* for a detailed explanation).

15	14	13	12	11	10	9	8	7 6 5 4	3 2 1 0
1	0	1	1	1	1	1	1	Test Condition	If-Then Mask

Figure A-2. Encoding of an `IT` instruction

Code	Condition	Meaning
0000	EQ	**EQ**ual
0001	NE	**N**ot **E**qual
0010	HS/CS	unsigned **H**igher or **S**ame (Carry Set)
0011	LO/CC	unsigned **Lo**wer (Carry Clear)
0100	MI	**MI**nus (Negative)
0101	PL	**PL**us (Positive or Zero)
0110	VS	o**V**erflow **S**et
0111	VC	o**V**erflow **C**lear
1000	HI	unsigned **HI**gher
1001	LS	unsigned **L**ower or **S**ame
1010	GE	signed **G**reater or **E**qual
1011	LT	signed **L**ess **T**han
1100	GT	signed **G**reater **T**han
1101	LE	signed **L**ess than or **E**qual
1110	AL	Always

Table A-5. Encoding of condition code

A-3. Mixing C and Assembly

The basic format of inline assembly is

```
asm volatile ( assembly code
       : output operands                /* optional */
       : input operands                 /* optional */
       : list of clobbered registers    /* optional */
       );
```

Example A-4 shows inline assembly code with only one assembly instruction. This example does not include the list of clobbered registers. The list of clobbered registers is explained later. In the C program, `src1`, `src2`, and `dst` are three local integer variables. The `volatile` keyword helps compilers avoid optimizing away or reordering the assembly code. The `%[rd]` refers to the register `rd`. The symbolic name `rd` is defined in the output operand statement as `[rd] "=r" (dst)`. This statement names the register that holds the value of the C variable `dst` as `rd`.

```
int src1 = 1, src2 = 2, dst;
// The inline assembly instructions below perform the following C statement:
// dst = src1 + src2;

asm volatile ("add %[rd], %[rs], %[rt]"
    : [rd] "=r" (dst)
    : [rs] "r" (src1), [rt] "r" (src2) );
```

Example A-4. Simple inline assembly code performs "dst = src1 + src2".

The inline assembly code is explained below. "=r" refers to the register to write to, and "r" refers to the register to read from, where "r" stands for a register.

```
Prevent compiler from                              =: write-only operand
optimizing the assembly                            +: read-write operand
code away or moving it                             &: output operand only

asm volatile ("add %[rd], %[rs], %[rt]" : [rd] "=r" (dst) : [rs] "r" (src1), [rt] "r" (src2));

              Assembly                Output                          Input
              Instructions            Operands                        Operands

                                    Use a register
                                    for the operand
```

The list of clobbered registers is used to inform the compiler that additional registers (excluding the output operands) or the memory are to be modified but are not guaranteed to be preserved by the inline assembly. There is no need to add the output operands to the clobbered list. While it is not mandatory to specify the clobbered register list, it is highly recommended to add the list so that the compiler better or correctly performs optimization. In Example A-5, the clobbered list indicates that register r5, memory, and the program status register (psr) are overwritten. The "cc" stands for condition code registers, which let the compiler know that the assembly code will change the processor status flags. In this example, the instruction adds modifies the processor status flags.

```
int array[10];
// The inline assembly instructions below perform the following C statement:
//    array[0] += 1;
asm volatile (
    " lw   r5, #0(%[rs])  \n\t"  /* r5 is modified */
    " adds r5, r5, #1     \n\t"  /* processor flags are modified */
    " sw   r5, #0(%[rs])     "  /* memory is modified */
    :                            /* No output operands */
    : [rs] "r" (array)           /* Input operand */
    : "memory", "r5", "cc");     /* Memory, r5, and psr are modified */
```

Example A-5. Demo of the list of clobbered registers

Software can instruct the compiler to use a specific register to store a C variable by using the register keyword, as shown below.

```
register int t asm("r0");
```

Example A-6 shows the difference between ARM and GNU syntax when inline assembly accesses local variables.

ARM In-line Assembly	GNU In-line Assembly

<pre>int sum3(int a, int b, int c){
  int t;
  __asm {
    ADD t, a, b; // virtual registers
    ADD t, t, c;
  }
  return t;
}
 	
int main(void){
  int s = sum3(1, 2, 3);
  while(1);
}</pre>
	<pre>int sum3(int a, int b, int c){
	  register int t asm("r0");
	  asm volatile(
	    " ADD r0, r0, r1 \n\t" /* a + b */
	    " ADD r0, r0, r2 " /* add c */
	  );
	  return t;
	}
	
	int main(void){
	  int s = sum3(1, 2, 3);
	  while(1);
	}</pre>

Example A-6. Accessing local variables

A C function can be implemented by using only assembly instructions, as shown in Example A-7. We can declare a function using "__asm" for the ARM assembler and "__attribute__ ((naked))" for the GNU assembler. Be careful that, in both cases, the compiler does not insert any *prolog* (initial code in a function that preserves registers) and any *epilog* (final code in a function that recovers registers before the function returns). Therefore, if necessary, the assembly function body must push registers onto the stack at the beginning, retrieve input arguments from the stack, and pop register values off the stack at the end.

ARM In-line Assembly	GNU In-line Assembly

<pre>__asm int sum3(int a, int b, int c){
  ADD r0, r0, r1 ; a + b
  ADD r0, r0, r2 ; add c
  BX lr   ; return
}
 	
int main(void){
  int s = sum3(1, 2, 3);
  while(1);
}</pre>
	<pre>__attribute__ ((naked)) int sum3(int
	a, int b, int c){
	  asm volatile(
	    " ADD r0, r0, r1 \n\t" /* a + b */
	    " ADD r0, r0, r2 \n\t" /* add c */
	    " BX lr" /* return */
	  );
	}
	
	int main(void){
	  int s = sum3(1, 2, 3);
	  while(1);
	}</pre>

Example A-7. Implementing a C function body by using assembly instructions only

A-4. Linker Script

When the linker combines object files and library files into a single executable file, a linker script provides the linker two critical types of instructions regarding (1) how data and code sections are merged, and (2) where each section should be placed in memory.

A linker script is a text file that contains two major components: MEMORY{} and SECTIONS{} (see Example A-8). The MEMORY{} describes the type, the starting address, and the size of various memory devices on a chip. The SECTIONS{} specifies the location of different sections of memory. All sections are placed in sequential order in their target memory device. Table A-6 summarizes the content of each section.

```
ENTRY(Reset_Handler)   /* Specify the entry point of the program */


_estack = 0x20017FFF   /* Place the stack at the top end of RAM */


/* Define memory areas */
MEMORY
{
  FLASH (rx): ORIGIN = 0x08000000, LENGTH = 1024K /* read, execute */
  RAM (xrw) : ORIGIN = 0x20000000, LENGTH = 96K   /* execute, read, write */
}


/* Define output sections */
SECTIONS
{
  /* ISR vector table should be at beginning of FLASH */
  .isr_vector : {...} > FLASH

  /* Program code and some constant data go into FLASH */
  .text : {...} > FLASH

  /* Read-only data section goes into FLASH */
  .rodata : {...} >  FLASH

  /* Read-write initialized data section goes into RAM and FLASH */
  .data : {...} > RAM AT> FLASH      /* AT means both */

  /* Read-write uninitialized data section goes into RAM */
  /* bss = Block Started by Symbol */
  .bss : {...} > RAM

  /* Allocate a heap section in RAM */
  ._user_heap_stack: {...} > RAM
  ...
}
```

Example A-8. The linker script for STM32L4 that stores a program in flash memory.

Section	Content	Memory Region
`.isr_vector`	Stack address, interrupt address vector	Flash
`.text`	Program code, some constants	Flash
`.rodata`	Constant data, strings	Flash
`.data`	Global initialized variables, local initialized static variables	RAM and Flash
`.bss`	Global un-initialized/zero-initialized variables, local un-initialized/zero-initialized static variables	RAM
heap	Dynamically allocated variables	RAM
stack	Local non-static variables	RAM

Table A-6. Memory layout of a C or assembly program

The ENTRY keyword specifies the first instruction to be executed when the program starts is Reset_Handler. The linker script also defines a constant named _estack, which is the largest memory address in RAM. Note that the stack pointer descends to lower memory addresses when data are pushed onto the stack. The Reset_Handler initializes the stack pointer as follows:

```
LDR    sp, =_estack    /* Initialize the stack pointer */
```

The section .isr_vector is for ARM processors only. As defined in the startup file (such as startup_stm3214xxxx.s), it includes the memory address of the main stack, the memory address of the Reset_Handler function, and the memory address of interrupt service routines (also known as the *interrupt vector table*). The .isr_vector section, defined in Example A-9, is placed at the beginning of the flash memory. The special linker variable dot "." represents the current location counter, which is automatically incremented by section size when a section is added. The statement ". =" forces the linker to change the location counter to the expression assigned.

```
.isr_vector :
{
  . = ALIGN(4);          /* Align to words */
  KEEP(*(.isr_vector))   /* Instruct linker to keep it in executable */
  . = ALIGN(4);          /* Align to words */
} >FLASH                 /* Store this section in flash memory */
```

Example A-9. Definition of the .isr_vector section in the linker script

Another important section is the heap, which is placed immediately after all data sections in RAM, as shown in Example A-8. The heap grows upwards as space is allocated dynamically during run time.

A-5. Programming and Debugging the board

The debug interface of most development boards, such as STM32L4 Discovery Kit, often provides a USB mass storage interface. When a board is connected to a computer, it is automatically mounted as a USB drive. To program the board, we only need to copy the generated `.bin` file to the mounted USB drive.

If the USB mass storage interface is not available, we can use the open-source `st-flash` tool to program an STM board:

```
st-flash write myProgram.bin 0x8000000
```

To debug a program running on the board, we can use a user-friendly IDE such as Eclipse and TrueSTUDIO. In the following, we focus on how to debug via GNU `gdb` on the command line.

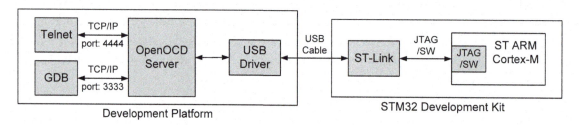

Figure A-3. Using OpenOCD to debug

As shown in Figure A-3, many development boards, such as STM32 discovery kits, integrate a hardware debugger. The hardware debugger, such as ST-Link, uses a serial communication interface to interact with the JTAG (Joint Test Action Group) or SW (Serial Wire) debug port of ARM Cortex-M processors.

OpenOCD (Open On-Chip Debugger) is an open-source software that is widely used for debugging and downloading executables to microprocessors. OpenOCD runs as a server (also known as a *daemon*) on a host computer and serves two purposes:

1. It receives commands from either Telnet or `gdb` via a TCP/IP connection.
2. It translates commands received to JTAG/SW commands, and sends them to the target ARM Cortex-M processor via the hardware debugger.

OpenOCD and ST-Link communicate via USB. By default, Linux only allows privileged users to access an USB device using `libusb`. To enable unprivileged users to run OpenOCD, we need to create a rule file named "`stlink.rules`" and copy it to the directory `/etc/udev/rules.d/` as root.

```
# libusb device nodes
KERNEL=="tty[A-Z]*[0-9]", MODE="0666"
SUBSYSTEM=="usb", ATTRS{idVendor}=="0483", MODE="0666"
```
Example A-10. stlink.rules

In the following, we focus only on debugging via gdb and OpenOCD.

On one terminal window, we run the following command:

```
openocd -f board/stm32l4discovery.cfg -f interface/stlink-v2.cfg
```

On another terminal window, we start gdb. The OpenOCD server listens for gdb connections on TCP port 3333 by default.

```
arm-none-eabi-gdb myProgram.elf
(gdb) target remote localhost:3333
(gdb) monitor reset halt
(gdb) load
(gdb) continue
```

"monitor [commands]" means that these commands are issued to the OpenOCD server; they are not commands executed by gdb. These commands are called *remote commands*. OpenOCD translates remote commands to JTAG commands.

While OpenOCD works for a verity of ARM Cortex chips from different companies, one alternative to OpenOCD for STM32 ARM Cortex chips is the open-source tool st-util.

On one terminal, run the following command:

```
st-util
```

On another terminal, you can start to debug the code:

```
arm-none-eabi-gdb myProgram.elf
(gdb) target extended localhost:4242
(gdb) load
(gdb) continue
```

You can stop the execution by pressing ctrl + c in the gdb command window. You can also set up breakpoints and watchpoints, execute the code step by step, examine code and data, and print variables. Refer to *GNU gdb documentation* for details.

Appendix B: Cortex-M3/M4 Instructions

Instruction	Operands	Description and Action
ADC, ADCS	{Rd,} Rn, Op2	Add with Carry, Rd ← Rn + Op2 + Carry, ADCS updates N,Z,C,V
ADD, ADDS	{Rd,} Rn, Op2	Add, Rd ← Rn + Op2, ADDS updates N,Z,C,V
ADD, ADDS	{Rd,} Rn, #imm12	Add Immediate, Rd ← Rn + imm12, ADDS updates N,Z,C,V
ADR	Rd, label	Load PC-relative Address, Rd ← <label>
AND, ANDS	{Rd,} Rn, Op2	Logical AND, Rd ← Rn AND Op2, ANDS updates N,Z,C
ASR, ASRS	Rd, Rm, <Rs|#n>	Arithmetic Shift Right, Rd ← Rm>>(Rs|n), ASRS updates N,Z,C
B	label	Branch, PC ← label
BFC	Rd, #lsb, #width	Bit Field Clear, Rd[(width+lsb-1):lsb] ← 0
BFI	Rd, Rn, #lsb, #width	Bit Field Insert, Rd[(width+lsb-1):lsb] ← Rn[(width-1):0]
BIC, BICS	{Rd,} Rn, Op2	Bit Clear, Rd ← Rn AND NOT Op2, BICS updates N,Z,C
BKPT	#imm	Breakpoint, prefetch abort or enter debug state
BL	label	Branch with Link, LR ← next instruction, PC ← label
BLX	Rm	Branch register with link, LR←next instr addr, PC←Rm[31:1]
BX	Rm	Branch register, PC ← Rm
CBNZ	Rn, label	Compare and Branch if Non-zero; PC ← label if Rn != 0
CBZ	Rn, label	Compare and Branch if Zero; PC ← label if Rn == 0
CLREX	-	Clear local processor exclusive tag
CLZ	Rd, Rm	Count Leading Zeros, Rd ← number of leading zeros in Rm
CMN	Rn, Op2	Compare Negative, Update N,Z,C,V flags on Rn + Op2
CMP	Rn, Op2	Compare, Update N,Z,C,V flags on Rn - Op2
CPSID	i	Disable specified (i) interrupts, optional change mode
CPSIE	i	Enable specified (i) interrupts, optional change mode
DMB	-	Data Memory Barrier, ensure memory access order
DSB	-	Data Synchronization Barrier, ensure completion of access
EOR, EORS	{Rd,} Rn, Op2	Exclusive OR, Rd ← Rn XOR Op2, EORS updates N,Z,C
ISB	-	Instruction Synchronization Barrier
IT	-	If-Then Condition Block
LDM	Rn{!}, reglist	Load Multiple Registers increment after, <reglist> = mem[Rn], Rn increments after each memory access
LDMDB, LDMEA	Rn{!}, reglist	Load Multiple Registers Decrement Before, <reglist> = mem[Rn], Rn decrements before each memory access
LDMFD, LDMIA	Rn{!}, reglist	<reglist> = mem[Rn], Rn increments after each memory access
LDR	Rt, [Rn, #offset]	Load Register with Word, Rt ← mem[Rn + offset]
LDRB, LDRBT	Rt, [Rn, #offset]	Load Register with Byte, Rt ← mem[Rn + offset]
LDRD	Rt, Rt2, [Rn,#offset]	Load Register with two words, Rt ← mem[Rn + offset], Rt2 ← mem[Rn + offset + 4]
LDREX	Rt, [Rn, #offset]	Load Register Exclusive, Rt ← mem[Rn + offset]
LDREXB	Rt, [Rn]	Load Register Exclusive with Byte, Rt ← mem[Rn]
LDREXH	Rt, [Rn]	Load Register Exclusive with Half-word, Rt ← mem[Rn]
LDRH, LDRHT	Rt, [Rn, #offset]	Load Register with Half-word, Rt ← mem[Rn + offset]
LDRSB, LDRSBT	Rt, [Rn, #offset]	Load Register with Signed Byte, Rt ← mem[Rn + offset]
LDRSH, LDRSHT	Rt, [Rn, #offset]	Load Register with Signed Half-word, Rt ← mem[Rn + offset]
LDRT	Rt, [Rn, #offset]	Load Register with Word, Rt ← mem[Rn + offset]
LSL, LSLS	Rd, Rm, <Rs|#n>	Logic Shift Left, Rd ← Rm << Rs|n, LSLS update N,Z,C
LSR, LSRS	Rd, Rm, <Rs|#n>	Logic Shift Right, Rd ← Rm >> Rs|n, LSRS update N,Z,C
MLA	Rd, Rn, Rm, Ra	Multiply with Accumulate, Rd ← (Ra + (Rn*Rm))[31:0]
MLS	Rd, Rn, Rm, Ra	Multiply with Subtract, Rd ← (Ra - (Rn*Rm))[31:0]
MOV, MOVS	Rd, Op2	Move, Rd ← Op2, MOVS updates N,Z,C
MOVT	Rd, #imm16	Move Top, Rd[31:16] ← imm16, Rd[15:0] unaffected
MOVW, MOVWS	Rd, #imm16	Move 16-bit Constant, Rd ← imm16, MOVWS updates N,Z,C
MRS	Rd, spec_reg	Move from Special Register, Rd ← spec_reg
MSR	spec_reg, Rm	Move to Special Register, spec_reg ← Rm, Updates N,Z,C,V
MUL, MULS	{Rd,} Rn, Rm	Multiply, Rd ← (Rn*Rm)[31:0], MULS updates N,Z
MVN, MVNS	Rd, Op2	Move NOT, Rd ← 0xFFFFFFFF EOR Op2, MVNS updates N,Z,C

NOP	-	No Operation
ORN, ORNS	{Rd,} Rn, Op2	Logical OR NOT, Rd ← Rn OR NOT Op2, ORNS updates N,Z,C
ORR, ORRS	{Rd,} Rn, Op2	Logical OR, Rd ← Rn OR Op2, ORRS updates N,Z,C
POP	reglist	Canonical form of LDM SP!, <reglist>
PUSH	reglist	Canonical form of STMDB SP!, <reglist>
RBIT	Rd, Rn	Reverse Bits, for (i = 0; i < 32; i++): Rd[i] = RN[31-i]
REV	Rd, Rn	Reverse Byte Order in a Word, Rd[31:24]←Rn[7:0], Rd[23:16]←Rn[15:8], Rd[15:8]←Rn[23:16], Rd[7:0]←Rn[31:24]
REV16	Rd, Rn	Reverse Byte Order in a Half-word, Rd[15:8]←Rn[7:0], Rd[7:0]←Rn[15:8], Rd[31:24]←Rn[23:16], Rd[23:16]←Rn[31:24]
REVSH	Rd, Rn	Reverse Byte order in Low Half-word and sign extend, Rd[15:8]←Rn[7:0], Rd[7:0]←Rn[15:8], Rd[31:16]←Rn[7]*&0xFFFF
ROR, RORS	Rd, Rm, <Rs|#n>	Rotate Right, Rd ← ROR(Rm, Rs|n), RORS updates N,Z,C
RRX, RRXS	Rd, Rm	Rotate Right with Extend, Rd ← RRX(Rm), RRXS updates N,Z,C
RSB, RSBS	{Rd,} Rn, Op2	Reverse Subtract, Rd ← Op2 – Rn, RSBS updates N,Z,C,V
SBC, SBCS	{Rd,} Rn, Op2	Subtract with Carry, Rd ← Rn-Op2-NOT(Carry), updates NZCV
SBFX	Rd, Rn, #lsb, #width	Signed Bit Field Extract, Rd[(width-1):0] = Rn[(width+lsb-1):lsb], Rd[31:width] = Replicate(Rn[width+lsb-1])
SDIV	{Rd,} Rn, Rm	Signed Divide, Rd ← Rn/Rm
SEV	-	Send Event
SMLAL	RdLo, RdHi, Rn, Rm	Signed Multiply with Accumulate, RdHi,RdLo ← signed(RdHi,RdLo + Rn*Rm)
SMULL	RdLo, RdHi, Rn, Rm	Signed Multiply, RdHi,RdLo ← signed(Rn*Rm)
SSAT	Rd, #n, Rm{,shift #s}	Signed Saturate, Rd ← SignedSat((Rm shift s), n). Update Q
STM	Rn{!}, reglist	Store Multiple Registers
STMDB, STMEA	Rn{!}, reglist	Store Multiple Registers Decrement Before
STMFD, STMIA	Rn{!}, reglist	Store Multiple Registers Increment After
STR	Rt, [Rn, #offset]	Store Register with Word, mem[Rn+offset] = Rt
STRB, STRBT	Rt, [Rn, #offset]	Store Register with Byte, mem[Rn+offset] = Rt
STRD	Rt,Rt2,[Rn,#offset]	Store Register with two Words, mem[Rn+offset] = Rt, mem[Rn+offset+4] = Rt2
STREX	Rd, Rt, [Rn,#offset]	Store Register Exclusive if allowed, mem[Rn + offset] ← Rt, clear exclusive tag, Rd ← 0. Else Rd ← 1.
STREXB	Rd, Rt, [Rn]	Store Register Exclusive Byte, mem[Rn] ← Rt[15:0] or mem[Rn] ← Rt[7:0], clear exclusive tag, Rd ← 0. Else Rd ← 1
STREXH	Rd, Rt, [Rn]	Store Register Exclusive Half-word, mem[Rn] ← Rt[15:0] or mem[Rn] ← Rt[7:0], clear exclusive tag, Rd ← 0. Else Rd ← 1
STRH, STRHT	Rt, [Rn, #offset]	Store Half-word, mem[Rn + offset] ← Rt[15:0]
STRT	Rt, [Rn, #offset]	Store Register with Translation, mem[Rn + offset] = Rt
SUB, SUBS	{Rd,} Rn, Op2	Subtraction, Rd ← Rn – Op2, SUBS updates N,Z,C,V
SUB, SUBS	{Rd,} Rn, #imm12	Subtraction, Rd ← Rn-imm12, SUBS updates N,Z,C,V
SVC	#imm	Supervisor Call
SXTB	{Rd,} Rm {,ROR #n}	Sign Extend Byte, Rd ← SignExtend((Rm ROR (8*n))[7:0])
SXTH	{Rd,} Rm {,ROR #n}	Sign Extend Half-word, Rd←SignExtend((Rm ROR (8*n))[15:0])
TBB	[Rn, Rm]	Table Branch Byte, PC ← PC+ZeroExtend(Memory(Rn+Rm,1)<<1)
TBH	[Rn, Rm, LSL #1]	Table Branch Halfword, PC←PC+ZeroExtend(Memory(Rn+Rm<<1,2)<<1)
TEQ	Rn, Op2	Test Equivalence, Update N,Z,C,V on Rn EOR Operand2
TST	Rn, Op2	Test, Update N,Z,C,V on Rn AND Op2
UBFX	Rd, Rn, #lsb, #width	Unsigned Bit Field Extract, Rd[(width-1):0] = Rn[(width+lsb-1):lsb], Rd[31:width] = Replicate(0)
UDIV	{Rd,} Rn, Rm	Unsigned Divide, Rd ← Rn/Rm
UMLAL	RdLo, RdHi, Rn, Rm	Unsigned Multiply with Accumulate, RdHi,RdLo ← unsigned(RdHi,RdLo + Rn*Rm)
UMULL	RdLo, RdHi, Rn, Rm	Unsigned Multiply, RdHi,RdLo ← unsigned(Rn*Rm)
USAT	Rd, #n, Rm{,shift #s}	Unsigned Saturate, Rd←UnsignedSat((Rm shift s),n), Update Q
UXTB	{Rd,} Rm {,ROR #n}	Unsigned Extend Byte, Rd ← ZeroExtend((Rm ROR (8*n))[7:0])
UXTH	{Rd,} Rm {,ROR #n}	Unsigned Extend Halfword, Rd ← ZeroExtend((Rm ROR (8*n))[15:0])
WFE	-	Wait For Event and Enter Sleep Mode
WFI	-	Wait for Interrupt and Enter Sleep Mode

Appendix C: Floating-point Instructions (Optional on Cortex-M4 and Cortex-M7)

Instruction	Operands	Description and Action
VABS.F32	Sd, Sm	Absolute value of floats, Sd ← |Sm|
VADD.F32	{Sd,} Sn, Sm	Add floating points, Sd ← Sn + Sm
VCMP.F32	Sd, <Sm | #0.0>	Compare two floating-point registers, or one floating-point register and zero
VCMPE.F32	Sd, <Sm | #0.0>	Compare two floating-point registers, or one floating-point register and zero, and raise exception for a signaling NaN
VCVT{R}.S32.F32	Sd, Sm	Convert from single-precision to signed 32-bit (S32) or unsigned 32-bit (U32) integer. If R is specified, it uses the rounding mode specified by FPSCR. If R is omitted, it uses round towards zero.
VCVT{R}.U32.F32	Sd, Sm	
VCVT{R}.F32.S32	Sd, Sm	Convert to single-precision from signed 32-bit (S32) or unsigned 32-bit (U32) integer. See above for R.
VCVT{R}.F32.U32	Sd, Sm	
VCVT{R}.Td.F32	Sd, Sm, #fbits	Convert between single-precision and fixed-point. Td can be S16 (signed 16-bit), U16 (unsigned 16-bit), S32 (signed 32-bit), U32 (unsigned 32-bit). fbits is the number of fraction bits in the fixed-point number. See above for R.
VCVT{R}.Td.F32	Sd, Sd, #fbits	
VCVT{R}.F32.Td	Sd, Sm, #fbits	
VCVT{R}.F32.Td	Sd, Sd, #fbits	
VCVT<B|T>.F32.F16	Sd, Sm	Converts half-precision float to single-precision (B = bottom half of Sm, T = top half of Sm)
VCVT<B|T>.F16.F32	Sd, Sm	Converts single-precision float to half-precision (B = bottom half of Sd, T = top half of Sd)
VDIV.F32	{Sd,} Sn, Sm	Divide single-precision floats, Sd = Sn/Sm
VFMA.F32	{Sd,} Sn, Sm	Multiply (fused) then accumulate float, Sd = Sd + Sn*Sm
VFMS.F32	{Sd,} Sn, Sm	Multiply (fused) then subtract float, Sd = Sd - Sn*Sm
VFNMA.F32	{Sd,} Sn, Sm	Multiply (fused) then accumulate then negate float, Sd = -1 * Sd + Sn * Sm
VFNMS.F32	{Sd,} Sn, Sm	Multiply (fused) then subtract then negate float, Sd = -1 * Sd - Sn * Sm
VLDM.64	Rn{!}, list	Load multiple double-precision floats
VLDM.32	Rn{!}, list	Load multiple single-precision floats
VLDR.F64	<Dd|Sd>, [Rn]	Load one double-precision float
VLDR.F32	<Dd|Sd>, [Rn]	Load one single-precision float
VLMA.F32	{Sd,} Sn, Sm	Multiply float then accumulate float, Sd = Sd + Sn*Sm
VLMS.F32	{Sd,} Sn, Sm	Multiply float then subtract float, Sd = Sd - Sn*Sm
VMOV.F32	Sd, #imm	Move immediate to float-register
VMOV	Sd, Sm	Copy from float register to float register
VMOV	Sn, Rt	Copy ARM core register to float register
VMOV	Sm, Sm1, Rt, Rt2	Copy 2 ARM core registers to 2 float registers
VMOV	Dd[x], Rt	Copy ARM core register to a half of a double-precision floating-point register, where x is 0 or 1.
VMOV	Rt, Dn[x]	Copy a half of a double-precision floating-point register to ARM core register, where x is 0 or 1.
VMRS	Rt, FPSCR	Move FPSCR to ARM core register or APSR
VMSR	FPSCR, Rt	Move to FPSCR from ARM Core register
VMUL.F32	{Sd,} Sn, Sm	Multiply float, Sd = Sn * Sm
VNEG.F32	Sd, Sm	Negate float, Sd = -1 * Sm
VNMLA.F32	Sd, Sn, Sm	Multiply float then accumulate then negate float Sd = -1 * (Sd + Sn * Sm)
VNMLS.F32	Sd, Sn, Sm	Multiply float then subtract then negate float Sd = -1 * (Sd - Sn * Sm)
VNMUL.F32	{Sd,} Sn, Sm	Negate and multiply float, Sd = -1 * Sn * Sm
VPOP.64	list	Pop double registers from stack

VPOP.32	list	Pop float registers from stack
VPUSH.64	list	Push double registers to stack
VPUSH.32	list	Push float registers to stack
VSQRT.F32	Sd, Sm	Square-root of float
VSTM.64	Rn{!}, list	Store multiple double registers
VSTM.32	Rn{!}, list	Store multiple float registers
VSTR.64	Sd, [Rn]	Store one double register
VSTR.32	Sd, [Rn]	Store one float registers
VSUB.F32	{Sd,} Sn, Sm	Subtract float, Sd = Sn - Sm

Appendix D: DSP Instructions on Cortex-M4 and Cortex-M7

T = Top/high halfword, B = Bottom/low halfword
SQ = Signed saturation, UQ = Unsigned saturation

Instruction	Operands	Description and Action
PKHBT	{Rd,} Rn, Rm, Op2	Pack halfword. Rd = Rn[B]:(Rm, Op2)[T]
PKHTB	{Rd,} Rn, Rm, Op2	Pack halfword. Rd = Rn[T]:(Rm, Op2)[B]
QADD	{Rd,} Rn, Rm	Saturating add signed 32-bit integers Rd = SQ32(Rn + Rm)
QADD16	{Rd,} Rn, Rm	Saturating add 2 pairs of 16-bit signed integers Rd[T] = SQ16(Rn[T] + Rm[T]) Rd[B] = SQ16(Rn[B] + Rm[B])
QADD8	{Rd,} Rn, Rm	Saturating add 4 pairs of 8-bit signed integers Rd[31:24] = Rn[31:24] + Rm[31:24] Rd[25:16] = Rn[25:16] + Rm[25:16] Rd[15:8] = Rn[15:8] + Rm[15:8] Rd[7:0] = Rn[7:0] + Rm[7:0]
QASX	{Rd,} Rn, Rm	Saturating add and subtract with exchange Rd[T] = SQ16(Rn[T] + Rm[B]) Rd[B] = SQ16(Rn[B] - Rm[T])
QDADD	{Rd,} Rn, Rm	Saturating double and add Rd = SQ32(Rn + SQ32(Rm *2))
QDSUB	{Rd,} Rn, Rm	Saturating double and subtract Rd = SQ32(Rn - SQ32(2*Rm))
QSAX	{Rd,} Rn, Rm	Saturating subtract and add with exchange Rd[T]=SQ16(Rn[T]-Rm[B]), Rd[B]=SQ16(Rn[B]+Rm[T])
QSUB	{Rd,} Rn, Rm	Signed saturating subtract two 32-bit signed integers Rd = SQ32(Rn - Rm)
QSUB16	{Rd,} Rn, Rm	Signed saturating subtract 2 pairs of 16-bit signed integers, Rd[T]=SQ16(Rn[T]-Rm[T]), Rd[B]=SQ16(Rn[B]-Rm[B])
QSUB8	{Rd,} Rn, Rm	Signed saturating subtract 4 pairs of 8-bit signed integers
SADD16	{Rd,} Rn, Rm	Signed add 2 pairs of 16-bit integers Rd[T] = truncate16(Rn[T] + Rm[T]) Rd[B] = truncate16(Rn[B] + Rm[B])
SADD8	{Rd,} Rn, Rm	Signed add 4 pairs of 8-bit signed integers
SASX	{Rd,} Rn, Rm	Signed add and subtract with exchange Rd[T] = truncate16(Rn[T] + Rm[B]) Rd[B] = truncate16(Rn[B] - Rm[T])
SEL	{Rd,} Rn, Rm	Select bytes based on GE bits of CPSR
SHADD16	{Rd,} Rn, Rm	Signed halving add 2 pairs of 16-bit integers Rd[T] = (Rn[T] + Rm[T])/2, Rd[B] = (Rn[B] + Rm[B])/2
SHADD8	{Rd,} Rn, Rm	Signed halving add 4 pairs of 8-bit integers
SHASX	{Rd,} Rn, Rm	Signed halving add and subtract with exchange Rd[T] = (Rn[T] + Rm[B])/2, Rd[B] = (Rn[B] - Rm[T])/2
SHSAX	{Rd,} Rn, Rm	Signed halving subtract and add with exchange Rd[T] = (Rn[T] - Rm[B])/2, Rd[B] = (Rn[B] + Rm[T])/2
SHSUB16	{Rd,} Rn, Rm	Signed halving subtract 2 pairs of 16-bit integers Rd[T] = (Rn[T] - Rm[T])/2, Rd[B] = (Rn[B] - Rm[B])/2
SHSUB8	{Rd,} Rn, Rm	Signed halving subtract 4 pairs of 8-bit integers
SMLABB, SMLABT, SMLATB, SMLATT	Rd, Rn, Rm, Ra	Signed multiply accumulate long (halfwords) Rd = Ra + Rn[B/T]*Rm[B/T] e.g. BT, Rd = Ra + Rn[B]*Rm[T]
SMLALBB, SMLALBT, SMLATLB, SMLALTT	RdLo, RdHi, Rn, Rm	Signed multiply accumulate long (halfwords) RdHi:RdLo = RdHi:RdLo + Rn[B/T]*Rm[B/T] e.g. BT, RdHi:RdLo = RdHi:RdLo + Rn[B]*Rm[T]

SMLAD	Rd, Rn, Rm, Ra	Signed multiply accumulate dual Rd = Ra + Rn[T]*Rm[T] + Rn[B]*Rm[B]
SMLADX	Rd, Rn, Rm, Ra	Signed multiply accumulate dual with exchange Rd = Ra + Rn[T]*Rm[B] + Rn[B]*Rm[T]
SMLALD	RdLo, RdHi, Rn, Rm	Signed multiply accumulate long dual RdHi:RdLo = RdHi:RdLo + Rn[T]*Rm[T] + Rn[B]*Rm[B]
SMLALDX	RdLo, RdHi, Rn, Rm	Signed multiply accumulate long dual with exchange RdHi:RdLo = RdHi:RdLo + Rn[T]*Rm[B] + Rn[B]*Rm[T]
SMLAWB	Rd, Rn, Rm, Ra	Signed multiply accumulate (word by bottom halfword), Rd = Ra + (Rn*Rm[B])>>16
SMLAWT	Rd, Rn, Rm, Ra	Signed multiply accumulate (word by top halfword), Rd = Ra + (Rn*Rm[T])>>16
SMLSD	Rd, Rn, Rm, Ra	Signed multiply subtract dual Rd = Ra + Rn[B]*Rm[B] - Rn[T]* Rm[T]
SMLSDX	Rd, Rn, Rm, Ra	Signed multiply subtract dual with exchange Rd = Ra + Rn[B]*Rm[T] - Rn[T]* Rm[B]
SMLSLD	RdLo, RdHi, Rn, Rm	Signed multiply subtract long dual RdHi:RdLo = RdHi:RdLo + Rn[T]* Rm[T] - Rn[B]*Rm[B]
SMLSLDX	RdLo, RdHi, Rn, Rm	Signed multiply subtract long dual with exchange RdHi:RdLo = RdHi:RdLo + Rn[B]* Rm[T] - Rn[T]*Rm[B]
SMMLA, SMMLAR	Rd, Rn, Rm, Ra	Signed most significant word multiply accumulate, Rd = Ra + (Rn*Rm)>>32. If R exists, round to nearest; otherwise, truncate.
SMMLS, SMMLSR	Rd, Rn, Rm, Ra	Signed most significant word multiply subtract, Rd = Ra - (Rn*Rm)>>32. See above for R.
SMMUL, SMMULR	{Rd,} Rn, Rm	Signed most significant word multiply Rd = (Rn*Rm)>>32. See above for R.
SMULBB, SMULBT SMULTB, SMULTT	{Rd,} Rn, Rm	Signed multiply (halfwords), Rd = Rn[B/T]*Rm[B/T] e.g. BT, Rd = Rn[B]*Rm[T]
SMUAD	{Rd,} Rn, Rm	Signed dual multiply then add Rd = Rn[B]*Rm[B] + Rn[T]*Rm[T]
SMUADX	{Rd,} Rn, Rm	Signed dual multiply add with exchange Rd = Rn[T]*Rm[B] + Rn[B]*Rm[T]
SMULWB	{Rd,} Rn, Rm	Signed multiply word by bottom halfword Rd = (Rn*Rm[B])>>16
SMULWT	{Rd,} Rn, Rm	Signed multiply word by top halfword Rd = (Rn*Rm[T])>>16
SMUSD	{Rd,} Rn, Rm	Signed dual multiply then subtract Rd = Rn[B]*Rm[B] - Rn[T]*Rm[T]
SMUSDX	{Rd,} Rn, Rm	Signed dual multiply (with exchange) subtract Rd = Rn[B]*Rm[T] - Rn[T]*Rm[B]
SSAT16	Rd, #imm4, Rm	Signed saturate two 16-bit values #imm4 = saturation bit position, $-2^{imm4 - 1} \leq x \leq 2^{imm4 - 1} -1$
SSAX	{Rd,} Rn, Rm	Signed subtract and add with exchange Rd[T] = truncate16(Rn[T] - Rm[B]) Rd[B] = truncate16(Rn[B] + Rm[T])
SSUB16	{Rd,} Rn, Rm	Signed subtract 2 pairs of 16-bit integers Rd[T] = truncate16(Rn[T] - Rm[T]) Rd[B] = truncate16(Rn[B] - Rm[B])
SSUB8	{Rd,} Rn, Rm	Signed subtract 4 pairs of 8-bit integers
SXTAB	{Rd,} Rn, Rm{,ROR #}	Extend 8 bits to 32 bits and add Rd = Rn + sign_extend ((Rm, ROR #)[7:0])
SXTAB16	{Rd,} Rn, Rm{,ROR #}	Dual extend 8 bits to 16 bits and add Rd[T] = Rn[T] + sign_extend ((Rm, ROR #)[23:16]) Rd[B] = Rn[B] + sign_extend ((Rm, ROR #)[7:0])
SXTAH	{Rd,} Rn, Rm{,ROR #}	Extend 16 bits to 32 and add Rd = Rn + sign_extend ((Rm, ROR #)[15:0])
SXTB16	{Rd,} Rm {,ROR #n}	Signed extend byte to 16-bit value Rd[T] = sign_extend ((Rm, ROR #)[23:16]) Rd[B] = sign_extend ((Rm, ROR #)[7:0])

UADD16	{Rd,} Rn, Rm	Unsigned add 2 pairs of 16-bit integers Rd[T] = truncate16(Rn[T] + Rm[T]) Rd[B] = truncate16(Rn[B] + Rm[B])
UADD8	{Rd,} Rn, Rm	Unsigned add 4 pairs of 8-bit integers
UASX	{Rd,} Rn, Rm	Unsigned add and subtract with exchange Rd[T] = truncate16(Rn[T] + Rm[B]) Rd[B] = truncate16(Rn[B] - Rm[T])
UHADD16	{Rd,} Rn, Rm	Unsigned halving add 2 pairs of 16-bit integers Rd[T] = (Rn[T] + Rm[T])/2, Rd[B] = (Rn[B] + Rm[B])/2
UHADD8	{Rd,} Rn, Rm	Unsigned halving add 4 pairs of 8-bit integers
UHASX	{Rd,} Rn, Rm	Unsigned halving add and subtract with exchange Rd[T] = (Rn[T] + Rm[B])/2, Rd[B] = (Rn[B] - Rm[T])/2
UHSAX	{Rd,} Rn, Rm	Unsigned halving subtract and add with exchange Rd[T] = (Rn[T] - Rm[B])/2, Rd[B] = (Rn[B] + Rm[T])/2
UHSUB16	{Rd,} Rn, Rm	Unsigned halving subtract 2 pairs of 16-bit integers Rd[T] = (Rn[T] - Rm[T])/2, Rd[B] = (Rn[B] - Rm[B])/2
UHSUB8	{Rd,} Rn, Rm	Unsigned halving subtract 4 pairs of 8-bit integers
UMAAL	RdLo, RdHi, Rn, Rm	Unsigned multiply accumulate long RdHi:RdLo = Rn*Rm + RdHi + RdLo
UQADD16	{Rd,} Rn, Rm	Unsigned saturating add 2 pairs of 16-bit integers Rd[T] = UQ(Rn[T] + Rm[T]), Rd[B] = UQ(Rn[B] + Rm[B])
UQADD8	{Rd,} Rn, Rm	Unsigned saturating add 4 pairs of 8-bit integers
UQASX	{Rd,} Rn, Rm	Unsigned saturating add and subtract with exchange Rd[T] = saturate16(Rn[T] + Rm[B]) Rd[B] = saturate16(Rn[B] - Rm[T])
UQSAX	{Rd,} Rn, Rm	Unsigned saturating subtract and add with exchange Rd[T] = saturate16(Rn[T] - Rm[B]) Rd[B] = saturate16(Rn[B] + Rm[T])
UQSUB16	{Rd,} Rn, Rm	Unsigned saturating subtract 2 pairs of 16-bit integers Rd[T] = UQ(Rn[T] - Rm[T]), Rd[B] = UQ(Rn[B] - Rm[B])
UQSUB8	{Rd,} Rn, Rm	Unsigned saturating subtract 4 pairs of 8-bit integers
USAD8	{Rd,} Rn, Rm	Unsigned sum of absolute differences
USADA8	{Rd,} Rn, Rm, Ra	Unsigned sum of absolute differences and accumulate
USAT16	Rd, #imm4, Rm	Unsigned saturate two 16-bit integers #imm4 = saturation bit position, $0 \leq x \leq 2^{imm4} - 1$
USAX	{Rd,} Rn, Rm	Unsigned subtract and add with exchange Rd[T] = truncate16(Rn[T] - Rm[B]) Rd[B] = truncate16(Rn[B] + Rm[T])
USUB16	{Rd,} Rn, Rm	Unsigned subtract 2 pairs of 16-bit integers Rd[T] = truncate16(Rn[T] - Rm[T]) Rd[B] = truncate16(Rn[B] - Rm[B])
USUB8	{Rd,} Rn, Rm	Unsigned subtract 4 pairs of 8-bit integers
UXTAB	{Rd,} Rn, Rm{, ROR #}	Rotate, extend 8 bits to 32 bits and Add Rd = Rn + zero_extend ((Rm, ROR #)[7:0])
UXTAB16	{Rd,} Rn, Rm{, ROR #}	Rotate, dual extend 8 bits to 16 bits and add Rd[T] = Rn[T] + zero_extend ((Rn, ROR #)[23:16]) Rd[B] = Rn[B] + zero_extend ((Rn, ROR #)[7:0])
UXTAH	{Rd,} Rn, Rm{, ROR #}	Rotate, unsigned extend and add halfword Rd = Rn + zero_extend ((Rm, ROR #)[15:0])
UXTB16	{Rd,} Rm{, ROR #n}	Unsigned extend byte to 16-bit value Rd[T] = zero_extend ((Rm, ROR #)[23:16]) Rd[B] = zero_extend ((Rm, ROR #)[7:0])

Appendix E: Cortex-M0/M0+/M1 Instructions

Instruction	Operands	Description and Action
ADCS	{Rd,} Rn, Rm	Add with Carry, Rd ← Rn + Rm + Carry, update N,Z,C,V
ADD, ADDS	{Rd,} Rn, <Rm|#imm>	Add, Rd ← Rn + <Rm|#imm>, ADDS updates N,Z,C,V
ADR	Rd, label	Load PC-relative Address, Rd ← <label>
AND, ANDS	{Rd,} Rn, Rm	Logical AND, Rd ← Rn AND Rm, ANDS updates N,Z,C
ASR, ASRS	Rd, Rm, <Rs|#n>	Arithmetic Shift Right, Rd ← Rm>>(Rs|n), ASRS updates N,Z,C
B{cc}	label	Branch {conditionally}, PC ← label
BICS	{Rd,} Rn, Rm	Bit Clear, Rd ← Rn AND NOT Rm, BICS updates N,Z,C
BKPT	#imm	Breakpoint, prefetch abort or enter debug state
BL	label	Branch with Link, LR ← next instruction, PC ← label
BLX	Rm	Branch register with link, LR←next instr addr, PC←Rm[31:1]
BX	Rm	Branch register, PC ← Rm
CMN	Rn, Rm	Compare Negative, Update N,Z,C,V flags on Rn + Rm
CMP	Rn, <Rm|#imm>	Compare, Update N,Z,C,V flags on Rn - <Rm|#imm>
CPSID	i	Disable specified (i) interrupts, optional change mode
CPSIE	i	Enable specified (i) interrupts, optional change mode
DMB	-	Data Memory Barrier, ensure memory access order
DSB	-	Data Synchronization Barrier, ensure completion of access
EORS	{Rd,} Rn, Rm	Exclusive OR, Rd ← Rn XOR Rm, EORS updates N,Z,C
ISB	-	Instruction Synchronization Barrier
LDM	Rn{!}, reglist	Load Multiple Registers increment after, <reglist> = mem[Rn], Rn increments after each memory access
LDR	Rt, [Rn, <Rm|#imm>]	Load Register with Word, Rt ← mem[Rn + <Rm|#imm>]
LDRB	Rt, [Rn, <Rm|#imm>]	Load Register with Byte, Rt ← mem[Rn + <Rm|#imm>]
LDRH	Rt, [Rn, <Rm|#imm>]	Load Register with Halfword, Rt ← mem[Rn + <Rm|#imm>]
LDRSB	Rt, [Rn, <Rm|#imm>]	Load Register with Signed Byte, Rt ← mem[Rn + <Rm|#imm>]
LDRSH	Rt, [Rn, <Rm|#imm>]	Load Register with Signed Halfword, Rt ← mem[Rn+<Rm|#imm>]
LSLS	Rd, Rm, <Rs|#imm>	Logic Shift Left, Rd ← Rm << Rs|#imm, LSLS update N,Z,C
LSRS	Rd, Rm, <Rs|#imm>	Logic Shift Right, Rd ← Rm >> Rs|#imm, LSRS update N,Z,C
MOV, MOVS	Rd, <Rs|#imm>	Move, Rd ← <Rs|#imm>, MOVS updates N,Z,C
MRS	Rd, spec_reg	Move from Special Register, Rd ← spec_reg
MSR	spec_reg, Rm	Move to Special Register, spec_reg ← Rm, Updates N,Z,C,V
MULS	{Rd,} Rn, Rm	Multiply, Rd ← (Rn*Rm)[31:0], MULS updates N,Z
MVNS	Rd, Rm	Move NOT, Rd ← 0xFFFFFFFF EOR Rm, MVNS updates N,Z,C
NOP	-	No Operation
ORRS	{Rd,} Rn, Rm	Logical OR, Rd ← Rn OR Rm, ORRS updates N,Z,C
POP	reglist	Canonical form of LDM SP!, <reglist>
PUSH	reglist	Canonical form of STMDB SP!, <reglist>
REV	Rd, Rn	Reverse Byte Order in a Word, Rd[31:24]←Rn[7:0], Rd[23:16]←Rn[15:8], Rd[15:8]←Rn[23:16], Rd[7:0]←Rn[31:24]
REV16	Rd, Rn	Reverse Byte Order in a Half-word, Rd[15:8]←Rn[7:0], Rd[7:0]←Rn[15:8], Rd[31:24]←Rn[23:16], Rd[23:16]←Rn[31:24]
REVSH	Rd, Rn	Reverse Byte order in Low Half-word and sign extend, Rd[15:8]←Rn[7:0], Rd[7:0]←Rn[15:8], Rd[31:16]←Rn[7]*&0xFFFF
RORS	{Rd,} Rm, Rs	Rotate Right, Rd ← ROR(Rm, Rs), RORS updates N,Z,C
RSBS	{Rd,} Rn, #0	Reverse Subtract, Rd ← 0 - Rn, RSBS updates N,Z,C,V
SBCS	{Rd,} Rn, Rm	Subtract with Carry, Rd← Rn - Rm - NOT(Carry), updates NZCV
SEV	-	Send Event
STM	Rn{!}, reglist	Store Multiple Registers
STR	Rt, [Rn, <Rm|#imm>]	Store Register with Word, mem[Rn + <Rm|#imm>] = Rt
STRB	Rt, [Rn, <Rm|#imm>]	Store Register with Byte, mem[Rn + <Rm|#imm>] = Rt
STRH	Rt, [Rn, <Rm|#imm>]	Store Half-word, mem[Rn + <Rm|#imm>] ← Rt[15:0]
SUB, SUBS	{Rd,} Rn, <Rm|#imm>	Subtraction, Rd ← Rn - <Rm|#imm>, SUBS updates N,Z,C,V

SVC	#imm	Supervisor Call
SXTB	{Rd,} Rm	Sign Extend Byte, Rd ← SignExtend(Rm[7:0])
SXTH	{Rd,} Rm	Sign Extend Half-word, Rd ← SignExtend(Rm[15:0])
TST	Rn, Rm	Test, Update N,Z,C,V on Rn AND Rm
UXTB	{Rd,} Rm	Unsigned Extend Byte, Rd ← ZeroExtend(Rm[7:0])
UXTH	{Rd,} Rm	Unsigned Extend Halfword, Rd ← ZeroExtend(Rm[15:0])
WFE	-	Wait For Event and Enter Sleep Mode
WFI	-	Wait for Interrupt and Enter Sleep Mode

Appendix F: Cortex-M3 16-bit Thumb-2 Instruction Encoding

Instruction	15	14	13	12	11	10	9	8	7	6	5	4	3	2	1	0
LSL Rd, Rm, #imm5	0	0	0	0	0	imm5					Rm			Rd		
LSR Rd, Rm, #imm5	0	0	0	0	1	imm5					Rm			Rd		
ASR Rd, Rm, #imm5	0	0	0	1	0	imm5					Rm			Rd		
ADD Rd, Rn, Rm	0	0	0	1	1	0	0	Rm			Rn			Rd		
SUB Rd, Rn, Rm	0	0	0	1	1	0	1	Rm			Rn			Rd		
ADD Rd, Rn, #imm3	0	0	0	1	1	1	0	imm3			Rn			Rd		
SUB Rd, Rn, #imm3	0	0	0	1	1	1	1	imm3			Rn			Rd		
MOV Rd, #imm8	0	0	1	0	0	Rd			imm8							
CMP Rn, #imm8	0	0	1	0	1	Rn			imm8							
ADD Rdn, #imm8	0	0	1	1	0	Rdn			imm8							
SUB Rdn, #imm8	0	0	1	1	1	Rdn			imm8							
AND Rdn, Rm	0	1	0	0	0	0	0	0	0	0	Rm			Rdn		
EOR Rdn, Rm	0	1	0	0	0	0	0	0	0	1	Rm			Rdn		
LSL Rdn, Rm	0	1	0	0	0	0	0	0	1	0	Rm			Rdn		
LSR Rdn, Rm	0	1	0	0	0	0	0	0	1	1	Rm			Rdn		
ASR Rdn, Rm	0	1	0	0	0	0	0	1	0	0	Rm			Rdn		
ADC Rdn, Rm	0	1	0	0	0	0	0	1	0	1	Rm			Rdn		
SBC Rdn, Rm	0	1	0	0	0	0	0	1	1	0	Rm			Rdn		
ROR Rdn, Rm	0	1	0	0	0	0	0	1	1	1	Rm			Rdn		
TST Rm, Rn	0	1	0	0	0	0	1	0	0	0	Rm			Rn		
RSB Rd, Rn, #0	0	1	0	0	0	0	1	0	0	1	Rn			Rd		
CMP Rm, Rn	0	1	0	0	0	0	1	0	1	0	Rm			Rn		
CMN Rm, Rn	0	1	0	0	0	0	1	0	1	1	Rm			Rn		
ORR Rdn, Rm	0	1	0	0	0	0	1	1	0	0	Rm			Rdn		
MUL Rdm, Rn	0	1	0	0	0	0	1	1	0	1	Rn			Rdm		
BIC Rdn, Rm	0	1	0	0	0	0	1	1	1	0	Rm			Rdn		
MVN Rd, Rm	0	1	0	0	0	0	1	1	1	1	Rm			Rd		
ADD Rdn, Rm	0	1	0	0	0	1	0	0	DN	Rm				Rdn		
Unpredictable	0	1	0	0	0	1	0	1	0							
CMP Rm, Rn	0	1	0	0	0	1	0	1	N	Rm				Rn		
MOV Rd, Rm	0	1	0	0	0	1	1	0	D	Rm				Rdn		
BX Rm	0	1	0	0	0	1	1	1	0	Rm				(000)		
BLX Rm	0	1	0	0	0	1	1	1	1	Rm				(000)		
LDR Rt, [pc, #imm8<<2]	0	1	0	0	1	Rt			imm8							
STR Rt, [Rn, Rm]	0	1	0	1	0	0	0	Rm			Rn			Rt		
STRH Rt, [Rn, Rm]	0	1	0	1	0	0	1	Rm			Rn			Rt		
STRB Rt, [Rn, Rm]	0	1	0	1	0	1	0	Rm			Rn			Rt		
LDRSB Rt, [Rn, Rm]	0	1	0	1	0	1	1	Rm			Rn			Rt		
LDR Rt, [Rn, Rm]	0	1	0	1	1	0	0	Rm			Rn			Rt		
LDRH Rt, [Rn, Rm]	0	1	0	1	1	0	1	Rm			Rn			Rt		
LDRB Rt, [Rn, Rm]	0	1	0	1	1	1	0	Rm			Rn			Rt		
LDRSH Rt, [Rn, Rm]	0	1	0	1	1	1	1	Rm			Rn			Rt		
STR Rt, [SP, #imm8<<2]	1	0	0	1	0	Rt			imm8							
LDR Rt, [SP, #imm8<<2]	1	0	0	1	1	Rt			imm8							
STR Rt, [Rn, #imm5<<2]	0	1	1	0	0	imm5					Rn			Rt		
LDR Rt, [Rn, #imm5<<2]	0	1	1	0	1	imm5					Rn			Rt		
LDRH Rt, [Rn, #imm5<<1]	0	1	1	1	0	imm5					Rn			Rt		

Instruction	15	14	13	12	11	10	9	8	7	6	5	4	3	2	1	0
LDRB Rt, [Rn, #imm5<<1]	0	1	1	1	1	imm5					Rn			Rt		
STRH Rt, [Rn, #imm5<<1]	1	0	0	0	0	imm5					Rn			Rt		
LDRH Rt, [Rn, #imm5<<1]	1	0	0	0	1	imm5					Rn			Rt		
CPS iflags	1	0	1	1	0	1	1	0	0	1	1	im	0	0	I	F
ADD SP, SP, #imm7<<2	1	0	1	1	0	0	0	0	0	imm7						
SUB SP, SP, #imm7<<2	1	0	1	1	0	0	0	0	1	imm7						
CB{N}Z Rn, label	1	0	1	1	0	0	0	1	imm5					Rn		
CBZ i:#imm5:0	1	0	1	1	0	0	i	1	imm5					Rn		
SXTH Rd, Rm	1	0	1	1	0	0	1	0	0	0	Rm			Rd		
SXTB Rd, Rm	1	0	1	1	0	0	1	0	0	1	Rm			Rd		
UXTH Rd, Rm	1	0	1	1	0	0	1	0	1	0	Rm			Rd		
UXTB Rd, Rm	1	0	1	1	0	0	1	0	1	1	Rm			Rd		
REV Rd, Rm	1	0	1	1	1	0	1	0	0	0	Rm			Rd		
REV16 Rd, Rm	1	0	1	1	1	0	1	0	0	1	Rm			Rd		
REVSH Rd, Rm	1	0	1	1	1	0	1	0	1	1	Rm			Rd		
CBNZ i:#imm5:0	1	0	1	1	1	0	i	1	imm5					Rn		
POP registers	1	0	1	1	1	1	0	P	register list							
PUSH registers	1	0	1	1	0	1	0	M	register list							
BKPT #imm8	1	0	1	1	1	1	1	0	imm8							
IT{x{y{z}}} firstcond	1	0	1	1	1	1	1	1	firstcond				mask			
NOP	1	0	1	1	1	1	1	1	0	0	0	0	0	0	0	0
YIELD	1	0	1	1	1	1	1	1	0	0	0	1	0	0	0	0
WFE	1	0	1	1	1	1	1	1	0	0	1	0	0	0	0	0
SEV	1	0	1	1	1	1	1	1	0	1	0	0	0	0	0	0
B(cond) #imm8<<1	1	1	0	1	cond				imm8							
SVC #imm8	1	1	0	1	1	1	1	1	imm8							
B #imm11<<1	1	1	1	0	0	imm11										

The condition codes for the branch instruction B are listed as follows:

Condition	Suffix	Description
0000	EQ	EQual
0001	NE	Not Equal
0010	CS/HS	unsigned Higher or Same
0011	CC/LO	unsigned LOwer
0100	MI	MInus (Negative)
0101	PL	PLus (Positive or Zero)
0110	VS	oVerflow Set
0111	VC	oVerflow Clear
1000	HI	unsigned HIgher
1001	LS	unsigned Lower or Same
1010	GE	signed Greater or Equal
1011	LT	signed Less Than
1100	GT	signed Greater Than
1101	LE	signed Less than or Equal
1110	AL	ALways

Appendix G: Cortex-M3 32-bit Thumb-2 Instruction Encoding

Data processing (register)

31 - 24	23	22	21	20	19 - 16	15 - 12	11 - 8	7	6	5	4	3 - 0	Instruction
11111010	0	0	0	S	Rn	1111	Rd	0	0	0	0	Rm	LSL{S} Rd, Rn, Rm
11111010	0	0	1	S	Rn	1111	Rd	0	0	0	0	Rm	LSR{S} Rd, Rn, Rm
11111010	0	1	0	S	Rn	1111	Rd	0	0	0	0	Rm	ASR{S} Rd, Rn, Rm
11111010	0	1	1	S	Rn	1111	Rd	0	0	0	0	Rm	ROR{S} Rd, Rn, Rm
11111010	0	0	0	0	Rn	1111	Rd	1	0	rotate		Rm	SXTAH Rd, Rn, Rm, rotation
11111010	0	0	0	0	1111	1111	Rd	1	0	rotate		Rm	SXTH Rd, Rm, rotation
11111010	0	0	0	1	Rn	1111	Rd	1	0	rotate		Rm	UXTAH Rd, Rn, Rm, rotation
11111010	0	0	0	1	1111	1111	Rd	1	0	rotate		Rm	UXTH Rd, Rm
11111010	0	0	1	0	Rn	1111	Rd	1	0	rotate		Rm	SXTAB16 Rd, Rn, Rm, rotation
11111010	0	0	1	1	Rn	1111	Rd	1	0	rotate		Rm	UXTAB16 Rd, Rn, Rm, rotation
11111010	0	0	1	1	1111	1111	Rd	1	0	rotate		Rm	UXTB16 Rd, Rm, rotation
11111010	0	1	0	0	Rn	1111	Rd	1	0	rotate		Rm	SXTAB Rd, Rn, Rm, rotation
11111010	0	1	0	0	1111	1111	Rd	1	0	rotate		Rm	SXTB Rd, Rm
11111010	0	1	0	1	Rn	1111	Rd	1	0	rotate		Rm	UXTAB Rd, Rn, Rm, rotation
11111010	0	1	0	1	1111	1111	Rd	1	0	rotate		Rm	UXTB Rd, Rm, rotation

- rotate: 00 = no rotation; 01 = ROR #8; 10 = ROR #16; 11 = ROR #24;

Data processing with shifted register

31 - 25	24	23	22	21	20	19 - 16	15	14 - 12	11 - 8	7	6	5	4	3 - 0	Instruction
1110101	0	0	0	0	S	Rn	0	imm3	Rd	imm2		type		Rm	AND{S} Rd, Rn, Rm, shift
1110101	0	0	0	0	1	Rn	0	imm3	1111	imm2		type		Rm	TST Rn, Rm, shift
1110101	0	0	0	1	S	Rn	0	imm3	Rd	imm2		type		Rm	BIC{S} Rd, Rn, Rm, shift
1110101	0	0	1	0	S	Rn	0	imm3	Rd	imm2		type		Rm	ORR{S} Rd, Rn, Rm, shift
1110101	0	0	1	1	S	Rn	0	imm3	Rd	imm2		type		Rm	ORN{S} Rd, Rn, Rm, shift
1110101	0	0	1	1	S	1111	0	imm3	Rd	imm2		type		Rm	MVN{S} Rd, Rm, shift
1110101	0	1	0	0	S	Rn	0	imm3	Rd	imm2		type		Rm	EOR{S} Rd, Rn, Rm, shift
1110101	0	1	1	0	S	Rn	0	imm3	Rd	imm2	0		T		Rm	PKHBT Rd,Rn,Rm,LSL #imm
1110101	0	1	1	0	S	Rn	0	imm3	Rd	imm2	1		T		Rm	PKHTB Rd,Rn,Rm,ASR #imm
1110101	1	0	0	0	S	Rn	0	imm3	Rd	imm2		type		Rm	ADD{S} Rd, Rn, Rm, shift
1110101	1	0	0	0	1	Rn	0	imm3	1111	imm2		type		Rm	CMN Rn, Rm, shift
1110101	1	0	1	0	S	Rn	0	imm3	Rd	imm2		type		Rm	ADC{S} Rd, Rn, Rm, shift
1110101	1	0	1	1	S	Rn	0	imm3	Rd	imm2		type		Rm	SBC{S} Rd, Rn, Rm, shift

- shift amount (5 bits) = imm3:imm2
- shift type: 00 = LSL, 01 = LSR, 10 = ASR, 11 = ROR (if shift amount is non-zero), 11 = RRX (if shift amount is 0)
- PKHBT, PKHTB: A Pack Half-word instruction combines one halfword of its first operand with the other halfword of its shifted second operand. B stands for the bottom half. T stands for the top half.

Data processing (modified immediate)

31 - 25	24	23	22	21	20	19 - 16	15	14 - 12	11 - 8	7 - 0	Instruction
11110i0	0	0	0	0	S	Rn	0	imm3	Rd	imm8	AND{S} Rd, Rn, #const
11110i0	0	0	0	0	1	Rn	0	imm3	1111	imm8	TST Rn, #const
11110i0	0	0	0	1	S	Rn	0	imm3	Rd	imm8	BIC{S} Rd, Rn, #const
11110i0	0	0	1	0	S	Rn	0	imm3	Rd	imm8	ORR{S} Rd, Rn, #const
11110i0	0	0	1	0	S	1111	0	imm3	Rd	imm8	MOV{S} Rd, #const
11110i0	0	0	1	1	S	Rn	0	imm3	Rd	imm8	ORN{S} Rd, Rn, #const
11110i0	0	0	1	1	S	1111	0	imm3	Rd	imm8	MVN{S} Rd, #const
11110i0	0	1	0	0	S	Rn	0	imm3	Rd	imm8	EOR{S} Rd, Rn, #const
11110i0	0	1	0	0	1	Rn	0	imm3	1111	imm8	TEQ Rn, #const
11110i0	1	0	0	0	S	Rn	0	imm3	Rd	imm8	ADD{S} Rd, Rn, #const
11110i0	1	0	0	0	1	Rn	0	imm3	1111	imm8	CMN Rd, Rn, #const
11110i0	1	0	1	0	S	Rn	0	imm3	Rd	imm8	ADC{S} Rd, Rn, #const
11110i0	1	0	1	1	S	Rn	0	imm3	Rd	imm8	SBC{S} Rd, Rn, #const
11110i0	1	1	0	1	S	Rn	0	imm3	Rd	imm8	SUB{S} Rd, Rn, #const
11110i0	1	1	0	1	1	Rn	0	imm3	1111	imm8	CMP Rn, #const
11110i0	1	1	1	0	S	Rn	0	imm3	Rd	imm8	RSB{S} Rd, Rn, #const

- imm12 = i:imm3:imm8
- #const = ThumbExpandImm(imm12, carry_in)

```
ThumbExpandImm(imm12, carry_in){
  if imm12<11:10> == '00' {
    switch(imm12<9:8>){
      case '00':
        imm32 = ZeroExtend(imm12<7:0>, 32);
      case '01':
        imm32 = '00000000' : imm12<7:0> : '00000000' : imm12<7:0>;
      case '10':
        imm32 = imm12<7:0> : '00000000' : imm12<7:0> : '00000000';
      case '11':
        imm32 = imm12<7:0> : imm12<7:0> : imm12<7:0> : imm12<7:0>;
    }
    carry_out = carry_in;
  else {
    unrotated_value = ZeroExtend('1':imm12<6:0>, 32);
    (imm32, carry_out) = ROR_C(unrotated_value, UInt(imm12<11:7>));
  }
  return (imm32, carry_out);
}
```

Multiply, multiply accumulate, and absolute difference

31 - 23	22	21	20	19 - 16	15 - 12	11 - 8	7	6	5	4	3 - 0	Instruction
111110110	0	0	0	Rn	Ra	Rd	0	0	0	0	Rm	MLA Rd, Rn, Rm, Ra
111110110	0	0	0	Rn	1111	Rd	0	0	0	0	Rm	MUL Rd, Rn, Rm
111110110	0	0	0	Rn	Ra	Rd	0	0	0	1	Rm	MLS Rd, Rn, Rm, Ra
111110110	0	0	1	Rn	Ra	Rd	0	0	0	0	Rm	SMLABB Rd, Rn, Rm, Ra
111110110	0	0	1	Rn	Ra	Rd	0	0	0	1	Rm	SMLABT Rd, Rn, Rm, Ra
111110110	0	0	1	Rn	Ra	Rd	0	0	1	0	Rm	SMLATB Rd, Rn, Rm, Ra
111110110	0	0	1	Rn	Ra	Rd	0	0	1	1	Rm	SMLATT Rd, Rn, Rm, Ra
111110110	0	0	1	Rn	1111	Rd	0	0	0	0	Rm	SMULBB Rd, Rn, Rm
111110110	0	0	1	Rn	1111	Rd	0	0	0	1	Rm	SMULBT Rd, Rn, Rm
111110110	0	0	1	Rn	1111	Rd	0	0	1	0	Rm	SMULTB Rd, Rn, Rm
111110110	0	0	1	Rn	1111	Rd	0	0	1	1	Rm	SMULTT Rd, Rn, Rm
111110110	0	1	0	Rn	Ra	Rd	0	0	0	0	Rm	SMLAD Rd, Rn, Rm, Ra
111110110	0	1	0	Rn	Ra	Rd	0	0	0	1	Rm	SMLADX Rd, Rn, Rm, Ra
111110110	0	1	0	Rn	1111	Rd	0	0	0	0	Rm	SMUAD Rd, Rn, Rm
111110110	0	1	0	Rn	1111	Rd	0	0	0	1	Rm	SMUADX Rd, Rn, Rm
111110110	0	1	1	Rn	Ra	Rd	0	0	0	0	Rm	SMLAWB Rd, Rn, Rm, Ra
111110110	0	1	1	Rn	Ra	Rd	0	0	0	1	Rm	SMLAWT Rd, Rn, Rm, Ra
111110110	0	1	1	Rn	1111	Rd	0	0	0	0	Rm	SMULWB Rd, Rn, Rm
111110110	0	1	1	Rn	1111	Rd	0	0	0	1	Rm	SMULWT Rd, Rn, Rm
111110110	1	0	0	Rn	Ra	Rd	0	0	0	0	Rm	SMLSD Rd, Rn, Rm, Ra
111110110	1	0	0	Rn	Ra	Rd	0	0	0	1	Rm	SMLSDX Rd, Rn, Rm, Ra
111110110	1	0	0	Rn	1111	Rd	0	0	0	0	Rm	SMUSD Rd, Rn, Rm
111110110	1	0	0	Rn	1111	Rd	0	0	0	1	Rm	SMUSDX Rd, Rn, Rm
111110110	1	0	1	Rn	Ra	Rd	0	0	0	0	Rm	SMMLA Rd, Rn, Rm, Ra
111110110	1	0	1	Rn	Ra	Rd	0	0	0	1	Rm	SMMLAR Rd, Rn, Rm, Ra
111110110	1	0	1	Rn	1111	Rd	0	0	0	0	Rm	SMMUL Rd, Rn, Rm
111110110	1	0	1	Rn	1111	Rd	0	0	0	1	Rm	SMMULR Rd, Rn, Rm

- **SMLA<x><y>** Rd, Rn, Rm, Ra   ; Signed Multiply Accumulate (halfwords)
- **SMUL<x><y>** Rd, Rn, Rm   ; Signed Multiply Accumulate (word by halfword)
- **SMLAW<y>** Rd, Rn, Rm, Ra   ; Signed Multiply Accumulate (word by halfword)
- **SMULW<y>** Rd, Rn, Rm   ; Signed Multiply (word by halfword)
  - If <x> is B, then the bottom half (Rn[15:0]) is used as the first multiply operand.
    If <x> is T, then the top half (Rn[31:16]) is used as the first multiply operand.
  - If <y> is B, then the bottom half (Rm[15:0]) is used as the second multiply operand.
    If <y> is T, then the top half (Rm[31:16]) is used as the second multiply operand.
- **SMLAD{X}** Rd, Rn, Rm, Ra   ; Signed Multiply Accumulate Dual
- **SMLSD{X}** Rd, Rn, Rm, Ra   ; Signed Multiply Subtract Dual
- **SMUAD{X}** Rd, Rn, Rm   ; Signed Dual Multiply Add
- **SMUSD{X}** Rd, Rn, Rm   ; Signed Multiply Subtract Dual
  - If X is present, then the multiplication results are Rn[15:0]) × Rm[31:16] and Rn[31:16] × Rm[15:0].
  - If X is omitted, then the multiplication results are Rn[15:0] × Rm[15:0] and Rn[31:16] × Rm[31:16].
- **SMMLA{R}** Rd, Rn, Rm, Ra   ; Signed Most Significant Word Multiply Subtract
- **SMMUL{R}** Rd, Rn, Rm   ; Signed Most Significant Word Multiply
  - If R is present, then the multiplication result is rounded.
  - If the R is omitted, then the multiplication result is truncated.

Long multiply, long multiply accumulate, divide

31 - 23	22	21	20	19 - 16	15 - 12	11 - 8	7	6	5	4	3 - 0	Instruction
111110111	0	0	0	Rn	RdLo	RdHi	0	0	0	0	Rm	SMULL RdLo, RdHi, Rn, Rm
111110111	0	0	1	Rn	1111	Rd	1	1	1	1	Rm	SDIV Rd, Rn, Rm
111110111	0	1	0	Rn	RdLo	RdHi	0	0	0	0	Rm	UMULL RdLo, RdHi, Rn, Rm
111110111	0	1	1	Rn	1111	Rd	1	1	1	1	Rm	UDIV Rd, Rn, Rm
111110111	1	0	0	Rn	RdLo	RdHi	0	0	0	0	Rm	SMLAL RdLo, RdHi, Rn, Rm
111110111	1	0	0	Rn	RdLo	RdHi	1	0	0	0	Rm	SMLALBB RdLo, RdHi, Rn, Rm
111110111	1	0	0	Rn	RdLo	RdHi	1	0	0	1	Rm	SMLALBT RdLo, RdHi, Rn, Rm
111110111	1	0	0	Rn	RdLo	RdHi	1	0	1	0	Rm	SMLALTB RdLo, RdHi, Rn, Rm
111110111	1	0	0	Rn	RdLo	RdHi	1	0	1	1	Rm	SMLALTT RdLo, RdHi, Rn, Rm
111110111	1	0	0	Rn	RdLo	RdHi	1	1	0	0	Rm	SMLALD RdLo, RdHi, Rn, Rm
111110111	1	0	0	Rn	RdLo	RdHi	1	1	0	1	Rm	SMLALDX RdLo, RdHi, Rn, Rm
111110111	1	0	1	Rn	RdLo	RdHi	1	1	0	0	Rm	SMLSLD RdLo, RdHi, Rn, Rm
111110111	1	0	1	Rn	RdLo	RdHi	1	1	0	1	Rm	SMLSLDX RdLo, RdHi, Rn, Rm
111110111	1	1	0	Rn	RdLo	RdHi	0	0	0	0	Rm	UMLAL RdLo, RdHi, Rn, Rm
111110111	1	1	0	Rn	RdLo	RdHi	0	1	1	0	Rm	UMAAL RdLo, RdHi, Rn, Rm

- **SMLAL**<x><y> RdLo, RdHi, Rn, Rm   ; Signed Multiply Accumulate Long (halfwords)
  - <x> = B → Rn[15:0] is used.   <x> = T → Rn[31:16] is used.
  - <y> = B → Rm[15:0] is used.   <y> = T → Rm[31:16] is used.
- **SMLALD**{X} RdLo, RdHi, Rn, Rm   ; Signed Multiply Accumulate Long Dual
- **SMLSLD**{X} RdLo, RdHi, Rn, Rm   ; Signed Multiply Subtract Long Dual
  - If X is present, then the multiplication results are Rn[15:0]) × Rm[31:16] and Rn[31:16] × Rm[15:0].
  - If X is omitted, then the multiplication results are Rn[15:0] × Rm[15:0] and Rn[31:16] × Rm[31:16].

Branches and miscellaneous control

31 - 27	26	25 - 22	21	20 - 16		15 - 12	11 - 8			7 - 0		Instruction
11110	0	1110	0	Rn		1000	mask	0	0	SYSm		MSR
11110	0	1110	1	0	1111	1000	0000			00000000		NOP
11110	0	1110	1	0	1111	1000	0000			00000001		YIELD
11110	0	1110	1	0	1111	1000	0000			00000010		WFE
11110	0	1110	1	0	1111	1000	0000			00000011		WFI
11110	0	1110	1	0	1111	1000	0000			00000100		SEV
11110	0	1110	1	0	1111	1000	0000			1111	option	DBG
11110	0	1110	1	1	1111	1000	1111			00101101		CLREX
11110	0	1110	1	1	1111	1000	1111			0100	option	DSB
11110	0	1110	1	1	1111	1000	1111			0101	option	DMB
11110	0	1110	1	1	1111	1000	1111			0110	option	ISB
11110	0	1110	1	0	1111	1000	Rd			SYSm		MRS
11110	S	cond		imm6		1 0 J1 0	J2			imm11		B
11110	S	imm10				1 0 J1 0	J2			imm11		B
11110	S	imm10				1 1 J1 1	J2			imm11		BL

- Unconditional Branch:
  - I1 = NOT(J1 EOR S);   I2 = NOT(J2 EOR S);   PC = PC + SignExtend32(S:I1:I2:imm10:imm11:'0');
- Conditional Branch and Branch and Link (BL)
  - I1 = NOT(J1 EOR S);   I2 = NOT(J2 EOR S);   PC = PC + SignExtend32(S:I1:I2:imm10:imm11:'0');

Load/store multiple

31 - 25	24	23	22	21	20	19 - 16	15	14	13	12 - 0	Instruction
1110100	0	1	0	W	0	Rn	0	M	0	register_list	STM Rn{!},<registers>
1110100	0	1	0	W	1	Rn	P	M	0	register_list	LDM Rn{!},<registers>
1110100	0	1	0	1	1	1101	P	M	0	register_list	POP <registers>
1110100	1	0	0	W	0	Rn	0	M	0	register_list	STMDB Rn{!},<registers>
1110100	1	0	0	W	0	Rn	0	M	0	register_list	STMFD Rn{!},<registers>
1110100	1	0	0	1	0	1101	0	M	0	register_list	PUSH <registers>
1110100	1	0	0	W	1	Rn	P	M	0	register_list	LDMDB Rn{!},<registers>
1110100	1	0	0	W	1	Rn	P	M	0	register_list	LDMEA Rn{!},<registers>

- registers = '0':M:'0':register_list or registers = P:M:'0':register_list.
- If W (writeback) = 1, R[n] = R[n] + 4*BitCount(registers).
- LDMIA and LDMFD are pseudo-instructions for LDM.
- STMEA and STMIA are pseudo-instructions for STM.

Load/store dual or exclusive, table branch

31 - 25	24	23	22	21	20	19 - 16	15 - 12	11 - 8	7	6	5	4	3 - 0	Instruction
1110100	0	0	1	0	0	Rn	Rt	Rd		imm8				STREX Rd, Rt, [Rn, #imm8 << 2]
1110100	0	0	1	0	1	Rn	Rt	1111		imm8				LDREX Rt, [Rn, #imm8 << 2]
1110100	1	U	0	0	0	Rn	Rt	Rt2		imm8				STRD Rt, Rt2, [Rn, #+/-imm8<<2]
1110100	0	U	1	0	0	Rn	Rt	Rt2		imm8				STRD Rt, Rt2, Rn, #+/-imm8<<2
1110100	1	U	1	1	0	Rn	Rt	Rt2		imm8				STRD Rt, Rt2, [Rn, #+/-imm8<<2]!
1110100	1	U	0	0	0	1111	Rt	Rt2		imm8				LDRD Rt, Rt2, [Rn, #+/-imm8<<2]
1110100	0	U	1	0	0	1111	Rt	Rt2		imm8				LDRD Rt, Rt2, Rn, #+/-imm8<<2
1110100	1	U	1	1	0	1111	Rt	Rt2		imm8				LDRD Rt, Rt2, [Rn, #+/-imm8<<2]!
1110100	0	1	1	0	0	Rn	Rt	1111	0	1	0	0	Rd	STREXB Rd, Rt, [Rn]
1110100	0	1	1	0	0	Rn	Rt	1111	0	1	0	1	Rd	STREXH Rd, Rt, [Rn]
1110100	0	1	1	0	1	Rn	1111	0000	0	0	0	0	Rm	TBB [Rn, Rm]
1110100	0	1	1	0	1	Rn	1111	0000	0	0	0	1	Rm	TBH [Rn, Rm, LSL #1]
1110100	0	1	1	0	1	Rn	Rt	1111	0	1	0	0	1111	LDREXB Rt, [Rn]
1110100	0	1	1	0	1	Rn	Rt	1111	0	1	0	1	1111	LDREXH Rt, [Rn]

- If U = 1, then the memory address is [Rn, #imm8 << 2]. Otherwise, it is [Rn, #-imm8 << 2].

Store single data item

31 - 24	23	22	21	20	19 - 16	15 - 12	11 - 6	5	4	3 - 0	Instruction
11111000	1	0	0	0	Rn	Rt		imm12			STRB Rt, [Rn, #imm12]
11111000	0	0	0	0	Rn	Rt	000000	imm2		Rm	STRB Rt, [Rn, Rm, LSL #imm2]
11111000	1	0	1	0	Rn	Rt		imm12			STRH Rt, [Rn, #imm12]
11111000	0	0	1	0	Rn	Rt	000000	imm2		Rm	STRH Rt, [Rn, Rm, LSL #imm2]
11111000	1	1	0	0	Rn	Rt		imm12			STR Rt, [Rn, #imm12]
11111000	0	1	0	0	Rn	Rt	000000	imm2		Rm	STR Rt, [Rn, Rm, LSL #imm2]

Load byte, memory hints

31 - 25	24	23	22 - 20	19 - 16	15 - 12	11	10	9	8	7	6	5	4	3 - 0	Instruction
1111100	0	U	011	1111	Rt	imm12									LDRBRt, #+/-imm12
1111100	0	1	011	Rn	Rt	imm12									LDRB Rt, [Rn, #imm12]
1111100	0	0	011	Rn	Rt	1	1	1	0	imm8					LDRBT Rt, [Rn, #imm8]
1111100	0	0	011	Rn	Rt	0	0	0	0	0	0	imm2		Rm	LDRB Rt, [Rn, #imm12]
1111100	1	U	011	1111	Rt	imm12									LDRSB Rt, #+/-imm12
1111100	1	1	011	Rn	Rt	imm12									LDRSB Rt, [Rn, #imm12]
1111100	1	0	011	Rn	Rt	1	1	1	0	imm8					LDRSBT Rt, [Rn, #imm8]
1111100	1	0	011	Rn	Rt	0	0	0	0	0	0	imm2		Rm	LDRSB Rt, [Rn, #imm12]
1111100	0	0	001	Rn	1111	0	0	0	0	0	0	imm2		Rm	PLD [Rn, Rm, LSL #imm2]
1111100	0	0	001	Rn	1111	1	1	0	0	imm8					PLD [Rn, #-imm8]
1111100	0	U	001	1111	1111	imm12									PLD #+/-imm12
1111100	0	1	001	Rn	1111	imm12									PLD [Rn, #imm12]
1111100	1	0	001	Rn	1111	1	1	0	0	imm8					PLI [Rn, #-imm8]
1111100	1	0	001	Rn	1111	0	0	0	0	0	0	imm2		Rm	PLI [Rn, Rm, LSL #imm2]
1111100	1	U	001	1111	1111	imm12									PLI #+/-imm12
1111100	1	1	001	Rn	1111	imm12									PLI [Rn, #imm12]

- If U = 1, use #imm12. Otherwise, use #-imm12.
- PLD (Preload Data) and PLI (Preload Instruction) are the only memory hint instructions

Load halfword

31 - 25	24	23	22 - 20	19-16	15-12	11 - 8				7	6	5	4	3 - 0	Instruction
1111100	0	U	011	1111	Rt	imm12									LDRH Rt, #+/-imm12
1111100	0	1	011	Rn	Rt	imm12									LDRH Rt, [Rn, #imm12]
1111100	0	0	011	Rn	Rt	0	0	0	0	0	0	imm2		Rm	LDRH Rt, [Rn, Rm,LSL #imm2]
1111100	0	0	011	Rn	Rt	1	0	1	0	imm8					LDRHT Rt, [Rn]
1111100	0	0	011	Rn	Rt	1	1	U	0	imm8					LDRHT Rt, [Rn,#imm8]
1111100	0	0	011	Rn	Rt	1	0	U	1	imm8					LDRHT Rt, Rn,#imm8
1111100	0	0	011	Rn	Rt	1	1	U	1	imm8					LDRHT Rt, [Rn,#imm8]!
1111100	1	1	011	Rn	Rt	imm12									LDRSH Rt, [Rn, #imm12]
1111100	1	U	011	1111	Rt	imm12									LDRSH Rt, #+/-imm12
1111100	1	0	011	Rn	Rt	0	0	0	0	0	0	imm2		Rm	LDRH Rt, [Rn, Rm,LSL #imm2]
1111100	1	0	011	Rn	Rt	1	1	1	0	imm8					LDRSHT Rt, [Rn,#imm8]

- If U = 1, use #imm; oherwise, use #-imm.

Load word

31 - 25	24	23	22 -20	19 - 16	15-12	11 - 8				7	6	5	4	3 - 0	Instruction
1111100	0	1	101	Rn	Rt	imm12									LDR Rt, [Rn, #imm12]
1111100	0	0	101	Rn	Rt	1	1	1	0	imm8					LDRT Rt, [Rn, #imm8]
1111100	0	0	101	Rn	Rt	0	0	0	0	0	0	imm2		Rm	LDR [Rn, Rm, LSL #imm2]
1111100	0	U	101	1111	Rt	imm12									LDR Rt, #imm12

- Load Register Unprivileged (LDRT)

Coprocessor instructions

31 - 26	25	24	23	22	21	20	19-16	15-12	11 - 8	7-5	4	3-0	Instruction
111011	0	P	U	N	W	0	Rn	CRd	coproc	imm8			STC
111111	0	P	U	N	W	0	Rn	CRd	coproc	imm8			STC2
111011	0	P	U	D	W	1	Rn	CRd	coproc	imm8			LDC (immediate)
111111	0	P	U	D	W	1	Rn	CRd	coproc	imm8			LDC2 (immediate)
111011	0	P	U	D	W	1	1111	CRd	coproc	imm8			LDC (literal)
111111	0	P	U	D	W	1	1111	CRd	coproc	imm8			LDC2(literal)
111011	0	0	0	1	0	0	Rt2	Rt	coproc	opc1		CRm	MCRR
111111	0	0	0	1	0	0	Rt2	Rt	coproc	opc1		CRm	MCRR2
111011	0	0	0	1	0	1	Rt2	Rt	coproc	opc1		CRm	MRRC
111111	0	0	0	1	0	1	Rt2	Rt	coproc	opc1		CRm	MRRC2
111011	1	1	0	opc1			CRn	CRd	coproc	op2	0	CRm	CDP
111111	1	1	0	opc1			CRn	CRd	coproc	op2	0	CRm	CDP2
111011	1	0	opc1			0	CRn	Rt	coproc	op2	1	CRm	MRC
111111	1	0	opc1			0	CRn	Rt	coproc	op2	1	CRm	MRC2
111011	1	0	opc1			1	CRn	Rt	coproc	op2	1	CRm	MRC
111111	1	0	opc1			1	CRn	Rt	coproc	op2	1	CRm	MRC2

- Store Coprocessor (STC)
- Load Coprocessor (LDC)
- Move to Coprocessor from two ARM Registers (MCRR)
- Move to two ARM Registers from Coprocessor (MRRC)
- Move to Coprocessor from ARM Register (MCR)
- Move to ARM Register from Coprocessor (MRC)
- Example Instruction formats:
  - MRC coproc, opc1, Rt, CRn, CRm,opc2
  - LDC{L} coproc, CRd, [Rn,#+/-imm}]   ; Offset. P = 1, W = 0.
  - LDC{L} coproc, CRd, [Rn,#+/-imm>]!   ; Pre-index. P = 1, W = 1.
  - LDC{L} coproc, CRd, [Rn],#+/-imm   ; Post-index. P = 0, W = 1.
  - LDC{L} coproc, CRd, [Rn],   ; Unindexed. P = 0, W = 0, U = 1.
  - LDC{L} coproc, CRd, label   ; Normal form with P = 1, W = 0
  - LDC{L} coproc, CRd, [PC,#-0]   ; Alternative form with P = 1, W = 0

Appendix H: HID Codes of a Keyboard

Code	Usage	Code	Usage	Code	Usage	Code	Usage	Code	Usage
0x00	Reserved	0x23	6 and ^	0x46	Print Screen	0x69	F14	0x8C	International 6
0x01	Error Roll Over	0x24	7 and &	0x47	Scroll Lock	0x6A	F15	0x8D	International 7
0x02	POST Fail	0x25	8 and *	0x48	Pause	0x6B	F16	0x8E	International 8
0x03	Error Undefined	0x26	9 and (	0x49	Insert	0x6C	F17	0x8F	International 9
0x04	a and A	0x27	0 and)	0x4A	Home	0x6D	F18	0x90	LANG1
0x05	b and B	0x28	Return	0x4B	Page Up	0x6E	F19	0x91	LANG2
0x06	c and C	0x29	ESCAPE	0x4C	Delete Forward	0x6F	F20	0x92	LANG3
0x07	d and D	0x2A	Backspace	0x4D	End	0x70	F21	0x93	LANG4
0x08	e and E	0x2B	Tab	0x4E	Page Down	0x71	F22	0x94	LANG5
0x09	f and F	0x2C	Spacebar	0x4F	Right Arrow	0x72	F23	0x95	LANG6
0x0A	g and G	0x2D	- and _	0x50	Left Arrow	0x73	F24	0x96	LANG7
0x0B	h and H	0x2E	= and +	0x51	Down Arrow	0x74	Execute	0x97	LANG8
0x0C	i and I	0x2F	[and {	0x52	Up Arrow	0x75	Help	0x98	LANG9
0x0D	j and J	0x30	] and }	0x53	Keypad Num Lock and Clear	0x76	Menu	0x99	Alternate Erase
0x0E	k and K	0x31	\ and		0x54	Keypad /	0x77	Select	0x9A	SysReq Attention
0x0F	l and L	0x32	Non-US # and ~	0x55	Keypad *	0x78	Stop	0x9B	Cancel
0x10	m and M	0x33	; and :	0x56	Keypad -	0x79	Again	0x9C	Clear
0x11	n and N	0x34	' and "	0x57	Keypad +	0x7A	Undo	0x9D	Prior
0x12	o and O	0x35	` and ~	0x58	Keypad Enter	0x7B	Cut	0x9E	Return
0x13	p and P	0x36	Keyboard, and <	0x59	Keypad 1 and End	0x7C	Copy	0x9F	Separator
0x14	q and Q	0x37	. and >	0x5A	Keypad 2 and Down Arrow	0x7D	Paste	0xA0	Out
0x15	r and R	0x38	/ and ?	0x5B	Keypad 3 & Page Down	0x7E	Find	0xA1	Oper
0x16	s and S	0x39	Caps Lock	0x5C	Keypad 4 & Left Arrow	0x7F	Mute	0xA2	Clear/Again
0x17	t and T	0x3A	F1	0x5D	Keypad 5	0x80	Volume Up	0xA3	CrSel/Props
0x18	u and U	0x3B	F2	0x5E	Keypad 6 & Right Arrow	0x81	Volume Down	0xA4	ExSel
0x19	v and V	0x3C	F3	0x5F	Keypad 7 and Home	0x82	Locking Caps Lock	0xE0	Left Control
0x1A	w and W	0x3D	F4	0x60	Keypad 8 & Up Arrow	0x83	Locking Num Lock	0xE1	Left Shift

0x1B	x and X	0x3E	F5	0x61	Keypad 9 & Page Up	0x84	Locking Scroll Lock	0xE2	Left Alt
0x1C	y and Y	0x3F	F6	0x62	Keypad 0 and Insert	0x85	Keypad Comma	0xE3	Left GUI
0x1D	z and Z	0x40	F7	0x63	Keypad . and Delete	0x86	Keypad Equal Sign	0xE4	Right Control
0x1E	1 and !	0x41	F8	0x64	\ and		0x87	International 1	0xE5	Right Shift
0x1F	2 and @	0x42	F9	0x65	Application	0x88	International 2	0xE6	Right Alt
0x20	3 and #	0x43	F10	0x66	Power	0x89	International 3	0xE7	Right GUI
0x21	4 and $	0x44	F11	0x67	Keypad =	0x8A	International 4		
0x22	5 and %	0x45	F12	0x68	F13	0x8B	International 5		

Appendix I: GPIO Alternate Functions (STM32L4)

Software can program a GPIO pin to map this pin internally to the input or output of some on-chip peripheral. Thus, a GPIO pin usually can support more than one hardware functions, which are called *alternate functions*. The alternate function is selected by programming the AFSEL[3:0] bits defined in the Alternate Function Low or High Register. Alternate functions allow embedded system designers to better tailor the processor chip to the application's need.

Alternate Function Low Register

31 30 29 28	27 26 25 24	23 22 21 20	19 18 17 16	15 14 13 12	11 10 9 8	7 6 5 4	3 2 1 0
AFSEL7[3:0]	AFSEL6[3:0]	AFSEL5[3:0]	AFSEL4[3:0]	AFSEL3[3:0]	AFSEL2[3:0]	AFSEL1[3:0]	AFSEL0[3:0]
AF of Pin 7	AF of Pin 6	AF of Pin 5	AF of Pin 4	AF of Pin 3	AF of Pin 2	AF of Pin 1	AF of Pin 0

Alternate Function High Register

31 30 29 28	27 26 25 24	23 22 21 20	19 18 17 16	15 14 13 12	11 10 9 8	7 6 5 4	3 2 1 0
AFSEL15[3:0]	AFSEL14[3:0]	AFSEL13[3:0]	AFSEL12[3:0]	AFSEL11[3:0]	AFSEL10[3:0]	AFSEL9[3:0]	AFSEL8[3:0]
AF of Pin 16	AF of Pin 15	AF of Pin 14	AF of Pin 13	AF of Pin 12	AF of Pin 11	AF of Pin 9	AF of Pin 8

The following tables list all alternate functions supported by each GPIO pin on STM32L4. All alternate functions are divided into the following 16 categories. For example, the alternate function 11 (AF11) is to set a GPIO pin to drive an LCD.

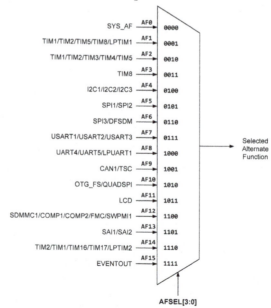

In the following tables, processor pins that have been extended to board pins on the STM32L4 discovery kit are shaded. To interface on-board peripherals, the alternative functions that should be selected are also shaded.

Appendix I: GPIO Alternate Functions (STM32L4)

Port A: Alternate Functions (STM32L4)

Pin	AF0 SYS_AF	AF1 TIM1/TIM2/TIM5/TIM8/LPTIM1	AF2 TIM1/TIM2/TIM3/TIM4/TIM5	AF3 TIM8	AF4 I2C1/I2C2/I2C3	AF5 SPI1/SPI2	AF6 SPI3/DFSDM	AF7 USART1/USART2/USART3	AF8 UART4/UART5/LPUART1	AF9 CAN1/TSC	AF10 OTG_FS/QUADSPI	AF11 LCD	AF12 SDMMC1/COMP1/COMP2/FMC/SWPMI1	AF13 SAI1/SAI2	AF14 TIM2/TIM1/TIM16/TIM17/LPTIM2
PA0		TIM2_CH1	TIM5_CH1	TIM8_ETR	-	-	-	USART2_CTS	UART4_TX	-	-	-	-	SAI1_EXTCLK	TIM2_ETR
PA1	-	TIM2_CH2	TIM5_CH2	-	-	-	-	USART2_RTS_DE	UART4_RX	-	-	LCD_SEG0	-	-	TIM15_CH1N
PA2	-	TIM2_CH3	TIM5_CH3	-	-	-	-	USART2_TX	-	-	-	LCD_SEG1	-	SAI2_EXTCLK	TIM15_CH1
PA3	-	TIM2_CH4	TIM5_CH4	-	-	-	-	USART2_RX	-	-	-	LCD_SEG2	-	-	TIM15_CH2
PA4	-	-	-	-	-	SPI1_NSS	SPI3_NSS	USART2_CK	-	-	-	-	-	SAI1_FS_B	LPTIM2_OUT
PA5	-	TIM2_CH1	TIM2_ETR	-	-	SPI1_SCK	-	-	-	-	-	-	-	-	LPTIM2_ETR
PA6	-	TIM1_BKIN	TIM3_CH1	TIM8_BKIN	-	SPI1_MISO	-	USART3_CTS	-	-	QUADSPI_BK1_IO3	LCD_SEG3	TIM1_BKIN_COMP2	TIM8_BKIN_COMP2	TIM16_CH1
PA7	-	TIM1_CH1N	TIM3_CH2	TIM8_CH1N	-	SPI1_MOSI	-	-	-	-	QUADSPI_BK1_IO2	LCD_SEG4	-	-	TIM17_CH1
PA8	MCO	TIM1_CH1	-	-	-	-	-	USART1_CK	-	-	OTG_FS_SOF	LCD_COM0	-	-	LPTIM2_OUT
PA9	-	TIM1_CH2	-	-	-	-	-	USART1_TX	-	-	-	LCD_COM1	-	-	TIM15_BKIN
PA10	-	TIM1_CH3	-	-	-	-	-	USART1_RX	-	-	OTG_FS_ID	LCD_COM2	-	-	TIM17_BKIN
PA11	-	TIM1_CH4	TIM1_BKIN2	-	-	-	-	USART1_CTS	-	CAN1_RX	OTG_FS_DM	-	TIM1_BKIN2_COMP1	-	-
PA12	-	TIM1_ETR	-	-	-	-	-	USART1_RTS_DE	-	CAN1_TX	OTG_FS_DP	-	-	-	-
PA13	JTMS/SWDIO	IR_OUT	-	-	-	-	-	-	-	-	OTG_FS_NOE	-	-	-	-
PA14	JTCK/SWCLK	-	-	-	-	-	-	-	-	-	-	-	-	-	-
PA15	JTDI	TIM2_CH1	TIM2_ETR	-	-	SPI1_NSS	SPI3_NSS	-	UART4_RTS_DE	TSC_G3_IO1	-	LCD_SEG17	-	SAI2_FS_B	-

Appendix I: GPIO Alternate Functions (STM32L4)

Port B: Alternate Functions (STM32L4)

Pin	AF0 SYS_AF	AF1 TIM1/TIM2/TIM5/TIM8/LPTIM1	AF2 TIM1/TIM2/TIM3/TIM4/TIM5	AF3 TIM8	AF4 I2C1/I2C2/I2C3	AF5 SPI1/SPI2	AF6 SPI3/DFSDM	AF7 USART1/USART2/USART3	AF8 UART4/UART5/LPUART1	AF9 CAN1/TSC	AF10 OTG_FS/QUADSPI	AF11 LCD	AF12 SDMMC1/COMP1/COMP2/FMC/SWPMI1	AF13 SAI1/SAI2	AF14 TIM2/TIM1/TIM16/TIM17/LPTIM2
PB0	-	TIM1_CH2N	TIM3_CH3	TIM8_CH2N	-	-	-	USART3_CK	-	-	QUADSPI_BK1_IO1	LCD_SEG5	COMP1_OUT	-	-
PB1	-	TIM1_CH3N	TIM3_CH4	TIM8_CH3N	-	-	DFSDM_DATIN0	USART3_RTS_DE	-	-	QUADSPI_BK1_IO0	LCD_SEG6	-	-	LPTIM2_IN1
PB2	RTC_OUT	LPTIM1_OUT	-	-	I2C3_SMBA	-	DFSDM_CKIN0	-	-	-	-	-	-	-	-
PB3	JTDO/TRACESWO	TIM2_CH2	-	-	-	SPI1_SCK	SPI3_SCK	USART1_RTS_DE	-	-	-	LCD_SEG7	-	SAI1_SCK_B	-
PB4	NJTRST	-	TIM3_CH1	-	-	SPI1_MISO	SPI3_MISO	USART1_CTS	UART5_RTS_DE	TSC_G2_IO1	-	LCD_SEG8	-	SAI1_MCLK_B	TIM17_BKIN
PB5	-	LPTIM1_IN1	TIM3_CH2	-	I2C1_SMBA	SPI1_MOSI	SPI3_MOSI	USART1_CK	UART5_CTS	TSC_G2_IO2	-	LCD_SEG9	COMP2_OUT	SAI1_SD_B	TIM16_BKIN
PB6	-	LPTIM1_ETR	TIM4_CH1	TIM8_BKIN2	I2C1_SCL	-	DFSDM_DATIN5	USART1_TX	-	TSC_G2_IO3	-	-	TIM8_BKIN2_COMP2	SAI1_FS_B	TIM16_CH1N
PB7	-	LPTIM1_IN2	TIM4_CH2	TIM8_BKIN	I2C1_SDA	-	DFSDM_CKIN5	USART1_RX	UART4_CTS	TSC_G2_IO4	-	LCD_SEG21	FMC_NL	TIM8_BKIN_COMP1	TIM17_CH1N
PB8	-	-	TIM4_CH3	-	I2C1_SCL	SPI2_NSS	DFSDM_DATIN6	-	-	CAN1_RX	-	LCD_SEG16	SDMMC1_D4	SAI1_MCLK_A	TIM16_CH1
PB9	-	IR_OUT	TIM4_CH4	-	I2C1_SDA	SPI2_NSS	DFSDM_CKIN6	-	-	CAN1_TX	-	LCD_COM3	SDMMC1_D5	SAI1_FS_A	TIM17_CH1
PB10	-	TIM2_CH3	-	-	I2C2_SCL	SPI2_SCK	DFSDM_DATIN7	USART3_TX	LPUART1_RX	-	QUADSPI_CLK	LCD_SEG10	COMP1_OUT	SAI1_SCK_A	-
PB11	-	TIM2_CH4	-	-	I2C2_SDA	-	DFSDM_CKIN7	USART3_RX	LPUART1_TX	-	QUADSPI_NCS	LCD_SEG11	COMP2_OUT	-	-
PB12	-	TIM1_BKIN	-	TIM1_BKIN_COMP2	I2C2_SMBA	SPI2_NSS	DFSDM_DATIN1	USART3_CK	LPUART1_RTS_DE	TSC_G1_IO1	-	LCD_SEG12	SWPMI1_IO	SAI2_FS_A	TIM15_BKIN
PB13	-	TIM1_CH1N	-	-	I2C2_SCL	SPI2_SCK	DFSDM_CKIN1	USART3_CTS	LPUART1_CTS	TSC_G1_IO2	-	LCD_SEG13	SWPMI1_TX	SAI2_SCK_A	TIM15_CH1N
PB14	-	TIM1_CH2N	-	TIM8_CH2N	I2C2_SDA	SPI2_MISO	DFSDM_DATIN2	USART3_RTS_DE	-	TSC_G1_IO3	-	LCD_SEG14	SWPMI1_RX	SAI2_MCLK_A	TIM15_CH1
PB15	RTC_REFIN	TIM1_CH3N	-	TIM8_CH3N	-	SPI2_MOSI	DFSDM_CKIN2	-	-	TSC_G1_IO4	-	LCD_SEG15	SWPMI1_SUSPEND	SAI2_SD_A	TIM15_CH2

Appendix I: GPIO Alternate Functions (STM32L4)

Port C: Alternate Functions (STM32L4)

Pin	AF0	AF1	AF2	AF3	AF4	AF5	AF6	AF7	AF8	AF9	AF10	AF11	AF12	AF13	AF14
	SYS_AF	TIM1/TIM2/TIM5/TIM8/LPTIM1	TIM1/TIM2/TIM3/TIM4/TIM5	TIM8	I2C1/I2C2/I2C3	SPI1/SPI2	SPI3/DFSDM	USART1/USART2/USART3	UART4/UART5/LPUART1	CAN1/TSC	OTG_FS/QUADSPI	LCD	SDMMC1/COMP1/COMP2/FMC/SWPMI1	SAI1/SAI2	TIM2/TIM1/TIM16/TIM17/LPTIM2
PC0	-	LPTIM1_IN1	-	-	I2C3_SCL	-	DFSDM_DATIN4	-	LPUART1_RX	-	-	LCD_SEG18	-	-	LPTIM2_IN1
PC1	-	LPTIM1_OUT	-	-	I2C3_SDA	-	DFSDM_CKIN4	-	LPUART1_TX	-	-	LCD_SEG19	-	-	-
PC2	-	LPTIM1_IN2	-	-	-	SPI2_MISO	DFSDM_CKOUT	-	-	-	-	LCD_SEG20	-	-	-
PC3	-	LPTIM1_ETR	-	-	-	SPI2_MOSI	-	-	-	-	-	LCD_VLCD	-	SAI1_SD_A	LPTIM2_ETR
PC4	-	-	-	-	-	-	-	USART3_TX	-	-	-	LCD_SEG22	-	-	-
PC5	-	-	-	-	-	-	-	USART3_RX	-	-	-	LCD_SEG23	-	-	-
PC6	-	-	TIM3_CH1	TIM8_CH1	-	-	DFSDM_CKIN3	-	-	TSC_G4_IO1	-	LCD_SEG24	SDMMC1_D6	SAI2_MCLK_A	-
PC7	-	-	TIM3_CH2	TIM8_CH2	-	-	DFSDM_DATIN3	-	-	TSC_G4_IO2	-	LCD_SEG25	SDMMC1_D7	SAI2_MCLK_B	-
PC8	-	-	TIM3_CH3	TIM8_CH3	-	-	-	-	-	TSC_G4_IO3	-	LCD_SEG26	SDMMC1_D0	-	-
PC9	-	TIM8_BKIN2	TIM3_CH4	TIM8_CH4	-	-	-	-	-	TSC_G4_IO4	OTG_FS_NOE	LCD_SEG27	SDMMC1_D1	SAI2_EXTCLK	TIM8_BKIN2_COMP1
PC10	-	-	-	-	-	-	SPI3_SCK	USART3_TX	UART4_TX	TSC_G3_IO2	-	LCD_COM4/LCD_SEG28/LCD_SEG40	SDMMC1_D2	SAI2_SCK_B	-
PC11	-	-	-	-	-	-	SPI3_MISO	USART3_RX	UART4_RX	TSC_G3_IO3	-	LCD_COM5/LCD_SEG29/LCD_SEG41	SDMMC1_D3	SAI2_MCLK_B	-
PC12	-	-	-	-	-	-	SPI3_MOSI	USART3_CK	UART5_TX	TSC_G3_IO4	-	LCD_COM6/LCD_SEG30/LCD_SEG42	SDMMC1_CK	SAI2_SD_B	-
PC13	-	-	-	-	-	-	-	-	-	-	-	-	-	-	-
PC14	-	-	-	-	-	-	-	-	-	-	-	-	-	-	-
PC15	-	-	-	-	-	-	-	-	-	-	-	-	-	-	-

Appendix I: GPIO Alternate Functions (STM32L4)

Port D: Alternate Functions (STM32L4)

Pin	AF0	AF1	AF2	AF3	AF4	AF5	AF6	AF7	AF8	AF9	AF10	AF11	AF12	AF13	AF14
	SYS_AF	TIM1/TIM2/TIM5/TIM8/LPTIM1	TIM1/TIM2/TIM3/TIM4/TIM5	TIM8	I2C1/I2C2/I2C3	SPI1/SPI2	SPI3/DFSDM	USART1/USART2/USART3	UART4/UART5/LPUART1	CAN1/TSC	OTG_FS/QUADSPI	LCD	SDMMC1/COMP1/COMP2/FMC/SWPMI1	SAI1/SAI2	TIM2/TIM1/TIM16/TIM17/LPTIM2
PD0	-	-	-	-	-	SPI2_NSS	DFSDM_DATIN7	-	-	CAN1_RX	-	-	FMC_D2	-	-
PD1	-	-	-	-	-	SPI2_SCK	DFSDM_CKIN7	-	-	CAN1_TX	-	-	FMC_D3	-	-
PD2	-	-	TIM3_ETR	-	-	-	-	USART3_RTS_DE	UART5_RX	TSC_SYNC	-	LCD_COM7/LCD_SEG31/LCD_SEG43	SDMMC1_CMD	-	-
PD3	-	-	-	-	-	SPI2_MISO	DFSDM_DATIN0	USART2_CTS	-	-	-	-	FMC_CLK	-	-
PD4	-	-	-	-	-	SPI2_MOSI	DFSDM_CKIN0	USART2_RTS_DE	-	-	-	-	FMC_NOE	-	-
PD5	-	-	-	-	-	-	-	USART2_TX	-	-	-	-	FMC_NWE	-	-
PD6	-	-	-	-	-	-	DFSDM_DATIN1	USART2_RX	-	-	-	-	FMC_NWAIT	SAI1_SD_A	-
PD7	-	-	-	-	-	-	DFSDM_CKIN1	USART2_CK	-	-	-	-	FMC_NE1	-	-
PD8	-	-	-	-	-	-	-	USART3_TX	-	-	-	LCD_SEG28	FMC_D13	-	-
PD9	-	-	-	-	-	-	-	USART3_RX	-	-	-	LCD_SEG29	FMC_D14	SAI2_MCLK_A	-
PD10	-	-	-	-	-	-	-	USART3_CK	-	TSC_G6_IO1	-	LCD_SEG30	FMC_D15	SAI2_SCK_A	-
PD11	-	-	-	-	-	-	-	USART3_CTS	-	TSC_G6_IO2	-	LCD_SEG31	FMC_A16	SAI2_SD_A	LPTIM2_ETR
PD12	-	-	TIM4_CH1	-	-	-	-	USART3_RTS_DE	-	TSC_G6_IO3	-	LCD_SEG32	FMC_A17	SAI2_FS_A	LPTIM2_IN1
PD13	-	-	TIM4_CH2	-	-	-	-	-	-	TSC_G6_IO4	-	LCD_SEG33	FMC_A18	-	LPTIM2_OUT
PD14	-	-	TIM4_CH3	-	-	-	-	-	-	-	-	LCD_SEG34	FMC_D0	-	-
PD15	-	-	TIM4_CH4	-	-	-	-	-	-	-	-	LCD_SEG35	FMC_D1	-	-

Appendix I: GPIO Alternate Functions (STM32L4)

Port E: Alternate Functions (STM32L4)

Pin	AF0 SYS_AF	AF1 TIM1/ TIM2/ TIM5/ TIM8/ LPTIM1	AF2 TIM1/ TIM2/ TIM3/ TIM4/ TIM5	AF3 TIM8	AF4 I2C1/ I2C2/ I2C3	AF5 SPI1/ SPI2	AF6 SPI3/ DFSDM	AF7 USART1/ USART2/ USART3	AF8 UART4/ UART5/ LPUART1	AF9 CAN1/ TSC	AF10 OTG_FS/ QUADSPI	AF11 LCD	AF12 SDMMC1/ COMP1/ COMP2/ FMC/ SWPMI1	AF13 SAI1/ SAI2	AF14 TIM2/ TIM1/ TIM16/ TIM17/ LPTIM2
PE0	-	-	TIM4_ETR	-	-	-	-	-	-	-	-	LCD_SEG36	FMC_NBL0	-	TIM16_CH1
PE1	-	-	-	-	-	-	-	-	-	-	-	LCD_SEG37	FMC_NBL1	-	TIM17_CH1
PE2	TRACECK	-	TIM3_ETR	-	-	-	-	-	-	TSC_G7_IO1	-	LCD_SEG38	FMC_A23	SAI1_MCLK_A	-
PE3	TRACED0	-	TIM3_CH1	-	-	-	-	-	-	TSC_G7_IO2	-	LCD_SEG39	FMC_A19	SAI1_SD_B	-
PE4	TRACED1	-	TIM3_CH2	-	-	-	DFSDM_DATIN3	-	-	TSC_G7_IO3	-	-	FMC_A20	SAI1_FS_A	-
PE5	TRACED2	-	TIM3_CH3	-	-	-	DFSDM_CKIN3	-	-	TSC_G7_IO4	-	-	FMC_A21	SAI1_SCK_A	-
PE6	TRACED3	-	TIM3_CH4	-	-	-	-	-	-	-	-	-	FMC_A22	SAI1_SD_A	-
PE7	-	TIM1_ETR	-	-	-	-	DFSDM_DATIN2	-	-	-	-	-	FMC_D4	SAI1_SD_B	-
PE8	-	TIM1_CH1N	-	-	-	-	DFSDM_CKIN2	-	-	-	-	-	FMC_D5	SAI1_SCK_B	-
PE9	-	TIM1_CH1	-	-	-	-	DFSDM_CKOUT	-	-	-	-	-	FMC_D6	SAI1_FS_B	-
PE10	-	TIM1_CH2N	-	-	-	-	DFSDM_DATIN4	-	-	TSC_G5_IO1	QUADSPI_CLK	-	FMC_D7	SAI1_MCLK_B	-
PE11	-	TIM1_CH2	-	-	-	-	DFSDM_CKIN4	-	-	TSC_G5_IO2	QUADSPI_NCS	-	FMC_D8	-	-
PE12	-	TIM1_CH3N	-	-	-	SPI1_NSS	DFSDM_DATIN5	-	-	TSC_G5_IO3	QUADSPI_BK1_IO0	-	FMC_D9	-	-
PE13	-	TIM1_CH3	-	-	-	SPI1_SCK	DFSDM_CKIN5	-	-	TSC_G5_IO4	QUADSPI_BK1_IO1	-	FMC_D10	-	-
PE14	-	TIM1_CH4	TIM1_BKIN2	TIM1_BKIN2_COMP2	-	SPI1_MISO	-	-	-	-	QUADSPI_BK1_IO2	-	FMC_D11	-	-
PE15	-	TIM1_BKIN	-	TIM1_BKIN_COMP1	-	SPI1_MOSI	-	-	-	-	QUADSPI_BK1_IO3	-	FMC_D12	-	-

[This page intentionally left blank]

Bibliography

1. ARM Limited. http://www.arm.com/
2. STMicroelectronics. http://www.st.com/
3. Texas Instruments. http://www.ti.com/
4. Freescale. http://www.freescale.com/
5. Cypress Semiconductor. http://www.cypress.com/
6. NXP Semiconductors. http://www.nxp.com/
7. Nordic Semiconductors. http://www.nordicsemi.com/
8. Nuvoton Technology Corporation. http://www.nuvoton.com/
9. STMicroelectronics. *Reference manual, STM32L151xx, STM32L152xx and STM32L162xx Advanced ARM-based 32-bit MCUs*, July 2012
10. STMicroelectronics. *Reference Manual STM32F405xx/07xx, STM32F415xx/17xx, STM32F42xxx and STM32F43xxx advanced ARM-based 32-bit MCUs.* May 2014
11. STMicroelectronics. *UM1079 User Manual, STM32L-DISCOVERY*, Doc ID 018789 Rev 2, June 2011
12. STMicroelectronics. *UM1472 User Manual, Discovery kit for STM32F407/417 lines*, DocID022256 Rev 4, January 2014
13. STMicroelectronics. *STM32L151xx STM32L152xx Data Sheets.* January 2012
14. STMicroelectronics. *STM32F405xx STM32F407xx Data Sheets.* DocID022152 Rev 4. June 2013
15. STMicroelectronics. *STM32F3 and STM32F4 Series Cortex-M4 programming manual*, DocID022708 Rev 4, May 2014
16. ARM Limited. *ARMv6-M Architecture Reference Manual*, rev C, 2008
17. ARM Limited. *ARMv7-M Architecture Reference Manual*, Fourth release, 2010
18. ARM Limited. *Cortex-M0 Technical Reference Manual*, Revision: r0p0, 2010
19. ARM Limited. *Cortex-M0+ Technical Reference Manual*, Revision: r0p0, 2012
20. ARM Limited. *Cortex-M3 Technical Reference Manual*, Revision: r1p1, 2006
21. ARM Limited. *Cortex-M4 Technical Reference Manual*, Revision: r0p1, 2013
22. ARM Limited. *Cortex-M7 Technical Reference Manual*, Revision: r1p0, 2015
23. ARM Limited. *Cortex-M0 Devices Generic User Guide*, 2009
24. ARM Limited. *Cortex-M0+ Devices Generic User Guide*, 2012
25. ARM Limited. *Cortex-M3 Devices Generic User Guide*, 2010
26. ARM Limited. *Cortex-M4 Devices Generic User Guide*, 2010
27. ARM Limited. *Cortex-M7 Devices Generic User Guide*, 2015
28. ARM Limited. *CMSIS - Cortex Microcontroller Software Interface Standard*, http://www.arm.com/products/processors/cortex-m/cortex-microcontroller-software-interface-standard.php, retrieved 2013, 2014 and 2015

29. ARM Limited. *ELF for the ARM Architecture*, ARM IHI 0044D, 10/28/2009

30. ARM Limited. *Application Binary Interface for the ARM Architecture*, The Base Standard, ARM IHI 0036B, 11/30/2010

31. ARM Limited. *Procedure Call Standard for the ARM Architecture*, ARM IHI 0042D, 8/16/2009

32. ARM Limited. *ARM Compiler Toolchain, Version 5.02, Assembler Reference*, ARM DUI 0489H (ID070912), 2010-2012

33. ARM Limited. *ARM Compiler Toolchain, Version 5.02, Compiler Reference*, ARM DUI 0491H (ID070912), 2010-2012

34. ARM Limited. *ARM Developer Suite, Version 1.2, Developer Guide*, ARM DUI 0056D, 1999-2001

35. ARM Limited. *Cortex-M4(F) Lazy Stacking and Context Switching*, Application Note 298, March 2012

36. ARM Limited. *Application Note 33 Fixed Point Arithmetic on the ARM*, 1996

37. ARM Limited. *Keil Embedded Development Kit*, http://www.keil.com/

38. Shyam Sadasivan, *ARM Limited. White paper, Developing optimized signal processing software on the Cortex-M4 processor*. November 2010

39. Peter Wegner. *A Technique for Counting Ones in a Binary Computer*, Communications of the ACM, Page 322, 1960

40. IEEE Std 754 – 2008, *IEEE Standard for Floating-Point Arithmetic*, IEEE Computer Society, 2008

41. *USB Device Class Definition for Human Interface Devices (HID)*, Firmware Specification, 6/27/2001, Version 1.11, www.USB.org

42. *USB HID Usage Tables*, 10/28/2004, Version 1.12, www.USB.org

43. *Universal Serial Bus Specification*, Revision 2.0, 5/27/2000, www.USB.org

44. *USB in a Nutshell. Making Sense of the USB Standard*. www.beyondlogic.org, 3/10/2014

45. Jan Axelson, *USB Complete, The Developer's Guide*, Fourth Edition, ISBN 978-1931448086, June 2009

46. ATMEL Application Note, *AVR065: LCD Driver for the STK502*, Rev. 2530E-AVR-07/08

47. Newhaven Display International, Inc., NHD-0216K1Z-NSW-BBW-L, Character Liquid Crystal Display Module, 2011

48. Sumsung. *16COM/40SEG Driver & Controller for Dot Matrix LCD*. KS0066U, retrieved March 2015

49. STMicroelectronics. *AN4032 Application note, Interfacing an HD44780 2-line LCD display with the STM8SVLDISCOVERY*, Doc ID 022651 Rev 1, February 2012

50. Hitachi. HD44780U (LCD-II), *Dot Matrix Liquid Crystal Display Controller/Driver*, ADE-207-272(Z), '99.9, Rev. 0.0

51. Microchip. *AN907 Stepping Motors Fundamentals*, DS00907A, 2004
52. Texas Instruments. *Data Sheet of ULN2803N Darlington Transistor Array*, July 2007
53. STMicroelectronics. *AN2604 Application note*, STM32F101xx and STM32F103xx RTC calibration, August 2007
54. STMicroelectronics. *AN3371 Application note, Using the hardware real-time clock (RTC) in STM32 F0, F2, F3, F4 and L1 series of MCUs*, Doc ID 018624 Rev 5, September 2012
55. STMicroelectronics. *AN4044 Application note, Using floating-point unit (FPU) with STM32F405/07xx and STM32F415/417xx microcontrollers*, Doc ID 022737 Rev 1, March 2012
56. Robert H. Walden, *Analog-to-Digital Converter Survey and Analysis, IEEE Journal on Selected Areas in Communications*, VOL. 17, NO. 4, APRIL 1999
57. Walt Kester, *ADC Architectures II: Successive Approximation ADCs*, Analog Devices, MT-021 Tutorial, Rev.A, 10/08, WK
58. ATMEL, *Atmel AVR127: Understanding ADC parameters*, Application Note Rev. 8456A-AVR-11/11, 2011
59. Walt Kester, *Which ADC Architecture Is Right for Your Application?* Analog Dialogue 39-06, June 2005
60. STMicroelectronics. *AN3126 Application note, Audio and waveform generation using the DAC in STM32 microcontroller families*, Doc ID 16895 Rev 1, May 2010
61. Walt Kester, *Basic DAC Architectures II: Binary DACs*, Analog Devices MT-015 Tutorial, Rev.A, 10/08, WK, 2008
62. Phillip L. De Leon, *Computer Music in Undergraduate Digital Signal Processing*, Annual Conference on Interactive Learning in Engineering Education, Session 76A3, 2000
63. Miller Puckette. *The Theory and Technique of Electronic Music*. World Scientific Publishing Co., Inc., River Edge, NJ, USA. 2007
64. Leens, F., *An introduction to I²C and SPI protocols, Instrumentation & Measurement Magazine*, IEEE , vol.12, no.1, pp.8,13, February 2009
65. STMicroelectronics. *AN2824 Application note, STM32F10xxx I2C optimized examples*, Doc ID 15021 Rev 4, June 2010
66. Microchip, *TC74 Datasheet, Tiny Serial Digital Thermal Sensor*, DS21462C, 2002
67. John R. Hauser. 1996. *Handling floating-point exceptions in numeric programs*. ACM Trans. Program. Lang. Syst. 18, 2 (March 1996), 139-174.
68. NXP Semiconductors, *UM10204 I2C-bus specification and user manual*, Rev. 6, 4 April 2014 User manual
69. UBICOM, *Serial Peripheral Interface (SPI) and Microwire/Plus implementation Using the SX Communications Controller*, Application Note 20, November 2000

70. Motorola, Inc. *SPI Block Guide V03.06*, Original Release Date: 21 JAN 2000, Revised: 04 FEB 2003

71. STMicroelectronics. *AN2159 Application note, SPI protocol for STPM01/STPM10 metering devices*, Doc ID 11400 Rev 3, July 2010

72. FTDI Chip. *FT232R USB UART IC Datasheet Version 2.09*, Document No.: FT_000053, 2010

73. Microchip, Section 18. USART, DS31018A, 1997

74. STMicroelectronics. *AN3155 Application note*, USART protocol used in the STM32 bootloader, Doc ID 17066 Rev 2, April 2010

75. Joseph Yiu and Andrew Frame, *ARM Cortex-M3 Processor Software Development for ARM7TDMI Processor Programmers*, White Paper, July 2009

76. Tyler Gilbert, *Make the most out of Cortex-M3's preemptive context switches*, EE Times-India, 2011

77. Micriµm. *µC/OS-II and ARM Cortex-M3 Processors*, Application Note AN-1018, 2006

78. Albert Huang and Larry Rudolph, *Bluetooth for Programmers*, http://people.csail.mit.edu/rudolph/Teaching/Articles/BTBook.pdf, Retrieve in Jan. 2014

79. connectBlue, *AT Command Specification - Bluetooth EPA*, http://www.connectblue.com, 2009

80. HC, *HC-03/05 Embedded Bluetooth Serial Communication Module AT command set*, http://www.wavesen.com/, April 2011

81. STMicroelectronics. xxxx-*TOUCH-LIB, STMTouch library*, DocID023933 Rev 4, February 2014

82. Cytron Technology, *Product User's Manual – HCSR04 Ultrasonic Sensor*, V1.0, May 2013

83. Gutierrez-Osuna, R.; Janet, J.A; Luo, R.C., *Modeling of ultrasonic range sensors for localization of autonomous mobile robots*, Industrial Electronics, IEEE Transactions on, vol. 45, no. 4, pp.654-662, Aug 1998

84. Microsoft, *Keyboard Scan Code Specification*, Revision 1.3a — March 16, 2000

85. Silicon Laboratories, *AN249 Human Interface Device*, Rev. 0.5 3/11

86. Robert Murphy, *AN57294 USB 101: An Introduction to Universal Serial Bus 2.0*, Document No. 001-57294 Rev. *D, www.cypress.com

87. STMicroelectronics. *STM32L Discovery Firmware Pack V1.0.2*, www.stm.com

88. MacKenzie, S., *A structured approach to assembly language programming," Education*, IEEE Transactions on, vol.31, no.2, pp.123,128, May 1988

89. Barry Donahue. 1988. *Using assembly language to teach concepts in the introductory course*. In Proceedings of the nineteenth SIGCSE technical symposium on

Computer science education (SIGCSE '88), Herbert L. Dershem (Ed.). ACM, New York, NY, USA, 158-162.

90. Actel. *Application Note AC161. Using Schmitt Triggers for Low Slew-Rate Input.* November 2002

91. E. Dijkstra. 1979. *Go to statement considered harmful.* In Classics in software engineering, Edward Nash Yourdon (Ed.). Yourdon Press, Upper Saddle River, NJ, USA 27-33.

92. C. K. Koç, T. Acar, Kaliski, and Jr. B.S., *Analyzing and Comparing Montgomery Multiplication Algorithms*, Micro, IEEE, Vol. 16, Issue 3, 1996, pp. 26-33

93. S. R. Dusse and B. S. Kaliski Jr. *A cryptographic library for the Motorola DSP56000.* In I. B. Damgard, editor, Advances in Cryptology - EUROCRYPT 90, Lecture Notes in Computer Science, No. 473, pages 230-244, New York, NY, 1990. Springer-Verlag.

94. J. Goodacre and A.N. Sloss, *Parallelism and the ARM instruction set architecture*, Computer, vol. 38, no. 7, pp.42-50, July 2005

95. Gene Frantz and Ray Simar, *Texas Instruments. Comparing Fixed- and Floating-Point DSPs.* http://www.ti.com/lit/wp/spry061/spry061.pdf, retrieved Jan. 2015

96. Alexandru Bârleanu, Vadim Băitoiu, Andrei Stan, *FIR Filtering on ARM Cortex-M3*, Page 490, Advances in Computer Science, Proccedings of the 6th WSEAS European Computing Conference, 2012, ISBN: 978-1-61804-126-5

97. S. Vassiliadis, E.A. Hakkennes, J.S.S.M. Wong, and G.G. Pechanek, G.G., *The sum-absolute-difference motion estimation accelerator*, Euromicro Conference, 1998. Proceedings. 24th, vol.2, no., pp.559-566 vol.2, 25-27 Aug 1998

98. J. Goodacre, and A.N. Sloss, *Parallelism and the ARM instruction set architecture*, Computer, vol. 38, no. 7, pp. 42-50, July 2005

99. ARM Limited. *Application Note 209 Using Cortex-M3 and Cortex-M4 Fault Exceptions*, June 2014

100. ARM Limited. *CMSIS DSP Software Library*, http://www.keil.com/pack/doc/CMSIS/DSP/html/index.html

101. STMicroelectronics. *AN4736 Application note: How to calibrate STM32L4 Series microcontrollers internal RC oscillator*, Doc ID 028052 Rev 2, August 2016

102. STMicroelectronics. *AN4566 Application note, Extending the DAC performance of STM32 microcontrollers*, Doc ID 026799 Rev 2, August 2015

103. STMicroelectronics. *AN4235 Application note: I2C timing configuration tool for STM32F3xxxx and STM32F0xxxx microcontrollers*, Doc ID 024161 Rev 2, August 2013

104.   STMicroelectronics. *AN4261 Application note: STM32L4 ultra-low-power features overview*, Doc ID 027173 Rev 1, July 2015

105.   STMicroelectronics. *AN2606 Application note: STM32 microcontroller system memory boot mode*, Doc ID 13801 Rev 29, December 2016

106.   STMicroelectronics. *AN4777 Application note: Implications of memory interface configurations on low-power STM32 microcontrollers*, Doc ID 28482 Rev 2, October 2016

107.   STMicroelectronics. *AN4013 Application note: STM32 cross-series timer overview*, Doc ID 22500 Rev 6, July 2016

108.   Joseph Yiu, *Optimizing a processor design for low power control applications*, ARM White Paper, 2013

109.   ARM Limited. Application Note 321: *ARM Cortex-M Programming guide to memory barrier instructions*, 17 September 2012

110.   Joe Bungo. 2008. *The use of compiler optimizations for embedded systems software*. Crossroads 15, 1 (September 2008), 8-15

111.   Jack G. Ganssle, *A Guide to Debouncing*, Rev 3, June 2008, https://www.researchgate.net/publication/228957558_A_Guide_to_Debouncing

Index

E

eabi, 667
EABI, 178, 230, 232
electromagnetic interference, 350
ELF, 3, 4, 25, 665, 706
embedded assembly in C programs, 229
EMI, 350
END, 70
end of packet, 583
endian, 89, 129, 247
ENDP, 70
endpoint, 578, 581, 583, 584, 585, 587, 590, 593
ENTRY, 70
enumeration, 588
EOP, 582, 583, 584
EPSR, 75, 92, 93
EQU, 71, 358
equal, 112
even parity, 529
event generation register, 382
EXC_RETURN, 601
exception, 238, 243
exception handling, 266
executable and linkable format, 3
executable file, 1
executable interface, 3
execution program status register, 75
execution view, 4
export, 175, 230
EXPORT, 73
extern, 231, 233
external voltage reference, 487

F

factorial numbers, 141, 194
FAULTMASK, 14, 92, 253
FHSS, 543
FILL, 71
find maximum, 144
fixed-point numbers, 270
    accuracy, 274
    addition, 276
    division, 278
    multiplication, 277
    Qm.n format, 271
    range, 274

resolution, 274
    subtraction, 276
flash memory, 7
floating-point numbers, 279
    addition, 293
    biased exponent, 281
    double precision, 281
    fraction field, 281
    half precision, 281
    IEEE 754, 279
    normalized notation, 279
    overflow, 285
    range, 287
    rounding rules, 289
    rounding to even, 290
    sign bit, 281
    single precision, 281
    special values, 284
    subnormal numbers, 286
    underflow, 285
floating-point register, 299
floating-point unit, 270
flowcharts, 136
for loop, 122
FPCAR, 299, 304, 305, 316, 321
FPCCR, 299, 306, 307, 316
FPSCR, 299, 302, 303, 304, 309, 311, 312, 314, 315, 316, 680
FPU, 299, 512
    alternative half-precision, 303
    arithmetic instructions, 310
    comparison, 311
    copy, 309
    CPACR, 301
    default NaN mode, 303
    divide-by-zero exception, 304
    exception handling, 314
    exceptions, 304, 314
    flushing-to-zero, 303
    FPCA, 305
    FPCAR, 304
    FPCCR, 306
    FPSCR, 302
    inexact exception, 304
    input denormal cumulative exception, 304
    invalid operation exception, 304
    lazy stacking, 307
    load and store, 308